KING BENJAMIN'S SPEECH

FARMS Publications

Teachings of the Book of Mormon

The Geography of Book of Mormon Events: A Source Book

The Book of Mormon Text Reformatted according to Parallelistic Patterns

Eldin Ricks's Thorough Concordance of the LDS Standard Works

A Guide to Publications on the Book of Mormon: A Selected Annotated Bibliography

Book of Mormon Authorship Revisited: The Evidences for Ancient Origins

Ancient Scrolls from the Dead Sea: Photographs and Commentary on a Unique Collection of Scrolls

LDS Perspectives on the Dead Sea Scrolls

Images of Ancient America: Visualizing Book of Mormon Life

Isaiah in the Book of Mormon

Periodicals

Insights: An Ancient Window

FARMS Review of Books

Journal of Book of Mormon Studies

FARMS Reprint Series

Book of Mormon Authorship: New Light on Ancient Origins

The Doctrine and Covenants by Themes

Copublished with Deseret Book Company

An Ancient American Setting for the Book of Mormon

Warfare in the Book of Mormon

By Study and Also by Faith: Essays in Honor of Hugh W. Nibley

The Sermon at the Temple and the Sermon on the Mount

Rediscovering the Book of Mormon

Reexploring the Book of Mormon

Of All Things! Classic Quotations from Hugh Nibley

The Allegory of the Olive Tree

Temples of the Ancient World

Expressions of Faith: Testimonies from LDS Scholars

Feasting on the Word: The Literary Testimony of the Book of Mormon

The Collected Works of Hugh Nibley

Old Testament and Related Studies

Enoch the Prophet

The World and the Prophets

Mormonism and Early Christianity

Lehi in the Desert; The World of the Jaredites; There Were Jaredites

An Approach to the Book of Mormon

Since Cumorah

The Prophetic Book of Mormon

Approaching Zion

The Ancient State

Tinkling Cymbals and Sounding Brass

Temple and Cosmos

Brother Brigham Challenges the Saints

Published through Research Press

Pre-Columbian Contact with the Americas across the Oceans: An Annotated Bibliography

New World Figurine Project, vol. 1

A Comprehensive Annotated Book of Mormon Bibliography

KING BENJAMIN'S SPEECH

"That Ye May Learn Wisdom"

Edited by John W. Welch and Stephen D. Ricks

Foundation for Ancient Research and Mormon Studies
Provo, Utah

Foundation for Ancient Research and Mormon Studies
P.O. Box 7113
University Station
Provo, Utah 84602

Library of Congress Cataloging-in-Publication Data

King Benjamin's speech : "that ye may learn wisdom" / edited
    by John W. Welch and Stephen D. Ricks
        p.   cm.
    Includes bibliographical references and index.
    ISBN 0-934893-30-6
    1. Book of Mormon. Mosiah I–VI—Criticism, interpretation,
etc. 2. Benjamin, King (Book of Mormon figure) I. Welch,
John W. (John Woodland) II. Ricks, Stephen David. III. Book of
Mormon. Mosiah I–VI
BX8627.K47
289.3'22—dc21   97-49375
                                                           CIP

To Colleen Maxwell and
Phyllis Nibley

CONTENTS

INTRODUCTION

With the exception of the words of Christ himself, no speech in sacred literature, in our opinion, surpasses that of King Benjamin. Delivered at the temple in the city of Zarahemla around 124 B.C., this text is a treasure trove of inspiration, wisdom, eloquence, and profound spiritual experience and insight. Little wonder that Mormon saw fit to include this speech as he compiled the most significant Nephite records into the Book of Mormon. Mormon abridged many Nephite sources, but not Benjamin's speech. Mormon may well have copied the text directly from Benjamin's original or from one of the copies that Benjamin caused to be "written and sent forth among those who were not under the sound of his voice" (Mosiah 2:8). That oration was a landmark in its own day, and it still stands as a shining beacon of truth and goodness in our day.

In this lengthy collection of studies, we approach this classic text from many angles. What kind of a text is Benjamin's speech? Is it a prophetic text? A coronation text? A covenant renewal text? A farewell speech? Is it religious exhortation? A doctrinal discourse? A judgment speech? A temple text? Is it a royal confession? A personal testimony? It is all of these things, and more.

Professor Hugh W. Nibley was likely the first scholar to sense the extraordinary historical and literary richness of the words found in Mosiah 1–6. Nibley's discussion of Benjamin's speech in the 1957 Melchizedek Priesthood manual opened many doors and invited multifaceted studies of the ways in which these chapters reflect Old World ritual and experience. Many students over the ensuing forty years have pursued various avenues of research that radiate from this ancient text.

This volume began to come together over a decade ago. The work of gathering and refining these materials eventually culminated in a FARMS symposium, held in Provo and repeated in Oakland, California, in April 1996. All the contexts of this book are related to the speeches presented at that symposium, drawing together and expanding the research that stood behind those studies about Benjamin's speech.

Elder Neal A. Maxwell first discusses the main spiritual messages and personal character of Benjamin and sees the speech as a manual for discipleship. He focuses his attention on removing stumbling blocks, on prayer and revelation, and on virtues of submissiveness, consecration, lovingkindness, and meekness.

Two essays by John W. Welch next examine Benjamin's place in Nephite history and the qualities of Benjamin's speech that make it a masterful oration. Of particular interest are Benjamin's lineage, name, chronology, roles, and responsibilities. The speech itself displays numerous qualities that make it a masterful oration and consummate work of sacred literature.

A study by Welch and Daryl R. Hague examining these words as a classic speech of a departing leader near the time of his death displays an array of elements that positions this speech alongside the most famous farewell speeches of ancient Judeo-Christian and Greco-Roman literature.

Great orations are spawned by great occasions, and annual assemblies of entire populations were awe-inspiring events in the ancient world. As Hugh W. Nibley shows, coming together in assemblies was no perfunctory formality, but was the essence of unification, typifying the coming atonement that would reconcile and unify God and his people.

Annual convocations were mandated anciently under the law of Moses, which prescribed a detailed set of regulations that the Nephites continued to observe strictly until the coming of the resurrected Christ. Accordingly, Terrence L. Szink and Welch explore the distinct possibilities, detected and researched by several scholars, that Benjamin's speech occurred during a traditional Israelite festival season, most likely sometime near the beginning of the ancient calendar year, when the all-important festivals of the Day of Atonement and the Feast of Tabernacles were celebrated. Although it is difficult to know with certainty very much about the ancient observance of such holy days either in Lehi's Jerusalem or in Benjamin's Zarahemla, primary evidence from the Bible, supplemented with secondary evidences from later, but related, Jewish texts and traditions provides a rich field against which Benjamin's speech can be favorably compared on many counts.

The beginning of the autumn season was also often a time of covenant renewal and coronation, especially during sabbatical years. On such occasions, the leaders of the Israelites called their people to repentance and renewed their requirements of social justice. Hence Benjamin's speech may also be viewed as a "prophetic lawsuit," in which this Nephite leader called the Nephite and Mulekite peoples to judgment in ways that took full advantage of the popular, royal, and sacred domains of law and justice that existed in ancient Israel.

Ancient celebrations typically also had much to do with kingship, coronation, treaty making, covenant renewal, and promises of temporal and divine blessings or curses. Stephen D. Ricks demonstrates a broad range of Nephite and Israelite attitudes toward kingship, royal ideologies, coronation ceremonies, and treaty-covenant patterns detectable in Benjamin's speech, consistent with what many scholars have perceived as basic elements in the ideology of kingship from the ancient Near East.

Delivered within the sacred precinct of the Nephite temple in Zarahemla, Benjamin's speech also reaches deeply into the domain of sacral experience. M. Catherine Thomas illuminates the clear religious messages and subtle spiritual allusions in Mosiah 1–6 as she reflects on the mysteries unfolded by Benjamin to the minds and hearts of his people. For those who have ears to hear and eyes to see, more is going on here than an initial conversion of neophyte investigators. Readers of Benjamin's speech are made privy to a higher election and deeper covenantal commitment than the ordinary reader often assumes.

It follows appropriately from the temple setting of Benjamin's speech that the sacred words used by Benjamin in consummating that covenant should persist down through the years in other covenant-making and covenant-renewing texts found within the gospel of Jesus Christ. As Welch next shows, several key words and elements in Benjamin's covenant terminology in Mosiah 5 are closely aligned with the words that the resurrected Jesus used when he administered the sacrament in 3 Nephi 18. These same words in turn formed the basis of the Nephite sacrament prayers found in Moroni 4–5, which are used each week in the LDS Church today.

Words were obviously of great importance to Benjamin. He selected his words with precision and crafted his statements to convey his brilliant doctrinal messages and powerful spiritual testimony. Benjamin's use of various forms of parallelism, and in particular chiasmus, communicated potent contrasts and created sharp points of emphasis. A comprehensive treatment of Benjamin's implementation of these various literary forms is offered by Welch, assisted by Claire Foley. This study displays many intricate and skillful literary qualities in the composition of Benjamin's elaborate text.

Few passages of scripture have had a richer influence on the preaching and doctrinal awareness of the modern church than Benjamin's speech. Bruce Van Orden's contribution to this book catalogues and classifies all general conference talks that have quoted or paraphrased the words of King Benjamin. Benjamin is a primary source of revealed truth on dozens of points, most notably with respect to the theology of service and the centrality of the atonement of Jesus.

Finally, we conclude this volume by presenting the complete text of Benjamin's speech along with detailed notes and textual commentary. The full text of the speech is divided into sections. The notes following each section offer information on such data as the numerous scriptural cross-references that can be drawn between Benjamin's speech and other passages in the four standard works, summaries or quotations of insights given by dozens of Latter-day Saint commentaries on Benjamin's speech, information about biblical scholarship pertinent to verbal or cultural elements in the speech, and references that direct the reader to specific information contained in this volume concerning the particular words, phrases, concepts, or patterns present in Mosiah 1–6. At the end of these textual annotations is a bibliography of LDS writings about Benjamin's speech to which the textual annotations refer. This textual supplement has been developed mainly by Alison V. P. Coutts, together with the editors and other FARMS researchers.

This volume is full of many details and much information. We hope that this collection of studies will serve its readers as a valuable reference tool, a source of inspiration, and a book that can be read and enjoyed either one piece at a time or as a grand tour that opens up broad views and allows the mind to contemplate Benjamin's speech as a whole. Our objective is to know as much as possible about Benjamin and the message, methods, and moment of his speech, and to participate in that event almost as if we were present to hear and understand the words which he spoke. Although we have tried to deal with our topics as well as possible, we know that our modest effort leaves much more to be said about Benjamin's speech. We fully expect a classic text of its order to wear us out long before we will wear it out. We hope that each reader will appreciate and enjoy the rich blessings that can be claimed through further study of Benjamin's scripture.

Many points have deeply impressed us about Benjamin's speech. Our studies have convinced us that if a person were to sit down to write such a speech, that person would need to know hundreds of facts and details; and after years of research seeking to grasp all of those details correctly, that author would still be left with the staggering task of embedding all that information fluently and purposefully into an organized composition that accomplishes simultaneously multiple objectives and does so in an unassuming and artistically lucid manner. Benjamin's speech is not a creation that just happened. Its very existence, with all that it enfolds, testifies of God, that he is, that he loves his children despite their weaknesses, and that he blesses those that keep his commandments.

We conclude, both on spiritual and intellectual grounds, that Benjamin's speech bears true and valuable testimony of the prophesied atonement of Jesus Christ, the son of God, the creator of the heavens and the earth and all things that in them are. We apologize if it takes readers more than a day and a half to read this book, but we remind the impatient that Joseph Smith took only about that long to translate this section in the Book of Mormon containing King Benjamin's speech.

Many people have assisted us in bringing this volume to publication. We express our deep appreciation to Shirley S. Ricks for her editing, with the assistance of Alison V. P. Coutts; to S. Kent Brown for his careful review and useful suggestions; to Claire Foley for her assistance in research and drafting; to Marc-Charles Ingerson for his meticulous source checking; to Mara L. Ashby, Jeromy R. Caballero, Rebecca M. Flinders, Robyn M. Patterson, Wendy C. Thompson, and Anita C. Wells for their proofreading; to Mary Mahan for her design and typesetting skills; to Jessica Taylor for her indexing macros; and to our many other colleagues and associates at Brigham Young University and FARMS who have enriched and promoted our quest to fathom the treasures of Benjamin's speech.

John W. Welch and Stephen D. Ricks
Provo, Utah
December 1997

ABBREVIATIONS

ABD   David N. Freedman, ed., *Anchor Bible Dictionary* (New York: Doubleday, 1992)

ANET   James B. Pritchard, ed., *Ancient Near Eastern Texts Relating to the Old Testament*, 3rd ed. (Princeton: Princeton University Press, 1969)

BDB   Francis Brown, S. R. Driver, and Charles A. Briggs, *A Hebrew and English Lexicon of the Old Testament* (Oxford: Oxford University Press, 1974)

JBL   *Journal of Biblical Literature*

JBMS   *Journal of Book of Mormon Studies*

JD   *Journal of Discourses*

JSOT   *Journal for the Study of the Old Testament*

M   Mishnah

TB   Babylonian Talmud

TDOT   G. Johannes Botterweck and Helmer Ringgren, eds., *Theological Dictionary of the Old Testament*, trans. John T. Willis (Grand Rapids: Eerdmans, 1974–)

TY   Jerusalem Talmud

ZAW   *Zeitschrift für die altestamentliche Wissenschaft*

CHAPTER 1

KING BENJAMIN'S SERMON:
A MANUAL FOR DISCIPLESHIP

Elder Neal A. Maxwell

First of all, my congratulations to FARMS for sponsoring this celebration of King Benjamin's special sermon.[1] This celebration will be carried out most effectively by those who speak after me and will help us understand even more the ways in which, as we sang together, we "have been given much."[2]

I should have been more careful in selecting the title of this talk. Using the word *manual* suggests something stodgy and very lengthy, which this sermon clearly is not. King Benjamin's sermon is anything but stodgy and lengthy, especially with what phrases like "lively . . . guilt" and "bright testimony" (Mosiah 2:38; 3:24) signify, and with inspired interrogatories like "Are we not all beggars?" (Mosiah 4:19).

Almost fifty years ago, I arrived at the mission home in Toronto, Canada. The first assignment given to all of us who arrived, by what seemed to me a very stern mission president, Octave W. Ursenbach, was to memorize and recite orally and in unison Mosiah 2:20–25. I could not appreciate back then the significance of what we were reciting.

Furthermore, the ending words of that particular selection about how even the dust of the earth from which we were created belongs to him who created us also seemed quite stern. But it didn't take long for me to appreciate and love that stern mission president and to love those stern words of Benjamin, words that were just what I needed as I came home from World War II as a first sergeant in the infantry after the battle at Okinawa and many months in the Pacific.

We have no biography of King Benjamin; nevertheless, we have his words, which are what we most need for our discipleship. The combined efforts of the angel who inspired King Benjamin and King Benjamin himself, together with the selectivity of Mormon as editor have given us high relevancy amid the paucity of the Benjamin pages. Of course, while a special portion of King Benjamin's sermon was directed by an angel, angels, in turn, "speak by the power of the Holy Ghost" in what is a seamless process (2 Nephi 32:3).

Since the Book of Mormon itself "shall go from generation to generation as long as the earth shall stand" (2 Nephi 25:22), this means, much as we appreciate them today, that the words of King Benjamin will have their widest and greatest influence—personal and global—in the decades ahead.

Benjamin's Character

As for his own exemplification of discipleship, we begin to learn of Benjamin's character well before his sermon. Just as this special king labored to produce his own necessities, he personalized his leadership in other ways. As a warrior-king, he "did fight with the strength of his own arm, with the sword of Laban" in putting down unrest (Words of

Mormon 1:13), to which false Christs, false prophets, and false preachers doubtless contributed (see Words of Mormon 1:16). In this challenging context he was not alone, for there were "many holy men in the land" who assisted him (Words of Mormon 1:17). Thus, well before the great sermon, King Benjamin had been involved with typical single-mindedness in his successful efforts to deal with contention and dissension. He acted, as was his pattern, "with all the might of his body and the faculty of his whole soul" and established peace in the land (Words of Mormon 1:18).

Even with all this turbulence, King Benjamin did not become jaded, nor was he preoccupied with or defined by his role as a warrior-king. Clearly, he knew that his was a spiritual ministry. Even a cursory cruise through modern political and military history attests to how often lesser individuals are both confined and defined by their contemporary events. We never would have had the great King Benjamin sermon if he had been confined and defined by such prior events. Likewise, we would never have had the sermon and his example if he had become desensitized by his victories and achievements. Benjamin's meekness in the face of his many accomplishments marks this man.

Ours is an age when we yearn for more consistency and for more correct character in the private and public behaviors of secular leaders. Benjamin was Benjamin, whether he was in his garden, on the battlefield, with his family, or practicing statecraft. For him there was no such thing as a public persona. Moreover, how many other warrior-kings, for instance, would have chosen to regard themselves as teacher more than king?

So concerned was Benjamin with his major sermon that he sent among the people to see if they really believed in his words (see Mosiah 5:1). Benjamin was much more concerned over connecting with his spiritual constituency than with his political constituency. He was continually concerned about communicating. For example, Benjamin did not want his people to forget the name by which they were called (see Mosiah 5:14). Illustratively, too, he was anxious to complete the covenant with them, yet he concluded it only when he was sure that their hearts had been touched and that they understood clearly what he had taught (see Mosiah 5:6–7). Such is the great teaching style of this remarkable man whose sermon we celebrate.

Additionally, though the information on the subject is scanty, we know that Benjamin was a special father. Significantly, his own lack of interest in status and power was apparently successfully transmitted to his sons. Evidently they were not power hungry and did not vie with one another for ascendancy, as so often has happened in the process of political succession. Their father-king had set the example for those whom he affectionately addressed as "O my sons" (Mosiah 1:6). His successor son even tilled the soil just as his father had done, signaling to the people that they were not required to sustain him either (see Mosiah 6:7).

King Benjamin's tutorial efforts not only included encouraging his sons, but also teaching them in the language of his fathers, as well as teaching them how to appreciate and search sacred records (see Mosiah 1:2–3). "And many more things did king Benjamin teach his sons, which are not written in this book" (Mosiah 1:8). "Many more things" which we do not have, it says. Intriguing, is it not?

In contrast to Benjamin's effective fatherhood, one cannot help but remember Eli, whose sons "knew not the Lord" and in their iniquity were not restrained (1 Samuel 2:12; see 3:13). With no desire whatsoever to be judgmental, one ponders those comparative implications.

Removing Stumbling Blocks

The general substance of the Book of Mormon itself, of course, encapsulates this rich and special sermon, which is like a sparkling, doctrinal diamond that can be approached and appreciated in so many different ways. Surely King Benjamin kept his promise not to "trifle" with words (Mosiah 2:9), for his was a rich and whole-souled sermon.

Earlier, Nephi wrote of how the Lord would, "in word, and also in power," remove stumbling blocks in order to help some people believe (1 Nephi 14:1). In our time, the prevailing intellectual pattern is secular, and an "exceedingly great many do stumble" over and experience difficulty in accrediting and taking seriously revelations and sacred records (1 Nephi 13:29). Nephi also advised that the Lord will stir, even "shake," the kingdom of the devil in order to help bring some therein to repentance (2 Nephi 28:19). For the meek, however, the Book of Mormon removes some very large stumbling blocks, including the clear pattern of revelation set forth therein:

> And after God had appointed that these things should come unto man, behold, then he saw that it was expedient that man should know concerning the things whereof he had appointed unto them;
> Therefore he sent angels to converse with them, who caused men to behold of his glory.
> And they began from that time forth to call on his name; therefore God conversed with men, and made known unto them the plan of redemption, which had been prepared from the foundation of the world; and this he made known unto them according to their faith and repentance and their holy works. (Alma 12:28–30)

This, of course, is the very pattern featured in the great latter-day restoration, which is so rich in revealed knowledge about God's plan of salvation. Brigham Young was, as usual, "spot on" in noting how strange the doctrine of modern revelation was in his setting of religious revival, saying:

> The first Elders can recollect, when we commenced preaching "Mormonism," that present revelation and a Prophet of God on the earth were the great stumbling blocks to the people, were what we had to contend against, and were, seemingly, the most potent obstacles in our way to the introduction of the Gospel.[3]

George Q. Cannon confirmed:

> There was a day in our history when it was considered a crime for us to believe in revelation from God. I do not know that that day is entirely past. There was a day in our history when it was considered very improper for us to believe in Prophets or Apostles—that is, to believe that they ought to be in the Church. There was a time when we were indicted by a mob in its written proclamation for believing in miracles. . . . You have doubtless thought, all of you, about the character of the men whom Jesus chose to be His Apostles. They were men who were stumbling-blocks to their generation, for they did not belong to the popular classes. They were not learned men, they were not rich men—that is in the worldly sense of the word— they were not dignified men; and Jesus Himself, the Lord of life and of glory, was a constant stumbling-block to His generation.[4]

After all, revelations do tell us, as Jacob said, of "things as they really will be" (Jacob 4:13), just as the angel revealed to King Benjamin things about the impending Messiah (see Mosiah 3:2, 5–9).

Given the multifaceted richness of King Benjamin's sermon, it is instructive to note the one thing another prophet cited ninety years later. Helaman chose this passage out of Benjamin's rich and resplendent sermon:

O remember, remember, my sons, the words which king Benjamin spake unto his people; yea, remember that there is no other way nor means whereby man can be saved, only through the atoning blood of Jesus Christ, who shall come; yea, remember that he cometh to redeem the world. (Helaman 5:9)

As we see from the content of Benjamin's sermon, the so-called mysteries referred to by King Benjamin are actually the plain but precious things required for salvation and for exaltation:

I say unto you, my sons, were it not for these things, which have been kept and preserved by the hand of God, that we might read and understand of his mysteries, and have his commandments always before our eyes, that even our fathers would have dwindled in unbelief, and we should have been like unto our brethren, the Lamanites, who know nothing concerning these things, or even do not believe them when they are taught them, because of the traditions of their fathers, which are not correct. (Mosiah 1:5)

Wise King Benjamin knew personally of the importance of sacred records. Just a few years before Benjamin's reign, some of the people of Zarahemla ended up denying "the being of their Creator" (Omni 1:17). Why? Because they had no sacred record. Within one generation of Benjamin's great sermon, it was reported that:

There were many of the rising generation that could not understand the words of king Benjamin, being little children at the time he spake unto his people; and they did not believe the tradition of their fathers.

They did not believe what had been said concerning the resurrection of the dead, neither did they believe concerning the coming of Christ. (Mosiah 26:1–2)

How ironic that the last words of King Benjamin were lost on "many" of the first generation after him!

The very things a secular society in any age is so quick to discount or to deny are the existence of God and the reality of the resurrection. No wonder King Benjamin prophesied that the reactions of so many to Jesus would be merely to "consider him a man" (Mosiah 3:9). For the Jews, Jesus was and is a "stumblingblock," and for the Greeks and their philosophical heirs, he is "foolishness" (1 Corinthians 1:23). Some continue to demand a sign, while others emphasize secular wisdom, with each of these tendencies deflecting or rejecting Christ's divinity.

In Wisdom's Paths: Prayer and Revelation

Benjamin, who twice pointedly mentions his "clear conscience" (Mosiah 2:15, 17), did not do so to be legalistic; instead, he wanted to do everything he could to keep his people "in wisdom's paths" (Mosiah 2:36). But the path of wisdom he cited is sharply distinguished from the "world and the wisdom thereof" (1 Nephi 11:35). Benjamin knew that without revelations, prophets, and sacred records, mankind must settle for "preach[ing] up . . . their own wisdom" (2 Nephi 26:20), which is not much of an offering. Only the Holy Ghost can keep us on the strait and narrow path, which is wisdom's path (see Mosiah 2:36).

It is no safer, therefore, to rely on the mind of flesh than on the arm of flesh. Unfortunately, many pridefully make that mistake. I cite as an example an "ancient retiree from the Research Department of the British Foreign Office [who] reputedly said, after serving from 1903–50: 'Year after year the worriers and fretters would come to me with awful predictions of the outbreak of war. I denied it each time. I was only wrong twice' "[5]—World War I and World War II!

Of course, the world's wisdom can be helpful—but only like a lighthouse that works some of the time. Observe, for instance, how America currently tries to solve what is becoming the massive challenge of illegitimacy without meaningful concern over the importance of chastity and fidelity. It would be comic if it were not so tragic! Thus the need for revelation and its refreshment is so fundamental.

Mentioned earlier was the seamless web of revelation. Given this reality, one should not be surprised by all the correlations and parallels among various prophetic utterances. Consider, for example, how many sincerely believe that if they simply ask for something in prayer, God will grant it, especially if they ask with at least a modicum of faith. King Benjamin counseled us, however, that while we are to pray in faith, it should be for "that [which] is right" (Mosiah 4:21). The resurrected Jesus so confirmed, saying: "And whatsoever ye shall ask the Father in my name, which is right, believing that ye shall receive, behold it shall be given unto you" (3 Nephi 18:20).

The phrase *which is right* is correlated. Not surprisingly, Paul also understood the need for inspired prayers, saying, "Likewise the Spirit also helpeth our infirmities: for we know not what we should pray for as we ought: but the Spirit itself maketh intercession for us with groanings which cannot be uttered" (Romans 8:26). I hope I am not the only one in this audience who has sometimes wondered what to pray for. Therefore, how much, in the complexities of life's situations, we need to have our very prayers inspired!

When the resurrected Savior viewed his devout followers engaged in prayer, "they did not multiply many words, for it was given unto them what they should pray, and they were filled with desire" (3 Nephi 19:24). Inspired prayers

do not require the multiplying of words. Rather, true peti-
tioners are filled with desire. This role of desire in discipleship is another topic for another time. Can God give us desire or is it something only we can bring to the altar of faith?
In any case, we worship an omniscient God, as Benjamin
emphatically reminded us:

> Believe in God; believe that he is, and that he created
> all things, both in heaven and in earth; believe that he has
> all wisdom, and all power, both in heaven and in earth;
> believe that man doth not comprehend all the things
> which the Lord can comprehend. (Mosiah 4:9)

In the face of that pleading, that heartfelt entreaty from
Benjamin, our need is great for submissiveness to God's
will, especially since from time to time you and I, if only
innocently, will ask most earnestly for something that is not
expedient or right. When it is not granted, this can adversely affect our faith or at least our feelings about God.
This may seem to be a minor matter, but in day-to-day discipleship each must work his way through this recurring
reality. I find it is more difficult to do when our unanswered
but heartfelt petitions involve those we love. Here again
we see the instructive practicality and the spirituality of
Benjamin.

Submissiveness

The submissiveness of Benjamin in all things tells us
how far along he was in his discipleship. In the aggregate,
his attributes gave him the impressive authority of example
to accompany his holding of the Holy Priesthood. Though
to a lesser degree than Jesus, their perfect Master, prophets
like Benjamin can with some justification echo his entreaty,
"Come, follow me" (Luke 18:22). Such was the case with
Benjamin as he followed the Lord's example. Benjamin's

adoration of the Lord led to his emulation of the Lord attribute by attribute. Therefore, he was not only a model king and father, but he was also correspondingly a model disciple, being a "holy" and a "just man" (Words of Mormon 1:17 and Omni 1:25, respectively).

King Benjamin both counted and weighed his blessings. He had a sense of the proportion between large and small blessings, but he also had gratitude for all blessings. On this point, the eminent historian Will Durant wrote of the human need for perspective and proportion, pleading "to know that the little things are little, and the big things big, before it is too late; we want to see things now as they will seem forever—'in the light of eternity.'"[6] King Benjamin understood the difference between the large and the small blessings. He understood how God's generosity and graciousness are expressed in what he and a fellow prophet termed God's "infinite goodness" and his "immediate goodness" (Mosiah 5:3; 25:10), thus distinguishing between the strategic and tactical blessings, respectively, that he bestows on us.

A second searching interrogatory is eloquently expressed by Benjamin in his superb sermon: "For how knoweth a man the master whom he has not served, and who is a stranger unto him, and is far from the thoughts and intents of his heart?" (Mosiah 5:13).

Discipleship requires extensive thinking about, praying to, and serving the Lord. Otherwise, distance develops. There can be no deep discipleship if we do not think about him, serve him, and have heartfelt intentions concerning him; otherwise, estrangement will engulf us.

If one "mind[s] the things of the flesh," one cannot "have the mind of Christ" (Romans 8:5; 1 Corinthians 2:16). One such person's thought patterns are thereby focused "far from" Jesus, as are the desires and "intents of his heart" (Mosiah 5:13).

Jesus said, "Take my yoke upon you, and learn of me; for I am meek and lowly" (Matthew 11:29). If we go un-yoked very long, there will be no real understanding on our part. However, when a person combines this divine instruction of Jesus with the answers implicit in the query of King Benjamin, then he or she has exposed the totality of what is required of serious disciples.

Consecration

Benjamin is such a superb example of consecration. He did things with the "faculty of his whole soul" (Words of Mormon 1:18). Such is the very "heart . . . might, mind, and strength" required in connection with keeping the first great commandment (D&C 59:5; see Matthew 22:37). No wonder Benjamin urged us to be sufficiently consecrated to give all that we "have and are" (Mosiah 2:34). How appropriate that his sermon was given near a temple.

However, without consecration, we may be "honorable," but we are not "valiant" (D&C 76:75, 79). Honorable individuals are certainly not wicked, nor are they necessarily unhappy; they are just unfulfilled. It is not usually what is done but what is left undone that is amiss. In King Benjamin's consecration, there was no holding back, and it must become the same with us.

The spirit of consecration pervades the lines of King Benjamin's speech as he urges followers, for instance, "to render to [God] all that you have and are" (Mosiah 2:34), thus touching a raw and reminding nerve in each of us insofar as we hold back some of ourselves.

Ironically, if the Master is a stranger to us, then we will merely end up serving other masters. The sovereignty of these other masters is real, even if it is sometimes subtle. They do call their cadence, for "we are all enlisted,"[7] if only in the ranks of the indifferent. To the extent that we are not willing to be led by the Lord, we will, instead, be driven by our appetites and be preoccupied with the lesser things and the pressing cares of the day.

So many of us are kept from eventual consecration because we mistakenly think that somehow, by letting our will be swallowed up in the will of God, we lose our individuality. Abinadi cited the key example, for he spoke of how Jesus let his will be "swallowed up in the will of the Father" (Mosiah 15:7).

What we are really worried about, of course, is not giving up self, but rather selfish things—like our roles, our time, our preeminence, and our possessions. No wonder we are instructed by the Savior to lose ourselves (see Luke 9:24). He is only asking us to lose the old self in order to find the new self. This is part of what Benjamin's sermon is all about—to put off the natural man in order to come into our spiritual inheritance. So, it is not a question of losing one's identity but of finding it. Ironically, so many people already lose themselves anyway—but in their consuming hobbies and preoccupations.

Loving-Kindness

Benjamin stressed knowing God's attributes. Again, he touched firmly though subtly on a profound point. As we come to know the attributes of God, this can awaken us, as King Benjamin said, to our comparative fallen state (see Mosiah 4:5–6). It is true, as you know, that God's goodness actually draws us to him and thus leads us to repentance. Paul confirmed this (see Romans 2:4). God's gravitational pull is real. This was well expressed by Jeremiah, speaking for the Lord: "Yea, I have loved thee with an everlasting love: therefore with lovingkindness have I drawn thee" (Jeremiah 31:3). Surely the Psalmist was correct in declaring, "Whoso is wise . . . shall understand the lovingkindness of the Lord" (Psalm 107:43). And Benjamin drove that point home. No wonder the Prophet Joseph would say that unless we comprehend the character of God, we do not comprehend ourselves.[8] Thus, as we read in *Lectures on Faith,* we must first gain a correct idea of the character of God in order to have real faith.[9] In all these ways, as we come to know God, he draws us to him.

The apogee of Benjamin's address is the atonement. Benjamin's foretelling of Jesus' ministry revealed that Christ would bleed at every pore, "so great shall be his anguish for the wickedness . . . of his people" (Mosiah 3:7). It was real blood, pore by pore, removing any reason to think of the precious liquid as only being symbolic sweat. Benjamin's reference to Jesus' great anguish parallels the later-revealed words about how Jesus experienced "the fierceness of the wrath of Almighty God" (D&C 76:107) and, likewise, how Jesus "descended below all things, that he comprehended all things" (D&C 88:6; see D&C 122:8). The perfected personal empathy of Jesus includes his knowing our sicknesses as well as our sufferings as a result of sin (see Alma 7:11–12).

Of the characteristics of a true disciple, given to us by Benjamin, we are not surprised that Benjamin emphasized having no intent to injure others, living peaceably with them, rendering unto others what is due, and not suffering people to be in hunger or poverty. Each of these expressions, of course, branches from the second great commandment. Brigham Young put the various attributes in perspective with these words: "There is one virtue, attribute, or principle, which, if cherished and practised by the Saints, would prove salvation to thousands upon thousands. I allude to charity, or love, from which proceed forgiveness, long-suffering, kindness, and patience."[10]

Though it may seem obvious, these varied expressions do grow out of genuine love for others. Such concern is not possible if one is selfish or lacking in either empathy or meekness. The fact that the expressions of love occur in such variety is almost incidental to the basic and underlying attribute of love. Thus, for instance, love would clearly and quickly veto stealing from a neighbor, but it would also keep one from withholding from that same neighbor needed and deserved praise. Hence, as Benjamin said, just as it is impossible to catalogue the many ways in which we can sin (see Mosiah 4:30), it is likewise impossible to set forth the many ways we can love and serve others. Therefore, when we engage in various expressions of loving service, we are merely in the service of our God. The second great commandment is really part of the first commandment. Who would care to try to fix the precise border between these two commandments?

Other Virtues

Benjamin was so poignant in his sharp, one-liner inquiry, "For behold, are we not all beggars?" (Mosiah 4:19). In stressing our continuing dependence on God for all the necessities of life, Benjamin moved quickly to note our spiritual dependence—especially our dependence on the atonement, the only means by which we can have a remission of our sins (see Mosiah 4:19–20). Since we are utterly and totally dependent on the Lord, Benjamin urged us to be especially sensitive to others and to impart to them. In the spiritual domain, those who are rich spiritually have a duty to impart to and nurture those who are weak. While Benjamin stressed the imparting of material and physical substance to the poor, he would doubtless agree with Isaiah about the need to clothe others as well in "the garment of praise" (Isaiah 61:3). Those who have enough bread may shiver for recognition and yearn for the succor of deserved commendation.

Yet in the intensity of King Benjamin's discipleship, there is also balance. After his exhortation on caring for the poor, he nevertheless urged that we do things "in wisdom and order" (Mosiah 4:27). How like the counsel of the Lord to the Prophet Joseph Smith: "Do not run faster or labor more than you have strength and means provided to enable you to translate" (D&C 10:4). A lack of balance can burn out discipleship. Hence we have Benjamin's wisdom and order test, and we have the strength and means test given to Joseph Smith by the Lord. I wonder if, in this connection, Benjamin's time spent gardening and farming in order to avoid being a burden might also have provided him with much-needed therapy and with time for unhurried reflection.

Much emphasis was given by King Benjamin to retaining a remission of our sins (see Mosiah 4:26). We do not ponder that concept very much in the church. We ought to think of it a lot more. Retention clearly depends on the regularity of our repentance. In the church we worry, and should, over the retention of new members, but the retention of our remissions is cause for even deeper concern.

What King Benjamin said with such clarity and humility about becoming more saintly and childlike, in my opinion, has a fulness and specificity unrivaled in all of scripture. In my opinion, if King Benjamin had uttered only the words in Mosiah 3:19, the verse would still rank among the great gems in all our scriptures. This verse is so succinct. By way of comparative illustration, if needed, today's missionary handbook could be further compressed into these lines from Alma: "Use boldness, but not overbearance; and also see that ye bridle all your passions, that ye may be filled with love; see that ye refrain from idleness" (Alma 38:12). In a similar way, the goals and the process of discipleship could be compressed into that precious verse 12. Its concision and compression are in such stark contrast to the repetition and multiplication we often see in so many human communications.

Granted, the adjuration for us to be childlike also occurs in the New Testament: "Verily I say unto you, Except ye be converted, and become as little children, ye shall not enter into the kingdom of heaven" (Matthew 18:3). But contextuality is given in King Benjamin's sermon:

> For the natural man is an enemy to God, and has been from the fall of Adam, and will be, forever and ever, unless he yields to the enticings of the Holy Spirit, and putteth off the natural man and becometh a saint through the atonement of Christ the Lord, and becometh as a child, submissive, meek, humble, patient, full of love, willing to submit to all things which the Lord seeth fit to inflict upon him, even as a child doth submit to his father. (Mosiah 3:19)

It is noteworthy that twice in that verse *submissiveness* is mentioned, since it is the crowning quality needed for consecration.

Yes, Paul wrote helpfully, "[See] that ye have put off the old man with his deeds" (Colossians 3:9). However, King Benjamin parallels and exceeds what is preserved from Paul. Brigham Young, such a careful student of the Book of Mormon, was quick to see and use numerous times in his teachings counsel concerning the natural man, for instance:

> How difficult it is to teach the natural man, who comprehends nothing more than that which he sees with the

natural eye! . . . Talk to him about angels, heavens, God, immortality, and eternal lives, and it is like sounding brass, or a tinkling cymbal to his ears; it has no music to him; there is nothing in it that charms his senses, soothes his feelings, attracts his attention, or engages his affections, in the least.[11]

Brigham understood the natural man, as did King Benjamin and the apostle Paul. Paul concurred, of course, noting that to the natural man the things of the Spirit "are foolishness" (1 Corinthians 2:14).

Meekness

Meek King Benjamin could have wallowed in public esteem. He could have worried over how to preserve and keep his image intact. Instead, he was concerned with having Christ's image in his countenance (see Alma 5:14). Being meek, he quickly deflected praise, as we all should, giving glory to God and deferring to our heavenly King (see Mosiah 2:19).

Benjamin's impressive meekness actually mirrors the majestic and mutual meekness of the Father and the Son, on which I have reflected lately. So I share these brief thoughts with you. Consider these illustrations of the majestic mutual meekness of the Father and the Son.

Deferential Jesus said:

- "There is none good but one, that is, God" (Matthew 19:17).
- "My doctrine is not mine, but his that sent me" (John 7:16).
- "The Son can do nothing of himself, but what he seeth the Father do: for what things soever he doeth, these also doeth the Son likewise" (John 5:19).

The Father said:

- "This is my beloved Son, in whom I am well pleased" (Matthew 3:17; Jesus would have known intellectually how well he had done, but to have his Father say it is something else again).
- "And I heard a voice from the Father, saying: Yea, the words of my Beloved are true and faithful" (2 Nephi 31:15; the Father meekly testified to the truthfulness of his Son).
- The Father's very voice, as we all know, was "small" but penetrating, not "harsh" or "loud" (3 Nephi 11:3).

There is a majestic mutual meekness about the Father and the Son, and we should learn from it. We certainly see meekness in the life and sermon of King Benjamin.

With our joy as their objective, God and Jesus, though profoundly meek, are determined to bring to pass their purposes, for "there is nothing that the Lord thy God shall take in his heart to do but what he will do it" (Abraham 3:17). Indicatively, after completing their vast creative activities, they "watched those things which they had ordered [i.e., their creations] until they obeyed" (Abraham 4:18). What doing that meant, astrophysically, we do not know—but affectionately and determinedly they pursued their "work and . . . glory" in behalf of God's spirit children (Moses 1:39). Actually, the Lord meekly understates his cosmic competency twice in the Book of Mormon by saying simply, "I am able to do mine own work" (2 Nephi 27:20, 21). Is he ever!

God has foreseen all the details in human wickedness, and he has made "ample provision" so that all his purposes will still come to pass.[12] No wonder Benjamin exhorted us to believe that God comprehends all things, including things we don't comprehend.

We are counseled by Benjamin to "continue in the faith even unto the end of [our lives]" (Mosiah 4:6). We can be sure that King Benjamin endured well and meekly in the remaining three years of his life after his great sermon (as he taught us to do; see Mosiah 4:30).

One wonders if he still worked in his garden, at least a little bit. If so, did passersby stop to greet him? Did they perhaps notice, near the end, that he was not in his garden anymore?

Revered as Benjamin was, what an engaging experience it must have been to hear him preach personally—especially while sitting in one's family circle in a tent facing the temple.

But we can hear him now. If we read him reverently, the intervening centuries soon melt away. His earnestness emerges, and his personableness almost caresses us, giving King Benjamin such immediacy and high relevancy as his example combines with such powerful words about discipleship. I wonder if, like meek President Spencer W. Kimball, meek Benjamin also did not realize how unique he was in the eyes of the Lord. How blessed we are to have such models.

Notes

1. The Ninth Annual FARMS Symposium on the Book of Mormon, featuring King Benjamin's speech, was held on 13 April 1996 in Provo, Utah.

2. "Because I Have Been Given Much," *Hymns* (1995), no. 219.

3. Brigham Young, in *JD*, 3:158.

4. George Q. Cannon, in *JD*, 22:261–62.

5. Thomas L. Hughes, *The Fate of Facts in a World of Men—Foreign Policy and Intelligence-Making* (New York: Foreign Policy Association, 1976), 48, cited in Richard K. Betts, "Analysis, War, and Decision: Why Intelligence Failures Are Inevitable," *World Politics* 31/1 (1978): 62 n. 2.

6. Will Durant, *The Story of Philosophy: The Lives and Opinions of the Great Philosophers* (Garden City, N.Y.: Garden City Publishing, 1927), 1.

7. "We Are All Enlisted," *Hymns*, no. 250.

8. See *The Teachings of the Prophet Joseph Smith*, comp. Joseph Fielding Smith (Salt Lake City: Deseret Book, 1976), 343.

9. See *Lectures on Faith* (Salt Lake City: Deseret Book, 1985), 33.

10. Brigham Young, in *JD*, 7:133–34.

11. Ibid., 1:2; see *Discourses of Brigham Young* (Salt Lake City: Deseret Book, 1954), 260.

12. *Teachings of the Prophet Joseph Smith*, 220.

CHAPTER 2

BENJAMIN, THE MAN:
HIS PLACE IN NEPHITE HISTORY

John W. Welch

King Benjamin's speech in Mosiah 2–5 is a classic in the world's library of religious literature. Unparalleled in many respects by anything else in the Book of Mormon, this document stands as a monument of Nephite civilization and spirituality. The text of this speech can be explored from many different angles—literary, historical, and theological, to name but a few. Only under close examination do the complexity, subtlety, beauty, truth, and wisdom of this inspired composition start to come to light. To introduce the study of this address, we begin with some background information about the remarkable man who authored it.

Because of the wide influence he had on his own subjects and subsequent generations in the Book of Mormon, Benjamin occupied a unique place in Nephite history. No other Nephite king was remembered in so many positive ways. While Lehi and Nephi were the founders of the Nephite civilization, it was Benjamin who preserved and revitalized the people at a time when they were perilously close to failure. Benjamin unified his people in the land of Zarahemla at a critical time in their history and gave them the spiritual strength they needed to flourish for the next several generations. His influence produced an important era of religious and political strength in Nephite history.

Who was Benjamin, the author of this masterpiece? When did he live? What challenges and tasks did he face? What do we know of him and his world?

Benjamin the King

Benjamin is almost always referred to in the Book of Mormon as King Benjamin. Although he was a multifaceted man and must have been many things to many people, he was remembered primarily as the greatest of all Nephite kings. Of the thirty-four times his name appears in the Book of Mormon, all but two of them identify him as *King* Benjamin. The first exception occurs before he was king (see Omni 1:23), and the second when his son Mosiah speaks of him as "my father Benjamin" (Mosiah 29:13).

He was remembered by his people as having been a very good king. As the records disclose, Benjamin was righteous, holy, inspired, just, frugal, loving, concerned, humble, articulate, and courageous. About thirty years after his death, his son and successor Mosiah$_2$ declared to the Nephites, "If ye could have men for your kings who would do even as my father Benjamin did for this people—I say unto you, if this could always be the case then it would be expedient that ye should always have kings to rule over you" (Mosiah 29:13). Striking a sharp contrast with the goodness of Benjamin, the book of Mosiah depicts King Noah, the nemesis of Abinadi, as typifying everything antithetical to King Benjamin (see Mosiah 29:18). Noah was wicked, abominable, indulgent, corrupt, extravagant, materialistic, selfish, and impatient. No doubt Benjamin's historical reputation benefited by this comparison. Compared with a king like Noah, such a sterling man as Benjamin looks even more magnificent, and deservedly so.

Genealogy

Benjamin's lineage and the date of his birth are not known. He was the son of a Nephite king, Mosiah₁, and while one may assume that this Mosiah was a descendant of Nephi, there is no indication that Nephite kingship necessarily passed down from father to son among Nephi's descendants. Jacob 1:11 prescribes that each Nephite king should be called by a coronation name of "Nephi," but begins with "*whoso* should reign . . . ," which seems to say that lineage was not a determining factor in the selection of these rulers. Mosiah₁ and Benjamin could, therefore, have been Nephites, Jacobites, Josephites, or Zoramites, but one suspects they were from the lineage of Nephi, especially since Amaleki, a descendant of Jacob, had no posterity himself to whom he could give the small plates before he died (see Omni 1:25).

The Name Benjamin

Benjamin's name is intriguing, although somewhat of a mystery. Benjamin was the name of the younger brother of Joseph (see Genesis 35:18; 46:19), and the tribe of Benjamin was known for being warlike. It is quite possible that Benjamin's name was meaningful to him and his people in the context of his kingship over the land of Zarahemla. This name may have been given to him at birth, or it may have been given to him as a coronation name. Indeed it is probable that Israelite kings were given a new name or a coronation name when they took the throne.[1] Either way, the name of Benjamin was probably meaningful to him as king.[2]

Since the Nephites were from the tribe of Manasseh (see Alma 10:2–3), and since the Mulekites were from the tribe of Judah (as descendants of royal fugitives from Jerusalem and their sailors), it is unclear why Benjamin would have been given the name of the head of another tribe in Israel. Several possibilities exist.

The first king over a united Israel was Saul. He was a Benjamite (see 1 Samuel 9:1) who made the site of Gibeah in the central Benjamite territory his capital. Saul ruled over all Israel until he was defeated by the Philistines. Similarly, King Benjamin ruled over a newly consolidated kingdom. In such circumstances, the name Benjamin could well have evoked politically neutral yet positive feelings among these diverse Book of Mormon descendants from both the southern kingdom of Judah and a northern Israelite tribe. While a royal name like David, from whom Mulek was descended, would probably have been politically uncomfortable for the Nephites, a name like Benjamin would have been conciliatory and unifying.

Furthermore, in ancient Israel the lands of the tribe of Benjamin lay immediately and strategically between the territory of the tribe of Judah to the south and the land of Manasseh to the north.[3] In this central territory the people of Israel "came up" to their judges to be judged (Judges 4:5); here also Samuel assembled all Israel to pray (see 1 Samuel 7:5–6). From traditional functions like these, the name and place of Benjamin symbolized to the Israelites a meeting place between Judah and Manasseh. In Nephite terms, one may conjecture that Benjamin's name (either as a birth name or a coronation name) could have similarly suggested a middle ground between the Mulekites (of Judah) and the Nephites (of Manasseh). Consistent with what his name suggests, Benjamin valiantly filled the role of unifier and moderator between these two separate populations over whom he ruled.[4]

The name Benjamin may mean literally "son of the right hand," although this etymology is not entirely certain. If the name was understood this way among the Nephites, it may have had significance to Benjamin and his people. Benjamin was surely a righteous son, found on the right hand of his father Mosiah. Moreover, Benjamin promised his people that he who knows "the name by which he is called" "shall be found at the right hand of God" (Mosiah 5:9). Benjamin's audience may well have noticed a similarity between Benjamin's name and this important phrase, "to be found at the *right hand* of God."

Chronology

Though nothing is known about Benjamin's birth, the year of his death is accurately recorded, and from that information several significant details can be extrapolated. Benjamin died in 119 B.C. (see Mosiah 6:5). At this time he was fairly old (see Mosiah 2:28–30), perhaps around the age of seventy or more.[5] Since Benjamin had been consecrated king by his father Mosiah (see Mosiah 2:11), who himself was probably reigning as early as 210 B.C. in the days of Amaleki (see Omni 1:23),[6] one can confidently assume that both Mosiah$_1$ and Benjamin ruled in Zarahemla for a long time, each probably reigning for more than forty years. Mosiah$_2$ reigned for thirty-three years (see Mosiah 29:46). In certain periods of history, other rulers have governed for such lengths of time or longer. Some lengthy reigns are noted among the Mayas, and other exceptional reigns longer than sixty years are found among the Egyptians.[7]

War and Peace

From all we can learn, Benjamin was a very effective and successful ruler. Despite considerable challenges, he maintained a stable government throughout his long lifetime and established peace in his lands. Judging by the brief account of Benjamin's reign given by Mormon (see Words of Mormon 1:10–18), Benjamin's first political challenge was that of consolidating control over the lands and people in Zarahemla.

Early in his reign, Benjamin had to protect the integrity of his lands. Under the leadership of his father Mosiah (200 B.C.), the Nephites had moved from the land of Nephi, traveling about 200 miles to the north, down into the lower land of Zarahemla in the Sidon river valley.[8] Surprisingly, no further Lamanite harassment of the fleeing Nephites is mentioned in the record during the reign of Mosiah$_1$, but shortly after Benjamin became king, a significant Lamanite invasion occurred (see Words of Mormon 1:13; Omni 1:24). This Lamanite invasion from the south, down into the land of Zarahemla, was launched in the middle of the second century B.C. Several reasons make it probable that the attack against Benjamin was related to the major Lamanite offensive being waged at that same time in the south against the Nephite colonists in the land of Nephi (see Mosiah 10:6–16). At that time, the Lamanites in the south were still angry because Nephi had "departed into the wilderness" four centuries earlier and had taken with him the plates of brass (Mosiah 10:16). Since the plates of brass were now in Zarahemla, it would have been logical for the Lamanites to have included that city as one of the military targets in their campaign.[9]

The date of this Lamanite offensive, known from the record of Zeniff, makes it likely that this campaign was related to the battles fought at that same time by Benjamin. The war began thirty-four years after Zeniff had arrived in the land of Nephi from Zarahemla in the early part of the second century B.C. (see Mosiah 9:11; 10:3–5). Since a reasonable date for Zeniff's departure from Zarahemla is around 195–185 B.C., the date of this war would be around 160–150 B.C., which is further corroborated by the facts that it pre-dated the trial of Abinadi (about 145 B.C.), that it shortly pre-ceded the reign of Noah (about 155 to 145 B.C.), and that it was fought by Noah's father Zeniff, a contemporary of Benjamin's father Mosiah, at a time when Zeniff was old (see Mosiah 9:11; 10:22). This war also came during the life-time of Amaleki, born in the days of Mosiah₁ (see Omni 1:23–24). If Benjamin was born between 195 and 187 B.C. and acceded to the throne like his own son Mosiah at the age of thirty,[10] then the first year of Benjamin's reign would have come between 165 and 157 B.C.—right around the time of this major Lamanite unrest.[11]

In this war, King Benjamin was the commander-in-chief. He assembled his armies and personally stood against the enemy. He fought with his "own arm," as was customary for kings in the ancient world and in the Book of Mormon.[12] He also used the sword of Laban—a symbolic artifact as well as an effective weapon—indicating his firm confidence in the sacred and traditional Nephite heritage. This campaign established Benjamin early in his reign as a victorious and successful military leader. The positive claim he modestly makes in his final speech that he had "kept [his people] from falling into the hands of [their] enemies" (Mosiah 2:31) was a feat Benjamin could assert persuasively and legitimately. As a protector of his people, Benjamin epitomized the blessing of Moses given to the tribe of Benjamin, King Benjamin's ancient namesake: "The be-loved of the Lord shall dwell in safety by him; and the Lord shall cover him all the day long, and he shall dwell between his shoulders" (Deuteronomy 33:12).

As a result of this war, Benjamin was able to "[drive the Lamanites] out of all the lands of [Nephite] inheritance"

(Words of Mormon 1:14), thereby protecting and affirming his territory as a land subject to his jurisdiction and governed by the prevailing Nephite laws. Benjamin thus administered a defined area, referred to as "the land of Zarahemla" (Omni 1:12; Mosiah 2:4), although the size of this territory is unknown. John Sorenson estimates that, while delivering his famous speech near the end of his reign, Benjamin spoke to a group of about 25,000 citizens,[13] but the population in the land of Zarahemla could have been much larger.[14]

Keeper of All the Records

Early in his reign, Benjamin received the small plates of Nephi from Amaleki. With these sacred plates came the obligation to keep records of the religious experiences of the Nephites. Since Benjamin also held the plates of brass and was one of the probable few who could read these ancient writings, he became the custodian and effective interpreter of all the scriptures and prophecies fundamental to the Nephite tradition. Benjamin held these records, along with the large plates of Nephi that had been entrusted to him by his father Mosiah (see Words of Mormon 1:10), thereby consolidating for the first time since Nephi these important elements of Nephite religious leadership and political power in the hands of a single individual.

This significant union of religious and political roles in a single leader marked a major change in Nephite politics and theocracy. This shift was apparently not accomplished without some resistance. Mormon mentions several false messiahs, false prophets, false preachers, and false teachers who arose at this time and had to be silenced and punished. This led to "much contention" in Zarahemla (Words of Mormon 1:16). While the origin of these dissenting groups is not disclosed, it is possible that this condition of religious instability and controversy occurred as a result of changes stemming from Benjamin. Members of the tribes of Jacob and Joseph, to whom the roles of prophet, priest, preacher, and teacher had traditionally belonged, might have been alienated by these developments (see 2 Nephi 5:26). They could have objected, as false "prophets," to the unprecedented dominance of Benjamin in both the political and religious affairs of his people. Undoubtedly Benjamin saw himself not only as carrying out a legitimate stewardship entrusted to him and his posterity by Amaleki, but also as taking steps necessary to the eternal welfare of his people. These steps were occasioned by the fact that descendants of Jacob such as Omni (who was "a wicked man" by his own admission; see Omni 1:2), as well as Amaron, Chemish, and Abinadom, had failed to provide spiritual leadership to the Nephites (see Omni 1:4–11). Amaleki's brother returned to the city of Nephi (see Omni 1:30), and as a result, this line of religious record keepers ended with Amaleki.

Prophet-Leader

In place of such religious leaders, Benjamin stood successfully as the spiritual leader of his people. He was a "holy man" who reigned "in righteousness" (Words of Mormon 1:17). He received revelation, presided over his temple precinct, and appointed priests. He controlled religious teaching with the "assistance of the holy prophets who were among his people" with the help of "many holy men in the land" (Words of Mormon 1:16–17; see 1:18). From such statements it appears that many men in Zarahemla were known as prophets and originally functioned independently of the king. Benjamin was apparently able to win their confidence and enlist their support in normalizing religious thought and practice. By the end of Benjamin's reign, the role of these prophets or holy men seems to have diminished; they are never mentioned in any of Benjamin's words, nor do they reemerge as part of the church in Zarahemla during the subsequent reign of Mosiah$_2$. Perhaps the need to fill the vacuum caused by the reduction in the role of these prophets, preachers, and teachers contributed to Mosiah$_2$'s eagerness to embrace Alma$_1$ and his group and to grant him very broad powers to establish Nephite churches shortly after he arrived in Zarahemla (Mosiah 25:19) only a few years after the commencement of Mosiah's reign. In any event, Benjamin seems eventually to have brought these holy men under his administration where their significance lessened because of Benjamin's own stature and righteousness, although one suspects that the tradition of independent prophets continued to play some role among these people, as had long been the case in ancient Israel[15] and as has been found to have existed among the Maya in later years.[16]

A Man for All Seasons

In his younger years, Benjamin was known as an impressive warrior, but he eventually became known as a devoted spiritual leader as well. This combination of strength and humility is precious and rare among men, and it allowed Benjamin to speak from substantial personal knowledge and experience. The fact that he had personally fought with the sword gives a flesh-and-blood sense of potency to his forceful words about the severe punishment of those who come out "in open *rebellion* against God" and who remain and die "an *enemy* to God" (Mosiah 2:37–38). His position of strength contrasts dramatically with the fact that he worked with his own hands to serve his people so that they would not be heavily taxed (see Mosiah 2:14). His personal knowledge of things of the spirit, particularly through the visitation to him by an angel from God (see Mosiah 3:2), gives an uncommon depth of feeling and perspective to his words about humility and submissiveness (see Mosiah 3:19), about God's patience and love (see Mosiah 4:6, 11), and about humanity and the universal obligation to care for one another (see Mosiah 4:13–26).[17]

Benjamin's message combined the best of concerns for both poles in the typical dichotomies of life: the group and the individual, temporal affairs and spiritual matters, politics and theology, power and pleading, and recognizing both strengths and weaknesses. He spoke from a rich and wide spectrum of personal experience gained from his youth to his old age. Like the biblical Jacob had said in his blessing to his own son Benjamin, "[He] shall ravin as a wolf: in the morning he shall devour the prey, and at night he shall divide the spoil" (Genesis 49:27). King Benjamin similarly combined power with magnaminity.

Student of the Scriptures

Benjamin had custody of both the large and small plates of Nephi as well as the plates of brass, and he held these scriptures in high regard. He taught his sons "the language of his fathers, that thereby they might . . . know concerning the prophecies which had been spoken by the mouths of their fathers, which were delivered them by the hand of the Lord" (Mosiah 1:2). He "taught them concerning the records which were engraven on the plates of brass" (Mosiah 1:3) because he felt that if it had not been for the commandments and teachings on these plates, their people would have "suffered in ignorance" (Mosiah 1:3), would not have understood the mysteries of God (see Mosiah 1:5), would have ended up with incorrect traditions as the Lamanites did (see Mosiah 1:5), and would not have prospered in the land (see Mosiah 1:7). He told his sons to search the plates "diligently" (Mosiah 1:7) and reminded the people that they had been taught concerning the sacred records (see Mosiah 2:34) and were now accountable to live by their precepts. Benjamin's use of Deuteronomy 17:14–20 in Mosiah 2:11–14, his affinity toward the virtues of social justice required in the Pentateuch, and his awareness of other ancient Hebrew texts give evidence that Benjamin himself had indeed searched the plates of brass and knew the words of Moses and his Israelite predecessors.

Moreover, Benjamin knew and also referred to several concepts that were found on the small plates or were traditional in Nephite culture. One example is found in Mosiah 2:27–28, in which Benjamin says he had served the people "that [their] blood should not come upon [him]," and that he had called them together that he "might rid [his] garments of [their] blood . . . that [he] might go down in peace." Jacob expresses the same idea in 2 Nephi 9:44 ("I . . . am rid of your blood"), in Jacob 1:19 ("by laboring with our might their blood might not come upon our garments; otherwise their blood would come upon our garments, and we would not be found spotless at the last day"), and in Jacob 2:2 ("I . . . magnify mine office with soberness, and that I might rid my garments of your sins"). Another example appears in Mosiah 4:8 (see also Mosiah 3:17), in which Benjamin says "there is none other salvation save this which hath been spoken of," which seems to quote 2 Nephi 31:21: "this is the way; and there is none other way nor name given under heaven whereby man can be saved in the kingdom of God." Further examples include Mosiah 2:32 ("beware lest . . . ye list to obey the *evil spirit*") and Mosiah 4:14 ("the devil, who is the master of sin, or who is the *evil spirit* which hath been spoken of by our fathers"), which appear to draw on 2 Nephi 32:8 ("for the *evil spirit* teacheth not a man to pray"); and also Mosiah 2:41 ("they are blessed in all things, both temporal and spiritual") which may be quoting from 1 Nephi 22:3 ("pertaining to things both temporal and spiritual"). Independent but similar use by Benjamin and Abinadi of the ideas of rebelling against God (see Mosiah 2:37; 15:26; compare 1 Samuel 12:13–15; Isaiah 1:20), of dying in one's sins (see Mosiah 2:33; 15:26), and of being an enemy to God (see Mosiah 2:37–38; 3:19; 16:5) show that both of these prophets drew faithfully on "all that has been spoken by our fathers until now" (Mosiah 2:35; see 15:11).

Conservator

Having worked hard to unify his political and religious control, Benjamin took great care to see that this situation continued into the reign of his son. To his son Mosiah he passed the Liahona, the sword of Laban, and all the plates (see Mosiah 1:16). These were customary symbols of kingship among the Nephites, and they relate to the orb, scepter, and book of the law used as royal symbols in many civilizations.[18] He also put the entire population under covenant to obey "the commandments of my son, or the commandments of God which shall be delivered unto you by him" (Mosiah 2:31; see 5:5). To assure a smooth transition of power to his son, Benjamin crowned him while well enough to live three more years (see Mosiah 6:5). Benjamin and his son probably functioned during these three years as coregents in order to facilitate the transition of power in a manner similar to ancient Israelite politics, which is not an unprecedented technique.[19] To secure his son's position over the priests, Benjamin, as his last recorded official act, "appointed priests to teach the people" (Mosiah 6:3), thus carrying out his policies of consolidation and centralization to the end.

Linguist

The most challenging domestic task faced by Benjamin was probably that of unifying his two culturally diverse peoples, the Nephites and Mulekites. Cultural assimilation would have been slow and painful since serious language barriers existed between them and since their religious traditions had diverged widely over the years (see Omni 1:17). One of the main projects Benjamin undertook in an attempt to bring these two populations together was to teach the Nephite language to the Mulekites, for Benjamin knew the importance of words. His father Mosiah had led the Nephites out of the land of Nephi, freeing them from the 250-year period of apparent cultural depression and literary inactivity—years that can almost be called a Dark Age, as reflected in the sparse books of Jarom and Omni. By witnessing what had happened to the Mulekites, who had not preserved their language and records, Benjamin could see in his youth how vulnerable his own people were to the same problem. He probably sensed how perilously close the Nephites had come to suffering a similar fate, judging by the marginal attention they had recently given to adding to their own sacred records kept on the small plates.

When he arrived in the city of Zarahemla, Mosiah$_1$ found that the teaching of language was needed as a first order of business. The Mulekites' language had become corrupted to such a great extent that communication was impossible (see Omni 1:17), and therefore "Mosiah caused that they should be taught in his language" (Omni 1:18). During this period of social formation in the city of Zarahemla, Benjamin would have been an impressionable young leader, no doubt acutely aware of these problems and intimately involved in the affairs of his father's kingdom, perhaps even as a high administrator instructing the people of Zarahemla in the Nephite language. This was not an insignificant chore or one unbecoming of a prince or priest. Writing was a powerful and closely cherished art in ancient Egypt; it was also of such importance among the Lamanites that the king of the Lamanites once engaged the former priests of Noah to teach his people the language of Nephi (see Mosiah 24:4). Perhaps Benjamin taught or supervised several of the scribes who later served in copying his speech for distribution to his people on his son's coronation day.

Benjamin's concerns about language extended beyond public education and official record keeping. The record gives Benjamin particular credit—more than any other Nephite leader—for having taught his three sons "all the language of his fathers, that thereby they might become men of understanding" (Mosiah 1:2). He taught them Hebrew, the language of his fathers, as well as Egyptian, which he himself knew (see Mosiah 1:4). One can assume that he knew and taught them not only vocabulary words, but also grammar, syntax, style, form, composition, and literary appreciation, for he taught them "*all* the language of his fathers."

Builder

One also assumes that during the reign of Benjamin's father the Nephites constructed or remodeled a temple in Zarahemla, probably similar to the one they had left in the city of Nephi, and that Benjamin was involved to some extent in its construction.[20] Benjamin's speech was delivered from that temple, whose immediate precincts the population had outgrown during Benjamin's long reign. The sentiments of love, devotion, sacrifice, and homeland must have filled Benjamin's heart as he said farewell to the place he had worked for and occupied all his life.

Parent

Of King Benjamin's three sons, the eldest, Mosiah, was born in 154 B.C., probably not many years after Benjamin became king, and died at the age of sixty-three in 91 B.C. (see Mosiah 29:46). We know nothing about Helorum and Helaman, Benjamin's two other sons, except that the name Helaman was later given by Alma$_2$ to his eldest son, the great prophet-warrior who led the Ammonite youths in battle. Alma$_2$ could have known and must have admired this Helaman, the son of Benjamin, who would have been a contemporary of Alma's father and also the uncle of the four sons of Mosiah$_2$ with whom Alma$_2$ was a very close friend. Benjamin took personal responsibility for the education of his sons and was a good father. He was also concerned about the children of his kingdom and exhorted parents to teach their children to live righteously (see Mosiah 4:15).

Classicist

The fact that Benjamin was concerned enough to teach his sons these ancient languages at a time when the spoken Nephite language had probably already begun to change shows Benjamin's great interest in classicism. Such a desire to perpetuate and rejuvenate an understanding of the classics typifies many renaissance men who, like Benjamin, lived at a time in their civilization's history when a reawakening and cultural reestablishment was taking place. Benjamin was deeply committed to seeing that the language and literature left behind by the prophets of Israel remained accessible to his posterity.

Given the fact that Benjamin was known to his people and to his sons as a great teacher of languages and literature, it would be unthinkable for him to deliver the greatest speech of his life at the coronation of his son in anything less than an eloquent style and exquisite form. Indeed, his speech shows clear signs of being carefully crafted and artistically composed.[21] Benjamin's interest in classicism may also explain why he crowned his son king in such a solemn and traditional manner. His ceremony followed the traditional patterns of coronation in ancient Israel,[22] and it was evidently scheduled and held at the highest and holiest festival time of the year under the law of Moses—the time when kings were traditionally installed and temples dedicated.

Legalist

Benjamin's intense interest in preserving, teaching, and following the traditional norms of ancient Israel is also reflected in the large number of legal terms or topics found in his speech. In Benjamin's role as a king of Israelites, one of his duties was to assure that justice was found among his people. Traditionally, kings were responsible for the overall administration of justice in their lands; consider, for example, King Jehoshaphat's legal leadership (see 2 Chronicles 19:8–11) or King Hammarubi's legal system in Mesopotamia.

In a few respects, it appears that Benjamin instigated new legal practices among his people. The fact that he mentioned his prohibition against imprisonment and slavery at the top of the list of the legal rules that he enforced during his regime suggests that he was the first to enact or emphasize

these two rules: "Neither have *I* suffered that ye should be
confined in dungeons, nor that ye should make slaves one
of another" (Mosiah 2:13). The use of dungeons or prisons
was apparently tolerated in Israel (see Jeremiah 37:15;
1 Nephi 7:14), generally in the land of Nephi (see Mosiah
17:5), in the land of Ammonihah (see Alma 14:18, 23), and
among the Lamanites (see Helaman 5:21); but by special
dispensation, the use of prisons was not allowed in Zarahemla under King Benjamin or in other lands by special
royal decrees (see Alma 23:2). Likewise, although slavery
was possible under the law of Moses, provided the slave
was given the opportunity to go free after six years (see
Exodus 21:2–6), Benjamin prohibited slavery, presumably
including involuntary debt servitude, compulsory enslave-
ment of prisoners of war, and all other forms of bondage. If
one looks for a social explanation for Benjamin's emphasis
on these two provisions, the answer is probably to be found
in Benjamin's need to maintain equality and social justice
between the Nephites and the Mulekites. The tendency on
the part of the ruling Nephites would have been to subju-
gate and confine the less-educated Mulekites; likewise, the
rich would have wanted to make their poor debtors serve as
slaves or bond servants. Obviously, Benjamin was opposed
to such developments on theological as well as social
grounds.

Other legal or administrative subjects mentioned by
Benjamin include murder, plundering, stealing, adultery,
and wickedness (see Mosiah 2:13); taxation (see Mosiah
2:14); witnesses (see Mosiah 2:14); the covenant formula
from the law of Deuteronomy (see Mosiah 2:31); contentions, which would include lawsuits (see Mosiah 2:32);
cursing (see Mosiah 2:33); ignorant sin (see Mosiah 3:11);
the legal innocence of little children (see Mosiah 3:21); the
bright testimony of judgment (see Mosiah 3:24); parental

duties to teach their children (see Mosiah 4:15; compare Deuteronomy 4); laws regarding the poor (see Mosiah 4:22–26); and borrowing and returning borrowed property (see Mosiah 4:28). It appears significant that Benjamin required the borrower to return the very object that he borrowed; otherwise disputes could arise about the valuation or acceptability of substitute property tendered in return.

In addition, Benjamin drew on legal analogies when he described the nature and consequences of the covenant (or contract) that his people entered into with the Lord: adoption, or becoming sons and daughters (see Mosiah 5:7); banishment, or being blotted out (see Mosiah 5:11–14); and sealing, or being marked with a seal (see Mosiah 5:15). The legal effects of sealing a document or container with a wax or clay seal in antiquity was to attest to the integrity and purity of the enclosed contents and to certify the ownership of the document or the sealed vessel. With similar force and effect, Benjamin blessed his people to the end that God would seal them his.

Founding Father

The legacy left by Benjamin in Nephite thought and culture combines a number of traditional elements with a significant degree of innovation. His major contribution in this area seems to have been to solidify the theology and culture of his people, much as he had consolidated the political power and territory in the land of Zarahemla. In so doing, he set the stage for the next 150 years of Nephite experience.

Judging from the prominence given to Benjamin by Mormon, it seems that Benjamin stood at the head of a great political and cultural reawakening in Nephite civilization. He lived at the beginning of a renaissance in Nephite culture that blossomed in the latter part of the second and the

early part of the first centuries B.C. At this time one sees
great creative forces at work among the Nephites, not only
in literature, but also in politics, theology, law, calendar,
weights and measures, and military technology. For example, great literary compositions were produced during
this period not only by Benjamin but also by Alma₂ and
Amulek. The major political reform in Nephite history, that
of shifting from a kingship to the chief judgeship (see
Mosiah 29:44), came thirty years after Benjamin's death (see
Mosiah 29:46). Theologically, the baptizing church that was
established in Zarahemla by Alma₁ became very influential
during this period, developing clearer doctrines concerning
God, the atonement, faith, and personal conversion. New
legislation was introduced regarding the judicial system,[23]
and the Nephite weights and measures were standardized
(see Alma 11:4–19). A new system for counting the years of
the judges was adopted, and the Nephites won battles
aided by improved breastplates and shields never mentioned earlier in the Book of Mormon. Even the Zoramites
did not yet have this equipment (see Alma 43:21) but would
soon copy it (see Alma 49:6). The solid cultural foundation
laid by King Benjamin made it possible for Nephite civilization to flourish during the three or four generations that followed his reign.[24]

A Lasting Legacy of Authoritative Words and Phrases

Benjamin's words were specifically remembered and
used by his people for years after. For instance, shortly after
his death, Benjamin's son Mosiah sent Ammon and fifteen
other emissaries from Zarahemla to the land of Nephi (see
Mosiah 7:1–6). There they found King Limhi and his people
in bondage to the Lamanites. After the sixteen messengers
were properly identified (see Mosiah 7:13–14), Limhi gath-

ered all his people together at the local temple, where he spoke of bondage and deliverance (see Mosiah 7:17–33). After that, Ammon "rehearsed unto them the last words which king Benjamin had taught them, and explained them to the people of king Limhi, so that they might understand all the words which he spake" (Mosiah 8:3). Soon thereafter,[25] the people of Limhi "entered into a covenant with God to serve him and keep his commandments" (Mosiah 21:31). Thus it appears that Limhi's people not only heard and understood Benjamin's words, but also entered into the covenant "to do [God's] will, and to be obedient to his commandments" (Mosiah 5:5), as Benjamin had desired of his people at the conclusion of his own speech.

An important political role was given to Benjamin's words in this distant assembly. Ammon's mission had a primary political objective—to learn the fate of Zeniff's colony and, apparently, to seek reunification with them. Ammon went prepared with the words of King Benjamin—the new document of Nephite polity. Once the people of Limhi had entered into the same covenant as had the people of Benjamin, the people of Limhi could be numbered again for political purposes among the Nephites. Conclusive evidence that Ammon's authority and use of Benjamin's words embraced political—but not priestly—functions is found in the fact that he had authority to cause the people to enter into the covenant of Mosiah 5:5 to obey the king, but lacked authority to baptize, purify, or establish a religious community (see Mosiah 21:33). Benjamin's words immediately provided authoritative language for political reunification even beyond the borders of Zarahemla.

Although Benjamin's foundational words soon seemed obscure to some young people (see Mosiah 26:1), his text remained important to Nephite religious and civic life for more than a century. Consider the following examples:

In establishing the church of God in the first years of the reign of judges, Alma₂ implemented many of the religious and social policies articulated by Benjamin. Alma required that all those who "had taken upon them the name of Christ" (Alma 1:19; compare Mosiah 5:9) should "impart of their substance" to the poor and the needy, "every man according to that which he had" (Alma 1:27; compare Mosiah 4:26); that no church leader should "[esteem] himself above his hearers" (Alma 1:26; compare Mosiah 2:26); that the names of all hardened transgressors "were blotted out" (Alma 1:24; compare Mosiah 5:11); that "every man receiveth wages of him whom he listeth to obey" (Alma 3:27; compare Mosiah 2:32); that all should strive to retain "a remission of their sins" (Alma 4:14; compare Mosiah 4:12), should have "experienced this mighty change in [their] hearts" (Alma 5:14; compare Mosiah 5:2); and that the people should be "humble, and . . . submissive and gentle; easy to be entreated; full of patience and long-suffering; being temperate in all things; being diligent in keeping the commandments" (Alma 7:23; compare Mosiah 3:19; 2:20). Speaking to the people in Ammonihah, Alma exhorted them to become "humble, meek, submissive, patient, full of love and all long-suffering" (Alma 13:28), essentially restating Mosiah 3:19. No one in the Nephite culture who was familiar with King Benjamin's speech would easily miss Alma's allusions to the order established by Benjamin. No doubt Alma was following the covenant pattern established by his father Alma at the waters of Mormon (see Mosiah 18), but the specific terminology that Alma₂ used around 90 B.C. in implementing that ecclesiastical order was Benjamin's.

Benjamin's founding legacy also endured in a Nephite legal formula that persisted to the end of Nephite civilization. When Benjamin gave his accounting of how he had faithfully discharged his governmental duties, he averred that he had not allowed his people to "*murder*, or *plunder*, or *steal*, or commit *adultery* . . . or *any manner of wickedness*" (Mosiah 2:13). This precise list of five public law requirements is found six other times in the Book of Mormon, and in every case this set measures the extent to which kings and rulers had discharged their legal duty of maintaining the public order. First, in Alma 23:3, the king of the Lamanites issued a proclamation that his people "ought not to *murder*, nor to *plunder*, nor to *steal*, nor to commit *adultery*, nor to commit *any manner of wickedness*." Benjamin's precise words in this regard were apparently taught to the Lamanite king by the four missionary sons of Mosiah, who, we can be sure, intimately knew the details of their grandfather's speech. Second, in Alma 30:10, Alma affirmed that he had carried out his public duties by punishing all those who "murdered, . . . robbed, . . . stole, . . . committed adultery, . . . yea for all this wickedness they were punished." Third, in relinquishing the kingship, Mosiah did likewise in Mosiah 29:14–15, 36. In the remaining three texts, the wickedness of the Gadianton rulers in Zarahemla and the corruption of the Jaredite king Akish were judged harshly by Nephi and Moroni because they sought to "murder, and plunder, and steal, and commit whoredoms and all manner of wickedness, contrary to the laws of their country and also the laws of their God" (Helaman 6:23; see 7:21; Ether 8:16). Benjamin's list appears in each of these scriptures, modified only slightly as the exigencies of the individual circumstances over time dictated.[26]

About 30 B.C. Helaman, the son of Helaman, exhorted his sons Nephi and Lehi to "remember, remember, my sons, the words which king Benjamin spake unto his people" (Helaman 5:9; compare Mosiah 3:18–19). Helaman taught his sons Nephi and Lehi the words of King Benjamin's speech, as seen in Helaman 5:9: "Yea, remember that there is no other way nor means whereby man can be saved, only through the atoning blood of Jesus Christ, who shall come; yea, remember that he cometh to redeem the world." Nephi also echoed Benjamin in Helaman 8:25 when he said, "ye have rejected the truth, and rebelled against your holy God."

The distinctive name spoken by the angel to Benjamin identified the coming Messiah as "Jesus Christ, the Son of God, the Father of heaven and of earth, the Creator of all things from the beginning" (Mosiah 3:8). Significantly, these exact words were used by Samuel the Lamanite at the center of his prophetic judgment speech, given from the walls of the city of Zarahemla in 6 B.C., 116 years after Benjamin's speech. Samuel declared that his intent was to preach "that ye might know of the coming of *Jesus Christ, the Son of God, the Father of heaven and of earth, the Creator of all things from the beginning,"* and believe on his name (Helaman 14:12). Although Samuel did not mention the name of Benjamin, as did Helaman, this second formulaic use of words from Benjamin's speech provides strong evidence that these sacred words, introduced by Benjamin into the Nephite religious idiom, probably became standard confessional language among the believing generations that succeeded him. It is quite conceivable that Nephi and Lehi followed the admonition of their father not only by remembering but also by teaching the words of Benjamin to their Lamanite converts, from whose ranks Samuel the Lamanite emerged. On hearing these most sacred words repeated by Samuel, some of the Nephites in Zarahemla must have been struck to the core, recognizing them as the very words King Benjamin had spoken years before in the same city.

Other texts in the Book of Mormon quote or paraphrase Benjamin, including 3 Nephi 6:18, which recalls Benjamin's speech in the phrases "sin ignorantly," and "wilfully rebel against God" (Mosiah 3:11, 12). In Mormon 7:7, such phrases as "sing ceaseless praises with the choirs above" and "a state of happiness which hath no end" again reflect Benjamin's lasting influence (see Mosiah 2:28, 41). Further similarities, such as those between Mosiah 5 and the Nephite sacramental covenant at the temple in 3 Nephi 18, also show how the words and phrases of Benjamin's speech remained useful, meaningful, and normative for years to come.[27] Clearly Benjamin's words were well-known to many people long after his speech was delivered. It remained a controlling, authoritative text—a primary scripture that the Nephites looked back on as a foundation of their faith. His words became the moral and political standard for many generations to come.

Benjamin's words remained the standard of Nephite faith and government for so many years for numerous reasons. He was a marvelously inspired man and the paragon of a benevolent monarch. The fact that Benjamin had distributed a written copy of his speech to all his people assured that his words would remain memorable and enduring. His people would have treasured these copies as precious memorabilia from the day they themselves were present at the coronation of King Mosiah. Since many people would have read and used this text for years to come, it is not surprising, as has been shown, that specific words spoken by Benjamin continued to surface significantly in several Nephite texts as time went by. Benjamin was succeeded as the Nephite leader for over 300 years by strong followers: first by his son Mosiah, who deeply admired his father, and then by Alma$_2$, who was the close friend of Benjamin's four grandsons. Alma's posterity remained in control of the Nephite government and church, succeeding from father to son for many years: Alma$_2$, Helaman, Helaman, Nephi, Nephi, Nephi, Amos, Amos, and his brother Ammaron, who finally hid up the records (see 4 Nephi 1:48). These rulers kept the traditions of their dynasty—including those established by Benjamin—in memory and in effect.

A Delicate Union

Benjamin's influence throughout Nephite history was impressive, but under the circumstances it was not indelible. The key function achieved by Benjamin's speech was to bring the entire population—both Nephites and Mulekites—under a single covenant of loyalty to God and to Mosiah, the new king. Benjamin counts both "the people of Zarahemla, and the people of Mosiah" among his people (Mosiah 1:10), and the record emphasizes that all of them entered into the covenant (see Mosiah 1:10–15; 6:2). This political and religious achievement appears to have been very successful at first, but it did not last. While the Mulekites had initially welcomed the arrival of the Nephites in Zarahemla (at least according to the Nephite version of that encounter, recorded in Omni 1:14), it is doubtful that the entire Mulekite population remained content under Nephite rule for long. Human experience says that it would have been extraordinary for an indigenous population to have relinquished control over its own city, to have forgotten all its loyalties to its own king, and to have lost its own cultural identity without some reluctance and eventual resistance. Indeed, several hints and clues in the Book of Mormon indicate that these two groups of people, though politically united for a while under the Nephite king (see Omni 1:19), did not merge into a homogeneous population. In the ensuing years, several political and religious conflicts were led by men *within* the land of Zarahemla who were opposed to the Nephite regime. Some were connected with the order of Nehor, and the names of other dissenters appear to have Mulekite or Jaredite origins (for example, Zerahemnah, Amlici, Nehor, and Korihor). It is tempting, therefore, to conclude that some of the political turmoil and civil wars that arose in the land of Zarahemla in the first century B.C. were instigated by disgruntled Mulekites who had grown weary of Nephite rule. These people, who were more numerous than the Nephites (see Mosiah 25:2), would have naturally sought more of a political role in the society as they became educated about their own royal heritage, which ran back to the Davidic kings of Jerusalem.

These conditions are consistent with the fact that around 90 B.C. a formidable subgroup in Zarahemla began asserting a claim to kingship (see Alma 2). Such a claim would have been most persuasive if it were made or supported by the surviving descendants of King Zarahemla, who himself could trace his legitimacy back to King Zedekiah and to the royal house of David as a recipient of the blessings of Judah. The Nephites, perhaps in part anticipating such a claim, abandoned the institution of kingship altogether (see Mosiah 29) and selected Alma$_2$ as chief judge. Perhaps his attractiveness as a leader was enhanced by the fact that his lineage was not of Mosiah or Mulek and that his family had not been in the city of Zarahemla during most of the second century B.C. His appointment may have been part of an attempt to work out a politically acceptable compromise. Undoubtedly, many Mulekites remained loyal to Benjamin's heritage, just as some of the Nephites defected from it. The lines were not rigid between these populations, and the ideal of a united people was one the Nephites never forgot.

Thus to Benjamin can be attributed many things: the monumental achievements of protecting and preserving the fledgling colony of Nephites in Zarahemla, unifying diverse populations for several generations, keeping the Nephites from fragmenting into heretical groups, establishing a benevolent but strongly centralized Nephite monarchy, and preserving traditions of literature, culture, and covenant. He combined the best of tradition and personal experience, scripture and vision, nation and individual, and prophet and king. His roles and achievements reflect the underlying character of a man who was long remembered as "a just man before the Lord" (Omni 1:25) and as a hard worker who labored "with all the might of his body and the faculty of his whole soul" to serve his people (Words of Mormon 1:18). Everything known about King Benjamin gives the distinct impression that he was a very Christlike man, whose life was characterized dominantly by humility, love, and service. His many sterling traits of character[28] were amplified as he used them to teach the gospel of Jesus Christ. He was a true father to his people—the father of one of the most flourishing periods in Nephite civilization.

Notes

1. Roland de Vaux, *Ancient Israel* (New York: McGraw-Hill, 1965), 1:108. De Vaux suggests, for example, that Shallum was the birth name of King Joachaz; that Azarias was the given name of Ozias; and Elhanan, that of David. De Vaux discusses other examples of coronation names being given in ancient Israel in connection with vassalage and as a regular royal practice in Egypt and Mesopotamia.

2. The sixth-century B.C. Nephite practice of calling the kings "second Nephi, third Nephi, and so forth" (Jacob 1:11) either did not survive or lost enough of its importance by the second century B.C. that no record of its continuing use was made. It is possible, of course, that Nephite kings bore several titles, one of which was always the name of Nephi. In Egypt, for example, each king had five titles or names (de Vaux, *Ancient Israel*, 1:107), and in a similar fashion multiple names could have been given to the Nephite kings.

3. Dennis R. Thompson, "The Strategic Significance of the Central Benjamin Plateau," Near Eastern Studies Student Symposium, Brigham Young University, 28 March 1987, 10 pp., available at FARMS.

4. Mosiah 25:2 provides evidence that these people kept their social and familial identities separate, at least to some extent, even after Benjamin's reign. See John L. Sorenson, "The Mulekites," *BYU Studies* 30/3 (1990): 6–22; and *An Ancient American Setting for the Book of Mormon* (Salt Lake City: Deseret Book and FARMS, 1985), 156.

5. Discussed further in John W. Welch, "Longevity of Book of Mormon People and the 'Age of Man,'" *Journal of Collegium Aesculapium* 3 (1985): 35–45, esp. 37–38.

6. Ibid.

7. See ibid., 45 n. 16. See also the Jewish traditions that report the life of an early judge in Israel named Kenaz, whose farewell assembly has much in common with Benjamin's (discussed below), and who reportedly ruled in Israel for 57 years. James H. Charlesworth, *Old Testament Pseudepigrapha* (Garden City: Doubleday, 1985), 2:341.

8. For a discussion of the distances and directions involved, see Sorenson, *Ancient American Setting*, 8–12.

9. See generally, John W. Welch, "Why Study Warfare in the Book of Mormon?" in *Warfare in the Book of Mormon*, ed. Stephen D. Ricks and William J. Hamblin (Salt Lake City: Deseret Book and FARMS, 1990), 6.

10. As discussed further in Welch, "Longevity of Book of Mormon People," 38–39.

11. Welch, "Why Study Warfare in the Book of Mormon?" 6–7.

12. King Zeniff fought despite his old age (see Mosiah 10:10); later, Alma as high priest and chief judge personally did battle with Amlici (Alma 2:29–31) and with the king of the Lamanites (see Alma 2:32).

13. Sorenson, *Ancient American Setting*, 157.

14. See James E. Smith, "How Many Nephites? The Book of Mormon at the Bar of Demography" in *Book of Mormon Authorship Revisited: The Evidence of Ancient Origins*, ed. Noel B. Reynolds

(Provo, Utah: FARMS, 1997), 255–93; see also John L. Sorenson's response to "I have heard that the sizes of the Nephite and Lamanite populations indicated in the Book of Mormon do not make sense. What do we know about their numbers?" I Have a Question, *Ensign* (September 1992): 27–28.

15. E. W. Heaton, *The Hebrew Kingdoms* (Oxford: Oxford University Press, 1968), esp. 86, 232–36. King Ahab, for example, consulted about four hundred prophets (see 1 Kings 22:1–40). These holy men were "institutional prophets" or "professional consultants" who served the ancient Israelite community in many ways. Different versions of this institution of prophecy were also known in Phoenicia (see 2 Kings 10:19) and at Mari; see ibid., 236; John F. Craghan, "Mari and Its Prophets," *Biblical Theology Bulletin* 5 (1975): 32–55; and sources cited in Paul Y. Hoskisson, "The Deities and Cult Terms in Mari: An Analysis of the Textual Evidence" (Ph.D. diss., Brandeis University, 1984).

16. See "Prophecy among the Maya," in *Reexploring the Book of Mormon*, ed. John W. Welch (Salt Lake City: Deseret Book and FARMS, 1992), 263–65.

17. See Neal A. Maxwell, "King Benjamin's Sermon: A Manual for Discipleship," in this volume.

18. Discussed further in Gordon Thomasson, "Mosiah: The Complex Symbolism and the Symbolic Complex of Kingship in the Book of Mormon," *JBMS* 2/1 (1993): 21–38.

19. Unlike the usual practice among European royalty, Egyptian and Assyrian kings apparently took their eldest son and successor "as a partner in the government during his lifetime." De Vaux, *Ancient Israel*, 1:101. Some Israelite kings seem to have done likewise. Solomon and Jotham both became king while their fathers were still alive (see 1 Kings 1:32–40; 2 Kings 15:5).

20. See John W. Welch, "The Temple in the Book of Mormon: The Temples at the Cities of Nephi, Zarahemla, and Bountiful," in *Temples of the Ancient World*, ed. Donald W. Parry (Salt Lake City: Deseret Book and FARMS, 1994), 348–49; and "Kingship and Temples in 2 Nephi 5–10," in *Reexploring the Book of Mormon*, 66–68.

21. Discussed further in John W. Welch, "Parallelism and Chiasmus in Benjamin's Speech," in this volume.

22. Compare de Vaux, *Ancient Israel*, 1:100–114; see also Stephen D. Ricks, "Kingship, Coronation, and Covenant in Mosiah 1–6," in this volume.

23. See "The Law of Mosiah," in *Reexploring the Book of Mormon*, 158–61.

24. This cultural wave crested and fell as the civilization was exhausted by the prolonged wars from 74 to 60 B.C. (see Alma 43–62), ending shortly before the deaths of Helaman in 57 B.C. (see Alma 62:52), of Captain Moroni in 56 B.C. (see Alma 63:3), and of Shiblon in 53 B.C. (see Alma 63:10), which abruptly deprived the Nephites of the core members of a generation of leaders.

25. Mosiah 8:4 does not say whether Limhi's people entered into the covenant before he "dismissed the multitude, and caused that they should return every one unto his own house," but it appears that they did so for two reasons: First, the same phrase describes how Benjamin "dismissed the multitude, [so] they returned, every one, according to their families, to their own houses" (Mosiah 6:3), immediately after his covenant-making and name-taking ceremony was completed; thus it seems likely that the identical formula is used in Mosiah 8:4 as a summary statement indicating that all the same covenants had been concluded in Limhi's case as well. Second, Mosiah 21:30–31 reports that Ammon and the people declared a time of mourning for those who had been lost; this mourning would likely have begun the next day. Whenever it began, by that time the people had already "entered into a covenant with God to serve him and keep his commandments" (Mosiah 21:31), and these words appear to describe the same covenant required by Benjamin's speech as it was delivered by Ammon to King Limhi's people.

26. Discussed further in John W. Welch, "Series of Laws in the Book of Mormon" (Provo, Utah: FARMS, 1987).

27. For further information, see John W. Welch, "Benjamin's Covenant as a Precursor of the Sacrament Prayers," in this volume.

28. Drawing from specific indications within his speech, one may conclude that, in his conduct toward his fellow beings, Benjamin's salient character traits included the following: he did not seek glory or honor; was submissive; was generous, committed

to civic justice in his kingdom, and promoted social justice for the poor; was inclusive, leaving no one out; was kind, gentle, sympathetic, compassionate, and concerned; listened to others and cared about their response; and was an understanding, attentive, and devoted parent. When his people fell down in fear, he picked them up with words of love and kindness.

Concerning his individual or personal traits, the record shows him as a man who desired above all to have a clear conscience and to be free from guilt before God; who was orderly and peace loving, dynamic, a doer, faithful, firm, wise, dedicated, attentive to personal duty, and obedient; and who was capable of experiencing deep happiness and expressing great joy.

As a writer and speaker, his speech further reflects the personality of a man who must have consistently been quite purposeful, logical, frank, clear, deliberate, determined, sure-minded, gentle-toned, attentive to detail, skillful, insightful, and intelligent. At the same time, he was very knowledgeable of the past, deeply appreciative of present traditions, and acutely mindful of future eventualities, both in this life and in the world to come.

I am grateful to my fall 1997 Honors Book of Mormon students, whose papers explored the personality traits of King Benjamin.

CHAPTER 3

BENJAMIN'S SPEECH: A MASTERFUL ORATION

John W. Welch

As a work of sacred literature and masterful oratory, Benjamin's speech deserves deep respect. After all that has been said about this speech over the years, it still invites further reflection and comment. Many readers have intuitively sensed the profundity of its message. Elder Bruce R. McConkie found that it contained "what well may be the greatest sermon ever delivered on the atonement of Christ the Lord."[1] Milton R. Hunter marveled at King Benjamin, observing that "perhaps no other teacher except the Master has given a more beautiful, humble sermon."[2] King Benjamin is frequently quoted in Latter-day Saint general conferences[3] —the April 1996 conference, for example, was no exception: Benjamin was quoted extensively by Elder Neal A. Maxwell in his talk on children and becoming childlike,[4] by Sister Susan Warner on the spiritual functions of remembering,[5] and by others.

In the previous chapter we have focused on Benjamin as a historical personality and his place in Nephite history. In this chapter, we turn our attention to the literary qualities of the speech itself. How does Benjamin's speech function as oratory? Does it have a deep aesthetic order? How does it compare with other texts of its kind? What are some of its unique or salient characteristics? How do we account for the popularity of this speech? What makes it so great? Such questions can be answered by pointing to twelve of the many features that make Benjamin's speech a masterful oration. Several of the characteristics introduced in this overview will be examined in greater detail in subsequent chapters.

1. An Embodiment of the Spirit of an Age

A great oration captures and distills the spirit of an age. Historically, significant literature often includes speeches, because these revealing discourses embody the essence of the particular culture. "The history of Britain," it is said, "is told in [its] speeches."[6] Under this criteron, Benjamin's speech qualifies as a major monument in its own culture and time. Delivered about 124 B.C., it was one of the most important and influential speeches ever given in Nephite history, being treasured by righteous Nephites for years thereafter and having a lasting impact on Nephite civilization.

In the histories of most cultures, certain speeches stand out as particularly stirring orations that distill, shape, and propel the spirit of their critical times. Benjamin's was such a speech. In a historical sense, it ranks with Lincoln's Gettysburg Address, Churchill's wartime speeches, Kennedy's inaugural address, Pericles' ancient funeral oration in Athens, and Martin Luther King's verbal shaping of a modern dream. Famous speeches like these are said to "embody and utter, not merely the individual genius and character of the speaker, but a national consciousness—a national era, a mood, a hope . . . —in which you listen to the spoken history of the time."[7] Such speeches depict "the crises and cruxes of history as seen from the [speaker's] platform and interpreted to a [timeless] audience."[8] Benjamin's speech similarly distills the eternal hopes and fears of a nation. It stands not only at a crucial turning point in Nephite history in the second century B.C., but it also speaks to generations down through the ages and into eternity.

No doubt Benjamin faced several crises during his lifetime. As has been discussed above, one of his most urgent needs was to promote unity among his people.[9] The first and last things said in reference to Benjamin in the Book of Mormon are about contentions. Judging by Benjamin's comments to the rich and the poor, class stratification was a problem that had developed among these people. To strengthen his community, Benjamin's first covenantal stipulation for the people was that parents should teach the youth that they should "not have a mind to injure one another, but to live peaceably" one with another (Mosiah 4:13).

Benjamin would have learned the importance of social unity firsthand. When establishing themselves in the land of Zarahemla, Benjamin and his father Mosiah must have faced many challenges. Unifying two groups of people who spoke different languages and had developed different religious and cultural practices would have been no simple task, especially since the indigenous Mulekite population outnumbered the people of Nephi. Benjamin melded together a pluralistic polity that was to thrive for generations. Only a leadership grounded firmly in the principles taught by Benjamin could have survived the next 150 years of rebellions, dissensions, wars, persecutions, reforms, factions, rameumptoms, robbers, and various comings and goings to preserve a remnant of a righteous people who eventually received the resurrected Christ. Benjamin's speech and the ideas that it embodied became a crucial force[10] in promoting unity and harmony at an important juncture in the history of the Nephites when every thread holding their world together threatened to unravel.

It appears that one of Benjamin's most creative political moves was to promote and solidly establish a strong element of popular egalitarianism in Nephite society. He proudly reported that he had not allowed any of his people in the land of Zarahemla to "make slaves one of another" (Mosiah 2:13). If we assume that prior Nephite and Mulekite practices followed the normal (if not necessary) realities and standard legal rules used in most ancient societies that were economically dependent on some form of slavery or involuntary debt servitude (compare Exodus 21:2–11; Leviticus 25:25–55; Deuteronomy 15:1–6), then we must conclude that Benjamin's abolition of slavery constituted a major innovation in Nephite political history. Only an effective and powerful leader could have made such a change that would have favored the populist poor and probably unsettled members of the upper class.

Moreover, in a world in which a new coronation name was typically given exclusively to the ascending monarch, it is politically significant that Benjamin decided to give the new name revealed at his son's coronation to every man, woman, and child in the crowd. Benjamin recognized that this move was unique—even remarkably daring. By giving the people a name, he said that they would thereby "be distinguished above all the people which the Lord God hath brought out of the land of Jerusalem" (Mosiah 1:11). Not only was the new name, found in Mosiah 3:8, uniquely and distinctively given for these particular people and for this specific occasion, but, even more importantly, this designation was given to the *people*, not just to the new king. In traditional Israelite coronations only the king entered into the covenant with God and thereby became his son (see Psalm

2:7). In Benjamin's kingdom, however, every person was allowed to enter into a covenant in connection with Mosiah's coronation (see Mosiah 5:1–5), and thereby they all became God's "sons, and his daughters" (Mosiah 5:7). Modern readers may have a hard time appreciating how expansive and egalitarian these simple, symbolic gestures must have seemed in the minds of the people who were allowed to receive these privileges from Benjamin. Perhaps openly sharing these previously restricted elements, along with publicly disclosing sacred revelations that would normally have been retained among the prophetic elite, contributed to the overwhelming, united reaction of the people who were deeply moved on this occasion by spiritual feelings of love and appreciation for their old and new kings. If these moves by Benjamin were as politically bold as they appear to have been, then Benjamin's recognition of the people in these ways would have given enormous impetus to democratization and popularization of Nephite government and society. Perhaps the ultimate elimination of kingship with the subsequent inauguration of the reign of the judges, which occurs at the end of the book of Mosiah, was already a political inevitability embedded in the spirit of this Nephite age and propelled by the expansive steps taken in Benjamin's oration at the opening of the book of Mosiah. Although we cannot document all this reconstruction and analysis as a historical certainty, the crux of these points can definitely be seen as a rhetorical reality in the political fabric of the book of Mosiah.

Benjamin's speech also addressed a significant theological crux: the melding of the Israelite heritage with the messianic expectation in Christ. Benjamin's speech describes a society in transition from its ancient Israelite heritage to its full Christian destiny. Many aspects of his speech capture the essence of the past and at the same time redirect his people's attention toward the coming Christ.[11] Benjamin did not repudiate his Mosaic heritage but infused it with a knowledge of Christ.[12] For example, Benjamin's theology was rooted in the Deuteronomic formula of keeping the commandments and prospering in the land according to the law of Moses. Affirming the righteousness of his own administration, Benjamin turned to Deuteronomy 17:14–20—the Paragraph of the King. In certifying that he had spent his days in the service of his people and had "not sought gold nor silver nor any manner of riches" (Mosiah 2:12), Benjamin drew straight from the Deuteronomy text, which limited the power of Israelite kings to multiply unto themselves gold, silver, or horses. Likewise, Benjamin's humanitarian ethics regarding the poor cannot be properly understood apart from the underlying principles of the Hebrew scriptures, for which it is axiomatic that everything belongs to God, that orphans and widows must be helped, that charity is a duty and not an optional kindness, and that the dignity of the poor must be preserved. Deuteronomy 15 reads: "There shall be no poor among you" (15:4) and "thou shalt not harden thine heart, nor shut thine hand from thy poor brother" (15:7). Benjamin not only assumed but transformed these Old Testament principles in light of his knowledge of the power of the atonement of Jesus Christ; thus he captured the essence of the old and infused it with the outlook of a new age.

The enduring value of Benjamin's classic speech in Nephite history can be confirmed in many ways by internal textual analysis of subsequent texts in the Book of Mormon that remember and draw on his words. Benjamin's influence on other Book of Mormon writers also serves as a subtle check on its historicity; after all, one would expect to hear echoes of this significant speech in later Book of Mormon language. Indeed, as has been shown in the preceding chapter, Benjamin's words were expressly quoted in the Nephite record for many generations to come. The fact that each family was given a copy of this speech must have facilitated its far-reaching impact. Shortly after Benjamin's death, his son Mosiah sent Ammon and fifteen other emissaries to the land of Nephi. When they found Limhi and his people, Ammon "rehearsed unto them the last words which king Benjamin had taught" (Mosiah 8:3), and the people of Limhi followed Benjamin's pattern and "entered into a covenant with God to serve him and keep his commandments" (Mosiah 21:31). Almost a century later, Helaman spoke to his sons Nephi and Lehi, admonishing them to "remember, remember, my sons, the words which king Benjamin spake unto his people" (Helaman 5:9). The fact that Samuel the Lamanite knew key words from Benjamin's speech suggests that Nephi and Lehi indeed remembered and used Benjamin's words among the Lamanites.

Benjamin's monumental speech also became a type of constitutional document in Nephite culture, and specific influences from Benjamin's speech are found in later Nephite law and society. As discussed above, Benjamin reports that he had not allowed his people to do five specific criminal things: they were not to "murder, or plunder, or steal, or commit adultery . . . [nor] any manner of wickedness" (Mosiah 2:13). This exact list appears several other times in the Book of Mormon. In Alma 23:3, the converted Lamanite king issued a proclamation that his people "ought not to murder, nor to plunder, nor to steal, nor to commit adultery, nor to commit any manner of wickedness." These words were evidently brought to the Lamanites by the four sons of Mosiah, who, of all people, would have remembered and used the words of their grandfather Benjamin. The fact that this five-part list surfaces again in Mosiah 29:36, Alma 30:10, and Helaman 6:23 shows that

Benjamin's speech was considered to be a foundational and authoritative oration in its own time and culture.

2. A Dramatic Occasion and Presentation

Memorable oratory is dramatic. "Truly great oratory," it is said, "is the result only of a great occasion."[13] The setting, timing, and delivery of Benjamin's speech make it no ordinary, off-the-cuff conversation. His counsel and testimony were delivered in a powerfully dramatic setting that even today attracts the reader's attention and contributes to its literary effectiveness. The drama of the situation mounts as readers learn about the preparations for the event, sharing the people's anticipation as Benjamin promised to reveal to them new names and new insights. One can easily imagine the construction of a special tower beside the temple, *upon* which, not beside which, the text correctly says Benjamin stood to proclaim his dramatic message.[14]

The sacred, festive mood of the occasion enhances the excitement, especially if Benjamin's speech was delivered in connection with anything like the year-rite ceremony that made such a deep impression on ancient peoples.[15] The solemnity of the occasion is heightened by Benjamin's tedious effort to write out his text, distribute copies, proclaim the covenant, and crown it all with the coronation of an earthly king as nothing less than a shadow of the heavenly king. Obviously, in all this something important is going on. This is not just an ordinary meeting or a routine state-of-the-union address of the king to his people. Benjamin's speech is not just another oration or campaign speech. All this drama attracts attention and draws the audience and reader into the text.

3. The Sincerity of a Farewell Setting

Much of the success of Benjamin's speech resides in its deep and honest sincerity: "The essential element in oratory is simply the ability to talk to the heart of the hearer."[16] The words of Demosthenes, the most classic of Greek orators, have been praised as "eminently plain and unadorned. His strength lies in his earnest sincerity and sterling character, coupled with remarkable sympathy for his audience, and great skill in appealing to the prejudices and passions as well as the reason of that audience."[17] All these descriptions can be aptly attributed to Benjamin's speech, which exudes sincerity and truthfulness born of a sterling character.

The quality of Benjamin's sincerity is magnified by the fairly obvious but very significant fact that he delivered his speech near the end of his life. It is interesting that many other important speeches in world literature and in the scriptures were also farewell speeches. Perhaps it is only natural that toward the end of his life a great, observant prophet like Benjamin should give his final assessment of what his life had amounted to. What does he see and include as he looks back on life and ahead to meeting God? What does he pass over and leave out? What a speaker omits on such an occasion often reveals as much as what he puts in. For example, Benjamin says nothing of his military victories or his political and administrative achievements, which must have been many.

Interestingly, literary analysts have identified and compared some twenty-two farewell speeches from Greco-Roman antiquity and from the Bible. William S. Kurz has developed a set of twenty elements that are found in this genre of notable literary farewell addresses.[18] On his list were farewell orations by Moses (Deuteronomy 31–34), Joshua (Joshua 23–24), David (1 Kings 2:1–10; 1 Chronicles 28–29), Samuel (1 Samuel 12), Socrates, and others. Based on this analysis, Benjamin's speech works well as a classic farewell address, containing at least as many elements of a typical farewell speech as any other text. Of course, no single speech contains all the elements identified by Kurz: Moses' contains the most, with sixteen; Paul's, fourteen; and Socrates's, eleven. As will be discussed in detail in a subsequent chapter of this book, Benjamin's features at least sixteen, with other elements implied.

4. A Humility That Instills Confidence

Another hallmark of a great oration is its delivery of "eternal truths uttered with disarming humility."[19] Throughout his speech, Benjamin's plain and simple language is effective in creating confidence and transmitting this powerful, stirring discourse. Love of audience is an essential key to penetrating oratory.[20] Benjamin understands this principle, and he communicates the tenderness of his relationship to his people, saying that he is no better than his audience: all people come from the dust and must have sincere concern for the poor and for the children, if everyone is to succeed. Benjamin's personable nature that is displayed through his humility endears him to his audience, both ancient and modern, and makes them take seriously his instructions to be humble.

5. A Voice of Pure Authority

In addition to speaking with humility, a charismatic orator must talk frankly, with power, and "as one having authority" (Matthew 7:29). Ralph Waldo Emerson once said, the "anecdote of eloquence . . . is a triumph of pure power, and it has a beautiful and prodigious surprise in it."[21] Combining the authority of his offices as king, teacher, and as representative and messenger of the Lord, Benjamin faithfully and triumphantly delivered the holy message from the angel of God of "glad tidings of great joy" (Mosiah 3:3) to his people. Benjamin spoke with divine power. His speech penetrated the hearts of his people, regenerating their souls. Using mostly simple, everyday words and phrases, Benjamin skillfully discharged his authorized assignment and communicated his thoughts with a surprising and overwhelming display of divine authority and power. William Norwood Brigance has described this manifestation of impact and power in oratory as follows:

> Not only is history written with words. It is made with words. Most of the mighty movements affecting the destiny of [nations] have gathered strength in obscure places from the talk of nameless men, and gained final momentum from leaders who could state in common words the needs and hopes of common people. Great movements, in fact, are usually led by men of action who are also men of words, who use words as instruments of power, who voice their aims in words of historic simplicity.[22]

Benjamin gathered not only verbal power but divine authority by using words and phrases given to him from a heavenly source. He shaped in the minds of the people vivid images of an ideal society by looking ahead with prophetic insight to a clearly envisioned world to come and by patterning his own message after the angel's revealed message. According to Chauncy Goodrich, "Rhetoric endeavors to describe the shape of an undiscovered country and, often as occasion affords, to alter or determine that shape."[23] Benjamin drew upon the intrinsic power of the words of the angel and was able to shape in the souls of his people the ultimate vision of the blessings of Jesus Christ.

King Benjamin's divine commission and extensive understanding of the nature of God, as well as his lifelong relationship with his people and his knowledge of sacred material, gave him an authority that was sensed by the people and inspired them to believe his words and act on them by committing themselves to serve and obey God. It is said that "the secret of [Lincoln's] success was simply this: he realized that power lay in doing what the occasion required and nothing more."[24] Benjamin too does not overadorn his key points, nor does he digress into tangents. The authority of his office, his style, and his message did not call for going beyond what was required.

6. A Purposeful and Effective Organization

A fine classic speech like Benjamin's doesn't happen accidentally. In my opinion, Benjamin prepared for many months or maybe even years to deliver this speech. And consistent with this notion, the entire speech manifests an extraordinarily purposeful and effective organization. Of Cicero, the paragon of Roman orators, it is said that he "dazzles us with the brilliancy of his rhetoric. His words roll out in perfect oratorical rhythm, his periods are nicely balanced, his figures of speech and his choice of words beautifully artistic, singing through the mind like music and enchanting the ear."[25] Benjamin's masterful oration was also carefully written and intricately orchestrated.

At the broadest level, several internal structural facets show that the speech consists of seven segments, with scheduled pauses between them for ceremonial actions and audience responses.[26] The structures within the seven main sections of this speech are analyzed in greater depth in another chapter below.[27] For the present purposes of this rhetorical overview, we note that the sections of the oration are distinctly divided and constructed. Because Benjamin usually placed key points at the center of each section of his speech, which gives the composition a focusing pattern, it helps to read and study the speech according to its natural divisions and central points.

Furthermore, the seven main sections of the speech may be arranged in a general chiastic manner—that is, as an inverted parallelism. Section 4 contains the central turning point of the speech; sections 3 and 5 are related to each other as testimonies about the works and attributes of God; and sections 1 and 7 are companions in detailing the relationships between God, king, and man. The announcement of the new king at the end of section 1 is paralleled by the covenant to obey the new king at the beginning of section 7. And the death of the Messiah in section 3 contrasts with the long-suffering goodness of the living God in section 5.

Moreover, seeing the overall structure of this oration exposes the brilliantly interwoven threads and highlights the echoes that reverberate through its passages. For example, readers often overlook the fact that Benjamin speaks about service not just once in the speech (see Mosiah 2:17), but three times (see Mosiah 2:17–19, 21; 5:13), and Benjamin's point remains unclear until all three references are put together. At the outset, Benjamin's intent is to show that man is less than the dust of the earth. People try to elevate themselves by serving other people, but Benjamin quickly reminds us that, as noble as that may be, "when ye are in the service of your fellow beings ye are *only* [or *merely*] in the service of your God" (Mosiah 2:17). Then, in Mosiah 2:21, the chiastic counterpart to Mosiah 2:17, Benjamin makes it clear that even if one "should serve him who has created you from the beginning, . . . if ye should serve him with all your whole souls yet ye would be unprofitable servants." So where does that leave us as mortals? We cannot say aught of ourselves, not by service to others (for that is only service to God) or by service to God (for he immediately blesses us, and we are still in his debt). So why serve? Benjamin gives us the answer, but not until the chiastic conclusion of this point in Mosiah 5:13.

In order to understand the rhetorical impact of this three-stage line of thought, an expanded explanation is called for. The initial key is found in the word *only* in Mosiah 2:16 and 17. One can well imagine that Benjamin placed heavy emphasis on that word as he spoke. Benjamin insisted that he had *"only* been in the service of God" ("I do not desire to boast, for I have only been in the service of God," Mosiah 2:16), and he hoped that his people might learn that by serving their fellow beings, they are *"only* in the service of [their] God" (Mosiah 2:17). The occurrence of the word *only* in these two statements has three possible implications. First, the word *only* may be simply a colloquial expression, unimportant to the main content of the statements. In other words, Benjamin may be saying, "I have *really* been in the service of God." Understood this way, the word *only* becomes an insubstantial word added only for casual embellishment. Second, the word *only* may have the logical force of the word *exclusively*. In other words, Benjamin could be understood as saying, "I have been *exclusively* in the service of God." Third, the word *only* may be a strong diminutive expression, similar in force to the word *merely*. In other words, Benjamin is saying, "I have *merely* been in the service of God, and this is in reality nothing to boast of."

A combination of the last two possibilities fits the context of Mosiah 2 the best and paves the way for the crowning point in Mosiah 5. The thrust of Benjamin's thought in that chapter is that when one serves one's fellowman one has no cause to boast, because that service is only (i.e., exclusively) service to God and that is only (i.e., merely) serving God. And one cannot boast of serving God because, as Benjamin made clear in Mosiah 2:20–21, all service to God is unprofitable service. Benjamin stated unequivocally that "if you should render all the thanks and praise which your whole soul has power to possess, . . . if ye should serve him with all your whole souls yet ye would be unprofitable servants" (Mosiah 2:20–21). In other words, Benjamin strikes here a double blow: first he reshapes our thinking about service by redefining it as exclusively service to God, and second, he reduces all service to God as ultimately unprofitable (see Mosiah 2:23–24). Even royal service is not exempt from this sobering reduction: "I [your king] . . . am [no] more than a mortal man . . . like as yourselves, subject to all manner of infirmities in body and mind; . . . I . . . am no better than ye yourselves are; for I am also of the dust" (Mosiah 2:10–11, 26).

In the end, Benjamin's point is this: The purpose of service is not to release us from our indebtedness to God but to increase our personal knowledge of him and his goodness: "For how knoweth a man the master whom he has not served, and who is a stranger unto him, and is far from the thoughts and intents of his heart?" (Mosiah 5:13).

Many other threads like these become visible when one examines the organization in each of the other sections of this grand oration. For instance, an ironic interplay exists in section 3 between Christ's power over evil spirits (see Mosiah 3:6) and its counterpart: men shall say "he hath a devil" (Mosiah 3:9). The all-important sacred name is given at the very center of section 3 (see Mosiah 3:8), and the crucial terms on which the efficacy of the atonement depend are stated at the precise center of section 4 (see Mosiah 3:18–19).

7. An Elegance of Verbal Detail and Arrangement

Another feature of literary achievement in Benjamin's speech is its verbal elegance: "In public speaking we have long and rolling sentences, words that fill the mouth, and sustained periods."[28] As is also demonstrated extensively below,[29] Benjamin was a master in the use of impressive expressions and memorable words. His words were carefully chosen and displayed with virtuosity, and this is what makes them memorable. Benjamin's use of chiasmus compares very favorably with the best examples of the important feature of that biblical style, which is a beautiful and memorable form of verbal organization.[30] An excellent instance of chiasmus is found in Mosiah 5:10–12. This was the first example of extended chiasmus discovered in the Book of Mormon. This superb example of composition—which I found in 1967 while serving as a missionary in Germany—in a style that was important in Hebrew literature, shows Benjamin's literary mastery. It comes at the very center of section 7 of the speech in which Benjamin presents six ideas, first in one order and then in the exact opposite order:

> Whosoever shall not take upon him the [1] *name* of Christ must be [2] *called* by some other name; therefore, he findeth himself on the [3] *left hand of God*. And I would that ye should [4] *remember* also, that this is the name that I said I should give unto you that never should be [5] *blotted out*, except it be through [6] *transgression*; therefore, take heed that ye do not [6] *transgress*, that the name be not [5] *blotted out* of your hearts. . . . I would that ye should [4] *remember* to retain the name written always in your hearts, that ye are not found on the [3] *left hand of God*, but that ye hear and know the voice by which ye shall be [2] *called*, and also, the [1] *name* by which he shall call you. (Mosiah 5:10–12)

This arrangement made Benjamin's words stylistically elegant, rhythmically flowing, and also easy to remember.

Another chiasm of virtually the same length is found in Mosiah 3:18–19. It is as if, by creating this second chiasm, Benjamin was trying to make it obvious that these two beautifully matched patterns had not been created by accident. Moreover, this second pattern comes at the very center of the middle section (4), and thus its words fall at the structural turning point of the entire speech—a point rarely noticed. There are 2,467 words of Benjamin—in the English translation, of course—before this midpoint (from Mosiah 2:9–3:18) and 2,476 words of Benjamin and the people after it (Mosiah 3:19–5:15)—the virtual middle of the speech.

In addition to many marvelous literary structures, Benjamin's facility with language is evident in his use of distinctive words and phrases. One study analyzed 470 phrases in Benjamin's speech; many of these phrases are sensible, insightful, and memorable verbal gems. Of those phrases, 84 appear for the first time in scripture on the lips of Benjamin; 28 appear to be entirely unique to Benjamin.[31] Interestingly, 27 of those 28 expressions occur in the verses written by Benjamin himself, with only one appearing in the words of the angel in Mosiah 3. Similarly, Benjamin spoke with originality; he does not quote Isaiah, Zenos, or other prophetic predecessors. The sound of Benjamin's new formulations may well have struck his immediate audience as highly creative and impressive.

Moreover, Benjamin's testimony of Jesus Christ was couched in distinctly personal terms.[32] For example, Benjamin, as a king himself, was especially concerned with God's kingship. Himself a strong, benevolent king, he referred favorably to the Lord as the "heavenly King" (Mosiah 2:19), a term unique to Benjamin. Consistent with Benjamin's personal interests and royal circumstances in life, he was the only Book of Mormon writer ever to use the word *omnipotent*. In fact, Benjamin spoke six times of God's omnipotence (see Mosiah 3:5, 17, 18, 21; 4:9; 5:15).

8. A Trove of Timeless Themes

Of course, sacred literature is not simply a matter of well-crafted words. The enduring classics and orations of world literature address timeless themes of human life and key values of society. They are veritable treasure troves of eternal truths and good sense. The golden art of speech making is "the steadfast use of a language in which truth can be told; a speech that is strong by natural force, and not merely effective by declamation; an utterance without trick, without affectation, without mannerism."[33] And so it is with Benjamin's speech. There is nothing trivial or affected here. Each segment goes directly to the essence of what life is all about. Benjamin reveals eternal doctrines of central importance. Sometimes they are so plainly stated that casual readers miss their theological import.

For example, Benjamin's ultimate concept of sinfulness is impressive. For Benjamin, sin is not merely the physical action of transgressing a commandment of God; it is even more than the mental or intentional commission of misconduct. The essence of sin, as Benjamin explained it (and this comes in the middle of section 2 of the speech), is coming out "in open rebellion against God" (Mosiah 2:37). Indeed, at the core of every sin one is saying to God, "I know you don't want me to do this, but I don't care. I don't care enough about you, or about what you want, for me to refrain. I'm going to do it anyway." How can a person love God and keep the greatest commandment but not care what God wants or feels? By recognizing that this state of rebellion is the essence of all sin, Benjamin helps thoughtful listeners resist temptation by affirming, "But I do care, I do love God, and I keep the great commandment."

Many other similar points can be made from the succinct

and incisive themes presented by King Benjamin. Many profound topics in almost every sentence of Benjamin's speech still wait to be pondered and elaborated. The bibliographic notes and comments provided in this volume list several articles or chapters in books that have clearly illuminated many of Benjamin's classic themes.

9. A Practical Approach in Touch with Real Life

Benjamin's speech is great oratory not only because it addresses great themes, but because it does so while remaining completely in touch with real life. Benjamin was a very practical man whose wisdom reflected a kind of good sense and keen judgment that comes only from a long life of concrete experience. His comments rise to the level of proverbial wisdom on such varied topics as service ("when ye are in the service of your fellow beings ye are only in the service of your God," Mosiah 2:17), leadership ("I, even I, whom ye call your king, am no better than ye yourselves," Mosiah 2:26), human nature ("the natural man is an enemy to God," Mosiah 3:19), responsibility ("but men drink damnation to their own souls," Mosiah 3:18), humility ("ye cannot say that ye are even as much as the dust of the earth; yet ye were created of the dust," Mosiah 2:25), indebtedness ("and ye are still indebted unto him, and are, and will be, forever," Mosiah 2:24), grace ("ye should remember, and always retain in rememberance, the greatness of God, and your own nothingness, and his goodness and long-suffering towards you, unworthy creatures," Mosiah 4:11), obedience ("watch yourselves, and your thoughts, and your words, and your deeds, and observe the commandments of God," Mosiah 4:30), gratitude ("if you should render all the thanks and praise which your whole soul has power to possess . . . yet ye would be unprofitable servants," Mosiah 2:20-21), the importance of children ("little children . . . they are blessed," Mosiah 3:16), human accountability ("[remember] . . . the awful situation of those that have fallen into transgression," "consider on the blessed and happy state of those that keep the commandments of God," Mosiah 2:40-41), peace ("ye will not have a mind to injure one another, but to live peaceably, and to render to every man according to that which is his due," Mosiah 4:13), contention ("beware lest there shall arise contentions among you," Mosiah 2:32), wealth ("For behold, are we not all beggars?" Mosiah 4:19), and charity ("ye yourselves will succor those that stand in need of your succor," Mosiah 4:16). Something as practical as the connection between thanking and praising illustrates Benjamin's sensible wisdom (see Mosiah 2:20). He rightly links these two ideas: You must render to God all your thanks *and* praise. Indeed, to thank someone truly means to praise that person, not just selfishly saying, "Thanks, I'm glad you gave that to me." Benjamin's attention to these themes shows that he was concerned with public issues, and like other skilled orators, wanted his listeners to "do something of a social or political kind."[34]

Many of Benjamin's words become even more potent in light of the real-life situations in the ancient world out of which they came. Consider, for example, the ancient catastrophe of indebtedness. That calamity sets the stage for those parts of the speech in which Benjamin spoke pointedly about debt, repaying debts, and acting generously in light of the burden of indebtedness. In ancient society, being in debt and unable to repay that burden meant more than just needing to run to the bank to take out a larger home equity loan. Indebtedness was next to death in terms of personal catastrophe: "Ancient Israel considered permanent slavery the most inhumane condition possible."[35] It usually meant the crippling loss of all one's assets—including one's children capable of gainful employment—complete social degradation, and involuntary debt servitude for the maximum allowable duration, even though many masters were caring and benevolent. Thus when Benjamin talked pointedly and practically about our being eternally indebted, modern readers probably do not sense the magnitude of the extreme disaster that this specter evoked in the ancient mind. Nor does the modern mind sense enough the liberation that comes in Benjamin's promise that under this head we are made free (Mosiah 5:8)—that is, not free to run around, but free from that eternal debt.

10. A Source of Unmistakable Instructions to Enable Success

Fortunately, with all this wisdom Benjamin's words are not broad platitudes, but like the best of meaningful oratory, his speech gives clear instructions and tells specifically how to achieve the desired spiritual objectives. "Great speeches are concerned chiefly and characteristically with matters of probability, with the taking of action in those questions on which policies must be formed and decisions made without benefit of all the facts"; yet "rhetorique will make [things that are] absent and remote . . . present to your understanding."[36] Although God's final judgment is "absent and remote," Benjamin made that eventuality "present to the understanding" and impelled choice and action by the influence of his instructive rhetoric.

For example, Benjamin wanted his audience, as much as anything else, to have access to God and to build faith in him. Benjamin taught his people eight steps, an early sort of the Articles of Faith (couched in a beautiful eight-part parallelism), which appear at the center of section 5 of the speech (see Mosiah 4:9–10). His eight incremental and sequential steps are (1) believe that he is, (2) believe that he created all things, (3) believe that he has all wisdom and power, (4) honestly admit that man does not comprehend all, (5) believe that you must repent and forsake your sins, (6) humble yourself before God, (7) ask in sincerity of heart for forgiveness, and (8) if you believe these things, see that you do them.

Likewise, the steps involved in claiming the benefits of the atonement are not left as a vague concept. Human beings access the atoning blood of Christ by acquiring seven primary virtues specifically listed as steps in becoming a saint: being childlike, submissive, meek, humble, patient, full of love, and willing to submit to whatever God might inflict on us (see Mosiah 3:19).

In order to help children, students, or other people, a skilled leader will do several things. Benjamin senses the need to help and applies wise counseling techniques in his speech: He discusses openly with the people their goals and ambitions; he recognizes the value of each individual, recording the name of each; he teaches them that increased freedom brings responsibility; he brings them to a realization that everyone in his audience old enough to understand is no longer innocent; he allows them to experience consequences of their actions, clearly stating that the names of wrongdoers will be blotted out; he shares his own struggles, work, and mortality; he acknowledges the positive changes he sees them making as they call for the atoning blood to be applied and enter into the covenant; and he expresses confidence in them, ending with a firm assurance that God will seal them his. Benjamin knows that a successful speech "must so stir a public body that something will be done";[37] therefore he employs every necessary technique in order to convey the clear instructions of a masterful teacher.

11. A Profound Ethical Logic

Persuasive and influential orations supply logical reasons for ethical behavior. And make no mistake—Benjamin was not just a fine social counselor, an energetic leader, or a friendly confidant. He was also blunt, direct, bold in testifying, and he drove home his instructions with very interesting and compelling forms of ethical logic.

Benjamin based moral obligation on the fact that, by serving his people, he had put them in debt—a debt they ought to repay by serving others and thanking God. For example, the question of why one should care about others or give freely to another is one of the most basic issues of moral philosophy. It is a question that Benjamin's speech answers like no other. Benjamin's logic of love, service, and charity is cogent, thorough, and persuasive. He offers at least eight answers to this crucial and persistent problem of ethics and morality.

We should serve one another because we have received benefits from the service of others. In Mosiah 2:18–19, at the central crux of section 1 of this speech, Benjamin informs his people that they are morally obligated to serve one another: "Behold, ye have called me your king; and if I, whom ye call your king, do labor to serve you, then ought not ye to labor to serve one another?" (Mosiah 2:18). Benjamin's logic can be described as following a law of transferred obligations. But one may wonder how this logic of transferred obligations works. Normally it is not logical for a person to say, "Because I went skiing Saturday, you should go skiing," or "Because I do not smoke, you should not smoke." But Mosiah 2:18 does not transfer moral obligation by simple fiat; instead, it creates obligation by indebtedness. It is axiomatic that a person should repay his or her debts. The creation of a moral obligation is implicit in the creation of the debt itself. Put another way, if there is no obligation to repay a debt, the debt simply does not exist. By serving his people, Benjamin has put them in debt, and by recognizing him as king his people have acknowledged the legitimacy of that debt. Thus the moral obligation of the people, according to Benjamin's premises, can be stated as follows: "Since you should thank God, and since the only way to thank God is to serve God, and since service to fellowman is service to God, then it follows that you ought to serve one another." Here the equation of serving man and serving God works in reverse. One discharges the obligation to serve God by serving one's fellowman. A similar gospel logic stands firmly and compellingly behind other vicarious moral transfers, including the transferred benefits that may be received through the atonement (Christ's suffering transfers benefits to other people), or in the dynamics of forgiveness (God will forgive a person as and if a person forgives others).

Moral situations along these lines arise frequently in everyone's daily life. To paraphrase Benjamin, one might say, "You should (are morally obligated to) serve because your parents have served you," or "You should serve others in your ward because your neighbors or roommates have served you," or, as we sing in hymn 219, "because I have been given much, I too must give." It is thus somewhat ironic that we do not always do people a favor by serving them, for we then place a burden of moral duty on them to do likewise for others. But this is also a true and righteous principle: God himself only puts us further in his debt when he blesses us (see Mosiah 2:23–24). What is most impressive about Benjamin's logic of generosity is that he does not say, "Since I have served you, you should now serve *me*." That would be inconsistent with his own acknowledgment that

his service was only service to God—completely service to
God—and thus Benjamin retained no reversionary or residu-
ary interest in it. Similarly, Benjamin instructs his people
not to thank him, but to thank God.

*We should serve others because we have been commanded to,
and by disobeying that command we come out in open rebellion
against God.* The logic of this imperative goes beyond a
simple command coupled with a threat of divine punishment for disobedience. Some people today feel that the law
of Moses is nothing but a series of wooden rules and that
commands (rules) are for kids (and Pharisees). But as Paul
has affirmed, the law serves righteous purposes even in
Christ: "wherefore the law is holy, and the commandment
holy, and just, and good" (Romans 7:12). The only problem
with rules comes when we lose sight, in our acts of obedience, of the weightier matters of the law or of the deeper
reasons behind the commands.

Underpinning the idea that we should obey God's commands is the ultimate commandment that we should love
God. As mentioned above, the problem in disobeying any
of God's commandments is that disobedient people essentially say that they simply do not care enough about what
God wants; such behavior breaks the great commandment
to love the Lord (see Deuteronomy 10:12), on which hangs
all the law and the prophets (see Matthew 22:40). Thus, as
Benjamin puts it, a person who disregards the commandments of God lists to obey the evil spirit and comes out in
open rebellion against God. The alternatives are clear.

*We should serve one another because through the atonement
of Christ we will stand before God to be judged according to our
works.* The law and logic of God embrace both mercy and
justice. Moral logic and mercy follow from the fact that one
should not expect to find justice in this life. Those who serve
their fellow beings will not be rewarded equitably by others,

and they should not expect to be. Equity and fairness can be approximated through social justice and by various efforts to redistribute wealth and other social benefits among people, but the only time that people will stand to be judged and rewarded, "every man according to his works, whether they be good, or whether they be evil" (Mosiah 3:24), is in the hereafter. The logical outcome of this knowledge is that we ought to serve now, because what we do now will largely determine the outcome of that judgment.

Christ's atonement places us eternally in his debt, and because of his atonement and generosity toward us we are given further reason to serve others. In Mosiah 3, Benjamin's speech does not address service or charity directly. In that chapter, the angel emphasizes the atoning blood that takes away all kinds of sin. That sacrifice of Christ creates the ultimate indebtedness that humans owe, which leads directly to Benjamin's next point: If we view our own nothingness and worthless state, if we recognize the great disparity between man and God that now exists (see Mosiah 4:4–11), and if we see our necessary dependence on Christ's atonement, we will see the logical consequences of our own position as beggars: "And has he suffered that ye have begged in vain?" No, he has not. "O then, how ye ought to impart of the substance that ye have one to another" (Mosiah 4:20, 21).

When we have been truly converted, we serve because we cannot do otherwise. Benjamin declares that if we remember the greatness of God, we will always rejoice, have no mind to injure one another, not suffer others to go hungry, impart our substance to the poor, return those things that have been borrowed (and repay all our debts), and in the end have (as Benjamin's people came to acknowledge that they had) "no disposition to do evil" (Mosiah 5:2; see 4:12–14, 16, 28). The questions of why birds fly or why fish swim or why good people serve others all call for the same answer: they do it by nature. When the natural man has been put off, another nature is taken on—a nature of service, love, righteousness, humility, and submissiveness. To such a person, service is natural. For such a person, it would not feel right to do otherwise.

We should serve because we have made a promise that we will do so. This is the heart and soul of morality and ethics, if not business and law. Regarding the covenants made within the gospel of Jesus Christ, covenanters agree to serve one another, "to bear one another's burdens, . . . mourn with those that mourn; yea, and comfort those that stand in need of comfort" (Mosiah 18:8–9), to sacrifice and consecrate for the common good. At Sinai, the Israelites similarly covenanted to serve one another, to watch out for the widow and orphan (see Exodus 22:22), and to love their neighbor as themselves (see Leviticus 19:18). Similarly, Benjamin adds the force of covenant (see Mosiah 5:5) in answer to the question why one should serve.

We serve each other because we come to view other people as a part of ourselves. This concept, in turn, adds an interpersonal reason to serve. One result of the covenant, according to Benjamin, is that the covenanters all become the sons and daughters of God, which means that they also become related to each other as if they were siblings. In this sense, one's self is not an isolated entity but an interconnected and composite being to which many people have contributed through associations and involvements that predate this existence and will postdate this life through a sealing that binds us together eternally (see Mosiah 5:15). Relationships such as these change the concept of service to others, who are in a sense part of ourselves, and we, of course, have no desire or reason to injure ourselves.

We serve in order to know the Master. As mentioned above, at the end of his speech Benjamin returns one last time to the theme of service. After laying all the foregoing logical groundwork flowing from obligation, commandment, judgment, generosity, nature, promise, and sociality, Benjamin is at last prepared to offer his final solution to the problem that he posed in the first paragraphs of his speech: If we are always going to remain unprofitable servants, why should one ever bother to serve? Mosiah 5:13 adds an eighth and crowning reason why one should serve: "For how knoweth a man the master whom he has not served?" One obtains an important kind of knowledge about the Master from books, the scriptures, manuscripts, and commentaries. But one gets another kind of knowledge from church service—a kind of unity, sympathy, and understanding that helps us understand the Master's will. People serve so that they may in the process come to know the Master whom they serve and that the Master will also know them; for without service, they will be "a stranger unto him" (Mosiah 5:13). Through service, Christ becomes more prominent in the thoughts and intents of our hearts. True service requires dedication and real intent. Through service the Master becomes a focal point of the thoughts and intents of our hearts. It is hard to imagine a more complete list of reasons why human beings should serve one another than that embedded in the principles set forth in Benjamin's speech.

12. A Compelling Presentation of Ultimate Human Choice

Benjamin posed ultimate human choices in bold relief. Like all great orations, Benjamin's speech sets forth the question and compels the audience to make a choice. It has been said that the most famous orations in world history have impelled people to critical action. One thinks of the speeches of Churchill or Lincoln. Speaking and hearing alone are not enough; righteousness requires doing.

Benjamin was a man of action who voiced his aims in words of historic simplicity. He stirred his people to repentance and induced "a mighty change" in them, so that they had "no more disposition to do evil, but to do good continually" (Mosiah 5:2). From a literary standpoint, Benjamin was able to accomplish this largely by presenting crucial issues in terms of stark contrasts that exposed two clear extremes.

Benjamin's speech is filled with such contrasts: he juxtaposed the mortal and the immortal; the king and the dust of the earth; kingship and servitude; indebtedness and freedom; drinking damnation and becoming a saint; coming out in open rebellion against God and walking with a clear conscience, fully submissive to his will; "the awful situation of those that have fallen into transgression" and "the blessed and happy state of those that keep the commandments" (Mosiah 2:40–41); works, whether they be good or evil; the greatness of God and man's own nothingness (see Mosiah 4:11); the rich and the poor; being found on the right hand (see Mosiah 5:9) or the left hand of God; and feeding among the flocks and being cast out (see Mosiah 5:14). Lehi had earlier taught that an opposition exists in all things (see 2 Nephi 2:11); the literary achievements of Benjamin's speech, filled with stark contrasts that expose these clear eternal extremes, are crowned by placing the ultimate choice of eternal life squarely before the listener—urgently but lovingly.

Conclusion

To recapitulate, twelve qualities stand out in King Benjamin's speech that make it a masterful oration and consummate work of sacred literature. This speech poses the ultimate human choices in bold relief, it employs a compelling and profound ethical logic, it gives unmistakable instructions to enable success, it addresses practical themes in touch with real life, it reveals eternal doctrines of central importance, it uses eloquent and impressive words and phrases, it manifests purposeful and effective organization, it is presented with authority and humility, it influences readers by its sincere farewell setting and its use of other impressive forms of speech, it attracts attention through dramatic presentation, and it stands as a monument in Nephite religious history. Undoubtedly, other qualities could also be mentioned. All these impressive features are found in an oration that contains only about 5,000 words and was translated and dictated by Joseph Smith in approximately a day and a half.

It has taken us as a people a long time for our understanding of this speech to mature. B. H. Roberts viewed the speech as an elementary discussion, as if given, he said, to "little children who were taking first lessons."[38] Sidney B. Sperry saw the speech as "remarkable in many respects," but he thought it was "highly improbable that Benjamin had received much instruction in the making of sermons or speeches."[39] Today careful students can see, even more clearly than ever before, that this masterful speech offers more than people have ever suspected. Benjamin makes his points so clearly that people may mistake his brilliance for something less. But it is the mark of all masters to make difficult feats look easy and to employ complex forms so fluently and fluidly that they draw no attention to themselves but flawlessly convey the intended message and result.

Oratory is the oldest of the arts. Few orations are of supreme merit. The best ones manifest a fluent command of language, superior powers of thought, logical consistency, quickness and brilliancy of conception, control of rhetorical expedients, personal magnetism, and control of the feelings as well as an appeal to the judgment of audience. To be fully appreciated an oration must be heard. "Much of what gave it force and effect is lost when it is committed to print."[40] Benjamin does all this; and even though his text is outstanding in print, it must have been superb when delivered.

Webster said that true eloquence is not merely in the speech but "in the man, the subject, and in the occasion."[41] Worthy though he might be to be called "a master of oratory," Benjamin would undoubtedly recognize that for any such tribute, he was indebted completely to God for everything in his speech that is magnificent, of good report, or praiseworthy.

Notes

This paper is a revised version of two similar talks delivered at the FARMS Annual Book of Mormon Symposium, first in Provo, Utah, 13 April 1996, and then in Oakland, California, 20 April 1996.

1. Bruce R. McConkie, *The Promised Messiah* (Salt Lake City: Deseret Book, 1981), 232.

2. Milton R. Hunter, *Conference Report* (October 1955): 65.

3. See Bruce A. Van Orden, "The Use of King Benjamin's Address by Latter-day Saints," in this volume.

4. Neal A. Maxwell, "Becometh as a Child," *Ensign* (May 1996): 68–70.

5. Susan L. Warner, "Remember How Thou Hast Received and Heard," *Ensign* (May 1996): 78–79.

6. Andrew Scotland, *The Power of Eloquence: A Treasury of British Speech* (London: Cassell, 1961), v.

7. Rufus Choate, quoted in Houston Peterson, *A Treasury of the World's Speeches*, rev. and enl. ed. (New York: Simon and Schuster, 1965), xxvii. For another collection of great speeches, see

Lord George-Brown, *The Voice of History: Great Speeches of the English Language* (London: Sidgwick and Jackson, 1979).

8. Peterson, *Treasury of the World's Speeches*, xxvii.

9. This theme is developed further in Neal A. Maxwell, "King Benjamin's Sermon: A Manual for Discipleship," and in John W. Welch, "Benjamin, the Man: His Place in Nephite History," both in this volume.

10. Bower Aly, quoted in Chauncey A. Goodrich, *Select British Eloquence* (Indianapolis: Bobbs-Merrill, 1963), xi. "Great speeches on great occasions [are] great events deserving the notice of historians. . . . Speechmaking [is] a force."

11. Ibid., xii. "Speeches are events that influence and are influenced by other events." Oratory is a bridge between the past and the future. "Speechmaking is to the future as history is to the past."

12. John W. Welch, "The Temple in the Book of Mormon: The Temples at the Cities of Nephi, Zarahemla, and Bountiful," in *Temples of the Ancient World*, ed. Donald W. Parry (Salt Lake City: Deseret Book and FARMS, 1994), 342.

13. Sherwin Cody, *A Selection from the World's Great Orations* (Chicago: McClurg, 1917), xvi.

14. See "Upon the Tower of Benjamin," FARMS Update, *Insights* (August 1995): 2.

15. See Hugh W. Nibley's chapter, "Assembly and Atonement," and Terrence L. Szink and John W. Welch's chapter, "King Benjamin's Speech in the Context of Ancient Israelite Festivals," both in this volume.

16. Cody, *World's Great Orations*, xvi.

17. Ibid., xiii.

18. For further information, see "Benjamin's Speech: A Classic Ancient Farewell Address," in *Reexploring the Book of Mormon*, ed. John W. Welch (Salt Lake City: Deseret Book and FARMS, 1992), 120–22; this topic is developed further in John W. Welch and Daryl R. Hague, "Benjamin's Speech as a Traditional Ancient Farewell Address," in this volume.

19. Peterson, *Treasury of the World's Speeches*, xxix.

20. Compare ibid., xviii.

21. Quoted in ibid., xxvii.

22. William N. Brigance, *A History and Criticism of American Public Address* (New York: Russell and Russell, 1960), 1:vii.

23. Goodrich, *Select British Eloquence*, xiii.

24. Cody, *World's Great Orations*, xxxi.

25. Ibid., xiii.

26. See "Chiasmus in the Book of Mormon," in *Chiasmus in Antiquity*, ed. John W. Welch (Hildesheim: Gerstenberg, 1981), 203.

27. See John W. Welch, "Parallelism and Chiasmus in Benjamin's Speech," in this volume.

28. Cody, *World's Great Orations*, xxiii.

29. See Welch, "Parallelism and Chiasmus," in this volume.

30. A good illustration of this form of inverted parallelism in the Bible can be found in Leviticus 24:17–21.

31. See Cory Chivers and John W. Welch, "Exact Words and Phrases in Benjamin's Speech in the Old Testament, New Testament, Book of Mormon and Other LDS Scriptures," unpublished FARMS research project (1988). The twenty-eight phrases unique to Benjamin's speech are as follows: "ye may hear" (2:9; 4:4), "I have been suffered" (2:12), "to spend my days" (2:12), "tell these things" (2:15; cf. 2:17), "clear conscience" (2:15, 27), "I, whom ye call" (2:18, 19, 26), "I answer you, Nay" (2:25), "mortal frame" (2:26), "I have caused that" (2:28, 29), "wo pronounced" (2:33), "receiveth for his wages" (2:33), "remaineth and dieth" (2:33, 38), "eternally indebted" (2:34), "have and are" (2:34; 4:21), "has no place" (2:37), "shrink from the" (2:38; 3:25), "call your attention" (3:1; 4:4), "Lord omnipotent" (words of the angel: 3:5, 17, 18; 5:2), "peace of conscience" (4:3), "ye will not suffer" (4:14, 16), "putteth up" (4:16, 22), "perhaps thou shalt" (4:17, 28), "end of . . . lives" (4:30; 5:8), "we are willing" (5:5), "remainder of our days" (5:5), "bring upon ourselves" (5:5), "ye shall be called" (5:7, 12), "left hand of God" (5:10, 12).

32. See John W. Welch, "Ten Testimonies of Jesus Christ from the Book of Mormon," in *Doctrines of the Book of Mormon*, ed. Bruce A. Van Orden and Brent L. Top (Salt Lake City: Deseret Book, 1992), 223–42.

33. Goodrich, *Select British Eloquence*, xiv.

34. Richard Crosscup, *Classic Speeches: Words That Shook the World* (New York: Philisophical Library, 1965), x.

35. Victor H. Matthews, "The Anthropology of Slavery in the Covenant Code," in *Theory and Method in Biblical and Cuneiform Law*, ed. Bernard M. Levinson (Sheffield: JSOT, 1994), 124.

36. Goodrich, *Select British Eloquence*, xii.

37. Cody, *World's Great Orations*, xi.

38. B. H. Roberts, "God's Great Men: Jacob and Benjamin," *Millennial Star* 50 (3 December 1888): 774.

39. Sidney B. Sperry, *Book of Mormon Compendium* (Salt Lake City: Bookcraft, 1968), 293.

40. Charles Morris, *Famous Orators of the Word and Their Best Orations* (Chicago: Clarkson and Cooper, 1902), ii.

41. Peterson, *Treasury of the World's Speeches*, xxviii.

CHAPTER 4

BENJAMIN'S SERMON AS A TRADITIONAL ANCIENT FAREWELL ADDRESS

John W. Welch and Daryl R. Hague

In many ways, Benjamin's speech (Mosiah 1–6) is bound up with ancient and venerable literary and religious traditions, drawing heavily on and conforming extensively to customary Israelite patterns and practices. To our understanding of Benjamin's speech can be added yet another significant dimension. It involves the literary pattern that can be seen in the farewell speeches that were given by several ancient political and religious leaders near the end of their lives. William S. Kurz has studied a large number of farewell speeches found in the Bible and in classical literature from the Greco-Roman world.[1] Kurz has abstracted from his collection of speeches twenty elements that appear regularly in most of these addresses. Because Benjamin's speech was also written and delivered in contemplation of Benjamin's own approaching death, the invitation seems natural, if not irresistible, to analyze Benjamin's discourse and several other farewell speeches in the Book of Mormon in terms of Kurz's list of typical farewell speech elements. The results of this study show that Benjamin's speech possesses as many or more of the characteristics of a traditional ancient Israelite farewell address than any other similar speech on record.

Ancient Farewell Speeches from the Old World

The Old Testament contains many reports of aging prophet-leaders who, at a time when it was obvious that they were about to die, called all or some of their people together one last time to teach them, to exhort them to righteousness, and to confer the responsibilities of leadership on their successors. Four of these accounts, which vary considerably in length, preserve what is known of the farewell speeches of Moses (Deuteronomy 31–34), Joshua (Joshua 23–24), David (1 Kings 2:1–10; compare 1 Chronicles 28–29), and Samuel (1 Samuel 12:1–25). In addition, several other farewell speeches were delivered by prominent religious and political leaders in the New Testament, the Apocrypha and Pseudepigrapha, and Greco-Roman literature. Certain themes appear regularly in all these farewell addresses, as if the speakers were consciously striving to conform their words to a customary prototype or to the traditional expectations of their audiences.

Furthermore, these ancient farewell addresses may be divided into two groups, each with their own distinctive patterns: (1) the Greco-Roman speeches and (2) the biblical addresses. In comparing these two groups, Kurz has found that, in the Greco-Roman literary tradition, the dying speaker was usually a philosopher or statesman, such as Socrates in Plato's *Phaedo*, whose speeches "are concerned with suicide, the meaning of death, questions about noble deaths, and life after death."[2] This emphatic preoccupation with death and dying, however, is absent in the biblical speeches. In biblical farewell addresses, the speaker is a man of God and his speech typically focuses on "God's plan, people and covenant, or on theodicy and theological interpretations of history."[3] David's instructions to Solomon (see 1 Kings 2:1–10) and Mattathias's last words to his sons (see 1 Maccabees 2:49–70) provide strong examples of the biblical tradition in this regard.

Despite this one fundamental difference in focus between these two main groups of texts, Kurz has found that twenty elements can be identified in these speeches and that many of these elements are generally common to all farewell addresses. While no single speech contains all twenty elements, most contain many of them. For example, Moses' speech contains sixteen of these elements (see Deuteronomy 31–34), Paul's fourteen (see Acts 20), Mattathias's ten, and David's nine.

Kurz's analysis creates a useful literary tool for dissecting, comparing, and assessing the components of farewell speeches. While other scholars might wish to point out further elements in this genre or might place different degrees of emphasis on the various features, Kurz's treatment offers a serviceable description of the standard literature that has emerged in farewell speeches in general. His descriptions of the attributes typical of these kinds of speeches can be summarized as follows:

1. *The summons.* The speaker calls his successors and followers together so they can receive his last instructions.

2. *The speaker's own mission or example.* A description of the speaker's life and calling is followed by a commandment that his followers should do as he has done.

3. *Innocence and discharge of duty.* The speaker declares that he has done his best and has fulfilled his obligations. He has accomplished what he intended to do and cannot be held liable for his people's actions in the future.

4. *Impending death.* The announcement of the speaker's impending death reveals no fear of death. Rather, the speaker

shows courage and an acceptance of his fate. Sometimes he commends his soul to God or the gods.

5. *Exhortation.* The listeners are encouraged to remember the teachings that the speaker has given previously and to obey the commands that he will give during his address. The people are also counseled to have courage during times of trial or difficulty. Exhortations help to solidify the lessons of the past and provide comfort for the future.

6. *Warnings and final injunctions.* Warnings about disobedience and its consequences are given. There may also be warnings concerning false teachers who will try to lead the people astray. Commandments and final instructions, designed to aid the people, accompany these warnings.

7. *Blessings.* The speaker usually pronounces or promises blessings in conjunction with his warnings and final instructions.

8. *Farewell gestures.* While the speaker may make some gesture to bid farewell, as seen especially in the Greco-Roman literature, only one of the twelve biblical addresses cited by Kurz mentions a farewell gesture. That instance occurs when Paul knelt down and prayed with the disciples at the end of his speech, after which the disciples fell on his neck and kissed him (see Acts 20:36–38).

9. *Tasks for successors.* Final orders may confer specific responsibilities to successors. Jesus, for example, gave final charges to the apostles at the last supper (see Luke 22:25–38); David commanded Solomon to take vengeance on Joab and Shimei (see 1 Kings 2:5–6, 8–9).

10. *Theological review of history.* A theological review of the past is given, often rehearsing events going back to the beginning of the world, the purpose of which is to emphasize the guidance, protection, and chastisement of God. Moses, for example, recounted the history of Israel and acknowledged God's hand in the protection and development of the children of Jacob (Deuteronomy 32).

11. Revelation of the future. Often the speaker is aware of future events that could threaten his reputation or might involve his followers. Jesus, for instance, predicted Judas's betrayal and Peter's denial (see Luke 22:21, 34).

12. Promises. Biblical farewell speeches typically promise the prospect of eternal glory. Thus both Jesus (Luke 22) and Mattathias (1 Maccabees 2) promised glory to their followers after teaching them about the importance of serving one another. This element does not appear in the speeches from the Greco-Roman tradition.

13. Appointment of or reference to a successor. The appointment of a successor is a very common feature of farewell speeches in the biblical tradition, and this designation serves to legitimize the authority of the new leader. For example, David's farewell address specifically endorsed Solomon's leadership (see 1 Kings 2:1–4).

14. Bewailing the loss. Often the account describes the mourning by the friends and followers of the speaker.

15. Future degeneration. Predictions and warnings concerning future heresies and disobedience often appear in biblical farewell speeches. Such predictions transfer responsibility for adverse developments in the future from the speaker to the coming generations. Moses, for example, declared that Israel would reject the Lord and turn to idolatry.

16. Covenant renewal and sacrifices. The listeners are enjoined to renew their covenant with God. David's instructions to Solomon ensured the fulfillment of David's covenant with God, and Jesus' actions at the last supper signaled a new covenant symbolized by the bread and wine. The covenant element is unique to the biblical tradition, and in Old Testament times sacrifices would generally accompany the covenant renewal.

17. Providing for those who will survive. Since the followers of the aged leader will require guidance and comfort after his death, instructions are given for providing such help. Jesus' command that Peter strengthen the brethren (see Luke 22:23) is an example of this element.

18. Consolation to the inner circle. Often, the speaker attempts to comfort his closest associates. Jesus did this at the last supper, when he and his most beloved followers were alone.

19. Didactic speech. The speaker may review certain principles to help the followers remember what they should do.

20. Ars moriendi or the approach to death. This element relates to the leader's approach to death itself. Kurz finds this element present only in Plato's *Phaedo,* although he suggests that it may also be implied in Josephus.

Benjamin's Farewell Speech

At least as complete as any farewell address that Kurz has analyzed is King Benjamin's speech.[4] This speech and the events related directly to it comprise a lengthy primary account. It is longer and more detailed than any of the biblical farewell speeches; only the speech of Moses comes close to it. In Benjamin's speech, sixteen elements of the farewell address typology are directly present, with two others clearly implied. Only the elements of bewailing the loss and *ars moriendi* (the least common factor and one evidenced only in the Greco-Roman tradition) fail to appear in Mosiah 1–6. No other single speech manifests more features of Kurz's pattern, and thus Benjamin's speech may well be the best example on record of this ancient rhetorical form of speech.

Kurz has singled out four of his twenty elements as fundamentally characteristic of addresses in the Old Testament and the Old Testament Apocrypha, as opposed to the Greco-Roman tradition: (1) the speaker's assertion of innocence and fulfillment of his mission, (2) the designation of

tasks for successors, (3) a theological review of history, and
(4) the revelation of future events. All four of these characteristically Israelite elements appear prominently in Benjamin's speech. Furthermore, Benjamin emphasizes the covenant relationship between God and man, and his text ends
with an express covenant renewal. No preoccupation with
death occurs here, as it does in the Greco-Roman texts.
Benjamin's speech is not only one of the most complete ancient
farewell addresses known anywhere, but it also strongly
manifests those elements that are most deeply rooted in
early biblical tradition.

Benjamin delivered his address about three years before
his death (see Mosiah 6:5). He called all the Nephites and
Mulekites together to impart his final teachings and appoint his son king (see Mosiah 1:10–18). The following overview summarizes and illustrates the elements in Kurz's
analysis of ancient farewell addresses as those factors appear
in Benjamin's speech:

1. *The summons.* The text begins by telling how Benjamin
summoned his people together:

> And it came to pass that after King Benjamin had
> made an end of teaching his sons, that he waxed old, and
> he saw that he must very soon go the way of all the earth;
> therefore, he thought it expedient that he should confer
> the kingdom upon one of his sons. Therefore, he had
> Mosiah brought before him. (Mosiah 1:9–10)

Following Benjamin's instructions, Mosiah "made *a proclamation* throughout all the land," and "the people gathered
themselves together throughout all the land, that they
might go up to the temple to hear the words which king
Benjamin should speak unto them" (Mosiah 2:1; see also
2:9). Benjamin's stated purposes were to appoint his successor, give his people a new covenantal name, remind
them that God had preserved them by his matchless power,

and unfold to their view the mysteries of God (see Mosiah 1:10–13; 2:9).

2. *The speaker's own mission or example.* Near the beginning of his speech, Benjamin pointed to his own life as an example of brotherly service that should be followed by those who would survive him. Having faithfully served many years as their king, Benjamin declared that he had spent his days in the service of his people. He further stressed that he had not sought riches but had worked with his own hands so he would not be a burden to them, and he affirmed that he had not allowed his people to break the law, but had fulfilled his mission and taught them to keep the commandments of God (see Mosiah 2:12–14). He was explicit that his people should follow his example: "Behold, ye have called me your king; and if I, whom ye call your king, do labor to serve you, then ought not ye to labor to serve one another?" (Mosiah 2:18).

3. *Innocence and discharge of duty.* After Benjamin reported his activities as king, he openly declared his innocence before God: "Yet my brethren, I have not done these things that I might boast, neither do I tell these things that thereby I might accuse you; but I tell you these things that ye may know that I can answer a clear conscience before God this day" (Mosiah 2:15). In the same spirit, Benjamin revealed that one of his purposes in calling his people together was that he might "be found blameless," "rid [his] garments of [their] blood," and die peacefully (Mosiah 2:27–28).

4. *Impending death.* Benjamin plainly acknowledged that he was close to death: "And I, even I, whom ye call your king, am no better than ye yourselves are; for I am also of the dust. And ye behold that I *am old*, and am *about to yield up this mortal frame* to its mother earth . . . at this period of time when I am about to go down to my grave" (Mosiah 2:26, 28; see also 1:9).

5. Exhortation. Benjamin's speech is filled with imperatives and strong exhortations. For example:

> Believe in God; believe that he is, and that he created all things, both in heaven and in earth; believe that he has all wisdom, and all power, both in heaven and in earth; believe that man doth not comprehend all the things which the Lord can comprehend. And again, believe that ye must repent of your sins and forsake them, and humble yourselves before God; and ask in sincerity of heart that he would forgive you; and now, if you believe all these things see that ye do them. (Mosiah 4:9–10; see also 2:9, 40–41, and 5:12)

6. Warnings and final injunctions. Mosiah chapter 4 concludes with the following general warnings of this aged leader:

> And finally, I cannot tell you all the things whereby ye may commit sin; for there are divers ways and means, even so many that I cannot number them. But this much I can tell you, that if ye do not watch yourselves, and your thoughts, and your words, and your deeds, and observe the commandments of God, and continue in the faith of what ye have heard concerning the coming of our Lord, even unto the end of your lives, ye must perish. And now, O man, remember, and perish not. (Mosiah 4:29–30)

Similarly, the words of the angel in Mosiah chapter 3 end with severe warnings and woes: "And if they be evil they are consigned to an awful view of their own guilt and abominations; . . . therefore they have drunk damnation to their own souls, . . . and their torment is as a lake of fire and brimstone" (Mosiah 3:25, 27). Several other sections in Benjamin's speech contain equally stern warnings (see Mosiah 2:32, 36–37, 39; 3:12; and 5:10–11).

In addition, Benjamin gave various injunctions to his people, especially including commands to care for the poor, the hungry, and the naked, both spiritually and temporally (see Mosiah 4:16–26). As a just king in ancient Israel, Benjamin had a particular responsibility to see that the weak and the poor in his society were cared for and not oppressed (see Psalm 72:1–4), and this helps to explain Benjamin's deep concern that his successors not ignore the needs of these vulnerable people. He also implored the assembly to care for their children's physical needs and to teach them to walk in the ways of the Lord (see Mosiah 4:14–15). His last words combined a final instruction with a message of comfort: "Therefore, I would that ye should be steadfast and immovable, always abounding in good works, that Christ, the Lord God Omnipotent, may seal you his, that you may be brought to heaven, that ye may have everlasting salvation and eternal life" (Mosiah 5:15).

7. *Blessings.* On several occasions, Benjamin mentioned or pronounced the blessings of God on his people (see Mosiah 2:22, 24, 31, 36, 41; 3:16). He promised that God would immediately bless and prosper his people for their righteousness (see Mosiah 2:22, 24), he exhorted his people to walk "in wisdom's paths that [they] may be blessed" (Mosiah 2:36), and he invited them to reflect on "the blessed and happy state of those that keep the commandments of God. For behold, they are blessed in all things, both temporal and spiritual; and if they hold out faithful to the end they are received into heaven, that thereby they may dwell with God in a state of never-ending happiness" (Mosiah 2:41).

8. *Farewell gestures.* Benjamin declared that he had called the assembly so that he might rid his garments of the people's blood (see Mosiah 2:28). It is possible that Benjamin ritually shook or cleansed these garments; Jacob, one of Benjamin's spiritual predecessors, actually took off his garment in front of a similar assembly and shook his clothes to

rid himself symbolically of the blood of his people (see 2 Nephi 9:44).

9. Tasks for successors. In the course of his speech, Benjamin assigned future tasks and roles to his son, his people, and the priests in his kingdom. For example, before delivering his address, Benjamin gave his son Mosiah "charge concerning all the affairs of the kingdom" (Mosiah 1:15), and he entrusted to Mosiah the care of the plates of brass, the plates of Nephi, the sword of Laban, and the Liahona (see Mosiah 1:16). Then, during his speech, Benjamin pronounced his son Mosiah to be king, publicly charging him with the task of teaching the law to the people; he also enjoined the people to "keep the commandments of my son, or the commandments of God which shall be delivered unto you by him" (Mosiah 2:31). After his address, Benjamin consecrated Mosiah as king, formally giving him "all the charges concerning the kingdom"; he then appointed priests to teach the people to "know the commandments of God and to stir them up in remembrance of the oath which they had made" (Mosiah 6:3).

10. Theological review of history. At two points in his speech, Benjamin briefly discussed historical topics. He reviewed the recent past by summarizing the character and history of his administration. Furthermore, after reminding the assembly that God had always sent prophets to the children of men, he recounted some of the more distant experiences of the early Israelites, describing how Moses showed the Israelites "many signs, and wonders, and types, and shadows" concerning the coming of Christ (Mosiah 3:15), as also did the prophets, but how the Israelites hardened their hearts. As Benjamin explained, the Israelites did not understand that the law of Moses availed nothing without the atonement of Christ (see Mosiah 3:13–15).

11. Revelation of the future. In Mosiah 3, Benjamin revealed things to come. He called special attention to his prophetic words:

> And again my brethren, I would call your attention, for I have somewhat more to speak unto you; for behold, I have things to tell you concerning *that which is to come.* And the things which I shall tell you are made known unto me by an angel from God. . . . For behold, the time cometh, and is not far distant, that with power, the Lord Omnipotent who reigneth, who was, and is from all eternity to all eternity, shall come down from heaven among the children of men, and shall dwell in a tabernacle of clay. (Mosiah 3:1–2, 5)

Verses 5–10 contain further revelations about the future mission of Jesus Christ.

12. Promises. Benjamin gave his people many promises. For instance, he promised that if they would remember the greatness and goodness of God and their own nothingness, if they would humble themselves and pray continually, and if they would remain strong in their faith in the advent of Christ, then they would "always rejoice, and be filled with the love of God, and always retain a remission of [their] sins; and [they should] grow in the knowledge of the glory of him that created [them], or in the knowledge of that which is just and true" (Mosiah 4:12). Furthermore, he told the people that as a result of their righteousness and belief in God, they would "not have a mind to injure one another, but to live peaceably, and to render to every man according to that which is his due" (Mosiah 4:13), and that parents would teach and care for their children and the needy in a righteous manner (see Mosiah 4:11–16). In Mosiah 2:22, 31, Benjamin promised his people that if they would obey Mosiah, the new king, they would receive the blessings of peace and prosperity; and in Mosiah 5:9, 15, he promised them salvation and eternal life. Such promises are conditioned upon obedience, and they are typical of literary formulations found in Moses' farewell speech in Deuteronomy.

13. *Appointment of or reference to a successor.* Before his farewell address, Benjamin privately announced that Mosiah would become his successor (see Mosiah 1:15–16), and during the speech he proclaimed his son the new king and commanded the people to keep Mosiah's commandments (see Mosiah 2:31). After the speech, Benjamin formally consecrated Mosiah as king (see Mosiah 6:3).

14. *Bewailing the loss.* The record makes no mention of mourning over Benjamin's death, probably because he was not on his deathbed at the time he delivered his speech. Perhaps, however, one may see in the response of the people another form of mourning: fearing for their own eternal lives, the people fell to the earth, overwhelmed, having "viewed themselves in their own carnal state, even less than the dust of the earth. And they cried aloud with one voice, saying: O have mercy, and apply the atoning blood of Christ that we may receive forgiveness of our sins, and our hearts may be purified" (Mosiah 4:2). Perhaps these cries reflected not only the people's sorrow for sin, but also their lament over the prophesied death of the Lord God Omnipotent, their awareness of Benjamin's approaching death, and their own mortality.

15. *Future degeneration.* Benjamin's speech, though serious and sober, is positive and optimistic. No pessimistic predictions about impending degeneration among his people as a whole are found. Benjamin does, however, implicitly acknowledge that future degeneration is possible. He realized that some of the individuals listening to him would not obey him but rather would obey the evil spirit and remain in a state of open rebellion against God. For them, judgment and punishment is in store:

> And thus saith the Lord: [These words] shall stand as a bright testimony against this people, at the judgment day. . . . And if they be evil they are consigned to an awful view of their own guilt and abominations, which doth cause them to shrink from the presence of the Lord into a state of misery and endless torment, from whence they can no more return; therefore they have drunk damnation to their own souls. (Mosiah 3:24–25)

Moreover, in Mosiah 4:14–15, Benjamin also spoke concerning the need to teach children properly, presumably in order to prevent future degeneration among his people.

16. Covenant renewal and sacrifices. These two factors are clearly visible in Mosiah 1–6. Shortly before Benjamin's address commenced, the people offered sacrifices and burnt offerings to God (see Mosiah 2:3). At the conclusion of his speech, Benjamin asked the people if they believed his words, and they replied that they desired to make a covenant with God: "We are willing to enter into a covenant with our God to do his will, and to be obedient to his commandments in all things that he shall command us, all the remainder of our days" (Mosiah 5:5; see 5:1–7).

17. Providing for those who will survive. In Mosiah 4, Benjamin commanded his people to care for the children and for the poor, both spiritually and temporally. He imposed these duties on all those who would survive him, and he made the act of providing for the poor a mandatory condition which the people must satisfy in order to retain a remission of their sins (see Mosiah 4:14–26). His reappointment of priests also provided for the spiritual needs of all those who could survive him (see Mosiah 6:3).

18. Consolation to the inner circle. In his preparations for transferring the kingdom to his son Mosiah, Benjamin met first with all his sons, his closest circle of family associates (see Mosiah 1). Benjamin extended comfort to the entire assembly at several points in his speech; he viewed his entire audience as family, as his "friends" and "kindred" (Mosiah 4:4), and as an eternal family, the sons and daughters of God (see Mosiah 5:7). In his closing words, Benjamin gave comfort and encouragement to all his people, assuring them that great blessings would be theirs if they lived as he had taught them (see Mosiah 5:15).

19. *Didactic speech.* Many didactic elements are present in Benjamin's speech. Benjamin taught the importance of such things as service, humility, charity, obedience, faith, the atonement of Jesus Christ, and many other practical and spiritual virtues.

20. Ars moriendi *or the approach to death.* This element is not found in Benjamin's speech, though it might be seen in Mosiah 2:28–30.

Based on this data, a strong case can be made in support of the fact that the pattern of ancient farewell addresses that has been detected by scholars in recent years was illustriously carried out by Benjamin in his classic farewell address. Almost every element found and enumerated by Kurz in a wide array of ancient sources—but especially the aspects pertinent to the biblical tradition—was included by Benjamin.

Was Benjamin Following Prior Patterns?

A logical inference from the foregoing data is that Benjamin was aware of the ancient farewell speech tradition and followed its pattern consciously. This raises the question: which prior precedents did Benjamin know about as he designed and orchestrated his final farewell sermon? Three possibilities present themselves: (1) precedents from previous Book of Mormon prophets and leaders; (2) biblical examples known to him from the plates of brass; and (3) cases in additional texts found on the plates of brass.

Several farewell speeches are contained in the Book of Mormon. Indeed, it seems that it became almost mandatory for a Book of Mormon prophet near the time of his death to deliver his parting words to his posterity, his people, or to future readers. It exceeds the scope of this study to compare all the elements of these farewell speeches in depth, but even a cursory survey shows that most of Kurz's farewell speech elements are present in these seven final statements or discourses in addition to Benjamin's: Lehi (2 Nephi 1–4), Nephi (2 Nephi 31–33), Jacob (Jacob 4–6), Enos (Enos 1:27), Mosiah (Mosiah 28–29), Mormon (Mormon 6:17–7:10), and Moroni (Moroni 10:34).

Benjamin would have been aware of the farewell texts of Lehi, Nephi, Jacob, and Enos. After Benjamin, the tradition continued in the Book of Mormon, though it became much less distinct. Benjamin's speech must be viewed as a part of this longstanding, venerable Nephite literary and rhetorical tradition, which very likely drew much of its strength from biblical sources. Two tables show the elements of the farewell speech protocol included by both Book of Mormon and Old Testament prophets. Four Old Testament accounts are old enough to have been on the plates of brass: Moses (Deuteronomy 31–34), Joshua (Joshua 23–24), David (1 Kings 2:1–10; compare 1 Chronicles 28–29), and Samuel (1 Samuel 12:1–25). Table 1 examines Book of Mormon speeches, and table 2 compares Old Testament speeches with that of Benjamin.[5] From the information on these tables we can examine the similarities and patterns found in the different records.

It is also possible that Benjamin was aware of other farewell speeches contained on the plates of brass that are not

Table 1
Farewell Speeches in the Book of Mormon

Kurz's Attributes of Typical Ancient Farewell Addresses	Lehi	Nephi	Jacob	Enos	Benjamin	Mosiah	Mormon	Moroni
1	◗	○	●	○	●	◗	○	●
2	●	●	●	●	●	●	○	○
3	●	●	●	●	●	○	●	●
4	●	●	●	●	●	●	◗	●
5	●	●	●	◗	●	●	●	●
6	●	●	●	◗	●	●	●	●
7	●	●	◗	◗	●	◗	●	●
8	○	◗	◗	○	◗	○	○	●
9	●	●	○	◗	●	●	○	○
10	●	○	●	○	●	●	●	○
11	●	●	●	◗	●	◗	◗	●
12	●	●	●	◗	●	●	●	●
13	●	○	○	○	●	●	○	○
14	○	○	○	○	○	◗	○	○
15	◗	●	●	○	◗	●	◗	◗
16	○	○	○	○	●	○	○	○
17	●	●	●	○	●	●	●	●
18	●	○	●	○	●	○	○	○
19	●	●	●	●	●	●	●	●
20	●	●	●	●	○	○	◗	●

● present
◗ implied
○ absent

Table 2
Farewell Speeches in the Old Testament and Benjamin's Speech

Kurz's Attributes of Typical Ancient Farewell Addresses	Moses	Joshua	David	Samuel	Benjamin
1	●	●	●	○	●
2	●	●	○	●	●
3	◗	●	○	●	●
4	●	●	●	○	●
5	●	●	●	●	●
6	●	●	●	●	●
7	●	○	○	○	●
8	○	○	○	○	◗
9	◗	○	●	○	●
10	●	●	○	●	●
11	●	●	○	○	●
12	●	●	●	○	●
13	●	○	●	◗	●
14	●	○	○	○	○
15	●	●	◗	●	◗
16	●	●	●	○	●
17	●	○	○	○	●
18	○	○	○	○	●
19	●	○	○	○	●
20	○	○	○	○	○

● present
◗ implied
○ absent

found in the Bible today. In a Hebrew text recorded at least as early as the time of Christ—and quite possibly containing materials that are considerably older—an account appears of a farewell speech delivered by an Israelite leader named Cenez.[6] Without necessarily arguing that this precise text was found on the plates of brass, the speech of Cenez (which was not included by Kurz) provides an excellent example of yet another ancient Israelite farewell sermon and perhaps is the kind of additional material Benjamin might have known about and used as a model.

The history of Cenez tells of a prophet-warrior-leader who succeeded Joshua as the first judge in Israel. The precise spelling of his name is shrouded in obscurity, and versions of it such as Cenez, Zenez, and Zenec have been used in various Latin manuscripts. D. J. Harrington, translator of the text in Charlesworth's *Pseudepigrapha*, spells the name as Kenaz. The traditions about him were known well enough that he is mentioned by Josephus, who knew him as Keniazos.[7] We shall call him Cenez, following the Latin manuscript (A).

According to *Pseudo-Philo*, Cenez ruled the Israelites for fifty-seven years—about the length of time that Benjamin probably reigned. During Cenez's lifetime he purged his people by burning all the self-confessing covenant-breakers. When the time came for him to die, Cenez called his people together in a large assembly and spoke to them about what the Lord was prepared to do for his people in the last days. Cenez reestablished God's covenant with the Israelites, and his priest Phinehas revealed to the people sacred things that had been shown one night to Phinehas's father in a dream.

In this text, the modern reader gets a close look at what an ancient Israelite farewell and covenant renewal assembly might have been like, or at least what one Jewish historian long ago understood it to have been. Because of the numerous points of similarity it has to the farewell and covenant-renewal assembly convened by Benjamin,[8] this text is worth examining in detail. The following consists of chapter 28 of *Pseudo-Philo* as translated by D. J. Harrington in the Charlesworth volume, with a few of the ancient Latin phrases included and explained. The italicized phrases indicate points of contact with Benjamin's speech and are discussed following the text itself:

> And when the days of Kenaz drew *near for him to die*, he *sent and summoned all* of them and Jabis and Phinehas the two prophets and Phinehas the son of Eleazar the priest, and he said to them, "Behold now the Lord has shown to me all his wonders that he is *ready to do for his people in the last days* (literally "the newest days," in novissimis diebus). And now I will *establish my covenant* (or "last will," testamentum) *with you today* so that you do not abandon the Lord your God after my departure. For you have seen all the wonders that came upon those who sinned and what they declared in *confessing their sins* voluntarily, or how the Lord our God destroyed them because they transgressed against his covenant. Now therefore *spare those of your household and your children*, and stay in the paths of the Lord your God lest the Lord destroy his own inheritance."
>
> And Phinehas the son of Eleazar the priest said, "If Kenaz the leader and the prophets and the elders command it, I will speak the word that I heard from my father when he was dying, and *I will not be silent* about the command that *he commanded me* while his soul was being taken away." And Kenaz the leader and the prophets said, "Speak, Phinehas. Should anyone speak before the priest who guards the commandments of the Lord our God, especially since truth goes forth from his mouth and a shining light from his heart?"
>
> And then Phinehas said, "While my father was dy-

ing, he commanded me, saying, 'These words you will say to the sons of Israel, "When you were gathered together in the assembly, *the Lord appeared to me three days ago in a dream by night* and said to me, 'Behold you have seen and also your father before you how much I have toiled among my people. But after your death this people will rise up and corrupt its ways and turn from my commands, and I will be very angry with them. But I will recall that time that was before the creation of the world, the time when man did not exist and there was no wickedness in it, when I said that the world would be created and those who would come into it would praise me. And *I would plant* (or "I shall plant for myself," plantabo mihi) *a great vineyard*, and from it I would choose a plant (or "planting," "cutting," plantationem); and I would care for it (or "put it in different places," disponam) and *call it by my name*, and it would *be mine forever* (or "always," semper). When I did all the things that I said, nevertheless my plant that was called by my name did not recognize (or "perceive, or acknowledge as genuine," agnoscet) me as its planter, but it destroyed its own fruit (or "corrupted its fruit," corrumpet fructum suum) and did not yield up its fruit to me (or "did not bring forth its fruit," non proferat fructum eius).'"' And this is what my father commanded me to say to this people."

And Kenaz and the elders and *all the people lifted up their voices and wept* ("together," unanimiter) with great lamentation until evening and said, "Will the Shepherd destroy his flock for any reason except that it has sinned against him? And now he is the one who will *spare us according to the abundance of his mercy*, because he has toiled so much among us."

And when they had sat down, a holy spirit ("the Holy Ghost," spiritus sanctus) came upon Kenaz and dwelled in him and put him in ecstasy, and he began to prophesy, saying, "Behold now I see what I had not hoped for, and I perceive that I did not understand. Hear now, you who dwell on the earth, just as those staying a while (or "dwelling, or tarrying," commorantes) on it prophesied before me and saw this hour even before the earth was corrupted (corrumperetur; compare nine appearances of *corrupt* or *corrupted* in Jacob 5), so all of you who dwell in it may know the *prophecies that have been fixed in advance* (or "decided, determined at a previous time," predestinatas). Behold now I see flames that do not burn, and I hear springs raised up out of a sleep for which there is no foundation, and I perceive neither the tops of the mountains nor the roof of the firmament, but everything has no appearance and is invisible and has no place whatsoever. And although my eye does not know what it sees, my heart will find what to say. Now from the flame that I saw not burning, I saw and behold a spark came up and, as it were, laid for itself a platform. And the floor was like what a spider spins, in the pattern of a shield. And when this foundation had been set, behold there was stirred up from that spring, as it were, boiling foam; and behold it changed itself into another foundation, as it were. Now between the upper foundation and the lower there came forth from the light of that invisible place, as it were, the images of men; and they were walking around. And behold a voice was saying, 'These will be a foundation for men, and they will dwell in between them for 7,000 years.' And the lower foundation was solid material, but the upper was of foam. And those who went forth from the light of the invisible place, they will be *those who will have the name 'man'*" (or "of a man," eius hominis). And when he will sin against me and the time will be fulfilled, the spark will be put out and the spring will stop, and so they will be transformed."

And when Kenaz had spoken these words, he was awakened, and his senses came back to him, but he did not know what he had said or what he had seen. But this alone he said to the people: "If the repose of the just after they have died is like this, we must die to the corruptible world so as not to see sins." And when he had said these words, Kenaz died and slept with his fathers. And the people mourned for him thirty days.[9]

The farewell speech of Cenez seems to manifest twelve of Kurz's elements, as enumerated below:

1. The summons. Cenez himself summoned all his people, along with two prophets and the son of the priest.

4. Impending death. His assembly occurred at a time when it was "near for him to die."

5. Exhortation and *17. Providing for those who will survive.* Cenez also admonished his people to spare those of their household and their children and to stay in the paths of the Lord.

6. Warnings and final injunctions. His people acknowledged his warning that the shepherd would destroy his flock only if it had sinned against God.

9. Tasks for successors and *13. Appointment of or reference to a successor.* Phinehas's dying father commanded his son (successor) to speak his final words. His father commanded him to tell the people certain things.

10. Theological review of history. Only those who remain diligent in keeping the commandments and covenant of the Lord will be preserved. Cenez recalled in his speech the wonders that came upon those who had sinned and those who had fallen into idolatry and adultery. When they voluntarily confessed their sins, the Lord destroyed them by burning 6,110 transgressors, according to events mentioned earlier in *Pseudo-Philo's* history of the time of Cenez.

11. Revelation of the future. Following this response by the people, Cenez began to prophesy, saying, "Behold now I have seen what I had not hoped for, and I perceive that I did not understand. Hear now you who dwell on the earth." In the middle of Cenez's assembly, Phinehas, the son of Eleazar the priest, reported an extraordinary vision received by Eleazar as he was about to die. Phinehas had been commanded by his father to reveal these things to Israel, and Phinehas did so at a special time when the people were "gathered together in the assembly." Otherwise, Phinehas was to remain silent about this revelation until commanded to speak. Cenez announced that his purpose was to tell that which the Lord had shown to him, particularly all the Lord's wonders and that which he was ready to do for his people "in the last days."

14. Bewailing the loss. After his death, Cenez's people mourned for thirty days. Also, as in the allegory of the olive tree in Jacob 5, Eleazar was told that the plant would not recognize God as its planter and would destroy its own fruit and not yield up fruit to God. Upon hearing these things the people of Cenez "lifted up their voices and wept with great lamentation until the evening."

16. Covenant renewal and sacrifices. Cenez was concerned to establish the covenant of God with the people on that day so they would not abandon the Lord after Cenez's departure.

19. Didactic speech. Much of his address takes on a didactic tone.

In addition to Cenez's conformity to the biblical tradition, many similarities can be found between the account of Cenez and the speech of Benjamin, including the following, which do not necessarily fit into any of Kurz's categories in particular:

- The command of Eleazar was a command given by a father to his son, just as Eleazar entrusted his son with sacred knowledge to be preserved and transmitted to subsequent generations. Commands from fathers also play a prominent role in the protection and transmission of sacred knowledge in the Book of Mormon. Following this same pattern, Benjamin commands his sons and gives them charge concerning the affairs of the kingdom and the sacred treasures as he is about to die.[10]

- The vision of Eleazar is extraordinary. The occasion of an annual assembly, when the people were "gathered together in the assembly," triggered a vision in which the Lord appeared to Eleazar "in a dream by night." Likewise, Benjamin reveals the very sacred words made known unto him "by an angel from God" who woke him up and stood before him and delivered a message (Mosiah 3:2).

- The words of the Lord to Eleazar began by acknowledging that the Lord had toiled long among the people. Benjamin also recognizes the great goodness of God to his people (see Mosiah 4:6).

- Eleazar was told that even though the Lord would be angry with his people because of their corruption, he would recall both the things that were planned before the creation of the world and the world's purpose as a dwelling place for those who would praise God. Of course, praising God occupies a prominent and important position in Mosiah 4:1–11.

- Eleazar was told how God would plant a vineyard and choose a particular plant that would become special to him. God would care for it and call it by his name and it would be God's forever. These words distinctively recall the allegory of the olive tree in Jacob 5. Moreover, Benjamin echoes the theme that his people are a "highly favored people of the Lord" (Mosiah 1:13), would be kept and preserved by God (see Mosiah 1:13; 2:31), and would specifically be called by his name (see Mosiah 1:12; 5:9–12), through all of which the Lord would seal them his (see Mosiah 5:15).

- Cenez declared that he had been privileged to see those

things which had been seen and established "even before the earth was corrupted," which were "fixed in advance," and also to know those things as they had been
"prophesied [by others] before" him. In a similar way,
Benjamin asserts that the substance of his prophecies
had been shown to previous generations, to Moses and
his people, and also to all the "holy prophets" who
spoke concerning the Lord's coming (Mosiah 3:15).

- The prophecy of Cenez foresaw the millennial day
  when, in his view, the world would become invisible.[11]
  From a spark there was laid a foundation and from a
  spring there emerged a firmament; between these
  two—the new heaven and the new earth—there came
  forth from the light of that place the images of men who
  would dwell there for 7,000 years. These are they who
  will have the name "man" or, according to a variant
  text, "they will be those who will dwell and [will have]
  the name of that man" (habitabunt et nomen hominis
  illius). For Benjamin, this is the name that should never
  "be blotted out, except it be through transgression"
  (Mosiah 5:11). Parenthetically, the blotting out of names
  was vividly a part of Cenez's early ministry, since Cenez
  wrote the names of sinners on books that were then
  blotted out of Israel when the books were consumed by
  divine fire.[12]

- The final statement of Cenez was that his people must
  "die to the corruptible world so as not to see sins."
  Benjamin's central admonition is that people must put
  off the natural man and become saints and that this is
  the only way to be found blameless (see Mosiah 3:19–22).

  Pseudo-Philo is a valuable text shedding light on the religious, cultural, and literary backgrounds of Benjamin's
speech. The valedictory words of Cenez and others capture
the essence of the traditional Israelite farewell sermon,

through which the Western mind can more deeply appreciate yet another dimension of the salutatory words and deeds of King Benjamin. Some of the foregoing similarities may be coincidental, but taken together they form an impressive array. The items on this list—the theology, imagery, protocol, and ritual—point consistently in the same direction, to the Hebrew background and Palestinian provenance of *Pseudo-Philo*.[13]

This chapter has considered several ideas. Above all, Benjamin's speech is the most complete example of a typical Israelite farewell speech known today. Benjamin's address epitomizes this genre of traditional Israelite literature, as recently defined in scholarly studies. The account of the funeral speech of Cenez is probably the next best example in existence, followed by Moses' concluding words in Deuteronomy 31–34. Given the obscurity of this information in *Pseudo-Philo* before the turn of this century, the remarkable affinities between the farewell assembly and address of Cenez and the final speech of Benjamin become even more impressive and highlight even further the strong conformity and congruence between King Benjamin's speech and the farewell speeches found in the biblical tradition.

Notes

1. William S. Kurz, "Luke 22:14–38 and Greco-Roman and Biblical Farewell Addresses," *JBL* 104 (1985): 251–68. See also William S. Kurz, *Farewell Addresses in the New Testament* (Collegeville, Minn.: Liturgical Press, 1990).

2. Kurz, "Luke 22:14–38," 261.

3. Ibid.

4. This information was briefly reported in "Benjamin's Speech: A Classic Ancient Farewell Address," in *Reexploring the Book of Mormon*, ed. John W. Welch (Salt Lake City: Deseret Book and FARMS, 1992), 120–22.

5. The data concerning the Old Testament prophets was found in Kurz, "Luke 22:14–38," 262.

6. An English translation of this work, which is titled *Biblical Antiquities* or *Liber Antiquitatum Biblicarum*, is available in James H. Charlesworth, ed., *Old Testament Pseudepigrapha* (Garden City: Doubleday, 1985), 2:297–377. Its unknown author is called Pseudo-Philo because the work was collected and found among a number of books written by Philo of Alexandria. For more information comparing and distinguishing elements in Cenez's life and what is known about the ancient prophet Zenos who was known to the writers of the Book of Mormon, see John W. Welch, "The Last Words of Cenez and the Book of Mormon," in *The Allegory of the Olive Tree*, ed. Stephen D. Ricks and John W. Welch (Salt Lake City: Deseret Book and FARMS, 1994), 305–21.

7. Josephus, *Antiquities* 5.3.3; compare Joshua 15:17.

8. Hugh W. Nibley first detected the fact that this account in *Pseudo-Philo* was relevant to the Book of Mormon; see *Since Cumorah* (Salt Lake City: Deseret Book and FARMS, 1988 [1st ed., 1967]), 286–89. He was interested in connecting Cenez (Zenez, Zenec, Kenaz, Cinez) with the Book of Mormon Zenos and with the author of the Thanksgiving Hymns from Qumran, but he does not mention Benjamin.

9. D. J. Harrington, "Pseudo-Philo: A New Translation and Introduction," in Charlesworth, *Old Testament Pesudepigrapha*, 2:341–42.

10. The pattern in the Book of Mormon begins with Nephi's commands to his brother Jacob (see Jacob 1:2) and then is continued by the commands of Jacob to his sons and grandsons. After Benjamin, Alma and his posterity follow the same pattern (see, for example, Alma 37). See John W. Welch, "The Father's Command to Keep Records in the Small Plates of Nephi" (Provo, Utah: FARMS, 1985).

11. Nibley, *Since Cumorah*, 288, understands the text otherwise. He sees the words of Cenez in 28:7 as "recall[ing] to his hearers' minds the state of things at the creation of the earth," whereas the response of Cenez's listeners in 28:10 strongly indi-

cates that this prophecy is describing the future "repose of the just after they have died." Nibley, *Since Cumorah*, 288, explains the awkwardness of his reading by concluding that "much of the vision is missing." Understanding the text from the outset as foreseeing the millennial or eschatological day seems more natural, however, and it is also consistent with the eschatology in the rest of *Pseudo-Philo*. See Harrington, "Pseudo-Philo," in Charlesworth, *Old Testament Pseudepigrapha*, 2:301.

12. *Pseudo-Philo* 26:3–4, 8.

13. See Harrington's comments in Charlesworth, *Old Testament Pseudepigrapha*, 2:298–300.

CHAPTER 5

ASSEMBLY AND ATONEMENT

Hugh W. Nibley

Public and Private

At a recent general conference we heard of plans for building a larger "tabernacle."[1] That word taken literally denotes the opposite of an assembly hall, where everybody meets. A tabernacle (Latin *tabernaculum*) is "a little house made of boards," a quick shelter or booth put together from boards, branches, and bits of clothing. The roots behind the English word *booth* describe its purpose: it is the Semitic *bayt* from the verb *bāta-yabītu* (Aramaic), meaning "to spend the night," and certainly suggests our word *bide* or *abide*. The Hebrew *sukkāh* is the same as the Egyptian *seh*, with an ideogram depicting the booth that provided shelter—"shadow in the daytime from the heat, and . . . covert from the storm and from rain" (Isaiah 4:6)—for an individual family living in the open during the Passover (see Leviticus 23:42–43; Nehemiah 8:17)—"Thou mayest not eat within thy gates" (Deuteronomy 12:17; compare 12:18).

The people whom Benjamin commanded to assemble "gathered themselves together throughout all the land" (Mosiah 2:1). And yet they all enjoyed a private family outing, for they "pitched their tents round about, every man according to his family, . . . every family being *separate* one from another" (Mosiah 2:5). This was the practice observed at the Feast of Tabernacles, and booths are one of the characteristic features of great national assemblies of the ancients throughout the world. At the culmination of the celebration we have both the vast unison of the hallelujah shouts and the private thoughts, secret names, and whispered exchanges of the initiation that preceded and followed with name, seal, mark, and personal registration.[2]

Some today have trouble making the distinction between what is strictly private in one's thinking—after all, we are commanded to pray in secret—and what is necessarily shared among members of the church. Some would have uniform political commitment required of all members, and some would have mission and stake presidents prescribe what books may be read and what music may be heard by the individual members. How far does free agency go? How far can individual tastes be assigned? No one was a more stalwart exponent of temperance than Brigham Young; yet when his father asked him to sign the Temperance Pledge, he resolutely refused. What he objected to of course was being officiously told what his principles were.[3]

Albert Einstein begins his book, *The World as I See It:* "A hundred times every day I remind myself that my inner and outer life depend on the labours of other men, living and dead, and that I must exert myself in order to give in the same measure as I have received and am still receiving."[4] And yet no one was ever more aloof, absorbed, private, and original than Einstein, and still his inner and outer life are not to be separated.

Committees do not think; they noodle, throw things around, drop suggestions, send up flags and signals in the hope that someone may react with an original idea. But

committees themselves contain nothing of the deep, prolonged, concentrated thought of the individual or the brilliant flashes of insight that may result. Solon, the wisest of
the Greeks, said that the Athenians were too smart by half
individually but collectively a lot of simpletons. It is always
gratifying to discover that the members of a quorum, board,
committee, or faculty are individually smarter than they are
collectively. That is necessarily the case because each has
certain ideas that would not be quite acceptable to everybody. Yet we still come together to consult; we still warm up
to each other's presence. I might say of family, friends, and
church members what St. Augustine said of God: *"Fecisti
nos ad te et inquietum est cor nostrum donec requiescat in te*—
You made us to be with you, and so our heart is restless
until we can be with you"[5] (and when we are all with you,
we are of course all together with each other—we are made
both to be together and to stand alone but too much of either
condition can drive one crazy).

The Great Assembly

Over the years, I have spoken about the "great assembly,"
or year-rite. People have asked me just what I mean by this.
I can best sum it up from an article I wrote forty-five years
ago, now beyond the statute of limitations:

> That is the *panegyris*, the great [New Year's] assembly
> of the entire race to participate in solemn rites essential to
> the continuance of its corporate and individual well-
> being. . . . At hundreds of holy shrines, each believed to
> mark the exact center of the universe and represented as
> the point at which the four quarters of the earth con-
> verged—"the navel of the earth"—one might have seen
> assembled at the New Year—the moment of creation, the
> beginning and ending of time—vast concourses of people,

each thought to represent the entire human race in the presence of all its ancestors and gods.

A visitor . . . could have witnessed ritual contests: foot, horse, and wagon races, . . . choral competitions, the famous Troy game, beauty contests, and . . . [especially] the now famous ritual year-drama . . . [in which] the king wages combat with his dark adversary of the under-world, emerging victorious after a temporary defeat from his duel with death, . . . as the worthy and recognized ruler of the new age.[6]

The drama celebrated the creation of the world, the marriage and coronation of the king, and the birthday of the human race. It culminated in a feast of abundance, the king having proven his capacity to bring prosperity and victory to the people. All these elements are present in Benjamin's celebration. "The 'origin' of the drama (both of Greek tragedy and of the dramatic spectacles of the ancient Near East and of Europe)," writes Mircea Eliade, "has been traced back to certain seasonal rituals which, broadly speaking, presented the following sequence: conflict between two antagonistic principles (Life and Death, God and the Dragon, etc.), tragic suffering of the God, lamentation at his death and jubilation to greet his 'resurrection.'"[7]

King Benjamin sums up the purpose of the meeting as *at-one-ment*, bringing together man with God and also men with each other, but men do not swear loyalty to each other; their common loyalty to God alone unites them in the most perfect possible unity (see Mosiah 5:2–5). In fact, Benjamin explains that the purpose of the meeting is "that they might give thanks to the Lord . . . , that they might rejoice and be filled with love towards God and *all men*" (Mosiah 2:4). That is the spirit of the great assembly everywhere; it recalls the Golden Age, when men and gods lived together in a heaven on earth.

The Coronation Assembly

Since treating the subject of ritual in the Melchizedek Priesthood manual for 1957 (lesson 23),[8] I have come upon more confirmation, such as in a particularly interesting writing of Nathan the Babylonian, a writer of the tenth century A.D. who has left us an eyewitness account of the coronation of the Prince of the Captivity or Exilarch in Babylonia. He speaks with the detachment of a gentile though he may have been a Jew.[9] Since we find no extended description of a coronation in the Old Testament, as we do in the Book of Mormon, and since no one showed interest in the remarkably uniform pattern of ancient coronations until the present century, Nathan's account provides us with strong evidence for the authenticity of Mosiah's account.

Because these Jews living in Babylonia had lost their real king and yet wished to continue their ancient customs, it was necessary to choose a candidate. The chief men of the community came together to appoint the new Exilarch from one of the most illustrious families. The elders then set him apart by the laying on of hands and sent out a proclamation that all should come to the coronation, bringing the most costly presents of gold, silver, and textiles that each could afford. Note that Benjamin, in a list of contrasts between himself and the conventional divine kings, expressly forbids that very thing: "I have . . . not sought gold nor silver nor any manner of riches of you" (Mosiah 2:12). In Babylonia, the day before the affair a wooden tower ten feet high and four and a half feet broad was erected as a speaker's platform, so the king could be seen and heard by the vast multitude. On the top was a throne covered by a *baldachin*, or tent, and on either side at a lower level were seats for two counselors—on the right the head of the School of Sura, on the left the head of the School of Pumbadetha. The tower was covered with costly materials, behind which at ground level a highly trained youth choir was concealed.[10]

When King Benjamin finishes his address, he says, "I am about to go down to my grave . . . in peace, and my immortal spirit may join the choirs above in singing the praises of a just God" (Mosiah 2:28). In the account of Nathan the Babylonian, the Exilarch's descent from the tower after his final speech was accompanied by the heavenly voices behind the veil. The *ḥazzān*, or cantor, representing the old king, began with a blessing on the congregation followed by the antiphonal hymn of praise by the congregation. The people arose and gave the Eighteen Benedictions. Then the king appeared on the tower and sat on his throne between the two lesser thrones. Then all the people sat. The cantor alone sang "Redeemer of Israel" and all the people stood for prayer; all the youths shouted "Holiness to the Lord." And then the *ḥazzān* put his head and shoulders into the *baldachin*, representing Moses' meeting with the Lord at the *kappōreṭ*, the tent of the covenant (later the veil of the temple), and exchanged words, including the secret name, in a whisper so that only those nearby could hear. When the blessing ended, the boys in the chorus shouted "Amen," all the people keeping silent until the blessings were completed. Then the Prince of the Captivity, having received his authority (he was now the king), spoke openly and taught on the subject of the lesson for that day; an interpreter or translator (Aramaic *meturgeman*) stood by because the people spoke Aramaic and the scripture was Hebrew. The king taught with great passion, keeping his eyes closed, his head wrapped in a *tallit*; as he talked for an hour there was not a peep in the congregation, for if anyone uttered a single word he uncovered his eyes and terror and dread fell upon all the people—even so does Benjamin hold his congregation spellbound in awe and humiliation.

The address was followed by a questioning period; a wise old man, very shrewd and instructed, acted as intercessor. The *ḥazzān* gave a New Year's greeting of long life: "Long live our Prince of the Captivity; may you all live long." We recall that Benjamin declares, "This day he hath . . . begotten you" (Mosiah 5:7)—it was the universal birthday, the day of creation, the *natalia*; to celebrate it the people bring the first fruits of the New Year and animals for sacrifice (see Mosiah 2:3). To mark the new birthday as a rebirth, King Benjamin gives the people a new name as a covenantal token. As in Mosiah's account, register was taken of the names of those present, acknowledging their donations. Then the Book of the Law was brought, and a priest and a Levite both read from it, after which the cantor—the old king—took the book to the new Exilarch, and all the people rose to their feet as the new Exilarch read to them from the Book of the Law. As in Mosiah's account, the main purpose of the event was to give a refresher course in the Law to the entire nation. To be the interpreter for the royal teacher was considered a very high honor indeed, and a rich and important man was chosen for the privilege. The prince was again blessed by the Book of the Law, which was returned to its place with blessings "forever and ever." The people then fell to and enjoyed the sumptuous feast; Nathan lays special emphasis on the dessert.

As in Mosiah, there were frequent exchanges between the king and the people, the latter reciting in unison. This explains the odd circumstance in which the people "all cried aloud with one voice" (Mosiah 4:2) and proceeded to recite in unison an ecstatic statement of some fifty words. How could they do it spontaneously "with one voice"? Throughout the world such acclamations were led by a special cheerleader, sometimes called a *stasiarch*, who stood before the crowd and received notes from important people or shouts from the audience requesting particular cheers. He would recite a sentence to the people and wave a flag to lead them in a uniform chant (compare Deuteronomy 27:14–26). Sometimes the king himself chose to lead the cheering, and some Roman emperors enjoyed it. There was no limit to what could be shouted in unison, and it could go on for hours.

The Nothingness of Man

Benjamin begins his talk on public policy by distancing himself from the once-conventional model of the divine year-king, disclaiming any supernatural status for himself. Not only is he not "more than a mortal man" (Mosiah 2:10), but he is a sadly typical one, "like as yourselves, subject to all manner of infirmities in body and mind" (Mosiah 2:11). What a confession! And yet we now find everywhere that the nothingness of man is the theme of the great year-drama.

Today the great year-rite is being examined even more closely. Professor Hornung, the most celebrated of today's Egyptologists, says that the coming together of the Egyptians to rehearse the creation of the world, the fall of man, and all that followed had three purposes. The first was to give some sort of explanation for the utterly wretched human condition on earth, which is always on the brink of failure and always looking forward to death.[11] Arthur Koestler and others conclude that "our race is . . . a very sick biological product," and there is nothing we can do about it; we are programmed for failure.[12] Koestler, after a lifelong search, solved the problem by suicide. But the ancients had a better way—they dramatized the situation. As uniform as the protocol of the feast itself was the drama that went with it. The drama began with the council in heaven discussing the creation, then continued with a dispute over leadership, the casting out of the adversary, the Garden of Eden, and the fall of man. These marvelous temple plays, some of which survive from very ancient times, give solace to our sorry state by lending it some majesty and dignity. The ancients went to the heart of the matter where our troubles are concerned, but tossed up their hands in despair when looking for a solution. It was simply beyond them. The choruses wail and lament; the lead players like the lyric poets wring their hands in despair: "O the human race!" says the chorus, "I have calculated your worth and find it sums up to exactly nothing."[13] Benjamin's sentiments exactly. A long tragic drama or trilogy of tragedies would be followed up by a slapstick comedy to make life endurable by laughing at ourselves.

Hornung's second point involves the question, Why does God leave men alone to suffer? Plato in the *Republic* accuses Aeschylus of charging God with *aporia*—failure to provide or falling short. Either God was helpless to save men or willingly stood by and let them suffer, an act which would make him either weak or vicious. The ancients never answered that one, as Omar Khayyam reminds us with wicked glee.

The third point was the utter cruelty of the abrupt curtailment of human life, long, long before any individual has had half a chance of using even a fraction of his potentialities—why are we so overendowed and then hustled from the scene before we can make proper use of our talents? It all seems so wrong.

Here, of course, we have the difference between Benjamin's teachings and those of the Greeks and Egyptians. Many recent studies have shown the close resemblance of the ancient Hebrew Wisdom Literature to that of the Egyptians. Both reach King Solomon's conclusion about this world:

> I have seen all the works that are done under the sun;
> and, behold, all is vanity and vexation of spirit. That
> which is crooked cannot be made straight: and that
> which is wanting cannot be numbered. . . . I gave my
> heart to know wisdom, and to know madness and folly: I
> perceive that this also is vexation of spirit. For in much
> wisdom is much grief and he that increaseth knowledge
> increaseth sorrow. (Ecclesiastes 1:14–15, 17–18)

Man is a born loser, but it is here that the ancients part company with Benjamin—they think they have seen it all, and so are guilty of both overrating and underrating themselves. The overrating is quite absurd: "And now I ask, can ye say aught of yourselves? . . . Nay. Ye cannot say that ye are even as much as the dust of the earth. . . . And I, even I, whom ye call your king, am no better than ye yourselves are; . . . I am old, and am about to yield up this mortal frame" (Mosiah 2:25–26). "For even at this time, my whole frame doth tremble exceedingly while attempting to speak unto you" (Mosiah 2:30). At the normal year-rite, the king was expected to be victorious in combat, majestic, irresistible, a rampant bull.

Then Benjamin really gets serious: "For the natural man is an enemy to God, and has been from the fall of Adam, and will be, forever and ever, unless he yields to the enticings of the Holy Spirit, and putteth off the natural man" (Mosiah 3:19). That is the key to the whole situation—we are dealing with the natural man and the natural man only. Jacob frankly admits that entropy is the fate of the natural man: "This flesh must have laid down to rot and to crumble to its mother earth, to rise no more" (2 Nephi 9:7). Moses, landing on earth as a natural man, is surprised to discover that "man is nothing, which thing I never had supposed" (Moses 1:10). But yet one verse later he announces that he is nothing less than "a son of God, in the similitude of his Only Begotten" (Moses 1:13).

After the Nephite king spoke, he saw that his people had come to view "themselves in their own carnal state, even less than the dust of the earth" (Mosiah 4:2). Benjamin rejoiced to see that "the knowledge of the goodness of God . . . has awakened you to a sense of your nothingness, and your worthless and fallen state" (Mosiah 4:5). "Ye should remember, and always retain in remembrance, the greatness of God, and your own nothingness, and his goodness and long-suffering towards you, unworthy creatures. . . . If ye do this ye shall always rejoice, and be filled with the love of God, . . . and ye shall grow . . . in the knowledge of that which is just and true. And ye will not have a mind to injure one another" (Mosiah 4:11–13). This definition of the real world makes a nice contrast to what we call "the real world" today, where everyone is advised to learn martial arts, both to avoid and to inflict injury. And then the cruelest cut of all, "For behold, are we not all beggars?" (Mosiah 4:19). If we become too much attached to our earthly carnal state, Benjamin reminds us, in effect, "There is nothing for you here. You can't stay here. You should be glad that this is not where you belong!"

During his life span on this earth, in which all are in the same situation, "the natural man is an enemy to God"—carnal, sensual, and devilish, or as we would say, oversexed, greedy, and mean, or perhaps lecherous, pampered, and vicious. Obviously things are out of order; but if we are really nothing, how can we save ourselves? Someone has to intervene, and here, with a sigh of relief, we learn that Benjamin has been tutored for this talk by an angel. This shocks us into realizing that we have not seen it all after all. There may be more to life than going to the office every day—this is *not* "all there is!"

Where did we get all those gifts and endowments with which we enter the world and then leave without ever using them? This question of Plato's was repeated by Lamarck—to

130 • *Hugh W. Nibley*

Darwin's immense annoyance; he called it an abominable mystery. If natural selection chooses only those defenses of which the creature has absolute need for survival, why has our brain capacity so outrageously exceeded our needs? Where did we develop it? Where did we need it, if not in a far more sophisticated environment than we have here, where the stupidest species have survived the longest? We are equipped for much greater things than we ever achieve, and we yearn for something better than we can ever expect here and yet envisage most positively. That is what Plato calls *anamnesis*, dim memories of a better world that give us intimations of immortality at the sight of the *kaloskagathos*, something good, true, and beautiful. We are living in a dismal swamp between two glorious uplands. Why this unhappy interruption? For life is an interruption which consists almost entirely of an unbroken succession of interruptions. All this is to try man and to tempt him. For in getting ready for the long pull ahead, we must learn to cope with the worst.

Principles of Government

After discounting all of man's boasted claims to independence—"of what have ye to boast? . . . can ye say aught of yourselves?" (Mosiah 2:24–25)—and declaring himself satisfied with a place in the choir above, while resigning his royal teaching job on earth, Benjamin lays down the first principle of government, which may appear very strange to us but is a corollary to the nothingness of man: there shall be no contentions among the people lest they "list to obey the evil spirit" (Mosiah 2:32). *Tendere* means to stretch a rope; *contendere* is a tug-of-war. The Lord's first words to the Nephites, after he had introduced himself to them and told them how to baptize, dealt with contention:

According as I have commanded you . . . there shall be no disputations among you, as there have hitherto been; neither shall there be disputations among you concerning the points of my doctrine, as there have hitherto been. For verily, verily I say unto you, he that hath the spirit of contention is not of me but is of the devil, who is the father of contention, and he stirreth up the hearts of men to contend with anger, one with another. Behold, this is not my doctrine, to stir up the hearts of men with anger, one against another; but this is my doctrine, that such things should be done away. (3 Nephi 11:28–30)

Does he want to do away with the adversarial method, two-party debate, and legal confrontation, which we consider the best means of settling an argument? Exactly. The trouble is that such methods settle nothing. As Karl von Clausewitz noted, political argument leads to war, which simply "continu[es] . . . political intercourse [argument] . . . by other means,"[14] until the exhausted powers fall back on diplomacy again, and so prepare for another war. I spent most of my mission teaching the gospel in villages in Baden, Germany, both in the Black Forest and the Rhine Plain. The villages were either Protestant or Catholic, and there was always tension, mistrust, and dislike between them. Why? Because some learned divines had held formal disputations on Christian doctrine some four hundred years before. Need we say more? The ancient plays likewise are endless discussion and argument with chorus and semichorus, protagonist and antagonist, constantly going at it and only making matters worse. The oldest surviving play begins with the king announcing his program: "My children, we must think this thing through."[15] But the play leaves us with the battle of the sexes, of the races, and nations all going full blast. The ladies' chorus—the Danaids—express their loathing of Egyptian-style marriage and can't stand men of darker skin, and the nations of Egypt and Argos exchange insults and go to war. Such was the result of their endless discussions in tireless debate, and their raging sexism, racism, and nationalism still flourish in the same countries.

How do we solve things then? Benjamin makes it clear:

> And now, my brethren, . . . as ye have kept my commandments, and also the commandments of my father, and have prospered, and have been kept from falling into the hands of your enemies [the two things which the king must guarantee], even so if ye shall keep the commandments of my son, or the commandments of God which shall be delivered unto you by him, ye shall prosper in the land, and your enemies shall have no power over you. (Mosiah 2:31)

This looks like autocratic monarchy and bald theocracy, but Benjamin has already settled that issue by his heavy emphasis on both his own mediocre qualifications and the right of the people in common with the royal family to receive revelation for themselves. They too can say, "And we, ourselves, also, through . . . the manifestations of his Spirit, have great views of that which is to come; and were it expedient, *we* could prophesy of all things" (Mosiah 5:3). Here the people receive their individual revelations. Prophesy means both to foretell and speak out, but here there is a contrary-to-fact or future-less-vivid condition: the individual is expected to receive and follow the promptings of the Spirit for himself, but *not* to introduce his personal revelations into public discussion. It is "expedient" for all to receive "great views" by revelation, but not expedient, unless so commanded, to teach them publicly.

Benjamin feels strongly that people have been on the wrong path in their confrontational politics (see Mosiah 2:32). If they continue that way, they will die in their sins and receive everlasting punishment (see Mosiah 2:33). In engaging in partisan debate, "ye do withdraw yourselves from the Spirit of the Lord, that it may have no place in you to guide you in wisdom's paths" (Mosiah 2:36). This is a real and omnipresent danger in society: "And now, O man, remember, and perish not" (Mosiah 4:30). The danger is perennial: "If ye do not watch yourselves, and your thoughts, and your words, and your deeds . . . even unto the end of your lives, ye must perish" (Mosiah 4:30). We are constantly liable to slip into partisan controversy.

This seems contrary to what we have been taught about such things as the importance of debate and the two-party system. But Benjamin is above all that; he wants to transfer our whole activity to another plane. "[Stand steadfast] in the faith of that which is to come," he says, "which was spoken by the mouth of the angel" (Mosiah 4:11). Benjamin puts it bluntly, "Believe that man doth not comprehend all the things which the Lord can comprehend" (Mosiah 4:9). What you have to do, he says, is to "believe that ye must repent of your sins . . . and humble yourselves before God; and ask in sincerity of heart that he would forgive you" (Mosiah 4:10). Does that sound authoritarian? We seem to forget that these words were handed not only to Benjamin but also to Joseph Smith by an angel from another sphere. Their purpose is to help prepare us for that other sphere. Do not expect the words of the angel to be like other texts, conservative or liberal. Benjamin pleads desperately, "all ye old men, and also ye young men, . . . and [even] you little children who can understand my words, . . . *awake* to a remembrance of the awful situation of those that have fallen into transgression" (Mosiah 2:40). Plainly, things among the Nephites had reached a dangerous state. The people had wandered from the road of keeping the commandments, "both temporal and spiritual" (Mosiah 2:41). What we should be after is not to gain advantage in this world but to "dwell with God in a state of never-ending happiness" (Mosiah 2:41). He knows that it will sound unrealistic. If that suggests our worldly vantage point as some faraway wishful thinking or fantasy, Benjamin brings us around: "O remember, remember that *these things are true*" (Mosiah 2:41). They are not imaginary; it is the everyday world, the light of common day, that is a deception. Far from being expected to accept these things on authority, the people presently are given to see it all for themselves.

The word *power* occurs over four hundred times in the Book of Mormon. Power is the essence of politics where the object of the game is to be the party or individual in power. This is true, even though few would challenge Lord Acton's famous maxim, "All power corrupts."[16]

But Benjamin, in his speech on government and national policy, uses the word only seven times, of which five refer to God, who "has . . . *all* power" (Mosiah 4:9). The other two passages speak only of powers which no man possesses, that is, the power to express our full obligation to God (see Mosiah 2:20) and the power which our enemies do *not* have over us if we obey the commandments of God (see Mosiah 2:31). What power does that leave to feeble man? There are only two sources of power. One is God, the other the evil one who covets power: "Satan . . . sought . . . that I should give unto him mine own *power*; by the *power* of mine Only Begotten, I caused that he should be cast down" (Moses 4:3). What he wanted was power over others, and so it has ever been with man. From Cain come "oaths . . . given by them of old who also sought *power*. . . . [The kinsmen of Akish] were kept up by the *power* of the devil to administer these oaths unto the people, to keep them in darkness, to help such as sought *power* to gain *power*. . . . Whatsoever nation shall uphold such secret combinations, to get *power* and *gain*, . . . they shall be destroyed. . . . Suffer not . . . that these murderous combinations shall get above you, which are built up to get *power* and *gain*" (Ether 8:15–16, 22–23).

How remarkable that a royal discourse on the subject of government and dominion never once refers to power and tells the people bluntly that the king never wanted their money—he could get what was sufficient for his needs by working on the farm! And this total shifting of values takes us directly to the subject of the atonement.

The Politics of Shame

The atonement requires a totally different state of mind from that which men suppose leads them to success. Benjamin makes direct appeal to the hearts of men. In case after case, he teaches what suggests "the politics of shame." The phrase has been revived in a recent book by Stuart Schneiderman,[17] and the word *shame* has suddenly come into general use by politicians against each other. It is a sense of shame that keeps people from stepping over the line and doing mean and ignoble things. Benjamin knew that when he said that every man's immortal soul should be awake "to a lively sense of his own guilt, . . . his breast [filled] with guilt, and pain, and anguish, . . . like an unquenchable fire" (Mosiah 2:38). The result is "never-ending torment" (Mosiah 2:39). But nothing could be farther from today's ethic, which is to feel shame only for what an opponent does and call public attention to it as a ploy to take over power. This relieves the inner tension on both sides, and since "the great American cultural revolution" of the 1960s, Schneiderman writes, "Ostentatious displays of wealth were good, as were exhibitionistic displays of one's sexual prowess. . . . Obnoxious and insulting behavior became acceptable. . . . Rude language became a sign of freedom."[18] Fame became more highly valued than shame: "Seeing omens of destruction everywhere we grasp at solutions offered by guilt culture: more police, more courts, more prisons, more litigation, more regulation, more lawyers."[19] And all that is shameful, and Benjamin turns away from it.

In pointing the way for his people, the king cites case after case where their own immediate reaction should be one of shame. "Believe that man doth not comprehend all the things which the Lord can comprehend" (Mosiah 4:9). This should make me feel cheap and ashamed of my own arrogance, and the reaction is "Believe that ye must repent . . . and humble yourselves before God; and ask in sincerity of heart that he would forgive you" (Mosiah 4:10). Does God have to argue his case? Not "if ye have known of his goodness and have tasted of his love" (Mosiah 4:11). That is another feeling: taste, like shame, is a final argument about which *non est disputandum*—there is no argument. We are the first, last, and only judges of our actions, and our clear and vivid recollection shall testify against us at the judgment. When you compare "the greatness of God, and your own nothingness, and his goodness and long-suffering towards you, unworthy creatures," the shame will bring you into "the depths of humility" (Mosiah 4:11). Is it not shameful that you should "have a mind to injure one another, . . . [that you should let] your children . . . go hungry, . . . transgress the laws of God, and fight and quarrel one with another, . . . [giving way to] the evil spirit?" (Mosiah 4:13–14). And how shameful to turn your back on the beggar, with some self-serving rationalization that "the man has brought upon himself his misery" (Mosiah 4:17). How do you know that? And you a beggar yourself! For shame! Is it necessary to pass a law against holding back on sharing what God has given you liberally? Or to use verse 27—that "all these things [be] done in wisdom and order, for it is not requisite that a man should run faster than he has strength" (Mosiah 4:27)—as an excuse for withholding your substance until a later time? What is it that prompts us to return what we have borrowed—fear of a lawsuit? (see Mosiah 4:28).

The Hard Question

Eight years ago I wrote a sixty-page article titled "The Meaning of the Atonement."[20] Some things were explained, but the great mysteries remain. "Mysterious, incomprehensible, . . . and inexplicable" are the workings of the atonement, according to the *Encyclopedia of Mormonism*.[21] The first question which such an admission raises is whether all "things which pertain to our religion are only appendages" to what Joseph Smith declared to be the center of our religion—the atonement.[22] Is it meant to remain mysterious? Not everything is incomprehensible to everybody: "It is given unto you to know the mysteries of the kingdom of heaven, but to them it is not given" (Matthew 13:11). As the Pearl of Great Price tells us, some mysteries "ought not to be revealed at the present time" (explanation to fac. 2, fig. 9); some are only "to be had in the Holy Temple of God" (fac. 2, fig. 8); some "will be given in the own due time of the Lord" (fac. 2, figs. 12–21). As to others: "If the world can find out these numbers, so let it be" (fac. 2, fig. 11).

The mysteries are on the borderline, depending on our own qualifications. Scientific writers in the 1920s told us there were no more mysteries; today it is all a mystery. Chapters 14 to 17 in the Gospel of John describe in matter-of-fact terms the comings and goings, departures and arrivals that ultimately put into effect the at-one-ment, or joining of the apostles and the Saints with the Father and the Son in heaven. Yet for conventional Christian theologians, all of this is quite unimaginable, without space or motion. So we see that mystery is knowledge not known to some: "He that hath ears to hear, let him hear" (Matthew 11:15). "Behold my beloved brethren, I will unfold this mystery unto you; if I do not, by any means, get shaken from my firmness in the Spirit, and stumble because of my over anxiety for you" (Jacob 4:18). A people are condemned who "will not search knowledge, nor understand great knowledge, when it is given unto them in plainness" (2 Nephi 32:7). We make our own mysteries; we are not meant to be kept in darkness, and the mysteries of heaven will be unfolded to us as we make an effort to understand them.

This is particularly true of the atonement. Students now beset me with searching questions. Some are genuinely perplexed, and others are set on challenging the rationality of the gospel. I am assailed by eight questions in particular. The first three are those Terrible Questions, listed by Professor Hornung, which the ancients left unanswered. The plan of atonement offers a clear explanation.

1.   First is the problem of evil. In our world, evil spoils everything, and it is everywhere, even ingrained into our own carnal, sensual, and devilish natures. Why is that? Answer: It was planned that way. We were once at one with the Father and hope to be so again. But in the meantime we are being prepared for a higher order of glory; our whole life here is a state of probation, as Jacob tells us (see 2 Nephi 2:21), and the adversary is permitted to try us and to tempt us. The existence of Satan is another of those points that leaves the clergy perplexed. Yet the existence of evil is at least as certain as the existence of gravitation; we must accept the reality of these two powerful forces whether we can explain them or not. We cannot proceed into the eternities in ignorance; we must know the worst if we are to cope with the worst and bring the atonement of the Father to others. We come down here to discover those weaknesses and vices that could not come out in the presence of God and

angels and to dig out the nitty-gritty of our earthly existence, recognize and acknowledge it in repentance, and wash it away in baptism.

2. Then there is that *aporia*—where is God when we need him? The explanation is to be found in the plan of salvation. The master of the house is one taking a far journey, leaving his servants on their own. He deliberately delays his return, and, when he does appear "like a thief in the night," catches them completely off guard, doing just what they normally do—some of them beating their fellow-servants to get more work out of them, while they enjoy their perks in drunken dinner parties (see Matthew 24:42–51; Joseph Smith—Matthew 1:46–54). If we are all to be at one again in the hereafter, King Benjamin reminds us, it is to be in a different spirit from that competitive neo-Darwinism, which he so vigorously condemns.

3. The third problem that distressed the ancients is the cruel curtailment of life, which shuts off the lives of almost all living things in midcourse. Why?—"Lest [Adam] put forth his hand and partake also of the tree of life, . . . and live forever [in his sins]" (Moses 4:28). After this life has been declared a vale of tears, we should only be too glad to get out of it as soon as possible, were it not for the uncertainty of the hereafter which gives us pause and makes us decide to stick it out here in this dismal place. Yet the atonement makes this life bearable, even delightful. The doctrine of the atonement gives us permission to enjoy ourselves to the fullest here and now, as we revel in the gospel; time and space drop out of the question, leaving us completely at ease and inexpressibly happy (see Mosiah 2:41; 3:4, 13; 4:11–12; 5:3).

4. How can we apply the blood of Christ to relieve our present condition? Answer: It redeems us from our sins. To redeem is to buy back, to ransom. We return to the other

world loaded with experience, some of it pretty bad, which can be turned to our advantage once we are purged of the vice in our nature. The scriptures use the language of business, of buying and selling, to make the problem clear to a money-minded people. We shall explain the blood presently.

5.   But why payment? Cannot we simply acknowledge that all make mistakes, write them off, and "get on with our lives," as the popular saying goes? Why must we pay the uttermost farthing? (see Matthew 5:26). That question was paramount with the ancients. The great tragedies begin with something seriously wrong in the land—plague, famine, war, etc. Someone has done foolish or wicked things and all are paying the price. We must find the culprit and payment must be made, both to put an end to disaster and to pay for the damage already done. Who shall it be? The king, because he is responsible for the welfare and safety of the state? The periodic sacrifice of kings, whom old age had rendered a liability to their people, was commonplace in primitive and ancient societies. "The king must die!" Oedipus was a king who refused to pay the price and instead placed himself at the head of the investigation and proceeded to accuse everyone else. The chorus reminds him that we are all in this together, and Oedipus admits, "we are all sick, none more than myself." All are to blame. But how do we assess the blame individually and calculate the penalty? In a lump sum for all, choosing one scapegoat out of the whole community by impartial lottery? Is that fair? Yes, if we all share the suffering, and there is a very real way in which all do.

6.   But before we consider sharing, we must ask why the payment must be painful. Why all the agony, on which Benjamin dwells so disturbingly? The Greek *poinē* is the clue. It is blood money, the payment of a debt, the evening up of accounts, according to the *Lexicon*,[23] and it is always painful. The English word *pain* is borrowed from the ancient legal

terms *pains* and *penalties,* referring to the payment of a debt. Note that the words *pain, punish, penalty, repentance, penitence, penitentiary,* and *penal* all imply a feeling of discomfort and at the same time of paying back, the pain remaining until the debt is cleared.

7. But why the emphasis on blood? Benjamin goes to the limit here. Answer: The blood makes it clear that (a) it is a real sacrifice and (b) it goes all the way. Even the interrupted sacrifice of Isaac required the token, but real, shedding of blood in circumcision of the covenant. Benjamin tells us that the Lord would sweat blood from every pore, not from the physical brutality of the Roman soldiers, but because "so great shall be his anguish for the wickedness and abominations of his people" (Mosiah 3:7). There is a limit to physical suffering but not to spiritual. And this answers the final questions.

8. Why should one innocent person, Christ, suffer so horribly for the sins he did not commit? How can all that suffering be transferred from one person to another? Is that justice? The answer: Do not think that anyone is getting off easy. Each suffers to his capacity in time for his own sins: "there could be nothing so exquisite and so bitter as were my pains," Alma reports (Alma 36:21). And worst of all, "we shall be brought to stand before God, knowing even as we know now, and have a bright recollection of all our guilt" (Alma 11:43). Physical suffering has its limits at which the body shuts off, but not spiritual suffering, which requires the atoning blood of Christ more than any theory or abstraction. "God so loved the world, that he gave his only begotten Son, that whosoever believeth in him should not perish, but have everlasting life" (John 3:16). "So loved the world," says the cynic, that he sacrificed somebody *else*? When you consider who that somebody was, or even who Abraham's sacrifice was—far dearer to him than his own

life, which Abraham had often put on the line—this makes the sacrifice of the Father equal to that of the Son.

But it was only when the angel said "Now I know" (Genesis 22:12) that the ram was substituted—Abraham did not have to make the supreme sacrifice, and although his own life was spared on the altar, he must be given full faith and credit for having been prepared to sacrifice what was more precious to him than his life. Even so, we are expected to "do the works of Abraham" (D&C 132:32) and go all the way—eternal life is not cheaply bought.

All this is made possible by the principle of substitution or proxy or vicarious work, so well-known to Latter-day Saints. It should be clear how one can suffer for another. The work we do for our dead calls for a measure of trouble, inconvenience; we must take some pains in behalf of those for whom we feel responsible as they anxiously await our action for release from long confinement. They are, where possible, our closest relatives for whom we feel most responsible. And we can take further pains in long hours of searching the records, writing the histories, going to the temple at dawn—all very minor sacrifices—but for someone else. The leaders of all the great dispensations—Adam, Enoch, Noah, Abraham, Moses, and Joseph Smith—suffered greatly for others, but there was only *one* who could suffer for all. The word *suffer* is from *sub-ferre*, "to bow under" or "to bear a load." Only *one* has the capacity, strength, and greatness to bear the load of all. This is a mystery, but it is a mystery that anyone can understand. Who can deny that "if there be two spirits, . . . one shall be more intelligent than the other," and, that being the case, that "there shall be another more intelligent than they" (Abraham 3:18–19)? Jesus Christ bore our load because he and only he was able to, his work and his glory being "to bring to pass the immortality and eternal life of man" (Moses 1:39). He shares all he has, as his Father does, with all who will receive it. That there is such a being is as certain as the proposition that one person can be greater than another.

The ancients saw light and life coming from the sun, and every creature that receives that life and light must pass it on to others. Benjamin insists that all who have received the bounty of God must also pass it on. "Are we not all beggars?" is more than a rhetorical question; we receive what we have not produced. It is a pure gift from God; even by working day and night, no one could hope to earn it. We must pass it on and not divert all the water of the canal to our own use: "For the earth which drinketh in the rain that cometh oft upon it, and bringeth forth herbs meet for them by whom it is dressed, receiveth blessing from God" (Hebrews 6:7); "Wherefore receive ye one another, as Christ also received us to the glory of God" (Romans 15:7).

The sun is only one of countless participants in the pouring forth of energy into the cosmos, according to Moses and Abraham—"worlds without number" (Moses 1:33), "I could not see the end thereof" (Abraham 3:12), and so forth. And all are dependent on each other so that when one perishes "the heavens [shall] weep, yea, and all the workmanship of mine hands" (Moses 7:40), and God himself weeps, so closely are they bound in each other's affections. "I . . . [gave them a] commandment, that they should love one another . . . ; but, behold, they are without affection, and they hate their own blood" (Moses 7:33). This is the reverse of atonement. In the eternal order of things, we are all assembled and bound together, at-one, if only by the laws of nature—the four mysterious forces. It can easily be seen how sin—ego-centered, inconsiderate, spiteful—can loosen the bonds of affection, in the manner of entropy. These are far more than imaginary forces. Only the intervention of God himself who "possesses all power" can reverse the process (2 Nephi 9:7). Jacob tells us this in that other great address given by royal sanction in 2 Nephi 6–10, which should always be read along with the great words of Benjamin.

Notes

1. Gordon B. Hinckley, "This Glorious Easter Morn," *Ensign* (May 1996): 65.

2. For such assemblages celebrating both individual covenants and national unity, see Hugh W. Nibley, *The Ancient State* (Salt Lake City: Deseret Book and FARMS, 1991), 8–9, 41–43, 150–51, and passim.

3. Brigham Young, in *JD*, 14:225.

4. Albert Einstein, *The World as I See It* (New York: Philosophical Library, 1949), 1.

5. St. Augustine, *Confessions* 1.6.

6. Hugh W. Nibley, "The Hierocentric State," in *Ancient State*, 99–100, reprinted from *The Western Political Quarterly* 4/2 (1951): 226.

7. Mircea Eliade, *The Forge and the Crucible* (Chicago: University of Chicago, 1978), 10.

8. See Hugh W. Nibley, "Old World Ritual in the New World," in *An Approach to the Book of Mormon*, 3rd ed. (Salt Lake City: Deseret Book and FARMS, 1988 [1st ed., 1957]), 295–310.

9. See Benzion Halper, *Postbiblical Hebrew Literature* (Philadelphia: Jewish Publication Society of America, 1946), 1:37–38.

10. See ibid., 39.

11. See Erik Hornung, *Der ägyptische Mythos von der Himmelskuh* (Goettingen: Vandenhoeck & Ruprecht, 1982), x.

12. Arthur Koestler, *Janus: A Summing Up* (London: Hutchinson, 1978), 2.

13. Sophocles, *Oedipus Rex*, lines 1186–89.

14. Karl von Clausewitz, *War, Politics, and Power: Selections from* On War, *and* I Believe and Profess, tr. and ed. Edward M. Collins (Chicago: Gateway, 1967), 83.

15. Aeschylus, *The Suppliant Maidens,* line 176.

16. "Power tends to corrupt and absolute power corrupts absolutely" (Lord Acton, letter to Bishop Mandell Creighton, 3 April 1887).

17. See Stuart Schneiderman, *Saving Face: America and the Politics of Shame* (New York: Knopf, 1995).

18. Ibid., 124.

19. Ibid., 288–89.

20. See Hugh W. Nibley, "The Meaning of the Atonement," in *Approaching Zion* (Salt Lake City: Deseret Book and FARMS, 1989), 554-614.

21. Jeffrey R. Holland, "Atonement of Jesus Christ," in *Encyclopedia of Mormonism,* 1:86, citing John Taylor, *The Mediation and Atonement* (Salt Lake City: Deseret News, 1882), 148–49.

22. *The Teachings of the Prophet Joseph Smith,* comp. Joseph Fielding Smith (Salt Lake City: Deseret Book, 1976), 121, cited in Holland, "Atonement of Jesus Christ," 83.

23. See Henry G. Liddell and Robert Scott, *Greek-English Lexicon,* 7th ed., s.v. "poinē."

CHAPTER 6

KING BENJAMIN'S SPEECH
IN THE CONTEXT OF
ANCIENT ISRAELITE FESTIVALS

Terrence L. Szink and John W. Welch

Years of research have identified many threads of evidence in the Book of Mormon that tie back into the observance of ancient Israelite festivals. While traces of several preexilic Israelite festivals have been found in various places in the Book of Mormon, no source has been more fertile than King Benjamin's speech. To a greater degree than most people might have suspected, characteristics of the speech that mark the occasion as a day of holy Israelite observances are both rich and specific. Several texts and surrounding contexts highlight the importance of this public occasion as a significant religious event.

During the first two weeks of each fall season, all the people living under the law of Moses kept certain days holy, marking the celebration of the turn of a new year, the continuation of God's reign, and the abundance of God's goodness. Although it is impossible to reconstruct with precision what transpired in antiquity on those days, it appears that such Israelite celebrations probably included religious convocations, rituals, and festivals that served to renew the allegiance of the people to their heavenly and earthly kings, to purify the group from all unholiness, and to strengthen their commitment to revealed principles of personal and community righteousness. Several kings in ancient Israel selected this time of the year for the official inauguration of their reign or the installation of their successor to the throne. From several similar indications, it would appear that King Benjamin likewise planned to celebrate the culminating day of his life—the coronation of his firstborn son Mosiah—on or around this high and holy season in the traditional Israelite religious calendar. No other time of the year would have been more suited for the installation of a new regent or for renewing the covenant relationship between God, king, and people—the essence of any Israelite monarchy.

The discoveries reported and developed in this chapter are attributable to the research, collaboration, and combined criticism of many people. As early as 1957, Hugh W. Nibley proposed the theory that Benjamin's speech was an ancient year-rite festival,[1] a theme that he develops further in his newly prepared chapter in this volume. His 1939 doctoral dissertation drew on Roman and other pagan sources to apply a typology of the classical year-rite festivals to the Roman games,[2] and his intense familiarity with these popular religious or quasi-religious practices in diverse parts of the ancient world readily led him in 1957 to identify certain parallels between the typical annual pagan ritual and Benjamin's speech.[3] Nibley's genius for drawing cultural associations broke new ground forty years ago by inviting Book of Mormon scholars to view Benjamin's speech in an entirely new light.

However, even though Nibley's initial approach included a few references to the Israelite Feast of Tabernacles in connection with his analysis of the standard year-rite phenomenon of many ancient civilizations,[4] his original pagan year-rite theory attracted few fully settled followers. More research and further investigation was invited and needed. The main question Nibley left unresolved was why an inspired king in the house of Israel would ever be inclined to mimic or dignify the practices of a pagan year-rite cult.

A possible answer to this question began to emerge in the 1970s and took clearer shape in the 1980s. Rather than ranging far afield among widely scattered ancient civilizations, but without rejecting the value of comparative cultural studies, Latter-day Saint scholars in those years focused their attention more extensively on the Old Testament as well as many features of subsequent related Jewish history, literature, and ceremony grounded in the Hebrew Bible. Interesting bonds were discovered between Benjamin's speech and the laws, statutes, and ordinances revealed by Jehovah to the prophets of Israel who preceded and influenced Lehi and Nephi. The following chapter consolidates the results of this research and reports ideas contributed by many individuals.[5] In writing and editing this chapter, we express appreciation for the collegial willingness of this group to explore and share the many possibilities that seem, in our best judgment, to shed light on the setting and significance of Benjamin's address.

Israelite Festivals in the Book of Mormon: General Considerations and Caveats

Every civilization or culture, it seems, enjoys holidays or special times of the year. Christmas, Thanksgiving, Easter, Halloween, and the Fourth of July are among the main holidays celebrated in the United States. Other nations have similar holidays. Certain traditions associated with each of these days are of characteristic importance to their native cultures, especially as these celebrations perpetuate and reinforce the main institutions of that society, whether in the domain of church, state, or family. As important as such secular and religious holidays may be in the modern world, religious festivals and holy days carried even greater significance in the ancient world, particularly in Israel.

Under the law of Moses, Israelites were required to observe three main holy days each year (see Exodus 23:14–19). The first was the well-known spring festival of *Pesach* (Passover), which began the Feast of Unleavened Bread. The second was *Shavuot* (Pentecost), occurring fifty days after Passover. The third was an autumn festival complex that later developed into the composite two- or three-week-long observance of the three related celebrations of *Rosh ha-Shanah* (New Year and Day of Judgment), *Yom Kippur* (Day of Atonement), and *Sukkot* (Feast of Tabernacles).

These holy days held enormous religious, political, and family significance, especially since God had commanded their observance: "Three times thou shalt keep a feast unto me in the year" (Exodus 23:14). Details concerning the celebration of each holiday are found in a number of festival calendars and instructions in the Old Testament (for example, see Exodus 23:14–17; 34:18–23; Leviticus 23; Numbers 28–29; Deuteronomy 16). Accordingly, no person could claim to keep the law of Moses and not observe these special holy days, which would have been kept at least as intently as the strictly observed regular weekly sabbaths.

As guided by the Lord and his prophets, Lehi and his people diligently kept the law of Moses. Nephi affirmed, in the sixth century B.C., that his people "did observe to keep the judgments, and the statutes, and the commandments of the Lord in all things, according to the law of Moses" (2 Nephi 5:10), and that they did "keep the law of Moses, and look forward with steadfastness unto Christ, until the law shall be fulfilled" (2 Nephi 25:24). In 74 B.C., some fifty years after Benjamin's speech, the Nephites were still keeping the law of Moses: "Yea, and the people did observe to keep the commandments of the Lord; and they were strict in observing the ordinances of God, according to the law of Moses" (Alma 30:3). The Nephites were to continue to keep the law of Moses until it was fulfilled entirely by the death and resurrection of Christ (see 3 Nephi 1:24–25), and the Lamanites observed the law of Moses in the days of their righteousness (see Alma 25:15; Helaman 13:1). It stands to reason, therefore, that the Nephites in Benjamin's day would have kept holy observances that were appropriately similar to the festivals and holy days required by the Old Testament texts that the Nephites possessed on the plates of brass.

How the Nephites and Lamanites understood and applied those ancient biblical regulations, however, remains obscure. Jewish practices evolved, at least to some degree, during the period of the Babylonian captivity that began after Lehi and his family left the Holy Land. We do not mean to imply that the Nephites or Lamanites followed "the later varieties of Jewish law that proliferated among various Jewish communities several centuries after Lehi left Jerusalem,"[6] but it is still logical to conclude that these Nephites and Lamanites were committed to observe the ancient holy days as best they could in the essential forms in which those festivals were known under the preexilic law of Moses. Indeed, as has been argued extensively elsewhere, "the prophets of the Book of Mormon present a thoroughly Christian theology and religion" but all "against a background of ancient Israelite law and culture."[7] For example, Benjamin prepared his people for the end of the law of Moses when he stressed the importance of the atonement of Jesus Christ, repentance, and charity. Benjamin realized, as would the Jews eventually on the destruction of their temple in Jerusalem by the Romans, that "without repentance no sacrificial rites were of any avail. With the cessation of sacrifices, therefore, repentance was left as the sole condition of the remission of sins,"[8] placing emphasis on prayer and charity. Nevertheless, Benjamin and his subjects still recognized that the end of the law would not come until God himself would announce that momentous transition, as finally occurred in 3 Nephi 9:17–22.

In the meantime, the Nephites kept careful calendrical watch of their times and seasons, a necessary precondition in any society for the timely observance of specific days as legal holidays or annual festivals. Abundant evidence in the Book of Mormon shows that the people in the Nephite culture generally paid great attention to their calendar. In his editing, Mormon carefully kept track of years, months, and even days; the years from the time Lehi left Jerusalem, the years of the reign of the judges, the years from the appearance of the sign of Jesus' birth, and sometimes the months and days within those years were meticulously noted.[9] Throughout Jewish history, one of the most important reasons for keeping an accurate standardized calendar was to regulate and facilitate the observance of specific holidays,[10] especially since the law of Moses stipulated a precise day for most of the festivals. Bitter and divisive arguments over who had the right calendar in fact became deep and fundamental points of theological dispute among the Pharisees, the Essenes at Qumran, and other Jewish groups of that period.[11] Into the modern period, Jewish law still concerns itself with calendrical issues, such as what happens in regard to the observance of a festival when a Jew crosses the international date line and gains or loses a day.[12] Thus, one of the unstated reasons why the Nephites kept such careful track of their days, months, and years may well have been to create a strict framework within which they could properly observe their weekly sabbaths, annual holy days, sabbatical years, and jubilee releases, as well as identifying certain anniversaries in their individual lives that had legal significance under the law of Moses (such as retirement from routine priestly duties at age fifty according to Numbers 8:25).

While the Book of Mormon never mentions Passover, the Feast of Tabernacles, or any other religious holiday specifically by name, several reasons can be suggested to explain this omission. The ancient writers may have assumed that their readers would naturally understand. A person does not have to say the word *Christmas* to refer implicitly to that special day. Even a casual mention of "wise men" or "decorating a tree" is enough. In just the same way, the words *Passover* or *Pentecost* do not need to appear in the Book of Mormon to evoke images alluding to the Israelite holidays.[13] Alternatively, Mormon may have found such points to be irrelevant to his purposes, since he was writing after the time when the law of Moses had been fulfilled in Christ. Moreover, one must remember that the Book of Mormon was not designed to be prescriptive in the same way as are the codes found in the Torah. Thus, although Mosaic festivals receive only indirect attention in the Book of Mormon, this does not mean that they lacked importance in Nephite society, only that further details about them were not chosen for inclusion in the final abridgments of the narratives or speeches preserved in the Book of Mormon. Other Nephite records also existed, and they may well have contained extensive descriptions of their religious and social observances. Indeed, the weekly sabbath is rarely mentioned in the Book of Mormon (see only Jarom 1:5; Mosiah 13:16–19; 18:23), yet is it unthinkable that the righteous Nephites, throughout their history, did not remember to keep the sabbath day; and one must remember that the annual holy days and sabbatical years were also part of the ancient law of the sabbath.

While the annual festivals are not mentioned expressly in the Book of Mormon, perhaps allusions to these festival names were more apparent in the original Nephite languages than they are in the English translation. For example, these Hebrew names have meanings: in Hebrew, *Pesach* literally means "exemption"; *Sukkot* means "tabernacles" or "booths"; *Yom Kippur* is "day of atonement." Thus the reference to the word *tents*[14] in Mosiah 2:5 and the repeated mention of *atonement* in Mosiah 3 may well have caused a Nephite to think of the respective names of those holidays.

Whether expressly mentioned or not, evidence located in the Book of Mormon, particularly in King Benjamin's speech, supports the claim that those particular festivals which were most likely known to Israel in Lehi's day were indeed observed in the lands of Nephi and Zarahemla. Of course—and we repeat—it is difficult to determine which festivals were observed in preexilic Israel before the destruction of Jerusalem in 587/586 B.C., and how those religious feasts were celebrated in that era of Israelite history. No person alive today, of course, has ever witnessed an ancient Israelite celebration, and biblical scholars differ considerably in their views about the nature of the festivals in ancient civilizations, let alone the possible connections or borrowings between them.

Nevertheless, considerable evidence about ancient Israelite practices can be gleaned from many biblical passages. If those biblical texts were written before the time of Lehi, they become particularly useful and relevant to the study of Book of Mormon world views. It must be noted, however, that some biblical passages may reflect Jewish customs or practices that were influenced or modified in Babylon or Palestine only after Lehi's departure. In that case their value for understanding the Book of Mormon is diminished, although to address the theories and uncertainties involved in Old Testament chronological criticism exceeds the scope of this chapter. Accordingly, as various features of these festivals are discussed below, emphasis will be placed on those practices that can be traced most clearly to the earlier biblical periods, although later Jewish sources are not considered completely irrelevant to the discussion of King Benjamin's speech.

We are aware that it would simplify and tighten our presentation if we were to limit our sources to the preexilic materials; indeed, we believe that most of our points are supported by early data. We have chosen, however, to include later Israelite and Jewish sources, both for the sake of completeness and because research in this area may enrich our understanding. Moreover, many of the detailed and elaborate descriptions of Jewish festivals found in the Talmud and other later Jewish literature may well reflect long-standing Israelite traditions, even though it is not always possible to know which texts or details are archaic and which emerged as later innovations. Thus, while we are keenly aware that these later sources are much weaker than the earlier texts for our purposes, they still offer useful information. Even today, most of the basic elements in Jewish observances of these festivals strive to follow the instructions and patterns found in the ancient Torah scrolls pertaining to these festivals. For this reason, when one reads popular Jewish guides to the prayer services of these festival days today, numerous themes and even some phrases jump out at the reader as points of commonality between the Bible, long-standing Jewish tradition, and parts of Benjamin's speech. For example, during Yom Kippur and Rosh ha-Shanah, prayers praising him "who has granted us life" (She-hecheyanu), prayers signifying "the acceptance of

God's sovereignty" (the *Shema*), prayers recognizing the commandment to love (*Vəʾahavta*), and prayers describing thirteen attributes of God (*El melech yoshev*) are recited.[15] All these modern prayers are grounded in ancient biblical texts and several similar features are also prominent in Benjamin's speech, sometimes being expressed in quite similar terminology and phraseology.

General observations and caveats such as these lead us to the following position regarding the comparative use of biblical and Jewish sources in studying Benjamin's speech:

- When Book of Mormon concepts and practices are consistent with well-established early biblical materials, the relevance of these parallels to Benjamin's speech seems relatively clear. In these cases, one may fairly confidently assert that Benjamin was aware of those early biblical texts and traditions, which he consciously followed.

- When features of ancient biblical routines and institutions are unclear, it becomes impossible, of course, to determine with certainty whether Benjamin's speech resembled or differed from actual ancient Israelite concepts and practices. Nevertheless, in such cases it is interesting to study the possible reconstructions that have been advanced by biblical researchers and to compare their proposals with elements in Benjamin's speech, many of which are consonant with those sophisticated theories and scholarly results.

- With respect to the use of later rabbinic and Jewish traditions that were first committed to writing long after Lehi left Jerusalem, it may sometimes be argued that the origins of those rules and regulations found in the oral law can be dated back to the time of Lehi, even though the archaic written sources may be silent on the particular point involved.[16] If materials found in the oral Jewish tradition are similar to factors in Benjamin's speech, it becomes even more plausible that the oral tradition dates back far enough for it to have been known by Lehi, although one cannot rule out the possibility that the Jewish and Nephite practices simply developed independently along parallel lines.

There are many possibilities here, and we wish neither to overstate nor understate the possible significance of these Jewish comparisons in probing the context of Benjamin's assembly. Thus, in presenting the findings reported below, we usually will identify or signal the time period or source from which each piece of evidence derives. The biblical texts are the earliest and most relevant; the Mishnah (first and second century A.D.) and Talmud (second through fifth centuries A.D.) are later and constitute secondary evidence; Jewish traditions, customs, and liturgies are more recent and are less probative yet, but still interesting. Readers are free to weigh these bits of information as they wish in determining the degree to which these details may shed light on the festival celebration that was observed and enjoyed by King Benjamin and his people.

Finally, caution must be employed in dealing with evidence not only from the Old World, but also from the New. Beyond the problem of tracing the origins and identifying the elements of ancient Israelite and Jewish festivals, additional difficulties arise because it is not clear exactly what form of the law of Moses appeared on the plates of Laban and was brought to the New World by Lehi and his descendants, nor is it known how those rules were implemented.[17] The version of law found on the plates of brass may not have been exactly the same as the legal provisions—found mainly in the books of Exodus, Leviticus, Numbers, and Deuteronomy—that have come down to us in the Bible today.[18] Nevertheless, sufficient evidence is available to support a strong presumption that Lehi and his descendants had written legal materials quite similar to many passages in the King James Version of Exodus and Deuteronomy (for example, in Mosiah 13, Abinadi quotes the Ten Commandments from Exodus 20 and Deuteronomy 5). Accordingly, unless a good reason exists for doubting that the Nephites knew of a particular passage in the Torah, one may cautiously proceed on the tentative assumption that they adequately understood and appropriately followed that provision.

In spite of these challenges and uncertainties, attempting to identify the possible ancient Israelite holy days or festival season on which or during which a Book of Mormon speech or event may have taken place is significant and rewarding for several reasons: First, finding evidence of such observances tends to confirm the internal consistency of the Book of Mormon by showing that its peoples kept the law of Moses as they claimed. Second, knowing something of the potential background or context of a passage from the Book of Mormon promotes a better understanding of the possible meanings of its words and phrases. Third, because much of the following information about ancient Israelite or Jewish festivals pertinent to King Benjamin's speech was simply unknown by and—as far as we can discover—unknowable to Joseph Smith in 1829,[19] such accuracy supports the claim that the Book of Mormon was translated from an ancient Israelite record, as Joseph Smith explained.

With these general comments and caveats in mind, and without claiming to be exhaustive in our coverage or dispositive in our conclusions, we turn our attention to the exploration of specific details that link King Benjamin's speech to the main fall festivals celebrated in ancient Israel.

The Autumn Festival Complex

Of the three annual festival times in ancient Israel, the autumn festival complex was the most important and certainly the most popular in ancient Israel.[20] In early times it apparently was called the Feast of Ingathering. According to many scholars, the various components of the autumn festival were celebrated as a single season of celebration in the earliest periods of Israelite history.[21] Its many elements were not sharply differentiated until later times, when the first day of the seventh month became Rosh ha-Shanah (New Year), followed by eight days of penitence, then followed on the tenth day of the month by Yom Kippur (Day of Atonement) and on the fifteenth day by Sukkot (Festival of Tabernacles), concluding with a full holy week.

As this study will show, it appears to us that Benjamin's speech touches on all the major themes of these sacred days, treating them as parts of a single festival complex, consistent with what one would expect in a preexilic Israelite community in which the fall feasts were not sharply differentiated but were still closely associated as parts of one large autumn festival. That the elements of the three Israelite fall festivals appear in one integrated text in the book of Mosiah provides circumstantial evidence agreeing with the scholarly conclusion that the divisions into distinct Jewish festivals may have taken place after Lehi and his family left Israel.[22]

Many pieces of evidence support the view that an ancient Israelite autumn festival was observed at the time of King Benjamin. Although Benjamin's assembly may have involved only some of the features of these holy days, we believe that it makes good sense if one understands Benjamin's speech as taking place during the season of the year when the Nephites would have been turning their hearts and minds to the kinds of themes and concerns that characterized this time of annual religious renewal and activity in ancient Israel. The purpose of this study is to facilitate this inquiry. The later designations of New Year, Day of Atonement, and Feast of Tabernacles will be used, though this distinction need not have been clear in the minds of the Nephites, and, as will be indicated, many of the themes associated with these holy days apply to one or more of the individual festivals.

The New Year

Of the elements of the autumn festival in ancient Israel, one of the most interesting but least certain is the observation of the New Year.[23] In postexilic Judaism, the New Year became known as Rosh ha-Shanah, literally the "head of the year." However, this phrase appears only once in the Old Testament (Ezekiel 40:1), and in this case it does not appear to be referring to a New Year but rather to "the beginning of the year."[24] Many scholars even deny the existence of a New Year feast day in preexilic Israel.[25] Others reconstruct an Israelite New Year on indirect evidence and on the basis of New Year festivals in surrounding cultures.[26] Several important elements in the Jewish celebration, however, were probably not like New Year celebrations in other cultures; it was "not a time of revelry, but an occasion of the deepest religious import."[27] We will proceed on the assumption that a New Year festival existed in some form in ancient Israel and then compare Benjamin's speech with materials from both its proposed preexilic reconstructions and the postexilic Jewish traditions.

The first point to be made with regard to the New Year is that ancient calendar systems are extremely complex and have been the object of a great deal of study. The Nephite New Year was apparently set in the "first" month;[28] however, the dating of this festival in Israel was not always so defined. Exodus 12:2 appears to introduce a change from earlier practices. Later, Rosh ha-Shanah was celebrated on the first day of the seventh month. There appears to be evidence for years starting both on the first month and on the seventh month in preexilic Israel.[29] D. J. A. Clines examined all the evidence and concluded that no strong arguments exist for either a spring or autumn calendrical New Year.[30]

However, a distinction is made for many social purposes between the calendrical year and the agricultural year. Since the Feast of Tabernacles is an agriculturally based festival, it would follow the agricultural calendar. The reckoning of the sabbatical and jubilee years is also based on the agricultural year. Since the New Year is associated with both the Feast of Tabernacles and the sabbatical and jubilee years, it seems likely that it also would have been based on the agricultural year rather than the calendrical year,[31] which would argue for its observance, in some form, together with the other agricultural festivals that clearly belonged to the seventh month of the calendrical cycle. This may sound strange until we realize that in modern Western culture we also encounter various "years," the academic and fiscal years being two examples.

Leaving aside the calendrical issue, we can proceed to isolate some of the themes and traditions probably associated with the New Year. Unlike New Year's Day in most Western cultures, the beginning of a New Year's cycle in the ancient Near East was the occasion of a sacred religious celebration, one of the most important religious days of the year. The following are among the main traditions that have come to characterize the ancient Israelite New Year: the blowing of horns, sacrifice of burnt offerings, a day of judgment, the kingship of God, creation and renewal, remembrance and memorial, and the king's humility.

Horns. The blowing of horns was certainly a common part of Israelite culture and worship, and the most characteristic ritual of the later Rosh ha-Shanah was the sounding of the *shôfār*, the straight horn of a wild ram (see Numbers 29:1).[32] This is likely related to the "memorial of blowing of trumpets," specifically prescribed for the first day of the seventh month in Leviticus 23:24. Horns are never mentioned in connection with Benjamin's speech, but one would not necessarily expect this detail to have accompanied Benjamin's written script or to have been preserved.[33] Nevertheless, there is reason to believe that some kind of cue, such as the blowing of a horn or the announcement of an acclamation, would have been given to assemble the people (see Mosiah 2:9), to call them again to attention (see Mosiah 3:1), to call the people to fall simultaneously to the ground (see Mosiah 4:1), and to cry aloud all with one voice (see Mosiah 4:2; 5:2).

Furthermore, Jewish literature gives several commonly cited reasons for blowing the *shôfār*.[34] Most of these circumstances pertain to parts of Benjamin's speech that would have offered several occasions for the sounding of horns, namely when: (1) hailing God as King[35] (see Mosiah 2:19), especially at a coronation (see Mosiah 2:30; see also 2 Kings 9:13); (2) heralding the season of repentance (see Mosiah 2:9; 4:1; and possibly 4:26); (3) remembering the giving of the law on Mt. Sinai to Moses (which is mentioned in Mosiah 3:14; see also Exodus 19:19); (4) declaring the words of the prophets (prophetic declarations are referred to in Mosiah 3:3 and 3:13); (5) causing the people to tremble (see Mosiah 2:30; 4:1); (6) announcing the judgment of God (see

Mosiah 3:18, 24–25) and sounding the horn of warning or alarm (see Exodus 20:18; Amos 3:6), or calling the troops to arms (see Judges 3:27); (7) heralding the coming messianic age (see Isaiah 27:13 and Mosiah 3:5; see also Revelation 8–9); and (8) marking the resurrection of the dead (see Mosiah 3:10). The sounding of the horn in much later Judaism eventually came to be known as a reminder of the following:

> A call to contrition and penitence, as a reminder of the Shofar-sound of Sinai; and the Day of Memorial, the beginning of the Ten Days of Repentance which culminate in the Day of Atonement, as a time of self examination and humble petition of forgiveness. "The Scriptural injunction of the Shofar for the New Year's Day has a profound meaning. It says: Awake, ye sleepers, and ponder over your deeds; remember your creator and go back to Him in penitence. Be not of those who miss realities in their pursuit of shadows and waste their years in seeking after vain things which cannot profit or deliver. Look well to your souls and consider your acts; forsake each of you his evil ways and thoughts, and return to God so that He may have mercy upon you" (Maimonides).[36]

Though all these connections may not have been familiar in the days of Lehi, similar sentiments may well have existed already, to be expressed both by his descendants in the New World and by the posterity of his surviving relatives in Jerusalem. Since most of these traditional occasions and purposes for sounding the *shôfār* are so clearly manifest at the ceremonial sectional dividing points in Benjamin's speech, one can easily envision their being accompanied by the sounding of the *shôfār*.

Further evidence that the horn (*shôfār*) or the trumpet (*yōḇēl*) may have been used among the Nephites as a liturgical instrument, blown at the New Year to herald a season of repentance or on other similar occasions, may be garnered from Alma's wish that he might speak with the "trump of God, with a voice to shake the earth, and cry repentance unto every people" (Alma 29:1). Alma's psalm may well have been written for a New Year festival, because it appears in the text immediately after the ending of the fifteenth year (see Alma 28:9) and near the time of "the days of fasting, and mourning, and prayer" that seem to mark the beginning of the sixteenth year (Alma 30:2).[37]

Sacrifice. The typical New Year, like most festivals,[38] evidently began with burnt offerings of animals of "the first year." "In the seventh month, in the first day of the month . . . ye shall offer an offering made by fire unto the Lord" (Leviticus 23:24–25). Consistent with this, Benjamin's people brought "the firstlings of their flocks, that they might offer sacrifice and burnt offerings according to the law of Moses" (Mosiah 2:3).[39]

Judgment. A characteristic theme in both ancient Near Eastern and later Jewish sources is that the New Year is a day of judgment. In Babylonia and Assyria, the New Year festival took place in the month of Nisan in the spring.[40] An important aspect of the festival was the "Decreeing" or "Determining of Fates," by which the success or failure of the following year was determined.[41] Because of the importance and danger of this ominous period of the year, a certain uneasiness was in the air. Frankfort describes it as follows: "The mood of the Babylonians at the beginning of the year was peculiar. They not only felt uncertainty as regards the future but feared that their own inadequacy and guilt might have incurred divine wrath."[42] Baruch Halpern adds: "At the start of the feast, a certain insecurity, a cosmic paranoia, seems to have pervaded the air. Fearing for their destinies, perhaps afraid that nature stood in an inchoate or malevolently chaotic state, the people cleansed themselves, to prepare the way, and perhaps to search, for their savior."[43]

The idea of the New Year as a time of judgment is also found in Judaism. According to the Mishnah, it is the day when all mankind is judged.[44] In the face of this judgment, God is "entreated to show mercy to his creatures," and confidence in the mercy of God is expressed.[45] This is the only day on which modern Jews are permitted to "kneel and fall upon their faces."[46] On this day, people in the Talmudic era wore white garments, and books of judgment were opened:

> The completely righteous are immediately inscribed in the book of life. The completely wicked are immediately inscribed in the book of death. The average persons are kept in suspension from Rosh ha-Shanah to the Day of Atonement. If they deserve well, they are inscribed in the book of life, if they do not deserve well, they are inscribed in the book of death.[47]

Furthermore, Gaster suggests that the symbolism of judgment by fire (compare Ezekiel 38:18–39:16) draws upon imagery pertinent to the fall festivals.[48] Corresponding to the mood of the Mesopotamian New Year, the celebration of the Jewish New Year "has no traces of joy, for these are profoundly serious days, with a feeling of the heavy moral responsibility which life puts on all."[49]

Similarly, Benjamin's people faced a day of judgment. In his speech, Benjamin lays bare the fate of those who remain and die in their sins—enemies to God (see Mosiah 2:37–38); he spells out the nature of God's judgment, "for behold he judgeth, and his judgment is just" (Mosiah 3:18); he makes it clear that all men are subject to this judgment (see Mosiah 3:17), except little children (see Mosiah 3:21); and he declares that these ceremonial words shall stand to judge the people (see Mosiah 3:24–25) "like an unquenchable fire" (Mosiah 2:38).

Just as the Mesopotamians and the Jews were awed by the seriousness of the day, so too were the people of

Zarahemla when they heard Benjamin speak about the judgment: "Behold they had fallen to the earth, for the fear of the Lord had come upon them. And they had viewed themselves in their own carnal state, even less than the dust of the earth" (Mosiah 4:1–2). Yet in the face of this judgment, mercy was sought. Benjamin's people cried out in unison, "O have mercy" (Mosiah 4:2). Mercy is mentioned by Benjamin several other times (see Mosiah 2:39; 3:26; 5:15). There is also mention of cleansing of garments (see Mosiah 2:28)[50] and of writing down the names of all the righteous who have entered into the covenant to keep God's commandments (see Mosiah 6:1).

The later Jewish liturgy for this "Day of Awe" provides further interesting points of comparison. Although this liturgy cannot be dated confidently before the time of the Crusades,[51] some of its elements could, of course, have been drawn from the substantially older traditions discussed above. Schauss gives the following account; parallels to King Benjamin's speech are italicized and referenced in brackets, with citations to earlier biblical precedents:

> The greatest and most exalted moment of the services comes when the Ark of the Torah is opened. . . . An unnatural *fear* grips the hearts of the worshipers [compare Mosiah 4:1; Exodus 3:6; Deuteronomy 28:58] [who] recite the words in a *loud voice* [Mosiah 4:2; Deuteronomy 27:14] with tears and sobs: "We will declare the *greatness* [Mosiah 4:11; Deuteronomy 5:24] and the holiness of this Day, for thereon, Thy kingdom is exalted, Thy throne established in mercy and Thou judgest in truth. It is true that *Thou art the judge* [Mosiah 3:18; Genesis 31:53], Thou reprovest; *Thou knowest all* [Mosiah 4:9; 1 Samuel 2:3; 1 Chronicles 28:9], Thou bearest *witness* [Mosiah 3:24; Isaiah 55:4], *recordest and sealest* [Mosiah 6:1; 5:15; Isaiah 8:16]. Thou also rememberest all things that seem to be

forgotten; and *all that enter the world must pass before Thee* [Mosiah 3:24], even as the *shepherd* [Mosiah 5:14; Psalms 23:1; 80:1] causes his sheep to pass under his rod. Thou *numberest* [Mosiah 6:1; Daniel 5:26] and countest, and visitest every living soul, appointest the limitations of all Thy creatures, and *recordest* [Mosiah 6:1; Deuteronomy 30:19] the sentence of their judgment." The moans die down and the congregation calms itself somewhat at the words: "But *repentance* [Mosiah 3:21; Proverbs 28:13; Jeremiah 35:15; Ezekiel 18:30], prayer, and *charity* [Mosiah 4:26; Leviticus 19:18] avert the evil decree."[52]

Moreover, the accompanying Jewish prayer does not end here but concludes with a sharp reminder of the shortness and impotence of man's life, contrasted with the greatness of God, and expressed in ancient biblical idioms:

> *How weak is man* [Mosiah 2:25; Psalm 8:4]! He comes from the *dust* [Mosiah 2:25–26; Genesis 2:7] and returns to the dust; must *toil* [Mosiah 2:14; Genesis 3:19] for his sustenance; passes away like withered grass, a vanishing shadow, a fleeting dream. But Thou, O God, art eternal; Thou art *King* [Mosiah 2:19; Psalms 47:7; 89:18; Jeremiah 10:10] everlasting![53]

Kingship of God. Part of the New Year festival in Mesopotamia involved reciting the epic poem *Enuma Elish*.[54] In this tale the god Marduk slays Tiamat (goddess of the salt-water ocean), uses the body to create the world, and thus attains suzerainty. He then takes his throne at the head of the gods.[55] This festival has served for some as one of the foundations for reconstructing the New Year festival in Israel. As noted above, Mowinckel's attempted reconstruction of the New Year had as its central ritual the enthronement of God.[56] Although the ritual in which God *becomes* king has been the subject of debate,[57] "Mowinckel's arguments have carried the greatest support in locating the celebration of

Yahweh's kingship at the great autumnal festival of the New Year in the Jerusalem temple."[58] Even if no direct connection existed between Mesopotamian and Israelite practices, many of the psalms were probably sung on occasions in Israel when God's kingship was openly celebrated and venerated. Generally God's kingship is celebrated in the Bible because he is able to subdue people and nations (see Psalm 47:3), has power over chaos as represented by the floods (see Psalm 93:3), and is to be the judge of all (see Psalms 96:13, 99:4). In several instances in the psalms cited, God's kingship is celebrated by the sounding of trumpets, characteristic of the New Year, and in many of these "God-is-king" psalms, the people are told to sing unto the Lord (see Psalm 47:5–7, for example). In the Talmud and in later Jewish literature, the ideas of the kingship and judgment of God are also linked to the New Year: "The theme of God as King is particularly stressed on *Rosh Ha-Shanah* because of the day's association with His judgment."[59]

The idea that God, not Benjamin or Mosiah his son, is truly the king is expressly found in Benjamin's words, "If I, whom ye call your king, . . . do merit any thanks from you, O how you ought to thank your heavenly King" (Mosiah 2:19), and in his instruction that the people should obey "the commandments of my son, or the commandments of God which shall be delivered unto you by him" (Mosiah 2:31). The same reasons for celebrating God's kingship, as cited above, are also given by Benjamin, and the power of God is acknowledged in close association with Benjamin's declaration that God is king (see Mosiah 2:11, 20–21), and the role of God as judge is proclaimed (see Mosiah 3:18). As noted above, the kingship of God was celebrated by singing, thanksgiving, and rejoicing in Israel, and similarly in his speech Benjamin hoped that his spirit "may join the choirs above in *singing* the praises of a just God" (Mosiah

2:28), and he admonished his people to "thank your heavenly King" (Mosiah 2:19) and to "render all the thanks and *praise* which your whole soul has power to possess" (Mosiah 2:20).

Creation. The New Year was also a day on which the creation of the earth was typically celebrated. As noted above, during the New Year festival in Mesopotamia, the *Enuma Elish* was read. The principal theme of this epic is the creation of the world. Lambert noted with regard to the *Enuma Elish*: "There is the fundamental presupposition that myths which we should suppose were regarded as having happened once and for all in the remote past, in fact were conceived to be recurring at regular intervals in the world in which the Babylonian authors lived."[60] The repetition of the creation generally took place at the New Year.[61]

The New Year has also been the time when some Jews have observed the renewal of the creation. "In the beginning" was the creation (Genesis 1:1), and thus it was natural for the Israelite mind to think of the creation at the beginning of each new year's cycle. Psalm 148 would have made a fine hymn for such an occasion. According to Jewish traditions found in the Talmud, the world was created in the first month in the fall, Ethanim (Tishri), and the New Year was an appropriate time to recall the creative work of God in forming a new earth.[62] Gaster has summarized: "The world is reborn from year to year—even, in an extended sense, from day to day and from minute to minute; and the primary message of the festival is that the process of creation is continuous, that the breath of God moves constantly upon the face of the waters."[63]

Perhaps this adds context to the angel's reference in the Book of Mormon to Christ as "the Creator of all things from the beginning" (Mosiah 3:8), and to the people's appellation of Christ as "the Son of God, who created heaven and earth, and all things" (Mosiah 4:2). Benjamin's statement that God has "created you, . . . and is preserving you from day to day, by lending you breath . . . from one moment to another" (Mosiah 2:20–21), as well as his other frequent references to God's creative powers (see Mosiah 4:9, 12; 5:15), fit well into these Israelite contexts that highlighted God's creative works. Likewise, the rebirth of the people—"this day he hath spiritually begotten you" (Mosiah 5:7)—is evidence that one of the main purposes of Benjamin's ceremony was to see that the people's relationship with God and each other was renewed and reborn.[64]

Remembrance. Few themes are stressed more emphatically by Benjamin than that of remembrance.[65] The word appears with repeated emphasis throughout the text. For example: "My sons, I would that ye should remember" (Mosiah 1:3, 6, 7); "stir them up in remembrance" (Mosiah 1:17); "ye should awake to a remembrance" (Mosiah 2:40); "O remember, remember that these things are true" (Mosiah 2:41); "I would that ye should remember, and always retain in remembrance" (Mosiah 4:11); "O man, remember, and perish not" (Mosiah 4:30); "I would that ye should remember also, that this is the name. . . . I would that ye should remember to retain the name" (Mosiah 5:11–12). The Nephite priests were even appointed to stir the people up "in remembrance of the oath which they had made" (Mosiah 6:3; compare the *Kol-nidre* liturgy of the Day of Atonement).

In Leviticus 23:23–25, the holy sabbath convocation celebrated on the first day of the seventh month is called a *zikkārôn* (memorial, remembrance).[66] This ancient observance, represented as the New Year,[67] involved the blowing of trumpets, a holy assembly, and the avoidance of work.

King. The king himself is frequently associated with New Year festivals. This was apparently the preferred time for the coronation of the king and the renewal of the people's covenant to obey him and God. According to John Eaton, at such great Israelite assemblies, the king served in several ways: he would "exhort men in God's way," and admonish them to worship God (compare Mosiah 2:18–19); he would "[testify] to the marvels of Yahweh's salvation and [assert] his superiority to other gods" (compare Mosiah 2:40–41; 3:5, 17; and many others); and he would be God's witness, appearing "as an evidential sign, an abiding token and reminder of God's work in the midst of the nations" (compare Mosiah 2:24, 27, 29; 4:5–9).[68] Scholars feel that "the king's function as witness was represented and indeed rooted in the ceremonies of his ordination and its renewal . . . addressed to a great assembly representing Israel and all peoples, indeed all creatures."[69] Psalm 40 mentions all these roles of the king, especially the king's duty to call the people to worship God (compare Mosiah 2:22), and also declares God's status as King and Creator (compare Mosiah 3:8) who will rise from the dead (compare Mosiah 3:10).[70] Benjamin fulfills all the responsibilities of a king that are outlined in tradition and scripture.

For purposes of comparison, among the Sumerians the responsibilities of the *akītu* (or *zagmuk*) festival belonged to the king.[71] In the first millennium B.C., the king's participation in the *akītu* / New Year festival was "obligatory."[72] It was through this participation that his kingship was renewed.[73] Scholars have identified six elements of this festival: (1) a reenactment of the myth of creation issuing in the renewal of the cosmos, (2) a triumphal procession of the god, (3) the death and resurrection of the god, (4) the humiliation and reinstallation of the king, (5) the sacred marriage, and (6) the determination of destiny.[74] Though scholars feel (3) is "highly controversial," and (5) and (6) are absent in Psalms, all elements except (5) are clearly present in Benjamin's speech.[75] Mosiah 2:20–23 and 4:7 refer to creation and the cosmos; the angel describes Christ's triumphal procession in Mosiah 3:5–9 and his death and resurrection in Mosiah 3:9–11; Benjamin refers numerous times to his own status as a subject to God ("I am also of the dust" Mosiah 2:26) and chooses his son to be his successor (see Mosiah 1:10); and throughout his speech he discusses the consequences and the rewards of one's actions (see, for example, Mosiah 2:31, 40–41; 4:11–12).

Regarding the king's personal participation in the Mesopotamian temple program for the New Year's festival at Babylon, the king was led to the temple, where his royal regalia were taken away; he was made to bow down and to declare before the god that he had neither been neglectful in the worship of the god nor had harmed the city or the people. The text of this negative confession is as follows: "I did not sin, lord of the countries. I was not neglectful of the requirements of your godship. I did not destroy Babylon; I did not command its overthrow; I did not . [broken] . . the temple Esagil, I did not forget its rites; I did not rain blows on the cheek of a subordinate. . . . I did not humiliate them. I watched out for Babylon; I did not smash its walls."[76] He was then struck on the cheek and if tears flowed the god was appeased.[77] The king's restoration to the throne symbolized his continuing ability to stabilize the society and the elements. Some scholars have suggested that certain psalms imply that the king in Israel underwent a similar type of ritual humiliation as part of an Israelite New Year festival.[78] Johnson suggests that, as part of this humiliation, Psalm 101 was an "affirmation of the rule which he (the king) is wont to exercise" and compares it to the negative confession in Babylon.[79]

In Israel the situation, although not identical, was apparently similar. A. R. Johnson has concluded that the New Year festival "was used in Jerusalem for the important purpose of binding the people in loyalty not only to the national deity but also to the reigning house."[80] J. B. Segal concurs: "The autumn New Year festival in Israel was a formal occasion at which the authority of King or High Priest was proclaimed or renewed."[81] De Moor notes that the official beginning of the king's reign was connected with the New Year[82] and provides a brief reconstruction:

> The celebration of New Year did not differ much from what we have found earlier. The people made a pilgrimage to Jerusalem. The king sacrificed burnt- and peace-offerings of sheep and oxen. He recited ancient songs, recalled the name of his dead ancestor David, praised the Lord and prayed for the prosperity of his dynasty and his people. He also prayed for rain and asked JHWH to judge his servants, condemning the wicked and vindicating the innocent.[83]

With these concepts of the king's participation in the New Year festival in Mesopotamia and Israel as points of comparison, one may now better appreciate parts of King Benjamin's speech and actions in Mosiah 1–6. Clearly the New Year festival time was an appropriate time for Benjamin to effect his son's coronation.[84] It also seems plausible that Benjamin's frequent and sincere statements of humility and the accounting of his stewardship as king are in some way related to the general genre of humiliation and negative confession of the king found in other ancient cultures.[85] Benjamin asserts that he is like the people and "subject to all manner of infirmities" (Mosiah 2:11) and is "also of the dust" (Mosiah 2:26), and in rendering the accounting of his stewardship he follows very closely the so-called Paragraph of the King (Deuteronomy 17:14–20), which set standards by which the king's performance was judged in Israel.[86]

Thus the spirit of the Israelite New Year—as far as that may be known and defined—is reflected with considerable clarity in King Benjamin's speech. The persistence of these traditions carries down even to the level of customary sayings and greetings. Even today, one greets friends on this occasion with "May you be inscribed (in the book of life) and sealed for a good year."[87] Suitably, Benjamin gives his people a name that cannot be "blotted out [of the book of life]" except by transgression (Mosiah 5:11), and he hopes that God will seal them his. With possible parallels to Benjamin's speech, the following traditional Jewish New Year's prayer expresses sentiments that Benjamin himself would have whole-heartedly concurred with: "Now, therefore, O Lord our God, impose Thine awe upon all Thy works, and Thy dread upon all that Thou hast created, that all works may revere Thee and all creatures prostrate themselves before Thee, that they may all form a single band to do Thy will with a perfect heart."[88]

These factors indicate that the themes of King Benjamin's speech and the themes of the traditional Israelite New Year were indeed very similar. This discussion also supplies further reasons to believe that many Jewish traditions remained quite stable over the centuries, and that the Nephites were indeed conscientious and "strict" (Alma 30:3) in observing and perpetuating the law of Moses as they knew it.

Day of Atonement (Yom Kippur)[89]

The next festival aspect of the month of the Feast of Ingathering in preexilic Israel was the all-important Day of Atonement,[90] a day of holy convocations and ritual atonement at the temple. It would later become the most sacred day in the Jewish liturgical year.[91] The hypothesis that Benjamin's speech was held on or in connection with the Day of Atonement finds initial plausibility in Benjamin's seven explicit references to the atonement. This number seven may be purely coincidental, but doing something seven times is characteristic of rituals performed on the Day of Atonement and during other biblical purification ceremonies prescribed in the book of Leviticus.[92] Benjamin speaks of (1) "the atonement of his blood" (Mosiah 3:15), (2) the "atoning blood" (Mosiah 3:18), (3) the blood which "atoneth" (Mosiah 3:11), (4) the blood of Christ which "atoneth for [their] sins" (Mosiah 3:16), (5) the "atonement of Christ the Lord" (Mosiah 3:19), (6) the "atonement" prepared from the foundation (Mosiah 4:6), and (7) the "atonement" prepared for all mankind (Mosiah 4:7). Examining the speech further reveals substantial cumulative evidence that the rituals and traditions manifest in the Day of Atonement are also to be seen in Benjamin's words and deeds.[93] These elements involve special preparations, blood sacrifices, sin removal, the holy name of God, fasting, repentance, confession, giving to the poor, repaying debts, rejoicing, and blessing.

Preparations. Special preparations were in order for such a great day, particularly for those in charge, such as the high priest. Rabbinic writings report special efforts taken to keep the high priest awake during the night of Yom Kippur, and pious men followed this example.[94] Benjamin's preparations also were substantial; coincidentally, he was awakened, apparently during part of the night, by the visitation of an angel from God: "Awake; and I awoke. . . . Awake and hear" (Mosiah 3:2–3). Several points in the Jewish ceremony draw on biblical precedents: for example, the priest would wash and change his garments (compare Exodus 19:14).[95] Perhaps this relates to Benjamin's saying that he has assembled his people that he "might rid [his] garments of [their] blood" (Mosiah 2:28). Yom Kippur is the anniversary of Moses' second descent from Mount Sinai after having received the Ten Commandments. This day was declared one of forgiveness and pardon for the Israelites, and this event is remembered each year even to this day.[96] In Mosiah 3:14–15,

Benjamin also remembered this event and the law that was received, and throughout his speech can be seen the themes of forgiveness and pardon.

Sacrifice and blood purifications. On this day in Israel, sacrifices were made. First, a special atonement was made by one designated priest. In ancient Israel he would purify various parts of the temple by daubing and then sprinkling blood (see Leviticus 16:16–20), for it was necessary to purify the temple once each year (see Hebrews 9:7). The theme of temple purification is also found during the week of New Year's observances in Mesopotamia. As part of the *akītu* festival a priest would purify the temple and all its environs by sprinkling water on it from the Tigris and the Euphrates.[97]

If such a temple purification had just taken place in Zarahemla—or was about to take place—this would have given concrete contextual impact to Benjamin's saying that the Lord "dwelleth not in unholy temples" (Mosiah 2:37). Assuming that Benjamin had followed the rules in Leviticus 16 and had used blood to purify the temple in Zarahemla, his several references to the cleansing power of "the atoning blood of Christ" (Mosiah 3:18) could hardly have been set more vividly in the minds of his people.

Second, the priest would cleanse the people from certain kinds of iniquities and transgressions (see Leviticus 16:21, 33), particularly sins against God: "This shall be an everlasting statute unto you, to make an atonement for the children of Israel for all their sins once a year" (Leviticus 16:34). Of primary concern on this particular day were the sins of inadvertence. Even though a transgression occurred unconsciously, the ancient Israelites still viewed this as a transgression that defiled the temple and the people, and thus it was necessary to make an atonement (see Numbers 15:27–29). In addition, of grave import were the sins of rebelliousness, or *pəshāʿîm*.[98] Those who "brazenly rebel" are not eligible to have their transgression forgiven through sacrifice (see Numbers 15:30–31). Later, the Talmudic sages made the same distinction and expressed similar concern regarding the different types of sin that were to be expiated on the Day of Atonement.[99]

In much the same way, Benjamin expressed concerns regarding sin and the need for atonement. He explained that the atoning power of the blood of Christ covers inadvertent sins and sinners: "those who have died not knowing the will of God concerning them, or who have ignorantly sinned" (Mosiah 3:11),[100] while he who sins "contrary to his own knowledge" (Mosiah 2:33) receives the harshest condemnation (see Mosiah 2:38–40). Likewise, Benjamin spoke adamantly about the great seriousness of rebellious sin: "Wo unto him who knoweth that he rebelleth against God!" (Mosiah 3:12). "The man that . . . cometh out in open rebellion against God, . . . the Lord has no place in him" (Mosiah 2:37). Moreover, Benjamin's theology is accurately Israelite when he explains that "salvation cometh to none such" rebellious sinners (compare Numbers 15:30–31), except through the extraordinary redemptive powers of Christ (see Mosiah 3:12). Conventional animal sacrifice could not expiate such sin.

Scapegoat. Leviticus 16:7–10 prescribes the well-known and distinctive scapegoat ritual[101] in which the high priest, on the Day of Atonement, took two goats; by casting lots one goat was declared to be "for the Lord" and the other "for Azazel."[102] A similar dichotomy appears in Mosiah 5:7–12, in which the people are called either by the name of Christ and found belonging at the right hand of God, or are called "by some other name" and found at the left hand of God. According to later rabbinic tradition, if the lot "For the Lord" came up in the left hand it was permissible to switch the lots with their respective goats so that although the determination of which goat was the Lord's was made by lot, the Lord's goat would be on the right hand while Azazel's goat would be on the left.[103]

As the goat was set before the high priest, he drew a lot in each hand from an urn. The high priest then actually placed the lots upon the heads of the goats.[104] A metaphorical connection of this "head" (Christ) that can make one free appears in Mosiah 5:8.

The goat for the Lord was sacrificed, but the high priest placed his hands on the scapegoat and confessed all the sins of Israel, thereby transferring them to Azazel's goat, which was then taken off into the desert.[105] The man who carried the goat out to the empty wilderness became impure and could not come back into the camp until he burned his clothes and washed himself.[106] Similarly, any individual who breaks the covenant was, in Benjamin's mind, to be "consigned to an awful view" of his guilt and "into a state of misery and endless torment" (Mosiah 3:25); he would find himself to be "worthless," in a state of "nothingness" (Mosiah 4:5), and ultimately Benjamin compared those who "know not the name by which [they] are called" to an ass that belongs to a neighbor and is not suffered to feed among the flocks but is driven away and cast out (see Mosiah 5:14–15).

Had Benjamin said that the sinner would be driven out like a goat instead of an ass, these connections with the Day of Atonement would have been more direct.[107] But in fact, the kind of animal used in such settings was not critical among Israel's neighbors in the ancient Near East. Similar Hittite expiatory rituals drove out bulls, rams, mice, and vermin of the ground.[108] Furthermore, asses were commonly used in covenant-making ceremonies during the second millennium B.C. in Mesopotamia.[109] Because Benjamin is using the ass as a symbol of excommunication or banishment, not of purification or impurity removal, it makes sense that he referred to a different animal than a goat.

The name. So holy was the Day of Atonement that on this day the ineffable name of God, YHWH, could be pronounced. During the Yom Kippur service at the temple, the priest could pronounce this sacred name aloud. Later Jewish tradition seems to have the priest utter this name ten times during the Yom Kippur liturgy, and to a similar degree, Benjamin employs the expanded names *Lord God* and *Lord Omnipotent* seven and three times, respectively.[110]

Seven of these utterances are in the reported words of the angel to Benjamin (see Mosiah 3:5, 13, 14, 17, 18, 21, 23). It seems more than coincidental[111] that it is in the mouth of an angel that such names appear seven times and that the number seven reflects a "spiritual" perfection. The other three utterances come in the words of Benjamin (see Mosiah 2:30, 41, and 5:15). These three utterances come at important ceremonial breaking points in the speech, not merely at random or inconsequential places.[112]

The response of the people to the pronouncement of the sacred name was singular. According to the Mishnah, each time the people at the temple in Jerusalem heard the sacred name they would fall prostrate on the ground.[113] This can be compared with the reactions to King Benjamin's speech in Zarahemla. When he finished reciting the words of the angel, "he cast his eyes round about on the multitude, and behold they had fallen to the earth, for the fear of the Lord had come upon them" (Mosiah 4:1). It is possible that Benjamin's people would have fallen down in profound reverence and awe several times when Benjamin spoke the holy name of God, as the Israelites did on hearing the tetragram, according to the Mishnah.[114]

Indeed, Benjamin declared that one of the main purposes

of the assembly was to "give this people a name" (Mosiah 1:11). Associated with pronouncing the name of God was the giving of his name to the people. In great solemnity and literary emphasis,[115] Benjamin revealed the name of the Messiah as the following expression: "Jesus Christ, the Son of God, the Father of heaven and earth, the Creator of all things from the beginning." He also revealed Mary as the name of Christ's mother (see Mosiah 3:8). He concluded his speech, telling the people, "this [the sacred name of Christ] is the name that I said I should give unto you" (Mosiah 5:11; see 5:9–14).

Fasting. On this day, according to the ancient custom, all were required to "afflict" their souls (see Leviticus 16:29–31; 23:27–32). Traditionally this has been understood to mean fasting (see Psalm 35:13; Isaiah 58:3, 5); however, it has been argued that this term should not be limited to fasting but should include other forms of self denial.[116] Fasting is not specifically mentioned in Mosiah 1–6. Nevertheless, evidence exists in the book of Alma that fasting was practiced in Zarahemla around the beginning of the New Year (see Alma 30:2; 44:24–45:1). Thus fasting may have been a regular part of the Day of Atonement among the Nephites. If Benjamin spoke on a day when the people were afflicting their souls, his deprecating descriptions of humans as being not even "as much as the dust of the earth" (Mosiah 2:25) and an "enemy to God" (Mosiah 3:19), whose "nothingness" makes them "unworthy creatures" (Mosiah 4:11), would have fit powerfully into that context.

If an ancient Israelite did not "afflict" his soul on this day, he was "cut off" from among the people (Leviticus 23:29). Benjamin speaks of blotting such a person out (see Mosiah 5:11) and of casting him out (see Mosiah 5:14), but since all his people complied with the requirement of making the covenant (see Mosiah 6:2), none had to be expelled.[117]

Repentance. Benjamin implored his people to repent before God and to settle with their neighbors: to "live peaceably, and to render to every man according to that which is his due" (Mosiah 4:13); and to "return [any]thing that he borroweth" (Mosiah 4:28). This, along with prayer, was a necessary condition of obtaining remission of sins: "calling on the name of the Lord daily" (Mosiah 4:11), and imparting of your substance, "for the sake of retaining a remission of your sins from day to day" (Mosiah 4:26). Benjamin's exhortations in this regard, as well as his decrees about giving liberally to the poor, reconciling with your neighbor, and realizing that we are "all beggars" (Mosiah 4:19; see also 4:20–28) would be especially pertinent at the time of a Day of Atonement celebration, when people were seeking forgiveness for sin. The Mishnah explicitly teaches that the scapegoat's atonement is effective only when it is accompanied by repentance[118] and that transgressions against one's fellowman must first be resolved before the atonement can have a beneficial effect.[119]

Confession. Also associated with the Day of Atonement and naturally connected with repentance was the process of confession. According to the Talmud, the priest would confess the iniquities of the people—the confessions generally consisting of acknowledging sins and trespasses—and a corresponding expression of remorse from the people would follow.[120] This is to be compared with the confession of the people of King Benjamin of their carnal and sinful state (see Mosiah 4:2, 5), specifically adopting the king's own acknowledgment of his "worthless and fallen state" (Mosiah 4:5): "I am also of the dust, . . . [an] unprofitable servant" (Mosiah 2:26, 21). According to one source, forgiveness is granted to all on this day who thus confess and repent (see Jubilees 34:17–18; see also Mosiah 3:16; 6:2).

Giving to the poor or repaying debts. Over the years, Jewish traditions of asking forgiveness of one another, giving gifts to the poor, and generally appeasing one's neighbor developed from these ancient teachings in connection with the Day of Atonement.[121] On the eve of the Day of Atonement "it is customary to send gifts to the poor, and a duty to ask forgiveness from one another and to appease each other."[122] "Ye should impart of your substance to the poor," says Benjamin, "administering to their relief, both spiritually and temporally" (Mosiah 4:26). Expressing the natural human feeling of gratitude and debt that comes with any occasion of profound forgiveness and reconciliation, Jews today recite at Yom Kippur the *Avinu Malkaynu* prayer, which speaks of the deep indebtedness of all humans to God.[123]

Joy. The Day of Atonement was apparently in all eras a time of "true joy."[124] Similarly, Benjamin and his people experienced "exceedingly great joy" (Mosiah 4:11) and rejoiced (see Mosiah 4:12) abundantly. On the Day of Atonement, Israelites came to feel God's close association with his creatures,[125] just as Benjamin exulted in the "goodness of God, and his matchless power, and his wisdom, and his patience, and his long-suffering towards the children of men" (Mosiah 4:6). In this same spirit, the great Nephite celebrations at the beginning of the nineteenth year of the reign of the judges were marked with "exceedingly great joy" (Alma 45:1).

Blessings. On many occasions in Jewish life, but especially on this day, blessings were pronounced. In Benjamin's case, several blessings were mentioned: "he doth bless and prosper you" (Mosiah 2:22); "ye shall prosper in the land, and your enemies shall have no power over you" (Mosiah 2:31); and remember "the blessed and happy state of those that keep the commandments" (Mosiah 2:41). At the end of the Day of Atonement, Jewish people exchange blessings such as "May you be inscribed for life [in the book of life] and merit many years."[126] Likewise, at the conclusion of his speech, Benjamin took "the names of all those who had entered into a covenant with God to keep his commandments" (Mosiah 6:1). In some cases the Israelites immediately began constructing their booths (*sukkot*) in preparation for the next phase of this season's celebrations.[127]

The Feast of Tabernacles (Sukkot)

The next aspect of the great fall celebrations in ancient Israel was the Feast of Tabernacles (Sukkot).[128] The earliest sources refer to it as the Feast of Harvest or Feast of Ingathering (see Exodus 23:16; 34:22).[129] Later it was called the Feast of Tabernacles or Feast of Booths in reference to the booths or huts in which the Israelites dwelt during this celebration. It was also called the "feast unto the Lord" (Leviticus 23:39; Numbers 29:12); "feast to the Lord" (Exodus 12:14); or simply "the feast" (1 Kings 8:2; 2 Chronicles 7:8). Of the three yearly festivals, it is often considered the most significant.[130] This portion of the festival eventually came to be observed on the fifteenth of Tishri, the seventh month of the year, five days after the Day of Atonement. Probably an agricultural festival originally, it eventually came to celebrate historical events associated with the exodus.[131] The Feast of Tabernacles is mentioned frequently in the Bible (see Leviticus 23:33–44; Numbers 29:12–38; Deuteronomy 16:13; 31:9–13; Zechariah 14:16, 18–19; Ezra 3:4; 2 Chronicles 8:13; John 7:2), and many details about the particular customs associated with this day can be found in these biblical accounts. The description of the Feast of Tabernacles as drawn from the Bible compares very favorably and significantly with further elements in Benjamin's speech. Other important information about this festival is given in the Mishnah, Talmud, and later Jewish writings.

While it is not always possible to know exactly which of these later details were already part of the observance of the Feast of Tabernacles in Lehi's day, many intriguing parallels to Benjamin's festival in Zarahemla are found throughout this material as well. The basic aspects of this celebration encompass the following: pilgrimage to the temple, sitting in booths or tents, sacrifices, reading the law, renewing the covenant, coronation of kings, God's heavenly kingship, and praise and thanksgiving.

Pilgrimage. The Feast of Tabernacles was a day of national assembly, a great pilgrimage festival.[132] The Mosaic law specified that "all . . . males shall appear before the Lord God" (Exodus 23:17), and in Deuteronomy the entire family was expected to participate: "And thou shalt rejoice in thy feast, thou, and thy son, and thy daughter, and thy manservant, and thy maidservant, and the Levite, the stranger, and the fatherless, and the widow, that are within thy gates" (Deuteronomy 16:14; compare 31:10–12).[133] The people were to congregate at one of Israel's sanctuaries or "in the place which [God] shall choose" (Deuteronomy 31:11).

Similarly, at the occasion of King Benjamin's address, whole families were present. Benjamin caused all the people in his land to "gather themselves together" (Mosiah 1:18) and to assemble together (see Mosiah 2:9, 27), both Nephites and Mulekites (Mosiah 1:10): "every man according to his family, consisting of his wife, and his sons, and his daughters, and their sons, and their daughters, from the eldest down to the youngest, every family being separate one from another" (Mosiah 2:5). They assembled specifically "round about" the main Nephite sanctuary in the days of Benjamin, the temple in Zarahemla (Mosiah 2:6).[134]

Booths/tents. In Zarahemla, Benjamin's people "pitched their tents round about the temple, every man having his tent with the door thereof towards the temple, that thereby they might remain in their tents and hear the words which king Benjamin would speak unto them" (Mosiah 2:6). During the Feast of Tabernacles in the Old World, the ancient Israelites sat in booths or huts made from branches and vines (see Leviticus 23:41–44). According to Leviticus 23:43 the purpose of the booths was to remind the children of Israel that they had been "made . . . to dwell in booths (*sukkot*)" when they were brought out of Egypt.[135] The relationship between such booths and tents has received a fair amount of comment. In particular, the word "booths" (*sukkot*) does not appear in the account of the exodus. Instead we find that the people lived in tents. For example, in Exodus 33:8, "and it came to pass, when Moses went out unto the tabernacle (*hā-ʾōhel*), that all the people rose up, and stood every man at his tent (*ʾōhel*) door, and looked after Moses, until he was gone into the tabernacle."[136]

Tents were specifically mentioned in connection with the celebration of Solomon's dedication of the temple: "And at that time Solomon held a feast, and all Israel with him, a great congregation. . . . On the eighth day he sent the people away: and they blessed the king, and went unto their tents (*ləʾohōleyhem*) joyful and glad of heart" (1 Kings 8:65–66). This feast, in which tents were used, was held in the seventh month (see 1 Kings 8:2) and has generally been thought of as a Feast of Tabernacles.[137] A passage in Hosea also refers to tents: "And I that am the Lord thy God from the land of Egypt will yet make thee to dwell in tabernacles (*baʾōhālîm*), as in the days of the solemn feast" (Hosea 12:9). The Hebrew word *ʾōhālîm*, translated in the King James Version as "tabernacles," is most often rendered "tents."[138] To the Nephites, their festival use of tents may also have symbolized the time when Lehi and his family had "dwelt in a tent" (1 Nephi 10:16),[139] for Benjamin convenes his celebration in part to remember the distinctiveness of his people, whom "the Lord God hath brought out of the land of Jerusalem" (Mosiah 1:11).

It is evident in Benjamin's speech that the tents are ceremonially significant. Each family had a "tent with the door thereof towards the temple, that thereby they might remain in their tents and hear the words which king Benjamin should speak unto them" (Mosiah 2:6). Everyone had a tent, not just those who had come from out of town and needed a place to stay. Furthermore, they all remained in their tents during the speech, surely for ceremonial reasons. If it had not been religiously and ritually important for them to stay in their tents, the crowd could have stood much closer to Benjamin and been able to hear him, obviating the need for written copies of his words to be prepared and circulated (see Mosiah 2:8). Apparently Benjamin considered it more important for the people to remain in their tents than to have them stand within close hearing distance of the speaker. The relationship between booths and tents is not yet entirely clear,[140] but the use of the word *tents* instead of *booths* in Mosiah 2 does not appear out of place.

Sacrifice. Numbers 29:12–34 lists the sacrifices connected with the Feast of Tabernacles. These sacrifices were greater in number than those connected with the two previous celebrations.[141] The Book of Mormon has relatively few references to sacrifices and burnt offerings. Two are found in 1 Nephi during the journey in the wilderness from Jerusalem to the new land (see 1 Nephi 5:9; 7:22). Another is in 3 Nephi 9:19, in which the Lord commands that sacrifices and burnt offerings no longer be performed. It is significant, then, that sacrifices and burnt offerings are mentioned in the prologue to King Benjamin's address: "And they also took of the firstlings of their flocks, that they might offer sacrifice and burnt offerings according to the law of Moses" (Mosiah 2:3).

Law and covenant. During the Feast of Tabernacles, the Israelites celebrated the giving of the law to Moses on Mount Sinai.[142] Ancient Israelites profoundly venerated their laws. Every seven years at the Feast of Tabernacles, the law was read, and a statement of the people's commitment to the law took place.[143] In postexilic times, this ancient element became so prominent that the ninth day of the feast came to be known as *Simḥat Torah* ("Joy-of-the-Torah"), in commemoration of the revelation of the law at Sinai. Today, the annual reading cycle of the Torah for the Jews ends at *Simḥat Torah*. This expanded practice of reading assigned portions of the law each week during each year is traditionally dated to the time of Ezra the Scribe (fifth century B.C.), who renewed the celebration of Sukkot after the Babylonian captivity and the return of the Jews to Jerusalem; but originally the law was read all at one time (see Deuteronomy 31:11). It has been suggested that the reading of the law on Sukkot "not only gives us a relatively early basis for the development of the Joy-of-the-Law observance on the ninth day, but also hints at a connection between the Feast of Booths and a formal covenant ceremony at which the reading of the laws of the covenant was a standard feature."[144] Thus not only do King Benjamin's constant references to keeping the commandments of God (see Mosiah 2:13, 22, 31, 41; 4:6, 30) and to God's appointment of the law of Moses to a stiffnecked people during the exodus (see Mosiah 3:14) fit the Feast of the Tabernacles perfectly, but also in both Jerusalem and Zarahemla this day was a day of covenant renewal. In Israel, on this day the people renewed their covenant with God to be his people and to obey his laws.[145] Benjamin's people also enter into such a covenant, and they follow the form of covenant renewal in Israel in detail.[146] Through this covenant, the people became the sons and daughters of God (see Mosiah 5:1–7; compare Exodus 19:5;

Jeremiah 31:33; Nehemiah 7:73–8:18; 9:1–13:31). The fact that Benjamin's people simultaneously fell down and spoke certain words in unison (see Mosiah 4:1–3; 5:1–5) strongly suggests a ritual or ceremonial response. The words that the people spoke may well have been prescribed. This does not detract from the profound spiritual state of the people as they uttered them. Solemn covenant renewals can have a profound impact on both hearers and participants, especially when they are beautifully and eloquently presented.

Earthly king. The figure of the king seems to have played an important part in the ancient Feast of Tabernacles. As noted above, King Solomon chose this time to dedicate his temple. To do so, he had to wait eleven months—from the eighth month until the seventh month (1 Kings 6:38; 8:2), indicating the importance he placed on waiting until a specific time in the fall. Later Jewish texts attest to the association between the king and the Feast of Tabernacles. The king's responsibility was to read the law every seven years during the Feast of Tabernacles. The Mishnah gives a good description of the activities of the king: [147] the king stands upon a specially constructed platform, [148] and he is given a copy of the law from which he reads various passages from Deuteronomy, including the Paragraph of the King [149] and other texts dealing with the law and covenant-making. John Tvedtnes has examined these passages in depth and draws numerous comparisons between its particulars and the text of King Benjamin's address. [150] In view of the role of the king in the Feast of Tabernacles it is not surprising that this was the time for the coronation of a new king both in Israel and among the Nephites. [151]

Heavenly king. Not only did the earthly king play an important part in the Feast of Tabernacles, but God as the Heavenly King is also implied in early sources. [152] The prophet Zechariah, who looked strongly toward the heavenly Lord of Hosts as the eternal king, prophesied that the Messiah would come on the Feast of Tabernacles and that the people would venerate him as king after his coming: "And it shall come to pass, that every one that is left of all the nations which came against Jerusalem shall even go up from year to year to worship the King, the Lord of hosts, and to keep the feast of tabernacles" (Zechariah 14:16). Thus the royal aspects of the Feast of Tabernacles also served as reminders that Jehovah rules as king (see Psalms 93:1; 96:10; 97:1). Such references to God as king call to mind Benjamin's reference to God as the "heavenly King" (Mosiah 2:19) and also Benjamin's discussion of the coming of the Messiah (see Mosiah 3:1–10).

Thanksgiving and praise. Finally, prayers of thanksgiving and praising God were an important part of all ancient Israelite holy days. Over the years, a standard thanksgiving prayer known as the *She-hecheyanu* has been handed down among the Jews. This prayer is recited when eating the first-fruits, offering sacrifices, doing things for the first time (or for the first time in a long time), and at certain other prescribed times, including the beginning of every festival. The words of this prayer today are: *Barukh ʾattah YHWH ʾEloheinu melekh ha-ʿolam she-hecheyanu ve-kiyemanu ve-higiyanu laz-zəman ha-zeh,* which is "Praised (or blessed) art Thou, Lord our God, King of the universe, who hast kept us alive, and hast preserved us, and enabled us to reach this [festival] season."[153] Although it is impossible for us today to know when the specific words of this short traditional prayer were composed, its sentiments are all found in the Psalms and thus some formulation of this kind may resemble the words used by Jews long ago to express their feelings of praise and thanksgiving to God, especially at the beginning of their important festivals. Indeed, the oral law required the recitation of this blessing in Israel: the Mishnah mentions the prayer in a matter-of-fact manner, as if it were a long-standing tradition.[154]

Interestingly, King Benjamin's speech contains many of the elements found in the *She-hecheyanu*.[155] Immediately after referring to God as "your heavenly King" (Mosiah 2:19), Benjamin soberly instructs his people to render "*thanks and praise . . . to that God* who has created you, and *has kept and preserved you*" (Mosiah 2:20–21). As the traditional prayer emphasized "*this* festival season," Benjamin also spoke several times of his assembly "*this* day," which may reflect a Hebrew idiom referring to the arrival of a festival moment.[156] When Benjamin told his people that even by thanking and praising God with all they possessed they would still be unprofitable servants, he implied that they customarily offered such prayers of thanks and praise to God, their Creator, for keeping and preserving them, and causing them to have joy and peace. This deprecating reminder of Benjamin to his people would have been especially impressive to them if they offered this kind of prayer often in their religious worship, and thought it beneficial. Understanding that they may even have uttered such a prayer only shortly before the commencement of Benjamin's speech gives his words a cultural context, provides his message with immediate bearing on his people, and helps explain the powerful impact these words of Benjamin had on his people.[157]

In sum, many elements in King Benjamin's address and the events surrounding it correspond to the Feast of Tabernacles as practiced in ancient Israel and as those celebrations gradually developed in Jewish history.

Sabbatical Years[158]

In addition to perhaps scheduling his speech during the fall festival, Benjamin seems to have timed this great assembly to occur in connection with the conclusion of a sabbatical year, which came once every seven years. Four of the major themes of the sabbatical year can be found embedded in biblical legislation concerning land, debt, slaves (also servants or service), and the public reading of the law.[159]

Land, debt, and servitude. Under the law of Moses, in every seventh year beginning at the Feast of Booths, the fields had to lie fallow and their yield was left to the poor (see Exodus 23:10–11). According to the law set out in Deuteronomy, "at the end of every seven years" the covenant people of Israel were required to "make a release," namely that "every creditor that lendeth ought unto his neighbour shall release it; he shall not exact it of his neighbour, or of his brother" (Deuteronomy 15:1–2). This law may have involved either a full release or a one-year suspension, and it applied so long as any poor inhabited the covenant land; debts owed by foreigners were not subject to this release (see Deuteronomy 15:3–4), for God intended Israel to "lend unto many nations" but not to "borrow" (Deuteronomy 15:6). Moreover, in the year of release all Hebrew slaves were to be set at liberty, particularly those who were enslaved for the nonpayment of debts (see Exodus 21:2–6; Deuteronomy 15:7–18; Jeremiah 34:8–16).[160] The reason for this was that no one could "claim as his own private property a fellow Israelite, who belonged by right of purchase to God alone."[161]

Many of these factors are relevant to Mosiah 1–6. If Benjamin's speech came at the end of a sabbatical year, this would explain why King Mosiah, at the end of his coronation, "did cause his people that they should till the earth" (Mosiah 6:7). This royal act would seem to mark specifically the end of the sabbatical year and the ceremonial beginning of a new agricultural period, for it would be odd for a king to command his people to begin tilling the ground unless there had been some reason to cease, or some need to commence this common activity anew. It would also give new significance to the fact that Benjamin affirms that he has not allowed his people to "make slaves of one another" (Mosiah 2:13) and insists that all people belong to God by virtue of his having created them (see Mosiah 2:24). Furthermore, in the context of a sabbatical year celebration it makes good sense for Benjamin to speak so extensively about service, giving to the poor, and the realization that all people are beggars (see Mosiah 4:15–23). In addition, Benjamin commanded his people to settle their debts with their neighbors and not remain borrowers (see Mosiah 4:28). The absence of permanent servitude in his kingdom would have been immediately proven by a royal proclamation releasing all debtors who were working off debts through involuntary servitude.

Similarly, continuing the moral and ethical regime of Benjamin, his son Mosiah would later be remembered as a king who "had granted unto his people that they should be delivered from all manner of bondage" (Mosiah 29:40). It seems likely that such a "grant" would also have involved either a specific decree or the periodic implementation of the sabbatical laws, and that his "deliverance from all manner of bondage" would have included a sabbatical-like release from economic debts as well as all kinds of compulsory servitude.

The reading of the law. As discussed already above, associated with the celebration of the Feast of Tabernacles on the sabbatical year was the reading of the law. The stipulations regarding the reading of the law are found in Deuteronomy 31:9–13. The numerous similarities between that passage and the account of Benjamin's assembly present considerable evidence that Benjamin was consciously following the Deuteronomic regulations in observing just such a seventh-year Feast of Tabernacles. Deuteronomy 31:10–13 (with emphasis added) reads:

> And Moses *commanded* them, saying, At the end of every seven years, in the *solemnity* of the year of release [compare Mosiah 2:9], in the feast of tabernacles, When all Israel is come to appear before the Lord thy God in the *place* which he shall choose [compare Mosiah 1:18], thou shalt read this law before all Israel *in their hearing* [compare Mosiah 2:8]. *Gather* the people together, *men, and women, and children* [compare Mosiah 2:5], *and thy stranger* that is *within thy gates* [compare Mosiah 1:10], that they *may hear*, and that they *may learn* [compare Mosiah 2:9], and *fear the Lord* your God [compare Mosiah 4:1], and observe *to do all the words* of this law: and that their *children*, which have *not known* any thing, may hear, and learn to fear the Lord your God [compare Mosiah 3:21–22; 4:15].

The completeness and precision with which Benjamin appears to be fulfilling these technical Mosaic requirements lends weighty evidence to the conclusion that it was at just such a seventh-year Deuteronomic Feast of Tabernacles that Benjamin's speech was delivered.

The Jubilee

Moreover, every seventh sabbatical year was a jubilee year.[162] It is possible that Benjamin not only selected a sabbatical year on which to crown his son king, but that this great occasion also fell on a jubilee year, as the following factors may indicate:

A time of return. The jubilee year was a time when property was returned to its hereditary owner: "Ye shall return every man unto his possession, and ye shall return every man unto his family" (Leviticus 25:10). De Vaux summarizes:

"Consequently transactions in land had to be made by calculating the number of years before the next jubilee: one did not buy the ground but so many harvests. . . . Religious grounds are given for these measures: the land cannot be sold absolutely, for it belongs to God."[163] On a jubilee year, one could expect a king to comment on this extraordinary time of return, as Benjamin indeed does: "Whosoever among you borroweth of his neighbor should *return the thing* that he borroweth, according as he doth agree, or else thou shalt commit sin; and perhaps thou shalt cause thy neighbor to commit sin also" (Mosiah 4:28). Benjamin's concern, under one possible reading of this text, is that the very thing that has been transferred should be returned. Substituted property of equivalent value, or money, was apparently not acceptable to Benjamin on this occasion. One wonders why not—perhaps because during a jubilee year the people had to "return every man unto *his possession*" (Leviticus 25:10, emphasis added). Furthermore, Benjamin expresses concern that the lender might commit sin[164] as well as the borrower. Are we to imagine that Benjamin fears that the lender might commit sin by somehow injuring the delinquent debtor in anger?[165] Or is this more a reflection of the public nature of the obligation to fulfill the requirements of the jubilee wherein the possession of specific property itself had to be relinquished, and both parties were required to participate or else "commit sin"?

Underlying the jubilee laws was the idea that the land and all the world belongs to God. Private ownership of land in Israel was effectively limited, at least in theory, by the jubilee redemption and fallow laws. A similar concept is also expressly recognized by King Benjamin, who declares concerning the dust of the earth: "behold, it belongeth to him who created you" (Mosiah 2:25). The recognition of God's ownership of the earth would have been as powerfully felt on a jubilee year as at any time on the ancient Israel-ite calendar.

Jubilee texts. The jubilee text of Leviticus 25 compares closely with two sections of Benjamin's speech.[166] Leviticus 25 reflects the words and phrases associated with the jubi-lee in ancient times. A considerable density of phrases and ideas from these chapters can be found in the latter portions of Mosiah 2 and 4, sufficient to indicate a textual depen-dency of Benjamin's words on these or similar jubilee texts. The main parallels between these passages and Benjamin's speech can be outlined as follows:

- Benjamin's "*return* the thing" (Mosiah 4:28) recalls "*re-turn* every man unto his possession" (Leviticus 25:10).
- His injunction "Ye will *not* have a mind to *injure* one an-other" (Mosiah 4:13) echoes "Ye shall *not oppress* one another" (Leviticus 25:14, 17).
- At the jubilee, it was required: "He shall reckon with him" (Leviticus 25:50; compare 15–16). Similarly, Ben-jamin said: "Render to every man according to that which is his due" (Mosiah 4:13).
- "And if thy brother be waxen poor, and fallen in decay with thee; then *thou shalt relieve* him: yea though he be a stranger or a sojourner; that he may live with thee" (Leviticus 25:35) has the same import as "*Ye . . . will suc-cor* those that stand in need, . . . ye will not . . . turn him out to perish" (Mosiah 4:16).
- "I am the Lord your God, which brought you forth" (Leviticus 25:38) implies the same conclusion as "Do we not all depend upon the same Being, even God, for all the substance which we have" (Mosiah 4:19).
- The promise in Leviticus reads: "Wherefore ye shall do my statutes and keep my judgments, and do them; and ye shall dwell in the land in safety. And the land shall yield her fruit" (Leviticus 25:18–19); and in Benjamin,

"If ye would keep his commandments ye should *prosper in the land*" (Mosiah 2:22).

These relatively specific parallels, coupled with similarities in the overall tone and concerns of the jubilee texts and Benjamin's speech, indicate Benjamin's intense feelings about helping the poor, establishing God's covenant among his people, being conscientious in walking in the paths of righteousness, and realizing man's utter dependence on God for life and sustenance. These may well be attributable to the heightened sense of these principles felt by the ancient Israelites during the jubilee season.

A further parallel, expressing the spirit behind all sabbatical and jubilee laws, is found in Deuteronomy 15:9: "Beware that there be not a thought in thy wicked heart, saying, The seventh year, the year of release, is at hand; and thine eye be evil against thy poor brother, and thou givest him nought; and he cry unto the Lord against thee, and it be sin unto thee." This compares closely with Benjamin's injunctions to his people to impart freely of their substance to the poor without grudging (see Mosiah 4:22–25).

A time of beginning anew. While the jubilee laws served primarily to protect the lives and real property of small individual families from the horrors of bondage and disinheritance, these provisions also expressed powerful ideological values that helped periodically to set the community back on an even keel. Ancient economies were largely unregulated. In such societies, the rich tend to get richer and the poor become steadily poorer; land ownership becomes more and more concentrated in the hands of a few, and debts accumulate and compound without any hope of relief coming from such modern inventions as bankruptcy laws or government subsidies.

Babylonian kings in the second millennium B.C. dealt with this broad economic problem by issuing special edicts at the commencement of their reign or periodically as the need arose.[167] These so-called *mishârum* decrees forgave classes of people their outstanding debts and canceled taxes, and introduced various reforms,[168] thereby setting everyone in the kingdom, to an extent, back on an equal or equitable footing. This often involved the return of land or property that had been seized as collateral or was being held to produce revenue to pay off a debt.[169]

During its formative years, however, Israel had no kings. In the ancient Israelite world, no decrees would ever be forthcoming through the coronation edict of a generous new ruler seeking to garner political popularity, putting aside all the old obligations legitimized under his predecessor's authority in favor of giving his new administration a clean slate. Perhaps the jubilee laws were understood, in part, to fill this ancient need for periodical recalibration of Israelite economy and society. Whereas the kings of the ancient Near East reestablished their economic order at the time of their coronation and provided occasional subsequent reenactments throughout their reigns, Jehovah, the king of heaven and earth, decreed as a part of his perpetual reign that order should be regularly adjusted every seven years and then substantially re-created at the commencement of every new fifty-year cycle, approximately once in every lifetime. Obviously, religious and moral as well as economic and political purposes are served by this program.[170]

With this background, it is easy to imagine why King Benjamin would turn to the jubilee texts and sabbatical principles at the end of his reign and the commencement of the regency of his son Mosiah. Benjamin wanted his son to start afresh; he wanted old claims to be settled before new administrators and officers were put into office (see Mosiah 6:2), who would not necessarily know the terms of prior commitments or arrangements. Moreover, the ethical content of the jubilee strongly promoted such ideas as showing mercy (see Mosiah 4:16), forgiving indebtedness (see Mosiah 2:23), making people free (see Mosiah 5:8), proclaiming good news to the poor (see Mosiah 3:3; Isaiah 42:1–7; 61:1), settling accounts and returning borrowed property (see Mosiah 4:28), and retaining one's inheritance and favored condition (compare "retain" in Mosiah 4:12 and 26). These precepts are further bound up tightly with such theological themes as obtaining relief from one's debt to God through his mercy and goodness, being redeemed through the atonement of Christ, being held accountable at God's final judgment, and repenting and retaining a remission of forgiveness—doctrines that appear prominently in Benjamin's speech.

A time of peace. Another clue indicating that Benjamin's speech was delivered at the end of a jubilee year is found in Nephite history half a century later. Every seventh seven-year time period ideally occasioned a jubilee celebration, a time of peace. Mosiah reigned a total of thirty-three years after King Benjamin's speech (see Mosiah 29:46). Interestingly, in the sixteenth year of the reign of judges (the forty-ninth year after Benjamin's speech), "there began to be continual peace throughout all the land" (Alma 30:2). This peace lasted all through the seventeenth year of the reign of the judges (the fiftieth year); "there was continual peace" (Alma 30:5). During this time the people were especially "strict in observing the ordinances of God, according to the law of Moses" (Alma 30:3). Since the Hebrew word *yōḇēl* (jubilee) literally means "trumpet," and indeed the jubilee was so called because it was opened with the sound of the trumpet,[171] we may further conclude that Alma's wish that he might speak with the voice of "the trump of God" (Alma 29:1) is present and especially appropriate in this second identifiable jubilee season in Nephite history, as well as on the typical New Year occasion as discussed above.

Conclusion

The cumulative effect of all the foregoing information, in our opinion, points toward the idea that King Benjamin's speech was delivered in the fall, at the time of the year when all ancient Israelites, including peoples of the Book of Mormon, would have been celebrating their great autumn festival season, which included many ancient elements that later became enduring parts of the Jewish holidays of Rosh ha-Shanah, Yom Kippur, and Sukkot. Most of the known or surmised ancient elements of these festivals are represented in the text of the Book of Mormon. A very substantial percentage of the total number of words and topics found in Benjamin's speech are clearly found in the Israelite or Jewish literature associated with these sacred observances.

The setting for King Benjamin's speech was profoundly religious. On this occasion Benjamin disclosed sacred knowledge to his people about the true nature of divine kingship, the atonement of Christ, and the judgments of God. In addition, Benjamin performed the coronation of his son Mosiah and conducted his covenant renewal celebration—the most important ceremonial day of his life. It appears that he deliberately held this sacred assembly at the holy time of the year when such events were typically performed in ancient Israel, and possibly during a sabbatical or jubilee year. Just as the Israelite traditions shed considerable light on Benjamin's words, his speech represents a Nephite version of the ancient Israelite fall celebration, and as such it may add to our understanding of preexilic Israelite religion.

Thus it may be reasonably asserted that the ancient Israelite traditions connected with these festivals provided much of the fabric from which Benjamin fashioned his presentation of many of his revealed and revealing Christian expectations. This address ranks as one of the most spiritual and humanitarian sermons ever recorded in holy books the world over. Benjamin's speech contains numerous elements pertinent to the New Year holy day, the Day of Atonement observances, the Feast of Tabernacles, and the sabbatical or jubilee year. These elements account for the vast majority of themes or topics found in Benjamin's speech.

Benjamin's speech addresses many fundamental religious principles, and none of these topics can be considered out of place in a speech delivered by a king to a group of observant Nephites during their fall festival season. When viewed in light of the holy setting of this speech, its penetrating and revealing themes shine through especially bright and clear. King Benjamin's carefully chosen words and the angel's marvelously articulated messages could hardly have been more timely.

Some of Benjamin's Main Themes Appropriate to the Time of the Israelite New Year

admonitions	the long-suffering of God
the attributes of God	the Lord omnipotent
being sealed to God	man's nature and nothingness
covenant making	preaching and prophecy
creation	rebirth and resurrection
divine judgment	remembrance
forsaking sin	reverence and fear of God
God's involvement in history	sacrifice
guilt before God	testimony against the people
kingship of God	warnings against sin
law	wisdom

Some of Benjamin's Main Themes Appropriate to the Season of the Day of Atonement

atonement
balancing order and diligence
being made free from sin
belief in the Messiah
belief in God
blood
blotting out the names of transgressors
the commandments of God
confession and repentance
conversion
joy and blessings
eternal rewards and punishments
faith
the fall of Adam
the fallen state of humanity
foundation of the world
giving to the poor
the goodness of God
humility
ignorant sin
indebtedness to God
inscribing the names of the righteous
knowing the divine name
left hand
the means of salvation
the name of God
pride
purification
rebellion against God
repentance
right hand
service to God and fellowman
submission
the suffering and works of the Messiah
unintentional sin

Some of Benjamin's Main Themes Appropriate to the Season of the Feast of Tabernacles

becoming sons and daughters of God
booths/tents
coronation
deliverance
the effect of knowing God
family
giving thanks and praise
joy in the commandments
keeping the commandments
kingship
knowing God by serving God
law and order
one's accountability after being warned
praise
remembrance
rejoicing and thanksgiving
sacrifice
temple assembly

Some of Benjamin's Main Themes Appropriate to Sabbatical and Jubilee Years

blessings	prosperity
debt	purification and renewal
forgiveness	rendering to each his due
freedom	returning things borrowed
land	riches and generosity
love	service and servants
peaceful living	slaves released

Notes

1. See Hugh W. Nibley, *An Approach to the Book of Mormon*, 3rd ed. (Salt Lake City: Deseret Book and FARMS, 1988 [1st ed. 1957]), 295–310.

2. See Hugh W. Nibley, "The Roman Games as a Survival of an Archaic Year-Cult" (Ph.D. diss., University of California, Berkeley, 1939).

3. Nibley supported his claim by pointing out thirty-six elements present in Benjamin's assembly, potentially identifiable as part of a typical ancient year-rite: Benjamin's speech involves a proclamation, assembly, census, sacrifice, *silentium* (call to attention), a dramatic form of instruction, hailing of the king, homage, gifts, signs of submission, divine kingship, the king's farewell, a heavenly choir, promises of victory and prosperity, records, divination of the future, judgment, *acclamatio* (crying out), *proskynesis* (falling to the ground), recalling the condition of mankind in the Golden Age before the fall, caring for the poor, making a covenant, receiving a new name, recording the names in a register symbolic of the heavenly Book of Life, and dismissal. Each such element is identified as an "unfailing part" or "important aspect of the year-rites." Nibley, *Approach to the Book of Mormon*, 304.

4. See ibid., 299–300.

5. These include David E. Boruchowitz, Richard Erickson, Jerome Horowitz, Stephen D. Ricks, John L. Sorenson, Terrence L. Szink, Gordon C. Thomasson, John A. Tvedtnes, Benjamin Urrutia,

John W. Welch, and Stephen Wood. Many of the ideas expressed in this chapter can be found in the following publications: John A. Tvedtnes, "King Benjamin and the Feast of Tabernacles," in *By Study and Also by Faith: Essays in Honor of Hugh W. Nibley*, ed. John M. Lundquist and Stephen D. Ricks (Salt Lake City: Deseret Book and FARMS, 1990), 2:197–237; "The Ideology of Kingship in Mosiah 1–6," "This Day," "Benjamin's Speech: A Classic Ancient Farewell Address," and "The Coronation of Kings," in *Reexploring the Book of Mormon*, ed. John W. Welch (Salt Lake City: Deseret Book and FARMS, 1992), 114–26; Stephen D. Ricks, "King, Coronation, and Covenant in Mosiah 1–6," in *Rediscovering the Book of Mormon*, ed. John L. Sorenson and Melvin J. Thorne (Salt Lake City: Deseret Book and FARMS, 1991), 209–19; Gordon C. Thomasson, "Mosiah: The Complex Symbolism and Symbolic Complex of Kingship in the Book of Mormon," *JBMS* 2/1 (1993): 21–38.

6. John W. Welch, "The Temple in the Book of Mormon," in *Temples of the Ancient World*, ed. Donald W. Parry (Salt Lake City: Deseret Book and FARMS, 1994), 316–17.

7. Ibid., 309–10. Welch marshals arguments explaining the strict observance of the law of Moses by the Nephites, including sabbaths (the main festival days were also treated as sabbaths even if they fell on a regular day of the week), and daily sacrifice, as well as civil and criminal law; Nephite practices and teachings blended elements from both the Old Testament and the revealed knowledge of the coming Messiah (ibid., 301–19).

8. J. H. Hertz, "Sabbath, Festival and Fast in Judaism," in *The Babylonian Talmud*, ed. Isodore Epstein (London: Soncino, 1938), 1:xx.

9. See John P. Pratt, "Book of Mormon Chronology," in *Encyclopedia of Mormonism*, 1:169–71.

10. J. B. Segal, "The Hebrew Festivals and the Calendar," *Journal of Semitic Studies* 6 (1961): 76, has written: "The calendar must not be alienated from the periodic festivals, nor the periodic festivals from the calendar, if both are to survive. If the two systems are separated one from another, one or both will wither and die."

11. See R. T. Beckwith, "The Earliest Enoch Literature and Its Calendar," *Revue de Qumran* 39 (1981): 365–403; "The Significance of the Calendar for Interpreting Essene Chronology and Eschatology," *Revue de Qumran* 38 (1980): 167–202; Julius Morgenstern, "The Three Calendars of Ancient Israel," *Hebrew Union College Annual* 1 (1924): 13–78.

12. See J. David Bleich, "Sefirat Ha-Omer and the Observance of Shavuᶜot for Travellers Crossing the Dateline," *Tradition: A Journal of Orthodox Jewish Thought* 21/4 (1985): 62–66.

13. See "Abinadi and Pentecost" and "Sons of the Passover," in *Reexploring*, 135–38, 196–98. In the New Testament a similar thing happens: Matthew, assuming that the reader understands Judaism, offers no explanation of Jewish practices, but Luke stops to point out Jewish customs to his Greek audience. Compare, for example, Matthew 26:17 with Luke 2:40–41.

14. A strong association can be drawn between the "tabernacles" or "booths" of the Feast of Tabernacles and "tents"; see discussion of the Feast of Tabernacles, below.

15. See Moshe I. Sorscher, *Companion Guide to the Yom Kippur Prayer Service* and *Companion Guide to the Rosh Hashanah Prayer Service* (Brooklyn: Judaica, 1994).

16. A similar methodological assumption is made by Reuven Yaron, "Prolegomena to the Study of Biblical Law," in *Jewish Law in Legal History and the Modern World*, ed. Bernard S. Jackson (Leiden: Brill, 1980), 27–44, arguing that rabbinic sources can shed light on the state of the law in the early biblical period in which the rabbinic rules and the prevailing ancient Near Eastern law codes are consistent on a point of law, but the biblical rule on the subject is lacking.

17. For further discussion of this topic, see Welch, "Temple in the Book of Mormon," 314–16.

18. Current Old Testament scholarship has placed the final editing of the books from Genesis to Chronicles, as we know them today, in the middle of the sixth century B.C. in Babylon. The final records would have been written from early sources. See David

Noel Freedman, "The Formation of the Canon of the Old Testament: The Selection and Identification of the Torah as the Supreme Authority of the Post-Exilic Community," in *Religion and Law: Biblical-Judaic and Islamic Perspectives*, ed. Edwin B. Firmage, Bernard G. Weiss, and John W. Welch (Winona Lake: Eisenbrauns, 1990), 315–31.

19. See Robert E. Paul, "Joseph Smith and the Manchester (New York) Library," *BYU Studies* 22/3 (1982): 333–56.

20. See Menahem Haran, *Temples and Temple-Service in Ancient Israel* (Winona Lake, Ind.: Eisenbrauns, 1985), 297–98; H. J. Kraus, *Worship in Israel*, trans. Geoffrey Buswell (Richmond: Knox, 1966), 208.

21. The fall Feast of Ingathering "had many rites that are now associated with Rosh Hashanah, Yom Kippur, and Sukkot. It appears that it was only later, after the Babylonian Exile, that the autumn festival was divided into three separate holidays." Hayyim Schauss, *The Jewish Festivals* (New York: Schocken, 1962), 113. See also John Bright, *A History of Israel*, 3rd ed. (Philadelphia: Westminster, 1981), 171; Robert Martin-Achard, *Essai biblique sur les fêtes d'Israel* (Geneva: Labor et Fides, 1974), 73; Johannes C. de Moor makes the connection between the Canaanite New Year festival and the Israelite Feast of Tabernacles in *TDOT*, 2:191; for his discussion of possible reasons for the divisions of the feasts, see Johannes C. de Moor, *New Year with Canaanites and Israelites* (Kampen: Kok, 1971), 1:24–25. Even conservative scholar R. K. Harrison seems to accept "the three festivals of Tishri" as the preexilic counterpart to the Feast of Ingathering; see R. K. Harrison, *Introduction to the Old Testament* (Grand Rapids: Eerdmans, 1991), 52. For purposes of comparison, we may find a parallel to this idea of an ancient festival season in the common practice of celebrating Christmas, the New Year, and Hanukkah by sending Season's Greetings, a practice that combines several holidays in one.

22. Kraus, *Worship in Israel*, 208, writes "the division of the autumn festival into three parts must have taken place in the short

period of time between the reformation of king Josiah and the Babylonian exile." More specifically, he dated the division of the festival into three parts to "about 600 B.C." Ibid., 66.

23. On the New Year festival in general, see de Moor, *New Year with Canaanites and Israelites*. Martin-Achard, *Les fêtes d'Israel*, 93–104; Helmer Ringgren, *Israelite Religion*, trans. David E. Green (Philadelphia: Fortress, 1966), 185–200. Book of Mormon research in this area has been cultivated and advanced by several scholars; for example, in "New Year's Celebrations," in *Reexploring*, 209–11. The materials in this section have been developed particularly by Terrence L. Szink.

24. De Vaux, *Ancient Israel*, 502–3; Abraham Bloch, *The Biblical and Historical Background of the Jewish Holy Days* (New York: KTAV, 1978), 20. On the other hand, Haran, *Temples and Temple-Service*, 291 n. 7, argues that neither the New Year nor the Day of Atonement were mentioned in the nonpriestly sources because they were not designated as a *ḥag*, or festival, although they indeed did exist. It is also possible that the reason the New Year festival is not mentioned by name is that it was still part of the united autumn festival. This might also be why it was not identified by name in the Book of Mormon. Later it was differentiated, received a name, and developed further as a festival.

25. De Vaux, for example, in *Ancient Israel*, 2:502–3, wrote that "under this name [Rosh ha-Shanah], . . . the feast never existed in Old Testament times." He notes that "the feast held on the first of the seventh month was simply an unusually solemn new moon, the first day of a month which, at that time, was full of feasts." Kraus, *Worship in Israel*, 67, wrote "neither the older regulations concerning the autumn festival nor the cultic traditions in the Old Testament which presuppose the feast day on the first day of the seventh month make it possible to prove that there was a New Year festival in Israel"; compare Schauss, *Jewish Festivals*, 117.

26. De Moor reconstructs an Israelite New Year on the basis of Ugaritic material in *New Year with Canaanites and Israelites*. Many scholars combine passages from Psalms with parallels drawn from the Babylonian *akītu* (New Year) festival for reconstruction. In his

reconstruction, Sigmund Mowinckel saw the New Year festival as the "enthronement of Yahweh." *Psalmenstudien, II, Das Thronbesteigungsfest Jahwäs und der Ursprung der Eschatologie* (Oslo: Christiania, 1922). Von Rad and Weiser, on the other hand, saw it as a "covenant renewal festival." Gerhard von Rad, "The Form-Critical Problem of the Hexateuch," in *The Problem of the Hexateuch and Other Essays,* trans. E. W. Trueman Dicken (New York: McGraw-Hill, 1966), 33–40; Artur Weiser, *The Psalms,* trans. Herbert Hartwell (Philadelphia: Westminster, 1962), 35–52. For a discussion of these two theories, see Ringgren, *Israelite Religion,* 192–200, and Ringgren, "Enthronement Festival or Covenant Renewal?" *Biblical Research* 7 (1962): 45–48. For a rejection of the historical anthropology that stands behind these comparative approaches, see Harrison, *Introduction to the Old Testament,* 50–53.

27. Hertz, "Sabbath, Festival and Fast," xvii.

28. See "New Year's Celebrations," in *Reexploring,* 209–11. For a study of the Nephite calendar system, see John L. Sorenson, "Seasonality of Warfare in the Book of Mormon and in Mesoamerica," in *Warfare in the Book of Mormon,* ed. Stephen D. Ricks and William J. Hamblin (Salt Lake City: Deseret Book and FARMS, 1990), 445–77. Note that Sorenson suspects that the Nephites followed more than one calendar system (p. 449), which would mean that the timing of the festival is not as clear as we would like it to be.

29. In the past, many scholars have suggested that in preexilic times the New Year was observed in autumn and that the spring New Year developed after the exile, perhaps as a result of contact with Babylon, where the New Year was celebrated in spring. Jacob Klein, in his article "Akitu," in *ABD,* 1:138, notes that among the Sumerians a shift in the celebration of the *akītu* festival from the seventh to the first month also took place (this is not to imply a relationship between the two shifts). Another theory argues that the kingdoms of Israel and Judah simultaneously maintained opposing and overlapping year systems. See James C. Vanderkam, "Calendars: Ancient Israelite and Early Jewish," in *ABD,* 1:814–20, for a discussion and bibliography of this problem.

30. See D. J. A. Clines, "The Evidence for an Autumnal New Year in Pre-exilic Israel Reconsidered," *JBL* 93 (1974): 22–40.

31. Vanderkam, "Calendars," 817, explains that the festive calendar deals with an "agricultural cycle which is not necessarily the same as a calendar year." He notes that the Gezer calendar (presumably based on an agricultural cycle) begins with the ingathering, which would have been the seventh month; in a similar way among the Sumerians, "the *akītu* festival marked the beginning of the agricultural year." Klein, "Akitu," 138. The Mishnah notes not one or two, but four "New Year days" (*Rosh ha-Shanah* 1:1), each one having a different purpose.

32. See M *Rosh ha-Shanah* 3:3.

33. Similarly, Josephus makes no mention of the *shôfār* in his description of the holiday in *Antiquities* 3.10. Alternatively, it is possible that the blowing of the horns was not specifically known to Benjamin, since the form of Leviticus 23:24 that we know may well belong to "the last edition of the Pentateuch," which could have postdated Lehi. See de Vaux, *Ancient Israel*, 503. This would not rule out the possibility, however, that some kind of similarly functioning sound or instrument was used in preexilic Israelite festivals before being finally incorporated into their written traditions, as de Vaux himself suggests. Ibid., 254.

34. See Albert L. Lewis, "Shofar," in *Encyclopedia Judaica* (Jerusalem: Keter, 1972), 14:1442–47.

35. See "Kingship of God," below in this section.

36. Hertz, "Sabbath, Festival and Fast," xviii.

37. This suggestion was made by Gordon Thomasson.

38. See Bloch, *Jewish Holy Days*, 13.

39. This was an ancient practice with which Lehi would have been familiar. See Genesis 4:4 (Abel sacrificed the "firstlings of his flock"); Deuteronomy 12:6 ("And thither ye shall bring your burnt offerings, and your sacrifices, . . . and the firstlings of your herds and of your flocks"). The firstling males were eaten before the Lord "year by year"; see Deuteronomy 15:19–20.

40. "The fact that the Babylonian akitu was celebrated in the spring does not contradict the theory of an Israelite New Year's festival in autumn; as is well known, any new beginning in the

annual cycle can be observed as a New Year's festival." Ringgren, *Israelite Religion*, 200.

41. Klein, "Akitu," 138–39; W. G. Lambert, "Myth and Ritual as Conceived by the Babylonians," *Journal of Semitic Studies* 13/1 (1968): 107; de Vaux, *Ancient Israel*, 505.

42. Henri Frankfort, *Kingship and the Gods* (Chicago: University of Chicago Press, 1948), 331.

43. Baruch Halpern, *The Constitution of the Monarchy in Israel* (Chicago: Scholars Press, 1981), 57.

44. See M *Rosh ha-Shanah*, 1:2. "On New Year's Day all that come into the world pass before him like legions of soldiers, for it is written, He that fashioneth the hearts of them all, that considereth all their works."

45. *Leviticus Rabbah* 29:4; see TY *Rosh ha-Shanah*, 1:3; Louis Jacobs, "Rosh ha-Shanah," in *Encyclopedia Judaica*, 14:307, 309.

46. T. H. Gaster, *Festivals of the Jewish Year* (New York: Morrow Quill, 1978), 121.

47. TB *Rosh ha-Shanah* 16b; Jacobs, "Rosh ha-Shanah," 307.

48. See Gaster, *Festivals of the Jewish Year*, 93.

49. Schauss, *Jewish Festivals*, 112.

50. This may be distantly connected with the ritual of throwing one's sins into the sea (Micah 7:19), acted out in the *Tashlich* custom. See Schauss, *Jewish Festivals*, 148. The wearing of a long white cloak was customary and was a symbol of purity; Gaster, *Festivals of the Jewish Year*, 121.

51. See Schauss, *Jewish Festivals*, 300 n. 135.

52. Ibid., 147–48.

53. Ibid., 148.

54. As Lambert has pointed out, this poem was also read at other times during the year, "Myth and Ritual," 108.

55. See *ANET*, 501–3.

56. See Mowinckel, "Erster Teil: Die Thronbesteigungspsalmen und das Thronbesteigungsfest Jahwäs," in *Psalmenstudien, II, Das Thronbesteigungsfest*, 3–145.

57. Both Kraus, *Worship in Israel*, 205–8, and de Vaux, *Ancient Israel*, 504–6, reject the idea.

58. Keith W. Whitelam, "King and Kingship," in *ABD*, 4:44.

59. TB *Berakhot* 12b; Jacobs, "Rosh ha-Shanah," 307. See also Gaster, *Festivals of the Jewish Year,* 120.

60. Lambert, "Myth and Ritual," 112. Creation themes were often found in temple contexts; compare Stephen D. Ricks, "Liturgy and Cosmogony: The Ritual Use of Creation Accounts in the Ancient Near East," in *Temples of the Ancient World,* 118–25.

61. See Frankfort, *Kingship and the Gods,* 314.

62. See TB *Rosh ha-Shanah* 10b–11a.

63. Gaster, *Festivals of the Jewish Year,* 109. To this effect, Gaster cites generally Mircea Eliade, *The Myth of the Eternal Return,* trans. Willard R. Trask (Princeton: Princeton University Press, 1954), 51–92.

64. This was likewise the time of temple dedication in a Canaanite context. Frank M. Cross, "The Priestly Tabernacle in the Light of Recent Research," in *The Temple in Antiquity,* ed. Truman G. Madsen (Salt Lake City: Bookcraft, 1984), 93; compare Solomon's temple dedication at the Feast of Tabernacles (1 Kings 8:2–66).

65. See Louis Midgley, "The Ways of Remembrance," in *Rediscovering the Book of Mormon,* 168–76.

66. *BDB,* 272.

67. See Gaster, *Festivals of the Jewish Year,* 81.

68. John H. Eaton, "The King as God's Witness," *Annual of the Swedish Theological Institute,* ed. Hans Kosmala (Leiden: Brill, 1970), 7:27, 29, 31. This third duty is further divided into proclaiming peace, teaching one to look "to God as his rock, crag and fortress, his father who accepted him from the womb and who taught him as he grew," that "from the very netherworld God will bring him up and indeed increase his princely greatness," and also declaring at great length that he as king will stand as a witness for God "such as he has hitherto rendered daily and will continue to render in the future, proclaiming God's mighty work and righteousness to succeeding generations, affirming his incomparability" (p. 31).

69. Ibid., 32–33.

70. See ibid., 34.

71. See Klein, "Akitu," 138; John H. Eaton, *Kingship and the Psalms*, 2nd ed. (Sheffield: JSOT, 1986), 88.

72. Klein, "Akitu," 138; see also Eaton, *Kingship and the Psalms*, 88.

73. See Halpern, *Constitution of the Monarchy in Israel*, 53.

74. See Helmer Ringgren, "Enthronement Festival or Covenant Renewal," *Biblical Research* 7 (1962): 45.

75. See ibid.

76. *ANET*, 334.

77. See Klein, "Akitu," 139. In the Babylonian New Year festival, on the second day of the month, the king asked the all-seeing god (line 19; compare Mosiah 4:9) to have mercy on his people (line 24; compare Mosiah 4:2, 6) and to make them free (line 32; compare Mosiah 5:8) as god's subordinates (or servants, line 32; compare Mosiah 2:17). On the third day he offered additional prayers. On the fourth day he blessed and purified the temple and offered prayers to the God of heaven and earth, before being humiliated by having his scepter, circle, and sword (lines 420–25; compare Mosiah 1:16) taken from him and being slapped on the cheek until the tears flowed. On the sixth day the king raised two images, one in his right hand and the other in his left hand, knocked off their heads, and threw them into a fire (line 215; compare Mosiah 2:38). *ANET*, 331–34. Obviously, one may find in this ritual some similarities and several dissimilarities with Benjamin's speech as well as with certain elements in the Bible. Not much can be made of such comparisons, and we do not claim that the Israelites or Nephites celebrated a year-rite in the pagan sense; but texts such as the rare New Year's liturgy from Babylon help modern readers at least to imagine the general kinds of ceremonies that existed in the ancient Near East.

78. See Johnson, *Sacral Kingship in Ancient Israel*, 22–25; Eaton, *Kingship and the Psalms*, 133–34; Ringgren, *Israelite Religion*, 236–37. On the other hand, Tryggve N. D. Mettinger, *King and Messiah: The Civil and Sacral Legitimation of the Israelite Kings* (Lund: Liber Läromedel, 1976), 307, declares that "there is a lack of positive evidence for such a practice in ancient Israel," although he admits that "cultic suffering on the part of the king in a yearly renewal of

kingship would perhaps not constitute a wholly inconceivable element in Israelite kingship."

79. Johnson, *Sacral Kingship in Ancient Israel*, 106.

80. Aubrey R. Johnson, *Sacral Kingship in Ancient Israel* (Cardiff: University of Wales Press, 1955), 47.

81. J. B. Segal, *The Hebrew Passover: From the Earliest Times to* A.D. *70* (New York: Oxford Press, 1963), 267.

82. See De Moor, *The New Year with Canaanites and Israelites*, 1:20.

83. Ibid., 18.

84. See discussion of the "Earthly King" under the Feast of Tabernacles, below. See also "Kingship and Temple in 2 Nephi 5–10," in *Reexploring*, 66–68.

85. For people in a culture such as this, an actual killing of a king on New Year's Day would have caused absolute fear and terror, as if their world had just fallen apart. Thus it was surely no accident that Teancum chose New Year's Eve to steal into the tent of King Amalickiah and kill him (perhaps under the guise of some ritual). When his subjects found him dead "on the first morning of the first month" (Alma 52:1), it is no wonder that they "were affrighted" (Alma 52:2), abandoning all military plans and retreating in search of protection.

86. See Tvedtnes, "King Benjamin and the Feast of Tabernacles," 224–26, and pp. 34, 60, 188, and 248 in this volume.

87. Schauss, *Jewish Festivals*, 146; see also Jacobs, "Rosh ha-Shanah," 309.

88. Jacobs, "Rosh ha-Shanah," 310. For "awe" of God and lowliness of man as God's "creation," see Mosiah 2:20–26; 4:5–11. For "prostrating" oneself before God, see Mosiah 4:1 and Gaster, *Festivals of the Jewish Year*, 121. For achieving harmonious unity among the people, see Mosiah 4:13; 5:2. For doing God's will with a perfect heart, see Mosiah 5:2–5.

89. The biblical prescriptions for the rites of the Day of Atonement are noted in Leviticus 16; 23:26–32; Numbers 29:7–11. Their relevance to Benjamin's speech was first developed by John W. Welch. On the Day of Atonement see generally David P. Wright,

"Day of Atonement," in *ABD*, 2:72–76; Jacob Milgrom, *Leviticus 1–16* (New York: Doubleday, 1991), 1009–84; Kraus, *Worship in Israel*, 68–70; Jacob Milgrom, "Day of Atonement as Annual Day of Purgation in Temple Times," in *Encyclopedia Judaica*, 5:1384–87; Moshe D. Herr, "Day of Atonement," in *Encyclopedia Judaica*, 5:1376–84. Regarding the use of the term *kipper*, see Baruch A. Levine, *In the Presence of the Lord* (Leiden: Brill, 1974), 55–77.

90. The Day of Atonement was certainly preexilic. Kraus writes, "We can conclude that the special 'Day of Atonement' that is laid down for the first time in Lev. 23:26 was part of the autumn festival from the earliest period and points back even as far as the desert period." *Worship in Israel*, 69. Milgrom, *Leviticus 1–16*, 1071, closely examines the question of dating the Day of Atonement and concludes that "the tenth of Tishri, as the annual event for the purgation of the Temple, was observed in preexilic times."

91. The Mishnah devotes an entire tractate (*Yoma*, lit. "The Day") to the ceremony and prescriptions of the Day of Atonement.

92. Welch, "The Temple in the Book of Mormon," 353. Milgrom, *Leviticus 1–16*, 1039, notes that the septenary system was operative in the rites of the Day of Atonement. See Leviticus 4:6, 17; 8:11; 14:7, 16, 27, 51; 16:14, 19. In their response to his seven references to atonement, Benjamin's people speak once of the "atoning blood" (Mosiah 4:2).

93. That Benjamin seems to serve as the high priest, or at least describes actions taken by the high priest, is not unusual. Ringgren, *Israelite Religion*, 234, has written: "We are probably justified in assuming that the king officiated at certain atonement ceremonies in the context of the New Year festival." See also Mettinger, *King and Messiah*, 306; Eaton, *Kingship and the Psalms*, 172–77.

94. See M *Yoma* 1:7.

95. For example, see M *Yoma* 3:3 (31b); 3:4 (34b).

96. See Sorscher, *Companion Guide to the Yom Kippur Prayer Service*, xi.

97. See *ANET*, 333. Milgrom notes both the similarities and

differences between the two rites, *Leviticus 1–16*, 1067–70; note again this association between the Day of Atonement and the New Year celebration.

98. Leviticus 16:21 mentions three terms describing types of misdeeds: (1) ʿăwōnôt, "iniquities," which were deliberate wrong-doings but not quite as serious as (2) pəshāʿîm (translated by the KJV as "transgressions"), which were rebellious acts and the most serious type of sin, and (3) ḥaṭṭʾōtām, "sins," a general term that covered all types of misdeeds except the pəshāʿîm. See *BDB*, 306–10, 730–31, 833, and Milgrom, *Leviticus 1–16*, 1034, 1043.

99. M *Yoma* 3:5.

100. See "Unintentional Sin in Benjamin's Discourse," FARMS Update, *Insights* (April 1996): 2.

101. On the scapegoat rite and comparative Near Eastern rites, see David P. Wright, *The Disposal of Impurity: Elimination Rites in the Bible and in Hittite and Mesopotamian Literature* (Atlanta: Scholars, 1987), 15–74.

102. The term ʾAzazel most likely refers to a demon. Milgrom, *Leviticus 1–16*, 1020–21; Hayim Tawil, "ʾAzazel, the Prince of the Steepe [Steppe]: A Comparative Study," *ZAW* 92 (1980): 43–59.

103. See M *Yoma* 4:1.

104. See Milgrom, *Leviticus 1–16*, 1019. The placing of the lots on the heads of the goats is to mark them for identification only.

105. Interestingly, in the course of King Benjamin's speech he uses the term "evil spirit(s)" four times (Mosiah 2:32, 37; 3:6; 4:14), while it appears in the rest of the Book of Mormon only once (2 Nephi 32:8). Perhaps his references to the "evil spirit" are to be connected with "ʾAzazel" of Leviticus 16:8. Three of the references to the evil spirit in Benjamin's speech are associated with sins of rebellion, the type of sins the scapegoat carried to Azazel. In Benjamin's fourth reference, the evil spirits are to be "cast out," as was the scapegoat.

106. See generally, de Vaux, *Ancient Israel*, 508–9. Scapegoat analogy is not complete, of course. In Benjamin's words, the one

who is driven out does not bear the sins of any other people, only his own.

107. Benjamin might have preferred the ass over the goat for several reasons: availability, for the symbolic value of its fabled stubbornness, from connections between the ass and the Nephites' progenitory Lehi (whose name means "jawbone [of an ass]," compare Judges 15:15–17) and Joseph (Speiser's translation of Genesis 49:22 sees Joseph as a wild ass colt, although his analysis may be weak), and because the ass was uniquely "redeemable" by the slaying of a lamb (see Exodus 13:13; 34:20). These points were first explored by John W. Welch and Gordon C. Thomasson, "Ritual Use of the Ass in the Ancient Near East and in the Book of Mormon," unpublished manuscript.

108. See Wright, *The Disposal of Impurity*, 50–72.

109. See Delbert R. Hillers, *Covenant: The History of a Biblical Idea* (Baltimore: Johns Hopkins, 1969), 40–41.

110. The occurrences are Mosiah 2:30, "Lord God doth support me"; 2:41, "Lord God hath spoken it"; 3:5, "Lord Omnipotent who reigneth"; 3:13, "Lord God hath sent his holy prophets"; 3:14, "Lord God saw that his people were a stiffnecked people"; 3:17, "Lord Omnipotent [only means of salvation]"; 3:18, "Lord Omnipotent [atoning blood of]"; 3:21, "Lord God Omnipotent [name of]"; 3:23, "Lord God hath commanded me"; 5:15, "Lord God Omnipotent may seal you his." Moreover, only in Benjamin's speech do "Lord God Omnipotent" or "Lord Omnipotent" ever appear in the Book of Mormon, indicating cultic usage here. On the Jewish practice, see Schauss, *Jewish Festivals*, 135, who counts ten such occurrences, representing completeness and perfection. In addition, just as the people responded by saying the word *atone* once in Mosiah 4:12, they pronounce the name *Lord Omnipotent* once in Mosiah 5:2.

111. The use of these words is remarkable, especially since the angel also uses the name *Christ* exactly seven times, and Benjamin uses the root *atone* seven times in this seven-part speech.

112. The holy name is given at the endpoints of three of the chiastic sections of Benjamin's speech. Mosiah 2:30 is the breaking point between sections 1 and 2. Mosiah 2:41 is the breaking point between sections 2 and 3. The final utterance of the holy name is in Mosiah 5:15, the final verse of the speech.

113. "And when the priests and the people which stood in the Temple court heard the Expressed Name come forth from the mouth of the High Priest, they used to kneel and bow themselves and fall down on their faces and say, 'Blessed be the name of the glory of his kingdom for ever and ever!'" M *Yoma* 6:2.

114. It is quite plausible that the people would have fallen or bowed down in respect when they heard Benjamin pronounce the holy name of God as he announced his son Mosiah to be their new king (see Mosiah 2:29–30). It is possible that the people would have fallen down again when they heard Benjamin pronounce the holy name in Mosiah 2:41, as he imposed the judgment of God upon the people at the end of that section of his speech. Since Benjamin observes in Mosiah 4:1 that the people "had fallen to the earth," and since the sacred name is mentioned seven times in rapid succession in Mosiah 3:1–27, it seems probable that they remained in a fallen position throughout Benjamin's words about the fall of Adam (see Mosiah 3:11, 16, 19) and the atonement of Christ (see Mosiah 3:13, 17–21). Finally, the people could well have fallen or bowed down one last time as Benjamin spoke his doxology of God and as he sealed the people unto God at the conclusion of his speech (see Mosiah 5:15).

115. This revelation comes at the chiastic center of the third section of Benjamin's speech. The Talmud indicates that some men had the name of God written on their bodies, TB *Yoma* 88a, as a slave might have been branded with the name or mark of his owner.

116. See Milgrom, *Leviticus 1–16*, 1054. Chapter 8 of *Yoma*, the section of the Mishnah dealing with the Day of Atonement, deals with the regulations regarding fasting on that day. Fasting, of course, should not be misunderstood as afflicting one's soul in the sense of suffering but in the sense of developing piety and empathy (see Isaiah 58:5, 10; Matthew 6:16–18).

117. Milgrom notes that the reason for the public fast is a threatened calamity either from man or God, *Leviticus 1–16*, 1066. He goes on to cite the words of the king of Nineveh in Jonah 3:7–9.

118. "The Day of Atonement effect[s] atonement if there is repentance." M *Yoma* 8:8; Maimonides, *Yad* (*Mishneh Torah*), *Teshuvah* 1:2–4.

119. See M *Yoma* 8:9: "For transgressions that are between man and God the Day of Atonement effects atonement, but for transgressions that are between a man and his fellow the Day of Atonement effects atonement only if he has appeased his fellow."

120. See TB *Yoma* 87b.

121. See Herr, "Day of Atonement," 1378, 1381; Schauss, *Jewish Festivals*, 132.

122. Herr, "Day of Atonement," 1381.

123. See Sorscher, *Companion Guide to the Yom Kippur Prayer Service*, 50.

124. Herr, "Day of Atonement," 1382, especially citing Philo.

125. See ibid., 1383.

126. Ibid., 1382.

127. See ibid., again evidencing the close connection between Rosh ha-Shanah, Yom Kippur, and Sukkot, which in preexilic Israel were probably not distinct holidays. Schauss, *Jewish Festivals*, 119, discussed above.

128. The insights in this section were first developed in depth by John A. Tvedtnes. See Tvedtnes, "King Benjamin and the Feast of Tabernacles," 197–237; see also de Vaux, *Ancient Israel*, 495–502; Kraus, *Worship in Israel*, 61–66; Martin-Achard, *Les fêtes d'Israel*, 75–92; Gaster, *Festivals of the Jewish Year*, 80–104; Abraham Bloch, *Jewish Customs and Ceremonies*, 181–209; Bloch, *Jewish Holy Days*, 39–48; J. Coert Rylaarsdam, "Booths, Feast of," in *The Interpreter's Dictionary of the Bible*, ed. George A. Butterick et al. (New York: Abingdon, 1962), 1:455–58.

129. See Ringgren, *Israelite Religion*, 189; de Vaux, *Ancient Israel*, 495; Haran, *Temples and Temple-Service*, 296.

130. See Schauss, *Jewish Festivals*, 171; de Vaux, *Ancient Israel*, 495; Haran, *Temples and Temple-Service*, 297–98.

131. Ringgren, *Israelite Religion*, 190, suggests that anciently it

may have been a type of vintage celebration that featured excessive drinking, on which he blames the behavior of Eli's sons in 1 Samuel 2; also de Moor, *New Year with Canaanites and Israelites*, 1:28–29. Perhaps King Benjamin's thrice-mentioned "drinking damnation to souls" (see Mosiah 2:33; 3:18, 25) is an allusion to this. See also Gaster, *Festivals of the Jewish Year*, 84; de Vaux, *Ancient Israel*, 501. Kraus, *Worship in Israel*, 128–34, 173–78, on the other hand, suggests that an original "tent festival" was held while the Israelites were still in the desert (an example of which he saw in Exodus 33:7–11), which was either displaced by the agricultural "booth festival" or changed to fit the customs of the indigenous population. Against Kraus, see de Vaux, *Ancient Israel*, 502.

132. See Schauss, *Jewish Festivals*, 170–74; Haran, *Temples and Temple-Service*, 293–94; von Rad, "Problem of the Hexateuch," 35.

133. Haran, *Temples and Temple-Service*, 294, notes that "even in the early period" the feasts included the participation of the whole family.

134. The fact that the people *surrounded* the temple (see also Mosiah 4:1) may be insignificant. On the other hand, it may have ceremonial meaning. The Mishnah has a description of circumambulation of the altar during Sukkot: "Each day (for the first six days) they went in procession a single time around the Altar, saying 'Save now, we beseech thee, O Lord! We beseech thee, O Lord, send now prosperity.' . . . But on that day (the seventh) they went in procession seven times around the Altar." M *Sukkah* 4:5.

135. According to Rylaarsdam, "Booths, Feast of," 456–57, the use of the booth most likely is related to the use of similar types of structures during harvest time. De Moor notes the use of booths in the Ugaritic New Year festival, which he connects to the Israelite Feast of Tabernacles, in *TDOT*, 2:191. See also de Vaux, *Ancient Israel*, 501.

136. Gaster, *Festivals of the Jewish Year*, 84, notes that "the cold fact is that people who wander through deserts live in tents, not booths, wood and green leaves being unavailable except at rare and intermittent oases."

137. See de Vaux, *Ancient Israel*, 496; Martin-Achard, *Les fêtes d'Israel*, 79. Hugh W. Nibley, "Tenting, Toll, and Taxing," in *The Ancient State* (Salt Lake City: Deseret Book and FARMS, 1991), 41–46.

138. See *BDB*, 13–14.

139. The exodus from Egypt is a "type" of God's deliverance. The comparison between Lehi's deliverance from the Babylonian captivity and the Israelites' deliverance from Egypt is specifically mentioned in 1 Nephi 17:23–43 and Alma 36:28–29. On the exodus motif in the Book of Mormon generally, see George S. Tate, "The Typology of the Exodus Pattern in the Book of Mormon," in *Literature of Belief*, ed. Neal E. Lambert (Provo: Religious Studies Center Monograph Series, 1978); Terrence L. Szink, "Nephi and the Exodus," in *Rediscovering*, 38–51; S. Kent Brown, "The Exodus: Seeing It as a Test, a Testimony, and a Type," *Ensign* (February 1990): 54–57; S. Kent Brown, "The Exodus Pattern in the Book of Mormon," *BYU Studies* 30/3 (1990): 111–26; and "Nephi and the Exodus," *Ensign* (April 1987): 64–65.

140. Schauss, *Jewish Festivals*, 200, considers the idea of booths as a symbol of the wilderness, "a forced interpretation . . . evolved in later times; . . . besides, the Jews resided in tents during their wanderings in the desert, and there is quite a difference between a tent and a booth." Kraus, *Worship in Israel*, 64, quoting Alt, says that the interpretation of booths as representing the structures of the exodus was an "anachronism." As noted above, he believes there was originally a "tent festival" that was replaced by a booth festival.

141. See Haran, *Temples and Temple-Service*, 298.

142. Von Rad, "Problem of the Hexateuch," 35, wrote "The Feast of Booths was in earlier times pre-eminently the festival to which the community came on pilgrimage. It is therefore inconceivable that the festival of the renewal of the covenant between Yahweh and the people should not be identified with this very same festival."

143. See the discussion of the sabbatical/jubilee year, below.

Von Rad suggests that the reading of the law might have taken place not only every seven years, but annually, "Problem of the Hexateuch," 36.

144. Rylaarsdam, "Booths, Feast of," 456. See also Ringgren, *Israelite Religion*, 192–95, for a discussion of the covenant renewal as part of the autumn festival.

145. John Tvedtnes has interpreted the covenant-making ceremony at the base of Mount Sinai (Exodus 24) as a Feast of Tabernacles ceremony, "King Benjamin and the Feast of Tabernacles," 199. Although at the Feast of Tabernacles covenants were most likely made and renewed, note also the royal covenant of the third month in 2 Chronicles 15:10–15 (compare verse 13 with Mosiah 6:2).

146. See Ricks, "King, Coronation, and Covenant in Mosiah 1–6," 215–19, and his related materials in "Kingship, Coronation, and Covenant in Mosiah 1–6," in this volume.

147. See M *Sotah* 7:8.

148. T. Raymond Hobbs, *2 Kings* (Waco: Word Books, 1985), 142, suggests that the object stood on or was by "some kind of column, podium, or platform." Kraus, *Worship in Israel*, 224, notes that in the ceremonies of enthronement the king was lifted on to an *ʾammud* where he received the homage of the congregation.

149. See Tvedtnes, "King Benjamin and the Feast of Tabernacles," 224–26.

150. See ibid., 207–9.

151. Discussed further below.

152. For the link between the Heavenly King and the New Year, see the section on the New Year celebration, above.

153. See, for example, *Ha-Sidur ha-Shalem (Daily Prayer Book)*, translated and annotated with an introduction by Philip Birnbaum (New York: Hebrew Publishing, 1949), 678; this prayer is recited on the first day of waving the *lulav* during Sukkot.

154. See Sorscher, *Companion Guide to the Yom Kippur Prayer Service*, 5.

155. David Boruchowitz was primarily responsible for this discovery.

156. See "This Day," in *Reexploring,* 117–19.

157. The semantics of the Hebrew in the *She-hecheyanu* also fit the context of Benjamin's speech. The principal verb in the prayer is the *hiphil* form of the root *ḤYH, meaning "to preserve alive, let live, quicken, revive, restore to life." *BDB,* 311. From the same root come the verb *ḥāyāh* ("to live") and the noun *ḥayyîm* ("life: as consisting of earthly felicity combined often with spiritual blessedness"), ibid., 31. Benjamin elegantly elaborates on this main theme of the *She-hecheyanu* when he says that God has caused the people to rejoice and live in blessed peace and has lent them breath that they may live. The repeated occurrence of words derived from this root would have structurally reinforced his message and conveyed a pleasing alliteration. Other references to life (see Mosiah 4:6, 22; 5:15), and to joy and rejoicing (see Mosiah 3:3, 4, 13; 4:11, 12, 20; 5:4) occur plentifully throughout his speech.

158. Research on Benjamin's speech in the context of a sabbatical or jubilee year was initiated by John W. Welch. For general background information, see Christopher J. H. Wright, "Jubilee, Year of," in *ABD,* 3:1025–32; Christopher J. H. Wright, "Sabbatical Year," in *ABD,* 5:857–61; de Vaux, *Ancient Israel,* 173–77; Kraus, *Worship in Israel,* 70–76.

159. See Wright, "Sabbatical Year," in *ABD,* 5: 857. See generally Niels-Erik A. Andreasen, *The Old Testament Sabbath: A Tradition-Historical Investigation* (Missoula: Scholars Press, 1972); Bernard R. Goldstein and Alan Cooper, "The Festivals of Israel and Judah and the Literary History of the Pentateuch," *Journal of the American Oriental Society* 110/1 (1990): 19–31, and Timothy K. Hui, "The Purpose of Israel's Annual Feasts," *Bibliotheca Sacra* 147 (1990): 143–54.

160. A "release" similar to the Israelite practice of the sabbatical/jubilee year has been shown to occur in Mesopotamia, although it was not based on fixed intervals but declared arbitrarily by the monarch, usually (and interestingly) upon his ascension to the throne. See Julius Lewy, "The Biblical Institution of Dᵉrôr in the Light of Akkadian Documents," *Eretz Israel* 5 (1958): 21–31.

161. Wright, "Jubilee, Year of," in *ABD,* 3:1026. See generally,

Niels P. Lemche, "The Manumission of Slaves—The Fallow Year—The Sabbatical Year—The Jobel Year," *Vetus Testamentum* 26/1 (January 1976): 38–59; and Robert North, *Sociology of the Biblical Jubilee* (Rome: Pontifical Biblical Institute, 1954).

162. The inclusive mode of sometimes counting the last year as the first of the next jubilee cycle accounts for the frequent confusion between 49- and 50-year jubilee counts. Walter Wifall, "God's Accession Year According to P," *Biblica* 62/4 (1981): 532–33 (cf. Leviticus 25:10, *11QMelch* 3:2); Ben Zion Wacholder, *Essays on Jewish Chronology and Chronography* (New York: KTAV, 1976), 250. See also generally, Raymond Westbrook, "Jubilee Laws," *Israel Law Review* 6 (1971): 209–26.

163. De Vaux, *Ancient Israel*, 175.

164. A delinquent debtor was considered a thief under Nephite law (see Alma 11:2) as well as under early Jewish law; see Bernard S. Jackson, *Theft in Early Jewish Law* (Oxford: Clarendon, 1972), 91, but is not considered as such under Anglo-American law. See generally John W. Welch, "Theft and Robbery in the Book of Mormon and Ancient Near Eastern Law" (Provo, Utah: FARMS, 1985).

165. A lender under ancient Near Eastern law could also commit an offense by not accepting proper repayment of the debt. Since disputes arose over the adequacy of precious metal equivalents or substitute property, the laws, especially in cases of noncommercial borrowing, protected the right of the lender to receive repayment of the debt in exact kind. Systems of weights and measures and exchange equivalents were instituted, in part, to remedy this commercial difficulty. Jewish law also expresses grave concerns about exchanges of property: since no two pieces of property (especially of different kinds) can be assumed to have exactly the same value, one party to the exchange can be assumed to be getting less and the other more than is deserved. Such problems are averted by returning "the thing" that was borrowed.

166. Although the final composition of these chapters in Leviticus has often been dated during the exile, jubilee practices are much older, as Raymond Westbrook demonstrates in his "Jubilee Laws," *Israel Law Review* 6 (1971): 224–26; see also Cyrus

Gordon, "Sabbatical Cycle or Seasonal Pattern?" *Orientalia* 22 (1953): 81.

167. See Raymond Westbrook, "Jubilee Laws," *Israel Law Review* 6/2 (1971): 216.

168. See ibid., 217.

169. See ibid., 216–17.

170. See Wright, "Jubilee, Year of," in *ABD*, 3:1028–29.

171. See de Vaux, *Ancient Israel*, 175.

Chapter 7

Benjamin's Speech as a Prophetic Lawsuit

John W. Welch

Legal terminology and judicial patterns have found their way into the daily life and ordinary language of virtually all peoples.[1] The speech forms and imagery of Bible and Book of Mormon prophets, including King Benjamin, are no exception.

To illustrate this point, one may approach Benjamin's speech through form criticism, a branch of literary analysis that seeks to identify various forms within a body of literature. In the study of the Old Testament, form-critical scholars have defined and identified instances of several forms or genres of prophetic speech involving oracles, threats, reproaches, accusations, messenger formulas, and salvation speeches; judgment speeches to Israel, individuals, or other nations; the cry of woe, the legal procedure, the disputation, the parable, the lament, or the prophetic torah.[2] One of these speech forms is generally known to scholars as the "prophetic lawsuit," sometimes referred to as the "judgment speech," the "covenant lawsuit," or the "trial speech." In passages of this type, the prophet accuses, indicts, or prosecutes the people as if he were bringing an action against them in a court of law.[3] Gunkel argues that the prophetic lawsuit was a convenient form, because "the trial was a concrete situation with which everyone was familiar,"[4] and Julien Harvey maintains that the prophets used this literary form in order to explain the disasters that Israel had experienced, presenting their explanations in a way that would emphasize the justice and moral correctness of Yahweh's actions.[5]

On some occasions, the form of the prophetic lawsuit appears to have closely paralleled a typical civil or criminal legal proceeding. Other times, however, the form was utilized less rigidly. Nielsen suggests that four elements capture the essence of the so-called prophetic lawsuit: (1) the calling of witnesses, (2) the lodging of an accusation, (3) the consideration of a defense, and (4) the issuance of a judgment.[6] Biblical passages regularly identified as prophetic lawsuits include Isaiah 1:2–3, 18–20; Jeremiah 2:4–13; Micah 6:1–8; and Hosea 4:1–3. Furthermore, one wonders what type of trial the ancient prophet might have had in mind as he composed his speech. Three types of proceedings are possible: civil, international, and ritual, or perhaps a combination of all three.[7] For example, Gunkel sees the prophetic lawsuit as an imitation of a civil proceeding at the town gate. Julien Harvey argues that the formal setting of the prophetic lawsuit is found in international law, in an action for breach of treaty between a lord and a vassal. Finally, this form of speech may have reminded Israelite audiences of other forms of indictment or reprimand connected with some religious ceremony, although this possibility is the least documentable of the three and thus has the smallest number of adherents among biblical scholars.

While several Book of Mormon texts may be analyzed as prophetic lawsuits, Benjamin's speech presents an especially interesting case. Although the legal elements are not particularly obvious in Benjamin's sermon—mainly because his speech features so many other literary forms—all the basic elements of the prophetic lawsuit can be found in the text.

On first impression, it may seem odd to think of Benjamin's speech as a prophetic lawsuit, for his address is not heavily accusatory or legalistic. At no time does Benjamin enumerate a specific list of sins or transgressions committed by his people. Indeed, it appears that Benjamin's people were fairly righteous and well prepared to receive spiritual instructions from Benjamin and to enter into a covenant that required of them a high level of consecration of their resources and a mature degree of Christian devotion to God and their fellow beings. Moreover, when Benjamin told his people about his accomplishments as their king and the fulfillment of his duties as their leader, he went out of his way to say that he had not made these declarations to his people in order to accuse them: "I have not done these things that I might boast, neither do I tell these things that thereby I might accuse you" (Mosiah 2:15).

These facts, however, do not mean that Benjamin absolved his people from all possible indictments. On the contrary, he mentioned their guilt on several occasions. He shook their blood from his garments (see Mosiah 2:28), and they perceived his admonitions as a call to personal repentance. The people viewed themselves in their sinful state and cried out that they might be forgiven of their sins (see Mosiah 4:2). The effect of Benjamin's speech was so plain that even the little children could not misunderstand that they were subject to the rules and principles of God's justice and mercy (see Mosiah 2:40). Thus Benjamin made his people aware of the inevitable judgments of God, their own culpability before him, and the only way by which they might stand blameless at the judgment day. These are the same results that the Israelite prophets sought to achieve through the rhetorical force of the prophetic lawsuit.

Viewed from a Rhetorical Civil Lawsuit Setting

The fact that Benjamin's address makes frequent use of several standard legal terms and regular trial concepts is consistent with seeing his speech as a prophetic lawsuit from the perspective of a civil proceeding. The speech begins with a summons: "Hearken unto me, and open your ears that ye may hear, and your hearts that ye may understand" (Mosiah 2:9). Possibly, in light of Benjamin's further declaration, this language constitutes a legal summons for the people to serve as witnesses: "And of all these things which I have spoken, ye yourselves are witnesses this day" (Mosiah 2:14). Apparently, Benjamin anticipated that his people would become fearful that they themselves might be accused by the prophet Benjamin when they heard him use the word *witnesses* and various other terms relating to criminal law topics (see Mosiah 2:13). However, he immediately reassures them that he had not told them those things to accuse them (see Mosiah 2:15).

In terms of their public behavior, Benjamin had no accusation or complaint against his people. This is not to say, however, that they had nothing to fear or that they were absolved from all liability. Indeed, at the center of his speech, Benjamin gives repeated notice to his people that the Lord Omnipotent would judge, "and his judgment is just" (Mosiah 3:18; see 3:17). Moreover, he legally warns them that the words of the angel would stand as a "bright" (or indisputably clear) legal "testimony" against them "at the judgment day," when the wicked would stand "no more blameless" with "an awful view of their own guilt" and would be condemned to a mandatory sentence of "endless torment," having "drunk out of the cup of the wrath of

God" (Mosiah 3:22–26). Benjamin, of course, did not need to issue a formal indictment or accusation, for the people all confessed their guilt voluntarily (see Mosiah 4:2) and agreed that none of them should "be found blameless before God" (Mosiah 3:21) and that all were without defense or excuse (see Mosiah 3:22). The people were convicted of their guilt both in the present as they acknowledged their guilt that day (see Mosiah 4:5), and also in the future, for they were told that all "shall be judged, every man according to his works" (Mosiah 3:24; see also 2:33–41; 3:18–25). Mercifully, however, the impending judgment was suspended, and the people were told that the execution of the penalties mentioned in Mosiah 2:38–39 would be averted so long as the people continued to live righteously and kept their contract with God (see Mosiah 5:5), so that they might "remain guiltless . . . from day to day" and "walk guiltless before God" (Mosiah 4:25–26).

Viewed from the Rhetorical Setting of International Relations

From the realm of international relations and the understanding of prophetic lawsuits associated with that domain, all the legal elements of treaty making, covenant renewal, and covenant maintenance can also be found in Benjamin's speech, as Stephen Ricks has demonstrated and as others have concurred.[8] Although nothing in Benjamin's speech indicates that his people had breached the basic covenant between God and Israel and were thus being accused by Benjamin as having violated that agreement, Benjamin clearly saw himself as a vassal of the Lord for having discharged his stewardship and was eager to "answer a clear conscience before God" himself (Mosiah 2:15; compare 2:28). Consistent with that aim, his speech reflects the additional elements of the prophetic lawsuit viewed from the standpoint of international law and ancient Near Eastern treaty enforcement. A written copy of his speech was circulated and later read in public, fulfilling the typical treaty requirement that a written copy be deposited in the temple and periodically read in public. Treaty and covenant functions are emphasized by Benjamin in part because his people consisted of Nephites and Mulekites, and the covenant renewal would have served political purposes in further uniting this combined population under the leadership of Benjamin's son, the new king. The covenant renewal process probably took the form of a formal oath (see Mosiah 6:3; 5:5), combined with a solemn ceremony. Language describing the benevolence and blessings of the "heavenly King" to his people (see Mosiah 2:19–25; 4:9–12, 19–21) parallels the historical prologue of Hittite treaties. Furthermore, Benjamin's entire speech is replete with the expected stipulations (see Mosiah 2:22, 32; 3:19; 4:13–16, 26) and cursing or blessing formulas (see Mosiah 2:22, 31, 33, 36–41; 3:24–27; 4:23, 25).

Viewed from a Rhetorical Ritual Setting

Ritual or ceremonial elements are especially prevalent in Benjamin's speech. The actual *Sitz im Leben*, or real-life context, of King Benjamin's speech can unambiguously be identified as ceremonial, since the people gathered around their temple to hear the speech (see Mosiah 2:5–6). If more were known today about ancient Israelite rites, more could be said about the ritual dimensions of the prophetic lawsuit in general, as well as the rhetorical significance of these factors in Benjamin's speech in particular. Under the circumstances, however, it is possible to assume that Benjamin's speech drew further rhetorical power from its use of ceremonial terms that were part of the covenant renewal process that occurred under the law of Moses on the Israelite Day of Atonement. Both Benjamin's speech and the Day of Atonement rituals occurred at the temple (see Mosiah 2:5–6); both used animal sacrifice (see Mosiah 2:3) to induce an awareness of sinfulness, guilt, mortality, confession, and repentance, resulting in the deferral of God's judgment, the remission of sins, forgiveness, reconciliation, and joy (see Mosiah 2:25; 4:2–3, 10). In the end, the people pledged to believe in God and obey his commandments (see Mosiah 5:5–8; 6:1–3). Thus many factors support the idea that Benjamin's speech used judgment motifs also found in the ritual practices of Israel, which biblical commentators have argued may well be related to the idea of the prophetic lawsuit.

In conclusion, biblical scholars have identified the prophetic lawsuit as a form of speech in which the Lord takes legal action through his prophets against his people, delivering a formal complaint or legal warning of impending judgments. Several examples of the prophetic lawsuit are found both in the Bible and the Book of Mormon, and Benjamin's speech appears to draw effectively on this traditional form of speech—a type of speech that was probably familiar to the writers of the Bible and the Book of Mormon, as well as to their respective audiences. By including the elements of the prophetic lawsuit and by making use of judicial phraseology and precepts in his speech, Benjamin was able to emphasize concretely the justice and power of God's judgments. Indeed, Benjamin's speech not only draws strength from all three types of lawsuits that scholars have detected in the Bible, but it also forms one of the best illustrations of a prophetic lawsuit in an actual ritual setting found anywhere in sacred literature.

Notes

1. See, generally, John Barton, "Form Criticism (OT)," in *ABD*, 2:838–41. This chapter draws on research by Richard McGuire, a student in my ancient law class at the J. Reuben Clark

Law School in 1983. Several other law students have worked with me in developing this material. An early version of McGuire's paper has been circulated by FARMS. For further discussion of other prophetic lawsuits in the Book of Mormon, see the chapter on prophetic lawsuits in my forthcoming study on law in the Book of Mormon.

2. See Robert R. Wilson, "Form-Critical Investigation of the Prophetic Literature: The Present Situation," *Society of Biblical Literature* (1973): 100–127.

3. Kirsten Nielsen, *Yahweh as Prosecutor and Judge* (Sheffield, England: JSOT, 1978), 1. Nielsen's monograph provides an excellent survey of biblical scholarship on the prophetic lawsuit, including a very useful bibliography.

4. Cited in ibid., 6.

5. See Julien Harvey, "Le 'Rîb-Pattern' requisitoire prophétique sur la rupture de l'alliance," *Biblica* 43 (1962): 192, cited in Nielsen, *Yahweh as Prosecutor and Judge*, 18.

6. See Nielsen, *Yahweh as Prosecutor and Judge*, 27. Her four elements are a depiction of the scene of the trial, an accusation, a proffered defense, and a reference to a judgment; compare Psalm 82.

7. See Nielsen, *Yahweh as Prosecutor and Judge*, 22.

8. See Stephen D. Ricks, "The Treaty/Covenant Pattern in King Benjamin's Speech," *BYU Studies* 24/2 (1984): 151–62; see also his discussion of this subject, "Kingship, Coronation, and Covenant in Mosiah 1–6," in this volume; and Terrence L. Szink, "Israelite Festivals and Benjamin's Speech," presentation at the Ninth Annual FARMS Symposium on the Book of Mormon, 13 April 1996 (video available).

CHAPTER 8

KINGSHIP, CORONATION, AND COVENANT IN MOSIAH 1–6

Stephen D. Ricks

The first six chapters of Mosiah contain King Benjamin's farewell address—one of the most memorable sermons on record. These chapters also portray for us the succession of Mosiah₂ to the Nephite throne. Many features of this coronation ceremony reflect ancient Israelite culture. First is the significance of the office of king. Second is the coronation ceremony for the new king—the details of which have parallels in both Israel and other ancient Near Eastern societies and even in other parts of the world. Third, the order of events reported in these chapters reflects the "treaty / covenant" pattern well-known in ancient Israel and the ancient Near East. Finally, an interrelated cluster of concepts in Israelite religion connects the themes of rising from the dust, enthronement, kingship, and resurrection. My discussion of these four sets of features will show how faithfully the Book of Mormon reflects these Old World practices and beliefs.

Kingship

The Meaning of Kingship

Although kingship is a political institution whose origins are lost to history, nearly every ancient and medieval civilization had a king who was believed to have been appointed by heaven. The Egyptians held that kingship had existed as long as the world itself;[1] to the Sumerians, this form of rule was a gift from the gods.[2] The Israelites also believed that the king was appointed and adopted by God and that "he mediated between God and the people and represented them before each other."[3] Although the Nephite king was never viewed as a divine being (which would be inconsistent with Deuteronomy 17:15), he was closely connected with God in the sense that, as an intermediate, he too modeled and represented God to his people (as in Mosiah 2:19).

In the ancient view of God's conferral of governmental power upon the king, the traditional code of royalty—which stipulates that the monarch receive sacred names and powers—allows him to stand in the place of God before his people. That ceremony "contained in particular the ancient titles and sovereign rights and duties conferred on Pharaoh by the god, in brief, the king's authority to rule as the surrogate of the god."[4] In the case of Benjamin's speech, a similar ideology is to an extent operational: Benjamin conferred upon Mosiah, and also upon the people, a new name (see Mosiah 5:8); he entrusted Mosiah with other insignia of his royal office (see Mosiah 1:15–16), and he mentioned Mosiah's right and duty to deliver to his people the commandments of God and to lead them in the ways of peace and well-being (see Mosiah 2:31; see also 5:5).

If the king represented the person of God, *a fortiori*, he

also embodied the will and word of God or, in other words, the law of God. According to Moshe Weinfeld, "law is embodied in the person of the king. The king is 'the living law.'"[5] Similarly, a strong element in Benjamin's discourse is his role as an example. At several important junctures in the speech, Benjamin cites his own behavior or function as a role model to the people, thus embodying the principles of divine righteousness that were incumbent upon his people to obey. For example, if Benjamin had labored to serve other people, then how much more should they do likewise (see Mosiah 2:18).

The role of king in Hebrew times

> was based on two covenants which defined the duties of the crown towards God and towards the people. The king's relationship to the divinity was conceived as that of a vassal towards his overlord. He was installed in the office by divine election, on condition that he remain loyal to God and keep his laws (II *Sam.* xxiii 5; *Ps.* cxxxii 12). The other covenant defined the king's obligations towards the nation and fulfilled the function of a modern constitution (II *Sam.* iii 21, v 3; II *Chron.* xxiii 3). The various conditions were probably recited at the accession to the throne.[6]

In the case of Benjamin's and Mosiah's kingship, we see clearly that they both stood between God and the people (see Mosiah 2:31; 5:5) and that the king was one who acted as a vassal or steward over God's people (see Mosiah 1:10) and who accepted the king's commands by way of covenant (see Mosiah 5:5).

In Israel, kingship came to be a vital element of the society's organization through the four hundred years leading up to Lehi's departure from Jerusalem. In the American promised land, among the Nephites, Lamanites, and people of Zarahemla, kings were again an essential part of political life for many centuries. Mosiah 1–6 gives us some of the clearest information on the ideals of royal government in the Book of Mormon. For example, as a practical matter, the ancient king had two fundamental obligations: namely, to maintain peace and to establish justice. "Clearly, the function of the king was twofold: to ensure the safety of his people by 'force of arms' against [the] internal threat of rebellion or external threat of invasion and to ensure the 'well-being' of the nation through the establishment of justice. This dual function of the king as both warrior and judge is evident throughout the ancient Near East."[7] These two roles transcended the particular form of rulership in Israel or in the ancient world and endured from era to era: Whether an early judge or a later monarch in Israel, the ruler "was the leader in the Holy War chosen by Yahweh. He was also the man who had been given wisdom to act as a Judge of the people: to see that honesty flourishes in the kingdom."[8] As Falk has observed, the Hebrew king was responsible for the "functions of judicial and political administration"; he acted as judge, and was also "called upon to fulfill a political task, in the course of which he also took upon himself the religious functions"; and he was "commissioned by God to administer justice."[9] Benjamin clearly filled these perennial roles: as warrior, he had led the Nephites into victorious battle against invading troops and quelled rebellion in his own lands (see Words of Mormon 1:12–16); as judge, it is evident that he had established justice and enforced the laws against slavery, murder, theft, adultery, and "any manner of wickedness" (Mosiah 2:13); and as religious leader, he received revelation from God and inspired his people in righteousness.

Especially prominent in the ancient meaning of kingship was the king's domestic role as the one in society primarily responsible for the internal peace, fairness, and equity within his realm. This royal function stands out in several Old Testament texts. For example, as Keith Whitelam remarks on Psalm 72: "The whole psalm is a testimony to the importance of the ideal of monarchical judicial administration which guarantees both the cosmic harmony, fertility and prosperity of the nation."[10] Thus to Benjamin is attributed primary credit for the condition of peace in his land: "by laboring with all the might of his body and the faculty of his whole soul," he and his prophets were able to "establish peace in the land" (Words of Mormon 1:18).

Whitelam identifies three additional points as being common to the ancient Near Eastern and Israelite royal ideologies: (1) the king's administration of justice was seen as essential for cosmic harmony; (2) this ensured the fertility and prosperity of the nation; and (3) the ideal king was often concerned with providing for the needs of the poor and the underprivileged.[11] While Benjamin recognizes these characteristics of kingship, he attributes them primarily to God and is only vicariously involved in caring for the poor. For Benjamin, the order of the world depends, not on himself as king, but solely on God's sustaining power that maintains life and the world order from day to day (see Mosiah 2:21). Likewise, Benjamin affirms that the eternal well-being of mankind is solely contingent on the atonement of Jesus Christ and the omnipotent goodness of God—not on the king's power as ruler (see Mosiah 3:18; 4:8–11). It is on the third point that Benjamin focuses his personal emphasis: just as God is kind and generous to all individuals who are impoverished beggars in the sight of God (see Mosiah 4:21), so too Benjamin expresses deep concern and takes specific steps to see that the poor and the underprivileged in his kingdom are cared and provided for (see Mosiah 4:14, 22–23).

Choosing the King

The Book of Mormon presents a pattern of choosing kings that matches customs in ancient Israel. In Israel, as in the ancient Near East generally, kingship was a divine election.[12] It was considered necessary that God choose the man to be king. Thus Solomon, not his older brother Adonijah, succeeded his father David as king, since, as Adonijah himself said, "it [the kingship] was [Solomon's] from the Lord" (1 Kings 2:15).[13] De Vaux observes that "accession to the throne (of Judah) implies a divine choice: a man is 'king by the grace of God' not only because God made a covenant with the dynasty of David, but because his choice was exercised at each accession."[14] Following this pattern of divine election of the king, King Benjamin believed that God had called Mosiah, his son: "On the morrow I shall proclaim . . . that thou art a king and a ruler over this people, *whom the Lord our God hath given us*" (Mosiah 1:10).

In Israel, the eldest son of the king usually became the next ruler, although the king was not obligated to choose him if he believed God desired otherwise. Jehoshaphat gave the kingdom to Jehoram "because he was the firstborn" (2 Chronicles 21:3). However, at a later time Joachaz succeeded Josiah even though Joachaz had an older brother (see 2 Kings 23:31, 36). The Book of Mormon does not say whether Mosiah was Benjamin's firstborn son, though this was probably the case since his name is given first in the list of names of Benjamin's sons (see Mosiah 1:2).

In Israel, both Solomon and Jotham became king while their fathers were still alive, because their fathers were old or ill (see 1 Kings 1:32–40; 2:1–10; 2 Kings 15:5). This is also apparently why Benjamin installed Mosiah when he did: "[Benjamin] waxed old, and he saw that he must very soon go the way of all the earth; therefore, he thought it expedient that he should confer the kingdom upon one of his sons" (Mosiah 1:9). After he "had consecrated his son Mosiah to be a ruler and a king over his people, . . . king Benjamin lived three years and he died" (Mosiah 6:3, 5).

Conflicting Views of Kingship

In Mesopotamia and Egypt, kingship was the only form of government, as far as we know. There the king was viewed as having descended from a god, or he had at least been adopted as an offspring of deity.[15] To the writers of history in those lands, no other type of rule was conceivable. Some ancient Israelites took a very positive view of kingship, seeing the king as a necessary and elevated representative of God, even as an adopted son of God; other writers took a limited view of monarchy, seeing the king as "ultimately subject to the law given to the people by Yahweh. . . . The king represents more than just his person, he also represents the future of the nation and more especially his own dynasty."[16]

On the other hand, some people in Israel objected to kingship categorically on the ground that God alone was to rule over his people. For this reason, Gideon refused the invitation to become a hereditary monarch in Israel: "And Gideon said unto them, I will not rule over you, neither shall my son rule over you: the Lord shall rule over you" (Judges 8:23).

Others considered kingship permissible but warned against it. Samuel recognized the dangers of kingship. When the Israelites demanded of the prophet Samuel, "Make us a king to judge us like all the nations," Samuel painted a grim picture of what would happen under a king:

> He will take your sons, and appoint them for himself, for
> his chariots, and to be his horsemen; and some shall run

before his chariots. And he will appoint him captains over thousands, and captains over fifties; and will set them to ear [plant] his ground, and to reap his harvest, and to make his instruments of war, and instruments of his chariots. And he will take your daughters to be confectionaries, and to be cooks, and to be bakers. And he will take your fields, and your vineyards, and your oliveyards, even the best of them, and give them to his servants. And he will take the tenth of your seed, and of your vineyards, and give to his officers, and to his servants. And he will take your menservants, and your maidservants, and your goodliest young men, and your asses, and put them to his work. He will take the tenth of your sheep: and ye shall be his servants. And ye shall cry out in that day because of your king which ye shall have chosen you; and the Lord will not hear you in that day. (1 Samuel 8:11–18)

In dealing with kingship, biblical authors, like people everywhere, were torn by the divergence between theory and practice. What a king was supposed to be and what a king in reality became were not often one and the same: "In general, the ideal position is presented in the Psalms and Prophets, whereas the historical books often witness to the practical problems involved in the administration of monarchical judicial authority and the failures to attain this ideal."[17]

The Nephites were also torn between conflicting views of kings. The Book of Mormon presents a similar variety of perspectives on kingship. The descendants of Nephi$_1$ found kings to be desirable, declaring that "whoso should reign in [Nephi's] stead were called by the people, second Nephi, third Nephi, and so forth, according to the reigns of the kings" (Jacob 1:11). Zeniff and his people willingly recognized the Lamanite king of the land (see Mosiah 9:5) and then proceeded to set up their own kingdom nearby. When Zeniff died, he conferred his kingdom upon his son, Noah.

Though Noah "did not walk in the ways of his father" (Mosiah 11:1), he was still recognized and obeyed as king by the people. There was rarely a time when there was not a king of the Lamanites.

A second view presented by the Book of Mormon is that kingship is undesirable. After Lehi died, Nephi's supporters desired him to rule over them. However, Nephi opposed this idea, saying: "I, Nephi, was desirous that they should have no king" (2 Nephi 5:18). Other Nephites developed this stance even further, declaring that kings are trouble:

> Because all men are not just it is not expedient that ye should have a king or kings to rule over you. For behold, how much iniquity doth one wicked king cause to be committed, yea, and what great destruction! . . . ye cannot dethrone an iniquitous king save it be through much contention, and the shedding of much blood. For behold, he has his friends in iniquity, and he keepeth his guards about him; and he teareth up the laws of those who have reigned in righteousness before him; and he trampleth under his feet the commandments of God; And he enacteth laws, and sendeth them forth among his people, yea, laws after the manner of his own wickedness; and whosoever doth not obey his laws he causeth to be destroyed; and whosoever doth rebel against him he will send his armies against them to war, and if he can he will destroy them; and thus an unrighteous king doth pervert the ways of all righteousness. (Mosiah 29:16–17, 21–23)

Benjamin's description of how he ruled could hardly contrast more with Samuel's or Mosiah's description of the problems caused by wicked kings:

> I . . . have not sought gold nor silver nor any manner of riches of you; Neither have I suffered that ye should be confined in dungeons, nor that ye should make slaves one of another. . . . And even I, myself, have labored with

mine own hands that I might serve you, and that ye should not be laden with taxes, and that there should nothing come upon you which was grievous to be borne. (Mosiah 2:12–14)

Mosiah followed his father Benjamin in farming "the earth, that thereby he might not become burdensome to his people" (Mosiah 6:7). He took great pains to avoid abusing the royal power. Yet, near the end of his reign, Mosiah gives the most damning criticism to be found anywhere in scripture on the perils of kingship: "Because all men are not just it is not expedient that ye should have a king or kings to rule over you. For behold, how much iniquity doth one wicked king cause to be committed, yea, and what great destruction!" (Mosiah 29:16–17; see all of 29:5–36).

The Nephites had many different models of rulership to choose from as they consulted the precedents in the records they had brought with them from Jerusalem. Many types of rulers were found in Israel over the centuries: priest-kings like Melchizedek; patriarchs like Abraham and Jacob; family and tribal leaders of various types; lawgivers like Moses; high priests like Aaron; prophets like Samuel; military leaders like Joshua and Sampson; judges like Gideon and Deborah; powerful kings like Saul, David, and Solomon; and reform-minded kings like Hezekiah and Josiah. From this wide array of options, it is little wonder that no single theory of kingship or rulership emerges among the Nephites, who at diverse times and under changing circumstances found themselves led by rulers such as Nephi, hereditary kings such as Nephi's successors, good kings such as Benjamin, wicked kings such as Noah, chief judges such as Nephihah, military captains such as Moroni, governors such as Lachoneus, and prophets such as Alma. All this generated conflicting ideologies of kingship and leadership among the Nephites and helps explain the dichotomy in Benjamin's kingship, which featured both power and humility.

The King as Guardian of the Covenant of the Lord

The king in the ancient Near East was obliged to maintain justice generally and to protect the rights of the weakest members of society.[18] King Benjamin did not discuss this responsibility directly, but it is implied at several points in his sermon that he understood and observed the principle of protecting the rights of the weak (for example, see Mosiah 2:17–18; 4:13–16, 24).

The king in Israel had an added responsibility of acting as guardian of the covenant between the Lord and his people—a concept that seems to have no parallel among neighboring peoples. He was expected to be an obedient follower of God and to lead his people in obeying this covenant.[19] Accordingly, "both Joshua and Josiah mediate covenants between Israel and God, [and] promise obedience to the book of the Torah."[20] As guardian of the covenant and of the law, the Israelite king took "special measures in his capacity of teacher of the torah, being the highest responsible authority in all matters appertaining to the department of the law."[21]

Kingship and covenant are also closely connected in Mosiah 1–6. Benjamin's command to his son to prepare for this grand occasion had two parts to it—to proclaim his son the new king and to "give this people a name" (Mosiah 1:11; see 1:10). The name was "the name of Christ"; this was to be accepted by all "that have entered into the covenant with God that [they] should be obedient unto the end of [their] lives" (Mosiah 5:8). The association of the two concepts in King Benjamin's agenda indicates that they were linked in

244 • *Stephen D. Ricks*

Nephite thinking. In Mosiah 2:13, Benjamin clearly declares ways in which he had discharged his obligations as teacher and administrator in all matters of law.

Kingship and the covenant of the people with God are again combined in Mosiah 6:3. After Mosiah had been consecrated king, he "appointed priests to teach the people, that thereby they might hear and know the commandments of God, and to stir them up in remembrance of the oath [or covenant] which they had made." The record notes that following Benjamin's death, Mosiah very strictly observed the covenant and the commandments that his father had passed on to him (see Mosiah 6:6).

Coronation

The coronation of the king is the most important ritual act associated with kingship in the ancient Near East. A comparison of Mosiah 1–6 with coronation ceremonies recorded in the Old Testament and with such rites among other ancient Near Eastern peoples reveals striking parallels.[22]

The Sanctuary as the Site of the Coronation

A society's most sacred spot is the location where the holy act of royal coronation takes place. For Israel, the temple was that site. So we read that during his coronation Joash stood "by a pillar [of the temple], as the manner was" (2 Kings 11:14). However, the temple had not been built when Solomon became king, so he was crowned at Gihon (see 1 Kings 1:45). Although Gihon may have been chosen because water was available for purification rites,[23] it was made sacred by the presence of the ark of the covenant (which contained the sacred objects from Moses' day) in the special tabernacle that David had made to shelter it at Gihon.

The priest Zadok took "out of the tabernacle" the horn containing oil with which he anointed Solomon (1 Kings 1:39). Thus scholars have concluded that the covenants made in connection with Israelite coronations were "made in the Temple. . . . The king went up into the House of Yahweh, he had his place by, or on, the pillar . . . and he concluded the covenant before Yahweh."[24]

In the specifically Nephite case of Mosiah, all the people gathered at the temple at Zarahemla, the site chosen for Benjamin's address to the people and for the consecration of his son Mosiah as king (see Mosiah 1:18). The Nephite formalities, as had been the case in ancient Israel, took place in stages: "the coronation ceremony was divided into two parts, the anointing in the sanctuary and the enthronement in the royal palace."[25] Mosiah was first designated king in a private setting, presumably at the royal palace (see Mosiah 1:9–12), and then presented to the people in the public gathering at the temple (see Mosiah 2:30).

The Royal Dais

Benjamin had a tower constructed from which he spoke and, presumably, presented Mosiah to the people (see Mosiah 2:7). Not only was the king crowned in the temple, but in a specific place within the temple complex. In 2 Kings 11:14 we read that at the time of his coronation, King Joash "stood *by a pillar* (Hebrew ʿal ha-ʿammûḏ), as the manner was" (emphasis added). According to Welch and Szink, "The preposition ʿal can be translated 'by,' but it is much more often rendered 'on' or 'upon.'"[26] Similarly, in 2 Kings 23:3, when King Josiah rededicates the temple, he gathers all the elders of Judah and Jerusalem and reads the law before all the people. He then stands "by" or "on the pillar"—ʿal ha-ʿammûḏ—and makes a covenant to keep all the commandments.[27]

De Vaux connects these pillars with the "brasen scaffold" that Solomon built (2 Chronicles 6:13), upon which he stands and kneels "before all the congregation of Israel," and from which he offers the dedicatory prayer for the temple; further, de Vaux suggests that the phrase *near the pillar* be translated "on the dais."[28]

Another such structure is mentioned in Nehemiah 8:4. On the occasion of the reading of the law by Ezra the scribe, the religious leader of the people, we are again told that, during the Sukkot feast, Ezra "stood upon a pulpit of wood" in order to read the law to the people who were living "in booths for seven days following their return to Jerusalem from Babylon."[29] Commenting on the pillars in 2 Kings, Gerhard von Rad wrote, "It is certainly to be understood in any case that the place where the king stood was a raised one. The king would have had to be visible to the crowd which had gathered for the solemnities, so that one may probably think of some sort of pillar-like platform."[30] Widengren added,

> We therefore conclude that at least towards the end of the pre-exilic period, but possibly from the beginning of that period, the king when reading to his people on a solemn occasion from the book of the law and acting as the mediator of the covenant making between Yahweh and the people had his place on a platform or a dais.[31]

In confirming the Old Testament documentation of the use of the dais, the Mishnah also supports the evidence found in the Book of Mormon. Together these illustrate that platforms are (1) located in the temple precinct, (2) associated with the coronation of new kings, (3) used by the king or another leader to read the law to the people, (4) used to offer dedicatory prayers for the temple, and (5) associated with the Festival of Booths. In view of these considerations, one can conclude that Benjamin's tower was more than just a way to communicate to the people—it was part of an Israelite coronation tradition in which the king stands on a platform or pillar at the temple before the people and before God.

Installing in Office with Insignia

At the coronation of Joash, Jehoiada the priest conferred upon him two objects, called the *nēzer* and the *ʿēḏûṭ*. "It would seem that the diadem and the protocol were the two items of sacral and legal insignia, conferment of which constituted the essential act of coronation."[32] The meaning of the first term is certain; it means "crown" (2 Kings 11:12). What *ʿēḏûṭ* means is far less certain. Von Rad connected the *ʿēḏûṭ* with the idea of covenant and also with the Egyptian protocol that were given to the Pharaoh upon his ascent to the throne.[33] In other words, it refers to a list of laws or regulations by which the king was to govern.[34] Geo Widengren, on the other hand, believes that the *ʿēḏûṭ* refers to the whole law. He notes:

> It is highly important that according to all traditions the leader of the people of Israel, in older times chieftains of the charismatic type, like Moses and Joshua, in the period of the monarchy the king—and this right down into Hellenistic-Roman times—*always* had the law handed over to him, and thus was the real possessor of the Torah, in the concrete meaning of the word.[35]

Ringgren cites Psalm 132:12 to support this claim:

> If your sons keep my covenant
>   and my testimonies [*ʿēḏōṭai*] which I shall teach them,
> their sons also for ever
>   shall sit upon your throne.[36]

The king, as possessor of the law, would then "read out to the assembly the commandments of the book of the covenant and then . . . make the covenant between Yahweh and his people."[37] The medieval Jewish commentator Rashi opined that the ʿēḏûṭ was a law, connecting it with the injunction in Deuteronomy 17:18–20, which specifies that the king should keep a copy of the law with him, that he might always remember the commandments of God, "to the end that he may prolong his days in his kingdom."[38] In like manner, Benjamin told his sons, including Mosiah, his successor, "I would that ye should keep the commandments of God, that ye may prosper in the land according to the promises which the Lord made unto our fathers" (Mosiah 1:7). Thus not only may Mosiah's receipt of the law as part of the regalia of kingship be similar to the procedure at the coronation of the kings in Israel, but the purpose for which it was given was also similar.

The royal documents were the most important records in the kingdoms of the ancient world, and a sword was a frequent sign of kingship in Europe and Asia. In addition, from early modern times at least back to the Roman Empire, an orb or ball was commonly held in the hand of Old World rulers; although the Bible does not mention such an object, it still might have been part of the Israelite set of artifacts copied from their neighbors.[39]

With the transfer of power, Benjamin gave Mosiah similar objects.[40] He passed on the official records of the people (the plates of brass and the plates of Nephi), the sword of Laban, and the miraculous ball (called the director or Liahona; see Mosiah 1:15–16).

Moreover, the king donned sacred garments: "His sacral garment, his ecclesiastical garb, so to speak, meant that he wore the breast-plate of judgement, and in the pouch of judgement carried the Urim and Tummim, the symbols of the tablets of the law, corresponding exactly to the tablets of destiny worn by the ruler in Mesopotamia."[41] Benjamin's concern about his garments (see Mosiah 2:28) and the fact that King Mosiah was known to possess "two stones" (Mosiah 28:13) by means of which he could translate the twenty-four plates of Ether may be evidence that similar items were present in the Nephite coronation.

Anointing

To anoint the king with oil was a significant part of coronation ceremonies in ancient Israel and in the ancient Near East generally. The Bible records the anointing of six kings: Saul, David, Solomon, Jehu, Joash, and Jehoahaz.[42] "The anointing is a ritual religious act, which marks the candidate for kingship as the Lord's elected."[43] Indeed, the name Messiah, which was used to refer to several of the kings of Israel, means "anointed," no doubt referring to the rite of anointing the king during his installation as ruler.[44]

The Hittites, a northern neighbor of the Israelites, also had a ceremony that included anointing the king with oil.[45] Although no clear evidence exists that the Egyptian king was anointed at his accession to the throne, he apparently was anointed every morning before entering the temple where he performed daily chants.[46]

Following Benjamin's address and the renewal of the covenant by the people, Benjamin "consecrated his son Mosiah to be a ruler and a king over his people" (Mosiah 6:3). In the Book of Mormon the verb *to consecrate* occurs mostly in connection with priests or teachers (see 2 Nephi 5:26; Mosiah 11:5; 23:17; Alma 4:4, 7; 5:3; 15:13; 23:4), but also appears in three instances in association with kings. (1) Benjamin says that he was "consecrated" to be king by his father (Mosiah 2:11), (2) Mosiah was "consecrated" by Benjamin his father (Mosiah 6:3), and (3) Amlici was "consecrate[d]" by his followers to be their king (Alma 2:9).

The verb *to anoint* is more commonly used in the Book of

Mormon record with the setting apart of kings. Nephi "anointed" his successor (Jacob 1:9); interestingly, the word is used nine times in the Jaredite record, perhaps in a formulaic fashion (see Ether 6:22, 27; 9:4, 14–15, 21–22; 10:10, 16). In the Bible, only the verb *to anoint* (from the root *MŠḤ) is used exclusively with reference to kings.[47] In the enthronements of both Solomon (see 1 Kings 1:34, 39) and Joash (see 2 Kings 11:12) an anointing occurs. Furthermore, Saul, David, Jehu, and Jehoahaz were all anointed.[48] The verb *to consecrate* (from the root *QDŠ) is restricted to priests in the Old Testament. The two terms are similar but not identical in meaning. *To anoint* means to set apart by applying oil to the body, specifically the head, and *to consecrate*, a more general term, means to make holy. Consecrating could be done by anointing, but is not limited to it. It is possible that the consecration of Mosiah included anointing, which would have been in accordance with the practices in ancient Israel and the ancient Near East.

Presentation of the New King

Mosiah is presented to the people as their king in Mosiah 2:30. In 1 Kings 1:34, 39, Solomon is presented to the people, "and they blew the trumpet; and all the people said God save king Solomon." At the coronation of Joash "the princes and the trumpeters [were] by the king, and all the people of the land rejoiced, and blew with trumpets" (2 Kings 11:14). The blowing of the trumpet *(shôfār)* bears an interesting connection with the New Year festival discussed above. Returning to the enthronement of the Assyrian king Esarhaddon cited above, we find that he too was presented to the people:

> He (i.e., Sennacherib [Esarhaddon's father]) heeded their [the gods'] important pronouncement and called to-

gether the people of Assyria, young and old, my brothers
(and all) the male descendants of (the family of) my father and made them take a solemn oath in the presence of
(the images of) the gods of Assyria: Ashur, Sin, Shamash,
Nebo, (and) Marduk, (and) of (all) the (other) gods resid-
ing in heaven and in the nether world, in order to secure
my succession.[49]

It should also be noted that Esarhaddon's enthronement
took place during the Babylonian month of Nisan, which,
being the first month of the year, was the month when the
Babylonian New Year festival was celebrated. Similarly,
presentation and acclamation were formal parts of the enthronement in Israel and the ancient Near East.[50]

One reason for the public proclamation of the new king
was to avoid disputes over the throne. In fact, it is most
likely that we have detailed accounts concerning the coronation of Solomon and Joash specifically because both
kingships were challenged.[51] Despite his father's efforts, the
Assyrian Esarhaddon had serious problems with his brothers who also wanted to be king. With this in mind, Benjamin's statements immediately following the presentation of
his son take on new meaning: "If ye shall keep the commandments of my son, or the commandments of God
which shall be delivered unto you by him, ye shall prosper
in the land, and your enemies shall have no power over
you. But, O my people, beware lest there shall arise contentions among you, and ye list to obey the evil spirit, which
was spoken of by my father Mosiah" (Mosiah 2:31–32). The
use of the word *contention* is significant. A quick study of its
context in the Book of Mormon reveals that it is often tied to
wars and that the principal cause of those wars was dissension and rebellion against the king by individuals. Hence
the need for public designation of the king.

As Nibley has pointed out, there is a twist in the Nephite

enthronement ceremony, for although Mosiah was proclaimed king, more attention is devoted to God as king.[52]
Benjamin repeatedly reminds the people that he too is human (see Mosiah 2:11, 26) and that God is the real king (see
Mosiah 2:19). The idea of God-as-king is frequently found
in the Old Testament, especially in Psalms.[53] As a final part
of the proclamation of the coronation of the new king, "in a
fresh act of the drama," the king himself would next speak;
"claiming the authority of a divine revelation made to him,
he proclaims to the city and to the world (in a more or less
threatening speech) the nature of the overlordship which
has been conferred upon him."[54] At this point, the people
respond by accepting the king's declarations (see Mosiah
4:2; 5:2–4), and their acclamation "signalizes the people's
approval and contributes to the reciprocal feeling of close-
ness between the king and his citizens."[55] The public proclamation of the kingship of Mosiah evidently follows the ancient pattern closely.

Receiving a Throne Name

In many societies, a king received a new name or throne
name when he was crowned king.[56] Several Israelite kings
had two names, a "birth name" and a throne name. It may
be that all the kings of Judah received a new name when
they came to the throne.[57] During the "royal protocol Yahweh
addresses the king in direct speech, calls him his son, in-
vests him with sovereign rights, confers upon him his coronation name, and so on."[58] During the Middle Kingdom period, each king of Egypt had no less than five names and
received a throne name at the time he became king.[59] Kings
in Mesopotamia also received a new name. All Parthian
kings (in ancient Iran) assumed the same throne name,

"Arsak," at their crowning—a fact that has made it hard for historians to identify one ruler from another.[60]

Use of the same royal title also marks the early Nephite kings. Jacob wrote that, "The people having loved Nephi exceedingly, . . . Wherefore, the people were desirous to retain in remembrance his name. And whoso should reign in his stead were called by the people second Nephi, third Nephi, and so forth, according to the reigns of the kings; and thus they were called by the people, let them be of whatever [original] name they would" (Jacob 1:10–11). While it is true that we do not know that this new name was given to the rulers over the Nephites as part of the coronation rite, there is every reason to expect that it was.

Divine Adoption of the King

Based on relating various Psalms (2, 89, 110) or passages in Isaiah (9:6–7) to the coronation, many scholars include as part of the enthronement procedure the divine adoption of the king.[61]

> As "son" of God, the king belongs to the sphere in which God in a specific manner manifests his fatherly concern and exercises fatherly authority. Both a privilege and an obligation are thus involved. As "son", the king enjoys divine protection and help. This feature is found in all the most important texts. As "son", the king also participates in the power of God and exercises delegated divine power. His sovereignty on earth is a replica of that of God in heaven (Ps 89 and 110). But divine sonship also implies filial obedience, although this obedience is not a *sine qua non* for the legitimacy of the king.[62]

Typically, Latter-day Saints have interpreted these passages as referring to Christ. In them the king is called a son of

God. In one passage, however, the Lord through Nathan the prophet, referring directly to Solomon, declares, "I will be his father, and he shall be my son" (2 Samuel 7:14). Benjamin's actual bestowal of the name on the people is recorded in Mosiah 5:6–12. Note particularly verse 7:

> And now, because of the covenant which ye have made ye shall be called the children of Christ, his sons, and his daughters; for behold, this day he hath spiritually begotten you; for ye say that your hearts are changed through faith on his name; therefore, ye are born of him and have become his sons and his daughters.

Again we can find a similar idea in the enthronement of Joash. "And Jehoiada made a covenant between the Lord and the king and the people, that they should be the Lord's people" (2 Kings 11:17). What was once reserved for kings at coronation has now been extended in Nephite culture to the people generally. These last two themes—new name and divine adoption—are included in the coronation ritual and further confirm the ancient antecedents of King Benjamin's address.

The Assembly of Mosiah 1–6 as a Covenant Renewal

Mosiah 1–6 mentions three notable features of this assembly: the pilgrimage of whole families to the temple site, the sacrifice of animals, and the people's dwelling in tents. These elements are so typical of the Israelite Feast of Tabernacles that they strongly suggest that the events recorded in these chapters took place during a Nephite observance of that festival.[63] From the Old Testament it appears that the Feast of Tabernacles was the time when the Israelites renewed their covenant with God,[64] which is what the Nephites appear to have been doing in the assembly reported in Mosiah 1–6.

Six elements of covenant renewal can be found in Exodus, Deuteronomy, and Joshua: the record (1) gives a preamble in which God is introduced as the one making the covenant or in which his prophet is introduced as spokesman for God; (2) gives a brief review of God's relations with Israel in the past; (3) notes the terms of the covenant, listing specific commandments and obligations that God expected Israel to keep; (4) records that the people bear witness in formal statements that they accept the covenant; (5) gives a list of blessings and curses for obedience or disobedience to the covenant; and (6) records that provisions are made for depositing a written copy of the covenant in a safe and sacred place and for reading its contents to the people in the future.

In addition, the ideal was that the new king take office before the death of the old one,[65] and this transfer of power was connected with the ceremony in which the people make or renew their covenant with God. Interestingly, each of these features is found in Mosiah 1–6 (see table 1 and its comparisons of Mosiah 1–6 and Old Testament covenant passages). This basic structure of the covenant is further nuanced by a comparison with Hittite treaties composed in the fourteenth and thirteenth centuries B.C., approximately the same period of time as the Israelite exodus from Egypt.[66] The fundamental elements common to both the Hittite treaties and the covenant passages in the Old Testament include the preamble, the antecedent history, individual stipulations, witness formulas or oaths of acceptance, blessings and curses, and provisions for the recital of the covenant and deposit of the text.[67]

Table 1
Treaty/Covenant Pattern in the Old Testament and in Mosiah

Elements	Exodus 19:3b–8	Exodus 20–24	Deuteronomy	Joshua 24	Mosiah 1–6
Preamble	19:3b	20:1	1:5 (1:1–5)	24:2a (24:1–2a)	2:9a (1:1–2:9a)
Antecedent History	19:4	20:2	1:6–3:29	24:2b–13, 16b–18a	2:9b–21, 23–24a, 25–30
Terms of the Covenant	19:5–6	20:3–23:19	chapters 4–26	24:14, 18b, 23	2:22, 24b, 31–41; 4:6–30
Formal Witness	19:8	24:3	31:19	24:16a, 19a, 21–23	5:2–8
Blessings and Curses	19:5	23:20–33	27:9–28:68	24:19b–20	5:9–15 (3:24–27)
Recital of the Covenant and Deposit of the Text	19:7	24:4–8	27:1–8; 31:9, 24–26	24:25–27	(2:8, 9a) 6:1–3, 6

1. Preamble

In the Hittite treaties, the preamble contains the name, as well as other titles and attributes, of the suzerain making the treaty: "These are the words of the Sun, Muwatallis, the Great King, King of the land of Hatti, Beloved of the Weather-God."[68] The passages in the Bible that deal with the renewal of the covenant sometimes introduce God as the maker of the covenant: "And God spake all these words saying . . ." (Exodus 20:1). At other times, a prophet is introduced to act for God: "And Joshua said unto all the people, Thus saith the Lord God of Israel . . ." (Joshua 24:2). Similarly, Benjamin's covenant assembly in the book of Mosiah begins: "And these are the words which [Benjamin] spake and caused to be written, saying . . ." (Mosiah 2:9). Although Benjamin is speaking, he is clearly acting as the mouthpiece of God. In fact, a sizable part of his address consists of words that had been made known to him "by an angel from God" (Mosiah 3:2).

2. Review of God's Relations with Israel

This part of the typical Hittite treaty acknowledges the past kindnesses that had been shown by the suzerain toward his vassal, providing the rationale for the great king's appeal (in the following section, which contained specific stipulations) to his vassal to render future obedience in return for past benefits: "When, in former times Labarnas, my grandfather, attacked the land of Wilusa, he conquered [it]. . . . The Land of Wilusa never after fell away from the land of Hatti but . . . remained friends with the king of Hatti."[69] At this point in the covenant renewal, according to the Bible, the people hear of God's mighty acts on behalf of his people Israel. For example, "Ye have seen what I did unto the Egyptians, and how I bare you on eagle's wings, and brought you unto myself" (Exodus 19:4; compare Exodus 20:2; Joshua 24:12–13). The Mosiah passage includes a long account of the past relations between King Benjamin and his people and uses the thanks the people owe him for his contributions to their welfare as an *a fortiori* argument for the greater thanks they owe to God:

> And behold also, if I, whom ye call your king, who has spent his days in your service, . . . do merit any thanks from you, O how you ought to thank your heavenly King!
> . . . who has created you from the beginning, and is preserving you from day to day, by lending you breath, . . . and even supporting you from one moment to another. (Mosiah 2:19, 21)

3. Terms of the Covenant

In the Hittite treaties, this section includes the specific obligations that the vassal had to his overlord: "Thou, Alaksandus, shalt protect the Sun as a friend. . . . If anyone says an unfriendly word about the Sun and you keep it secret from the Sun . . . then thou, Alaksandus, sinnest before the oath of the gods; let the oath of the gods harry [thee]!"[70] Each of the biblical covenant passages stipulates the commandments that God expects his people Israel to keep. A prime example is in Exodus 20–23 where God first briefly lists the Ten Commandments (see Exodus 20:3–17) and then spells out in greater detail what the people are to obey (see Exodus 21:1–23:19). Benjamin's address also contains numerous commandments; for example, "Believe in God. . . . And again, believe that ye must repent of your sins and forsake them, and humble yourselves before God; and ask in sincerity of heart that he would forgive you" (Mosiah 4:9–10).

4. Formal Witness

The Hittite treaties contain clauses in which the gods are invoked to witness and act as guarantors of the treaties: "The Sun God of heaven, lord of the lands, Shepherd of men, the Sun Goddess of Arinna, the Queen of the lands, the Weather-God [are called to witness this treaty]."[71] Clearly, such a clause would have been unacceptable in a covenant in monotheistic Israel. At one time in the Old Testament, an object, a particular stone, is made witness to the covenant, "for it hath heard all the words of the Lord which he spake unto us: it shall be therefore a witness unto you, lest ye deny your God" (Joshua 24:27). In general, though, the people themselves were the witnesses; for instance, they say "All that the Lord hath spoken we will do" (Exodus 19:8). Following King Benjamin's address, the people express their desire "to enter into a covenant with [their] God to do his will, and to be obedient to his commandments" (Mosiah 5:5). They further witness their willingness to obey by allowing their names to be listed among those who have "entered into a covenant with God to keep his commandments" (Mosiah 6:1).

5. Blessings and Cursings

The end of a biblical covenant ceremony often contains a list of curses and blessings for those who enter into the covenant:

> Cursed be the man that maketh any graven or molten image. . . . And all the people shall answer and say, Amen. Cursed be he that setteth light by his father or his mother. And all the people shall say, Amen. (Deuteronomy 27:15–16)

> Blessed shalt thou be in the city, and blessed shalt thou be in the field. Blessed shall be the fruit of thy body,

and the fruit of thy ground, and the fruit of thy cattle. (Deuteronomy 28:3–4)

More often the Old Testament just implies the curses and blessings:

And Joshua said unto the people, . . . If ye forsake the Lord, and serve strange gods, then he will turn and do you hurt, and consume you, after that he hath done you good. (Joshua 24:19–20)

The curses and blessings in Benjamin's speech are also implied rather than stated outright:

And . . . whosoever doeth this shall be found at the right hand of God. . . . And now . . . whosoever shall not take upon him the name of Christ must be called by some other name; therefore, he findeth himself on the left hand of God. (Mosiah 5:9–10)

6. Reciting and Depositing the Covenant

The Bible frequently mentions that the covenant was read aloud: "And he [Moses] took the book of the covenant, and read in the audience of the people" (Exodus 24:7). Other passages mention that the covenant was written and put in a safe and sacred place: "And Joshua wrote these words in the book of the law of God, and took a great stone, and set it up there under an oak, that was by the sanctuary of the Lord" (Joshua 24:26). The words of King Benjamin were written and sent out among the people, not only so they could study and understand what had gone on, but also as a permanent record of the assembly (see Mosiah 2:8–9). At the end of Benjamin's address, when all the people expressed a willingness to take upon themselves Christ's name, their names were recorded (Mosiah 6:1).

From Dust to Exaltation

The ideology of kingship in ancient Israel extended beyond coronation rituals and covenant patterns. Biblical scholars have found that the ideas associated with becoming a king or a queen also came to serve as religious images, symbolizing the ascent of mortal beings from dust to exaltation.

"Recent studies," according to Walter Brueggemann, "have suggested an intersection in the motifs of covenant-making, enthronement, and resurrection."[72] For example, the resurrection of Jesus was conjoined in early Christianity with his messianic enthronement, and descriptions of his glorification were substantiated through Old Testament passages about Davidic kingship. And just as mortal kings were created out of the dust of the earth and yet could be elevated by God to become a leader in Israel, so all human beings could be raised from their mortal state to resurrected glory.

Thus, in Israelite thought, "the motifs of covenant-renewal, enthronement, and resurrection cannot be kept in isolation from each other but they run together and serve to illuminate each other."[73] And with this matrix in mind, it becomes all the more significant that Benjamin intertwines the themes of dust, kingship, covenant, enthronement, and resurrection throughout his speech.

The use of the word *dust* is a first important indicator of the possible presence of royal language. In a telling declaration, God told the Israelite king Baasha that divine power had raised him to kingship from the dust: "Since I exalted you out of the dust and made you leader over my people Israel . . . " (1 Kings 16:2, translation by author; see also the combination of dust and kingship in 1 Samuel 2:6–8; Psalm 113:7). Brueggemann argues that the creation account and

Adam's elevation from the dust should be understood as having enthronement overtones, for Adam "is really being crowned king over the garden with all the power and authority which it implies."[74] Thus it is significant that King Benjamin began his royal speech by reminding his people that he too was "of the dust" (Mosiah 2:26) and was dependent on God for his power, that he had been "suffered by the hand of the Lord . . . [to] be a ruler and a king over this people" (Mosiah 2:11).

The operative vehicle that takes any man from the dust and installs him in a position of authority or favor is the power of covenant, according to Brueggemann. Hence, texts that speak of being in the dust can refer to situations in which the covenant relationship between Jehovah and the king or his people has been broken (see Psalm 7:6), while its opposite, coming to life, is connected with making and keeping the covenant. For instance, in Psalm 104:29–30, covenant and creation "are closely related."[75] In the case of Benjamin's people, they first viewed themselves as "even less than the dust of the earth" (Mosiah 4:2), but through the force and effect of their covenant they became spiritually begotten, born, free, and positioned on the right hand of God (see Mosiah 5:7–10). It was the covenant that raised them from the dust, both ceremonially and spiritually.

The idea that God elevates the righteous king from the dust brings with it two counter sides. First is the realization that if the king is wicked the Lord will utterly sweep away the ruler who breaks the covenant, returning him to the dust and sweeping him out of the house (compare 1 Kings 16:3). Although Benjamin does not turn explicitly to dust imagery when he warns his people against breaking their covenant, he takes it for granted throughout his speech that mortals owe to God everything that they have and are (see Mosiah 2:20–25), and therefore it is to be expected that they will be returned to the dust, utterly blotted out, driven away, and cast out if they are not true and faithful to their God (see Mosiah 5:11, 14).

The second counterpoint is a motif that frequently occurs in connection with the ascension of a righteous king, namely the logical presumption that, conversely, one king "can be raised from the dust to power only when the alternative rulers are sent to the dust."[76] Thus the Psalmist prays in a royal setting, "May his foes bow down before him, and his enemies lick the dust" (Psalm 72:9, translation by author; see also Micah 7:17; Isaiah 49:23). This imagery is sometimes "extended so that the whole people now share in the promise and hope of the royal tradition," as when Isaiah prophesies that the people of Israel will be raised to power as their enemies are brought low in the dust (see Isaiah 25:10–12; 26:5–6).[77] Benjamin seems attuned to this motif as well when he assures the ascendance of his son Mosiah by promising and instructing his people that "your enemies shall have no power over you" (Mosiah 2:31), and that the "enemy to all righteousness" (Mosiah 4:14) shall have "no place in you" (Mosiah 2:36), if they would obey Mosiah as king.

The ultimate victory over one's enemy, of course, is found in overcoming death through the resurrection of the dead. Here, also, the theme of rising from the dust becomes important in scripture: "Awake and sing, ye that dwell in the dust" (Isaiah 26:19); "many . . . that sleep in the dust of the earth shall awake, some to everlasting life, and some to shame and everlasting contempt" (Daniel 12:2). John H. Hayes has argued that New Testament texts about resurrection draw on enthronement imagery.[78] Brueggemann extends that argument into the Old Testament: "The resurrection of Israel is in fact the enthronement of Israel among the nations"; by building "an anthropology out of royal ritual," the ancient prophets affirmed "that man is bound for king-ship."[79] With equal confidence, King Benjamin took the symbols and promises of royal ritual and extended them to the common people in his domain. He delivered to them great promises of joy and confidence (see Mosiah 3:3–4), as-suring them that the dead will rise (see Mosiah 3:5, 10) and that the righteous will be lifted up and "brought to heaven" (Mosiah 5:15).

No one seems to dispute Brueggemann and others in their assertion that themes of kingship, covenant-making, rising from the dust, coronation, and resurrection were closely linked in the minds of ancient Israelites and early Christians, even though their findings have been detected and assembled only from bits and pieces in scattered texts throughout the Bible. Thus it may come as an unexpected verification that all their findings are illuminated and strongly exemplified in a single text—the Book of Mormon. Indeed, Benjamin's speech may be the best royal and reli-gious text that shows both king and common folk in relation to each of the elements in the precise set of interconnected themes of kingship, coronation, covenant, and being raised from the dust to eternal life.

Conclusion

As Hugh Nibley has noted on numerous occasions, one of the best means of establishing a text's authenticity lies in examining the degree to which it accurately reflects in its smaller details the milieu from which it claims to derive.[80] The Book of Mormon claims to derive from ancient Israel. The extent to which it correctly mirrors the culture of the ancient Near East in matters of religious practice, manner of life, methods of warfare, as well as other topics (especially those that were either unknown or unexamined in Joseph

Smith's time), may provide one of the best tests of the book's genuineness. In this study, we have found numerous elements in the ancient ideology of kingship that are reflected accurately in Benjamin's speech. Indeed, the full ceremonial life-setting of both the covenant renewal festivals— in the books of Exodus, Deuteronomy, and Joshua—and the coronation ceremonies have been identified with the Feast of Tabernacles. And its form (going back to what must have been a far more ancient Near Eastern pattern) has only in the past several decades been analyzed to include a preamble, antecedent history, stipulations, witness formulas, blessings and curses, and provisions for the recital and deposit of the text. That the covenant assembly in the book of Mosiah has been found—possibly—to have the same ritual setting (the Feast of Tabernacles) as the covenant renewal festivals and coronation assemblies in the Old Testament is remarkable. That the covenant ceremonies in both the Old Testament and the book of Mosiah reflect an ancient Near Eastern pattern prescribed for such occasions may provide another control for establishing the genuineness of the Book of Mormon.

Mosiah 1–6 reflects in considerable detail the Israelite customs and beliefs that are part of the process of choosing and seating a new king on the throne. This sermon ranks as one of the most important in scripture. It serves to fulfill one of the primary purposes of the Book of Mormon by placing central focus and highest importance on the life, mission, atonement, and eternal reign of the heavenly King, Jesus Christ, the Lord God Omnipotent.

Notes

1. See Henri Frankfort, *Kingship and the Gods* (Chicago: University of Chicago Press, 1948), 15.

2. See Cyril J. Gadd, *Ideas of Divine Rule in the Ancient Near East* (London: Oxford University Press, 1949), 21.

3. Zeʾev W. Falk, *Hebrew Law in Biblical Times: An Introduction* (Jerusalem: Wahrmann, 1964), 45.

4. Gerhard von Rad, "The Royal Ritual in Judah," in *The Problem of the Hexateuch and Other Essays*, trans. E. W. Trueman Dicken (New York: McGraw-Hill, 1966), 225.

5. Moshe Weinfeld, "The King as Servant of the People: The Source of the Idea," *Journal of Jewish Studies* 33/1–2 (1982): 189.

6. Falk, *Hebrew Law*, 45–46.

7. Keith W. Whitelam, *The Just King: Monarchical Judicial Authority in Ancient Israel* (Sheffield: JSOT, 1979), 17.

8. Hamish F. G. Swanston, *The Kings and the Covenant* (London: Burns & Oates, 1968), 169.

9. Falk, *Hebrew Law*, 43–45.

10. Whitelam, *The Just King*, 29.

11. Ibid.

12. On the ideology of kingship in the ancient Near East and in Israel, see John M. Lundquist, "The Legitimizing Role of the Temple in the Origin of the State," and Stephen D. Ricks and John J. Sroka, "King, Coronation, and Temple," in *Temples of the Ancient World*, 181, 236–38.

13. See Roland de Vaux, *Ancient Israel* (New York: McGraw-Hill, 1961), 1:100. Adonijah's statement in 1 Kings 2:15 should be compared with David's in 1 Chronicles 28:5: "And of all my sons, (for the Lord hath given me many sons,) he hath chosen Solomon my son to sit upon the throne of the kingdom of the Lord over Israel."

14. De Vaux, *Ancient Israel*, 1:100.

15. As was the case during the whole history of Mesopotamian kingship, until the New Kingdom the Egyptian king was seen as the offspring of deity rather than deity itself. Thus Dietrich Wildung, *Egyptian Saints: Deification in Pharaonic Egypt* (New York: New York University Press, 1977), 1–3, compares the pharaohs to saints in the normative Christian tradition; see also Georges Posener, *De la divinité du Pharaon* (Paris: Imprimerie nationale, 1960).

16. Victor H. Matthews, "The King's Call to Justice," *Biblische Zeitschrift* 35/2 (1991): 206.

17. Whitelam, *The Just King*, 18.

18. See F. Charles Fensham, "Widow, Orphan, and the Poor in Ancient Near Eastern Legal and Wisdom Literature," *Journal of Near Eastern Studies* 21/1 (1962): 129–39; Whitelam, *The Just King*, 17–37.

19. Compare Helen A. Kenik, "Code of Conduct for a King: Psalm 101," *JBL* 95/3 (1976): 391, 395.

20. Ray K. Sutherland, "Israelite Political Theories in Joshua 9," *Journal for the Study of the Old Testament* 53 (1992): 70.

21. Geo Widengren, "King and Covenant," *Journal of Semitic Studies* 2/1 (1957): 17.

22. The full pattern of common elements in the coronation rites in various cultures of the world was worked out in detail by Arthur Hocart, *Kingship* (London: Oxford University Press, 1969), especially 70–71. Hocart includes in his comparison twenty-six features, which I give in a somewhat different order, with brief explanations of each of the features and with the addition of one feature in Ricks and Sroka, "King, Coronation, and Temple," 236–71, esp. 260–63.

23. It is still uncertain whether ablutions—ceremonial washings that were believed to avert evil, give life and strength, and symbolize rebirth—were part of the ancient Israelite coronation ceremonies; thus Mircea Eliade, *The Sacred and the Profane*, trans. William R. Trask (New York: Harcourt Brace, 1959), 130; compare also Mircea Eliade, *Patterns in Comparative Religion* (Cleveland: World, 1963), 188–89, 193–94; Maurice A. Canney, *Newness of Life* (Calcutta: University of Calcutta Press, 1928), 67; W. B. Kristensen, *The Meaning of Religion* (The Hague: Nijhoff, 1960), 446–47; A. J. Wensinck, "The Semitic New Year and the Origin of Eschatology," *Acta Orientalia* 1 (1923): 166, 186; Robert A. Wild, *Water in the Cultic Worship of Isis and Sarapis* (Leiden: Brill, 1981), 125, 153. However, since purification in water is mentioned in Exodus 29:4 in connection with the anointing and investment of Aaron and his sons (compare Exodus 40:12), Geo Widengren, "Royal Ideology and the Testament of the Twelve Patriarchs," in *Promise and*

Fulfillment, ed. F. F. Bruce (Edinburgh: Clark, 1963), 207, thinks that "it is probable that certain water-purifications had a place in the Israelite royal consecration." In the fourth century A.D., Cyril of Jerusalem, "Catachesis XXI Mystagogica III de Chrismate 6 (Catechetical Lecture on the Chrism)," in *Patrologiae Graecae,* ed. J. P. Migne (Paris: Garnier, 1892), 33:1093, may have based his comments on an extrabiblical tradition when he wrote: "When the High Priest raised Solomon to the kingship, he anointed him after washing him in the waters of Gihon." Although there is no explicit mention in 1 Kings 1:38–39 of a ritual ablution in connection with King Solomon's coronation rites, TB *Horayoth* 12a records that "our Rabbis taught: The kings are anointed only at a fountain." The presumption in favor of the existence of ablutions in the Israelite coronation ceremony is strengthened by the symbolic placement of the temple—the site of many Israelite coronations (e.g., the coronation of Joash, 2 Kings 11:4–14)—over the center of the world, where the "Water of Life" flowed; see Geo Widengren, "Israelite-Jewish Religion," in *Historia Religionum,* ed. C. J. Bleeker and Geo Widengren (Leiden: Brill, 1969), 1:258–59. Such ablutions were a part of the coronation ceremonies in Egypt and the ancient Near East. According to Samuel A. B. Mercer, *The Pyramid Texts* (New York: Longmans, Green, 1952), 4:55, and Aylward M. Blackman, "An Ancient Egyptian Foretaste of the Doctrine of Baptismal Regeneration," *Theology* 1 (1920): 140–41, even as a child the Egyptian crown prince was sprinkled with water by officials in order that he might be endowed with divine qualities and be reborn. In his daily preparations for entrance into the temple, the pharaoh was sprinkled with holy water, an act that endowed him with life, good fortune, stability, health, and happiness. For the purpose of performing these ritual acts of ablution, a pool or lake was connected with many Egyptian temples. Blackman, "An Ancient Egyptian Foretaste," 135, 137–38; compare Aylward M. Blackman, "Some Notes on the Ancient Egyptian Practice of Washing the Dead," *The Journal of Egyptian Archaeology* 5 (1918): 124; Samuel A. B. Mercer, *The Religion of Ancient Egypt* (London: Luzac, 1949), 348–50; Wild, *Water in the Cultic Worship,*

145. According to Aylward M. Blackman, "The House of the Morning," *The Journal of Egyptian Archaeology* 5 (1918): 155; Frankfort, *Kingship and the Gods*, 83; and Eva L. R. Meyerowitz, *The Divine Kingship in Ghana and Ancient Egypt* (London: Faber and Faber, 1960), 159, during the Sed festival, the recurring feast celebrating the pharaoh's kingship, the pharaoh would have his feet ceremonially washed.

24. Widengren, "King and Covenant," 3.

25. Von Rad, "The Royal Ritual in Judah," 223.

26. John W. Welch, Terrence L. Szink, et al., "Upon the Tower of Benjamin," FARMS Update, *Insights* (August 1995): 2.

27. The Jewish historian Josephus, writing in *Antiquities* 9.7.3, also placed King Joash "by" or "on a pillar" at the time of his coronation.

28. De Vaux, *Ancient Israel*, 1:102–3; the preposition involved here (ʿal) certainly allows for such a translation; *BDB*, 752; T. Raymond Hobbs, *2 Kings* (Waco: Word Books, 1985), 142, suggests that the object stood on or was by "some kind of column, podium, or platform"; Hans-Joachim Kraus, *Worship in Israel: A Cultic History of the Old Testament* (Richmond: Knox, 1966), 224, notes that "in the ceremonies of enthronement the king was lifted on to an ʿammûd where he received the homage of the congregation."

29. Welch and Szink, "Upon the Tower," 2; compare Widengren, "King and Covenant," 11.

30. Von Rad, "The Royal Ritual in Judah," 224.

31. Widengren, "King and Covenant," 10. Later testimony of this structure is indicated by certain rabbis in M *Sotah* 7:8: "After the close of the first Festival-day of the Feast of Tabernacles, in the eighth year, after the going forth of the Seventh Year, they used to prepare for him in the Temple Court a wooden platform on which he sat, for it is written, 'At the end of every seven years in the set time . . .'" (compare Deuteronomy 31:10–13).

32. Von Rad, "The Royal Ritual in Judah," 228–29.

33. See ibid., 224–29.

34. See Hobbs, *2 Kings*, 141; *BDB*, 730. Tryggve N. D. Mettinger, *King and Messiah: The Civil and Sacral Legitimation of the Israelite*

Kings (Lund: Gleerup, 1976), 286–89, acknowledges this possibility and offers a quite speculative, alternative one: he suggests that the *ʿēḏûṭ* was an inscription on the crown indicating the king's close relationship with God.

35. Widengren, "King and Covenant," 21, emphasis in original. He also connects the king's receiving the law to the reception of the law by Moses and the Mesopotamian tradition that the king received the "tablets of the gods," or "tablets of destiny," upon his heavenly enthronement, 17.

36. Helmer Ringgren, *Israelite Religion,* trans. David E. Green (Philadelphia: Fortress, 1966), 223–24; Aubrey R. Johnson, *Sacral Kingship in Ancient Israel* (Cardiff: University of Wales Press, 1967), 67 n. 2.

37. Widengren, "King and Covenant," 7.

38. *Miqraot Gedolot,* vol. 3; note Rashi's comment on 2 Kings 11:12.

39. On this compare Gordon C. Thomasson, "Mosiah: The Complex Symbolism and the Symbolic Complex of Kingship in the Book of Mormon," *JBMS* 2/1 (1993): 21–38, and Stephen D. Ricks, "Olive Culture in the Second Temple Era and Early Rabbinic Period," in *The Allegory of the Olive Tree: The Olive, the Bible, and Jacob 5,* ed. Stephen D. Ricks and John W. Welch (Salt Lake City: Deseret Book and FARMS, 1994), 466–67, 474–75 n. 26.

40. See Brett L. Holbrook, "The Sword of Laban as a Symbol of Divine Authority and Kingship," and Daniel N. Rolph, "Prophets, Kings, and Swords: The Sword of Laban and Its Possible Pre-Laban Origin," *JBMS* 2/1 (1993): 39–72, 73–79, for a rich and detailed discussion of the religious and ceremonial significance of swords in the Book of Mormon and the ancient Mediterranean. The kings evidently kept the large plates; beginning only with Mosiah$_1$ did the small plates also go through the royal line.

41. Widengren, "King and Covenant," 21; see also John van Seters, "The Creation of Man and the Creation of the King," *ZAW* 101/3 (1989): 335–36.

42. Saul (1 Samuel 10:1); David (2 Samuel 5:3); Solomon (1 Kings 1:39); Jehu (2 Kings 9:6); Joash (2 Kings 11:12); Jehoahaz

(2 Kings 23:30). In addition, it is recorded in 2 Samuel 19:10 that the upstart Absalom was anointed to be king.

43. Zafrira Ben-Barak, "The Mizpah Covenant (I Sam 10:25)—The Source of the Israelite Monarchic Covenant," *ZAW* 91/1 (1979): 38.

44. See Ernst Kutsch, *Salbung als Rechtsakt im Alten Testament und im Alten Orient* (Berlin: Töpelmann, 1963), 52–63; compare also J. A. Soggin, *"maelaek,"* in *Theologisches Handwörterbuch zum Alten Testament,* ed. Ernst Jenni and Claus Westermann (Munich: Kaiser, 1971), 1:914–20. According to later Jewish legend, *Apocalypse of Moses* 9:3, cited in *The Apocrypha and Pseudepigrapha of the Old Testament in English,* ed. R. H. Charles (Oxford: Clarendon, 1976), 2:143, the idea of anointing began with the first man. According to this story, when Adam was 930 years old, he knew that his days were coming to an end. He therefore implored Eve: "Arise and go with my son Seth near to paradise, and put earth upon your heads and weep and pray to God to have mercy upon me and send his angel to paradise, and give me of the tree out of which the oil floweth, and bring it (to) me, and I shall anoint myself and shall have rest from my complaint."

45. See Oliver R. Gurney, "Hittite Kingship," in *Myth, Ritual, and Kingship,* ed. S. H. Hooke (Oxford: Clarendon, 1958), 118.

46. See Kutsch, *Salbung als Rechtsakt,* 41–52; Mercer, *Religion of Ancient Egypt,* 348.

47. See Baruch Halpern, *Constitution of the Monarchy in Israel* (Chico: Scholars Press, 1981), 14, has proposed that anointing was not directly associated with the king's coronation but rather with his divine election; for further on anointing, see de Vaux, *Ancient Israel,* 1:103–6.

48. See n. 44.

49. *ANET,* 289.

50. See de Vaux, *Ancient Israel,* 1:106; Geo Widengren, *Sakrales Königtum im Alten Testament und im Judentum* (Stuttgart: Kohlhammer, 1955), 49.

51. Solomon's by his half-brother Adonijah (see 1 Kings 1:5–10), and Joash's by his grandmother Athaliah (see 2 Kings 11:1–3).

52. See Hugh W. Nibley, *An Approach to the Book of Mormon*, 3rd ed. (Salt Lake City: Deseret Book and FARMS, 1988), 300–301.

53. On this see Halpern, *Constitution of the Monarchy*, 61–109; Herman L. Jansen, "The Consecration in the Eighth Chapter of Testamentum Levi," in *The Sacral Kingship, Contributions to the Central Theme of the VIIIth International Congress for the History of Religions*, Rome, April 1955 (Leiden: Brill, 1959), 361–62. More recently see John H. Eaton, *Kingship and the Psalms*, 2nd ed. (Sheffield: JSOT, 1986), for a comprehensive discussion of the issue. But this theory is not without its critics. See de Vaux, *Ancient Israel*, 2:504–6; Kraus, *Worship in Israel*, 205–8. Mowinckel and Widengren themselves have been discussed in J. de Fraine, "Mowinckel (Sigmund Olaf Plytt)," in *Dictionnaire de la Bible*, ed. Henri Cazelles and André Feuillet (Paris: Letouzey, 1957), 5:1387–90; Arvid S. Kapelrud, *God and His Friends in the Old Testament* (Oslo: Universitetsforlaget, 1979), 53–78; Arvid S. Kapelrud, "Sigmund Mowinckel 1884–1965," *Svensk Exegetisk Årsbok* 49 (1984): 66–73; John W. Jonsson, "Reflections on Geo Widengren's Phenomenological Method: Towards a Phenomenological Hermeneutic of the Old Testament," *Scriptura*, special issue S 2 (1986): 21–39.

54. Von Rad, "The Royal Ritual in Judah," 229.

55. Ben-Barak, "The Mizpah Covenant," 38.

56. See Arthur M. Hocart, "Initiation," *Folklore* 35 (1924): 312; compare Bruce H. Porter and Stephen D. Ricks, "Names in Antiquity: Old, New, and Hidden," in *By Study and Also by Faith: Essays in Honor of Hugh W. Nibley*, ed. John M. Lundquist and Stephen D. Ricks (Salt Lake City: Deseret Book and FARMS, 1990), 1:501–22, and Truman G. Madsen, "'Putting on the Names': A Jewish-Christian Legacy," in *By Study and Also by Faith*, 1:458–81.

57. See de Vaux, *Ancient Israel*, 1:108.

58. Von Rad, "The Royal Ritual in Judah," 229.

59. See Frankfort, *Kingship and the Gods*, 46–47; compare also John A. Wilson, *The Culture of Ancient Egypt* (Chicago: University of Chicago Press, 1951), 102.

60. See Widengren, "The Sacral Kingship of Iran," in *The Sacral*

Kingship/La regalità sacra (Leiden: Brill, 1959), 253–54. On the practice of assigning a new name at the time of the king's enthronement, see Ricks and Sroka, "King, Coronation, and Temple." Of course, kings were not the only ones to receive new names. Biblical history is full of examples of men (and in one case, a woman) who received new or changed names, frequently in association with a transition (usually, though not invariably, of a spiritual nature) in their lives. Thus Abram became Abraham (see Genesis 17:5), his wife Sarai became Sarah (see Genesis 17:15), Jacob was renamed Israel (see Genesis 32:28), and Joseph became Zaphnath-paaneah (see Genesis 41:45). In the New Testament, Jesus gave Simon the name Cephas (whose Greek reflex is Peter—see John 1:42; Matthew 16:17–18), while Saul took on the Latin name Paul, indicative of his role as missionary to the gentiles. The name Paul is first mentioned at Acts 13:9, at the beginning of his first missionary labors among the gentiles. The receipt of a new name is promised to all the faithful in Revelation: "He that hath an ear, let him hear what the Spirit saith unto the churches; To him that overcometh will I give to eat of the hidden manna, and will give him a white stone, and in the stone a new name written, which no man knoweth saving he that receiveth it" (Revelation 2:17).

61. See, for example, Ringgren, *Israelite Religion*, 225–27; Kraus, *Worship in Israel*, 181, 224; Halpern, *Constitution of the Monarchy*, 128–29; von Rad, "The Royal Ritual in Judah," 230–31; Eaton, *Kingship and the Psalms*, 146–49; on divine election in ancient Babylonia, see René Labat, *Le caractère religieux de la royauté assyro-babylonienne* (Paris: Maisonneuve, 1943), 53–69; on divine adoption in ancient Egypt, see Wildung, *Egyptian Saints*, 1–3.

62. Mettinger, *King and Messiah*, 291–92.

63. Compare von Rad, "The Problem of the Hexateuch," in *The Problem of the Hexateuch*, 35. Similarly, John Bright writes in *A History of Israel* (Philadelphia: Westminster, 1981), 171: "It is exceedingly probable . . . that there was a regular ceremony of covenant renewal—whether annually or every seven years (Deuteronomy 31:9–13)—to which the tribesmen would come with

their tribute to the God-King, to hear his gracious deeds recited and his commandments read, and then with blessings and curses to take anew their oath of allegiance to him."

64. "The idea of a covenant between a deity and a people is unknown to us from other religions and cultures [of the ancient Near East]." Moshe Weinfeld, "bᵉrîth," in *TDOT*, 2:278. Covenant renewal also appears to be unique to ancient Israel.

65. See Klaus Baltzer, *The Covenant Formulary*, trans. David Green (Philadelphia: Fortress, 1971), 82–83.

66. The constituent elements of the Hittite treaty were first isolated and analyzed by Viktor Korošec, *Hethitische Staatsverträge* (Leipzig: Weicher, 1931), 12–14. The structural link between the Hittite treaties and the Old Testament covenant passages was first suggested by Elias Bickerman in "Couper une alliance," *Archives d'histoire du droit oriental* 5 (1950–51): 153, reprinted with an additional note in Elias Bickerman, *Studies in Jewish and Christian History*, Part One (Leiden: Brill, 1976), 23, and later developed and expanded by George Mendenhall in "Covenant Forms in Israelite Tradition," *Biblical Archaeologist* 17/3 (1954): 50–76. The literature on the treaty/covenant in the Bible and the ancient Near East since Bickerman and Mendenhall has been considerable; see Dennis J. McCarthy's thorough analysis of ancient Near Eastern treaties and their structural relationship to the covenant pericopes in the Old Testament (as well as an extensive bibliography) in his recent *Treaty and Covenant* (Rome: Biblical Institute Press, 1978).

67. The specific names for these categories are, to an extent, my own, but they are similar to those in other treatments of the treaty/covenant pattern in the Bible, for example, J. A. Thompson, "The Near Eastern Suzerain-Vassal Concept in the Religion of Israel," *Journal of Religious History* 3 (1964): 4, and Mendenhall, "Covenant Forms in Israelite Tradition," 57–60, both of which are based ultimately on the analysis of the constituent elements of the Hittite treaty in Korošec, *Hethitische Staatsverträge*, 12–14. The biblical covenant passages which will be studied here include Exodus 19:3b–8, 20–24; Deuteronomy 1–31; and Joshua 24. Other passages may also be analyzed in light of this pattern, for example,

1 Samuel 12. This analysis was first published in Stephen D. Ricks, "The Treaty/Covenant Pattern in King Bemjain's Speech," *BYU Studies* 24/2 (1984): 151-62.

68. McCarthy, *Treaty and Covenant*, 1.

69. Ibid.

70. Ibid., 2.

71. Ibid.

72. Walter Brueggemann, "From Dust to Kingship," *ZAW* 84/1 (1972): 1.

73. Ibid.

74. Ibid., 12.

75. Ibid., 7.

76. Ibid., 8.

77. Ibid., 11.

78. See John H. Hayes, "The Resurrection as Enthronement and the Earliest Church Christology," *Interpretation* 22 (1968): 333–45.

79. Brueggemann, "From Dust to Kingship," 13, 17.

80. See, for example, Hugh W. Nibley, *Lehi in the Desert, The World of the Jaredites, There Were Jaredites* (Salt Lake City: Deseret Book and FARMS, 1988), 263, 378–79; Hugh W. Nibley, *Since Cumorah*, 2nd ed. (Salt Lake City: Deseret Book and FARMS, 1988), 152–53, 464 n. 121.

CHAPTER 9

BENJAMIN AND THE MYSTERIES OF GOD

M. Catherine Thomas

King Benjamin had been praying for his people; in response, an angel appeared with an important announcement. The king then summoned his people to the temple to receive the angel's message in connection with a sacred name. The people embraced the angel's message, were born again, and entered into a holy covenant.

In this simple statement of basic facts from the Book of Mormon account, we discover at least four interesting questions: (1) What was Benjamin's role in the rebirth experience at the temple, and for what was he praying? (2) What was it the angel came to announce? (3) How would the name the king gave his people distinguish them from earlier Nephites, who, for five hundred years, anticipated the coming of Christ? (4) What was the nature of the change that the people received, and what does it all have to do with the mysteries of God? In the pursuit of answers to these questions, we will explore the nature of priesthood and its relationship to the mystery of spiritual rebirth.

The Mysteries of God

The scriptures repeatedly invite the reader to inquire about and receive an understanding of the mysteries of God (see Alma 26:22; D&C 6:11; 42:61). *Mysteries* are spiritual realities that can be known and understood only by revelation because they exist outside man's sensory perception; but our scriptures record them, our prophets teach them, and the Holy Ghost reveals them to the diligent seeker. In fact, the whole gospel is a collection of mysteries—truths pertaining to salvation that would not be known by men in the mortal probation did God not reveal them. Benjamin's address begins with an invitation to prepare to view the mysteries of God:

> My brethren, all ye that have assembled yourselves together, . . . I have not commanded you to come up hither to trifle with the words which I shall speak, but that you should hearken unto me, and open your ears that ye may hear, and your hearts that ye may understand, and your minds that the *mysteries of God* may be unfolded to your view. (Mosiah 2:9)

The particular mystery that draws our attention here is the mystery of spiritual rebirth and the role that Benjamin's priesthood played in that experience. With respect to the revelation of mysteries and the power of the priesthood, the Lord has said:

> The power and authority of the higher, or Melchizedek Priesthood, is to hold the keys of all the spiritual blessings of the church—To have the privilege of *receiving the mysteries* of the kingdom of heaven, to have the heavens opened unto them, to commune with the general assembly and church of the Firstborn, and to enjoy the communion and presence of God the Father, and Jesus the mediator of the new covenant. (D&C 107:18–19)

In the first part of this paper we will examine Benjamin's priesthood role as a prelude to understanding his prayer, the angel's response, and the spiritual rebirth of his people.

Benjamin's Priesthood Role in the Prophetic Pattern: The Power to Bless

A study of Benjamin's role gives opportunity to look at Benjamin's priesthood work in particular, but also at priesthood in general. Priesthood is the great governing authority of the universe. It unlocks spiritual blessings of the eternal world for the heirs of salvation. The power to play a saving role is the most sought-after power among righteous priesthood holders in time or in eternity. The greater the soul, it seems, the deeper the desire to labor to bring souls to Christ through causing them to take his name upon them (see, for example, Abraham 1:2–3). "What was the power of Melchisedeck?" Joseph Smith asked.

> Twas not the priesthood of Aaron etc., [but it was the power of] a king and a priest to the most high God. [That priesthood was] a perfect law of Theocracy holding *keys of power and blessings*. [It] stood as God to give laws to the people, administering endless lives to the sons and daughters of Adam.[1]

The Prophet Joseph further explained:

> [Priesthood] is the channel through which all knowledge, doctrine, the plan of salvation and every important matter is revealed from heaven. . . . It is the channel through which the Almighty commenced revealing his glory at the beginning of the creation of this earth and through which he has continued to reveal himself to the children of men to the present time and through which he will make known his purposes to the end of time.[2]

A brief look at the history of the priesthood on the earth reveals that men like Benjamin have stood in this priesthood channel unlocking the blessings of salvation for their people since the days of Adam. Adam, in fact, was the great prototype of priesthood holders who strove to bring their communities and their posterity into at-one-ment with the Lord Jesus Christ. Adam blessed his posterity because, the Prophet Joseph taught, "he wanted to bring them into the presence of God. They looked for a city . . . 'whose builder and maker is God' (Hebrews 11:10)."[3]

After Adam, Enoch labored with his people and succeeded in bringing to pass not only their sanctification, but also their translation (see Moses 7:21), a function of the higher priesthood.[4] Following Enoch, Melchizedek, king and high priest of Salem, brought many into the fullness of the priesthood and the presence of God. His people also received translation, "obtained heaven, and sought for the city of Enoch" (Genesis 14:34 JST).

After Melchizedek, Moses strove for the same blessings for his people. The Lord said to them: "If ye will obey my voice indeed, and keep my covenant, then ye shall be a peculiar treasure unto me above all people. . . . And ye shall be unto me a kingdom of priests, and an holy nation" (Exodus 19:5–6), touching again on this idea of the holy city. Moses "sought diligently to sanctify his people that they might behold the face of God; But they hardened their hearts and could not endure his presence; therefore, the Lord . . . swore that they should not enter into his rest while in the wilderness, which rest is the fulness of his glory" (D&C 84:23–24). The Prophet Joseph explained: "Moses sought to bring the children of Israel into the presence of God, through the power of the Priesthood, but he could not."[5]

In this dispensation, Joseph Smith showed great anxiety to see the temple completed before his death, saying:

> Hurry up the work, brethren. . . . Let us finish the temple;
> the Lord has a great endowment in store for you, and I
> am anxious that the brethren should have their endow-
> ments and receive the fullness of the Priesthood. . . . Then
> . . . the Kingdom will be established, and I do not care
> what shall become of me.[6]

Our modern prophets strive in the same manner as Benjamin did to sanctify the members of the church and to un-
lock these priesthood powers in their behalf. Elder David B.
Haight made reference to this power as he recounted a sacred experience in which he viewed the Savior's ministry
and came to a greater understanding of the power of the
priesthood:

> During those days of unconsciousness I was given,
> by the gift and power of the Holy Ghost, a more perfect
> knowledge of His mission. I was also given a more com-
> plete understanding of what it means to exercise, in His
> name, the *authority to unlock the mysteries of the kingdom of
> heaven* for the salvation of all who are faithful.[7]

Thus Benjamin, as a prophet, seer, revelator, king, and
priest, held the keys of power and blessing for his community. He had received all the accoutrements of the high
priesthood: the sacred plates, the sword of Laban, the ball
or director, and the Urim and Thummim.[8] A priesthood
holder's office is to sanctify himself and stand as an advo-
cate before God seeking blessings for his community in the
manner of the Lord Jesus Christ himself (see John 17:19),
whether the community be as small as a family or as large
as Benjamin's kingdom. A righteous priesthood holder can
work by faith to provide great benefits to his fellow beings
(see Mosiah 8:18). He can, in fact, exercise great faith in behalf of others of lesser faith, "filling in" with faith for them;
thus a prophet and a people together can bring down blessings for even a whole community (for example, see Ether

12:14). The Lord seems to be interested not only in individuals but also in groups of people who wish to establish holy cities and unite with heavenly communities. Like the ancients, one who holds the holy priesthood is always trying to establish a holy community, is always "look[ing] for a city" (Hebrews 11:10, 16). So it was with Benjamin.

Priesthood Power over Enemies

In analyzing the scriptural accounts of priesthood work, we discover that one major task of priesthood holders, in unlocking the blessings of salvation for their people, is to triumph over the powers of evil—over "enemies." Of this task, Joseph Smith said,

> Salvation is nothing more nor less than to triumph over all our enemies and put them under our feet. And when we have power to put all enemies under our feet in this world, and a knowledge to triumph over all evil spirits in the world to come, then we are saved.[9]

This is the pattern: the priesthood holder labors with all his faculties to rout Satan from his loved ones as that enemy is manifested in contention, mental warfare, and physical violence among the people. For any Melchizedek priesthood holder to become a prince of peace, he must in some degree wrest his kingdom, great or small, from the adversary and halt the plans of the destroyer on behalf of his loved ones.[10] The Book of Mormon's description of Melchizedek reflects this pattern:

> Now this Melchizedek was a king over the land of Salem; and his people had waxed strong in iniquity and abomination; yea, they had all gone astray; they were full of all manner of wickedness; But Melchizedek having exercised mighty faith, and received the office of the high priesthood according to the holy order of God, did

preach repentance unto his people. And behold, they did repent; and Melchizedek did establish peace in the land in his days; therefore he was called the prince of peace. (Alma 13:17–18)

In this priesthood pattern, Benjamin labored against manifest evil and spiritual entropy to save his people in the manner of Christ himself. He contended with the adversary at three main points: He waged war against the destroying Lamanites—using the sword of Laban, going forth in the strength of the Lord (see Words of Mormon 1:13–14); he waged another battle against false prophets, preachers, and teachers; and then he put down contention among his people with the assistance of other holy prophets. The record says, "King Benjamin, by laboring with all the might of his body and the faculty of his whole soul, . . . did once more establish peace in the land" (Words of Mormon 1:18). *Peace*, that essential condition for spiritual progress, is evidence of the triumph of spiritual principle and also of the preparation of the people in any size group to receive greater spiritual blessings.

Benjamin then was not an anomaly; he acted in the tradition of all true prophets before and after him in drawing down spiritual blessings on his people as he strove to prepare them to return to God. He was therefore the very person in Zarahemla who had the power to pray that spiritual blessings would be poured out on this community of saints that they might be born again.

Benjamin's People, the Angel, and the Spiritual Rebirth

Benjamin's people were descendants of those righteous Nephites who fled from the land of Nephi under Benjamin's father, King Mosiah₁, and were led by the power of God to the land of Zarahemla, where they united with Zarahemla's people. Mosiah$_1$ restored the gospel among them and reigned over them. The important point here is that Benjamin's people were not spiritually ignorant; they were not hearing about the Lord Jesus Christ for the first time. The record states clearly that they were "a diligent people in keeping the commandments of the Lord" (Mosiah 1:11); it states that there were not any among them, except little children, who had not been taught "concerning the . . . prophecies which have been spoken by the holy prophets" and all that the Lord commanded their fathers to speak (Mosiah 2:34; see 2:35).[11] I assume here that Benjamin's people, having been taught the gospel, had been previously baptized in the name of Jesus Christ.

In addition, we might infer that Benjamin's people came up to the temple with some preparation for and in some anticipation of a spiritual event. They would have been aware of what their kings had been trying to do for them according to the ancient pattern. They knew there was a blessing awaiting them. They came up to the temple, in part, to give thanks to God for their king "who had taught them to keep the commandments of God, that they might rejoice and be filled with love towards God and all men" (Mosiah 2:4).

The phrases, *to rejoice and be filled with love* and *to be filled with joy*, seem to have a technical meaning in scripture. They appear to be alternative ways of describing being *born again*. Scripture abounds with references to being filled with this transforming joy and love under the influence of the Holy Ghost. Nephi said, for example, "[God] hath *filled me with his love*, even unto the consuming of my flesh" (2 Nephi 4:21); the Lamanites were "*filled with that joy* which is unspeakable and *full of glory*. . . . The Holy Spirit of God did come down from heaven, and did enter into their hearts, and they were *filled as if with fire*" (Helaman 5:44–45); the

Nephites with the resurrected Christ "were *filled with the Holy Ghost* and with fire" (3 Nephi 19:13); Mormon taught us to pray to be *filled with this love,* which is charity, or perfect love, which makes one pure like Christ (see Moroni 7:48).

Compare now the account of Benjamin's people:

> The Spirit of the Lord came upon them, and they were filled with joy, having received a remission of their sins, and having peace of conscience, because of the exceeding faith which they had in Jesus Christ who should come, according to the words which king Benjamin had spoken unto them. (Mosiah 4:3)

It seems that being filled with joy, love, and glory are all ways of describing being born again. Benjamin clearly identified for the people what they had experienced: "Behold, this day he hath spiritually begotten you; for ye say that your hearts are changed through faith on his name; therefore, ye are born of him and have become his sons and his daughters" (Mosiah 5:7). He said that they had "come to the knowledge of the *glory of God,*" as they "tasted of his love" (Mosiah 4:11). Elsewhere the Lord connects being born again with being a partaker of the *glory of God.* He says, "All those who are begotten through me are partakers of the glory of the same, and are the church of the Firstborn" (D&C 93:22).

One of the blessings of the priesthood is that it can bring others to be partakers of the glory of God. The Prophet Joseph taught that "being born again comes by the Spirit of God through ordinances."[12] Angels, as priesthood holders, can also play a part. Indeed, as Alma taught, angels can be commissioned by God to cause "men to behold of [God's] glory" (Alma 12:29). Thus the angel said to Benjamin,

> I am come to declare unto you the glad tidings of great joy. For the Lord hath *heard thy prayers,* and hath judged of thy righteousness, and hath sent me to declare unto thee that thou mayest rejoice; and that thou mayest declare

unto thy people, that they may also be *filled with joy*. (Mosiah 3:3–4)

If to be *filled with joy* is closely related to being *born again*, then it would seem that the angel had come from God to authorize Benjamin to proceed with the endowment of the name and the rebirth. The angel declared that the time had come that these people might literally be "filled with joy" (Mosiah 4:3) and that "whosoever should believe that Christ should come, the same might receive remission of their sins, and *rejoice with exceedingly great joy*" (Mosiah 3:13).

It was not just the news that the Savior would minister on the earth in the near future that filled them with joy—because they already knew all the prophecies of the holy prophets with respect to the Savior's ministry—but that the atonement was about to become very personal to *them*. Their faith in the Lord was about to become knowledge (see Mosiah 5:4). This joy announced by the angel was not to be just a momentary experience. If they were diligent unto prayer (see Moroni 8:26) and obedient to other instructions their king would give them, they would be changed forever, could retain this perfect love and joy in their hearts, and would even "grow in the knowledge of the glory of [God]" (Mosiah 4:12). We might infer then that these two parties—the king and the people—had been praying and preparing for the time when the whole community, in the ancient tradition, might be redeemed and born again.

Without doubt, Benjamin knew what was going to transpire as he told his son to summon the people to the temple. He said, "I shall give this people a name . . . that never shall be blotted out, except it be through transgression" (Mosiah 1:11–12). Giving them the name forever is equivalent to causing them to be born again into the family of Christ. Because of the greater responsibility inherent in the formal taking of the name, Benjamin prefaced this spiritual endowment with warnings that if they proceeded with taking the name but then turned away in disobedience, they would have to drink of the cup of the wrath of God (see Mosiah 3:26) and they would drink damnation to their souls (see Mosiah 3:18, 25). Benjamin quoted the angel's words, "When thou shalt have taught thy people the things which the Lord thy God hath commanded thee, even then are they found no more blameless in the sight of God" (Mosiah 3:22). In addition, it may be that Benjamin's words were especially binding on the people (as were the words of the later Nephi in 3 Nephi 7:17–18) because, in delivering the words of the angel, Benjamin spoke with the tongue of angels (see also 2 Nephi 31:13–14; 32:2–3) and "the word of God with power and with authority" (Words of Mormon 1:17).

Notwithstanding the warning, the people crossed the threshold of spiritual experience into a fearsome, spiritually induced view of the *reality* of their fallen condition, confronting their own carnal state, even less than the dust of the earth. At the height of their distress, united under the influence of the Spirit, they cried aloud on the Lord's name and begged for a remission of sins (see Mosiah 4:20). In response, the Spirit of the Lord descended upon them, and they were "filled with joy," the record says, fulfilling the exact words and promise of the angel. Their hearts were purified as they received a remission of their sins and peace of conscience because of their "exceeding faith . . . in Jesus Christ" (Mosiah 4:3). Benjamin observed, "He has poured out his Spirit upon you, and has caused that your hearts should be filled with joy, and has caused that your mouths should be stopped that ye could not find utterance, so exceedingly great was your joy" (Mosiah 4:20).

The Nature of Spiritual Rebirth

In trying to comprehend the nature and extent of the spiritual experience described here in Mosiah, our own experience tells us, as do the scriptures, that spiritual experience can range from the gentle impressions of the Holy Spirit to dramatic encounters with heavenly powers. Thus, spiritual rebirth may begin at baptism, but without doubt additional degrees of spiritual rebirth and sanctification lie ahead for the true disciple, even a consummate change in which he has received the power to yield his heart entirely to God (see Helaman 3:35). The description in Mosiah suggests such a change. In addition, based on other scriptures about being born again, it seems that the people partook of the following blessings:

1. As a result of the mighty change wrought in their hearts (see Mosiah 5:2), they received Christ's image in their countenances; they could "sing the song of redeeming love," their hearts having been "stripped of pride" and enmity (see Alma 5:12, 19, 26, 28).

2. Through the power of the Holy Ghost they were immersed in the heavenly fire, becoming one in God, attaining to a new order, as did Adam who, "born of the Spirit, and . . . quickened in the inner man, . . . heard a voice out of heaven, saying: Thou art baptized with fire, and with the Holy Ghost. . . . Thou art after the order of him who was without beginning of days or end of years, from all eternity to all eternity. Behold, *thou art one in me*, a son of God; and thus may all become my sons" (Moses 6:65–68).

3. To be born again is to be filled with "the Spirit of the Lord." Alma defined this mighty change when he proclaimed: "I had been born of God. Yea, and from that

time even until now, I have labored without ceasing, that I might bring souls unto repentance; that I might bring them to taste of the exceeding joy of which I did taste; that they might also be born of God, and be *filled with the Holy Ghost*" (Alma 36:23–24).

4. They enjoyed a degree of sanctification (see Mosiah 5:2). Their sins having been remitted, they could not look upon sin save with abhorrence; they also entered that spiritual dimension called "the rest of the Lord" (Alma 13:12).

5. The apostle John wrote, "Whosoever is born of God doth not continue in sin; for the Spirit of God remaineth in him; and he cannot continue in sin, because he is born of God, *having received that holy Spirit of promise*" (1 John 3:9 JST, emphasis added). This verse suggests that spiritual rebirth at a certain level is associated also with receiving the Holy Spirit of Promise or having one's calling and election made sure. It is not clear from the account in Mosiah whether this blessing was extended at this time to Benjamin's people.

6. They became, as mentioned above, candidates for the church of the Firstborn (see Mosiah 5:7; D&C 93:22).

The full reception of the Holy Ghost is the key to rebirth. Elder Bruce R. McConkie wrote:

> Mere compliance with the formality of the ordinance of baptism does not mean that a person has been born again. No one can be born again without baptism, but the immersion in water and the laying on of hands to confer the Holy Ghost do not of themselves guarantee that a person has been or will be born again. The new birth takes place only for those who actually enjoy the gift or companionship of the Holy Ghost, only for those who are

fully converted, who have given themselves without re-
straint to the Lord.[13]

These Nephites were "alive in Christ because they enjoy[ed]
the companionship of the Spirit";[14] they were immersed in
the Spirit, which they had received as a constant possession.[15]

Brigham Young taught that when one has been proved,
and labored, and occupied himself sufficiently upon obtaining the Spirit, if he would adhere to the Spirit of the Lord
strictly, it should become in him a fountain of revelation.

> After a while the Lord will say to such, "My son, you
> have been faithful, you have clung to good, and you love
> righteousness, and hate iniquity, from which you have
> turned away, and now you shall have the blessings of the
> Holy Spirit to lead you, and be your constant companion,
> from this time henceforth and forever." *Then the Holy
> Spirit becomes your property*, it is given to you for a profit,
> and an eternal blessing. It tends to addition, extension,
> and increase, to immortality and eternal lives.[15]

What is impressive here is that Benjamin's people were
already commandment keepers. It is not a mighty change
from evil to goodness that they have undergone, like Alma
or Paul, but a profound transformation from basic goodness
to something that exceeded their ability even to describe.
This much they did say, "The Spirit of the Lord Omnipotent
. . . has wrought a mighty change in us, or in our hearts, that
we have no more disposition to do evil, but to do good continually" (Mosiah 5:2).

Receiving the Name

What then distinguished Benjamin's community "above
all the people which the Lord God hath brought out of the
land of Jerusalem" (Mosiah 1:11)? Perhaps this was the first

time among all the people brought out from the land of Jerusalem that a king and priest—in the tradition of Adam,
Enoch, and Melchizedek—had succeeded in bringing his
people to this point of transformation: he had caused them
as a community actually to receive the name of Christ.

But what does it mean to receive the name of Christ? We
remember that when we take the sacrament, we signify not
that we have fully taken the name, but that we are willing to
take the name (see Moroni 4:3; D&C 20:77; compare Mosiah
5:5). Elder Dallin Oaks emphasized the word *willingness*,
pointing to a future consummation:

> The Lord and his servants referred to the . . . *temple* as a
> house for "the name" of the Lord God of Israel (see 1 Kgs.
> 3:2; 5:5; 8:16–20, 29, 44, 48; 1 Chr. 22:8–10, 19; 29:16; 2 Chr.
> 2:4; 6:5–10, 20, 34, 38).
>
>   . . . In the inspired dedicatory prayer of the Kirtland
> Temple, the Prophet Joseph Smith asked the Lord for a
> blessing upon "thy people upon whom thy name shall be
> put in this house" (D&C 109:26).
>
>   . . . [B]y partaking of the sacrament we witness our
> willingness to participate in the sacred ordinances of the
> temple and to receive the highest blessings available
> through the name and by the authority of the Savior
> when he chooses to confer them upon us.[16]

Elder Bruce R. McConkie also wrote about the meaning of
receiving the divine name: "God's name is God. To have his
name written on a person is to identify that person as a god.
How can it be said more plainly? Those who gain eternal
life become gods!"[17] On another occasion Elder McConkie
linked becoming a son or daughter of God with temple ordinances: "The ordinances that are performed in the temples
are the ordinances of exaltation; they open the door to us to
an inheritance of sonship; they open the door to us so that we

may become sons and daughters, members of the household of God in eternity. . . . They open the door to becoming kings and priests and inheriting all things."[18]

In connection with being born again, Benjamin's people may have received something of a temple endowment. In fact, we find in Benjamin's discourse essential temple themes pertaining to the creation, fall, atonement, consecration, and covenant making. Benjamin's last words pertain to being "sealed" to Christ and receiving eternal life (see Mosiah 5:15). Of course, important endowment elements are missing from the record, but had they been administered on this occasion, or at some later point, they would not, because of their sacred nature, have been included in our present Book of Mormon account. Nevertheless, King Benjamin's people received an endowment of spiritual knowledge and power which took them from being good people to Christlike people—all in a temple setting. What they experienced through the power of the priesthood was a revelation of Christ's nature and the power to be assimilated to his image.

Conclusion

For all the questions that may remain unanswered, the account of Benjamin's people is compelling in its promise of that which awaits the diligent seeker of Christ. Ultimately, many spiritual questions are answered only after one's own personal experience, to which experience the Lord generously extends invitation. The Lord said on one occasion to a group of saints, "Ye are not able to abide the presence of God now, neither the ministering of angels; wherefore, continue in patience until ye are perfected" (D&C 67:13); but he also taught: "Seek the face of the Lord always, that in patience ye may possess your souls, and ye shall have eternal life" (D&C 101:38). The message encourages diligence as well as patience for the fulfillment of the promise.

It is the privilege and responsibility of a community's priesthood leader, through exercising mighty faith and laboring with his people, to bring them to a higher spiritual plane in their quest to return to God. Benjamin had been praying that the Lord would send his power to bring to pass a spiritually transforming experience for his people. The Lord sent his angel to declare to the king that power would be given to cause the people to be spiritually reborn, to become sons and daughters of Christ, and to receive the sacred name forever. The spiritual rebirth as a community and the taking of the name in a temple setting distinguished them from those whom the Lord had previously brought out of Jerusalem. The people tasted the glory of God and came to a personal knowledge of him; through the power of the Holy Spirit they experienced the mighty change of heart and the mystery of spiritual rebirth.

Much of the Book of Mormon is devoted to that comprehensive and *mighty* change described here in Mosiah. That may be the reason President Benson pled with us to feast on this book. He wrote, "When we awake and are born of God, a new day will break and Zion will be redeemed. May we be convinced that Jesus is the Christ, choose to follow Him, be changed for Him, captained by Him, consumed in Him, and born again."[19]

Notes

1. *Words of Joseph Smith,* comp. and ed., Andrew F. Ehat and Lyndon W. Cook (Orem, Utah: Grandin Book, 1991), 244, corrections and emphasis added.

2. Ibid., 38–39.

3. *The Teachings of the Prophet Joseph Smith,* comp. Joseph Fielding Smith (Salt Lake City: Deseret Book, 1976), 159.

4. See *Words of Joseph Smith*, 41.

5. *Teachings of the Prophet Joseph Smith*, 159.

6. George Q. Cannon, quoted in *Words of Joseph Smith*, 306 n. 30.

7. David B. Haight, "The Sacrament—and the Sacrifice," *Ensign* (November 1989): 60, emphasis added.

8. Although not mentioned among the things that he entrusts to his son Mosiah (Mosiah 1:16), Mosiah₁ had the interpreters, alluded to in Omni 1:20. Mosiah₂ had them according to Mosiah 28:11; Mosiah 28:14 notes that they were handed down from generation to generation.

9. *Teachings of the Prophet Joseph Smith*, 297.

10. See Mosiah 4:14 on keeping evil out of one's family.

11. From Mosiah 2:35, we might understand that Benjamin's people were familiar with what was on the small plates of Nephi.

12. *Words of Joseph Smith*, 12; see also Doctrine and Covenants 84:19–25 and Exodus 34:1–2 JST.

13. Bruce R. McConkie, *Mormon Doctrine*, 2nd ed. (Salt Lake City: Bookcraft, 1966), 101.

14. Bruce R. McConkie, *A New Witness for the Articles of Faith* (Salt Lake City: Deseret Book, 1985), 285.

15. Brigham Young, in *JD*, 2:135, emphasis added.

16. Dallin H. Oaks, "Taking upon Us the Name of Jesus Christ," *Ensign* (May 1985): 81, emphasis added.

17. Bruce R. McConkie, *Doctrinal New Testament Commentary* (Salt Lake City: Bookcraft, 1973), 3:458; see also Revelation 3:12; 14:1.

18. Bruce R. McConkie, *Conference Report* (October 1955): 12–13.

19. Ezra Taft Benson, "Born of God," *Ensign* (July 1989): 5.

CHAPTER 10

Benjamin's Covenant as a Precursor of the Sacrament Prayers

John W. Welch

King Benjamin's covenant language in Mosiah 5 figures seminally as an early text to which Jesus was apparently alluding when he articulated in 3 Nephi 18 words that provided the basis for the final form of the Nephite sacrament prayers in Moroni 4–5. A historical, textual relationship exists between the words of the Nephite covenant text of King Benjamin, the words of Jesus in 3 Nephi 18, and the phrases used in the Nephite sacrament prayers; the precision and persistence of basic terms throughout all three of these texts, separated from each other by many years and pages of Nephite history, speak highly of the faithful and logical orderliness, the linguistic sensitivity, and the progressing revelation and inspiration present in this history.

Benjamin's Words and Moroni 4–5

At the conclusion of Benjamin's speech (Mosiah 5), his people entered into a covenant. The event began with a declaration by the people of their faith in the king's words, an affirmation of their disposition to do good continually, and an acknowledgment that the goodness of God had filled them with the spirit of prophecy and with joy. In effect, the people declared how they had been blessed and sanctified: "Yea, we believe all the words which thou hast spoken unto us; . . . we have no more disposition to do evil, but to do good continually" (Mosiah 5:2–4). The people then, in the following words, expressed their willingness to enter into a covenant. (The emphasized phrases contain words similar to those appearing in Moroni 4–5.) "And we *are willing* to enter into a covenant with our God to do his will, and *to be obedient to his commandments in all things that he shall command us,* all the remainder of our days, that we may not bring upon ourselves a never-ending torment, as has been spoken by the angel, that we may not drink out of the cup of the wrath of God" (Mosiah 5:5).

Benjamin responded by accepting the words of the people as a "righteous covenant" (Mosiah 5:6). He explained the resultant relationship the people would enjoy with their God as a consequence of their covenant and then affirmed the next requirement: "And now, because of the covenant which ye have made ye shall be called the children of Christ, his sons, and his daughters. . . . Therefore, I would *that ye should take upon you the name of Christ, all you that* have entered into the covenant" (Mosiah 5:7–8).

Benjamin explained how all those who know the sacred name by which they are called shall be found on the right hand of God, but those who do not shall be found on the left. Accordingly, he instructed his people further that they should "remember also, that this is the name that I said I should give unto you that never should be blotted out . . . [and that you] should *remember to retain the name written always* in your hearts" (Mosiah 5:11–12). Provided that they knew and remembered the name, the people were promised that they would not be driven away or cast out; if they remained steadfast in good works, they would have everlasting salvation (Mosiah 5:13–15).

The sacrament prayers in Moroni 4–5 contain several phrases that are similar to these words of King Benjamin:

Moroni 4–5	Mosiah 5
O God, the Eternal Father, we ask thee in the name of thy Son, Jesus Christ, to bless and sanctify this bread to the souls of all those who partake of it; that they may eat in remembrance of the body of thy Son, and witness unto thee, O God, the Eternal Father, that they *are willing* to	And we *are willing* (5:5)
take upon them the name of thy Son,	*take upon you the name of* Christ (5:8)
and *always remember him,*	*remember* to retain the name written *always* (5:11)
and *keep his commandments* which he	to be *obedient to his commandments* (5:5)
hath given them, that they may always have his Spirit to be with them, Amen.	
O God, the Eternal Father, we ask thee in the name of thy Son, Jesus Christ, to bless and sanctify this wine to the souls of all those who drink of it, that they may do	

it in remembrance of the
blood of thy Son, which was
shed for them; that they may
witness unto thee, O God,
the Eternal Father, that they
do *always remember* him,

remember to retain the name
written *always* (5:11)

that they may have his Spirit
to be with them. Amen.

The text of Mosiah 5 indicates that by making this covenant, Benjamin's people witnessed that they were willing to keep God's commandments, after which they took upon themselves the name of Christ and the obligation to remember to keep that name always written in their hearts. These promises similarly comprise the essential elements of the Nephite sacramental prayers as they eventually appeared in Moroni's day and as they are used among Latter-day Saints today.[1]

Jesus' Words in 3 Nephi 18 as the Bridge between Benjamin and Moroni 4–5

With the coming of the risen Jesus to the Nephites gathered at their temple in Bountiful, the law of Moses was fulfilled, and Nephite laws and ordinances were changed. The voice of Christ had announced at the time of his crucifixion that the old law had been done away (3 Nephi 9:19–20). Thus as the Nephites gathered at their temple following Christ's crucifixion (3 Nephi 10:18; 11:1), they could well have wondered which parts of their old law and temple ritual they should continue to observe and which they should not.[2] As the people conversed, "wondering . . . about this Jesus Christ" (3 Nephi 11:1–2), the answer came.

Through the teachings and ministry of Jesus, they learned how "all things [had] become new" (3 Nephi 12:47; 15:2). One of the former elements that took on a new character at this time would have been the Nephite personal covenant language. The main instructions regarding the administration of the sacrament appear in 3 Nephi 18:5–12, a text that bears a close relationship to the wording of the sacrament prayers in Moroni 4–5.[3]

Jesus taught and ministered the sacrament to those assembled in Bountiful following a rich outpouring of the spirit. As was the experience of the people of Benjamin, those gathered in Bountiful were given, immediately before their covenant experience, great prophecies of things to come (see 3 Nephi 16:1–20), and they too had had their souls "filled" (3 Nephi 17:17). "So great was the joy of the multitude that they were overcome" (3 Nephi 17:18). They knelt down upon the earth (see 3 Nephi 17:13), and Jesus instructed them to "arise" (see 3 Nephi 17:19). Jesus blessed them because of their faith (see 3 Nephi 17:20), and after a profound spiritual manifestation (see 3 Nephi 17:24), the people bore record that what they had seen and heard was true (3 Nephi 17:25). Each of these aspects in the experience at the temple in Bountiful has a counterpart in Mosiah 5:1–4.[4]

The words which Jesus then spoke in 3 Nephi 18 are as follows:

> He said unto the disciples: Behold there shall one be ordained among you, and to him will I give power that he shall break *bread* and *bless* it and give it unto the people of my church, unto *all those who* shall believe and be baptized in my name. And this shall ye always observe to do, even as I have done, even as I have broken bread and blessed it and given it unto you. And this shall ye *do in remembrance of my body*, which I have shown unto you. And it shall be a *testimony unto the Father that ye do always*

remember me. And if ye do always remember me *ye shall have my Spirit to be with you.*

And it came to pass that when he said these words, he commanded his disciples that they should take of the *wine* of the cup and *drink of it,* and that they should also give unto the multitude that they might drink of it. . . . And when the disciples had done this, Jesus said unto them: Blessed are ye for this thing which ye have done, for this is fulfilling my commandments, and this doth *witness unto the Father that ye are willing to do that which I have commanded you.* And this shall ye always do to those who repent and are baptized in *my name;* and ye shall do it *in remembrance of my blood, which I have shed for you,* that ye may *witness unto the Father that ye do always remember me.* And if ye do always remember me *ye shall have my Spirit to be with you.* (3 Nephi 18:5–11)

The textual similarities between these words of Jesus and the Nephite sacrament prayers in Moroni 4–5 are abundant and apparent. (For purposes of this study, I assume that one of the twelve disciples, most likely Nephi, prepared the texts of the sacrament prayers based on the words of Jesus, perhaps under his direct supervision; I have explored this assumption and other such possibilities previously.)[5]

Less obvious but equally significant, it is evident that a clear continuity between the words of Jesus in 3 Nephi and the traditional Nephite covenant language known from the time of Benjamin is also visible, especially in the events preparing the people to participate in the rite, and also in the phrases "take upon you the name of Christ," "remember to retain the name always," and "be obedient to his commandments," which appear in Mosiah and are echoed in 3 Nephi. These connections demonstrate one way in which Jesus took the old Nephite covenant text and made it new. The promises and allegiance to Christ remained basically the same, but the tokens of his resurrected body and atoning blood were presented as Jesus himself stood in their midst and provided the pattern that his repentant followers should observe from that time forth. The result would have appeared to the Nephites both marvelously familiar and revealingly innovative.

Thus significant similarities exist between the words of the Nephite sacrament prayers and the covenant language of Mosiah 5. People in both instances witness their willingness, take upon themselves the name of Christ, and promise to remember him always and keep his commandments. Several subtle differences between Christ's words and King Benjamin's, however, can also be observed:

Clear reference to God as the Eternal Father. It is important and interesting that the sacrament prayers address God as "the Eternal Father" and clearly distinguish him from Jesus Christ, his Son.

In their covenant language, however, Benjamin's people initially referred to their God only as "our God" (Mosiah 5:5), not as their "father." In a covenantal sense, God (Christ) became their Father as a result of their conversion, as they were thereby spiritually begotten of him that day and were thus called "the children of Christ, his sons, and his daughters" (Mosiah 5:7). For the people to have spoken of God as their Father before uttering the words that created or renewed that relationship would have been premature.[6]

In Moroni 4–5, of course, God is addressed at the outset as "God the Eternal Father." Here, God's fatherhood is not dependent on the people becoming his sons and daughters through the covenant process. The language of the sacrament prayers focuses on the everlasting relationship between God the Father and Jesus Christ his Son. Here, God's fatherhood is called "eternal," which may reflect the point that God's fatherhood is not conditioned in any ultimate sense on the existence of covenant relationships with mortals (compare Hebrews 7:1–24).

Also, the distinction between God's fatherhood and

302 • *John W. Welch*

Christ's sonship is clearly stated in the prayers in Moroni 4–
5. After Jesus' appearance to them, the Nephites as a whole
would have become more explicitly sensitive to the relationship between the Father and the Son, especially in light
of the fact that Jesus taught them that he would ascend to
his Father (for example, 3 Nephi 15:1; 28:1). He expounded
on the distinct roles of the Father many times as he taught at
the temple in Bountiful. In the earlier portions of the Book
of Mormon, the distinctions between God the Father and
his son Jesus Christ, though basically understood by the
prophets in those eras, do not always appear so clearly
stated.[7] But in the sacrament prayers, this distinction is
more clearly defined, which may have helped standardize
the post-Easter Nephite usage.[8]

Asking the Father in the name of the Son, Jesus Christ. When
the prayers in Moroni 4–5 request a blessing and sanctification, they petition, "We ask thee in the name of thy son, Jesus
Christ." In so doing, they follow a specific instruction given
by Jesus in 3 Nephi 18:20, immediately following his administration of the sacrament. The use of this phrase in 3 Nephi
18 may represent a change from the time of Benjamin, making this form of asking God explicitly part of the covenant
text for the first time. On the other hand, in the early portions of the Book of Mormon, many things were done in the
name of Christ.[9] Nevertheless, the precise concept of "asking the Father in the name of Christ" appears to have taken
on broader significance in Nephite usage only after it appears in full and is emphasized four times by the resurrected Jesus in 3 Nephi (see 3 Nephi 16:4; 17:3; 18:20; 27:28).
Since Jesus had specifically instructed the Nephite disciples
to ask in his name (see 3 Nephi 18:20), it is no wonder that
this phrase was expressly incorporated into the sacrament
prayers.

Blessing and sanctifying. Benjamin's text mentions no sacramental emblems being blessed or sanctified as his people made their covenant. The people themselves, nevertheless, first recited the ways in which *they* personally had been blessed and sanctified by the spirit of God, making their desires pure. Likewise, Jesus pronounced the people in Bountiful "blessed" because of their faith (3 Nephi 17:20) before he administered the sacrament to them. In the prayers in Moroni 4–5, the bread and wine were sanctified. While the holiness of the people is not thereby diminished, the focus on Christ's sanctity is a meaningful addition.

Bread and wine. From the words of Jesus, above all, came the eucharistic aspects of the prayers in Moroni 4–5. The bread was eaten "in remembrance of" the body which Jesus *"show[ed] unto"* them (3 Nephi 18:7), thus adding a new and profound dimension to the sacrament symbolism over and above that found in the New Testament. There the bread represents the body "given for you" (Luke 22:19; compare 3 Nephi 18:6) and "broken for you" (1 Corinthians 11:24; compare 3 Nephi 18:6), but the idea of the body "shown unto" you is never mentioned. The wine here, as in the New Testament, was "in remembrance of" the blood which was shed (3 Nephi 18:11; Luke 22:20). A substitute for blood was appropriate, since the old law pertaining to the "shedding of blood" (3 Nephi 9:19) had been superseded.

Although probably remote, a connection between the texts of Mosiah 5 and 3 Nephi 18 may be found in the fact that another cup was mentioned in the covenant text of Benjamin. Previously, the cup was the cup of God's wrath (see 2 Nephi 8:17; Mosiah 3:26; 5:5; Alma 40:26; 3 Nephi 11:11). In 3 Nephi 18:8, the cup became the cup of Jesus' blood. All God's wrath had been poured, as it were, into that cup of the new covenant. One may drink of it, a bitter cup of blood turned through Christ's atonement into something as sweet as wine; otherwise, one will suffer the dregs of the wrath of God on one's own.

The covenantors. Both Benjamin and Jesus allowed only certain people to complete the covenant. Benjamin permitted only those who had entered into the covenant, "all you that have entered into the covenant with God" (Mosiah 5:8), to take upon them the name of Christ. Using Benjamin's words, as revealed to him by an angel, we know that those who then transgressed knowingly "drink damnation to their own souls" (Mosiah 3:18) and are "no more blameless" (Mosiah 3:22). In similar words, Christ allowed only those "who shall believe and be baptized in my name" to receive the sacrament. Anyone unworthy was not to be allowed to "eat and drink damnation to his soul" (3 Nephi 18:29). Moreover, the phrase *all you that* is found in the words of Benjamin (Mosiah 5:8) and the phrase *all those who* appears in the words of Jesus (3 Nephi 18:5), with the word *souls* appearing in this context in Mosiah 6:2, perhaps together contributing to the formulation of Moroni 4–5, "to the souls of all those who . . ."

The witness of willingness. In all three of these texts, the word *willing* appears. People entering or renewing their covenant with God must do so willingly, voluntarily, eagerly, and resolutely. The people of Benjamin expressed their willingness to enter into a covenant. They covenanted to do whatever God might command them all the rest of their lives. In terms that were rigorous and broad, the people entered into a covenant promising "to do his will" (Mosiah 5:5). Moreover, they promised to keep whatever commandments he might ever give them, now or in the future, all the days of their lives. Their promise was one of loyalty to God in general, and they expected that their king would yet deliver to them further commandments from

God (see Mosiah 2:31), which they would be equally bound to follow.

Moroni 4 also requires one's loyalty, but the orientation is more on the present than the future, for with the appearance of Jesus the law was already fulfilled. Thus the covenant obligation became to keep the commandments "which he *has* given them." "Therefore blessed are ye if ye shall keep my commandments, which the Father hath commanded me that I should give unto you" (3 Nephi 18:14), namely the commandments found primarily in 3 Nephi 11–14. Furthermore, by this new covenant, people expressly affirm their desire to keep the commandments, beyond their willingness to enter into a covenant. Benjamin's people said: "We are willing *to enter* into a covenant with our God to do his will, and to be obedient to his commandments in all things that he *shall* command us" (Mosiah 5:5). In slightly more direct terms than Benjamin had used, Jesus explains in 3 Nephi 18 that with the partaking of the sacrament comes a "witness unto the Father that ye are willing *to do* that which I *have* commanded you" (3 Nephi 18:10).

Requirements of the covenant. The prayer in Moroni 4 lists three requirements: that the people (1) be willing to take upon them the name of Christ, (2) always remember him, and (3) keep his commandments. In these regards, the prayers in Moroni 4–5 are particularly close to Benjamin's speech. After Benjamin's people had promised that they were *willing* to do whatever might be the will or *command* of their God, King Benjamin imposed on them two requirements: (1) they should "take upon [them] the *name* of Christ" (Mosiah 5:8), and (2) they "should *remember* to retain the name written always in [their] hearts" (Mosiah 5:12). These aspects of the covenant appear in this same order in Moroni 4. The phrase *take upon them the name* does not appear in 3 Nephi 18; rather, baptism "in my name" is mentioned as a prerequisite to partaking of the sacrament (3 Nephi 18:5, 11). The presence of these phrases in Moroni 4, therefore, seems to look back even more literally to the covenant language of Benjamin than to the words in 3 Nephi 18.

Moreover, the three requirements of Benjamin's covenant have been consolidated in Moroni 4 into a shorter single text, whereas the bread and wine were administered by Jesus with separate requirements. The bread was given and received expressly as a "testimony unto the Father that ye do always remember me" (3 Nephi 18:7). The wine was ministered as a "witness unto the Father that ye are willing to do that which I have commanded you" (3 Nephi 18:10). With the wine, however, Moroni 5 only has the people witness that "they do always remember him"; keeping the commandments is mentioned explicitly only with respect to the bread in Moroni 4—by ellipsis it is assumed with respect to the wine. Having all these requirements in the first of the sacrament prayers in Moroni 4–5 may be another way in which Benjamin's pattern contributed to the shape and consolidation preserved in Moroni 4–5 of the words of Jesus in 3 Nephi 18. Moreover, Moroni 4 and 5 both end with the requirement that "they do always remember him." This was also the final condition imposed by Benjamin upon his people. Similarly, in conjunction with the fact that the last words Jesus spoke regarding the wine were "if ye do always remember me ye shall have my Spirit to be with you," this phrase was placed as the sole final aspect of the sacrament prayer on the wine.

On the other hand, it is possible that the order of the three requirements in Moroni 4 is related only to 3 Nephi 18. Baptism in the "name" of Christ appears in 3 Nephi 18:5 and is also mentioned in 18:11, 16, and 30; "always remembering" him appears in 18:7 and again in 18:11; and "keeping the commandments" is enjoined in 18:10 and likewise in

18:14. These three conditions are each mentioned at least twice in 3 Nephi 18:5–14, and they appear for the most part in the same order as they appear in Moroni 4. Although it is uncertain what specific influence either Benjamin's text or the words of Jesus may have had on the sequence of phrases in the text of Moroni 4, it is apparent that all three texts coalesce beautifully.

The promise. Finally, in the different promises extended to the people by Benjamin and Jesus, a shift in emphasis may be discerned. The promises of Benjamin were that God would seal the people his, that they would have "everlasting salvation and eternal life," and that they would be the beneficiaries of God's wisdom, power, justice, and mercy (see Mosiah 5:15). Benjamin's object was to bring well-being to his people "in heaven and in earth" (Mosiah 5:15). Benjamin's promise, therefore, was not just one of the companionship of the spirit. He promised life and munificence in God—a spiritual counterpart to the secular blessing of victory and prosperity which he had earlier promised to the people if they would be obedient to their new king, his son (see Mosiah 2:31).

By contrast, the promise extended by both prayers in Moroni 4–5 is that the people will have the spirit of Jesus "to be with them." This promise comes directly from the words of Jesus, spoken twice earlier in the Book of Mormon: "And if ye do always remember me ye shall have my Spirit to be with you" (3 Nephi 18:7, 11). These words of Jesus shift the blessing from a longer-term blessing of future salvation to a more immediate personal appreciation of the continual presence of Jesus among his righteous followers. Earlier the Nephites had hoped and prayed, in several sublime moments, to have "the love of God always" in their hearts (Alma 13:29), and they had experienced a number of outpourings of his Spirit on particular occasions (see Mosiah 4:20; Alma 16:16; 17:10;

19:36; Helaman 6:36). But the culminating blessing of always having the companionship of this Spirit came more intensely with the fulfillment of all things in Jesus.

Israelite Antecedents

The foregoing discussion suggests that the sacrament instituted by Jesus would not have seemed wholly unfamiliar to the believers at the temple in Bountiful. Their traditional covenant texts dating from the time of Benjamin set the stage well for their experience with Jesus and his sacrament. In addition to that Nephite background, even more ancient Israelite antecedents may have supplied further contextual prologues for 3 Nephi 18.

One fertile source of studying all Israelite rituals and symbols is the ancient temple. Since Nephite temples were modeled—at least at the outset—after the Temple of Solomon (2 Nephi 5:16) and were places where the Nephites strictly observed the ordinances of God according to the law of Moses (Alma 30:3),[10] one may well surmise that the Nephites had shewbread in their temples. It is possible that the table with twelve loaves of shewbread set before the Lord in the Israelite temple was a conscious antecedent of the Christian sacrament.[11] The shewbread of the temple was known as the *leḥem ha-pānîm* in Hebrew, literally the "bread of the face [or presence] of [God]," or as the *maʿăreket*, the bread "arrayed," and in Greek, *prothesis tōn artōn* or *hoi artoi tēs protheseos*, the bread "set forth."[12] Derived from this ancient typology, the text in Romans 3:25 describes Christ as one whom God "displayed publicly" (*proetheto*) as a propitiation. Similarly, the Nephites may also have seen a substantial relationship between the shewbread of their temple and the bread symbolizing Jesus' body which Jesus said he had *"shewn unto"* them (1st ed. 3 Nephi 18:7), or which he set forth before them. The ancient Israelite shewbread and the manna kept in a gold bowl in the temple have been widely recognized as early Jewish antecedents to the Christian sacrament.[13] Additionally, the shewbread of the ancient temple, like the bread of the sacrament of Jesus' presence among the Nephites, "provided both a sacrifice and a communion," since it was presented before God but also consumed by the priests.[14] For this reason the Nephites may have seen yet another connection between the bread that Jesus asked the Nephite twelve to bring and the ancient Israelite traditions of the twelve loaves of the shewbread, which custom may still have been observed at the Nephite temple in Bountiful.

Another ancient Israelite precedent may be found in Numbers 6:27. Here Moses, Aaron, and the sons of Aaron were told to bless the people of Israel (see Numbers 6:24–26) and were instructed to have the children of Israel take upon themselves the name of God: "And they shall *put my name upon the children of Israel*; and I will bless them."[15] This preexilic source may well have given literal scriptural support for what Benjamin did when he had his people take upon them the name of God. Indeed, the Israelites may have overtly taken upon themselves the name of God. Proverbs 6:20–21 admonishes, "My son, keep thy father's commandment, and forsake not the law of thy mother: Bind them continually upon thine heart, and tie them about thy neck." The recent discovery of small silver scrolls that were worn around the neck inscribed with the benediction from Numbers 6:24–26 and dating to the seventh century B.C. in Jerusalem may give us some idea of how literally the expressions of Numbers 6 and Proverbs 6 may have been carried out anciently (compare Deuteronomy 6:8; Proverbs 3:3; 7:2–3).

Additional antecedents for the Christian sacrament

have been sought by various scholars in other Jewish sources, including (1) the "pure offering"[16] or the "offering in righteousness" prophesied by Malachi (1:11; 3:3, quoted by Jesus in 3 Nephi 24:3 shortly after he introduced the sacrament for the second time to the Nephites), (2) the offering of Melchizedek (see Genesis 14:18–20),[17] (3) the messianic feast or ritual meal eaten by Moses and seventy elders on Mount Sinai (see Exodus 24:11) and expected by Isaiah (see Isaiah 55:1–3),[18] (4) the manna,[19] (5) the sacrificial blood of the Old Testament,[20] and (6) the *bərākhāh* or regular blessing on the food spoken in thanksgiving (*eucharistein*) by Jews before eating.[21] Another possibility is in Isaiah 49:26 (see 1 Nephi 21:26; 22:13; 2 Nephi 6:18), which prophesies that those who oppress the righteous shall be fed in defeat "with their own flesh; and they shall be drunken with their own blood, as with sweet wine." By this shall all flesh know "that I the Lord am thy Saviour and thy Redeemer, the mighty One of Jacob" (1 Nephi 21:26). Although Isaiah says that the wicked will be humiliated by having to eat their *own* flesh and blood, this scripture associates eating flesh and blood (which in the prophecy has the intoxicating effect of wine) with the people's recognition and confession that the Lord is their Savior and Redeemer. It is possible that the Nephites, therefore, would have connected their eating of the bread and wine—symbolizing *Christ's* flesh and blood—with this scripture, as they were spared the eating of their own flesh and saw and bore record that Jesus was their Redeemer (see 3 Nephi 16:4; 17:25).

The texts of the sacrament prayers in Moroni 4–5 have a rich and meaningful background. Whenever these prayers are read or heard, they should bring to mind the spiritual power of the words and ministrations of Jesus himself at the meridian of time in Palestine and in Bountiful and, before that, the enduring influence of the words of King Benjamin in Zarahemla. The continuity and consistency from Mosiah 5 to 3 Nephi 18 and to Moroni 4–5 reflects an inspired and detailed textual history, one that remarkably evinces precise usage of particular phrases over several centuries of religious experience, as well as several subtle transformations from earlier points of spiritual emphasis by incorporating the words and symbols of Israelite and Nephite religious experience into the Nephite covenant-making texts.

Notes

1. See "Our Nephite Sacrament Prayers," in *Reexploring the Book of Mormon*, ed. John W. Welch (Salt Lake City: Deseret Book and FARMS, 1992), 286–89.

2. For a discussion of the timing of this gathering, as well as the dilemma of the Nephites who would not have known what to do next at their temple, see John W. Welch, *The Sermon at the Temple and the Sermon on the Mount* (Salt Lake City: Deseret Book and FARMS, 1990), 27–32.

3. The relationship between 3 Nephi and Moroni 4–5 is discussed in detail in John W. Welch, "From Presence to Practice: Jesus, the Sacrament Prayers, the Priesthood, and Church Discipline in 3 Nephi and Moroni 2–6," *JBMS* 5/1 (1996): 119–39.

4. See the stirring prophecies of Mosiah 3 and the phrase "we could prophesy of all things" (Mosiah 5:3), along with the rejoicing of the people with "exceedingly great joy" (Mosiah 5:4), falling down to the earth (see Mosiah 4:1; compare also 3 Nephi 11:12), being blessed with a great spiritual change (Mosiah 5:2), and testifying of the surety and truth of the words which had been spoken (Mosiah 5:2).

5. Welch, "From Presence to Practice," 126.

6. This is not to imply that Benjamin or his people did not refer to God as "Father" before the covenant making reported in Mosiah 5. The early Nephites referred to God (sometimes with reference to Heavenly Father, other times with respect to Christ) as "Father," for example, in 1 Nephi 14:17; Jacob 7:22; Mosiah

2:34. From the point of view of the ceremonial text itself, however, Benjamin may have preferred to have the people refer to Christ as their Father only after the covenant with him was in place.

7. This appears to be reflected in the terminology they used. An exhaustive treatment of Nephite terminology regarding God has yet to be made. Consider, however, the following scriptures in which the language used is not quite as clear as it is in Moroni 4–5: Isaiah taught that Christ would be called the "everlasting father" (2 Nephi 19:6). Nephi referred to Jesus as "the eternal Father" (1 Nephi 11:21, original manuscript, printer's manuscript, and 1830 edition; 1 Nephi 13:40, printer's manuscript and 1830 edition). Later, when Nephi spoke of Jesus as the "only begotten of the Father," he followed this by calling Jesus "even the Father of heaven and of earth" (2 Nephi 25:12). Likewise, Abinadi knew Jesus Christ as "the very eternal Father" (Mosiah 15:4; 16:15)—and he articulated senses in which Jesus could be both Father and Son (Mosiah 15:2–3). The phrase "Father of heaven and earth" may be a euphemism for Creator of the physical universe. For King Benjamin, "the Lord Omnipotent" who reigneth, who would come down, namely Jesus Christ, was known as "the Son of God, the Father of heaven and earth, the Creator of all things from the beginning" (Mosiah 3:5, 8). See also Alma 11:39, where Amulek affirms, "Yea, he [the Son of God] is the very Eternal Father of heaven and of earth," and Helaman 14:12, in which Samuel the Lamanite uses Benjamin's formulaic title for Jesus Christ, "the Son of God, the Father of heaven and of earth, the Creator of all things from the beginning." Helaman's words in Helaman 5:11–12 especially show that the basic distinction between the "Father" and the "Son of God" was understood among the Nephites before the appearance of Jesus among the Nephites, despite any possible ambiguity in their terminology elsewhere.

8. The late Nephite texts of Mormon and Moroni most often use the appellation the *Eternal Father* for God the Father. Mormon, for example, speaks of the "Father" and of "the Son of the living God, . . . his most Beloved" (Mormon 5:14). Mormon and Moroni refer to God the Father several times as "the *Eternal* Father" (see

Mormon 6:22; Moroni 4:3; 5:2; 10:4; 10:31), distinguishing him from Jesus Christ, who, however, is also referred to as "Jesus Christ, even the Father and the Son" (Mormon 9:12).

9. For instance, the Nephites worshiped God (see Jacob 4:5), baptized (see Mosiah 18:10), and prayed (see 2 Nephi 32:9) in the name of Christ. The only explicit reference before 3 Nephi to "asking" and receiving in the name of Christ is in Enos 1:15.

10. See John W. Welch, "The Temple in the Book of Mormon: The Temples at the Cities of Nephi, Zarahemla, and Bountiful," in *Temples of the Ancient World*, ed. Donald W. Parry (Salt Lake City: Deseret Book and FARMS, 1994), 301–19.

11. Alfred Adam, "Ein vergessener Aspekt des frühchristlichen Herrenmahles," *Theologische Literaturzeitung* 88 (1963): 9–20, cited in Hugh W. Nibley, *Since Cumorah*, 2nd ed. (Salt Lake City: Deseret Book and FARMS, 1988), 454 n. 114.

12. Roland de Vaux, *Ancient Israel* (New York: McGraw-Hill, 1964), 2:422; see Hermann L. Strack and Paul Billerbeck, *Kommentar zum Neuen Testament aus Talmud und Midrasch* (Munich: Beck, 1954), 718–33, on the Epistle to the Hebrews and Jewish descriptions of the shewbread.

13. See generally John 6; Revelation 2:17; Hebrews 9:4; see also Luke 15:17; Frank S. Gavin, *The Jewish Antecedents of the Christian Sacraments* (New York: Ktav, 1969).

14. LDS Bible Dictionary, s.v. "shewbread."

15. See also Deuteronomy 28:10: "And all the people of the earth shall see that thou art called by the name of the Lord."

16. Edward J. Kilmartin, *The Eucharist in the Primitive Church* (Englewood Cliffs, N.J.: Prentice-Hall, 1964), 2–4.

17. Ibid., 4–6; see also John W. Welch, "The Melchizedek Material in Alma 13:13–19," in *By Study and Also by Faith*, ed. John M. Lundquist and Stephen D. Ricks (Salt Lake City: Deseret Book and FARMS, 1990), 2:253.

18. Kilmartin, *The Eucharist in the Primitive Church*, 6–12. Consider also the motif of the messianic banquet of salvation on the world mountain found in ancient Near Eastern literature, for example, UT 67, 137, Krt, cited in John W. Welch, ed., *Chiasmus in*

Antiquity (Hildesheim: Gerstenberg, 1981), 43; Joachim Jeremias, *Jesu Mission für die Völker* (Stuttgart: Franz-Delitzsch-Vorlesung, 1956), cited in Frank M. Cross, *Ancient Library of Qumran and Modern Biblical Studies*, rev. ed. (Garden City, N.Y.: Doubleday, 1961), 90–92, as Robert F. Smith has suggested to me.

19. Kilmartin, *The Eucharist in the Primitive Church*, 12–16.

20. Ibid., 16–19. On the symbolic meaning of blood and life in ancient Israel and in the ancient Near East generally, see Dennis McCarthy, "The Symbolism of Blood and Sacrifice," *JBL* 88/2 (1969): 166–76, and Dennis McCarthy, "Further Notes on the Symbolism of Blood and Sacrifice," *JBL* 92/2 (1973): 205–10, as Stephen Ricks has pointed out to me. Although the idea of ceremonially drinking wine as a symbol of blood may have been new to the Nephites, and while the eating or drinking of blood was almost certainly taboo among righteous Nephites (see Jarom 1:6), as it was among the Israelites generally (see Genesis 9), the Nephites may have known something of the idea of drinking blood in connection with making vows. The drinking of blood or the symbolic use of blood in covenant making and in uniting with the gods has a widespread history among many cultures, notably in ancient Mesoamerica; see generally H. Clay Trumbull, *The Blood Covenant: A Primitive Rite and Its Bearings on Scripture* (New York: Scribner's Sons, 1885). Perhaps blood was involved in the making of certain oaths in the Book of Mormon: Amalickiah swore an oath that he would drink Moroni's blood (Alma 49:27; 51:9); Giddianhi swore an oath that he would annihilate the Nephites (3 Nephi 3:8) and then led his armies "dyed in blood" (3 Nephi 4:7). The role of blood symbolism here deserves further investigation.

21. Gavin, *Jewish Antecedents of the Christian Sacraments*, 59–114.

CHAPTER 11

PARALLELISM AND CHIASMUS IN BENJAMIN'S SPEECH

John W. Welch

A stunning array of literary structures appears in Benjamin's speech, purposefully and skillfully organized. Benjamin's use of chiasmus, all types of parallelisms, and many other forms of repeating patterns adds focus and emphasis to the main messages and the persuasive qualities of this text. The following discussions and textual figures attempt to identify, catalogue, and explore the main organizational and structural features of Benjamin's speech.

Facts known to us about King Benjamin indicate that he was a sensitive and articulate man. As will become evident, he was the kind of person who was interested in making the effort to arrange his words into a careful, artistic form. His speech, given at the coronation of his son and as part of a high and holy convocation of his people, does not appear to have been delivered extemporaneously. It was well thought out and, before it was distributed by Benjamin in written form, his text appears to have been beautifully polished. In Mosiah 2–5, one finds some superb examples of high literary achievement.

Above all, studying the structure of Benjamin's speech enhances appreciation for this composition as a literary masterpiece. Writing can be appreciated in its own right only in light of the literary tools and ideals available to the author. So understood, Benjamin's speech stands as a monumental literary composition, which unfortunately has long been underestimated. Mark Twain, speaking of the Book of Mormon in general, once called it "chloroform in print."[1] Even Sidney B. Sperry, one of the most astute Book of Mormon scholars of the previous generation, saw little literary value in Benjamin's text: "One likes to believe that King Benjamin was in effect the Wilford Woodruff of his time, a leader, a hard worker with his hands, a very spiritual man, but not an outstanding writer or orator."[2] In one sense, these commentators may be right: judged by the literary standards of Mark Twain's day or by the notions of modern rhetoric, Benjamin's speech may not measure up. But judged in light of the ancient conventions and stylistic preferences that were evidently operative in Benjamin's day, his speech shines again as it did on the ceremonious day when these words were spoken and received in public.

Parallelism and Repetition in General

Dominant features of Benjamin's style are parallelism and repetition. At least fourteen types of parallelism appear throughout the three chapters. Speaking of the style of parallelism, James Muilenburg has said:

> Persistent and painstaking attention to the modes of Hebrew literary composition will reveal that the pericopes exhibit linguistic patterns, word formations ordered or arranged in particular ways, verbal sequences which move in fixed structures from beginning to end. It is clear that they have been skillfully wrought in many different

ways, often with consummate skill and artistry. It is also apparent that they have been influenced by conventional rhetorical practices.[3]

King Benjamin created parallelisms to achieve a harmony or synthesis of his ideas. Donald W. Parry has demonstrated that "the Book of Mormon is replete with parallelisms. The poetic patterns serve, as they do in the Bible, to emphasize messages, define and expand them, make them more memorable, and structure them."[4] Over fifty times throughout his speech, Benjamin employed simple or extended synthetic parallelism, which is composed of two or more lines, the additional lines providing emphasis, explanation, or synthesis of the initial thought. Therefore, the idea or concept in the first phrase "thus receive[s] a double emphasis (the fundamental effect of most parallelisms)."[5] Muilenburg explains: "The parallel line does not simply repeat what has been said, but enriches it, deepens it, transforms it by adding fresh nuances and bringing in new elements, renders it more concrete and vivid and telling."[6]

Benjamin's speech features techniques such as simple and extended synonymy; simple, repeated, and extended alternates; synthetic parallelisms; climax, anabasis, catabasis; contrasting ideas and antithetical parallelism; detailing and working out. I will not take space here to define these varieties of parallelism, since basic definitions are readily available[7] and the rhetorical effect of each parallelism is fairly obvious once the arrangement is pointed out. A few illustrations and observations will be given here, and a full index of Benjamin's parallelisms appears below.

A prevalent stylistic form that King Benjamin drew on is simple, direct parallelism. For example, Mosiah 2:18 (all scriptural references in this study, unless otherwise noted, are to Mosiah) says,

a Behold, ye have *called* me your *king;*
a And if I, whom ye *call* your *king,*
  b do *labor* to *serve* you,
  b then ought not ye to *labor* to *serve* one another?

This passage is an example of poetic parallelism, or "words, phrases, or sentences that correspond, compare, contrast, or repeat."[8]

Likewise, Benjamin effectively taught the principle of humility by using synthetic parallelism in 2:24:

[God] doth immediately bless you; and therefore he hath paid you.
And ye are still indebted unto him, and are, and will be, forever and ever.

Benjamin's main thought in this passage was that God has been abundantly generous to his people, and through extended synthetic parallelism he went on to explain that people should show humility and gratitude on account of those many blessings.

Other types of parallelism in Benjamin's speech include antithetical parallelism:

ye will not have a mind to injure one another,
but to live peaceably (4:13);

alternates:

a the greatness of God,
  b and your own nothingness,
a and his goodness and long-suffering towards you,
  b unworthy creatures (4:11);

and contrasting ideas, such as yielding to the natural man versus becoming a saint (see 3:19). The feature of contrasting is most evident in Benjamin's parallelisms.

Another important feature of Benjamin's style consists of his repetition of key words that reverberate through the text and seem to be further evidence of deliberate organization. The index found at the end of this chapter, among other things, provides evidence of certain themes that echo through the speech. Such repeating themes provide continuity and structure to King Benjamin's message and again form an indication of structure. For example, the phrase *list to obey* occurs several times in section 2 of the speech (for definitions and descriptions of the seven main section divisions, see below). The concept of Benjamin's calling as king in 2:19 finds an echo in 2:26. Contention, serving the evil spirit, and becoming an enemy to all righteousness are themes that are found in section 2 and that surface again in section 4. The concept of the innocence or salvation of children appears three times in the speech. Keeping the commandments arises in sections 1, 2, 5, and 6. Remembrance characterizes sections 2, 5, 6, and 7; and salvation through Christ is a thread that runs through five of the seven sections: 3, 4, 5, 6, and 7.

Repetition is also an effective tool in Benjamin's teachings. Structures such as duplication ("remember, remember"), chiasmus, many *ands*, or even random repetition or the repetition of certain themes or key words that reverberate through the speech, all contribute to the stylistic continuity and coherence of Benjamin's message.

Chiasmus

Probably the most interesting literary device used in Benjamin's speech is the variety of parallelism known as chiasmus. The technique of presenting one set of words or ideas in one order and then retracing them in the opposite order operates in this text on several levels: in major structures, in extended word patterns, and also in smaller, simpler configurations. Benjamin's speech lends itself unusually well to chiastic analysis.

Chiasmus is a tool that has been appealed to quite commonly in recent years by literary analysts in studying the texts of the Bible and other literature. In light of that research, one may readily conclude that Benjamin's speech was composed with measured artistic control and with sustained precision, to as great an extent as one may find anywhere in the Old or New Testaments, or elsewhere in the Book of Mormon, in classical literature, or in any other composition written anciently when chiasmus was widely in use.[9] As such, Benjamin's composition deserves high praise and literary acclaim.

Defining Chiasmus

Before turning to Benjamin's text itself, a few introductory comments about chiasmus may be helpful. Literary analysis of this nature must be conducted cautiously if overstatement and misunderstanding are to be avoided. The following discussion briefly summarizes the characteristics of chiasmus and refers the reader to further publications on this subject.

One of the first steps is defining chiasmus. Chiasmus is the literary technique of creating double structures in which the second half of a composition mirrors and balances the first half, but in reverse order. In general, the device is useful for several literary purposes, especially for concentrating attention on the main point of the passage by placing it at the central turning point rather than in a topic sentence at the beginning of a paragraph, as is the trend with modern writers. King Benjamin was particularly effective in creating chiastic structures. Many of his chiasms have one clear central point (see 2:27; 3:11–16; 4:6–7; 5:6–8), while others contain a focal point of two or more lines, forming a parallelism at the center of the chiasm. One may assume that chiasmus served Benjamin's purposes in several ways, for it can aid memorization, teach by means of calculated repetition, and confer a sense of completeness or closure to a lengthy textual development. Chiastic structures can also convey the meaning of a passage in many ways beyond the meanings of isolated words and individual phrases.

In many cases the use of chiasmus is a conscious choice, but it need not always be intentional. Poets, authors, composers, and musicians create artistic works without being aware of every facet of their compositions. When the degree and precision of chiastic repetition is high enough, however—as in 3:18–19 and 5:10–12—it is likely that the author was aware of its existence. Thus it is plausible that Homer and the Homeric bards were aware that when Odysseus in the underworld asks the shade of his mother Anticleia seven things, she responds by addressing these seven questions in exactly the reverse order.[10] Nevertheless, one cannot speak with absolute certitude in attributing intentionality in all such cases.

When does it make sense to speak of a passage as being chiastic or not? Passages can manifest varying degrees of "chiasticity." Some passages are short, and their inverted order is obvious and noncontroversial. For example, Genesis 1:27 reads, "[a] God created man [b] in his own image; [b] in the image of God [a] created he him." The a–b–b–a order here is objectively verifiable. At least ten a–b–b–a chiasms occur in Benjamin's speech, while other parts of the text are longer, or the structure is less certain. Thus one must work and think in terms of degrees of chiasticity.[11]

Several conditions should be satisfied before one can speak meaningfully of chiasmus in a given passage. The more a particular text fulfills these criteria, the higher its degree of chiasticity. Chiasms are stronger when they consist of elements that are objectively observable in the text, when they are apparently placed in a passage intentionally for stylistic purposes, and if they are the dominant forms that operate across a literary unit as a whole and not merely upon fragments or sections that overlap or cut across significant organizational lines in the text. For example, the inverted parallel orders should be relatively self-evident in the passage. Many chiasms in Benjamin's speech consist of elements that are indeed objectively observable in the text and do not require imaginative explanations. Benjamin's text divides clearly into several distinct units within which his chiasms are found. Some of these patterns are quite solid: the strong structural chiasms are sections 1, 3, 5, and 7; weaker structural chiasmus may be found in the remaining sections—2, 4, and 6.

Strong extended chiasmus at the verbal level is found in 3:18–19, 5:10–12, and a few other places. These chiasms exhibit balance—having elements on both sides of the proposed focal point nearly equal in terms of number of words, lines, or elements—and create a convincing sense of return and completion from the beginning to the end. Similarly, the more compact the chiasm—or the fewer irrelevancies between its elements—and the longer the chiasm, the higher its degree of chiasticity. Benjamin has many examples of strong chiasmus throughout his speech.

Chiasmus is a dominant feature in a text when it is the only structuring device present, as appears to be the case in several passages in Benjamin's speech (see, for example, 2:26; 3:18–19). Of course, a powerful structural design revolves around major concepts, unique phrases, or focal words, and in some instances the only occurrences of a word or phrase in the Book of Mormon are found in two chiastically matched parts of Benjamin's speech ("natural man" 3:19; "have and are" 2:34 and 4:21; "left hand" 5:10 and 12). Moreover, because the crux of chiasmus falls generally at its central turning point,[12] it is significant that Benjamin often placed a well-defined centerpiece at the heart of his chiastic structures. These features also work comfortably and compatibly with his overall style, in which other forms of parallelism are also found. Many factors like these give evidence of a high degree of chiasticity in Benjamin's speech. His application of this form was fluid, consistent, and well balanced, yet it does not draw undue attention to itself.

Of course, chiasmus is not exclusive to ancient Hebrew texts, but has also been found in Akkadian, Ugaritic, Egyptian, Aramaic, Greek, and Latin texts.[13] Although chiasmus occurs in many ancient works of literature, and also to an extent in modern authors, it is employed more extensively and purposefully in the Hebrew Bible than anywhere else. Complex chiasms, such as those identified in Benjamin's speech, are recognized as a fairly salient characteristic of ancient Hebrew composition.[14]

All writers in the Book of Mormon do not use chiasmus equally. Benjamin and Alma appear to have employed it the most.[15] They lived in a golden era of Nephite civilization, when great creative forces in literature, politics, theology, law, calendar, weights and measures, and military technology were at work among the Nephites, and it would follow that chiastic writing would also flower among the Nephite authors at this time. But even prophets like Benjamin and Alma did not write chiastically all the time; chiasm was only one of several literary devices at their disposal.

Some chiasms are lost in the translation process, but larger chiastic patterns and parallelisms are usually preserved; the Book of Mormon is no exception to this rule. Of all poetical devices, extended chiasms and parallelisms are among the most likely to survive a translation. Although our knowledge is somewhat limited in this regard, it appears that several of these structures were faithfully preserved through Joseph Smith's translation process.

In Joseph Smith's day, not much was known about chiasmus. In England, two authors had written books in the 1820s about Hebrew literature in the Bible, and they explored the possibility of chiasmus in the Bible. But the idea took root slowly, and it was not until much later that biblical commentators endorsed chiasmus. Furthermore, those pioneering volumes of the 1820s do not seem to have found their way to the United States by Joseph Smith's day.[16] And even if they did, there is no evidence that Joseph Smith was aware of them. The chance that Joseph Smith unconsciously assimilated chiasmus through his familiarity with the Bible assumes a great deal about literary osmosis.

What does the presence of chiasmus in the Book of Mormon prove?[17] Although one cannot know absolutely whether Benjamin intentionally created the chiastic patterns observable in his speech, or whether they emerged as something second nature to his way of thinking and writing, the presence of various forms of parallelism and chiasm in Benjamin's speech is significant in any literary evaluation of its qualities. It demonstrates that this text was composed carefully, meticulously, purposefully, and elegantly, in a manner consistent with the basic parallelistic norms of ancient Hebrew style.

With these general principles in mind, the following thematic outlines and detailed configurations of the complete text of Benjamin's speech offer one possible approach to displaying and organizing all the words and concepts that comprise this literary document. Of course, other approaches to formatting this text are possible, but this particular proposal seems to me to offer several advantages and strengths of consistency and comprehensiveness.

The Main Divisions of Benjamin's Text

In overview, it is apparent that Benjamin's text divides naturally into seven sections, which are demarcated either by intervening ceremony or by abrupt shifts in subject matter. As can be seen below, after the preliminary account of preparations for the speech, section 1 (found in 2:9–28) is separated from section 2 (2:31–41) by the coronation ceremony itself (2:29–30). Between sections 2 and 3 (the latter of which is 3:2–10), Benjamin began as if anew: "And again my brethren I would call your attention [almost as if they had taken a break or he had lost their attention], for I have somewhat more to speak unto you" (3:1). After section 4 (covering 3:11–27), the people fall to the ground and are forgiven of their sins (4:1–3) in a purification ceremony. And after sections 5 and 6 (4:4–12 and 4:13–30, respectively) and before the final section 7 (namely, 5:6–15), the people enter into a covenant to continue living according to the will of God and to be obedient to the commandments, thereby honoring the new kings who should command them for the remainder of their days (5:1–5). Only the boundaries between sections 3 and 4 and between sections 5 and 6 are not delineated by explicit pronouncements. These, however, are formed by shifts in meaning and focus that are largely dictated by the fact that section 3 is the angel's testimony of the life of Jesus and section 5 is Benjamin's testimony of the necessity of faith in Jesus. The shift from section 3 to 4 is from a focus on Christ and his atonement to a focus on mankind and what mankind must do in order to take advantage of the atonement; the shift from section 5 to section 6 is basically from faith to works: again, from believing in God to acting consonant with that belief.

Overview of Benjamin's Speech

Preparations (1:1–2:8)
> Successor named and new name to be given
> People gathered but not yet numbered
> Tower constructed

1. All are indebted to God (2:9–28)

> God is the heavenly king
> God has physically created and sustains all people
> People should serve and thank God
> The hope of exaltation after death

First break (2:29–30)
> Coronation announcement

2. Consequences of obedience or disobedience (2:31–41)

> Obedience brings victory and prosperity
> Prohibition of contention (2:32)
> Rebellion and disobedience bring pain and anguish
> All are eternally indebted to heavenly Father

Second break (2:41–3:1)
> Remember, remember, the Lord has spoken
> Benjamin calls again for attention

3. The angel's testimony of Christ's deeds (3:2–10)

> Lord Omnipotent will come down in power and
>   goodness
> The sacred name of God
> The suffering and death of Jesus Christ

4. Sanctification by the atonement of Christ (3:11–27)

> The only possibility of reconciliation
> Putting off the natural man and becoming a saint
> People will be judged according to their works

Third break (3:27–4:4)
   Thus has the Lord commanded, Amen
   The people fall to the ground and confess
   Atoning blood is applied; joy and remission
   Benjamin begins to speak again

5. Benjamin's testimony of God's goodness (4:4–12)

   God is good, patient, long-suffering
   Believe in God
   God is all powerful, loving, and glorious
   Call upon the name of the Lord daily

6. Righteous behavior of the redeemed (4:13–30)

   Living in peace and social order
   Prohibition of contention (4:14)
   Because God imparts, all must give to those in
      need
   Avoid guilt and sin

Fourth break (4:30–5:6)
   Remember, and perish not
   Covenant response of the people
   Benjamin accepts their covenant

7. The sons and daughters of God (5:6–15)

   God has spiritually begotten you this day
   The only head to make you free from debt
   Excommunication upon breach of obligations
   Covenant people know God by serving him
   The hope of exaltation after death

Final acts (6:1–3)
   Names recorded of all who accepted the name
   Mosiah consecrated
   Priests appointed
   People dismissed

Although the interrelationships between these sections will not be discussed until their full texts have been examined below, the nature of the three ceremonies conducted during the course of the speech deserve attention at the outset. In the first ceremony, Mosiah₂ (Benjamin's son) was given charge over the people as their king and commander (2:29–30). In the second, staged at the middle of the speech, all the people were cleansed and forgiven of their wrongs (4:1–4).[18] The third placed the people under the obligation of covenant to obey the commandments of God (5:1–5) or, in other words, to obey the commandments given of the new king (2:31). Thus the pattern of the ceremonies is a–b–a, namely, establishing the king over the people, cleansing the people, establishing the people under the king. Therefore, the entire ceremony was more than just a coronation; it was a ritual that recognizes the reciprocity of relations and responsibilities between a ruler and his subjects, involving the entire nation, its purity, and its duty of civil obedience.

Certain general balances are achieved in the broad structure of these seven sections. First, their length is consistent: there are three long sections (1, 4, 6) containing 20, 17, and 18 verses respectively, and four short sections (2, 3, 5, 7) with 11, 9, 9, and 10 verses each. Second, the direction regularly alternates between expressing man's ultimate subservience to the king in heaven (1, 3, 5, 7) and formulating a humanistic basis of ethical behavior (2, 4, 6). In section 1, man was instructed to thank his heavenly king for the ultimate blessings of life; in 3, the ministry of Christ the King was prophesied; in 5, Benjamin testified of God; and in 7, the people took upon themselves the name of Christ through a covenant. In the even-numbered sections, however, the attention is directed to man, his accountability for his rebellious state, the necessity of putting off his natural state, and becoming charitable. We now turn to an analysis of the organization and structure of each of these seven individual sections.

Section 1

Outline. Benjamin started his speech with introductory material explaining why he had gathered the people together, and he reminded them—in chiastic form—of their responsibilities as citizens of the land and as subjects of God.

> A Purpose of the assembly
>   B What is man?
>   C The laws in Benjamin's kingdom
>   D Man cannot boast of service to fellowmen
>   E Imperatives to serve one another and thank God
>   D' Man cannot boast of service to God
>   C' The laws in God's kingdom
>   B' What is man?
> A' Purpose of the assembly

From the very beginning, then, Benjamin introduced his main form of organization—chiasmus—and also the fundamental point of his speech: people on earth are involved in a crucial relationship with God and with each other.

Detailed Analysis. When looking at the words and phrases in Benjamin's speech, one can readily see certain important elements. Many of the formal structural patterns found in the index below are found in this section: simple synonymous (2:9, ye that have assembled yourselves together, you that can hear my words), extended synonymous (2:11, chosen by this people, consecrated by my father, was suffered by the hand of the Lord), simple alternate (2:22, all that he requires of you is to keep his commandments and he has promised you that if ye would keep his commandments), detailing (2:14, why he has labored), climactic forms (2:9, 11, 13–14, etc.), like paragraph endings (2:16–17), repetition and duplication of words, and many other forms, including, of course, chiasmus. The full text of section 1 can be displayed as follows:

A Purpose of the assembly

2:9   a My brethren all ye that have *assembled yourselves together*[19]
      b you that can hear my *words which I shall speak* unto you this day
  a For I have not *commanded you to come up hither*
      b to trifle with the *words which I shall speak*

    1 but that you should hearken unto me
    2 and open your ears that ye may hear
    3 and your hearts that ye may understand
    4 and your minds that the mysteries of God may be unfolded to your view

2:10 a I have not *commanded you to come up hither*[20] that ye should fear me

B What is man?

  a Or that ye should think that *I of myself*[21]
      b am more than a *mortal man*[22]
2:11 a But I am *like as yourselves*[23]
      b subject to all manner of infirmities in *body and mind*

    1 Yet I have been chosen by this *people*
    2 and consecrated by *my father*
    3 and was suffered by the hand of *the Lord*
    4 that I should be a ruler and a king[24] over this *people*

And have been kept and preserved by his matchless power to serve you with all the might, mind, and strength[25] which the Lord hath granted unto me

C The laws in Benjamin's kingdom

2:12 a *I say* unto you that
    b as I have been suffered to spend *my days*
      c in your *service*
        d even up to *this time*
          e and have not sought *gold nor silver*
            f nor *any manner* of riches of you

2:13 1 Neither have I suffered that ye should be confined in dungeons
2 nor that ye should make slaves one of another
3 nor that ye should murder
4 or plunder
5 or steal
6 or commit adultery
7 nor even have I suffered that ye should commit any manner of wickedness
8 and have taught you that ye should keep the commandments of the Lord in all things which he hath commanded you

2:14 b And even I myself have labored with *mine own hands*[26]
  c that I might *serve* you
    e and that ye should not be laden with *taxes*
      f and that there should *nothing* come upon you which was grievous to be borne
a and of all these things which *I have spoken*
  d ye yourselves are witnesses *this day*

D Man cannot boast of service to fellowmen

2:15 a Yet, my brethren, I have not *done these things*[27] that I might *boast*
b neither do I *tell* these things that thereby I might *accuse* you
b but I *tell* you these things that ye may know that I can *answer* a clear conscience before God this day
2:16 a Behold I say unto you that because I said unto you that I had spent my days *in your service* I do not desire to *boast*[28]

a for I have *only* been *in the service of God*
2:17 b and behold I *tell* you these things that ye may *learn* wisdom
b that ye may *learn* that
a when ye are in the service of your fellow beings ye are *only in the service of* your *God*[29]

E Imperatives to serve one another and thank God

2:18 a Behold ye have called me *your king*
a and *if I whom ye call your king*
  b do *labor to serve* you
    c then *ought* not ye
  b to *labor to serve* one another?

2:19 a And behold also *if I whom ye call your king*
     b who has spent his days in your *service*
     b and yet has been in the *service* of God
       d do merit any *thanks* from you
      c O how you *ought*
      d to *thank*
  a *your heavenly King!*[30]

D' Man cannot boast of service to God

2:20 a I say unto *you* my brethren
     b that if you should render all the *thanks* and *praise*[31]
      c which your *whole soul* has power to possess

1 to that God who has *created you*
2 and has kept and *preserved you*
3 and has caused that ye should rejoice
4 and has granted that ye should *live* in peace one with another

2:21 a I say unto *you*
     b that if ye should *serve* him

5 who has *created you* from the beginning
6 and is *preserving you* from day to day
7 by lending you breath that ye may *live* and move and do according to your own will
8 and even supporting you from one moment to another[32]

     b I say if ye should *serve* him
      c with all your *whole souls*
  a yet *ye* would be unprofitable servants

C' The laws in God's kingdom

2:22 a And behold *all* that he requires of you is to keep his commandments
     b and *he has promised* you
      c that *if ye would keep his commandments*
       d ye should *prosper* in the land

  a and he *never* doth vary[33]
     b from that which *he hath said*
      c therefore *if ye do keep his commandments*
       d he doth bless you and *prosper* you

B' What is man?

2:23 And now in the first place
    he hath *created you*[34]
    and *granted*[35] unto you your lives
    for which ye are *indebted* unto him

2:24 And secondly he doth require
    that ye should do as he hath commanded you
    for which if ye do
      he doth immediately *bless you*
      and therefore he hath *paid* you[36]
      and ye are still *indebted* unto him[37]
    and are and will be forever and ever[38]
    Therefore of what have ye to boast?[39]

2:25 a And now *I ask*
    b can ye *say* aught of yourselves?
    a *I answer* you,
    b Nay. Ye cannot *say*[40]

    a that ye are even as much as the *dust of the earth*
      b yet ye were *created*
    a of the *dust of the earth* but behold *it belongeth*[41]
      b to him who *created* you

2:26 And I, even I, whom ye call your king[42]
    am no better than ye yourselves are[43]
    a for I am also of the *dust*
      b and ye behold that I am *old*
      b and am about to yield up this *mortal* frame[44]
    a to its mother *earth*[45]

A' Purpose of the assembly

2:27 Therefore as I said unto you that I had served you walking with a clear conscience[46] before God, even so I at this time *have caused that ye should assemble yourselves together*

1 that I might be found blameless
2 and that your *blood* should not come upon me when I shall stand to be *judged* of God of the things whereof he hath commanded me concerning you

2:28 I say unto you that I *have caused that ye should assemble yourselves together*

   3 that I might rid my garments of your *blood* at this period of
   time when I am about to *go down* to my grave
   4 that I might *go down* in peace and my immortal spirit may
   join the choirs above in singing the praises of a *just* God.[47]

Comments. Benjamin used a number of rhetorical techniques in section 1. One is balancing the equivalent words
and phrases. For example, "service" and "riches" in the first
part of C balance "serve" and "taxes" in the second part of
C. In E and D', serving fellowman and God balances thanking and praising God. The association between service and
thanksgiving was probably closer in Benjamin's mind than
it is in ours, since ancient Semitic languages speak of thanks
more in terms of grateful love, blessing, or praise (compare
2:20), which was to be rendered as service was rendered.[48]
Effective contrasts are also achieved in C, C', and E by
means of the contraposition of the king on earth against the
king in heaven.

   We also encounter here frequent emphatic uses of
quadripartite arrangements. Such figures are central in A,
B, C (twice), D' (twice), and A', and are consistently present
throughout the speech. This is not surprising, since four-
part arrangements are compatible with all parallel schemes.

   The continuity of this section was enhanced by Benjamin's astute bridging from one thought to the next. After
the initial order had been established from A to E, Benjamin
retreated, connecting each step with a previous one. In E,
two points were made, that man should serve his fellowman and that man should render thanks to his God. In D'
the same ideas appear, but in the reverse order. The central
quatrains of D' describe the source of man's indebtedness
and, as such, they prepare the audience for the interrogato-

ries of B'. The transition from C' to B' focuses on mortality, which leads back to Benjamin's preparations for his death and hence to the very purpose of the assembly in A'.

The chiastic outline exposes the development of Benjamin's thoughts as well as his style. When Benjamin repeated, he not only inverted but intensified what had previously been said. Accordingly, A' adds a new dimension to A, for he first tells the purpose of the assembly from the audience's viewpoint by indicating to them what they could expect to do and to receive at the assembly, but the second explains the purpose of the assembly from Benjamin's perspective and outlines his own purposes. Subsection B is a humble statement to be made by a king, but it is not nearly as abasing as the statements in B'. In B man is simply a mortal being subject to infirmities, while in B' he is irreparably in debt to God and is less than the dust of the earth. In C the topic is the civil order in Benjamin's kingdom, but in C' the operation of obligations under God's kingship is described. D asserts (and this is often misunderstood) that one cannot boast a record of service to other people because all service is unavoidably service to God.[49] D' then adds the further humiliation that one cannot boast a record of service to God because, despite our most diligent efforts, we are all unprofitable servants to him.

The turning point at E contains the two moral imperatives—to serve one another and to thank God—written in concise parallel form. The logic of verses 2:18–19 is discussed below in conjunction with similar reasoning found at 4:21. The shift that occurs at the center of this section moves from giving an accounting of benefits, which had been received by Benjamin (B) or by the people (C, D), to becoming profoundly aware of the obligations of gratitude and dependence that derive from the receipt of those blessings (D', B').

The ultimate reciprocation and fulfillment of these obligations does not, however, enter the ceremony until the covenant is consummated in section 7.

Section 2

Outline. In section 2, Benjamin explains in further detail the relationship between God and his children and the consequences of rebellion.

F Temporal blessings of obedience
 G Willful rebellion against God condemned
  H The accountability of the people
 G' Willful rebellion against God condemned
F' Eternal blessings of obedience

This section's central point, as seen in its chiastic structure, is the accountability of the people to their creator. Benjamin's purpose was to turn the focus of his people from the temporal blessings of obedience to the more important eternal blessings of dwelling in the presence of God and having "never-ending happiness" (2:41).

Detailed Analysis. The second section of the speech employs various arrangements of chiastic and alternating lines to create a meaningful formal basis on which a systematically complete message is imposed. The execution of chiasmus in this instance is carried out with substantial accuracy and, indeed, with several noteworthy variations that promote cohesion in the transitions from one subsection to the next. Benjamin showcased his versatility here, since while subduing the distinction between human and divine institutions that dominated the chiastic augmentations in the first section, he proceeded to new contrasts to display his thoughts.

F Temporal blessings of obedience

2:31 And now my brethren I would that ye should do as ye have hitherto done

a₁ As ye have kept *my* commandments
a₂ and also the commandments of *my father*
  b₁ and have *prospered*
  b₂ and have been kept from falling into the hands of your *enemies*
a₁ even so if ye shall keep the commandments of *my son*
a₂ or the commandments of *God* which shall be delivered unto you by him
  b₁ ye shall *prosper* in the land
  b₂ and your *enemies* shall have no power over you.

G Willful rebellion against God condemned

2:32 But, O my people, beware lest there shall arise contentions among you[50]

a and ye *list to obey*[51] the *evil spirit*[52]
  b which was *spoken*[53] of by my father Mosiah
2:33   b for behold there is a wo *pronounced* upon him
a who *listeth to obey* that *spirit*

for if he *listeth to obey* him
and *remaineth and dieth* in his sins
the same drinketh *damnation* to his own soul[54]
for he receiveth for his wages an *everlasting punishment*

H The accountability of the people

a having *transgressed* the law of God *contrary* to his own knowledge
2:34   b I say unto you that there are not any among you except it be your little children that have not been *taught* concerning *these things*
    c but what *knoweth*
      d that ye are eternally indebted to your heavenly *Father*
        e to render to him all that you *have* and *are*

2:35

　　　　1 and also have been *taught* concerning the records
　　　　which contain the *prophecies*
　　　　2 which have been *spoken* by the holy *prophets*
　　　　3 even down to the time our *father* Lehi left Jerusa-
　　　　lem
　　　　4 and also all that has been spoken by our *fathers*
　　　　until now[55]

　　d and behold also they spake that which was com-
　　manded them of the *Lord*
　　e therefore they are *just* and *true*[56]

2:36　c and now I say unto you my brethren that after ye have
　　known
　　b and have been *taught* all *these things*
　a if ye should *transgress* and go *contrary* to that which has
　been spoken

G' Willful rebellion against God condemned

　a that ye do *withdraw* yourselves from the Spirit of the Lord
　　b that it may have *no place* in you
　　　c to guide you in *wisdom's paths* that ye may be blessed,
　　　prospered, and preserved
2:37　　　d I say unto you that the man that doeth this the same
　　　cometh out in open *rebellion against God*[57]
　　　d' therefore he *listeth to obey the evil spirit*
　　　c' and becometh an enemy to all *righteousness*
　　b' therefore the Lord has *no place* in him
　a' for he *dwelleth not* in unholy temples

2:38　a therefore if that man repenteth not and *remaineth and dieth*
　　an enemy to God
　　b the demands of divine *justice* do awaken
　　　c his immortal soul to a lively sense of his own *guilt*
　　　which doth cause him to shrink from the presence of
　　　the Lord
　　　c' and doth fill his breast with *guilt* and pain and anguish
　　　which is like an unquenchable fire whose flame as-
　　　cendeth up forever and ever
2:39　　b' and now I say unto you that *mercy* hath no claim on that
　　man
　a' therefore his *final doom* is to endure a never-ending tor-
　ment[58]

F' Eternal blessings of obedience

2:40 O all ye old men and also ye young men and you little children who can understand my words[59]

a For I have *spoken* plainly unto you that ye might understand
b I pray that ye should awake to a *remembrance* of the awful situation of those that have fallen into transgression.
2:41 c and moreover I would desire that ye should consider on the *blessed* and *happy* state of those that keep the commandments[60] of *God*
c' for behold they are *blessed* in all things both temporal and spiritual[61] and if they hold out faithful to the end they are received into heaven that thereby they may dwell with *God* in a state of *never-ending*[62] *happiness*.
b' O *remember, remember* that these things are true
a' For the Lord God hath *spoken* it.

Comments. We can first observe that the general tone of this section is not negative or pessimistic, even though a fair amount of its material would add punch to any hellfire sermon. That material, however, does not occupy the prime positions of dominance in the balance of this passage. The middle and the extremes of section 2 are promissory, optimistic, and promote the righteous desires of the subjects to continue living in civil and spiritual obedience. The negative topics are introduced to create rhetorical opposition and emphasis.

The theme of section 2 is introduced in subsection F, directly following the coronation of Mosiah$_2$: the king promises victory and prosperity in reciprocation for loyalty and obedience. Subsection F is essentially an eight-line double structure naming four lawgivers, namely Benjamin, his father Mosiah$_1$, his heir Mosiah$_2$, and God. For Benjamin, political orders were sanctioned by two sources: the inherited right and the divine right. Thus Mosiah$_1$ stood to Benjamin as God stood to Mosiah$_2$ as the respective sources of these two sovereign rights (lines a$_2$). In b$_1$ and b$_2$ the blessings of the monarchy were reinstated in a continuation from the kingship of Benjamin to the reign of his son. Perpetuity of legal powers from one administration to the next is the crucial aspect of any succession.

In subsection F, physical blessings alone occupy the attention of the orator; but in F', he was concerned about blessings "in all things both temporal and spiritual." Subsection F', though not engaged in assuring the succession of the king's rights, is devoted to increasing the subjects' propensity to obey. Benjamin prayed that the people would remember the consequences of disobedience. The central lines in F' contrast the awful situation of those who disobey with the blessed and happy state of the righteous. Two lines (c and c') then repeat "blessed" and "happy," words that appear at the center of the first line, with the interesting gravitation of "blessed" toward the beginning of the following line and that of "never-ending happiness" toward the end of the same line. In good chiastic passages, frequently accentuated words tend to gravitate to opposite extremes of corresponding lines; this is a minor point, but it is in the details that art must meticulously measure up. In addition, "blessed" and "happy" in F' balance the ideas of prosperity and victory in F; Benjamin's words, contrasted with those of God in F', harmonize with the posture of the lawgivers in F. Thus F and F' form a well-matched pair in both content and structure. F' is slightly more elaborate, but this is the result of the impulse to embellish the second of each pair as it elevates the original idea. This elevation consistently occurs in section 2, since both F' and G' are considerably more elaborate than F and G.

Subsection G features a short chiastic section, followed by four lines that mention listing to obey the evil spirit, remaining and dying in sins, damnation, and everlasting punishment as coterminal ideas.

Subsection G introduces the topics that receive greater

treatment in G'. The bond between them is secured by the reoccurrence of the four elements: listing to obey the evil spirit, "remaineth and dieth" in opposition to God, the guilt and anguish of damnation, and a final doom. The first part of G' by itself exhibits a fine chiastic composition, made most apparent by the repetition of "no place" (b and b'). Significant is the association of "withdraw[ing] yourselves from the Spirit of the Lord"—which is done voluntarily, with the withdrawal of the Spirit—which is necessary, "for he dwelleth not in unholy temples" (a and a'). Being guided in wisdom's path is the obverse of following the evil spirit into antagonism against righteousness. The center of G' declares that a man who willingly withdraws from the spirit is in open rebellion against God. Thus the logic of the passage is: if you withdraw from God he must withdraw from you, for without any guidance of wisdom you become an enemy of all that is good, and this means you stand in rebellion against God. The "wo" that was announced in general terms in G (b) is then pronounced in specific language upon such a person in G'.

Subsection G' contains a mature psychological attitude toward punishment. Its central motif portrays two different reactions of the individual to the realization of his own culpability; these reactions appear to modify the two terms introduced in G—"damnation" and "everlasting punishment." Thus Benjamin seems to hold that the judgment will be self-executing, for "damnation" can be linked with "shrink[ing] from the presence of the Lord," and "eternal punishment" is identifiable with the anguish of the soul "which is like an unquenchable fire." In this picture, punishment is strictly internal and existential; no external decree or fiery torture is necessary for spiritual anguish.

In the second half of G', Benjamin made a successful effort to maintain equal lengths of lines in corresponding parts, even though the redundant addition of "and pain and anguish" was necessary in one case. The final line of G' also functions in a remarkable way, for while "never-ending" relates back to "remaineth" an enemy to God, it also looks ahead to the contrast with "never-ending happiness" created in the concluding passage.

The middle and turning point of section 2 is subsection H. It is chiastically framed by several lines (a, b, c, d, e) constructed around the key words "transgress," "contrary," "taught," "know," "Heavenly Father" or "the Lord," and "have and are" or "just and true." Pairing the words "have and are" with "just and true" shows keen conceptual association, for *justice* is the equitable distribution or retribution of things, privileges, or rights which people *have*, and *truth* is that whose referent is those things which ultimately *are*. At the very center, somewhat similar to the structure of the middle, E, in section 1, a quatrain is presented that is comprised of two couplets. The first couplet mentions, parallelistically in lines 1 and 2, the content and authorship of the records; the second couplet mentions, chiastically at the beginning and ending of lines 3 and 4, the two relevant time periods from which these records originate; the word "spoken" appears in the second and fourth lines, as in good form. The thought at the turning point is the accountability of the people, based upon the knowledge of their indebtedness to God, who is the source of their material existence and their holy writ.

The shift at the center is styled out of temporal elements, by dividing time periods before and after the departure from Jerusalem, and also out of the contrast between physical and spiritual indebtedness. But most important, H contains the thought that is indispensable to the logic of section 2, for it is axiomatic that a knowledge of one's obligations is prerequisite for any assignment of responsibility, which in turn is necessary for the ascription of either praise or blame. Blameworthiness is the condition on which punishment is predicated, and praiseworthiness is the condition of reward. Hence accountability, or responsibility, is the keystone in the structure of section 2, whose topic deals with blessings and punishments.

In sum, although this section is structurally complex, its underlying framework can be simplified and displayed by highlighting certain words that appear in one order in the first half of the section and whose counterparts are introduced in the opposite order in the second half:

> keep the commandments (31)
> > prospered (31)
> > > contention, listeth to obey, remaineth and dieth (32–33)
> > > > transgress contrary (33)
> > > > > taught these things (34)
> > > > > > knoweth (34)
> > > > > > > have and are (34)
> > > > > > > > prophecies, holy prophets (34)
> > > > > > > > father Lehi, fathers (34–35)
> > > > > > > just and true (35)
> > > > > > known (36)
> > > > > taught these things (36)
> > > > transgress contrary (36)
> > > rebellion, listeth to obey, remaineth and dieth (37–38)
> > blessed (41)
> keep the commandments (41)

The chiastic organization of this passage makes its central point quite clear and also renders the overall logic of the section coherent.

Section 3

Outline. The angel of the Lord delivered to Benjamin the information about Christ and his atonement found in sections 3 and 4.[63] It is interesting to see how Benjamin placed the words of the angel into the overall chiastic structure of his own speech.

> J The Lord has judged thy righteousness
>> K The Lord will descend
>>> L The Lord's works among men
>>>> M Christ's power over evil spirits
>>>>> N Christ will be divine and bring salvation
>>>> M' Christ will be accused of having an evil spirit
>>> L' Men's treatment of Jesus
>> K' The Lord will ascend
> J' The Lord will judge the world righteously

This section requires little exposition to elucidate its strong chiastic structure. Here Benjamin set forth his prophetic vision of the great marvels of the ministry of the Savior and then contrasted these marvels with the deep ironies of his rejection by his own chosen people. It should be readily evident that chiasmus was employed here to intensify those ironies, for it is ironic that Jesus' "own" should consider him merely a man after he has suffered more for them than any man of normal mortal frame can possibly suffer (N); that he should be accused of being possessed by a devil considering the fact that he drove out so many devils (M); and that the way he was put to death is rooted in the way that he blessed their sick and raised their dead (L).

Detailed Analysis. The important concepts dealt with in this section are righteousness, judgment, and the divinity and mission of Christ.

J The Lord has judged thy righteousness

3:3 Awake and hear the words which I shall tell thee:
  a for behold I am come to *declare* unto you
    b the glad tidings of great *joy*

3:4 for the Lord hath heard thy prayers and hath judged of thy righteousness

a and hath sent me to *declare* unto thee that
   b thou mayest *rejoice*
a and that thou mayest *declare* unto thy people that
   b they may also be filled with *joy*[64]

K The Lord will descend

3:5 For behold the time *cometh*
and is not far distant
   that with power
   the Lord omnipotent
     who reigneth
     who was and is
   from all eternity
   to all eternity
shall *come down* from heaven among the children of men
and shall dwell in a tabernacle of clay

L The Lord's works among men

And shall go forth amongst men
working mighty miracles such as
   healing the sick
   raising the dead
   causing the lame to walk
   the blind to receive their sight
   and the deaf to hear
   and curing all manner of diseases

M Christ's power over evil spirits

3:6 And he shall cast out devils or the evil spirits
which dwell in the hearts of the children of men

N Christ will be divine and bring salvation

3:7 1 *and lo* he shall *suffer temptations and pain* of body, hunger, thirst, and fatigue
2 even more than *man* can *suffer* except it be unto death
3 for behold blood cometh from every pore
4 so great shall be his *anguish* for the wickedness and the abominations of his *people*

3:8 and he *shall be called* Jesus Christ
　　the Son of God
　　the Father of heaven and earth
　　the Creator of all things from the beginning
　　and his mother *shall be called* Mary

3:9 5 *and lo*[65] he *cometh* unto *his own*
　　6 that salvation might *come* unto the *children of men*
　　7 even through faith on his name
　　8 and even after all this they shall consider him a *man*

M' Christ will be accused of having an evil spirit

and say that he hath a devil

L' Men's treatment of Jesus

and shall scourge him and shall crucify him

K' The Lord will ascend

3:10 and he shall *rise* the third day from the dead[66]

J' The Lord will judge the world righteously

and behold he standeth to *judge* the world
and behold all these things are done that a *righteous judgment*
　　might come upon the children of men.

Comments. This chiastic structure builds on the contrast between the eternal period of Christ's reign in heaven and the temporal duration of his spell with death, as well as the descension (K) and ascension (K') of God into earthly history. The center of K is constructed out of three pairs (power–omnipotent, who–who, eternity–eternity), while the elaboration in L contains two triads (healing–raising–causing, to walk–to receive–to hear). Also of significance is the appearance of "judgment" and "righteousness" in the J and J' subsections. This usage can be compared to a similar chiastic treatment of these ideas in certain psalms, such as Psalm 58. If this passage in Mosiah 3 is indeed following the pattern of Hebrew psalmody, we should recognize that "judgment" is used in the introduction and conclusion of several of the Psalms as a general desire and expectation of Israel, but not as a main point of the unit.

The turning point (N) is certainly the central idea of the passage. The divinity of Christ and his sacrifice on behalf of mankind falls distinctly at the center of intention and attention in this portion of the speech. The nomenclature at the center is also of note, for vocatives calling upon the Lord often appear at the center of chiastic systems (compare Psalm 58; Alma 36). Here the form is declarative but the idea of using the name to call upon the Lord is not far distant. The unusual brevity of M', L', and K' accentuates the stark contrasts they expose.

A nice effect is also achieved by means of the two closely interrelated quatrains that flank the names at the center. These two quatrains should be read together. The one ends (4) and the other begins (5) with reference to Jesus' own people; even after the extent of his bleeding and suffering (2), he shall be considered only a man (8); ironically, his sufferings bring the possibility of salvation to man (6); the offering of Christ was his blood (3), in response to which people offer faith on his name (7).

Section 4

Outline. This section of Benjamin's speech continues with the words of the angel and discusses the atonement and the law, judgment and salvation. Its components may be outlined as follows:

P The atonement covers the sins of the innocent
  Q Repentance is necessary for the rebellious
    R We may rejoice now as though Christ had already come
  Q' The atonement is necessary for the law of Moses
P' The atonement covers the sins of the innocent

S Salvation is exclusively in Jesus Christ
  T Putting off the natural man and becoming a saint
S' Salvation is universal in Jesus Christ

U The angel's words are witnessed by God
  W Final warning of God's judgment
U' The angel's words are witnessed by God

This is the central section of Benjamin's entire speech and covers the principles of repentance and the progression from one's natural state to becoming a saint.

Detailed Analysis. Section 4 is relatively difficult to parse, despite two unmistakable clues to its composition: First, this section is distinct from the foregoing section; section 3 dealt entirely with the mission of Christ, while section 4 discusses exclusively the human situation and the conditions related to it under which the atonement operates to absolve humans of sin. Second, section 4 contains one of the longest and most precise chiastic centerpieces in Benjamin's speech (subsection T, 3:18–19), which indeed occurs at the center of the central section of the whole speech. To this extent the structure and nature of section 4 is self-evident, but the organization of the materials that flank this monumental central passage is less obvious.

P The atonement covers the sins of the innocent

3:11 1 For behold and also *his blood atoneth* for the sins
      2 of those who have *fallen*
        3 by the transgression of *Adam*
          4 who have died *not knowing* the will of God concerning them or who have *ignorantly sinned*

Q Repentance is necessary for the rebellious

3:12   5 but wo, wo unto him who knoweth that he *rebelleth* against God
          6 for salvation cometh to *none* such

> 7 *except* it be through repentance and faith on the
> Lord Jesus Christ

R We may rejoice now as though Christ had already come

3:13 a and the Lord God hath sent his *holy prophets* among all the *children of men* to declare these things to every kindred, nation, and tongue that thereby

> b whosoever should believe that Christ should *come*
>   c the same might receive remission of their sins and rejoice
>   c with exceedingly great joy
> b even as though he had already *come* among them

3:14 Yet the Lord God saw that his *people*[67] were a stiffnecked people
>   d and he appointed unto them
>   e a law even the law of Moses
3:15 >   e And many signs and wonders
>   and types and shadows[68]
>   d showed he unto them

> b concerning his *coming*
> a and also *holy prophets* spake unto them
> concerning his *coming*

Q' The atonement is necessary for the law of Moses

> 5 And yet they *hardened* their hearts
>   6 and understood not that the law of Moses availeth *nothing*
>   7 *except* it were through the atonement of his blood

P' The atonement covers the sins of the innocent

3:16 > 4 and even if it were possible that *little children* could *sin* they could not be saved, but I say unto you they are blessed
> 3 for behold as in *Adam*
> 2 or by nature they *fall*[69]
> 1 even so the *blood* of Christ *atoneth for* their sins

S Salvation is exclusively in Jesus Christ

3:17 v *and moreover I say unto you that* there shall be no other name given nor any other way nor means whereby *salvation* can come unto the children of men

w *only* in and through *the name of* Christ *the Lord Omnipotent*

3:18 x for behold he *judgeth* and his judgment is just

y and the *infant* perisheth not that dieth in his *infancy*

z but men drink *damnation* to their own souls

T Putting off the natural man and becoming a saint

a except they *humble* themselves

b and become as little *children*

c and believe that salvation was and is and is to come in and through the *atoning* blood *of Christ the Lord* Omnipotent

3:19 d for the *natural man*

e is an enemy to *God*

f and *has been* from the fall of Adam

f and *will be* forever and ever

e unless he yields to the enticings of the *Holy Spirit*

d and putteth off the *natural man*

c and becometh a saint through the *atonement of Christ the Lord*

b and becometh as a *child*

a submissive, meek, *humble*, patient, full of love, willing to submit to all things which the Lord seeth fit to inflict upon him, even as a child doth submit to his father

S' Salvation is universal in Jesus Christ

3:20 v *And moreover I say unto you that* the time shall come when the knowledge of a *Savior* shall spread throughout every nation, kindred, tongue and people,[70]

3:21 x and behold, when that time cometh none shall be *found blameless* before God

y except it be *little children*

w *only* through repentance and faith on *the name of the Lord God Omnipotent*

3:22 z and even at this time when thou shalt have taught thy people the things which the Lord thy God hath commanded thee even then are they found *no more blameless* in the sight of God only according to the words which I have spoken unto thee

U The angel's words are witnessed by God

3:23 And now I have spoken the words which the Lord God hath *commanded* me
3:24 and thus saith the Lord

    W Final warning of God's judgment

    a They shall stand as a bright testimony against this people at the *judgment* day
    a whereof they shall be *judged*

      b every man according to his works *whether* they be good
      b or *whether* they *be evil*

3:25   c and if they *be evil* they are consigned to an awful view
        c of their own guilt and abominations

          d which doth cause them to shrink from the presence of the Lord into a state of misery
          d and endless *torment* from whence they can *no more* return;

    a therefore *they have drunk*
    a damnation to their own souls;

3:26   b therefore *they have drunk* out of the cup
    b of the wrath of God

      c which justice could *no more deny* unto them
      c than it could *deny* that Adam should fall because of his partaking of the forbidden fruit;

        d therefore mercy could have claim on them *no more forever*
3:27   d and their *torment* is as a lake of fire and brimstone whose flames are unquenchable and whose smoke ascendeth up *forever* and ever

U' The angel's words are witnessed by God

thus hath the Lord *commanded* me. Amen.

Comments. Working from the inside out, the turning point here (T) is exceptional. It is composed of six elements repeated in close proximity in reverse order. The phrase *natural man* is not only unique to this section of the speech, but these are its only two appearances in the entire Book of Mormon.[71]

The central chiasm found in 3:18–19 can be summarized and displayed as follows:

```
a humble themselves
  b become as little children
    c salvation through the atoning blood of Christ the Lord
      d natural man
        e enemy to God
          f has been from the fall of Adam
          f will be forever and ever
        e yieldeth to the Holy Spirit
      d natural man
    c become a saint through the atonement of Christ the Lord
  b become as a child
a submissive, meek, humble
```

In addition, 3:17–18 (S) can readily be identified with 3:20–22 (S'). Both are introduced by "moreover," and both qualify the preceding discussion of the general effects of the atonement of Christ. Benjamin taught that there shall be no other name upon which salvation is predicated (making the name of the Savior universal). Both S and S' mention salvation or being found blameless only through the name of Jesus Christ (W), the innocence of infants (Y), the responsibility of men for their own evil doing (Z), and the judgment (or in other words, being found blameworthy of God). These concepts are presented in nearly identical sequences in both groups, which, therefore, form alternating lines in contrast with the extensive chiastic centerpiece.

Two further groups remain on the extremities, namely verses 3:11–16 (P–Q–R–Q'–P') and verses 23–27 (U–W–U').

The two are related only by contrast, since the single direct link is one reference to Adam (3:26), which perhaps echoes P (3:11) and P' (3:16), the only other references to Adam in the speech. But the contrast between these two groups is sharp and most likely intentional, therefore being sufficient to justify aligning them. In 3:11–16, emphasis is placed on the merciful manifestations of the atonement and the blessings that are bestowed on souls by its effective operation. Thus, "his blood atoneth for the sins of those . . . who have died not knowing the will of God concerning them, or who have ignorantly sinned" (P). Likewise, little children are blessed (P'). For those who have rebelled or have hardened their hearts, the way is prepared for reconciliation through repentance and faith (Q) and the atonement (Q'). Above all, it was necessary for Benjamin's era to know that the atonement could be operative upon those who believe that the Christ should come, even though Christ had not yet received his mortal shroud.[72] Thus the key to the favorable, positive, and gracious working of the atonement among Benjamin's people is given at R: that they might "rejoice . . . even as though he had already come" and that the law itself is a sign, wonder, type, and shadow looking forward to his future coming. The structure of R itself is complicated by the occurrence of "holy prophets" at its beginning and end, followed by two minor chiasms, b–c–c–b in 3:13 and d–e–e–d 3:14–15. Although R manifests less discreteness of form, I prefer to leave it in a simple structural arrangement conjoining the futurity of Christ's coming and the presence of his atonement.

In contrast with the future working of the atonement, 3:23–27 focuses on the onerous responsibility that attaches to one's knowledge and awareness of the nature of the atonement. The mood is prepared for this stern warning as far back as 3:10: "all these things are done that a righteous judgment might come upon the children of men." The cadence of these lines is introduced when Benjamin charged his people unequivocally with responsibility for their own knowledge; they were "found no more blameless in the sight of God" (3:22). The eight segments that comprise W portray the nature of the judgment. For Benjamin, the judgment occurred internally in the separate soul, which views its own guilt and shrinks from the presence of the Lord of its own accord, thus being placed beyond the help even of mercy by the unrelenting self-view and guilt-awareness that cannot be deceived away. It may be that these eight strophes, each of which manifests an element of duplication, divide into the conventional arrangement of two halves of four strophes each (compare Alma 34:18–25), for judgment is the theme of lines one and five (a), and torment is the subject of lines four and eight (d); further associations may be drawn that are helpful but not necessarily binding.

Section 5

Outline. After the review of Christ's life and work, Benjamin's next section describes how a knowledge of the power of God leads to action and progression of the human spirit.

> **X Man's knowledge of the goodness of God**
>> **Y Articles of belief**
> **X' Man's knowledge of the goodness of God**

Section 5 contains the king's testimony of God and of the efficacy of the atonement of Christ, coupled with thoughts that accent mankind's need for the remission of sins in order to be redeemed from a state of "nothingness" and unworthiness. If it is correct that the general organization of the speech associates Benjamin's testimony of God with the angel's testimony of Christ's ministry, then we may secure the antecedent of the phrase "in the faith of that which is to come" (4:11) as being the ministry and atoning acts of the Savior. The chiasmus in this section as a whole and in its subsections is powerful and effective.

Detailed Analysis. This section contains a balance of negative and positive aspects of life and obedience and many forms of parallelisms.

X Man's knowledge of the goodness of God

4:5   k for behold, if the *knowledge of the goodness of God* at this time
     – has awakened you to a sense of your nothingness
     – and your worthless and fallen state

4:6   k I say unto you if ye have come to a *knowledge of the goodness of God*
     + and his matchless power and his wisdom
     + and his patience and his long suffering

     a towards the *children of men*
       b and also *the atonement which has been prepared from the foundation of the world*
         c that thereby *salvation* might come to him
           d that should put his *trust* in the Lord
             e and should be diligent in keeping his commandments
           d and continue in the *faith* even unto the end of his life
           I mean the life of the mortal body
4:7   c I say that this is the man who receiveth *salvation*
       b through *the atonement which was prepared from the foundation of the world*
     a for *all mankind*
     which ever were since the fall of Adam
       or who are
       or who ever shall be
     even unto the end of the world.

Y Articles of belief

4:8   1 and this is the means whereby *salvation* cometh,
     and there is none other *salvation* save this which hath been spoken of

2 neither are there any *conditions* whereby man can be saved
except the *conditions* which I have told you.

4:9   3 believe in God, believe that he is
and that he created *all* things both *in heaven and in earth*

4 believe that he has *all* wisdom
and all power both *in heaven and in earth*

5 believe that *man* doth not *comprehend* all the things
which the Lord can *comprehend*

4:10   6 and again believe that ye must *repent* of your sins
and *forsake* them

7 and *humble* yourselves before God
and *ask* in sincerity of heart that he would forgive you

8 and now if you believe all these things
see that ye do them

X' Man's knowledge of the goodness of God

4:11   And again I say unto you as I have said before[73]

k that as ye have come to the *knowledge* of the *glory* of God
k or if ye have *known* of his *goodness*

v and have tasted of his *love*
s and have received a *remission of your sins*
j which causeth such exceedingly great *joy* in your souls

r even so I would that ye should *remember*
r and always retain in *remembrance*
+ the greatness of God
– and your own nothingness
+ and his goodness and long suffering
– towards you unworthy creatures[74]

h and *humble* yourselves
h even in the depths of *humility*

n calling on the name of the Lord daily
f and standing steadfastly in the faith
f of that which is to come
n which was spoken by the mouth of the angel[75]

4:12 and behold I say unto you that
>   j if ye do this ye shall always *rejoice*
> v and be filled with the *love* of God
>   s and always retain a *remission of your sins*

k and ye shall grow in the *knowledge* of the *glory* of him that created you
k or in the *knowledge* of that which is *just* and *true*.

Comments. Section 5 is constructed of three subsections: X–Y–X'. Both X and X' manifest adept chiastic arrangements and are closely associated with each other by the repetition of many thoughts and phrases occurring in both instances. X is introduced by two references to the "knowledge of the goodness of God," a phrase that reappears in increasingly elaborate forms twice at the beginning of X' and twice at the end (k). The two negative aspects of mortal existence (– –) and the two companion positive traits of divine nature (+ +) gravitate from the beginning of X to the middle of X', with identical phrases recurring in alternating lines in the complementary passage (+ – + –). This gravitation accompanies a broader shift in emphasis from X to X', in that X discusses the atonement in terms of its being "prepared from the foundation of the world" and coming to mankind, while X' approaches the atonement from the standpoint of mankind coming to it through faith, humility, and cognizance of the human plight. Thus it furthered Benjamin's purposes to position the conditions of salvation in the middle of X (d–e–d) and to move the terms describing mankind's contribution to the saving process to the middle of X' (h–n–f).

Whereas little remains to be said about the chiastic characteristic of X—since a–b–c–d–e–d–c–b–a is straightforward—the material in X' is presented in a very creative form. The two pairs of k lines at the beginning and ending of this system make reference to the knowledge of the glory and goodness of God; they are interesting in light of Moroni

358 • John W. Welch

10:6, which reads: "whatsoever thing is good is just and true." The chiastic structure of X' links "goodness" in 4:11 with "that which is just and true" in 4:12. Thus it can be concluded that the roots of the definition in Moroni 10:6 date at least to the time of Benjamin (124 B.C.) in Nephite thought.

In X', three ideas appear grouped in nearly inverted order in the second positions. As is often present in good chiastic writing, these repetitions are also accompanied by a careful sense of intensification: the first instance (v) refers to tasting God's love (4:11), while the corresponding line in 4:12 makes the promise of being *"filled* with" that love. On one hand the remission of sins (s) is mentioned in 4:11, but on the other, its counterpart in 4:12 speaks of "always *retain[ing]* a remission of your sins"; likewise, line (j) first deals with feeling "great joy in your souls" now, but the intensification in 4:12 promises "ye shall *always* rejoice." The thrust of these climactic contrapositionings may be eschatological, so that we should understand Benjamin to be saying that the everlasting joy, the fullness of love, and the retention of remission will all come in the day of the Lord's final judgment. Or we may take the thrust of his comments to be more limited to events that are located in the scope of this-worldly experiences and expectations. According to the latter alternative, Benjamin expected the effects of salvation to become manifested in the field of this life. In light of Benjamin's general humanistic bent, and from the sense apparent in the line "if ye do this, ye shall always rejoice" (4:12), we may infer that Benjamin's perspective on the judgment of man was as much involved in events in this world as in the next.

In the center of X' we encounter an interesting pattern constructed of two couplets containing climactic parallelism in their second lines: "remember" becomes "always retain in remembrance," and "humble" becomes "the depths of humility." The first quatrain then alternates the positive and negative concepts (+ – + –) that occurred at the introduction of X (– – + +), while the second quatrain is one of straight parallelisms (n–f–f–n), in which the first two lines describe two righteous forms of behavior, "calling on the name of the Lord daily" and "standing steadfast in the faith," while the second two lines are relative clauses modifying the former two chiastically: the first and fourth lines (n) are linked because the angel gave the name that should be called upon daily, and the second and third lines (f) both associate with the idea of faith in future events.

Between X and X' the text includes an eight-part interlude in subsection Y. These eight lines form a magnificent declaration of faith and promise, to compare favorably with the eight-part exhortation of Alma 34:18–25 or with the structure of the Beatitudes in Matthew 5:2–9.

Subsection Y may be viewed from several angles. As paired couplets, it is apparent that 1 and 2 are closely connected, since both express common conditions of salvation and confirm the exclusive nature of this way to salvation. Lines 3 and 4 are joined by the phrase "both in heaven and in earth," which appears in each, and also by similar thoughts about God, his existence, and his power. Lines 5 and 6 deal with man's ignorance and iniquity. Lines 7 and 8 describe the way in which man can fulfill the requirements necessary to achieve the goal of salvation. These pairs then fall into two groups, namely 1–2–7–8, which all speak of the conditions of salvation, humble asking and doing; and 3–4–5–6, which all begin with the word *believe*, the first two in reference to God, the second two in reference to man. And beyond that, an alternation occurs within this structure: lines 1–2–6–7 describe specific events or are limited by phrases of exclusion ("none other," "except" and "must");

on the other hand 3–4–5–8 deal with generalities and universals and are especially detectable by the presence of the words "all things," "all wisdom," "all these things." Thus in the conventional pairing of couplets that occurs frequently in Hebrew literature, Benjamin incorporated an alternation of universal (U) and specific (S) features in the pattern SS–UU–US–SU in 4:9–10. This type of pattern has been encountered before, particularly at Mosiah 3:7, 9, the central panel of section 3 (this section's counterpart), where the pattern was the reverse of this one, i.e., ab–ba–aa–bb. It is also found in X and X', where the positive and negative aspects combine in the order – – + +; + – + –.

Section 6

Outline. The second to last section of Benjamin's speech describes in more detail the obligations of social justice that require members of the community to impart of their substance to those who are in need.

A Distribution of property
  B Teach your children the laws of God
    C Ministering to the poor
      D The rich man's excuse
        E Curse for not repenting
          F Imperative to impart substance to one another
        E' Curse for not repenting
      D' The poor man's excuse
    C' Ministering to the poor
  B' Adult approach to following the laws of God
A' Distribution of property
Final warning against sin

Here Benjamin draws an important parallel between our treatment of fellow human beings and God's treatment of us.

Detailed Analysis. Aside from two unusual departures from the standard form, namely, the logic at the center and the reiteration of the sanction, the basic organization of section 6 may be justifiably described as chiastic, even though Benjamin's style here has become more expositive and personal. In certain respects, it is as though Benjamin was writing from a broad chiastic outline only, with the imperative at the center. For he had no intention of discarding—in order to enhance the chiasmus at this point—important thoughts or even afterthoughts that bolstered the logic of the moral obligation he was issuing. But still his thoughts retraced themselves as the passage unwinds from the twice-pronounced dependence of man on God (major premise, 4:19, 21), the twice-invoked "wo" upon those who turn away their neighbor in need (E, E', 4:18, 23), and reference to the two states of mind in which the rich and the poor approach the beggar (4:17, 24). Verse 25 appears to be a refrain, repeating one of the central ideas of the passage (4:22). Verses 29 and 30 are somewhat parenthetical, and together they form an epilogue spoken as the final admonition before the ceremony in which the people answered the king and made their covenant with the Lord (5:1–5).

A Distribution of property

4:13 And ye will not have a mind to injure one another
but to live peaceably

and to render to every man
according to that which is his due[76]

B Teach your children the laws of God

4:14 a And *ye will not suffer* your children
b that they go hungry or naked
a *neither will ye suffer* that they transgress *the laws of God* and
b fight and quarrel *one* with *another*

and *serve* the devil
who is the master of sin or
who is the evil spirit
which hath been spoken of by our fathers
he being an enemy to all righteousness

4:15 a but *ye will teach* them
         b to walk in *the ways of truth* and soberness
      a *ye will teach* them
         b to love *one another* and to *serve one another*

C Ministering to the poor

4:16 and also ye yourselves will *succor*
      those that stand in need of *your succor*

      ye will administer of *your substance*
      unto him that standeth in *need*

      and ye will not suffer that the beggar putteth up his petition
      to you *in vain* and turn him out *to perish*

D The rich man's excuse

4:17 perhaps thou shalt say
         the man has brought upon himself *his misery*
            therefore I will stay my hand
            and will not give unto him of *my food*
            nor impart unto him of *my substance*
            that he may not suffer
         for *his punishments* are just

E Curse for not repenting

4:18 but I say unto you
         a O man, whosoever *doeth* this
            b the same hath great cause to *repent*
            b and except he *repenteth*
         a of that which he hath *done*
      he *perisheth*[77] forever
      and hath no interest in the kingdom of God

F Imperative to impart substance to one another

4:19 For behold, are we not *all* beggars
      Do we not *all* depend upon the same Being even God

      for all the substance which we have
         for both food and raiment and
         for gold and for silver and
      for all the riches which we have of every kind

4:20 and behold, even at this time
ye have been calling on his name
and *begging* for a remission of your sins
and has he suffered that ye have *begged* in *vain*?

Nay he has poured out his Spirit upon you
   and *has caused* that *your hearts* should be filled with *joy*
   and *has caused* that *your mouths* should be stopped that ye
      could not find utterance so exceedingly great was your *joy*

4:21 a And now, if God, who has created you, on whom you are
      dependent for your lives and for all *that ye have* and are
   b doth *grant* unto you
      c whatsoever ye *ask* that is right
         d in faith
         d believing
      c that ye shall *receive*
   b O then how ye ought to *impart*
a of the substance *that ye have* one to another

4:22 And if ye judge the man who putteth up his petition to you
for *your substance* that he perish not
   and *condemn* him
   how much more just will be your *condemnation*
for withholding *your substance*

a which doth not *belong*
   b to *you*
      c but *to* God
      c *to* whom also
   b *your* life
a *belongeth*

E' Curse for not repenting

and yet ye put up no petition
nor *repent* of the thing which thou hast done

4:23 I say unto you wo be unto that man
for his substance shall *perish*[78] with him
and now I say these things unto those who are rich
as pertaining to the things of this world[79]

D' The poor man's excuse

4:24   a and again I say unto the poor, ye who *have not*
      and yet have *sufficient* that ye remain from day to day
      I mean all you who deny the beggar because ye *have not*

      b I would that *ye say in your hearts*
        c that I *give* not
          d because I have not
          d but if I had
        c I would *give*
4:25   b and now, if *ye say* this *in your hearts*

      a ye remain guiltless, otherwise ye are condemned
      and your condemnation[80] is just
      for ye *covet*[81] that which ye *have not received*

C' Ministering to the poor

4:26 And now *for the sake of* these things which I have spoken unto you
      that is *for the sake of* retaining
      a *remission* of your sins from day to day
      that ye may walk *guiltless* before God
      I would that ye should impart of your substance[82] to the poor

      every man *according to* that which he hath
        such as feeding the hungry
        clothing the naked
        visiting the sick and
        administering[83] to their relief
        both spiritually and temporally
      according to their wants[84]

B' Adult approach to following the laws of God

4:27 And see that *all* these *things* are *done in* wisdom and *order*
      – for *it is not requisite*
        that a man should run faster
        than he has strength
      + and again *it is expedient*
        that he should be diligent
        that thereby he might win the prize
      therefore *all things* must be *done in order*

A' Distribution of property

4:28 And I would that ye should remember that
a whosoever among you *borroweth* of his *neighbor*
a should return the thing that he *borroweth*
according[85] as he doth agree
  b or else thou shalt *commit sin*
  b and perhaps thou shalt cause thy *neighbor* to *commit sin*
  also

Final warning against sin

4:29 a And finally *I cannot tell* you
  b *all the things* whereby ye may commit sin
  b for there are *divers ways and means*
a even *so many* that *I cannot* number them

4:30 but this much *I can tell* you
  that if ye do not watch yourselves
  and your thoughts and your words and your deeds
  and observe the commandments of God and continue in
    the faith of what ye have heard concerning the coming
    of our Lord even unto the end of your lives

  ye must *perish*
  And now, O man, remember,
  and *perish not*.[86]

Comments. Subsections A–B–C (4:13–16) balance C'–B'–A' (4:26–28), with important recurrences being "impart of your substance" (C, C', 4:16, 26), "the hungry" (4:14, 26), and "render to every man according to . . . his due" (4:13, compare "return the thing that he borroweth according as he doth agree" 4:28). By incorporating both halves of these related subsections into a single unit, we find that, in each case, Benjamin specifically stated both the types of behavior that he desired his people to avoid, and also the criteria he prescribed for remedying difficulties should they arise: in A, the desired behavior was the return of physical property, which would have been especially meaningful in connection with the restitution of property associated with the jubilee year rites (see note 18). The necessary criteria were first, having "no mind to injure one another" and ultimately to desire to avoid committing sin or causing one's neighbor to commit sin also. The remedy was found in rendering to each man according to his due, which appears to mean "according as he doth agree" (A', 4:28). Thus, A–A' instructed the people to keep their promises and agreements regarding the return of possessions at this time and as a general ethical rule.

In B, the desired behavior was to raise children by providing them sufficient temporal and spiritual support. The prerequisites were to avert the devil and to avoid contention (compare section 2.G, 2:32). This was to be accomplished in B by teaching them to obey "the laws of God," to "*walk* in the ways of truth and soberness" and to love and serve one another, and in B' all this is "done in wisdom and order," not *running* faster than one has strength.

In C, Benjamin desired to encourage charitable administration of substance to the needy. This is associated in C' with the retention of "a remission of your sins from day to day," which was achieved by feeding the hungry, clothing the naked, visiting the sick, and administering to those spiritually or temporally in need.

Although this section is softer in style than some of the earlier sections in Benjamin's speech, the flowing, almost lyrical passages in this section communicate a feeling of warmth, goodness, and assurance, conducive of engendering the spirit of generosity and humanitarian goodness that Benjamin wants to instill in the minds and spirits of his audience. The overall feeling of fullness and completeness in this section is enhanced by the use of chiasmus in several of its subsections: fine chiasms in subsections E (a–b–b–a), F (a–b–c–d–d–c–b–a, a–b–c–c–b–a), and D' (a–b–c–d–d–c–b–a) induce a natural sense of logical persuasion and moral closure. Moreover, to a greater degree than in other sections of his speech, Benjamin makes use of effective duplications in other parallelistic arrangements: suffer–suffer, teach–teach (B), succor–succor (C), my food–my substance (D), all the substance–all the riches, begging–begged, joy–joy, substance–substance, condemn–condemnation (F), have not–have not (D'), guiltless–guiltless (D', C'), sake of–sake of, according to–according to (C'), order–order (B'), borroweth–borroweth, commit sin–commit sin, cannot–cannot, perish–perish not (A'). The recurrence of these numerous two-part repetitions comports stylistically with the central theme of this section, which emphasizes reciprocity, mutual support, and balanced equality among individuals.

At the center, Benjamin's logic is intriguing. By drawing together certain relationships, he was able to derive a moral imperative by means of a conditional transitivity of obligations. The logic here, as discussed above in this volume (see chapter 2, subsection 11), is quite unlike traditional syllogistic or predicate logic, and in order to understand its operations on this occasion, it should be studied in conjunction with similar reasoning at 2:18–19 (1.E) and in terms of the structure of these passages. On all three occasions, the argument began with a statement of fact that, by its nature, entails certain rights, privileges, or obligations. A conditional or contingent premise then followed, through which an obligation was transferred to the people. Thus in 2:18 the lines of argument may be sketched as follows:

> I am your king (fact)
> You should serve me (entailed obligation from kingship)
> I serve you (condition)
> Therefore, you should serve one another (conclusion)

This conclusion follows logically only because Benjamin had voluntarily chosen to serve others, naming them

368 • *John W. Welch*

as the recipients of all his efforts and assets. Thus the obligation owed to him by the people transfers from him to "others" as his beneficiaries. Notice, however, that without the supplied entailment the argument will not go through, for

> I am your king
> I serve you
> Therefore you should serve one another

is not in the least persuasive and appears to derive an "ought" from an "is," a logical fallacy. From 2:19 we obtain:

> I am your king (fact)
> You should thank me for my service to you (entailment)
> My service to you is service to God (condition)
> Therefore you should thank God (conclusion)

Here, the king's right to thanks is dependent upon service which belongs to God. Benjamin, therefore, conveyed directly to God any credits that he might have earned in that service, and since the people still owed a debt of thanks, the obligation to pay that debt to Benjamin transferred to an obligation to thank God.

In 4:19–22, the reasoning employs the same methodology and structure:

> We are all dependent upon the same God for everything (major premise)
> You should recognize him as the source and controller of all (entailment)
> God grants whatever is asked of him and even what is not asked of him (conditional premise)
> Therefore, you ought to impart your substance to one another (conclusion).

Benjamin was not just saying here that he preferred people to be charitable one to another. Instead, he argued that an obligation to be charitable derives from man's obligation to recognize the immediate implication of the factual relationship asserted by the major premise. If there is a duty to recognize God as the controller, and God chooses to distribute benevolence universally, then people have an obligation to distribute their substance as the controller himself would distribute it. Just as the obligation is effectively transferred in 2:18 from one existing between the people and their king to one between the people and their fellowmen, here it transfers from a relationship between God and mankind to one between one human and another. In this way, Benjamin's arguments have merit and they form an unusual model of ethical deduction and presentation.

Section 7

Outline. Benjamin maintained the chiastic format to the very end of his epoch-making speech. Not only is each of the individual subsections well balanced and skillfully constructed, but section 7 as a whole is harmonic, contains an extensive chiastic turning point (Z, 5:10–12), and features additional chiasms in 5:7 and 5:8–9.

  X Born of Christ
    Y Obedience to the name of Christ
      Z Excommunication for transgression
    Y' Serving the master is the key to knowing his name
  X' Sealed by God

These elements contain Benjamin's final warnings against sin and describe the eternal blessings of obedience.

Detailed Analysis. The principles of covenants and freedom, of rebirth and worthiness discussed in this last section of Benjamin's speech were carefully encased in chiasms and parallelisms.

  X Born of Christ

5:6 Ye have spoken the words that I desired

    a and the *covenant* which ye have *made* is a righteous *covenant*
5:7   a and now because of the *covenant* which ye have *made* ye shall be called the children of Christ

   b his *sons* and his *daughters*
      c for behold this day he hath spiritually *begotten* you
         d for ye say that your hearts are changed through faith
            on his name
      c therefore ye are *born* of him
   b and have become his *sons* and his *daughters*

5:8 a and under this head ye are *made free*
    a and there is no other head whereby ye can be *made free*[87]

Y Obedience to the name of Christ

a there is no other *name* given whereby salvation cometh
a therefore I would that ye should take upon you the *name of
   Christ*
   b all you that have entered into the covenant with *God*
      c that ye should be *obedient* unto the end of your lives
5:9   c and it shall come to pass that whosoever doeth *this*
   b shall be found at the right hand of *God*
a for he shall know the *name* by which he is called
a for he shall be called by the *name of Christ*

Z Excommunication for transgression

5:10 a And now it shall come to pass that whosoever shall not take
     upon him the *name* of Christ
     b must be *called* by some other name
        c therefore he findeth himself on the *left hand of God*
5:11   d and I would that ye should *remember* also that this is
              the name that I said I should give unto you
              e that never should be *blotted out*
                 f except it be through *transgression*
                 f therefore take heed that ye do not *transgress*
              e that the name be not *blotted out* of your hearts
5:12   d I say unto you, I would that ye should *remember* to
              retain the name written always in your hearts
        c that ye are not found on the *left hand of God*
     b but that ye hear and know the voice by which ye shall be
        called
a and also the *name* by which he shall call you

Y' Serving the master is the key to knowing his name

5:13 a for how *knoweth* a man the master whom he has not served
and who is a stranger unto him and is far from the thoughts
and intents of his heart?

5:14 b and again doth a man take an ass which belongeth to his
neighbor and *keep him*?
    I say unto you nay.

    b he will not even suffer that he shall feed among his flocks
but will *drive him* away and cast him out

a I say unto you that even so shall it be among you if ye *know*
not the name by which ye are called

X' Sealed by God

5:15 Therefore I would
    1 that ye should be steadfast and immovable, always
abounding in good works
    2 that Christ the Lord God Omnipotent may seal you his
    3 that you may be brought to heaven
    4 that ye may have everlasting salvation and eternal life

through the
    1 wisdom
    2 and power
    3 and justice
    4 and mercy

of him
    who created *all* things
      in heaven and in earth
    who is God above *all*. Amen.

Comments. Regarding section 7, we note the following:
In X it is interesting that a double reference (a a) to making a
covenant (5:6–7) is contrasted with a double reference (a a)
to making people free (5:8). This direct association is confirmed by the integral connection between the ancient Israelite concept of freedom and the rights of liberty and the

notion of being a covenant people (Exodus 21:2; Jeremiah 35:9–10; John 8:33).

The rebirth of the multitude (5:7) appears to be the enactment of the central admonition and requirement of Benjamin's speech (3:18), that one must become as a child. This points to the conclusion that to Benjamin "becom[ing] as little children" meant being born of God.

The components of section 7 are almost exclusively constructed out of couplets and are matched with their corresponding elements in pairs. This technique seems to be executed in this culminating section of the speech more uniformly than in any other portion of the oration. The related couplets in X are nearly synonymous. In Y the (a) lines name the obligation and reward of obedience. Moreover, the (a) passages in Y relate to the (a) passages in Y', with the one addition that in Y the knowledge of the name is simply acquired by way of the ceremony but in Y' it is achieved by way of acquaintance through service.

Subsection X' invokes the final aspiration of the people of covenant, namely to be sealed or marked with a seal, certifying purity of quality and accurateness of measurement in preparation for receipt by the Lord. It may be that the four stages of exaltation mentioned in 5:15 were intended to be paralleled by the four attributes of God mentioned immediately thereafter. Sealing is a product of God's wisdom or his knowledge of the quality of a person's works; "that you may be brought to heaven" is effected by God's power; "that you may have everlasting salvation" results from the justice of the atonement; and "eternal life," which is the greatest of the gifts of God, is bestowed on mortals by the Father's mercy.

The central chiasm found in 5:10–12 can be summarized and displayed as follows:

a name of Christ
  b called by some other name
    c left hand of God.
      d remember the name
        e blotted out
          f transgression
          f transgress
        e blotted out
      d remember to retain the name
    c left hand of God
  b voice by which ye shall be called
a the name by which he shall call you

The sustained precision of form in these central verses merits comment. The length of this chiasm alone is impressive, equaled only by the central chiasm of the entire speech in 3:18–19. But even more meaningful is the successful integration of some unusual terms. For example, the phrase "left hand of God" appears twice in subsection Z (5:10, 12) and is a rare metaphor in the scriptures. Likewise, "blotted out" (5:11) occurs only in these verses in the Book of Mormon. This passage successfully builds to its climax and intensifies its final exhortation against transgression by the striking introduction of these carefully chosen and intentionally reiterated terms.

Chiasmus at the Level of the Entire Speech

We have so far examined the boundaries between the seven sections of the speech and the presence of chiasmus at the levels of main concepts and individual words as they appear throughout the seven main sections. One final level of overall analysis remains to be considered. When viewed as a whole and in detail, the seven major sections of Benjamin's speech associate with each other in a balancing and complementary fashion. The order is again chiastic, pairing sections 1 and 7, 2 and 6, 3 and 5, with 4 at the center. The subject matter of each section relates to that of its complementary section more advantageously than it does to any other section in the system.

    Section 1 (2:9–28)
      Section 2 (2:31–41)
        Section 3 (3:2–3:10)
          Section 4 (3:11–27)
        Section 5 (4:4–12)
      Section 6 (4:13–30)
    Section 7 (5:6–15)

Many links form a strong bond between the first and last sections of the speech. God's roles as heavenly king (2:19) and Heavenly Father (5:7) are brought to the audience's attention in 1 and 7. The first speaks of the physical creation, the latter of becoming spiritually begotten this day. At the end of 1.A' (2:28), Benjamin's thoughts turned to his death with the hope that his spirit will be raised up to praise God; the conclusion of 7.X' expresses the same hope for all people, "that you may be brought to heaven" (5:15). The turning point of 7.Z (5:10–12) impresses upon the audience the importance of the covenant (5:1–5), which placed the people under the rule of the king and God; likewise, the imperatives in 1.E (2:18–19) are emphatic about the obligations that devolved upon the people under the rule of God and their king. In 1.D–D', Benjamin disparages his own years of service, for one cannot boast of his service to his fellowmen, since that service is only in the service of God, but service to God is unavoidably unprofitable to God and therefore it too is not to man's credit. However, in 7.Y–Y', we learn that the purpose and benefit of service is not found in repaying God but in increasing our knowledge of the Lord, "for how knoweth a man a master whom he hath not

served?" (5:13). The idea that all service is service to God
(1.D, 2:16–17) is also related to the declarations in Leviticus
25:8–55, which forbid one child of the covenant from en-
slaving another after the beginning of the jubilee year, because "they are my servants, which I brought up from the
land of Egypt" (Leviticus 25:42; see 25:55). Thus all charity
is ultimately of God, and hence Benjamin explained "neither have I suffered that ye should be confined in dungeons
nor that ye should make slaves one with another" (2:13,
1.C). Leviticus 25:10 also required that because of this freedom and equality among the Israelites, at jubilee "ye
shall . . . proclaim liberty throughout all the land unto all
the inhabitants of the land." Accordingly, in 7.X (5:8), Benjamin proclaimed his people to be reviewed under the covenant, "and under this head ye are made free."

Sections 2 and 6 both strive to create a well-ordered
covenant community based on individual righteousness
and generosity that is motivated by God's goodness and
forgiveness. Both sections condemn contention and promote obedience. Benjamin warns in 2:32, "Beware lest there
shall arise contentions among you and ye list to obey the
evil spirit, which was spoken of by my father Mosiah," and
in 4:14, "neither will ye suffer that they . . . fight and quarrel
one with another, and serve the devil, who is the evil spirit
which hath been spoken of by our fathers." Enough allusions to the jubilee laws of Leviticus 25–26 occur in sections
2 and 6 that it is probable that Benjamin had this portion of
the Pentateuch in mind when he speaks of "the records"
(2:34, 2.H) and "the laws of God" (4:14, 6.B). For example,
Leviticus 25:10 says "Return every man unto his possession," and Mosiah 4:28 says each person "should return the
thing that he borroweth"; Leviticus 26:3 declares, "Walk in
my statutes, and keep my commandments, and do them,"
and Mosiah 2:31 encourages, "Keep the commandments of

my son, or the commandments of God." Accordingly, sections 2 and 6 are closely related by several factors, including the density of their simultaneous use of material from Leviticus 25–26.[88]

Sections 3 and 5 naturally complement each other as the angel proclaims of Christ's mission and Benjamin testified of God's goodness which provides the way for salvation.

Section 4, at the center, expresses the condition which all people must satisfy before they can be redeemed from their iniquities. This is clearly the turning point of a righteous relationship with God, the point of conversion, and the precondition of the covenant. Much the same condition is required in the Pentateuch: "If they shall confess their iniquity . . . if then their uncircumcised hearts be humbled . . . then will I remember my covenant with Jacob" (Leviticus 26:40–42; compare Mosiah 4:2; 3:18–19).

Conclusion

Since 1830, when the Book of Mormon was published, those who have believed in the book have asserted that its style reads like that of Hebrew texts.[89] Those who have not accepted the book have insisted that its style is "stilted, complicated, diffuse, meaningless or even brutal"[90] and that any resemblance between the style of the Book of Mormon and Hebrew is due solely to the passages in the Book of Mormon that have been "plagiarized from the Bible."[91] The book has been attacked frequently because of its repetitive and apparently redundant manner of speaking. For many years, the literary qualities of the Book of Mormon remained inadequately studied.[92] Even among its literary critics "the Book of Mormon has not been universally considered as one of those books that must be read in order to have an opinion on it."[93] Several recent publications, however, have made significant progress in reversing these dour assessments of the Book of Mormon as literature,[94] and this study takes one further step in that direction by examining the literary structure of a small but significant portion of that book. The results have shown that Benjamin achieved a substantially high and distinguished plateau of literary fluency and accomplishment in the use of ancient forms of parallelism and chiasmus. These attributes show Benjamin's speech as a marvelous example of chiastic literature.

It is impressive how fluently Benjamin employed chiastic orders and sustained precise balances of length and meaning in the related sections and subsections of his presentation. It is insightful to see how much these literary figures enhance and convey the messages and especially the practical applications of Benjamin's ethical principles; many details take on new significance in light of comparative and structural analysis. Interestingly, Benjamin frequently placed man and the human situation at the center of attention in his chiastic arrangements. This differs from Nephi, for example, who consistently placed the word of the Lord or revelations of the Lord at the focal point. In this regard, Benjamin's approach accords with his renaissance personality and his overall moment in Nephite history, when several democratic impulses were shifting important privileges to the ordinary members of society.

For all these reasons, I believe that careful literary analysis helps in many ways to understand Benjamin's speech itself. Seeing it against a background of Hebrew literature and formal artistry reveals an unmistakable congruence between Old World conventions, universal qualities, and the literary structure of King Benjamin's incomparable speech.

The following charts list and illustrate the many types of parallelisms and repetitions that can be identified in the English translation of Mosiah 2–5.

1. Index of Parallelistic Patterns in Benjamin's Speech

Simple Synonymous Parallelism (a/a)

2:9 ye that have assembled yourselves together/you that can hear my words

2:18 ye called me your king/whom ye call your king
I labor to serve you/ought not ye labor to serve

2:23 created you/granted unto you your lives

2:24 immediately bless you/hath paid you

2:27 that I might be found blameless/that your blood should not come upon me

2:28 I am about to go down to my grave/that I might go down in peace

2:31 kept my commandments/commandments of my father
prospered/kept from falling into the hands of your enemies
commandments of my son/commandments of God
prosper in the land/enemies shall have no power

2:39 mercy has no claim/doomed to endure never-ending torment

3:4 sent me to declare unto thee that thou mayest rejoice/thou mayest declare unto thy people that they may also be filled with joy

3:5 time cometh/is not far distant
who was and is/from all eternity to all eternity
shall come down from heaven among the children of men/shall dwell in a tabernacle of clay

3:9–10 he cometh unto his own that salvation might come unto the children of men/all these things are done that a righteous judgment might come upon the children of men

3:24 this people at the judgment day / they shall be judged

3:25 consigned to an awful view / their own guilt and abominations
state of misery / endless torment

3:26–27 justice could no more deny / it could deny
mercy could have claim on them no more forever / their torment ascendeth up forever and ever

4:5 your nothingness / your worthless and fallen state

4:9 believe in God / believe that he is
he created all things both in heaven and in earth / he has all wisdom and all power both in heaven and in earth

4:11 knowledge of the glory of God / ye have known of his goodness
remember / retain in remembrance
humble yourselves / depths of humility

4:12 knowledge of the glory of him / knowledge of that which is just and true

4:14 transgress the laws of God / fight and quarrel

4:16 succor those that stand in need / administer of your substance unto him that standeth in need

4:20 calling on his name / begging for a remission of your sins
has caused that your hearts should be filled with joy / has caused that your mouths should be stopped so exceedingly great was your joy

4:26 visiting the sick / administering to their relief

4:28 you borroweth / he borroweth
thou shalt commit sin / thou shalt cause thy neighbor to commit sin

4:30 observe the commandments of God / continue in the faith

5:6–7 covenant which ye have made is a righteous covenant / because of the covenant which ye have made ye shall be called the children of Christ

5:8   under this head ye are made free/there is no other head whereby ye can be made free
name given whereby salvation cometh/name of Christ

5:9   the name by which he is called/he shall be called by the name of Christ

5:14   not suffer that he shall feed among his flocks/drive away and cast him out

Extended Synonymous Parallelisms (a/a/a)

2:9   open your ears that ye may hear/your hearts that ye may understand/your minds that the mysteries of God may be unfolded to your view

2:11   chosen by this people/consecrated by my father/suffered by hand of the Lord

3:3–4   I come to declare unto you the glad tidings of great joy/sent me to declare unto thee that thou mayest rejoice/thou mayest declare unto thy people that they may also be filled with joy

3:5   working mighty miracles/healing sick/raising dead/causing lame to walk/blind to receive sight/deaf to hear/curing all manner of diseases

3:8   Jesus Christ/the Son of God/the Father of heaven and earth/the Creator of all things from the beginning

3:11   fallen by the transgression of Adam/died not knowing the will of God concerning them/ignorantly sinned

4:8   and there is none other salvation/save this which hath been spoken of/neither are there any conditions whereby man can be saved/except the conditions which I have told you

4:11   come to the knowledge of the glory of God/known of his goodness/tasted of his love/received a remission of sins
humble yourselves/calling on the name of the Lord daily/standing steadfastly in the faith

4:12   always rejoice / be filled with the love of God / always retain a remission of sins / grow in the knowledge of the glory of him / in the knowledge of that which is just and true

4:13-14 not have a mind to injure / live peaceably / render to every man according to that which is due / not suffer your children that they go hungry or naked / neither suffer that they transgress the laws of God

4:14   master of sin / evil spirit / enemy to all righteousness

4:15   walk in the ways of truth and soberness / love one another / serve one another

4:17   stay my hand / not give unto him of my food / nor impart of my substance

4:26   feeding hungry / clothing naked / visiting sick / administering relief

4:30   watch yourselves / thoughts and words and deeds / observe the commandments of God / continue in the faith

5:13   how knoweth a man the master he has not served / a stranger unto him / far from the thoughts and intents of his heart

5:15   Christ may seal you his / be brought to heaven / have everlasting salvation and eternal life

Simple Alternate (a/b/a/b)

2:9   ye have assembled yourselves / words which I shall speak / commanded you to come up / words which I shall speak

2:10-11 I myself / mortal man / like yourselves / subject to all manner of infirmities in body and mind

2:11   I am subject to all manner of infirmities in body and mind / chosen by people / suffered by hand of the Lord / ruler and a king over this people
ruler and king over this people / kept and preserved by his matchless power / serve with all the might, mind, strength / Lord granted unto me

2:15   I have not done these things/that I might boast/neither do
I tell these things/that I might accuse you

2:22   requires of you/keep commandments/promised you/
keep commandments

2:23–24   granted unto you your lives/indebted unto him/he paid
you/indebted unto him

2:25   I ask/can ye say/I answer/ye cannot say
ye are dust of the earth/ye were created/dust of the earth/
him who created you

2:31   kept my commandments and the commandments of my
father/prospered and have been kept from falling into
hands of enemies/keep commandments of my son or the
commandments of God which shall be delivered unto
you by him/prosper in the land and your enemies will
have no power over you

2:34   have been taught/prophecies/have been spoken/holy
prophets

3:4   sent me to declare/thou mayest rejoice/thou mayest de-
clare/they may also be filled with joy

3:9–10   he cometh unto his own/salvation might come unto children of men/all these things are done/righteous judgment might come upon children of men

4:5–6   knowledge of goodness of God/your nothingness and
your worthless and fallen state/knowledge of goodness
of God/his matchless power, wisdom, patience, and
long-suffering

4:8   none other salvation/save this which hath been spoken of/
neither are there any conditions whereby man can be
saved/except the conditions I have told you

4:11   greatness of God/your nothingness/his goodness and
long-suffering/you unworthy creatures

4:14   ye will not suffer/they go hungry or naked/neither will ye
suffer/they transgress the laws of God and fight and
quarrel

4:15   teach them/walk in the ways of truth and soberness/teach them/love one another and serve one another

4:16   ye will succor/those that need your succor/ye will administer of your substance/unto him that standeth in need

Repeated Alternate (a/b/a/b/a/b)

2:9   ears/ye may hear/hearts/ye may understand/minds/ mysteries of God may be unfolded to your view

3:3–4   I am come to declare unto you/great joy/hath sent me to declare unto thee/thou mayest rejoice/thou mayest declare unto thy people/they may also be filled with joy

Extended Alternates (a/b/c//a/b/c)

2:12, 14   suffered to spend my days/in your service/have not sought gold nor silver/nor any manner of riches of you// labored with mine own hands/I serve you/ye should not be laden with taxes/nothing come upon you which was grievous to be borne

2:22   all that he requires of you/he has promised you/keep his commandments/prosper in the land//he never doth vary/from that which he hath said/keep his commandments/bless and prosper you

2:31   kept my commandments/commandments of my father/ prospered/kept from falling into hands of enemies// keep the commandments/commandments of God/prosper in the land/enemies shall have no power over you

3:3–4   I am come to declare/unto you/glad tidings of great joy// sent me to declare/unto thee/that thou mayest rejoice// thou mayest declare/unto thy people/that they may be filled with joy

3:12, 15   rebelleth against God/salvation cometh to none/except through repentance and faith//hardened their hearts/ law of Moses availeth nothing/except through atonement

4:20   has caused/your hearts/should be filled with joy//has caused/your mouths/should be stopped so exceedingly great was your joy

Simple or Extended Synthetic Parallelism (a/b or a/b//c/d)

2:10–11   I am [not] more than a mortal man/I am like yourselves subject to all manner of infirmities in body and mind//I have been chosen by this people/consecrated by my father//was suffered by hand of the Lord/I should be ruler and king over this people

2:14   I have labored with mine own hands/that I might serve you

2:17   I tell you these things that ye may learn wisdom/that ye may learn

2:19   spent his days in your service/has been in the service of God

2:20   God created you/kept and preserved you
caused ye should rejoice/granted ye should live in peace

2:21   ye should serve him/ye would be unprofitable servants

2:23   he hath created you/granted unto you your lives

2:24   he doth immediately bless you/he hath paid you//ye are still indebted/and are and will be forever and ever

2:25   ye were created of the dust of the earth/it belongeth to him who created you

2:26   I am no better than ye yourselves are/I am also of the dust

2:27–28   I have caused ye should assemble together/I might be found blameless//I have caused ye should assemble yourselves together/I might rid my garments of your blood

2:31   prosper in the land/enemies will have no power over you

2:32   lest there shall arise contentions among you/ye list to obey the evil spirit

2:33   wo pronounced upon him/listeth to obey that spirit//listeth to obey him and remaineth and dieth in sins/drinketh damnation to soul//drinketh damnation to soul/receiveth for wages an everlasting punishment

2:34   ye are eternally indebted to heavenly Father/render to him all you have and are

2:35   that which was commanded them of the Lord/they are just and true

2:38–39 repenteth not and remaineth and dieth an enemy to God/ final doom is to endure a never-ending torment

2:41   these things are true/Lord God hath spoken it

3:7   more than man can suffer/except it be unto death//he shall suffer even more than man can suffer except it be unto death/for behold blood cometh from every pore//great shall be his anguish/wickedness and abominations of people

3:11   fallen by transgression of Adam/died not knowing will of God or who have ignorantly sinned

3:12   rebelleth against God/for salvation cometh to none such except it be through repentance and faith on the Lord

3:16   in Adam or by nature they fall/the blood of Christ atoneth for their sins

3:17–18 salvation can come/in and through the name of Christ the infant perisheth not/men drink damnation to their own souls

3:21   none shall be found blameless/only through repentance and faith

4:8   means whereby salvation cometh/none other salvation save this

4:11   humble yourselves/depths of humility
calling on the name of the Lord daily/standing steadfastly in the faith
that which is to come/was spoken by the mouth of the angel

4:12   rejoice/filled with the love of God and retain a remission of
        your sins and grow in the knowledge
        knowledge of the glory of him that created you/knowl-
        edge of that which is just and true

4:13   live peaceably/render to every man that which is his due

4:15   teach them to walk in the ways of truth and soberness/
        teach them to love one another and to serve one another

4:16   administer of your substance/not suffer that the beggar
        putteth up petition in vain

4:18   he perisheth forever/hath no interest in the kingdom of
        God

4:20   calling on his name/begging for a remission of sins

4:23   wo be unto that man/his substance perish with him

4:24   the poor who have not/have sufficient that ye remain from
        day to day//I give not because I have not/if I had I
        would give

4:25   your condemnation is just/ye covet that which ye have not
        received

4:26   retaining a remission of your sins/ye may walk guiltless
        before God
        administering relief/both spiritually and temporally ac-
        cording to their wants

4:27   not requisite/man should run faster/than he has strength
        //expedient/he should be diligent/he might win the
        prize

4:28   borroweth of neighbor should return the thing he borrow-
        eth/or else thou shalt commit sin and perhaps cause thy
        neighbor to commit sin also

4:29   I cannot tell you all the things whereby ye may commit sin/
        there are divers ways and means even so many that I can-
        not number them

4:30   if ye do not watch yourselves/ye must perish

5:6–7   covenant is a righteous covenant/ye shall be called the
        children of Christ
        spiritually begotten you/your hearts are changed//your
        hearts are changed/ye are born of him
        ye are born of him/sons and his daughters

5:8   under this head ye are made free/is no other head whereby
        ye can be made free

Antithetical Parallelism (a/-a)

2:11   I am like as yourselves, subject to infirmities in body and
        mind/yet I have been chosen by this people

2:15   not done things that I might boast/neither tell things that I
        might accuse you/but that ye know I answer a clear con-
        science before God

2:25   can ye say aught of yourselves/ye cannot say ye are as
        much as the dust
        yet ye were created of dust/but it belongeth to him who
        created you

2:39   mercy hath no claim/therefore his final doom is never-end-
        ing torment

3:18   infant perisheth not/but men drink damnation to their
        own souls

3:24   whether they be good/or whether they be evil

4:13   ye will not injure one another/but live peaceably

4:14–15 not suffer children that they go hungry or naked neither
        will ye suffer that they transgress laws of God/but teach
        them to walk in the ways of truth

4:24   I give not/because I have not/but if I had/I would give

4:25   if ye say this in your hearts ye remain guiltless/otherwise
        ye are condemned

5:2   no more disposition to do evil/but to do good continually

5:9–10   whosoever doeth this shall be found at the right hand of
God for he shall know the name by which he is called for
he shall be called by the name of Christ / whosoever shall
not take upon him the name of Christ must be called by
some other name therefore he findeth himself on the left
hand of God

Detailing, Working Out (a₁, a₂, a₃, . . .)

2:9   why they have assembled to listen to Benjamin

2:11   why Benjamin is king

2:14   why King Benjamin has labored

2:17   what wisdom there is to learn from his teachings

2:18   why they ought to serve one another

2:19   why they should thank God

2:20–21   what God has done for the people

2:20–27   why they are indebted to God

2:28–29   why they were assembled

2:33–34   why they are indebted to God

2:34–35   what the people have been taught

2:36   why they are accountable
effects of withdrawing from the Spirit

2:37–39   why mercy hath no claim on some

2:41   blessings of righteous

3:5   amount of time before God comes
qualities of God
mission of Christ

3:5–10   mission of Christ

3:7   what Christ will suffer

3:8   titles of God

3:9   man's understanding and treatment of Christ

3:11   extent of atonement

3:12   warning to the rebellious

3:16   innocence of children

3:19   traits of righteous

3:24–25 the final judgment

3:25–27 punishment for the wicked

4:5–6   knowledge of God

4:9–10 what to believe, understand, do

4:11   what a knowledge of God is

4:12   what to remember

4:13   how to live

4:14–15 how to treat children

4:17   man's rationalization of treatment of poor

4:19–22 why we should serve others

4:24–25 what to do if you are poor yourself

4:26   mission of humans

5:7   how they relate to Christ

5:13   how a man knows the master

5:15   how to achieve eternal life
        attributes of God

Climactic Forms:

Climax

2:31   kept my commandments, commandments of my father,
        have prospered, have been kept from falling, keep com-
        mandments of my son, commandments of God, shall
        prosper, enemies will have no power

3:5   time cometh, not far distant, who was and is, eternity to
        eternity, come down among men, dwell in tabernacle of
        clay

4:9–10 believe God, believe he is, all things in heaven and earth, all
        power in heaven and earth

Staircase Parallelism Up (Anabasis)

2:9   hearken unto me . . . mysteries of God unfolded to your
        view

2:11 chosen by people . . . suffered by hand of Lord to be ruler and king

2:13 be confined . . . any manner of wickedness

2:18-19 your king . . . heavenly King

2:31 my commandments . . . commandments of God; prospered . . . shall prosper

2:40-41 I have spoken . . . Lord God hath spoken

4:9-10 believe . . . do

4:21 dependent for your lives . . . impart of substance ye have

5:15 abound in good works . . . have eternal life

Staircase Parallelism Down (Catabasis)

2:21 serve him . . . yet would be unprofitable servants

2:24-25 boast . . . dust of earth

2:32-33 contentions . . . everlasting punishment

2:36-39 blessed, prospered, preserved . . . guilt, pain, anguish, never-ending torment

3:24-27 good works . . . torment forever and ever

4:18 repent . . . perisheth forever

4:29-30 commit sin . . . perish

2. Index of Chiastic Patterns in Benjamin's Speech

Chiasmus

2:5-6 a b c d d c b a

2:7 a b c d d c b a

2:12, 14 a b c d e f b c e f a d

2:15 a b b a

2:16-17 a b b a

2:20	a b c b c a
2:26	a b b a
2:27	a b c b a
2:32–33	a b b a
2:33–36	a b c d e d e c b a
2:36–37	a b c d d c b a
2:38–39	a b c c b a
2:40–41	a b c c b a
3:11–12	a b c d e f g e f g d c b a
3:13	a b b a
3:13–15	a b c c b d e e d b a
3:14–15	a b b a
3:15–16	a b c d e f g e f g d c b a
3:17, 20	a b c d e a c d b e
3:18–19	a b c d e f f e d c b a
3:23–27	a b a
4:6–7	a b c d e d c b a
4:11	a b b a
4:11–12	a a b c d e e f f d b c a a
4:18	a b b a
4:19	a b b a
4:21	a b b a
	a b c c b a
	a b c d d c b a
4:22	a b b a
	a b c c b a
4:24	a b b a
4:24–25	a b c d d c b a
5:8–9	a a b c c b a a
5:10–12	a b c d e f f e d c b a
5:13–14	a b b a
5:15	a b a

Structural Chiasmus

2:9–28 A B C D E D C B A

2:31–41 F G H G F

3:2–10 J K L M N M L K J

3:11–16 P Q R Q P

3:17–22 S T S

4:4–12 X Y X

4:13–28 A B C D E F E D C B A

5:6–15 X Y Z Y X

2:9–5:15 A B C D C B A

3. Index of Other Repetitive Patterns in Benjamin's Speech

Contrasting Ideas

2:31 prospered/kept from falling
      prosper/your enemies shall have no power

3:19 putteth off natural man/becometh a saint

3:24 good/evil

4:5–6 your nothingness, worthless and fallen state/his matchless power and his wisdom and his patience and his long suffering

4:11 the greatness of God/your own nothingness
      his goodness and long suffering/you unworthy creatures

Duplication

2:21 day to day

2:24 forever and ever

2:41 remember remember

3:5 eternity to eternity

3:12 wo wo

3:27 forever and ever

Echoes

Adam: 3:11–26; 4:7

atonement: 3:11–19; 4:6–7

believing: 3:13–18; 4:9–21

Benjamin's calling as king: 2:11, 18–19, 26

blessed: 2:22–41; 3:16

blood: 2:27–28; 3:7–18

boasting: 2:15–16, 25

call/calling: 2:18–26; 3:8; 4:11, 20; 5:7–14

Christ: 3:8, 12–13; 3:16–19; 5:7–15

commandments: 2:9–13, 22–41; 3:22–27; 4:6, 30

contention, evil spirit, enemy to all righteousness: 2:32, 37–38; 3:6, 19; 4:14

created: 2:20–25; 4:9, 12, 21; 5:15

earth: 2:25–26; 3:8; 4:9; 5:15

evil: 2:32, 37; 3:6, 25; 4:14

faith: 2:41; 3:9, 12, 21; 4:6, 11, 21, 30; 5:7

fall: 3:11, 16, 19, 26; 4:5, 7

forever: 2:24, 38; 3:19, 27; 4:18

God: 2:9, 15–20, 27–31, 33, 36–38, 41; 3:8–14, 19–26; 4:5–30; 5:8–15

great/greatness: 3:3–13; 4:11–20

have and are: 2:34; 4:21

heart: 2:9; 3:6, 15; 4:10, 20–25; 5:7, 11–13

heaven: 2:19, 34, 41; 3:8; 5:15

innocence or salvation of children: 2:34; 3:16, 18–19, 21

joy: 3:3, 4, 13; 4:20

judging: 2:27; 3:4, 10, 18, 24; 4:22

just: 2:35, 38; 3:18, 26; 4:12–25; 5:15

keeping the commandments: 2:22, 24, 31, 41; 4:6, 30

law: 3:14–15; 4:14

list to obey: 2:32–33, 37

Lord: 2:11–13, 35–41; 3:– 5, 12–27; 4:6, 9, 11, 30; 5:15

name: 3:9, 17, 21; 4:11, 20; 5:7–14

obedience: 2:32–37; 4:30; 5:8

omnipotent: 3:5, 17–18, 21; 5:15

perish: 3:18; 4:16–30

power: 2:11, 20, 31; 3:5; 4:6, 9; 5:15

receive: 2:33, 41; 3:5, 13

rejoice: 2:20; 3:4, 13; 4:12

remember: 2:40–41; 4:11, 28, 30; 5:11–12

remission: 3:13; 4:11–12, 20, 26

repent: 2:38; 3:12, 21; 4:10, 18, 22

righteous: 2:37; 3:4, 10; 5:6

salvation through Christ: 3:9, 12, 17, 18; 4:6–8; 5:8, 15

salvation: 3:9, 12, 17–18; 4:6–8; 5:8, 15

service: 2:11–27; 4:15; 5:13

sin/transgress: 2:33, 36, 40; 3:11–16; 4:10-29

spirit/spiritual: 2:36, 41; 3:19; 4:20, 26; 5:7

suffer: 2:11–13; 4:6, 11, 14–20; 5:14

teaching: 2:13, 34–36; 3:22; 4:15

truth: 2:35, 41; 4:12, 15

wisdom: 2:17, 36; 4:6, 9, 27; 5:15

Like Beginnings (Anaphora)

3:7, 9   and lo/and lo

3:17, 20   and moreover I say unto you/and moreover I say unto you

3:20–22   the time shall come/when that time cometh none shall/at this time when thou shalt

4:9–10   believe (5)

Like Endings (Amoebaeon)

2:15   that I might boast

2:16–17   in the service of God/only in the service of your God

2:18–19 ye have called me your king/I whom ye call your king/
 your heavenly King

2:23–24 indebted unto him/indebted unto him

2:25 dust of the earth/dust of the earth

4:9 in heaven and in earth/in heaven and in earth

4:15 one another/one another

4:20 caused that your hearts should be filled with joy/so exceedingly great was your joy

4:27 see that all these things are done in wisdom and order/all
 things must be done in order

4:28 or else thou shalt commit sin/thou shalt cause thy neighbor to commit sin

4:30 perish/perish not

5:7 his sons and his daughters/his sons and his daughters

Many *And*s (Polysyndeton)

2:9	3:4	4:11
2:11	3:5	4:12
2:20	3:4–11	4:20
2:24	4:6–8	4:24–5
2:31	4:9–10	4:29–30

Nor, Or, Not, Neither, None (Paradiastole)

2:12–13 not sought gold/nor silver/nor any manner of riches of you
 Neither have I suffered/nor that ye should make slaves/
 nor that ye should murder/or plunder/or steal/ or commit adultery
 I have not suffered

2:15–16 I have not done these things that I might boast/neither do I
 tell these things that thereby I might accuse you

3:24 whether they be good / or whether they be evil

4:7 or who are / or who ever shall be

4:8 there is none other salvation / neither are there any conditions

4:12 ye shall grow in the knowledge of the glory / or in the knowledge of that which is just and true

Loose Repetition of Words

2:9–36 brethren (5)

2:11–26 king (6)

2:22–36 prosper (5)

2:22–41 blessed (5)

3:7–18 blood (5)

3:11–19 atonement (5)

3:11–26 Adam (4)
fall (4)

3:13–19 holy (3)

4:5–11 goodness (4)

4:10–14 sin (4)

4:14–19 suffer (5)

4:15 teach (2)

4:16–24 beg(ging) / beggar (5)

4:16–30 perish (4)

4:20–25 condemn(ation) (4)

5:7–14 called (5)
name (11)

Tight Repetition of Words

2:12–14 suffer(ed) (4)

2:15 I (6)

2:18–19 king (4)
serve/service (4)

2:20–21 you/ye/your (18)

2:22 prosper (2)

2:25–26 dust (3)

2:31 commandments (4)
prosper(ed) (2)
enemies (2)

2:33–36 list(eth) (2)
spirit (2)
transgress(ed) (2)
spoken (2)

2:40–41 remember/remembrance (3)

3:2–3 awake/awoke (3)

3:3–4 joy/rejoice (3)

3:7 suffer (2)

3:17–19 child(ren) (4)

3:18–19 submit (2)

3:24–27 torment (2)
evil (2)
justice/judgment/judged (3)

4:6–8 salvation (4)

4:9–10 believe (5)

4:10–11 humble/humility (3)

4:20–22 belong(eth) (2)
substance (3)

4:24 give (2)
have/had (2)

4:27–30 borroweth (2)
neighbor (2)
order (2)
perish (2)

5:6–8 covenant (4)

5:10–13 name (4)
call(ed) (3)
remember (3)
transgress(ion) (2)

5:15 heaven (2)

Repetition of Phrases

2:9 words which I shall speak (2)

2:9–10 commanded you to come up hither (2)

2:15–19 in the service of (your) God (5)

2:20–21 created you (2)
preserved you (2)
whole souls (2)

2:20–25 created you (5)

2:22 keep his commandments (3)

2:23–24 indebted unto him (2)

2:28–29 I have caused that ye should assemble yourselves together (2)

2:33 list(eth) to obey (2)

2:33–36 been taught (concerning / all) these things (2)

3:7–9 and lo (2)

3:8 shall be called (2)

3:18–19 natural man (2)
atoning blood of Christ / atonement of Christ (2)

3:22–23 I have spoken (2)

3:23–27 commanded me (2)

3:24–25 they be evil (2)

3:24–27 therefore they have drunk (2)
no more (2)

4:5–6 knowledge of the goodness of God (2)

4:6–7 atonement prepared from the foundation of the world (2)

4:9 man doth not comprehend all things / which the Lord can comprehend (2)

4:9–10   both in heaven and in earth (2)

4:11–12   remission of your sins (2)
          knowledge of the glory (2)

4:20–22   has caused (2)

4:24–25   have not (3)
          ye say (this) in your hearts (2)

4:26   for the sake of (2)
          according to (2)

4:27   see that all these things (are / must be) done in wisdom and
          order (2)

4:27–30   commit sin (3)

5:7   sons and daughters (2)
          made free (2)

5:10–13   left hand of God (2)

Repetition of Particles

behold / for behold: 2:16–19, 22, 33, 35, 41; 3:5, 11, 18; 4:5, 19, 20; 5:7

and lo: 3:7, 9

for: 2:7, 30; 3:4, 19; 5:13

O: 2:19, 32, 40, 41; 4:2, 18, 21, 30

and: 2:1–6, 8–9, 14, 23–26, 29, 31, 35, 36, 41; 3:1–3, 6–10, 13, 15–17,
    20–25, 27; 4:1, 3, 4, 8, 11–14, 16, 20–22, 24–29; 5:1–11, 14

yet / but / neither: 2:9, 11, 13, 15, 32; 3:12, 14, 18; 4:15, 18

I say unto you: 2:12, 16, 20, 21, 28, 29, 34, 36, 37, 39; 4:6, 11, 12, 23;
    5:12

Synonymous Elements

2:36   blessed, prospered, preserved

2:38   guilt, pain, anguish

3:5   miracles, healing the sick, raising the dead, etc.

3:7   temptations, pain, hunger, thirst, fatigue

3:8   Jesus Christ, Son of God, Father, Creator

3:13   kindred, nation, tongue

3:20   nation, kindred, tongue, people

4:4   friends, brethren, kindred, people

4:6   power, wisdom, patience, long-suffering

4:11   glory, goodness, greatness, etc.

4:29–30 selves, thoughts, words, deeds

5:15   wisdom, power, justice, mercy

Notes

1. Mark Twain, *Roughing It* (New York: Harper, 1899), 132.

2. Sidney B. Sperry, "The Book of Mormon as Literature," reprinted in *JBMS* 4/1 (1995): 44.

3. James Muilenburg, "Form Criticism and Beyond," *JBL* 88/1 (1969): 18.

4. Donald W. Parry, "Hebrew Literary Patterns in the Book of Mormon," *Ensign* (October 1989): 59.

5. Ibid.

6. James Muilenburg, "A Study in Hebrew Rhetoric: Repetition and Style," *Vetus Testamentum* Supp. 1 (1953): 98, quoted in David J. A. Clines, "The Parallelism of Greater Precision: Notes from Isaiah 40 for a Theory of Hebrew Poetry," in *Directions in Biblical Hebrew Poetry*, ed. Elaine R. Follis (Sheffield, England: JSOT, 1987), 87.

7. Defined in Donald W. Parry, *The Book of Mormon Text Reformatted according to Parallelistic Patterns* (Provo, Utah: FARMS, 1992), i–li. See also Donald W. Parry, "Poetic Parallelisms in the Book of Mormon" (FARMS, 1988); Donald W. Parry, "Parallelisms Listed in Textual Sequence" (FARMS, 1983); and Donald W. Parry, "Parallelisms according to Classification" (FARMS, 1988).

8. Parry, "Hebrew Literary Patterns," 59, citing Robert Lowth, *Isaiah: A New Translation* (London: Nichols, 1795), ix.

9. See John W. Welch, ed., *Chiasmus in Antiquity* (Hildesheim: Gerstenberg, 1981), and John W. Welch, "Chiasmus Bibliography" (Provo, Utah: FARMS, 1997). An early version of this re-

search was presented under the title "Chiasmus in King Benjamin's Speech" at the Brigham Young University Book of Mormon Symposium, 1970.

10. See *The Odyssey* 11:170. For further discussion see Welch, *Chiasmus in Antiquity*, 253–54.

11. For a list of fifteen important criteria, see John W. Welch, "Criteria for Identifying and Evaluating the Presence of Chiasmus," *JBMS* 4/2 (1995): 1–14.

12. Lund lists the following as the first two of his seven criteria for chiasmus in the Bible: "1. The centre is always the turning point. 2. At the centre there is often a change in the trend of thought and an antithetic idea is introduced." Nils W. Lund, *Chiasmus in the New Testament* (Chapel Hill, North Carolina: University of North Carolina, 1942; reprint Boston: Hendrickson, 1992), 40–41.

13. See the various chapters in Welch, *Chiasmus in Antiquity*.

14. For a popular acknowledgment of chiasm as "one of the writing styles of the Bible . . . [used by] many Bible authors," see James I. Packer, Merrill C. Tenney, and William White, eds., *The Bible Almanac* (Nashville: Nelson, 1980), 364. My recent bibliography of scholarly studies on chiasmus shows that many more large chiasms have been identified in the Bible than in any other body of literature.

15. See, for example, Alma 36; Alma 41:13–15.

16. At least they do not appear on any of the book lists that I have examined of holdings of libraries in the United States in the 1830s.

17. See John W. Welch, "What Does Chiasmus in the Book of Mormon Prove?" in *Book of Mormon Authorship Revisited: The Evidence for Ancient Origins*, ed. Noel B. Reynolds (Provo, Utah: FARMS, 1997), 199–224.

18. These ceremonies bear several resemblances to ancient year-rite festivals, particularly in the proclamations of peace and prosperity given by the king (Mosiah 2:31, 41). Purification was also associated with the Jewish calendar through the sabbatical year jubilee (Leviticus 25:8–17). It may be that the purification of

the nation conducted here at the beginning of this new monarch's reign resembles the sabbatical year cleansing, the abolition of debts, return to families, and redemption of property to the poor, etc. This would help explain the special reference to family gathering (Mosiah 2:5) and also the emphasis in 4:13–30 upon imparting one's substance to the needy.

19. Compare "assemble yourselves together" (2:27–28).

20. This phrase forms an *inclusio* at the beginning and end of Benjamin's call to attention.

21. Benjamin's lack of strength alone stands in contrast to the "strength which the Lord hath granted [him]" (2:11).

22. Compare "mortal frame" (2:26).

23. Compare "I . . . am no better than ye yourselves" (2:26).

24. Perhaps these lines contain the chiasm: people, my father (= king), Lord, ruler (= Lord), king, people.

25. By affirming that he has served his people with all of his God-given might, mind, and strength, Benjamin prepares the way for a powerful reinforcement of the duty of man to serve God with all one's might, mind, and strength (compare Deuteronomy 6:5). Because God through Benjamin has served man in this way, man comes under an obligation to serve God in the same way.

26. In this chiasm, Benjamin pairs the use of his time with the work of his hands.

27. In other words, been in your service.

28. The futility of boasting on account of one's service to fellowmen brackets the parallel enclosed statements about accusation in 2:15. Benjamin does not desire to accuse his people, just as he hopes that God will not accuse him.

29. The important declaration that serving fellowmen only constitutes service to God appears twice: first, with respect to King Benjamin's service; and second, as a general principle with respect to the service of all his people. These two points frame the two statements in the middle about learning wisdom.

30. Several features strengthen the parallelism of these two forceful statements that stand at the center of section 1. The words *thank* and *ought* each appear twice. The words *king* and *service* oc-

cur four times. With respect to service, the pattern is a–a–b–b: serve, serve, service, service. With respect to the word *king*, the sequence is itself chiastic, a–b–b–a: the middle two occurrences are identical conditionals, while the first and the last form an *inclusio* through a transformation of "your king" to "your heavenly King."

31. In the preceding subsection, Benjamin had spoken of *service*, then of *thanks* (mentioned twice); in this subsection, he reverses the order, speaking first of the unprofitability of *thanking* God (thanks and praise), and then of the unprofitability of *serving* God (mentioned twice).

32. In this eight-part structure, the first and third pairs (1, 2, 5, 6) and the second and fourth pairs (3, 4, 7, 8) are matched. The two halves are clearly separated by the shift from the idea of thanking God back to the idea of serving God. The first half is plainer than the second. The second half adds a strong temporal element ("from the beginning," "from day to day," "from one moment to another") that unifies the second quatrain. The entire sequence escalates from broad, general statements down to the present instant in time, and the blessings of God become graver in the progression: (3) to rejoice alone or together, (4) to live in peace one with another, (7) to live and move freely according to one's own will, and (8) to be alive at all.

33. The absolutely dependable rule that God will never vary from his promise matches the absolutely inclusive rule that all he requires is obedience to his commandments.

34. This resumptive repetition takes this phrase from elements 1 and 5 in subsection D' and uses it to introduce subsection B'.

35. This word echoes God's grant of might and strength to Benjamin in subsection B above (2:11).

36. "Bless" and "paid" in this second stanza seem to mirror "created" and "granted" in the first stanza.

37. In subsection D', mankind was merely unprofitable, but in subsection B', Benjamin sees mankind as indebted to God.

38. The words "forever and ever" reappear at the center (3:27) of the speech in section 4 below.

39. In subsection D, Benjamin was the one who sought not to

boast; in this part, D', he transfers the same condition to his people, for they also have nothing of which they should boast.

40. Structurally, these two rhetorical questions and two denials of any human claim to merit independent of God comprise the central point of subsection B'. The whole part features two propositions before the center (in the first place, mankind was created by God; and secondly God rewards obedience), and two segments after the center (in the first place, mankind was created of the dust which belongs to God; and moreover, the king also was created of the dust). Notice also the echo of *answer* in 2:25 back to *answer* in 2:15.

41. The idea of the dust belonging to God intensifies the idea in the first segment (2:23) of this section that mankind is indebted to God because of the creation, not only for the order and form of creation, but also the material substance of it as well.

42. This echoes back to the crux of this section in 2:19.

43. The expression "am no better than ye yourselves" recalls the phrase "like as yourselves" in subsection B (2:11).

44. Compare "mortal man" in subsection B above (2:10).

45. These lines bring Benjamin back into the picture. Like his people he is (1) of the dust and (3) in a mortal frame; he spans (2) his old age and approaching death with the idea of (4) birth and the mother earth.

46. See subsection D above (2:15).

47. The final segment of this section continues the typical parallel style found throughout this section. Twice, Benjamin mentions his having caused the people to assemble themselves. Twice, Benjamin speaks of going down into his grave. Twice, he refers to the blood of the people coming upon him. Twice, he envisions the judgment and justice of God. The earthly assembly in the first half becomes the heavenly assembly in the second half. In both subsections A and A', he appears to state four functions of the assembly. Whereas Benjamin's purpose in subsection A was to reveal the mysteries of God to his people, his purpose in subsection A' is to prepare himself to meet God; these two purposes, however, are connected by the concept that runs throughout this part of Benjamin's speech, namely the commonality and identity

between the circumstances of the king and of the people in the eternal scheme of God's plan.

48. Whereas a person can feel thankful without doing anything about it, blessing, praising, and honoring necessarily entail manifestations. The overt demonstration of gratitude, which verse 19 implies was shown to Benjamin, would have been traditional thank offerings presented to the king on such occasions and formal gatherings.

49. As in feudalism, all obligations are owed in the final analysis to the king. Mosiah 2:18 does not say, "If you want to serve God, do so by serving man." It says that you cannot avoid serving God even when you are not conscious of the true destination of the benefit of that service to him. Thus the admonition and imperative to serve one another in verse 19 must be derived from another source, namely Benjamin's example, not from the inherent relationship between service to man and service to God.

50. Fighting and quarreling (contending), serving the "evil spirit which hath been spoken of by our fathers" and becoming "an enemy to all righteousness" are themes also echoed in section 6 in 4:14.

51. *List to obey* occurs three times in subsection G and once in G'.

52. *Evil spirit* occurs once in subsection G and once in G'.

53. The word *spoken* occurs six times in section 2, namely, once in subsection G, three times in H, and twice in F'.

54. This expression occurs again in section 4 (3:25).

55. The theme of the "fathers" begins in subsection G with "father Mosiah" (2:32) and continues in subsection H with "father Lehi" (2:34) and "the fathers," (2:35) all of whom are tied to the Lord (d, 2:35) or "heavenly Father" (d, 2:34).

56. Although not identical, the word pair describing two main virtues of divine things, "just and true," may balance in verbal weight the previous pair describing the meager attributes of mortal man, "have and are" (2:34), echoed in 4:21.

57. The idea of coming out in open rebellion against God and the curse placed on such a person reappears in section 4 (3:12).

58. Subsection G introduced the concepts of "listing to obey the evil spirit," "remaining and dying" in one's sins, and reaping

a reward of "everlasting punishment." Subsection G' covers again the same ground in basically the same order, elaborating more fully on the meaning of "listing to obey the evil spirit," the consequences of "remaining and dying" in one's sins, and the resulting "never-ending torment."

59. This line is a balancing counterpart to 2:34, above, "I say unto you, that there are not any among you except it be your little children that have not been taught."

60. Recall "keep the commandments" in F (2:31).

61. The pair "temporal and spiritual" in this subsection balances the ideas of peace ("kept from falling into the hands of your enemies") and prosperity in F (2:31).

62. Connect "everlasting punishment" in G, with "never-ending torment" in G' and "never-ending happiness" in F'.

63. Sections 3 and 4 derive from the words of the angel, and thus it is natural to wonder how much flexibility Benjamin had in composing these parts of the message he delivered to his people. Although any conclusions about the mechanics of how Benjamin received and recorded his revelation must necessarily remain uncertain, it is clear that he purported to be drawing directly upon the words of the angel, for he wrote in the first-person singular on behalf of the angel (3:3, 17, 20, 22, 23, 27). We have at least three explanations we might wish to consider. The first asserts that Benjamin was repeating verbatim the words spoken by the angel. If this is the case, the angel was responsible for the chiastic order of the words in these sections of the speech, which was then carried over by Benjamin into the speech as a whole. Also, it provides a good illustration of the Lord speaking in the language and style of the prophet and the people receiving the revelation.

A second explanation suggests that since the sustained use of chiasmus in this passage corresponds precisely to the style of Benjamin's own writing in the other sections of his speech, one might assume that Benjamin was shown a great vision and told many things that he then presented in his own manner of speaking and writing. This explanation draws some support from the fact that Nephi received substantially the same vision as did Benjamin (compare Mosiah 3:5–9 with 1 Nephi 11:31–33), and yet their accounts differ widely: Nephi used direct parallelisms in straight narration, while Benjamin's words are chiastically ordered. In other respects, however, their accounts bear certain resemblances: Mosiah 3:13–14 compares closely with 2 Nephi 25:24–27, and the warning that these words shall stand as a testimony on which men will be judged is present in 2 Nephi 25:18, 28 and Mosiah 3:24. Thus we might conclude that whereas the essential spiritual experiences, which lie at the basis of such cognate religious insights, are very similar, the verbalization of that spiritual knowledge can differ from prophet to prophet.

A third possibility combines the first two. Perhaps Benjamin took the words of the angel and used them as building blocks which he moved around to suit his structural literary design.

64. Once again, the structure of this passage reflects the relationship of God to the king, and the king to his people.

65. The expression *and lo* occurs only twice in Benjamin's speech, with both instances in this part of section 3.

66. Compare "come down" (3:5) in subsection K.

67. The text offsets "the children of men" and "every nation, kindred and tongue" who were invited to believe, with "his people," namely the children of Israel who did not believe.

68. Benjamin parallels receiving a remission of sins with the laws or commandments of Moses, which were given to facilitate obedience and repentence; rejoicing and joy are related to receiving "many signs and wonders and types and shadows," which were the occasion of blessings and happiness.

69. Note the chiastic reversal: fallen–Adam (3:11), Adam–fall (3:16).

70. "Nation, kindred, tongue, and people" parallels "children of men" (3:17) in the corresponding section S above.

71. In these respects 3:18–19 should be compared with 5:10–12, the same lengthened six-element central chiasm of section 7 also containing a paired *hapax legomenon*, "left hand of God."

72. Compare 2 Nephi 25:24–27 for a chiastic counterpoint between the law of Moses and the fulfillment of the law in Christ.

73. Here is an explicit acknowledgment that these repetitions are intentional.

74. In subsection X, the pattern was − − + +, which becomes + − + − in subsection X'.

75. It is possible to see a faint a–b–b–a pattern in these four lines: (a) people should call upon the Lord with their mouths, (b) having faith, (b) in the future, (a) as the angel spoke with his mouth.

76. Compare "return" and "according as he doth agree" in 4:28 in subsection A' below.

77. This indictment mirrors the fact that this person has turned the beggar out "to perish" (4:16; see subsection C above). The concept of reciprocal justice common in biblical law and in the Book of Mormon would require the punishment to fit the crime. See also 4:23.

78. Compare the destruction of Achan and his property in Judges 7. Benjamin's sense of justice and logic required that if a person turned away a beggar to perish, God's justice would demand not only the person but also that his property should perish.

79. "This world" in subsection E' stands in contrast to the "kingdom of God" in subsection E.

80. The double occurrence of "condemn" here may balance the double occurrence of "day" in 4:24, the first part of this subsection.

81. The structure of this passage would indicate that the problem with coveting is desiring more than is sufficient for one's needs, since these two ideas are counterparts to each other.

82. See "your substance" in subsection C, above (4:16).

83. See "administer" in subsection C, above .

84. See "in need" in subsection C, above.

85. Compare "according to that which is his due" in subsection A in the section above (4:13).

86. The double occurrence of "perish" places an emphasis on the problem of sin equal to the double recognition at the beginning of this warning of the numberless ways in which a person may commit sin. Also, the order of the positives and negatives in this passage is chiastic: cannot tell, can tell, perish, perish not.

87. A direct connection is drawn between "making" the covenant and being "made" free, as sons and daughters are free from indebtedness or servitude to the father.

88. The details of a comparison between Leviticus and Mosiah can be found in chapter six, "King Benjamin's Speech in the Context of Ancient Israelite Festivals."

89. See Parley P. Pratt, *A Voice of Warning* (Salt Lake City: Deseret Book, 1920 [1st ed. 1837]), 105.

90. Bruce Kinney, *Mormonism, the Islam of America* (New York: Revell, 1912), 60.

91. Ibid.

92. See Douglas Wilson, "The Book of Mormon as Literature," *Dialogue* 3 (1968): 30.

93. Thomas F. O'Dea, *The Mormons* (Chicago: University of Chicago Press, 1957), 26.

94. See, for example, Richard Dilworth Rust, *Feasting on the Word: The Literary Testimony of the Book of Mormon* (Salt Lake City: Deseret Book and FARMS, 1997); Eugene England, "A Second Witness for the Logos: The Book of Mormon and Contemporary Literary Criticism," in *By Study and Also by Faith*, ed. John M. Lundquist and Stephen D. Ricks (Salt Lake City: Deseret Book and FARMS, 1990), 2:91–125; Alan Goff, "A Hermeneutic of Sacred Texts: Historicism, Revisionism, Positivism, and the Bible and Book of Mormon" (master's thesis, Brigham Young University, 1989); Bruce W. Jorgensen, "The Dark Way to the Tree: Typological Unity in the Book of Mormon," in *Literature of Belief: Sacred Scripture and Religious Experience*, ed. Neal E. Lambert (Provo, Utah: BYU Religious Studies Center, 1981), 217–31; Victor L. Ludlow, "Scribes and Scriptures," in *Studies in Scripture: 1 Nephi to Alma 29*, ed. Kent P. Jackson (Salt Lake City: Deseret Book, 1987), 196–204; Stephen P. Sondrup, "The Psalm of Nephi: A Lyric Reading," *BYU Studies* 21/3 (1981): 57–72; Robert K. Thomas, "A Literary Critic Looks at the Book of Mormon," in *A Believing People* (Provo, Utah: Brigham Young University Press, 1974), 213–19; John A. Tvedtnes, "Hebraisms in the Book of Mormon: A Preliminary Survey," *BYU Studies* 11/1 (1970): 50–60; Stephen C.

Walker, "More than Meets the Eye: Concentration of the Book of Mormon," *BYU Studies* 20/2 (1980): 199–205; Donald W. Parry, Jeanette W. Miller, and Sandra A. Thorne, eds., *A Comprehensive Annotated Book of Mormon Bibliography* (Provo, Utah: FARMS, 1996).

CHAPTER 12

THE USE OF KING BENJAMIN'S ADDRESS BY LATTER-DAY SAINTS

Bruce A. Van Orden

Benjamin's speech was a high point in Nephite history, as Mormon recognized when he compiled the ancient Nephite records. Mormon chose to summarize the king's lengthy career in only a few lines, but he dedicated a good deal of space to Benjamin's speech. Like Mormon, many Latter-day Saints recognize the exceptional spiritual and moral value of this address and often appeal to it as a source of doctrine and a guide to righteous living. While the preceding chapters in the present volume concentrate on textual, historical, and cultural aspects of the speech, this chapter examines Benjamin's role in Latter-day Saint doctrine and tradition, describing how Latter-day Saints have used, applied, and discussed Benjamin's speech since its publication in 1830.

While critical analysis may aid in understanding the historical setting of a passage, an examination of modern exegesis is necessary to discover what a particular passage means for contemporary readers. Apparently in the early years of the church, when the Saints were still initially exploring Book of Mormon texts, they rarely referred to

Benjamin's words. Over time, however, the speech has grown immensely in popularity, and recent generations have referred to it more often than any other section of scripture. To demonstrate this growth, I have compiled a table and the results of a survey. The first discusses the doctrines taught in general conference addresses that rely on Benjamin's speech for scriptural support. The second gives a chronological survey of many other commentaries by Latter-day Saint writers concerning the speech.

Doctrinal Statements

The following summary demonstrates how Benjamin's speech has been used by General Authorities and a few women leaders in general conference since 1897. After a short explanation of each doctrine or principle, a table shows every reference to a particular passage that relates to the principle. This table includes the chapter and verse(s) from Benjamin's address, the month and year of the modern speech, the name of the speaker, and the specific teaching. An asterisk (*) indicates the speaker elaborated on the scripture.

1. We should serve one another through daily actions and participation in church welfare programs. One of the main points in Benjamin's speech pertains to the Christian duty to serve one's fellowman. General Authorities, especially since 1960, have repeatedly referred to Mosiah chapters 2 and 4 while urging members to show true Christian love through daily charitable acts and participation in church welfare programs. Leaders often quote either Mosiah 2:17, "When ye are in the service of your fellow beings ye are only in the service of your God," or Mosiah 4:26, "For the sake of retaining a remission of your sins from day to day, that ye may walk guiltless before God—I would that ye should impart of your substance to the poor, every man according to that which he hath, such as feeding the hungry, clothing the naked, visiting the sick and administering to their relief, both spiritually and temporally, according to their wants."

In April 1947, Elder Harold B. Lee cited Mosiah 2:17 and observed, "The highest service that we can render here in mortal life [is] the willingness to sacrifice of our own self for the welfare of others. . . . Giving, then, . . . is an evidence of an abiding love in that individual who thus is willing to give."[1] During the two decades that followed Elder Lee's talk, the church placed heavy emphasis on service, and leaders often quoted Benjamin's statement to strengthen the point. In recent years, while leaders still continue to cite Benjamin's admonition on service, they have done so less frequently; in the April 1986 general conference, however, the entire Saturday afternoon session was dedicated to welfare principles and their practice in the church, and most speakers cited King Benjamin's speech to support their teachings.[2] Elder Jeffrey R. Holland, in 1996, focused on our obligation to care for those in need and to be involved in worthy causes since we are all beggars before God.[3]

Mosiah	Speaker/Date	On Service
2:16–17	Howard W. Hunter October 1978	*True religion means devotion to God, demonstrated by love and compassion for fellowmen, coupled with unworldliness.
2:16–17	Thomas S. Monson October 1989	*The importance of service is emphasized.
2:17	Russell M. Nelson April 1994	Obedience to the second great commandment facilitates obedience to the first.
2:17	Ben B. Banks October 1993	Service ranks high in bringing joy.

Mosiah	Speaker/Date	On Service
2:17	Thomas S. Monson April 1993	This passage in Mosiah is quoted.
2:17	Alexander B. Morrison April 1992	Service is the golden key that unlocks the doors to celestial halls.
2:17	Thomas S. Monson April 1991	This passage in Mosiah is quoted.
2:17	Joseph B. Wirthlin October 1990	King Benjamin taught the same idea as Jesus in Matthew 25:34–40.
2:17	Thomas S. Monson April 1990	A large magnitude of opportunity to serve exists.
2:17	Hans B. Ringger April 1990	That we are in the service of God when we are in the service of each other is reiterated.
2:17	Joseph B. Wirthlin October 1989	Service is what will give us genuine satisfaction and joy.
2:17	Robert L. Backman October 1985	*Service provides the key to happiness.
2:17	Dallin H. Oaks October 1984	*Service is an imperative.
2:17	A. Theodore Tuttle April 1984	Service is one of the highest virtues.
2:17	Franklin D. Richards April 1981	Developing and sharing talents is a way to serve one another.
2:17	George H. Durham April 1977	Service shows our love for God.

Mosiah	Speaker/Date	On Service
2:17	Franklin D. Richards October 1972	Service does not mean sacrifice.
2:17	David O. McKay October 1969	*True Christianity is love in action.
2:17	Franklin D. Richards October 1968	While developing talents, we should gain the spirit of sharing or giving, not only with those closest to us, but with all of God's children.
2:17	Victor L. Brown April 1968	The Saints should respond positively to calls from the bishop.
2:17	Thomas S. Monson October 1965	If we remember Mosiah 2:17 we will not suffer Jacob Marley's fate, whose ghost lamented lost opportunities.
2:17	Franklin D. Richards April 1964	The world today needs a spirit of brotherhood, and the church provides opportunities for all to serve.
2:17	Henry D. Taylor October 1963	*Service brings joy.
2:17	Marion G. Romney October 1954	*As we serve others we minister to Christ.
2:17	Harold B. Lee April 1947	Service is a saving principle. We must sacrifice ourselves for others.
2:17	Heber J. Grant April 1942	The Saints should serve one another.

Mosiah	Speaker/Date	On Service
2:17	Charles A. Callis October 1940	America needs the gospel of work. Man has obligations to man, country, and God; he must care for fellow-creatures.
2:17	Charles A. Callis October 1918	The sons, husbands, and brothers at war in France are serving their fellow-beings and their God. Human liberty, according to Joseph Smith, is a cause of God.
2:21–24	Eldred G. Smith October 1963	*The more we serve, the more blessings we receive; therefore, we can never put God in our debt.
2:38	Dallin H. Oaks October 1984	*Some people serve because they fear divine punishment, a lesser motive at best. True charity or perfect love marks the highest motive.
2:41	Elray L. Christiansen April 1975	*The obedient inherit a state of never-ending happiness.
2:41	Elray L. Christiansen April 1975	Mosiah 2:41 should be pondered often.
2:41	Elray L. Christiansen October 1971	The gospel constitutes the perfect plan for happiness.
3:18	Bruce R. McConkie April 1966	In order to become like God, we must first learn the laws of Christ and the gospel, then we must obey those laws.
3:19	Robert E. Sackley October 1988	*We should live outside ourselves and serve others.

Mosiah	Speaker/Date	On Service
4:4–12	Richard L. Evans October 1955	The Saints have a responsibility to share the greatest message in the world.
4:9–30	Joseph F. Smith April 1898	*The Saints must be willing to give from the heart.
4:12–16	Marion G. Romney October 1980	The welfare programs are the Savior's work.
4:12, 26–27	Marion G. Romney April 1981	Welfare services represent the gospel in action. The Saints should incorporate welfare principles into their lives.
4:16–18	H. Burke Peterson April 1981	Family members have a duty to care for each other both spiritually and temporally. All should avoid unfounded judgments and prejudice.
4:16–18	Vaughn J. Featherstone April 1973	Welfare provides opportunities for giving and receiving.
4:16, 19, 21, 26	Jeffrey R. Holland April 1996	*Impart of your substance to the poor; succor those in need. We are all beggars.
4:16–19	Theodore M. Burton April 1974	*If we obediently follow Christ and share with those less fortunate than we, God will keep his promise to watch over and care for us.
4:16–19	Vaughn J. Featherstone October 1973	Make wise use of the bishop's storehouse.
4:16–20	Melvin J. Ballard October 1931	*The Saints have an obligation to care for beggars. All men are beggars in God's view.

Mosiah	Speaker/Date	On Service
4:16–27	Russell M. Nelson April 1986	The Lord commands us to care for the poor.
4:17–18	Marion G. Romney October 1972	*We must learn to be both givers and receivers.
4:17–19	Melvin J. Ballard April 1937	Those who contribute material goods should not judge the recipients' worthiness.
4:18	Henry D. Moyle April 1956	*Those who withhold assistance from the poor and needy have great cause to repent. The welfare programs give us the opportunity to discharge our duty.
4:19	Elray L. Christiansen April 1953	*All men depend on God for existence.
4:19–20	Robert D. Hales April 1986	*No one is exempt from receiving.
4:24	Thomas S. Monson October 1996	Individuals will be blessed for their willingness to give, despite their capacity.
4:24	Robert D. Hales April 1986	*No one is exempt from giving.
4:24	H. Burke Peterson April 1985	In giving or wanting to give, we will be judged by the intent of our hearts.
4:24–25	Marion G. Romney October 1981	The Lord commands us to give.
4:26	Hartman Rector Jr. October 1990	The nicest thing we can do for the poor is impart of our substance.
4:26	Thomas S. Monson April 1986	God commands us to care for the poor.

Mosiah	Speaker/Date	On Service
4:26	James E. Faust April 1986	Our own well-being is bound up with the care of others.
4:26	L. Tom Perry April 1986	*The law of the fast requires that we donate the cost of two meals to the poor.
4:26	Jack H. Goaslind October 1983	*Perfect love comes as a direct result of having our sins remitted. Therefore, if we hope to retain a remission of sins, we must administer to the spiritual and temporal needs of our fellowmen.
4:26	Marion G. Romney October 1980	The Saints have an obligation to serve the needy.
4:26	Spencer W. Kimball October 1977	Welfare programs require a sincere love for one's neighbors.
4:26	Marion G. Romney October 1972	Caring for the poor aids in retaining a remission of sins and receiving forgiveness.
4:26	Harold B. Lee October 1964	The welfare applications of this verse now form part of the priesthood quorums' duties, particularly those of the elders quorums.
4:26	George Q. Morris April 1957	*The Saints should pay an honest and full fast offering. It is just as important as paying a full tithe.
4:26–27	Ronald E. Poelman April 1980	The Lord commands us to give.
5:2	Marion G. Romney October 1981	President Romney teaches how to give ungrudgingly.

Mosiah	Speaker/Date	On Service
5:13	Neal A. Maxwell April 1996	We cannot know the master if we have not served him. Children's thoughts often focus on the Savior.
5:13	Neal A. Maxwell April 1991	This passage in Mosiah is quoted.
5:13	Derek A. Cuthbert April 1990	*Service helps us to know the Savior.
5:13	Robert E. Wells October 1982	The Saints must be servants of the Savior.
5:13	Marion D. Hanks April 1980	Through service we manifest a willingness to receive the blessings of heaven.

2. Salvation can come only through the atonement of Christ. During recent years the church has come under increasing attack for allegedly not being Christian. The General Authorities have countered by affirming more frequently their testimony of Christ, the significance of the atonement, and Christ's position as head of the church. Key passages from Benjamin's speech about the role of Christ (Mosiah 3) have often been cited to bolster the church's devotion to the Savior. At one point, in his closing remarks during the October 1978 general conference, President Spencer W. Kimball said, "We know, and it is our testimony, and we also proclaim it to the world that to be saved men must 'believe that salvation was, and is, and is to come, in and through the atoning blood of Christ the Lord Omnipotent' (Mosiah 3:18)."[4] Four years after President Kimball's talk, Ezra Taft Benson, then president of the Council of the Twelve, testified, "The fundamental principle of our religion is faith in the Lord Jesus Christ." He then asked, "Why is it expedient that we center our confidence, our hope, and our trust in one solitary figure? Why is faith in Him so necessary to peace of mind in this life and hope in the world to come?"[5] To answer these questions, President Benson explained that Christ was the *Lord God Omnipotent*" (Mosiah 3:5). Then he declared, "[Christ] was chosen before He was born. He was the all-powerful Creator of the heavens and the earth. He is the source of life and light to all things. His word is the law by which all things are governed in the universe. All things created and made by him are subject to his infinite power."[6]

Mosiah	Speaker/Date	On the Atonement
3	F. Melvin Hammond April 1994	Jesus came to the earth to sacrifice himself for our sins.
3:4	David B. Haight April 1988	An angel prophesied to Benjamin of the coming of a Messiah.
3:5	John M. Madsen April 1993	Jesus condescended to dwell on earth, and is from all eternity to all eternity.
3:5	Ezra Taft Benson October 1983	*Christ is the Lord Omnipotent.
3:5	Bruce R. McConkie October 1982	Through obedience, righteousness, and faith, Christ progressed until he became the Lord Omnipotent.
3:5	Joseph Fielding Smith October 1953	Christ is our advocate and mediator.
3:5–7	Thomas S. Monson October 1965	Benjamin's prophetic declaration is proof of Christ's divinity.
3:5–7	George F. Richards April 1937	An angel predicts Christ's suffering throughout his mortal life.

Mosiah	Speaker/Date	On the Atonement
3:5, 8	Adney Y. Komatsu April 1987	*Benjamin prophesied of Christ's coming. We must look to the Savior for guidance.
3:5, 7–10	David B. Haight April 1988	Benjamin learned in a vision that Christ would atone for the sins of mankind and judge the world.
3:5, 11, 17	Anthony W. Ivins October 1923	The Book of Mormon is another witness of Christ.
3:7	F. Melvin Hammond April 1994	Jesus loved us so intensely that blood emitted from every pore.
3:7	Ezra Taft Benson October 1983	The Father's plan required that Jesus suffer all the difficulties and tribulations of mortal life.
3:7	Neal A. Maxwell October 1982	Full understanding is not necessary for believing participation. We cannot savor all that swirls around us. As Mary bathed the infant Jesus' pores, she could not have known that those same pores would sweat great drops of blood.
3:7	Milton R. Hunter April 1958	Christ's suffering was required by the atonement.
3:7	J. Reuben Clark Jr. April 1954	Christ literally sweat blood in Gethsemane as part of the atonement. Benjamin and the Doctrine and Covenants settle the debate.
3:7	Milton R. Hunter April 1953	Those who reject Christ must suffer as he did.

Mosiah	Speaker/Date	On the Atonement
3:7	George F. Richards October 1914	We should feel sorry for the sins of others and rejoice in others' righteousness as Christ does.
3:7, 9	Howard W. Hunter April 1988	This passage concerns Gethsemane and Christ's rejection by the Jews.
3:8–9	Joseph Fielding Smith October 1953	Christ is our advocate and mediator.
3:9	John M. Madsen April 1993	Jesus came into the world to bring about salvation through faith in his name.
3:9	Neal A. Maxwell April 1984	Many judge Jesus as a thing of naught or consider him merely a man, but for us he is our Lord and Savior.
3:11	Milton R. Hunter April 1958	Christ sanctifies those who had no mortal chance to receive the gospel but repent in the spirit world.
3:11–18	John M. Madsen April 1993	Jesus came to atone for the sins of the world.
3:13	M. Russell Ballard April 1995	The proclamation of the atonement is linked to the necessity of obedience.
3:13	David B. Haight April 1988	Benjamin was one of many prophets who testified of Christ.
3:15	Alexander B. Morrison April 1992	All truth testifies of Christ. There are signs, wonders, types, and shadows.
3:16	Russell M. Nelson April 1987	Salvation comes through the resurrected Christ.

Mosiah	Speaker/Date	On the Atonement
3:16	Milton R. Hunter April 1958	Benjamin says that little children will be cleansed and sanctified with Christ's blood.
3:17	Russell M. Nelson October 1993	Salvation comes through the name of Christ.
3:17	Hartman Rector Jr. October 1990	We are saved only through the name of Christ.
3:17	Dallin H. Oaks April 1986	This is one of several scriptures declaring that the name of Jesus Christ brings salvation to the children of men.
3:17	Hartman Rector Jr. October 1985	Salvation comes only through Christ.
3:17	Dallin H. Oaks April 1985	When we take the sacrament we should think about what it means to take Christ's name upon ourselves.
3:17	Spencer W. Kimball October 1982	Salvation comes only through Christ.
3:17	Marion G. Romney October 1979	Salvation comes only through Christ.
3:17	Marion G. Romney October 1979	Men need to have faith in Christ's ability to save them.
3:17	Spencer W. Kimball October 1978	Salvation comes only through Christ.
3:17	Richard L. Evans October 1963	The answers which yearning and lonely hearts seek are found in Christ.
3:17–18	Dallin H. Oaks October 1988	Salvation comes only through Christ.

Mosiah	Speaker/Date	On the Atonement
3:17–18	Bruce R. McConkie April 1973	Christ is the only way to salvation. He is the truth and the light.
3:17–18	Bruce R. McConkie October 1970	*Salvation comes only through Christ.
3:17–18	Bruce R. McConkie October 1964	*No other name but Christ's will save us.
3:18	Dallin H. Oaks October 1990	Salvation comes only through the atoning blood.
3:18	Russell M. Nelson April 1984	Salvation comes only through Christ.
3:18	Spencer W. Kimball October 1982	The testimony of the brethren is that salvation comes only through Christ.
3:18	Spencer W. Kimball October 1978	Christ's is the only name by which we can be saved. He is the Lord Omnipotent.
3:18	Bruce R. McConkie April 1972	Salvation comes through Christ alone.
3:18	Bruce R. McConkie October 1951	Salvation comes through Christ alone.
3:20	John M. Madsen April 1993	The knowledge of the Savior will spread throughout the world.
4:2	Jeffrey R. Holland April 1996	Benjamin's people petition to apply the atoning blood of Christ.
4:2–3	Ronald E. Poelman October 1993	We can experience God's mercy through the atonement.

Mosiah	Speaker/Date	On the Atonement
4:19	Elray L. Christiansen April 1953	All men depend on the Lord. The riches of the earth are his and he gives them at his mercy. Pride and self-sufficiency would have us believe otherwise.
5:8	Russell M. Nelson October 1993	We should take upon ourselves the name of Christ via covenant.
5:10–13	Richard G. Scott October 1995	The consequences of the atonement have an impact on everyone.
5:13	Neal A. Maxwell April 1995	The remedy for not being driven by our appetites or being preoccupied with the lesser things is given by King Benjamin.
5:13	Neal A. Maxwell April 1986	One cannot have faith in a Christ whom he does not know.
5:13	Neal A. Maxwell April 1986	Not knowing Christ, we fail to hear him.
5:13	James E. Faust October 1976	The Saints should daily acknowledge the divinity of Christ.
5:13	Marion D. Hanks April 1973	Christ gives us hope and lifts us up.
6:2	Milton R. Hunter October 1952	*Benjamin's people accepted the name of Christ and so should the Saints.

3. What is the "natural man"? Mosiah 3:19, the most quoted passage from Benjamin in past years, describes carnal or "natural" man in this way:

> For the natural man is an enemy to God, and has been from the fall of Adam, and will be, forever and ever, unless he yields to the enticings of the Holy Spirit, and putteth off the natural man and becometh a saint through the atonement of Christ the Lord, and becometh as a child, submissive, meek, humble, patient, full of love, willing to submit to all things which the Lord seeth fit to inflict upon him, even as a child doth submit to his father.

Leaders have offered various descriptions of the natural man's character and explanations of why he is an enemy of God. Consensus seems to indicate that the natural man represents the selfishness that all people must overcome if they hope to return to the presence of God.

President Spencer W. Kimball has added his own simple definition of the natural man: "The 'natural man' is the 'earthy man' who has allowed rude animal passions to overshadow his spiritual inclinations."[7]

Mosiah	Speaker/Date	On the Natural Man
1:5	Neal A. Maxwell October 1986	If men go without spiritual truths too long, they may reject truth when it is presented.
2:17	Robert L. Simpson October 1962	Selfishness and ingratitude are tools of destruction.
3:19	Neal A. Maxwell April 1996	Become childlike, full of love, and willing to submit.
3:19	Richard G. Scott April 1996	The tempering effect of patience is required as we seek blessings.

Mosiah	Speaker/Date	On the Natural Man
3:19	Neal A. Maxwell April 1995	The natural man is turned away from God.
3:19	James E. Faust April 1994	Some people fall short of their potential because they do not rise above the natural man.
3:19	Neal A. Maxwell October 1994	Giving up on God and ourselves causes us to surrender to the natural man.
3:19	Waldo P. Call October 1990	This passage is quoted.
3:19	Neal A. Maxwell October 1990	*The natural man is selfish.
3:19	Charles A. Didier October 1983	*The natural or carnal man is the enemy of God.
3:19	Charles A. Didier October 1983	*The humble and submissive man is a friend of God.
3:19	Spencer W. Kimball October 1974	*Competition for our souls exists. The natural man allows animal passions to overshadow his spiritual inclinations.
3:19	Hartman Rector Jr. April 1970	*Benjamin bears strong testimony against man, and history confirms the truthfulness of that testimony.
3:19	Delbert L. Stapley April 1965	*Those who inquire of the Lord with faith, truly desire to be led by the Spirit, and willingly yield to the enticings of the Spirit cannot support a plan that goes contrary to moral convictions.

Mosiah	Speaker/Date	On the Natural Man
3:19	John H. Vandenberg October 1965	*Many of society's problems result from man's vain ambition to get gain and power, the desires of the natural man.
3:19	Marion G. Romney April 1964	Man is God's enemy only when he rejects spiritual promptings.
4:30	Carlos E. Asay April 1980	Men lose their savor when they contaminate their minds with unclean thoughts, tell lies, or commit immoral acts.

4. The natural man can be overcome. When explaining how the Saints can use Christ's atonement to overcome the natural man, General Authorities often quote Mosiah 3:19. Elder Bruce R. McConkie, for example, quoted this verse in 1950 and affirmed that the atonement of Christ was the most important event in world history. By making the atonement effective in their lives through repentance and humility, Elder McConkie explained, Saints can subdue and eventually defeat the natural man. Of course, those who overcome the natural man completely will become Christlike. General Authorities have emphasized the development of Christlike attributes so much over the last several years that they have quoted Mosiah 3:19 more than any other statement in Benjamin's speech.

Mosiah	Speaker/Date	Overcoming the Natural Man
3:7	Neal A. Maxwell April 1987	The Saints must overcome, even as Christ overcame.
3:18–19	Neal A. Maxwell October 1987	We can overcome the natural man through the atonement and become like Christ.

Mosiah	Speaker/Date	Overcoming the Natural Man
3:19	Spencer J. Condie October 1993	Yielding to the enticings of the Holy Spirit will enable us to overcome the natural man and thereby help in our quest for perfection.
3:19	Alexander B. Morrison April 1992	Undershepherds become as little children.
3:19	Derek A. Cuthbert April 1990	If we put off the natural man we will grow spiritually.
3:19	Ezra Taft Benson April 1989	*Putting off the natural man is what is needed to ward off pride.
3:19	Howard W. Hunter October 1988	If we yield to the enticings of the Spirit we can receive knowledge.
3:19	Gordon B. Hinckley April 1987	The brethren plead with people everywhere to live in accordance with the teachings of our Creator and rise above carnal attractions that often result in the tragedies that follow moral transgression.
3:19	Neal A. Maxwell April 1985	*We must offer childlike submissiveness to the Lord. This quality goes far beyond the bowed head or bended knee.
3:19	Neal A. Maxwell April 1985	*The Saints must willingly submit to God.
3:19	Neal A. Maxwell April 1985	*Additional tutoring and suffering appears to be the pattern for the Lord's most apt pupils when they enter earth life.

Mosiah	Speaker/Date	Overcoming the Natural Man
3:19	Robert L. Simpson April 1984	We need a child's implicit faith and sincerity in order to become more Christlike.
3:19	Neal A. Maxwell April 1983	*Elder Maxwell tells the story of a dying young mother who fits the portrait of a submissive Saint. She asks, "If I am about to die, then how can I help my husband and my parents as they watch me die?"
3:19	Neal A. Maxwell April 1983	*Benjamin describes what childlike and saintly submissiveness really means. Trials serve as divine tutorials.
3:19	Neal A. Maxwell October 1982	God deliberately gives us trials as divine tutorials. We must remain true even when we feel forsaken.
3:19	F. Enzio Busche April 1982	*We can overcome the natural self by listening to the Holy Ghost and making covenants with God.
3:19	Derek A. Cuthbert October 1982	Maturity requires the retention of certain childlike qualities, one of which is humility.
3:19	Adney Y. Komatsu October 1977	Those who listen to the Holy Ghost and submit themselves to God will receive great blessings.
3:19	Marion D. Hanks April 1975	*Like little children, we must be pure and open with the Lord.
3:19	Hartman Rector Jr. April 1974	*True conversion requires submission to the Lord.

Mosiah	Speaker/Date	Overcoming the Natural Man
3:19	Harold B. Lee October 1965	*We must sometimes learn obedience through suffering. This requires humility and submissiveness.
3:19	Elray L. Christiansen April 1953	Destroy pride and be humble.
3:19	Bruce R. McConkie April 1950	The atonement is the most important thing in the world. By making the atonement effective in their lives, people can overcome the natural man.
3:21	Marion D. Hanks April 1975	The purity and openness of little children in their relationship with the Lord points the way for all believers.
4:5, 8–10	John H. Vandenberg April 1976	The gospel in its fullness provides the help needed to "get yourself determined upon"—to find out what you are and what you are for.
4:29–30	W. Grant Bangerter April 1987	Although there are many ways to be imperfect, we should always strive for perfection and eternal life.
4:30	Joseph B. Wirthlin April 1982	Benjamin describes how we can become our best self.
4:30	Delbert L. Stapley October 1973	We need the Holy Ghost constantly in order to preserve our spiritual well-being.

5. *True humility is a characteristic of Christ's disciples and requires recognition of man's dependence on God.* When using Benjamin's teachings on humility, General Authorities of-

ten emphasize man's debt to God and the need to submit oneself to God. These teachings appear in Mosiah 2:20–24: "And now, in the first place, he [God] hath created you, and granted unto you your lives, for which ye are indebted unto him. And secondly, he doth require that ye should do as he hath commanded you; for which if ye do, he doth immediately bless you; and therefore he hath paid you. And ye are still indebted unto him, and are, and will be, forever and ever; therefore, of what have ye to boast?" In 1944, for example, Elder Joseph Fielding Smith cited Mosiah 2:20–24 and said that all people—and the LDS Church itself—were indebted to God.

Mosiah 3:19 also affirms the need for man to recognize his relationship to and dependence on God. In 1985 Elder Neal A. Maxwell quoted this verse and explained that true disciples offer childlike submissiveness to God, particularly when facing trials. This quality goes far beyond the "bended knee or bowed head."[8]

Mosiah	Speaker/Date	On Humility
2:17	Robert L. Simpson October 1962	Selfishness and ingratitude are tools of destruction.
2:20–24	Joseph Fielding Smith April 1944	*We are all indebted to God. The church is in debt to God.
2:21	Richard P. Lindsay April 1990	Even if we serve Christ with all our souls we are unprofitable servants.
2:21	Russell M. Nelson October 1986	Spiritual self-esteem comes by recognizing God's blessings.
2:21	Hartman Rector Jr. April 1979	Learning to sacrifice requires knowledge of our debt to God.

Mosiah	Speaker/Date	On Humility
2:21–24	Eldred G. Smith October 1963	The more we serve, the more blessings we receive; therefore, we can never put God in our debt.
2:23–25	Eldred G. Smith April 1955	Don't be too self-sufficient; stay humble and remember God's goodness.
3:19	Merlin R. Lybbert April 1994	Adults are expected to be as little children.
3:19	Robert L. Simpson April 1984	We need a child's implicit faith and sincerity in order to become more Christlike.
3:19	Derek A. Cuthbert October 1982	Maturity requires the retention of certain childlike qualities, one of which is humility.
3:19	Adney Y. Komatsu October 1977	Those who listen to the Holy Ghost and submit themselves to God will receive great blessings.
3:19	Marion D. Hanks April 1975	*Like little children, we must be pure and open with the Lord.
3:19	Hartman Rector Jr. April 1974	*True conversion requires submission to the Lord.
3:19	Harold B. Lee October 1965	*We must sometimes learn obedience through suffering. This requires humility and submissiveness.
3:19	Elray L. Christiansen April 1953	Destroy pride and be humble.

Mosiah	Speaker/Date	On Humility
3:21	Marion D. Hanks April 1975	The purity and openness of little children in their relationship with the Lord points the way for all believers.
4:10	Ezra Taft Benson April 1986	We must humble ourselves before God and avoid pride.
4:11	Angel Abrea April 1988	We can be effective in proclaiming the gospel to an insecure world if we are humble to the depths.
4:11–12	Henry B. Eyring October 1989	Gratitude comes from God's goodness to us in spite of our recognition of our own nothingness.
4:11–13	Marion D. Hanks October 1960	Those who give their hearts to God will enjoy numerous blessings.
4:11–15	Delbert L. Stapley April 1974	All should reflect on the goodness and graciousness of God; we can never repay him fully.
4:19	Elray L. Christiansen April 1953	*All men depend on Christ for existence.

6. Parents are responsible to teach and care for their children. Leaders have often quoted Benjamin while counseling parents. Of the following twenty-six references, however, only one occurs before 1960. This disparity reflects the greater emphasis on family home evening that occurred near the beginning of that decade. Generally, leaders have urged parents to follow Benjamin's instructions in Mosiah 4:14–15: "And ye will not suffer your children that they go hungry, or naked; neither will ye suffer that they transgress the laws of God, and fight and quarrel one with another, and serve the devil, who is the master of sin, or who is the evil spirit which hath been spoken of by our fathers, he being an enemy to all righteousness. But ye will teach them to walk in the ways of truth and soberness; ye will teach them to love one another, and to serve one another." In 1965, Elder Spencer W. Kimball noted that it was Benjamin, through these verses, who gave the scriptural appeal for the equivalent of home evenings.[9]

President Ezra Taft Benson gave an address at the priesthood session of October 1985 general conference on how "faithful fathers [in the Book of Mormon] constantly bore their testimonies to their sons."[10] He noted that "King Benjamin caused that his three sons 'should be taught in all the language of his fathers' and from the brass plates so that they would not suffer 'in ignorance' (Mosiah 1:2–3)."[11] After quoting Benjamin, President Benson asked, "Could the lack of teaching the scriptures in our homes be a source of our suffering in ignorance today?"[12] Elder Russell M. Nelson, in both 1989 and 1994, used Benjamin as a text to encourage parents to guide their children to love one another and relate well with each other; as a result, intolerance outside the home would decline.[13]

Mosiah	Speaker/Date	Duties of Parents
1:2–7	Ezra Taft Benson October 1985	*Righteous fathers teach their sons the gospel because God has commanded it. Poor or limited gospel training causes suffering in ignorance.
2:5	Gene R. Cook April 1984	*Once we become parents, we will always be parents.
2:12, 14	L. Tom Perry October 1986	Teach children the joy and value of work.

Mosiah	Speaker/Date	Duties of Parents
2:17	H. Burke Peterson April 1975	Teach children to read the scriptures.
3:19	Russell M. Nelson October 1985	*Initially, a child's physical needs take first priority, but parental concern eventually turns to helping a child reach his full spiritual potential.
4:14	Charles A. Didier October 1983	Parents should teach children gospel principles.
4:14	O. Leslie Stone April 1978	Parents take responsibility for their children's behavior.
4:14–15	Russell M. Nelson April 1994	*If parents taught their children to relate well with each other, intolerance outside of the home would decline.
4:14–15	Russell M. Nelson April 1994	*Parents are to give children appropriate guidance.
4:14–15	Joseph B. Wirthlin April 1993	Parents are to teach their children.
4:14–15	Russell M. Nelson April 1989	Parents are to guide their children to love one another.
4:14–15	Gene R. Cook April 1984	The family unit is the principal agency for the spiritual and temporal nurturing of the individual.
4:14–15	David B. Haight April 1978	Aurelia Rogers incorporated into her life Benjamin's teachings about parental responsibility.
4:14–15	H. Burke Peterson April 1977	Parents must give unconditional love.

Mosiah	Speaker/Date	Duties of Parents
4:14–15	H. Burke Peterson October 1972	Benjamin explains how parents can teach their children in a positive way.
4:14–15	David B. Haight April 1972	Concerning family home evening, how can we teach our children if we fail to meet together as a family?
4:14–15	A. Theodore Tuttle October 1971	*Parents teach by example.
4:14–15	Spencer W. Kimball April 1965	In our family home evenings, we should teach children through scripture.
4:14–15	Richard L. Evans October 1964	The responsibilities of parenting are ever-present and lifelong.
4:14–15	Marion D. Hanks October 1960	*Mosiah 4:14–15 contains Benjamin's promises and counsel to parents.
4:14–15	Sylvester Q. Cannon April 1939	Training children implies both instruction and application.
4:15	M. Russell Ballard April 1991	*Parents are to teach their children to love one another and serve.
4:15	Dallin H. Oaks April 1990	Parents who teach their children to love one another are working for peace.
4:15	Russell C. Taylor October 1984	Parents exert an eternal influence over their children.
4:15	A. Theodore Tuttle October 1979	Parents are responsible to teach their children.

Mosiah	Speaker/Date	Duties of Parents
4:16–18	H. Burke Peterson April 1981	Family members have a duty to care for each other both spiritually and temporally. All should avoid unfounded judgments and prejudice.

7. *Those who obey God's commandments will receive blessings both in heaven and in earth.* General Authorities frequently refer to the relationship between obedience and blessings. They quote Mosiah chapter 2, especially verses 22 and 41, to support this principle. Verse 22 reads: "And behold, all that he [God] requires of you is to keep his commandments; and he has promised you that if ye would keep his commandments ye should prosper in the land; and he never doth vary from that which he hath said; therefore, if ye do keep his commandments he doth bless you and prosper you." In 1987, Elder Charles A. Didier cited verse 41 to show that spiritual security is strengthened when one understands that blessings come to the obedient. Verse 41 reads:

> And moreover, I would desire that ye should consider on the blessed and happy state of those that keep the commandments of God. For behold, they are blessed in all things, both temporal and spiritual; and if they hold out faithful to the end they are received into heaven, that thereby they may dwell with God in a state of never-ending happiness. O remember, remember that these things are true; for the Lord hath spoken it.

Elder M. Russell Ballard quoted this verse in his 1995 address on finding answers to life's questions, with particular reference to receiving eternal happiness and joy.[14]

Mosiah	Speaker/Date	Blessings of Obedience
1:7	Russell M. Nelson April 1986	Obey and prosper.
1:7	Russell M. Nelson April 1985	Since abortion is a serious sin, those who condone it disobey the laws of God and therefore will not prosper.
2:4	Delbert L. Stapley October 1968	Obedience to God's commandments leads to rejoicing and love toward both God and fellowmen.
2:22	Hartman Rector Jr. April 1983	Tithing is a bedrock foundation principle of the gospel. Surely the Lord God has spoken it.
2:22	O. Leslie Stone October 1979	As we adhere to God's commandments we will reap the blessings promised to the faithful.
2:22	O. Leslie Stone October 1973	*Blessings come through obedience.
2:22	William J. Critchlow Jr. October 1961	The obedient will prosper in the land.
2:22–24	Delbert L. Stapley October 1977	Rewards come from obedience.
2:22, 31	Russell M. Nelson April 1985	Obey and prosper.
2:24	Henry B. Eyring April 1991	God is generous when we pray and obey.
2:41	M. Russell Ballard April 1995	*This passage is quoted in the context of receiving eternal happiness and joy.

Mosiah	Speaker/Date	Blessings of Obedience
2:41	Dallin H. Oaks October 1991	Those who obey commandments receive happiness and joy.
2:41	M. Russell Ballard October 1990	They are blessed and happy who keep the commandments.
2:41	Charles A. Didier April 1987	Spiritual security is strengthened by revelation that explains the results of observing the commandments.
2:41	Russell M. Nelson October 1986	*The obedient inherit a state of never-ending happiness.
2:41	Jack H. Goaslind April 1986	*Happiness is the destiny of those who obey the commandments.
2:41	Delbert L. Stapley April 1968	Happiness comes through obedience.
2:41	Elray L. Christiansen October 1966	Jesus has promised through his prophets that those who keep the commandments will be blessed in all things and eventually enjoy a state of never-ending happiness.
2:41	Elray L. Christiansen October 1960	Rewards come from obeying truth.
2:41	Elray L. Christiansen October 1956	We enjoy free agency, but when making choices we should remember Benjamin's counsel concerning the blessed state of the righteous.
2:41	Delbert L. Stapley April 1954	Faith and thoughtful obedience prepare the way to exaltation.

Mosiah	Speaker/Date	Blessings of Obedience
4:3	Dallin H. Oaks October 1991	The members of the audience of Benjamin's speech were filled with joy.
4:3, 20	Dallin H. Oaks October 1991	The joy that follows from a remission of sins comes from the Holy Spirit.
4:11	Dallin H. Oaks October 1991	The remission of sins causes joy.
4:21	Ezra Taft Benson April 1984	Obedience assures freedom from the bondage of sin. Pay an honest tithe and fast offering.
4:24–25	Dallin H. Oaks October 1989	When those who are trying to cope with life fall short, the Lord blesses them for their righteous desires.
5:6–10	Milton R. Hunter April 1953	By taking upon ourselves the name of Christ and obeying our covenants, we become the children of Christ.
5:7	Lynn A. Mickelsen October 1995	When we take upon ourselves the name of Christ through baptism, we become known as his children and promise to keep his commandments.
5:7–8	Milton R. Hunter October 1952	Christ's children will live on a celestial earth.
5:8	Dallin H. Oaks April 1985	Faith, repentance, and obedience qualify us to lay claim on Christ's atoning sacrifice.
5:8	Boyd K. Packer April 1983	*Willing disciples enjoy true freedom.

Mosiah	Speaker/Date	Blessings of Obedience
5:15	James E. Faust October 1996	When we remain steadfast and immovable, we can be sealed unto Christ.

8. True conversion results in a "mighty change" that removes the desire to do evil. Leaders often teach about the need to be truly converted, and some have referred to the "mighty change" experienced by Benjamin's people. Mosiah 5:2 reads: "And they all cried with one voice, saying: Yea, we believe all the words which thou hast spoken unto us; and also, we know of their surety and truth, because of the Spirit of the Lord Omnipotent, which has wrought a mighty change in us, or in our hearts, that we have no more disposition to do evil, but to do good continually." In 1898, President Joseph F. Smith spoke about the oath and covenant of the priesthood, as found in Doctrine and Covenants 84. President Smith likened that section to the covenant made by Benjamin's people and affirmed that those who are baptized and receive the gift of the Holy Ghost should experience a mighty change and strive to maintain the desire to do good constantly. This teaching applied especially to those who held the priesthood.

Leaders have not limited the need for true conversion to active members of the church. President Marion G. Romney, for example, has discussed several times the "mighty change" and its application to helping less active members. In 1975, he said that less active members would not want to return to full activity unless they experienced the profound change that true conversion effects. After explaining how Benjamin helped the people of Nephi and Zarahemla to desire the "mighty change," President Romney encouraged the Saints to follow Benjamin's example in their activation programs, as did Elder Richard G. Scott in 1990. Elder Scott reminded those who are seeking to come back that "any lasting improvement must come from your own determination to change."[15]

Mosiah	Speaker/Date	On Conversion
3:17–20	Richard G. Scott April 1990	*Priesthood leaders can help sinners to have a determination to change.
3:19	Lowell D. Wood April 1993	We will experience a mighty change as we yield to the Holy Ghost.
4:1–2	Milton R. Hunter October 1952	*Benjamin's address was so powerful that the people fell down and cried to God that he might purify their hearts and make Christ's atonement effective in their lives.
4:1–3	Marion G. Romney April 1967	Benjamin's people dramatically illustrate a community that experiences peace in a world of tribulation.
4:2	Marion G. Romney October 1975	Benjamin's people are an example of the profound change caused by conversion.
4:2, 9–10	Marion G. Romney October 1963	*As a result of Benjamin's powerful address, the people became truly converted.
4:3	Marion G. Romney October 1963	We are converted when we feel the power of the Holy Ghost heal our souls.
4:13	Dallin H. Oaks April 1990	Those who take advantage of the atonement have no desire to injure anyone, but to live peaceably.

Mosiah	Speaker/Date	On Conversion
4:13	L. Lionel Kendrick October 1988	*The admonition to live peaceably and not injure others is applied to kind communications.
5:1–9	Joseph F. Smith April 1898	*The mighty change experienced by Benjamin's people prepared them to make a righteous covenant with God. This covenant is very similar to the oath and covenant of the priesthood. Priesthood holders should review their standing continually.
5:2	Spencer J. Condie October 1993	We must undergo a mighty change of heart.
5:2	Rex D. Pinegar October 1991	We should rank Jesus first in our thoughts and deeds.
5:2	Marvin J. Ashton October 1988	The conversion process entails a mighty change of heart.
5:2	Neal A. Maxwell October 1980	The mighty change requires more than a slight change in schedule.
5:2	Marion G. Romney October 1975	The Saints must help the less active members to believe in the same way that Benjamin's people believed.
5:2	Theodore M. Burton October 1973	Those who are truly converted desire to become like God, both spiritually and physically.
5:2	Charles A. Callis October 1945	When Christ makes his glorious appearance to the Jews on the Mount of Olives, he will help them experience a "mighty change" of heart.

Mosiah	Speaker/Date	On Conversion
5:2, 5	Marion G. Romney October 1975	We need to help the less active members experience the mighty change.
5:2, 5	Marion G. Romney October 1963	*Although Benjamin's people seem to have been converted quickly from a disposition to do evil to a determination to do good continually, they evidently fully met the conditions for baptism.
5:2, 7	Ezra Taft Benson October 1985	President Benson describes the "mighty change."
5:6–8	Milton R. Hunter October 1952	Benjamin's people took upon themselves the name of Christ and covenanted to keep God's commandments. Thus they became the children of Christ and were spiritually begotten by him.
5:7	Robert E. Wells October 1982	We must live so as to be true children of Christ.
5:7	Joseph Fielding Smith October 1962	*Christ is our spiritual father. Salvation comes only through Christ.
5:7	Harold B. Lee April 1962	Those who receive baptism become the children of Christ.
5:7–8	Milton R. Hunter October 1952	Benjamin's people were spiritually begotten by Christ.
5:9	Dallin H. Oaks April 1985	We must repent to be called by Christ's name.

9. Those who are born again become the children of Christ. When one is "born again," one becomes a child of Christ. General Authorities sometimes quote Mosiah 5:7–10 concerning those who reach this state. In 1987, for example, Elder W. Grant Bangerter cited Mosiah 5:7 to explain what it meant to be spiritually begotten by Christ: "And now, because of the covenant which ye have made ye shall be called the children of Christ, his sons, and his daughters; for behold, this day he hath spiritually begotten you; for ye say that your hearts are changed through faith on his name; therefore, ye are born of him and have become his sons and his daughters." After quoting Benjamin, Elder Bangerter asked the Saints if their daily actions were those of a person redeemed of God, a true child of Christ. Leaders often ask such questions when discussing the need to be born again or to overcome the natural man. In April 1995, both Aileen H. Clyde and Bonnie D. Parkin, serving respectively in the Relief Society and Young Women general presidencies, cited Mosiah 5:7 in the context of reminding us to keep our covenants.

Mosiah	Speaker/Date	Children of Christ
5:7	Aileen H. Clyde April 1995	Covenants link us to God and loved ones.
5:7	W. Grant Bangerter April 1987	If we have truly been born again or redeemed of God, do we act like it?
5:7	Dallin H. Oaks April 1985	We take upon ourselves the name of Christ when we become members of the church.
5:7	Robert E. Wells October 1982	We must live so as to be true children of Christ.

Mosiah	Speaker/Date	Children of Christ
5:7	Joseph Fielding Smith October 1962	*Christ is our spiritual father. Salvation comes only through Christ.
5:7	Harold B. Lee April 1962	Those who receive baptism become the children of Christ.
5:7–8	Bonnie D. Parkin April 1995	Those who keep covenants are the children of Christ.
5:7–8	H. Burke Peterson April 1990	This passage is quoted.
5:8	Harold B. Lee April 1955	Benjamin best explains the meaning of baptism and the covenant of obedience asso- ciated with it.
5:8	Milton R. Hunter October 1952	*Benjamin's people received the name of Christ, just as the modern Saints do.
5:8–10	Joseph Fielding Smith October 1962	*Christ is our spiritual father.
5:9	Dallin H. Oaks April 1985	We must repent to be called by Christ's name.
6:2	Milton R. Hunter October 1952	*All Benjamin's people ac- cepted Christ's name and covenanted to obey God's commandments. Thus they became the children of Christ.

10. God will forgive our sins when we truly repent and serve others. Several General Authorities have quoted Mosiah 4 to explain the repentance process and how one can retain the remission of one's sins. In 1983, for example, Elder Jack H. Goaslind cited Mosiah 4:26 and said that perfect love comes from having one's sins remitted. Since "perfect love" or charity manifests itself through service, Elder Goaslind explained, those who hope to retain a remission of their sins must administer to the spiritual and temporal needs of their fellowmen. President Marion G. Romney has spoken in a similar vein while encouraging members in active support of welfare programs.

Mosiah 4:3 asserts that after Benjamin's people cried out for mercy, they were filled with a "peace of conscience." In 1973, President Harold B. Lee used this passage to explain to church members that they can know when the Lord has forgiven them: "In your soul-searching, if you seek for and you find that peace of conscience, by that token you may know that the Lord has accepted of your repentance. Satan would have you think otherwise and sometimes persuade you that now having made one mistake, you might go on and on with no turning back. That is one of the great falsehoods."[16]

Mosiah	Speaker/Date	On Repentance
2:36	Marion D. Hanks October 1973	Sin creates a separation between man and God. We must learn to forgive the offenses of others; if we fail to do so, we will create a separation between ourselves and God.
3:11	Milton R. Hunter April 1958	Christ sanctifies those who had no mortal chance to receive the gospel but repent in the spirit world.
4:1–3	Boyd K. Packer October 1995	Remember your sins no more.
4:1–3	Malcolm S. Jeppsen April 1994	We must plead for mercy, and we then can receive a peaceful conscience from the Holy Spirit, and the blood of Christ can remit our sins.

Mosiah	Speaker/Date	On Repentance
4:1–3	Marion G. Romney October 1980	Joy and peace of conscience come to those who receive a remission of sins.
4:2	F. Enzio Busche October 1993	*We may plead to God to be merciful and apply the atoning blood of Christ that our sins might be forgiven.
4:2	Dallin H. Oaks October 1988	We ask for mercy as we repent and keep commandments.
4:2–3	Harold B. Lee April 1973	*After repentance, a peace of conscience indicates that the Lord has forgiven us.
4:3	Ronald E. Poelman October 1993	Christ has power to forgive sins.
4:9–12	Bernard P. Brockbank October 1979	Prayer and repentance can prepare us to receive knowledge from the Lord.
4:12	Boyd K. Packer October 1995	Retain a remission of our sins.
4:10, 12	Bernard P. Brockbank October 1974	These verses contain Benjamin's counsel on how to repent.
4:10, 12	John H. Vandenberg October 1972	True repentance leads to forgiveness, which produces a cleansing joy that surges through us.
4:19, 21	Gordon B. Hinckley April 1990	We should have mercy on each other, because each of us needs God's mercy.
4:26	Thomas S. Monson October 1988	Retaining a remission of our sins is connected to welfare ideals.

Mosiah	Speaker/Date	On Repentance
4:26	Jack H. Goaslind October 1983	Perfect love comes as a direct result of having our sins remitted. Therefore, if we hope to retain a remission of sins, we must administer to the spiritual and temporal needs of our fellowmen.
4:26	Marion G. Romney October 1972	Caring for the poor aids in retaining a remission of sins and receiving forgiveness.
5:9	Dallin H. Oaks April 1985	We must repent to be called by Christ's name.
5:13	Richard G. Scott October 1992	God will help people overcome who do it his way.

11. Believe in God and be faithful. Leaders sometimes cite Mosiah 4 to encourage members to remain strong and stay confident in the Lord. Mosiah 4:9–10 reads:

> Believe in God; believe that he is, and that he created all things, both in heaven and in earth; believe that he has all wisdom, and all power, both in heaven and in earth; believe that man doth not comprehend all the things which the Lord can comprehend. And again, believe that ye must repent of your sins and forsake them, and humble yourselves before God; and ask in sincerity of heart that he would forgive you; and now, if you believe all these things see that ye do them.

Mosiah	Speaker/Date	On Faithfulness
2:9–13	Delbert L. Stapley April 1968	Benjamin exhorted his people to listen, understand, remember, and apply the principles of Christian living.

Mosiah	Speaker/Date	On Faithfulness
3:24	John H. Vandenberg April 1965	Although men will be judged by their works, no man stands alone. One man's words and acts may influence another man.
4:9	Loren C. Dunn April 1981	Faith is the ability to recognize God as all-powerful and the giver of all blessings.
4:9–10	Ezra Taft Benson October 1983	Benjamin explains God's solution to human problems.
4:9–10	Marion G. Romney October 1975	When Benjamin saw his people's humility, he asked if they believed his words. In the same way, when we see that a less active member appears humble, we should ask if he believes.
4:9–10	Elray L. Christiansen April 1961	Ours is a day of testimony and allegiance to God, a day of sifting. We must determine where we stand. Do we follow Benjamin's admonition?
4:9–10, 14–15	Richard L. Evans October 1963	Peace comes through finding purpose in life and feeling God's love.
4:10	Spencer W. Kimball October 1980	Obey if you believe.
4:10	Howard W. Hunter April 1967	Sincerity of belief must be demonstrated through action.
4:10	Marion D. Hanks October 1960	We cannot be impartial to the Book of Mormon. We must be faithful.
4:11–13	Francis M. Lyman October 1897	*Men must remain faithful and persevere.

Mosiah	Speaker/Date	On Faithfulness
4:26–30	Francis M. Lyman October 1897	*Men must remain faithful and persevere.
4:28	John H. Vandenberg April 1967	Every commandment requires that we be willing to live honestly and truthfully.
5:12–13	Henry B. Eyring April 1991	We may draw close to God by retaining his name in our hearts.
5:13	Kenneth Johnson April 1994	It is important to have a relationship with Christ.
5:13	James E. Faust October 1976	The Saints should daily acknowledge the divinity of Christ.

12. Run no faster than you have strength. When encouraging diligence tempered by thoughtfulness and order, some leaders have quoted Mosiah 4:27: "And see that all these things are done in wisdom and order; for it is not requisite that a man should run faster than he has strength." Elder M. Russell Ballard reminded us that King Benjamin counseled "that all these things are done in wisdom and order" (Mosiah 4:27) and urged focusing on a few basic objectives in order to keep life's demands in balance.[17]

Mosiah	Speaker/Date	On Practical Wisdom
4:27	Jeffrey R. Holland April 1996	It is not intended that we should run faster than we have strength; all things should be done in order.
4:27	Dallin H. Oaks October 1993	Do all things in wisdom and order.
4:27	Dallin H. Oaks October 1989	Do not run faster than you have strength.

Mosiah	Speaker/Date	On Practical Wisdom
4:27	M. Russell Ballard April 1987	*Maintain balance in life by remembering priorities.
4:27	Spencer W. Kimball April 1981	The Saints need to manage church growth with wisdom and order.
4:27	Franklin D. Richards October 1964	Order and diligence provide the key to happiness and success in any activity.
4:27	Franklin D. Richards October 1964	The Saints should exercise diligence in assignments and callings.

13. Benjamin exemplifies a great teacher. There are two instances in general conference in which a General Authority held up Benjamin as a paradigm for teachers.

Mosiah	Speaker/Date	On Good Teachers
4:11–15	David O. McKay April 1955	Teachers of the church can learn from Benjamin's teachings about humility and unconditional love.
5:1	H. Burke Peterson April 1990	Benjamin wanted to know what his audience thought of his speech.

14. Do not trifle with God's word. An interesting use of Benjamin's words occurred in 1975, when Elder Vaughn J. Featherstone quoted Mosiah 2:9 to instruct members that conference messages should not be taken lightly: "My brethren, all ye that have assembled yourselves together, you that can hear my words which I shall speak unto you this day; for I have not commanded you to come up hither to trifle with the words which I shall speak, but that you should hearken unto me, and open your ears that ye may hear, and your hearts that ye may understand, and your minds that the mysteries of God may be unfolded to your view." Elder Featherstone also proclaimed that Benjamin gave the second greatest discourse ever, the most important being Christ's first discourse to the Nephites after his resurrection.

Mosiah	Speaker/Date	Trifling with God's Word
2:9	Francisco J. Viñas October 1996	We are to listen to the Lord's servants and not trifle with their words.
2:9	Vaughn J. Featherstone April 1975	Conference messages should not be taken lightly.
5:2, 5	H. Burke Peterson April 1990	*We should respond to the messages of general conference just as the people of King Benjamin responded to his words of instruction.

15. Miscellaneous. Many General Authorities have employed Benjamin's teachings to encourage members of the church to improve their lives and draw nearer to the Lord.

Mosiah	Speaker/Date	Other Teachings
1:15	Boyd K. Packer April 1986	The scriptures preserve God's mysteries and commandments.
2:19	Robert D. Hales April 1992	We ought to be grateful to our heavenly king.
2:22	Hartman Rector Jr. October 1990	God does not vary.
2:36–37	L. Aldin Porter April 1992	It is serious to disobey the commandments.

Mosiah	Speaker/Date	Other Teachings
2:38	M. Russell Ballard October 1990	*Those guilty of sexual sin will feel pain and will shrink from the presence of the Lord.
2:41	Richard L. Evans October 1963	Remember that the gospel is true.
3:3	Russell M. Nelson October 1986	Scripture study brings "glad tidings of great joy."
3:7	Robert L. Backman October 1991	Christ suffered temptation and pain, more than man can suffer.
3:8	John M. Madsen April 1993	Jesus is the son of Mary after the manner of the flesh. He is also the father of heaven and earth.
3:10, 18	John M. Madsen April 1993	Jesus is the Eternal Judge.
3:13	John M. Madsen April 1993	Jesus is the Messiah of whom all prophets testified.
3:18	Merlin R. Lybbert April 1994	Children who die before the age of accountability are saved in the celestial kingdom as a result of the atonement.
3:19	James E. Faust October 1982	One way to overcome financial stress is to seek first the kingdom of God. The spiritual strength to do this comes from submission to the Lord.
3:19	Russell M. Nelson October 1991	*Tabernacle Choir members were submissive.
3:24	Russell M. Nelson October 1990	We are free to choose, but we are accountable.

Mosiah	Speaker/Date	Other Teachings
3:25	Dallin H. Oaks October 1991	Those who yield to Satan's enticings are in a state of misery.
4:5	F. Enzio Busche October 1993	*Benjamin brings to his audience's attention their worthless and fallen state.
4:6	Russell M. Nelson October 1991	*We may come to know the goodness of God and his patience.
4:11–12	Levi Edgar Young April 1931	The teachings of Jesus and his prophets will not pass away; they live on in the hearts of believers.
4:14	Harold B. Lee April 1956	The scriptures leave no doubt as to the author and the beginning of sin.
4:17–18	Glenn L. Pace October 1990	We should not judge in seeing the consequences of other people's sins.
4:21	Boyd K. Packer October 1991	We may ask and receive.
4:29	Richard L. Evans October 1971	The Saints should avoid quibbling about the gospel. The scriptures do not catalog every sin.

Chronological Survey of Secondary Commentaries on Benjamin's Speech

A review of other literature concerning Benjamin's speech reveals that few writers have concentrated on the text as a whole. Perhaps predictably, much of the commentary has been fairly superficial. In general, writers have used three methods of interpretation. First, many have noted in Benjamin a favorite doctrine or theme and have concentrated on that theme to the exclusion of others. Second, commentators have frequently seen themselves reflected in the text. For example, Elder B. H. Roberts, one of the finest intellectuals in the church, loved aphorisms and found the Book of Mormon an excellent source for them. One of his favorite aphorisms was from Mosiah 2:17: "When ye are in the service of your fellow beings, you are only in the service of your God."[18] Unfortunately, Roberts's commentary on Benjamin did not really go beyond this point. Third, some writers have freely interpolated words and meanings not found in Mosiah. A Sunday School lesson in 1898, for example, says that Benjamin taught about the *condescension* of God, a term Benjamin never used. While creative interpretation of this last sort cannot be justified, there is certainly nothing wrong with concentrating on a particular theme or seeing oneself in scripture. These two methods do not, however, allow analysis of the text as a whole. They cannot fully answer the question of what Benjamin wanted to say and why he said it. On the other hand, they do show that Benjamin's speech encompasses many truths that should not be treated lightly, a fact the following survey bears out.

Evidence reveals that during the pre-Utah period (1830–1846), the Saints rarely quoted the Book of Mormon in their books, pamphlets, and periodicals. Early Saints loved to study the Bible and were generally more familiar with its contents than with the Book of Mormon. Studies by Grant Underwood show that the early Saints cited biblical passages over those from the Book of Mormon by a ratio of nineteen to one, although the recently published journals of William E. McLellin show that the Book of Mormon was used in early LDS preaching to a greater extent than had been previously suspected.[19] Of the relatively few Book of Mormon references, none refers to Benjamin or his speech. In the first European edition of the Book of Mormon (1841), numerous index entries explained the chapter contents. The few references pertaining to Benjamin's address included "King Benjamin teacheth the people," "Their tent doors towards the temple," "Coming of Christ foretold," "Beggars not denied," and "Sons and daughters."[20]

Although the Saints apparently did not often cite Benjamin, they probably knew about his important convocation and saw themselves acting similarly. Brigham Young's remark at the beginning of his 8 August 1844 discourse indicates this. At that time, when he was transfigured in the appearance and voice of the Prophet Joseph Smith, Brigham declared: "*Attention all!* This congregation makes me think of the days of King Benjamin, the multitude being so great that all could not hear. I request the brethren not to have any feelings for being convened this afternoon, for it is necessary; we want you all to be still and give attention, that all may hear."[21] Brigham the leader saw his situation reflected in that of the ancient Nephite leader.

The Book of Mormon received relatively little treatment from Latter-day Saint writers until the appearance of the 1879 edition, which was divided into shorter chapters and verses and included numerous footnotes. This represented one of the culminating life works of Orson Pratt.

The year 1879 also saw the landmark Supreme Court ruling in the case of *Reynolds v. the United States*, which sent thirty-seven-year-old George Reynolds, a secretary to the First Presidency, to prison "for conscience sake" on polygamy charges. Reynolds—a longtime student of history, geography, and science—had also studied the potential of these disciplines to influence a person's understanding of the scriptures. He served as a member of the General Sunday

School committee on publications and frequently contributed to the magazine for youth, the *Juvenile Instructor*. He and his close friend George Q. Cannon, Deseret Sunday School Union superintendent and editor of the *Juvenile Instructor*, had long recognized the need for aids to help young people understand the Book of Mormon. While imprisoned in the Utah Territorial Penitentiary, George Reynolds wrote more than eighty articles for publication, over half on the Book of Mormon. He became so excited upon receiving a copy of the new 1879 edition that he also commenced his comprehensive concordance to the Book of Mormon, which was eventually published in 1904. The Saints received Reynolds's prison articles on the Book of Mormon so enthusiastically that friends convinced him to publish the articles together with additional material in a book that could be used in the Sunday Schools and in homes to understand the teachings, story, geography, and internal and external evidences of the Book of Mormon. *The Story of the Book of Mormon,* first published in 1888, was the first real commentary on the contents of the Book of Mormon. The book appeared in several subsequent editions.

Elder Reynolds wrote that Benjamin was "a mighty man in the midst of Israel," whose final teachings "were some of the most divine and glorious ever uttered by man." Reynolds further indicated that Benjamin taught his people "the pure principles of the gospel—the duty which men owed to their God and to their fellows. He also told them how he had been visited by an angel, and what wondrous things that angel had shown him concerning the coming of the God of Israel to dwell with men in the flesh."[22] George Reynolds went on to publish his *Dictionary of the Book of Mormon* in 1891 and included the same material under "Benjamin" as he had in *The Story of the Book of Mormon.*[23] Although he praised Benjamin's contributions, Reynolds did not specifically comment on the prophet-king's many teachings.

After Reynolds's work, no serious commentary on Benjamin's speech appeared for several decades, although General Authorities and church literature did refer to it occasionally. The *Deseret Sunday School Union Leaflets* (1898), for example, contain five lessons about Benjamin, several of which analyze him in a superficial way that often includes creative speculation and interpolation. Lesson 145, "Benjamin, King of the Nephites," gives a basic biography and says that Benjamin faced three major problems: contentions among his people, Lamanite invasions, and false religious teachers. Lesson 147, "King Benjamin's Vision of the Angel," concentrates on Mosiah 3:1–7 and the Savior's role. The following quotation contains some interesting material:

> Nowhere in the sacred scriptures have we a grander picture of the greatness, glory and everlasting mercy of *God, our Savior,* than in these memorable words of Benjamin's holy visitor. They are not the words of man but of an angel, and they describe to us the regard with which our Lord Jesus is held by the *heavenly hosts;* how he is Lord Omnipotent and reigns as such in heaven, yet with *condescension* beyond our comprehension he became man and suffered all that mortals can, that we, *his creatures,* may be saved and *become like unto him.*[24]

Several non-Book of Mormon phrases appear in this passage, as well as the word *condescension,* which Benjamin does not use. *Condescension* occurs only in 1 Nephi. The lesson places great emphasis on the heavenly kingdom and man's potential to become like God, neither of which can actually be found in Benjamin's speech. Lesson 148, "King Benjamin's Vision of the Angel (continued)," simply paraphrases Mosiah 3:8–12. Lesson 149, "Benjamin's Teachings Concerning the Poor," describes service and aid to the poor.

Lesson 150, "Organization of the Church of Christ," sets out the covenant established by Benjamin. By "organization," the lesson means that the covenant probably signaled the first time that the title of Christ was applied to a group in the New World.

In 1909, B. H. Roberts published his in-depth study on the Book of Mormon, *New Witnesses for God.* Surprisingly, Roberts did not comment on Benjamin at all, although, as stated earlier, one of Roberts's favorite aphorisms was Mosiah 2:17. Even in his major theological treatise, *The Truth, The Way, The Life,* Roberts quoted Benjamin to support only two propositions about the salvation of children and the omnipotence of God, besides recommending Mosiah 3–5 as general supplemental reading.[25]

Mother Stories from the Book of Mormon, by William A. Morton, appeared in 1911. Contrary to what one might think, the book did not tell stories about mothers in the Book of Mormon. Instead, it recounted the Book of Mormon through short stories that children could understand. (One assumes, perhaps, that "Mother" was telling the stories). The stories, unfortunately, do not even mention Benjamin. "Mother" tells about Nephi$_1$'s death and Jacob's appointment, then says that after many years Zeniff decided to visit the Lamanites. Apparently, Benjamin just did not seem exciting or important enough to be included in this book.

The Gospel Doctrine Sunday School lesson for 10 February 1929 teaches about Benjamin and the history of the priesthood. The lesson reports that Benjamin held the priesthood and served as a prophet to his people. Furthermore, "the proclamation, or address, of King Benjamin to the people was one given him by an angel from the Lord, who commanded him to give the people a 'name, that thereby they may be distinguished above all the people which the Lord God hath brought out of the land of Jerusalem.'" The writers of this lesson seem to think that Benjamin received his entire discourse from the angel. Also, the writers indicate that Benjamin received a commandment from the angel to give the people a new name. The Book of Mormon text does not confirm this. The last part of the lesson affirms that the priests and teachers appointed by Benjamin (see Mosiah 6:3) were "undoubtedly of the Melchizedek Priesthood." This appears to be a case of applying one's own situation to the scriptures. In other words, the lesson writers reasoned that since they had a prophet aided by Melchizedek priesthood holders, the priests of Benjamin the prophet necessarily held that priesthood too.

The Gospel Teachings lesson for 24 April 1932 contains the following introduction: "No writer in the Book of Mormon has spoken more plainly about the gospel and the plan of salvation than has King Benjamin." Clearly the church recognized the power of Benjamin's speech, yet there was still no major commentary. The lesson simply quoted Mosiah 1–4, followed by a few study questions.

An adult Sunday School lesson for 3 June 1934 presents Benjamin's account in story form and freely speculates about Nephite culture. A 1942 lesson, "Righteous King Benjamin," follows in a similar vein. Of course, neither of these lessons represents serious study.

Not until Sidney B. Sperry's *Our Book of Mormon* (1946) and *The Book of Mormon Testifies* (1952) did Benjamin receive some kind of textual analysis.[26] Sperry, a pioneer scholar in religious studies at Brigham Young University, focused on "literary forms" in the Book of Mormon. He wrote that Benjamin's speech was the only good example of "oratory" in the Book of Mormon.[27] Furthermore, Sperry characterized the speech as a triumph in rhetoric and described a successful religious orator, of whom Benjamin was an archetype, in this way:

The business of a speech-maker is to do something with his audience, to change the listeners or mold their opinions before they depart. Many *techniques* are used in doing this, and the true orator knows how to *employ them skillfully.* He may leave the audience better informed; he may cause an emotional change; or he may change a purely indifferent attitude to one of active interest. In any event, he must cause a change in the ideas and attitudes of his listeners, or he has failed as an orator.[28]

Immediately after the above statement, Sperry said that "it is highly improbable that Benjamin had received much instruction in the making of speeches or sermons"[29] and that most of Benjamin's speeches must have been religious. In a comment specifically directed to Mosiah 2:16–18, Sperry wrote that "the homely English of this scripture could be much improved, particularly the first sentence. Nevertheless, the sentiments expressed are lovely and sublime. One likes to believe that King Benjamin, the author, was in effect the Wilford Woodruff of his time, a leader, a hard worker with his hands, a very spiritual man, but not an outstanding writer or orator."[30] Sperry separated Benjamin's speech into three divisions: "the necessity of rendering service" (Mosiah 2:9–41); the message of an angel concerning the coming of the Savior, his atonement, and its consequent effects on mankind (see Mosiah 3); and the emphatic teaching of practical religious precepts following the assembly's acknowledgment of testimony (see Mosiah 4:4–30).[31]

Sperry's analysis presents several difficulties. First, it is not clear why Benjamin constitutes the "only good" example of oratory in the Book of Mormon. In his *Book of Mormon Studies*, a 1948 Sunday School lesson B manual, Sperry said that the "oration of Benjamin is really the *only* example of oration in the Book of Mormon."[32] Why does Sperry ignore Alma (Alma 5), Mosiah₂ (Mosiah 29), and Samuel

(Helaman 13–15)? Second, Sperry's judgment that Benjamin had little instruction in speechmaking lacks justification. Essays in the present volume demonstrate the complexity and craftsmanship of Benjamin's speech, as well as the fact that it follows traditional farewell patterns. In light of this understanding, Sperry's description of Benjamin as the "Wilford Woodruff of his time"—an unlettered but sincere and spiritual man—carries little credibility. Third, Sperry writes that "most of [Benjamin's] speeches were doubtless of a religious nature, if we may judge the spirit of the man in his last formal speech," but one may well wonder why the majority of a king's speeches would need to be religious. Fourth, Sperry emphasizes that a good orator knows and employs the proper techniques to persuade his audience. This makes Benjamin seem more like a rhetorician, although Sperry does point out that the speech is "characterized by dignity, simplicity, sincerity, and a warm religious feeling."[33] He adds that Benjamin's statements "are the words of a great religious soul . . . worthy of a high place in the scriptures," and deserve "more careful study than [they have] heretofore had."[34]

Despite its problems, *Our Book of Mormon* marked the first time that anyone tried to outline Benjamin's speech and comment on its parts comprehensively and systematically. *Our Book of Mormon* reflected a growing interest in the Book of Mormon generally and signaled the beginning of the transition that occurred in the 1950s. That transition was a veritable explosion of scholarly and ecclesiastical interest in the Book of Mormon. This led to increased study of Benjamin as well.[35]

As mentioned previously, Sidney B. Sperry published *The Book of Mormon Testifies* in 1952. Sperry's works, and those of Hugh Nibley, were more restrained than the other "scholarly" Book of Mormon studies that proliferated during

the 1950s. Nibley's *An Approach to the Book of Mormon* served
as the Melchizedek Priesthood lesson manual for 1957. Lesson 23, "Old World Ritual in the New World," examined
Benjamin's speech in detail and pronounced that the speech
and the Nephite assembly reflected the ancient year-rites
found in many civilizations.[36] Nibley cited various aspects
of ancient New Year festivals and found similar characteristics in the Benjamin account.

Both William E. Berrett (*Teachings of the Book of Mormon*)
and Daniel H. Ludlow (*A Combination Student and Teacher
Guide to the Reading of the Book of Mormon*) wrote lesson
manuals for Sunday School in the years 1960–62. These
manuals contain basic questions about Benjamin's teachings
on service, humility, practical religion, and the atonement.

In the early 1960s, George T. Boyd (a church educator)
and Sidney B. Sperry voiced opposing interpretations of the
"natural man" (Mosiah 3:19). Boyd explained that

> The term "natural man" as employed by Benjamin is
> equivalent to "the incorrigible sinner." It is also clear that
> all men are not included in this category. Furthermore, it
> is clear that those who are outside the class to which the
> "natural man" belongs include not only those who have
> not heard the gospel, but also all those who have not be-
> come enemies to God by the process he described. Sin,
> here, has to do with acts, not with an inherent condition
> of depravity due to the fall.[37]

Sperry, taking issue with Boyd, indicated that the context in Mosiah 3:19 "makes it clear Benjamin is making a
general statement which concerns all men," not merely "in-
corrigible sinners." He added:

> By "natural man" is meant man who is subject to the pen-
> alty placed upon Adam, unlike little children in this re-
> spect, and who, aware that salvation comes only through
> the atoning blood of Jesus Christ, does not yield to the

requirements of the gospel, "to the enticings of the Holy Spirit," in order to become a new man in Christ. He remains the "old man," (Romans 6:6) cut off by reason of Adam's fall "from the presence of the Lord." (2 Nephi 9:6) All men, regardless of how ethical or just they may appear to be on the surface, are in this fallen state unless, after proper teaching, they are "born of the spirit" and become "redeemed of the Lord." (Mosiah 27:24).[38]

In 1967, Hugh Nibley published *Since Cumorah*, a comprehensive study on the Book of Mormon. Nibley wrote only a few sentences about Benjamin, a half paragraph under the heading "Champions of Equality."[39] While Nibley obviously respected Benjamin's political and moral philosophy, he simply mentioned the king as a believer in equality and continued to a discussion of Mosiah$_2$'s constitutional equality.

Sperry's *Book of Mormon Compendium* appeared in 1968, but it contained the same Benjamin material as that found in *Our Book of Mormon*.

John L. Sorenson's *An Ancient American Setting for the Book of Mormon* (1985) was the first comprehensive work about the Book of Mormon to follow Nibley's *Since Cumorah*. Sorenson does not write about Benjamin's speech itself, but he uses the event to support the argument that Benjamin's people were a small group.[40] Other recent papers on Benjamin's speech are listed in the bibliography in this volume, indicating a sharp increase in interest in this text that has arisen in the current decade.

Concluding Comments

Obviously, King Benjamin's farewell speech has gained increased respect from a theological standpoint over the years. Scholars are gaining interest too, but the Latter-day

Saints have only begun to study and appreciate the speech. Benjamin had a powerful effect on his original listeners. They believed his teachings, and the Holy Ghost worked a "mighty change" on their hearts so that they had "no more disposition to do evil, but to do good continually" (Mosiah 5:2). In 1985, President Ezra Taft Benson similarly urged church members to undergo a change of heart. He said that "Christ changes men, and changed men can change the world."[41] Now that Benjamin's speech receives continuous attention in the church curriculum, within the teachings of modern apostles and prophets, and within scholarly studies, the Saints have a greater opportunity to prove the king's words for themselves.

In more recent years, Benjamin's speech as a whole has received more attention and further detailed commentary. My master's thesis in 1975 focused on the strategies of instruction used by prophets and teachers in the Book of Mormon and their application to present-day instructional settings. I described each teacher's preparation, outstanding character traits, internal feelings for his audience, and the teaching setting in which each found himself. King Benjamin emerged as one of the best examples of a successful teacher. I also urged current Latter-day Saint teachers to cultivate humility and sincere love toward their students, as Benjamin showed toward his people, and further suggested that teachers "recognize the teaching moments when students are most receptive. When the students are all repentant and desire to be fed spiritually, at this time especially should they be challenged to keep the commandments and make a covenant with God."[42]

The 1976 Book of Mormon Sunday School manual contained lessons on Mosiah 1–3 and 4–6. These lessons repeated basic doctrines such as service, the mission of Christ, obtaining and retaining forgiveness, and true conversion, as do the lessons in the 1984 manual (the Benjamin lessons are practically reprints from the 1976 manual).

In 1978 Elaine Cannon and Ed J. Pinegar published *The Mighty Change,* in which they described the process of how one may be born again and become a new soul in Christ, and how a righteous society can be achieved. They dedicated their work to "King Benjamin, from whom we gleaned the six principles of change, and to Alma the younger, from whom we learned that all of us may experience the mighty change by experimenting upon the Word and then in turn helping others to progress spiritually." The six principles of change drawn from Benjamin's speech include coming to truly know God, coming to know ourselves, feeling the need to change, acting upon righteous information, establishing new values, and making a commitment.[43]

In a regional representatives seminar in 1977, President Spencer W. Kimball mentioned Mosiah 4:19, which says that men should serve one another and avoid judging the poor, for all are beggars in God's view. President Kimball then asked, "Have we not all received from our Lord life and health and wealth and strength and power and food and clothing? Have we not all been blessed? How selfish and thoughtless would it be for a young man to grow to maturity, spend his time preparing for his life's work and his occupation and be unwilling to serve his Creator in this, the most important service [missionary service] in all the world."[44]

In 1979 the Church Educational System published a student manual on the Book of Mormon for college students enrolled in institute of religion classes and religion classes at church schools. This manual contained commentary, usually drawn from statements by General Authorities, on specific passages from Benjamin's speech. The manual also said that King Benjamin was "one of the few truly righteous monarchs of history," and his final address was "one of the most stirring and significant sermons in the Book of Mormon."[45] It described Benjamin as "the embodiment of faithfulness and service" and challenged its student readers: "Can you appreciate that the same is true today—that Latter-day Saints must endure in faithfulness to the end and rely upon the mercy of a just God in and through the Atonement of Jesus Christ?"[46]

When Benjamin completed the part of his sermon about Christ's atonement and the natural man, the multitude fell to the earth in deep humility, having recognized themselves "in their own carnal state" (Mosiah 4:1–2). With one voice they prayed that the atoning blood of Christ be applied in their behalf. Elder Maxwell used this passage to explain,

> We begin to appreciate the Atonement with more than passive intellectual acknowledgment only when, as in the words of one prophet, we accept the terms of his atonement and "apply the atoning blood of Christ." (Mosiah 4:2.) We do this by repenting of our sins and by having them washed away by the holy ordinance of baptism, an act of both cleansing and commitment, and by receiving the confirming witness of the Holy Ghost, the Comforter. Without this conversion and re-birth, and without its resulting childlike spiritual submissiveness, Christ has told us we can neither see nor enter his kingdom.[47]

Immediately following his charge to care for the needy, King Benjamin indicated that "all these things are done in wisdom and order; for it is not requisite that a man should run faster than he has strength. And again it is expedient that he should be diligent, that thereby he might win the prize; therefore, all things must be done in order" (Mosiah 4:27). Elder Neal A. Maxwell, in a masterful essay on pacing ourselves when we work in the kingdom of God, quoted the foregoing from Benjamin and added,

Running faster than we have strength "is not requisite." Doing things diligently but "in wisdom and order" is, in fact, necessary if one is to "win the prize." This balance between pace and diligence is a high and demanding exercise in the use of our time, talent, and agency. It is easy to be passive and withdrawn. In some ways it is likewise easy to fling ourselves thoughtlessly and heedlessly into a task that we then do not continue as we commenced. (See D&C 9:5.)

It takes, however, real wisdom, discipline, and judgment to do things in order. Only then do we "win the prize." True effectiveness requires the help of heaven, which is given only under certain conditions. The "dignity of causality" that attends genuine accomplishment is a result of *diligence with dignity* as we labor to bring about the accomplishment.[48]

In 1984 Elder Richard G. Scott maintained that the Book of Mormon "holds answers for the problems we face in everyday life." As one of his examples, he reminded us, "If you have a tendency to be overbearing in your calling and responsibility, remember King Benjamin, who taught us how to preside with humility in the work of the Lord. (See Mosiah 2.)"[49]

Benjamin himself insisted that service to God should not be reason to boast (see Mosiah 2:16) and that if we mortals "should serve [God] with all [our] whole souls [we] would be unprofitable servants" (Mosiah 2:21). The Church Educational System student manual thus indicates, "The debt to God is completely beyond our ability to repay. This is why Benjamin points out that even if we devoted our whole soul to Him we are still unprofitable servants. In other words, we can do nothing that puts God in our debt."[50] Elder Joseph Fielding Smith has also said, "We are told that we are unprofitable servants, and so we are, if we think of trying to pay our Savior back for what he has done for us, for that we never can do; and we cannot by any number of acts, or a full life of faithful service, place our Savior in our debt."[51]

One is struck by Benjamin's humility (see Mosiah 2:19–26). The Church Educational System student manual comments, "In this beautiful discourse on humility we find one of the keys to Benjamin's greatness. Humility is not a mental groveling about one's worthlessness. We are the children of God and the crown of his creations. True humility is a recognition of our actual position in relationship to God. If we truly sensed our total dependence upon God, as Benjamin did, it would profoundly affect our daily living."[52]

In 1965 Elder Spencer W. Kimball, addressing Brigham Young University students on the law of chastity, related the story of a young unmarried couple who had broken that law. Elder Kimball quoted Mosiah 2:36–39 to this couple, in which Benjamin said that people withdraw themselves from the Spirit of the Lord through their willful disobedience to commandments they know about. When this happens, divine justice awakens in the offender "a lively sense of his own guilt . . . and doth fill his breast with guilt, and pain, and anguish" (Mosiah 2:38). Elder Kimball further told the young couple, "Your very irresponsible act identifies you as most immature. . . . You made the choice when you broke the law of chastity and gave up your virtue. That hour, freedom was replaced with tyrannical fetters. You accepted shackles and limitations and sorrows and eternal regrets when you could have had freedom with peace."[53]

Benjamin concluded his address by admonishing his listeners to watch their thoughts, words, and deeds (see Mosiah 4:30). President Ezra Taft Benson wrote in April 1984 that a person is a product of his or her thoughts and used Benjamin's admonition to challenge members of the church to conquer thoughts of lust.[54] In like manner, a *Church News* editorial in 1985 cited Mosiah 4:29–30 and added, "This counsel is so timely in today's world as we struggle with the proliferation of pornography, obscenity, and indecency. These growing evils bombard us on every hand. At times it seems almost impossible to escape them because they appear to be everywhere. . . . Individually, we must remember the admonition of King Benjamin and watch ourselves, our thoughts, our words, and our deeds. If we keep the commandments and continue in the faith we will have power over the evils of pornography. Otherwise, we may succumb to its enticements and ultimately perish."[55]

King Benjamin's address had a profound effect on the people who listened to it. They believed his words, and the Holy Spirit wrought a "mighty change" on them to the point that they had "no more disposition to do evil, but to do good continually" (Mosiah 5:2). In 1985 President Benson urged church members similarly to undergo a change of heart.[56] Now that Benjamin's speech is receiving continuous attention in the curriculum of the church and in the teachings of modern-day apostles and prophets, one would hope that it is having a similar effect on the hearts of the members of the church today.

Notes

1. Harold B. Lee, in *Conference Report*, April 1947, 47–48.
2. See *Ensign* (May 1986): 22, 26, 30, 31, 63–64.
3. Jeffrey R. Holland, "A Handful of Meal and a Little Oil," *Ensign* (May 1996): 29–31.
4. Spencer W. Kimball, "An Eternal Hope in Christ," *Ensign* (November 1978): 72.
5. Ezra Taft Benson, "Jesus Christ: Our Savior and Redeemer," *Ensign* (November 1983): 6.

6. Ibid.

7. Spencer W. Kimball, "Ocean Currents and Family Influences," *Ensign* (January 1984): 4.

8. Neal A. Maxwell, "'Willing to Submit,'" *Ensign* (May 1985): 70.

9. Spencer W. Kimball, "Home Training—the Cure for Evil," *Ensign* (June 1965): 513.

10. Ezra Taft Benson, "Worthy Fathers, Worthy Sons," *Ensign* (November 1985): 36.

11. Ibid., 36–37.

12. Ibid., 37.

13. Russell M. Nelson, "The Canker of Contention," *Ensign* (May 1989): 68–70, and Russell M. Nelson, "'Teach Us Tolerance and Love,'" *Ensign* (May 1994): 69–71.

14. M. Russell Ballard, "Answers to Life's Questions," *Ensign* (May 1995): 22–24.

15. Richard G. Scott, "Finding the Way Back," *Ensign* (May 1990): 74.

16. Harold B. Lee, "'Stand Ye in Holy Places,'" *Ensign* (July 1973): 122.

17. M. Russell Ballard, "Keeping Life's Demands in Balance," *Ensign* (May 1987): 13–16.

18. See Truman G. Madsen, "B. H. Roberts and the Book of Mormon," *BYU Studies* 19/4 (1979): 434–35.

19. Grant Underwood, "Book of Mormon Usage in Early LDS Theology," *Dialogue* 17/3 (1984): 35–74; Jan Shipps and John W. Welch, eds., *The Journals of William E. McLellin, 1831–36* (Urbana: University of Illinois, 1994).

20. Underwood, "Book of Mormon Usage," 64; Grant Underwood, "Plumbling the 'Plain and Precious' from an Early Mormon Perspective," a paper delivered at the annual meetings of the Mormon History Association in Kansas City, Missouri, 4 May 1985.

21. *HC* 7:232.

22. George Reynolds, *The Story of the Book of Mormon* (Salt Lake City: Jos. Hyrum Parry, 1888), 79, 82.

23. George Reynolds, *A Dictionary of the Book of Mormon* (Salt Lake City: Jos. Hyrum Parry, 1891), 85–89.

24. Lesson 147, "King Benjamin's Vision of the Angel" in *Deseret Sunday School Union Leaflets* (Salt Lake City: Deseret Sunday School Union Board, 1898).

25. B. H. Roberts, *The Truth, The Way, The Life*, ed. John W. Welch (Provo, Utah: BYU Studies, 1994), quotation on 402, 414; see also 359, 403, 522.

26. On the rise of scholarship and emphasis on the Book of Mormon in the middle of the twentieth century, see Noel B. Reynolds, "The Use of the Book of Mormon in the 20th Century," presented at a symposium entitled "Ancient Scriptures and the Restoration," cosponsored by the Smith Institute for Church History, BYU, and FARMS on 8 June 1997.

27. Sidney B. Sperry, *Our Book of Mormon* (Salt Lake City: Bookcraft, 1946), 118; cf. Sidney B. Sperry, "Types of Literature in the Book of Mormon," *JBMS* 4/1 (1995): 88.

28. Sperry, *Our Book of Mormon*, 118–19, emphasis added; cf. Sperry, "Types of Literature," 88.

29. Sperry, *Our Book of Mormon*, 119; cf. Sperry, "Types of Literature," 88.

30. Sperry, *Our Book of Mormon*, 80; cf. Sidney B. Sperry, "The Book of Mormon as Literature," *JBMS* 4/1 (1995): 44.

31. Sperry *Our Book of Mormon*, 120–22; cf. Sperry, "Types of Literature," 89.

32. Sidney B. Sperry, *Book of Mormon Studies* (Salt Lake City: Deseret Sunday School Union Board, 1947), 54, emphasis added.

33. Sperry, *Our Book of Mormon*, 120; cf. Sperry, "Types of Literature," 89.

34. Sperry, *Our Book of Mormon*, 123–24; cf. Sperry, "Types of Literature," 93–94.

35. General conference addresses provide a striking example of this change. Between the years 1897 and 1949, General Authorities cited Benjamin only seventeen times. In the 1950s alone, however, they quoted Benjamin twenty-three times, and in the next

decade they nearly doubled that. General Authorities continued to increase their references to Benjamin, and between 1980 and 1989 they cited him one hundred and eighteen times, and in the nineties thus far, close to one hundred times (ninety-four by October 1996).

36. See Hugh W. Nibley, "Old World Ritual in the New World," in *An Approach to the Book of Mormon*, 3rd ed. (Salt Lake City: Deseret Book and FARMS, 1988), 295–310.

37. This quotation comes from an essay originally prepared for a convention of seminary and institute teachers held on the campus of Brigham Young University in the summer of 1962 and is now published in *Views on Man and Religion: Collected Essays of George T. Boyd* (Provo, Utah: Friends of George T. Boyd, 1979), 27.

38. Sidney B. Sperry, *The Problems of the Book of Mormon* (Salt Lake City: Bookcraft, 1964), 3–4.

39. Hugh W. Nibley, "Good People and Bad People," in *Since Cumorah* (Salt Lake City: Deseret Book, 1967), 396; reprinted in 2nd ed. (Salt Lake City: Deseret Book and FARMS, 1988), 359–60.

40. John L. Sorenson, *An Ancient American Setting for the Book of Mormon* (Salt Lake City: Deseret Book and FARMS, 1985), 156–57.

41. Ezra Taft Benson, "Born of God," *Ensign* (November 1985): 6.

42. Bruce A. Van Orden, "An Examination of the Strategies of Instruction Employed by Prophets and Teachers in the Book of Mormon and Their Potential Application to Current LDS Instructional Settings" (master's thesis, Brigham Young University, 1975), 164; see 54–60, 159–64.

43. Elaine Cannon and Ed J. Pinegar, *The Mighty Change* (Salt Lake City: Deseret Book, 1978).

44. Spencer W. Kimball, at Regional Representatives Seminar, 30 September 1977 (Salt Lake City), 13.

45. *Book of Mormon (Religion 121–122) Student Manual* (Salt Lake City: The Church of Jesus Christ of Latter-day Saints, 1979), 153.

46. Ibid., 156–57.

47. Neal A. Maxwell, "Our Acceptance of Christ," *Ensign* (June 1984): 72.

48. Neal A. Maxwell, *Notwithstanding My Weakness* (Salt Lake City: Deseret Book, 1981), 6, emphasis in original.

49. Richard G. Scott, "The Power of the Book of Mormon in My Life," *Ensign* (October 1984): 11.

50. *Book of Mormon (Religion 121–122) Student Manual*, 155.

51. Joseph Fielding Smith, *Doctrines of Salvation*, 3 vols. (Salt Lake City: Bookcraft, 1954–56), 1:15.

52. *Book of Mormon (Religion 121–122) Student Manual*, 155.

53. Spencer W. Kimball, "Love versus Lust," in *Brigham Young University Speeches of the Year* (Provo, Utah: Brigham Young University, 1965), 20–21.

54. Ezra Taft Benson, "Think on Christ," *Ensign* (April 1984): 10.

55. Editorial in *Church News*, 1 September 1985, 16.

56. Benson, "Born of God," 6.

Complete Text of Benjamin's Speech with Notes and Comments

Prologue (Mosiah 1:1–2:8)

Benjamin's Instructions to His Sons (Mosiah 1:1–8)

¹And now there was no more •contention in •all the land of Zarahemla, among all the people who •belonged to king Benjamin, so that king Benjamin had •continual peace •all the remainder of his days. ²And it came to pass that he had three sons; and he called their names •Mosiah, and •Helorum, and Helaman. And he caused that they should be taught in •all the language of his fathers, that thereby they might become •men of understanding; and that they might know concerning the •prophecies which had been spoken by the mouths of their fathers, which were •delivered them by the hand of the Lord. ³•And he also taught them concerning the records which were engraven on the •plates of brass, saying:

My sons, •I would that ye should remember that were it not for •these plates, which contain these records and these commandments, we must have •suffered in ignorance, even at this present time, not knowing the •mysteries of God. ⁴For it were not possible that our father, Lehi, could have remembered all these things, to have taught them to his children, except it were for the help of these plates; for •he having been taught in the language of the Egyptians therefore he could read these engravings, and teach them to his children, that thereby they could teach them to their children, and so fulfilling the •commandments of God, even down to this present time. ⁵I say unto you, my sons, were it not for these things, which have been kept and preserved by the hand of God, that we might read and •understand of his mysteries, and have his commandments always •before our eyes, that even our fathers would have •dwindled in unbelief, and we should have been like unto our •brethren, the Lamanites, who know nothing concerning these things, or even do not believe them when they are taught them, because of the •traditions of their fathers, which are not correct. ⁶O my sons, I would that ye should remember that •these sayings are true, and also that these •records are true. And behold, also the plates of Nephi, which contain the records and the sayings of our fathers from the time they left Jerusalem until now, and they are true; and we can •know of their surety because we have them before our eyes. ⁷And now, my sons, I would that ye should remember to •search them diligently, ˙that ye may profit thereby; and I would that ye should •keep the commandments of God, that ye may prosper in the land •according to the promises which the Lord made unto our fathers.

⁸And many more things did king Benjamin teach his sons, •which are not written in this book.

1:1 *contention.* Behind this word may stand the Hebrew word *rib*, which can refer to either physical battle or legal disputations. Compare W of M 1:16.

all the land of Zarahemla, all the people, all the remainder of his days. Note the inclusiveness: all space, all people, all time—a powerful introduction.

belonged to king Benjamin. The concept of people belonging to their king is found in 1 Sam. 21:7, "chiefest of the herdmen that belonged to Saul"; and in 1 Kgs. 1:8, "mighty men which belonged to David." In 1:10 Benjamin refers to the people in Zarahemla as "my people," and in 4:4, he expands this to read: "my friends and my brethren, my kindred and my people." In creating this sense of belonging to the king, Benjamin sets the stage for a realization of his people's dependence on their heavenly king: "King Benjamin's sermon about how God supports us from moment to moment as well as immediately blesses us (when we keep His commandments) was not designed to be a popular sermon in self-sufficient times like ours. For us to be called 'unprofitable servants' and to be reminded that even our bodies are made of the dust of the earth that also 'belongeth to him'—these are hard sayings that bruise our pride. Unless, through humility and obedience, we can transform feeling owned into a grand sense of belonging, and being purchased into gratitude for being rescued, and dependency into appreciation for being tutored by an omniscient God, which He does in order that we might become more dependable and have more independence and scope for service in the future." (Maxwell, *All These Things Shall Give Thee Experience,* 1980, 24). See the notes on Mosiah 4:4, *brethren.*

continual peace. This refers to the quality and depth of the peace, not necessarily the duration. It refers variously to just a year as in Alma 3:32, or for twenty-two years as in Mosiah 10:5; this expression is not found in the standard works outside of the Book of Mormon; see Mosiah 7:1; 19:29; 29:43; Alma 4:5; 16:12; 30:2, 5; 49:30; Hel. 3:23, 32; 3 Ne. 6:9.

all the remainder of his days. The phrase *remainder of . . . days* is unique to the Book of Mormon, occurring nine times: Mosiah 1:1; 5:5; 29:11; Alma 62:43; Hel. 5:4 (twice); Ether 10:30; 11:3, 18. A comparable phrase in the KJV is in Isa. 38:10 "residue of my years," and other phrases in biblical Hebrew express a parallel meaning. For example, after "land rests [root *ŠQT] from war" a specific number of years is often mentioned; *land rests* is often found at the end of an era (Josh. 11:23; 14:15; Judg. 3:11, 30; 5:31; 8:28). The compiler of Chronicles frequently uses this phrase at the end of the reign of a king (2 Chron. 14:1, 6; 20:30). The elements of these OT verses compare well with those of Mosiah 1:1, which mentions a cessation of war or contention in the land and looks forward to the end of a reign of a king.

1:2 *Mosiah.* Possibly related to the Hebrew *môšîaʿ,* "deliverer, savior," a divine and human epithet in Ps. 7:10 (MT 7:11); 17:7; 18:41 (MT 18:42); 106:21; 2 Sam. 22:42; Isa. 49:26; 60:16; Jer. 14:8; TB *Berakhot* 49a (God); Judg. 3:9 (Othniel), "deliverer"; Neh. 9:27. In biblical times, this name or title appears to have applied to a person or officer who was a victorious hero appointed by God; a liberator, one who delivered his people by nonviolent means, and who established justice. Benjamin's decision to name his son Mosiah after his own father Mosiah₁ signals a wish for the son to be a similar kind of king who "hearken[ed] unto the voice of the Lord" and was a savior for the righteous Nephites. "Indeed, the themes of God's salvation and the deliverance of his people are strong in the book of Mosiah," thus meaningfully reflecting the connotations of the word *môšîaʿ;* "in several respects, the Book of Mormon usage of this term is quite remarkable, meaningful, and wholly consistent with Hebrew usage" (Welch, *Reexploring,* 105–7). See the notes on Mosiah 5:8, *no other name,* and *take upon you the name of Christ.*

Helorum, and Helaman. Robert Smith suggests that the name could derive from the Hebrew *hlmm,* "hammer," while Joanne Hackett notes that the Bible name *Helem* has the meaning "yoke," and adds the possibilities of *ḤLM "to dream"; *hēlem* "strength." John Tvedtnes comments that although it is unlikely, we should consider the possibility that *he-* is the definite article (the expected form would be with *ha-*), which would allow a comparison of Helorum with the name Luram (Moro. 9:2). It should be noted that Alma$_2$, who was a friend and fellow missionary of the sons of Mosiah, apparently named his son after their uncle, Helaman. For more comments on these names, see this volume p. 38.

all the language of his fathers. The phrase *language of his fathers* does not occur in the Bible. In the Book of Mormon, *language* generally refers to speech or words (1 Ne. 1:15; 3:21; 5:3, 6, 8; 10:15; 17:22; Alma 5:61; 7:1; 26:24; 46:26; Hel. 13:37) and also in a more technical sense, to a system of written communication (1 Ne. 1:2; 3:19; 2 Ne. 31:3; Jacob 7:4; Enos 1:1; Omni 1:17–18, 22, 25; Mosiah 1:2, 4; 8:6, 11–12; 9:1; 24:4; 28:14, 17; 3 Ne. 5:18; Morm. 9:24; Ether 1:33, 35–36; 3:22, 24; 12:39; Moro. 10:16). Speculation as to what Benjamin meant by *the language of his fathers* has varied. Apparently Benjamin taught his sons Egyptian (see 1:4), just as the ancient "Jews adopted Greek, an international language, in preference to Hebrew, even as a vehicle of holy writ, for the purpose of commanding the widest possible hearing"; and so too did Nephi "choose to record his message . . . in a world language rather than in his own tribal Hebrew" (Nibley, *Lehi in the Desert/The World of the Jaredites/There Were Jaredites*, 1994, 17). He may also have taught them Hebrew or other languages: Sperry speculates on the limited persistence of Egyptian among the descendants of Nephi: "When the Nephites left Jerusalem they may have had an active speaking knowledge of Egyptian," but "within a few generations, . . . a knowledge of Egyptian would have been limited to comparatively few of their descendants. . . . I see few resemblances to either Egyptian or ancient Hebrew characters in the few lines of hieroglyphics copied from the plates and left us by the Prophet Joseph Smith" (*JBMS* 4/1, 1995, 210–11, but compare Ricks and Tvedtnes, who argue that although the "language," i.e., *script*, was Egyptian, the underlying language was Hebrew, *JBMS* 5/2, 1996, 156–63). The phrase *all the language of his fathers* would seem to imply more than Egyptian alone and thus that "the Nephites . . . had freely altered the Egyptian to suit their own purposes" (M.18, 129; for further discussion of Benjamin as a linguist, see this volume, pp. 36–37). In commenting on how he had educated his children, Benjamin reflects his awareness of the biblical requirement that parents should "teach [the commandments] diligently unto [their] children" (Deut. 6:7; see also Mosiah 4:14; notes on 4:15, *teach them*, below; and this volume p. 4). "It appears to be a characteristic of goodly parents to spend an adequate portion of their time and energy teaching their children the things of God" (Ogden, in *Studies in Scripture* 7, 17–18). Following Benjamin, Ezra Taft Benson emphasizes the importance of understanding the language of holy writ: "If they didn't know the right words, they wouldn't know the plan" (*Ensign*, Nov. 1985, 36).

men of understanding. This phrase occurs a number of times in the KJV OT: Ezra 8:16; Job 34:10, 34; Prov. 1:5; 10:23; 11:12; 15:21; 17:27–28; 20:5; 28:2; Eccl. 9:11. It appears most often in Proverbs, where the virtues of the man of understanding are extolled. The Hebrew term for *understanding* is from the common root *BYN, the basic meaning of which is "to discern." In Alma 17:2, the sons of Mosiah are referred to as "men of a sound understanding," following the tradition laid down by their grandfather Benjamin and his fathers. In the latter days, this phrase was used in connection with the organization of the Relief Society, "I again ask the sisters in every ward of the Territory to . . . get women of good understanding to be your leaders, and then get counsel from men of understanding" (Young, *JD*, 12:194); and also to describe returned missionaries, "They are broadened in their minds, they are enlarged in their capacities, they have increased in their experience, and they become men of understanding, because their faculties have been aroused and developed" (George Q. Cannon, *Collected Discourses* 4, 6 October 1895). Oliver Cowdery, however, used it in a derogatory fashion when describing anti-Mormon intellectuals of his day, who employed "the weak and vain excuse framed, either to justify themselves, or to blind the eyes of the more ignorant; for any man of principle or judgment might see at once, that these excuses in the minds of men of understanding would not weigh any thing" (*Evening and Morning Star*, Jan. 1834, 121).

prophecies which had been spoken by the mouths of their fathers. Evidently, these prophecies were found in the Nephite records, or they may have been handed down orally. See also the notes on Mosiah 1:2, *all the language of his fathers,* above.

delivered them by the hand of the Lord. The idea that the words of the prophets are not their own but come from the Lord is found often in the OT: Ex. 4:12; 24:12; Num. 23:5, 16; Deut. 5:22; 18:18; Isa. 59:21; Jer. 1:7–9; 25:30; 26:4; Ezek. 2:7; 3:27. See also D&C 1:38; 18:33–36. The duty of the messenger in the ancient world was to repeat precisely the words that he or she was entrusted to deliver. See the Ugaritic *Legend of Keret* A ii: 55–57; A iii 140–42 (message and repetition of a message); A ii: 62–71; A iii:156–64 (a command and a carrying out of a command), in Pritchard, ed. *Ancient Near Eastern Texts Relating to the Old Testament,* 1969, 143–44; compare *Iliad* 2.11–15, 28–34, 65–69; 4.192–96, 204–6; 6.87–98, 269–78; 9.122–57, 264–99; 11.187–94, 200–9, 793–802 (16.36–45); 12.343–50, 357–63; 15.159–67, 176–83; 23.113–16, 134–36; 24.113–16, 134–36, 146–58, 175–87.

1:3 *and he also taught them.* King Benjamin frequently ventured beyond the mere symbolic religious functions of ancient kings and personally taught his sons and his people concerning God's commandments (K.11, 114). On Benjamin as a father, see this volume, pp. 4, 38, 41.

plates of brass. Benjamin placed great importance on the plates of brass, "in spite of the fact that they had many prophets." A modern application of this would be, "don't get the idea that because we have a prophet we don't have to pay much attention to the scriptures" (N.25, 438). For a discussion of the king's responsibility to possess a copy of the law and read in it all the days of his life, see Deuteronomy 17:18–19 and this volume, pp. 192–93. Gary Sturgess suggests that the small plates of Nephi might also have been read during the ceremony (*JBMS* 4/2, 1995, 114, 131). For the term *plates of brass,* see 1 Kgs. 7:30; Sirach 50:3; 1 Ne. 3:3, 12, 24; 5:11, 14, 18–19; 2 Ne. 4:15; 5:12; Omni 1:14; Mosiah 28:11, 20; Alma 37:3–5; and the notes on Mosiah 1:16, *engraven on the plates of brass,* below.

I would that ye should. This subjunctive imperative carries a sense of urgency, but also gentleness, and is found fifty-three times in the Book of Mormon and the D&C, each with an injunction to remember or obey. Benjamin uses it thirteen times. See 1 Ne. 1:18, 22:30; 2 Ne. 2:28; 4:3; 31:4; Omni 1:2, 26; Mosiah 1:3, 6, 7 (twice), 10; 2:31; 4:11, 26, 28; 5:8, 11, 12, 15; 15:1; Alma 3:19; 5:43; 6:5; 7:23; 9:14; 12:5; 13:1, 13; 19:5; 32:22; 36:2; 37:43; 38:5, 10; 39:9; 44:3; 60:23, 34; Hel. 5:6, 7; 7:23; 8:19; 15:5; 3 Ne. 12:48; 13:1; 23:6; 26:13; 27:31; Morm. 1:3; D&C 9:1; 46:7, 10; 53:7.

these plates. The plates referred to are the plates of brass, see notes on *plates of brass,* above.

suffered in ignorance. Sin as a result of a lack of knowledge has special treatment. One type of sin referred to specifically in the law of Moses was a sin or transgression committed in error or ignorance (Lev. 4:2, 13, 22, 27; 5:15, 18; Num. 15:24–29; see also the notes on Mosiah 3:11, *ignorantly sinned,* below). Ancient Israel divided sin "into three categories in order of severity": (1) "*Khet* (inadvertent sin)," which is "'mark-missing,' [compare Jacob 4:14] on the analogy of X who draws the bow to shoot an arrow at Y, but instead of striking Y, strikes Z. Regardless of intention, X is held responsible for shooting Z." It is to this sin that Benjamin may have been referring, since without the stipulations of the law contained in the brass plates, they would not have been able to keep the law. (2) "*Avon* (advertent sin) . . . is often referred to as 'crookedness,' on the analogy of a Jew who eats pork. He knows he is not permitted according to the Torah, yet he chooses to eat pork in order to satisfy his appetite. This is a premeditated action to satisfy a human need with no regard for the culpability of his act." (3) "*Pesha* (demonstrative sin)" has to do with rebelliousness. "Surely included within [this] category would be the three cardinal sins of Judaism: bloodshed, adultery, and idolatry . . . but *pesha* is not limited to those three specific sins. *Pesha* is the ultimate proof of divine love; because we have the freedom to submit our wills to God, we have also the freedom to pit our wills against God" (Anderson and Culbertson, *Anglican Theological Review* 68/4, 1986, 308–9; see Milgrom on sacrifice or inadvertent sin in the notes on Mosiah 2:32, below). With regard to inadvertent sin, "the Hebrew Bible's connection between sin and ritual uncleanness, contracted through normal biological processes . . . or disease," then "corresponds to the contemporary experience of being 'stained' by circumstances for which we are not personally responsible, e.g., our complicity in the oppression brought about through the unjust structures of society" (Brown, *Union Seminary Quarterly Review* 44/1–2, 1990, 155). See further the notes on Mosiah 2:32, *list to obey;* 2:34, *eternally indebted;* 3:11, *ignorantly sinned;* 4:28, *cause thy neighbor,* below.

mysteries of God. The term *mystery* or *mysteries* does not appear in the KJV OT. However it is widely used in the NT (Matt. 13:11; Mark 4:11; Luke 8:10; Rom. 11:25; 16:25; 1 Cor. 2:7; 4:1; 13:2; 14:2; 15:51; Eph. 1:9; 3:3–4, 9; 5:32; 6:19; Col. 1:26–27; 2:2; 4:3; 1 Tim. 3:9, 16; Rev. 10:7), in the Book of Mormon (1 Ne. 1:1; 2:16; 10:19; Mosiah 2:9; Alma 12:9–10; 26:22), and elsewhere in early Jewish and Christian literature: Sirach 42:18–19; *Testament of Levi* 2:10; *1 Enoch* 16:3; *Sib. Or.* 12:64; *Odes of Solomon* 8:10; 1QH 11:10; 1Q27; Josephus, *Contra Apionem* 2.22 (189); 37 (266). The KJV OT has a comparable term *secret* or *secrets,* Hebrew *sôḏ* (see, for example, Job 15:8; 29:4; Ps. 25:14; Prov. 3:32; Amos 3:7). In its earliest contexts, the word *sôḏ* referred to the council of God in which the prophet learned the confidential and intimate and hence mysterious will of God (Welch, in *The Book of Mormon: First Nephi,* 1988, 46). Inasmuch as Benjamin will disclose to his people the words spoken to him by the angel of the Lord, his reference to the *mysteries of God* may relate back to the ancient Israelite concept of divine mystery. For more on *mysteries,* see this volume, p. 7, and generally chapter 9.

1:4 *he having been taught in the language of the Egyptians.* The *he* referred to is Lehi, who taught Nephi; see 1 Ne. 1:1–2. "Benjamin's three sons—Mosiah, Helorum, and Helaman—were taught to read the modified Egyptian script in which Laban's plates of brass and Nephi's plates of gold were written" (T.46, 207). "The Nephite record reflected the Hebrew culture and background of the Jews, but was written in Egyptian characters" (M.18, 130).

Nibley believes that the brass plates were probably written in the Hebrew language but by use of a demotic script that was introduced in Egypt around 750 B.C. (N.25, 438). The term *language of the Egyptians* can also be found in 1 Ne. 1:2; Morm. 9:32–34; see also notes on Mosiah 1:2, *all the langauge of our fathers,* above.

commandments of God. The specific commandment that parents teach their children the things of God is found most often in Deuteronomy: Deut. 4:9–10; 6:7; 11:19; 31:19, 22. It is also noted in Lev. 10:11 and Ps. 34:11.

1:5 *understand of his mysteries.* A similar expression is found in Eph. 3:4, "when ye read, ye may understand . . . the mystery of Christ"; *mysteries of God* is found in 1 Cor. 4:1; 1 Ne. 2:16; 10:19; Mosiah 1:3; 2:9; Alma 12:9–10; 26:22; D&C 6:7; 8:11; 11:7. Because the word *mysterion* could refer to sacred knowledge, Benjamin's use of this term may reflect the sacred temple setting in which he was speaking, or it may refer to the fact that all truths are myteries until they are understood: "There are in the gospel such things as mysteries. A mystery is, of course, some truth that is not understood. All the principles of the gospel and all truth pertaining to the salvation of men are simple when understood. Until it is understood, however, a simple truth may be a great mystery" (Smith, *Doctrines of Salvation* 1:296). The importance of understanding these mysteries is explained as follows, "The secular knowledge is to be desired; the spiritual knowledge is a necessity. We shall need all of the accumulated secular knowledge in order to create worlds and furnish them, but only through the mysteries of God and these hidden treasures of knowledge may we arrive at the place and condition where we may use that knowledge in creation and exaltation" (Kimball, *Faith Precedes the Miracle,* 1973, 280). See notes on Mosiah 1:3, *and he also taught them,* above. On mysteries and revelation, see this volume, pp. 5–8, and generally chapter 9.

before our eyes. This passage is reminiscent of the admonition to the Israelites to keep the law "as frontlets between thine eyes" (Ex. 13:8–10; cf. Deut. 6:6–9; 11:18–21); "for a memorial" (Ex. 13:14–16). It is unclear when this commandment began to be interpreted mechanically and phylacteries came into use, but from the beginning these biblical passages dealing with frontlets were associated with teaching religion to the children, as it is here. See also Matt. 23:5; Letter of Aristeas 158–59; *tefillin*, "phylacteries" from 1Q, 4Q, and Wadi Murabbaʿat (Midrash *Sifre Deut.* 6:4); see also Alma 3:16–18, "marking themselves in the foreheads."

dwindled in unbelief. This phrase is unique to the Book of Mormon: 1 Ne. 4:13; 12:22; 13:35; 2 Ne. 1:10; Alma 45:10, 12; 50:22; Hel. 6:34; 15:11; 3 Ne. 21:5; 4 Ne. 1:34, 38; Morm. 9:20. Interestingly 4 Ne. 1:38 distinguishes between dwindling in unbelief and willfully rebelling against God. In the KJV OT, apostasy is generally described as either *rebellion* or *forsaking*. Benjamin ensured the preservation of his people from ignorance by teaching them from the plates of brass, citing Lehi who taught his children Egyptian, so that they could read the engravings and pass knowledge on to further generations. Because he believed that without this knowledge, his "people would be no better off than the Lamanites," the "grand passion of Benjamin's life was the preservation intact of the mysteries and practices of his people as they went back to the beginning" (N.28, 298). Benjamin had a vivid example in front of him of one nation that had dwindled in unbelief: "The Mulekite civilization is a classic illustration of a nation without the anchor of scriptural writ going adrift in a troubled sea" (M.18, 130).

brethren. By referring to the Lamanites as their *brethren*, Benjamin includes them as family, part of the tribe of Israel and the house of Lehi. This tradition was carried on by the sons of Mosiah in Alma 17:9. See also Jac. 2:35: 3:5; 7:25; Enos 1:11; Jarom 1:2; Mosiah 11:19; 22:3; 25:11; 28:1; Alma 3:6; 17:9, 11; 19:14; 24:1, 20; 26:3, 27; 27:20; 43:11, 29; 48:21; Hel. 4:24; 15:4, 11, 12; 4 Ne. 1:43; Moro. 1:4; 10:1; D&C 3:18; 10:48; Testimony of Three Witnesses. See also the notes on Mosiah 1:1, *belonged to king Benjamin,* above; 1:13, *weak like unto their brethren;* and 3:1, *my brethren,* below.

traditions of their fathers. See Gal. 1:14, in which Paul was "zealous of the traditions of [his] fathers," and 1 Pet. 1:18, "by tradition from your fathers." Among the Israelites and Jews crucial debates often centered around the role of custom or tradition in contrast with the specific provisions of the written law. Benjamin favors the written law over oral traditions, objecting especially to any traditions that are not correct.

1:6 *these sayings are true.* Benjamin certifies as a witness the truthfulness of the words on the plates and the integrity of those ancient records. The phrases *these sayings are true, these records are true,* or *true sayings* and *true records* do not occur in the KJV OT. *True sayings* is found in 1 Tim. 3:1 and Rev. 19:9. The concept of true records is found in the writings of John: John 8:13–14; 19:35; 3 Jn. 1:12. *True words, word* or *words of truth* appear in the OT: 2 Sam. 7:28; 1 Kgs. 17:24; Ps. 119:43, 160, Prov. 22:21; Eccl. 12:10, as well as the NT: John 17:17; Acts 26:25; 2 Cor. 6:7; Eph. 1:13; Col. 1:5; 2 Tim. 2:15; James 1:18; Rev. 21:5. Reference is also made to *true law, true laws,* and *law of truth:* Neh. 9:13; Ps. 119:142; Mal. 2:6. The Book of Mormon contains several statements attesting to the truthfulness of records or words: 1 Ne. 1:3; 13:39; 2 Ne. 9:40; 11:3; 31:15; Mosiah 1:6; 5:2; 17:9, 20; 29:37; Alma 3:12; 5:47; 6:8; 30:43; 38:9; Hel. 9:37; 3 Ne. 5:9, 18; 8:1; 17:25; 18:37. Turner emphasizes the importance of the truthfulness of the records, "The contents of these three sets of plates provided the scriptural underpinnings of Nephite government and law" (T.46, 208). By bearing testimony to his sons, Benjamin highlights the importance of parents bearing testimony to their children: "It was human testimony . . . that excited this inquiry [after a knowledge of the glory of God] . . . . That inquiry frequently terminated . . . in the most glorious discoveries and eternal certainties" (A.01, 25). See the notes on Mosiah 5:2, *we know of their surety,* below.

records are true. Bearing witness of the truth of the Nephite records is an important task of the prophets of the Book of Mormon; see 1 Ne. 1:3; Alma 3:12; 3 Ne. 5:9, 18; 8:1; 17:25; 18:37; Ether 4:11; see also D&C 1:39; 67:8; 128:4; 138:60; John 8:13, 14; 19:35; 3 Jn. 1:12.

know of their surety. The phrase *know of a surety* occurs in Gen. 15:13; Acts 12:11; 1 Ne. 5:8.

1:7 *search them diligently.* The phrase *search diligently* is found in the KJV in Matt. 2:8. *A diligent search* is in the KJV Ps. 64:6; 77:6. In Psalm 64:6, the word *diligent* is a translation of a cognate accusative (literally "search a search"). *Search them diligently* appears twice more in the Book of Mormon, 3 Ne. 23:1 and Moro. 7:19, and also in D&C 84:94; 90:22, 24 (D&C 136:26 has *diligent search*).

that ye may profit thereby. The idea of teachings being profitable to the people can be found in 1 Ne. 19:23; 2 Ne. 2:14; 4:15; 5:30; W of M 1:2; often *profit* is linked with learning.

keep the commandments of God, that ye may prosper in the land. In many respects, Benjamin's words are consonant with the theology of Deuteronomy; compare "Keep therefore the words of this covenant, and do them, that ye may prosper in all that ye do" (Deut. 29:9). Obedience is of critical importance to Benjamin. "A knowledge of the things of God is inseparably connected with obedience to the commandments of God. . . . Prophets of all ages have taught that God cannot be known, nor can his gospel be understood by the carnally minded, the disobedient, or the rebellious" (M.18, 131). Keeping the commandments is also mentioned in Deut. 4:2; 6:17; 10:13; Ps. 119:115; 1 Chron. 22:12; Rev. 12:17; 14:12.; 1Q22 I–II. *Keep the commandments* is likewise found 36 times in the Book of Mormon, with 5 occurrences in Benjamin's speech: Mosiah 1:7; 2:13–14, 31, 41. Nibley sees in Benjamin's entire discourse a comparison with Moses' iteration of the law in Deuteronomy, according to which Benjamin offers in 1:7 a "conscious" echo of Deut. 7:9, for "the promised rewards are the same; . . . heaven and earth will bring forth in abundance, you will never have to fear a foreign enemy—success and security should be yours" (N.29, 223–24). See notes on Mosiah 2:13, 22, 31, *commandments,* below. For further information on *fear,* see the notes on Mosiah 2:10, *that ye should fear me;* 4:1, *fear of the Lord.*

according to the promises which the Lord made unto our fathers. Benjamin recognizes that his promises are the same as those given by other prophets. The idea that obedience to commandments leads to prosperity is widespread throughout the scriptures and is particularly prevalent in Deuteronomy, where it is often expressed in language similar to that of the Book of Mormon. Welch sees in this emphasis on Deuteronomy a possible reflection of the likelihood that the "book of law" found during Josiah's reign and during Lehi's day was all or part of the book of Deuteronomy. This book appears to have been the basis for religious reforms implemented at that time (*Ensign*, Sept. 1976, 28–29). In fact, in a ceremony somewhat similar to Benjamin's assembly, the newly discovered book was read before all Israel (2 Chron. 34:30). Certainly Lehi would have been greatly influenced by the concepts and even language of this "book of law." It is even conceivable that Lehi had been present at that ceremony. Prosperity involves more than material or physical well-being; it also involves a wide array of spiritual and divine blessings (see Deut. 28:1–14; Nibley, *Approaching Zion*, 1989, 196–97). On obedience leading to prosperity, see, for example, Deut. 29:9; Josh. 1:7; 1 Kgs. 2:3; 1 Chron. 22:13. On promises to the fathers, see Deut. 6:3; 19:8; Neh. 9:23. As widespread as this idea is in the Bible, it is expressed more strongly and more frequently in the Book of Mormon. See for example 1 Ne. 2:20; 4:14; 2 Ne. 1:9, 20; 4:4; Jarom 1:9; Omni 1:6; Mosiah 2:31; 26:37; Alma 1:31; 9:13; 36:1, 30; 37:13, 43; 38:1; 48:15, 25; 50:20; 62:51; Hel. 3:20; 4:15; 12:1; 3 Ne. 22:17. See notes on Mosiah 2:22, *prosper in the land,* below.

1:8 *which are not written in this book.* This verse is almost identical to John 20:30, which is in turn closely related to many other biblical texts. The Book of Mormon has other similar passages: 1 Ne. 10:15; Alma 9:34; 13:31; 3 Ne. 7:17; see also John 21:25. Compare references in the OT to the fact that additional words were spoken that could not be contained in the written record: 1 Kgs. 11:41; 14:29; 15:7, 23, 31; 16:5, 14, 20, 27; 22:39, 45; 2 Kgs. 1:18; 8:23; 10:34; 12:19; 13:8, 12; 14:15, 18, 28; 15:6, 21, 36; 16:19; 20:20; 21:17, 25; 22:13; 23:28; 24:5; 2 Chron. 9:29; 12:15; 25:26.

Benjamin Confers the Kingship on Mosiah (Mosiah 1:9–17)

⁹And it came to pass that made •an end of teaching his after king Benjamin had sons, that he •waxed old,

and he saw that he must very soon go •the way of all the earth; therefore, he thought it •expedient that he should •confer the kingdom upon one of his sons. [10]Therefore, he had Mosiah brought before him; and these are the words which he spake unto him, saying:

My son, I would that ye should •make a proclamation throughout all this land among all this people, or •the people of Zarahemla, and the people of Mosiah who dwell in the land, that thereby they may be gathered together; for •on the morrow I shall proclaim unto this my people •out of mine own mouth that thou art •a king and a ruler over this people, whom the •Lord our God hath given us. [11]And moreover, I shall •give this people a name, that thereby they •may be distinguished above all the people which the •Lord God hath •brought out of the •land of Jerusalem; and this I do •because they have been a diligent people in keeping the commandments of the Lord.

[12]And I give unto them a name that •never shall be blotted out, •except it be through transgression. [13]Yea, and moreover I say unto you, that if this •highly favored people of the Lord should fall into transgression, and become •a wicked and an adulterous people, that the Lord will •deliver them up, that thereby they become •weak like unto their brethren; and he will no more preserve them by his •matchless and marvelous power, as he has hitherto preserved our fathers. [14]For I say unto you, that if he had not •extended his arm in the preservation of our fathers they must have fallen •into the hands of the Lamanites, and become victims to their hatred.

[15]And it came to pass that after king Benjamin had made an end of these sayings to his son, that •he gave him charge concerning all the affairs of the kingdom. [16]And moreover, he also gave him charge concerning the records which were •engraven on the •plates of

brass; and also the plates of Nephi; and also, the sword of Laban, and the ball or director, which •led our fathers through the wilderness, which was •prepared by the hand of the Lord that thereby they might be led, every one according to the •heed and diligence which they gave unto him. ¹⁷There-

fore, as they were unfaithful they did not prosper nor progress in their journey, but were •driven back, and incurred the displeasure of God upon them; and therefore they were smitten with •famine and sore afflictions, to •stir them up in remembrance of their duty.

1:9 *an end*. The phrase *make* or *made an end* is found 45 times in the Book of Mormon and appears to be formulaic and to mark a transition, such as between Mormon's editorial commentary and his abridgment (Morm. 8:13). This leads to the proposition that Benjamin has delivered a formal period of instruction to his sons as he approaches the end of his life. See 1 Ne. 7:1; 10:2; 14:30; 16:1; 22:29; 30:18; 31:1; 2: Ne. 1:1; 4:3, 8, 10, 11; 30:18; 31:1; Jac. 2:22; 3:14; 7:27; Omni 1:3, 9, 11, 30; Mosiah 1:9, 15; 4:1; 6:3; 8:1, 19; 13:25; 25:7, 14, 17; Alma 6:1; 12:19; 14:1; 24:17; 35:1; 44:10; 3 Ne. 5:19; 10:19; 15:8; 17:18; 18:36; 19:35; 26:12; 28:24; Morm. 8:13; Moro. 1:1. See also notes on Mosiah 4:1, *made an end of speaking*, below.

waxed old. This phrase, meaning to grow old (see the comments on impending death, this volume, p. 91), appears several times in the OT and three times in the NT. Most often people are said to *wax old* (Gen. 18:12; Josh. 23:1; 2 Chron. 24:15; Ps. 32:3), but the phrase may also refer to garments (Deut. 8:4; Neh. 9:21), the root of a cut-down tree (Job 14:8), and a bag (Luke 12:33). People *wax old like a garment* (Ps. 102:26; Isa. 50:9; Heb. 1:11), as does the earth (Isa. 51:6). Interestingly, the old covenant is said to have *waxed old* (Heb. 8:13). Three Hebrew roots are rendered *wax old* in the OT: *ZQN, which means to become old; *BLH, meaning to become old and worn out with particular reference to clothing; and *ᶜTQ, which means to advance in years. The phrase also occurs in the Book of Mormon in 2 Ne. 4:12, referring to Lehi; in

2 Ne. 7:9 and 8:6, which are parallel to Isaiah; and in Jacob 5:3, where the allegorical olive tree waxes old.

the way of all the earth. This phrase appears in Josh. 23:14 and 1 Kgs. 2:2. The English is a literal translation of a Hebrew expression. In the Book of Mormon it is found in 2 Ne. 1:14; Alma 1:1; 62:37; and Hel. 1:2.

expedient. Benjamin uses the word *expedient* here and in Mosiah 4:27; 5:3; 6:1. Webster's 1828 dictionary defines *expedient* as "tending to promote the object proposed; fit or suitable for the purpose; proper under the circumstances." Benjamin's usage does not convey the sense of a practical shortcut, as in the modern meaning of the word, but more of being suitably necessary for reconciliation. See also notes on Mosiah 5:3, *expedient*, below.

confer the kingdom. Benjamin is conferring the kingdom on his son, rather than the heir assuming the throne on the death of the previous king. Further information on such a coregency is found in this volume, pp. 238–39.

1:10 *make a proclamation.* Proclamations and gathering together often occur together in the OT for various reasons. Proclamations are made (1) to gather people at the temple, (2) to celebrate feasts—specifically the feast of booths, (3) to declare liberty at the jubilee, and (4) to announce a new king (see this volume, pp. 167, 188–89). Proclamations are often, although not exclusively, made by kings. Examples of these four types of proclamations are (1) Hezekiah's proclamation to gather the people to observe the Passover in 2 Chron. 30:5. (2) Ex. 32:5, where Aaron "made a proclamation" and said, "To morrow is a feast to the Lord." Unfortunately, at this feast the golden calf was worshiped. In Lev. 23 a proclamation is made in association with feasts: "Speak unto the children of Israel, and say unto them, Concerning the feasts of the Lord, which ye shall proclaim to be holy convocations, even these are my feasts" (Lev. 23:2; see also 23:4, 21, 37). In 1 Kgs. 21:9 a fast is proclaimed by Jezebel. In 2 Kgs. 10:20 a solemn assembly is proclaimed for Baꜥal. Neh. 8:5 reads: "And that they should publish and proclaim in all their cities, and in Jerusalem, saying, Go forth unto the mount, and fetch olive branches, and pine branches, and myrtle branches, and palm branches, and branches of thick trees, to make booths, as it is written." This is directly tied to the festival of booths, although it is postexilic. (3) In Lev. 25:10 "liberty" is "proclaimed" as part of the jubilee. In Jer. 34:12–22 the people are condemned because they have not followed the commandment to "proclaim liberty," again as part of the jubilee. Thus this root is often associated with feasts (it is also used in a number of other ways). (4) A new king is proclaimed in Dan. 5:29: "Then commanded Belshazzar, and they clothed Daniel with scarlet, and put a chain of gold about his neck, and made a proclamation concerning him, that he should be the third ruler in the kingdom." Benjamin's listing of the recipients of this proclamation is unusual (Mosiah 1:10). He emphasizes that it is to go throughout all his land and among all his people, namely the Mulekites (the people of Zarahemla) as well as to the Nephites (the people of Mosiah). Biblical proclamations specify the following: "through Judah and Jerusalem" (2 Chron. 24:9); "throughout all Israel, from Beer-sheba even to Dan" (2 Chron. 30:5); "throughout Judah and Jerusalem unto all the children of the captivity" (Ezra 10:7); "in all their cities and in Jerusalem" (Neh. 8:15); "in the cities of Judah, and in the streets of Jerusalem" (Jer. 11:6). Some gatherings occur without specific mention of a proclamation, although it is likely that proclamations did occur in association with these gatherings. In Lev. 8:4, Moses gathers an assembly to dress Aaron in the clothing of the high priest (perhaps analogous to a coronation); in Ex. 35:1, Moses gathers the children of Israel to make covenants; see also 2 Chron. 30:5, "make proclamation throughout all Israel . . . that they should come to keep the passover unto the Lord God of Israel at Jerusalem"; 1 Esdras (3 Ezra) 9:3, "And there was a proclamation . . . that they should be gathered together at Jerusalem" (1 Esdras 5:47; see also Ezra 10:7; Mosiah 1:18; 2:1; 7:17;). See also this volume, p. 91, and notes on Mosiah 2:1, *proclamation.*

the people of Zarahemla. The Mulekites. See Omni 1:14, 18–19. They were more numerous than the Nephites. See Mosiah 25:2.

on the morrow. Although Benjamin is announcing the assembly for the next day, it should not be assumed that this was a hasty decision. Preparations had undoubtedly been underway for some time because of the necessity of constructing a tower, the need to distribute copies of the speech, and so forth. Because it probably would have taken all the people in the land of Zarahemla more than one day to assemble, it seems likely that they had already gathered at the temple, either for other festival purposes or in anticipation of the coronation announcement.

out of mine own mouth. Compare Job 9:20, which says "Mine own mouth shall condemn me," and Isaiah talks of words from his mouth in Isa. 45:23; 48:3; 55:11.

a king and a ruler. The combination of *king* and *ruler* occurs six times in the Book of Mormon: 1 Ne. 16:38; Jacob 1:9; Mosiah 1:10; 2:30; 23:39; 29:2. See also D&C 38:21, "no king nor ruler." Twice the phrase is turned around, "a ruler and a king" (Mosiah 2:11; 6:3), and once the phrase "king and leader" is found (Alma 47:6). No similar combination is found in the KJV. The context of the passages does not seem to uphold the supposition that this phrase might indicate that the two terms referred to two different aspects of the office, or even two different offices held at the same time by an individual. For example, in the first reference Laman uses these terms to speak of Nephi before kingship had been established. It has been suggested that Benjamin saw a distinction between *a king and ruler*, and *the king and ruler*, Christ being *the* king and *the* ruler (M.18, 132). For more information on the role of the king as intermediary between God and the people, see this volume, pp. 234–35.

Lord our God. This is a common phrase in the OT. The first term probably represents the tetragram YHWH and the second *ʾelōhênû*. These two words appear in the often recited verse, Deut. 6:4, "Hear, O Israel: the Lord our God is one Lord." See also *Lord God*, noted under Mosiah 1:11, below.

1:11 *give this people a name.* The full name is given to the people in Mosiah 3:8. Speaking generally, the name Benjamin gives his people is that of Christ (Mosiah 5:10), which "is a sacred title which means 'anointed' or 'anointed one.' . . . One does not have the right to assume it; rather, it must be conferred" (M.18, 132). "In becoming the sons and daughters of Christ, they took upon themselves both his *name* and his *nature*" (T.46, 223). For further references, see Mosiah 1:12; 5:7–13; 25:12; *Gospel of Philip* 58:17–59:6; 64:23–31 (Nag Hammadi Codex 2:3). See Madsen, in *By Study and Also by Faith*, 1990, 1:458–81. For further comments on the new name, see this volume, pp. 58, 243, 252–53, 286, 290–91, 296; and on covenant, see the notes on Mosiah 5:5, *enter into a covenant*, and this volume, pp. 243–44, 255, 258–59.

may be distinguished. In a recent article, Peter Machinist looks at how scholars have tried to find ways in which Israel was distinct from the other peoples in the Near East. Machinist examines two proposals: (1) in their individual traits and (2) in the way Israel "patterned and emphasized" cultural ideas. He suggests that neither of these features can be called distinctive. He investigates if and how the Israelites considered themselves distinct, and finds 433 examples of OT statements that show that distinctiveness was important to them. The reasons implicit in these passages concerning distinctiveness show that (1) "the core of Israel's claim to distinctiveness is her special relationship to her God," (2) "the unique relationship between Israel and Yahweh only underscores the uniqueness of Yahweh himself," (3) certain behavioral traits set Israel apart, and (4) because of this relationship and the behavior exhibited, Israel obtained a unique status from God, or in other words, she was blessed. Machinist notes the diversity on the placement in the Bible of the distinctiveness passages and suggests that they not only reflect the opinion of the canonical organizers but that of Israel as a whole. Benjamin and his people were equally conscious of their special status before God and among all the peoples of the earth. Interestingly, the Nephite concern over distinctiveness is specifically connected with their exodus from the land of Jerusalem (Mosiah 1:11); many of Machinist's passages establishing Israelite distinctiveness arise out of passages about Israel's exodus from Egypt (*Ah, Assyria—: Studies in Assyrian History and Ancient Near Eastern Historiography, Presented to Hayim Tadmor*, 1991, 196–212).

Lord God. The Hebrew expression used here would probably have been the Tetragrammaton YHWH for Lord (pronounced *adonai*) and *elohim* for God. See also notes on Mosiah 1:10, *Lord our God*, above.

brought out of the land of Jerusalem. See also notes on Mosiah 2:4, *who had brought them out of the land of Jerusalem*, above. Compare Ex. 32:7, "thy people, which thou broughtest out of the land of Egypt."

land of Jerusalem. "The land of Jerusalem is *not* the city of Jerusalem. Lehi 'dwelt at Jerusalem in all his days' (1 Ne. 1:4), yet his sons had to 'go down to the land of our father's inheritance' to pick up their property (1 Ne. 3:16, 22). The apparent anomaly is readily explained by the Amarna Letters, in which we read that 'a city of the land of Jerusalem, Bet-Ninib, has been captured.' It was the rule in Palestine and Syria from ancient times, as the same letters show, for a large area around a city and all the inhabitants of that area to bear the name of the city" (Nibley, *An Approach to the Book of Mormon*, 1988, 101–2).

because they have been a diligent people in keeping the commandments. See Deut. 6:17, "diligently keep the commandments of the Lord your God." See the notes on Mosiah 4:6, *diligent in keeping his commandments*. On the state of their worthiness: "One presumes that the people are previously baptized church members who are confident they are righteous" (R.41, 103). See also this volume, p. 290.

1:12 *never shall be blotted out.* In the KJV, *blotted out* is used in two ways. Sin or transgression is blotted out (Neh. 4:5; Ps. 51:1, 9; Isa. 43:25; 44:22; Jer. 18:23; Acts 3:19), and names or remembrances are blotted out from the book of life or from under heaven (Ex. 32:32–33; Deut. 9:14; 25:19; 29:20; 2 Kgs. 14:27; Ps. 109:13; Col. 2:14; Rev. 3:5; in Num. 5:23 a curse is blotted out from a writing). The Hebrew root here is *MḤH, and it is also translated "put out" in Deut. 25:6 and "wiped out" in 2 Kgs. 21:13. Brigham Young explained that "We receive the Gospel, not that we may have our names written in the Lamb's book of life, but that our names may not be blotted out of that book" (Widtsoe, comp., *Discourses of Brigham Young,* 1941, 7). See further the notes on Mosiah 5:11, *blotted out,* below.

except it be. This phrase appears frequently in Benjamin's speech (six times; once while addressing his sons and five times while speaking to the people). It appears only three other times in the Book of Mormon. On those three occasions, Christ and the atonement figure highly. Although the expression does not appear in the KJV OT, in the Hebrew OT a number of different words are used to express this idea: *lûlēʾ* = "except," *kî ʾim* = literally "that if" (this is most often used), *biltî* = a particle of negation, *ʾim lōʾ* = if not, *ʾim lōʾ kî* which is literally "if not that." Through such provisos, Benjamin makes it clear that the blessings promised in the covenant with God will never be revoked by God so long as his people do not fall into transgression.

1:13 *highly favored.* The term *highly favored* occurs seven times in the Book of Mormon: 1 Ne. 1:1; Mosiah 1:13; Alma 9:20; 13:23; 27:30; 48:20, and Ether 1:34. In the KJV it appears in the words of the angel Gabriel to Mary in Luke 1:28.

a wicked and an adulterous people. Wicked and adulterous occurs in the KJV only in Matt. 16:4, however adultery is repeatedly used as a figure of apostasy much earlier by Jeremiah (a contemporary of Lehi), Hosea, and other Israelite prophets.

deliver them up. Benjamin uses this phrase to mean "turn them over to destruction."

weak like unto their brethren. It is interesting to note that the Nephites referred to the Lamanites as "their brethren" throughout the Book of Mormon (see notes on Mosiah 1:5, and 3:1, *brethren*), and that the Nephite view characterized their Lehite relatives as *weak,* a relatively mild critique.

matchless and marvelous power. Although this phrase does not occur in the KJV, the Hebrew has an interesting phrase *kōaḥ gāḏôl* which means literally "great power" and is usually translated "great power" or "mighty power." See also notes on Mosiah 2:11 and 4:6, *matchless power,* below.

1:14 *extended his arm, preservation, into hands.* The words *extended . . . arm* do not appear in the KJV (*extended* usually appears with *mercy*), but *outstretched arm* or *stretched out arm* occurs sixteen times: Ex. 6:6; Deut. 4:34; 5:15; 7:19; 9:29; 11:2; 26:8; 1 Kgs. 8:42; 2 Kgs. 17:36; 2 Chron. 6:32; Ps. 136:12; 27:5; 32:17; 32:21; Ezek. 20:33, 34. The Hebrew verb used in these instances is *natah*, the very word which the KJV translators rendered as *extend*. The English *preservation* or *preserve* does not appear with *arm* or *arms outstretched*, neither does it occur with *from the hand[s]* or *into the hand[s]*. But a Hebrew root *NṢL, which means "to deliver," appears dozens of times with both *into the hands* and *out of the hands*. Most of the time when it is in association with *hands* it is translated by KJV as "to deliver" (once it is translated "rid" because it occurs in a passage in which it is parallel with a similar word that is translated "to deliver"). This verb is also translated "preserved" thirteen times in the KJV: Gen. 32:30; Ps. 12:7; 25:21; 31:23; 32:7; 40:11; 61:7; 64:1; 140:1, 4; Prov. 20:28; 22:12; Isa. 49:8; however, in none of these cases does it occur with *hands*. Accordingly, Joseph Smith's translation in this verse fits with the Hebrew use of these words but does not tie in with the KJV. See David Rolph Seely, "The Image of the Hand of God in the Exodus Traditions," Ph.D. diss., 1990; Seely, in *Fortunate the Eyes That See*, 1995.

into the hands of the Lamanites. David in 2 Sam. 24:14 talks of falling "into the hand of the Lord," rather than "into the hand of man."

1:15 *he gave him charge.* In the scriptures, this phrase is typically used for solemn instructions from kings and priests. See Gen. 28:6, Num. 27:23, Job 34:13, and 2 Sam. 18:5. Benjamin's instructions were for "things both temporal and spiritual"; the charge to Mosiah was to "care for [the Nephites'] spiritual records and their sacred relics (the sword of Laban and the Liahona)" (M.18, 134). For details of tasks for successors, see this volume, p. 99. In dating this coronation at or around the New Year, four references in the Book of Mormon support the convention of changing rulers at that time of the year: in Mosiah 29:44, Alma begins his reign at the commencement of the first year of the judges; in Alma 2:1, 6–7, 9, Amlici is consecrated by his supporters at the commencement of the fifth year; in Alma 4:20, the judgment seat was passed to Nephihah in the commencement of the ninth year; and in Alma 24:20, the Lamanites come up to the land of Nephi for the purposes of destroying the old king and installing a new one. In the last case, the Lamanite attempt failed, so they attacked the Nephites on the fifth day of the second month (Alma 16:1).

1:16 *engraven on the plates of brass; and also the plates of Nephi.* For similar concepts see the notes on Mosiah 1:3, *plates of brass,* above; 2:13. Compare 1 Kgs. 2:3; Deut. 17:18–19.

plates of brass, plates of Nephi (records); sword of Laban; ball or director (Liahona). Anciently, upon coronation, a typical king would have been given national treasures consisting of (1) a genealogy, (2) a symbol of power and rule, and (3) an orb—a symbol of royalty or power over the earth. The three tokens of Nephite kingship reflect those traditions—the plates of brass included a genealogy of Lehi back to Joseph (1 Ne. 5:14), and the sword of Laban was a symbol of power and rule (even more than that, it was used by Nephi and the kings after him, including Benjamin, as a literal weapon in defense of their people). The sword was often a symbol of kingship in Europe, Asia, and Africa (see *JBMS* 2/1, 1993, 39–79). Also, the Liahona was at one time not just a symbol, but a director of otherworldly power over the earth (T.45, 28–32; R.38, 213–14). For details of the insignia of the kings, see this volume, pp. 35, 247–49; for references to the Urim and Thummim, see this volume, pp. 281, 293 n. 8; Van Dam, *The Urim and Thummim: A Means of Revelation in Ancient Israel,* 1997.

led our fathers through the wilderness. Ps. 106:9, "he led them . . . through the wilderness"; Alma 37:39 refers to the Liahona showing "the course which they should travel in the wilderness."

prepared by the hand of the Lord. This phrase occurs only here and in 2 Ne. 5:12, where it also refers to the Liahona.

heed and diligence which they gave unto him. This phrase is also used in connection with the Liahona in 1 Ne. 16:28–29, where the heed and diligence are accorded to the Liahona or its pointers. Here, and in Mosiah 1:17, the Lord is the one whom they should heed. Likewise in Alma 37:40 the Nephites' faith in God is the catalyst. Alma 12:9 explains that the mysteries of God can be unfolded to people only "according to the heed and diligence which they give unto him." See also the notes on Mosiah 1:17, *stir them up in remembrance,* below.

1:17 *driven back.* This phrase makes specific allusion back to the time when Nephi used this distinctive phrase three times to describe the peril when his ship was driven back by the adverse winds that arose because of wickedness during the ocean crossing (1 Ne. 18:13–15). Later in the Book of Mormon it is used to describe the defeat of various armed groups. In the KJV it is found in Ps. 114:3, 5 to describe the parting of the waters of the Jordan at the time of the Israelite crossing.

famine and sore afflictions. This phrase also appears in Mosiah 9:3. In the KJV the phrase does not occur; rather, famines are often described as being sore (Gen. 41:56–57; 43:1; 47:4, 13; 1 Kgs. 18:2; Jer. 52:6).

stir them up in remembrance of their duty. 2 Pet. 1:13 reads "stir you up by putting you in remembrance." Benjamin's meaning is somewhat different: God uses famines and afflictions to motivate people to remember their duty to be faithful and obedient to God. In the Hebrew Bible, remembrance is itself an active concept that entails obedience. Louis Midgley points out that "to remember often means to be attentive, to consider, to keep divine commandments, or to act" (M.19, 128). The *Dictionary of New Testament Theology* adds these meanings: to mention in prayer; to proclaim, to celebrate, to solemnize; to believe, obey, become converted, turn about; and to confess. Thus, Benjamin does not use recollection to stir people up, as in 2 Peter, but rather outside pressures are used by God to stir people to do their duty. In Lev. 23:24, a festival rite of memorial is given. See also this volume, p. 170, and the notes on Mosiah 1:16; 2:41; 4:11, 30; 5:12; 6:3 on remembering.

The Gathering (Mosiah 1:18–2:8)

18And now, •it came to pass that Mosiah went and •did as his father had commanded him, and proclaimed

unto all the people who were in the land of Zarahemla that thereby they might gather themselves together, to go •up to the temple to hear the words which his father should speak unto them. ²:¹And it came to pass that after Mosiah had done as his father had commanded him, and had •made a proclamation •throughout all the land, that the people gathered themselves together throughout all the land, that they might go up to the temple to hear the words which king Benjamin should speak unto them. ²And there were a great number, even so many that they •did not number them; for they had multiplied exceedingly and waxed great in the land. ³And they also took of the •firstlings of their flocks, that they might offer sacrifice and burnt offerings according to the •law of Moses; ⁴And also that they might give thanks to the Lord their God, •who had brought them out of the land of Jerusalem, and who had •delivered them out of the hands of their enemies, and •had appointed •just men to be their teachers, and also a just man to be their king, who had established peace in the land of Zarahemla, and who had taught them to keep the commandments of God, that they might •rejoice and •be filled with love towards God and all men. ⁵And it came to pass that when they came •up to the temple, they •pitched their tents round about, every man •according to his family, consisting of his wife, and his sons, and his daughters, •and their sons, and their daughters, from the eldest down to the youngest, every family being separate one from another. ⁶And they pitched their tents round about the temple, every man having his tent with the door thereof •towards the temple, that thereby they might •remain in their tents and hear the words which king Benjamin should speak unto them; ⁷For the multitude being so great that king Benjamin could not teach them all within the walls of the temple, therefore he ˙caused a tower to be erected, that thereby his people might hear the words which he should speak unto them. ⁸And it came to pass that he began to speak to his people ˙from the tower; and they could not all hear his words because of the greatness of the multitude; therefore he caused that the words which he spake should be ˙written and sent forth among those that were not under the sound of his voice, that they might also ˙receive his words.

1:18 *it came to pass.* Ten elements of Mosiah 1:18 are repeated in exactly the same order in Mosiah 2:1: (1) it came to pass; (2) Mosiah; (3) did as his father had commanded him; (4) proclamation; (5) all the people; (6) all the land; (7) people gathered themselves; (8) up to the temple; (9) hear the words; (10) speak unto them. The significance of this precise phenomenon is unclear.

did as his father had commanded him. In Jacob 5:70, the servant in Zenos's allegory, "did as the Lord had commanded him." In Matt. 21:6, "the disciples went, and did as Jesus commanded them."

up to the temple. "A society's most sacred spot is the location where the holy act of royal coronation takes place" (R.38, 213). Israelites thought of their temple as the mountain of the Lord (Isa. 2:2; Ps. 24:3), and thus one always ascended *up* to the temple. Assembly at the temple is a feature associated with the Israelite Feast of Tabernacles and indicates the sanctity of the occasion. In addition, assembling at the temple reflects the assembly conducted by Ezra at the rebuilt temple on the return from Babylon, when they wished to recommit themselves to the law of Moses (T.49, 222). For information on the temple at Zarahemla, see Welch, in *Temples of the Ancient World*, 1994, 343–61, and this volume, pp. 244–47, 299–300.

2:1 *made a proclamation; gathered themselves together.* It was prescribed that Israel's feasts were to start by proclamations (Lev. 23:2, 4, 21, 37; 2 Chron. 30:5). Even unauthorized feasts began with proclamations (Ex. 32:5; 2 Kgs. 10:20). After the exile, when Ezra wanted to reestablish the law, he began with a proclamation that the people should gather themselves together to hear him read it to them (Ezra 10:7). To begin the Feast of Booths specifically, he sent forth a proclamation (Neh. 8:13–15). Israelites often gathered to go to battle, but also to make covenants and participate in feasts (Ex. 35:1; Lev. 8:3–4; Num. 8:9; Deut. 4:10; 31:12, 28; 1 Kgs. 8:1–2; 2 Chron. 5:1–3; Neh. 8:1); Ex. 32:1, "the people gathered themselves together unto Aaron"; 2 Chron. 30:3, "the people gathered themselves together to Jerusalem"; see the notes in Mosiah 1:10, *make a proclamation,* above; see also 1 Sam. 10:19–20; 11:14–15; 2 Kgs. 23:1–2; 2 Chron. 34:29–30; Ezra 3:1; Neh. 8:1; 1 Esdras 5:47; 9:3, 38. Other uses for proclamations include gathering to hear the announcement of a new king and to declare liberty at jubilee. "Apparently *all* King Benjamin's people have come together on short notice, eager to listen to their beloved king. . . . One presumes that the people are previously baptized church members who are confident they are righteous" (R.41, 103). See also the notes on Mosiah 1:18, *it came to pass,* above.

throughout all the land. This phrase is used thirty-two times in the Book of Mormon, nineteen times in the OT, and once in the NT. In Lev. 25:10, it refers to the proclamation of the jubilee.

2:2 *did not number them.* Censuses were often taken in the OT (Ex. 30:12; Num. 1:1–4, 26; 2 Sam. 24; 1 Chron. 21). Generally the purpose was to prepare for war, but censuses were also taken as preparation to serve God (Num. 4:1–3, 21–23). In 1 Chron. 23, some kind of census appears to have been associated with David making his son Solomon the king, a situation somewhat analogous to Benjamin's coronation of Mosiah. Although the Nephites were not numbered at this time, Nibley assumes that a census would have been a customary action at such an assembly, which he equates with the ancient year-rite. However, the names were taken of all those who entered into the covenant at the conclusion of King Benjamin's address (N.27, 502 n. 6). Compare Mosiah

25:12–13; Gen. 16:10; 32:12; 1 Kgs. 3:8; 2 Chron. 5:6; Rev. 7:9. For further comments on census taking, see this volume, pp. 120, 125, 144 n. 2.

2:3 *firstlings of their flocks; sacrifice; burnt offerings.* The firstlings belonged to the Lord, according to Ex. 13:1–16. Note that in these verses specific mention is made of giving thanks to the Lord who delivered them from Israel, as in Mosiah 2:4. Rules regarding burnt offerings are found in Lev. 1, 6:8–13. The sacrifice of the firstlings of the flock marks this as a New Year's offering. (N.28, 299). More animal sacrifices were prescribed for the Feast of the Tabernacles (Sukkot), which forms part of the New Year rites, than for any other of the festivals (T.49, 222; B.03, 2). For discussion on the autumn festival complex, see this volume, pp. 121–26, 150, 159–90, 254–55. Although firstlings were not used for burnt offerings, they were used along with other animals in the sacrificial peace offering and were clearly sacrificed at the temple (R.40, 171–72). Further, since the Nephites were not descended from Aaron—and therefore had no Aaronic priests to whom to bring the sacrifice—they, like Abel, would have presented the firstlings to the Lord to be completely consumed as a burnt offering. The Nephites themselves would have been forbidden by the law of Moses from making use of those sacrificial offerings as food since they did not have the Aaronic Priesthood (T.48, 230–31). Other references to firstlings can be found in Deut. 12:17, "the firstlings of thy herds or of thy flock"; "All the firstling males that come of thy herd and of thy flock thou shalt sanctify unto the Lord thy God: thou shalt do no work with the firstling of thy bullock, nor shear the firstling of thy sheep" (Deut. 16:19–20); "sacrifice to the Lord all that openeth the matrix, being males" (1 Esdras 5:47–53; 9:6, 38, 41; Ex. 13:15; compare Luke 2:23).

law of Moses. "And Moses said, Thou must give us also sacrifices and burnt offerings" (Ex. 10:25); "offer sacrifices and burnt offerings" (2 Kgs. 10:24; see also Jer. 7:22); "according to the law of Moses" (2 Chron. 30:16; Luke 2:22); "In the seventh month, in the first day of the month, shall ye have a sabbath, a memorial of blowing of trumpets, an holy convocation. Ye shall do no servile work therein: but ye shall offer an offering made by fire unto the Lord" (Neh. 8:1–18; see 1 Ne. 5:9; 7:22; 2 Ne. 25:25–30; Alma 30:3; 3 Ne. 15:2–10; Lev. 23:24–25; see also the section on horns in this volume, pp. 162–64); "Also on the tenth day of this seventh month *there shall be* a day of atonement: it shall be an holy convocation unto you; and ye shall afflict your souls, and offer an offering made by fire unto the Lord" (Ezek. 40:1; Lev. 23:27; 25:9–10; Jubilee [Luke 4:18–19]; TB *Rosh ha-Shanah* 8b [1:1]); "The fifteenth day of this seventh month shall be the feast of the tabernacles for seven days unto the Lord. On the first day shall be an holy convocation: ye shall do no servile work therein. Seven days ye shall offer an offering made by fire unto the Lord: on the eighth day shall be an holy convocation unto you; and ye shall offer an offering made by fire unto the Lord" (Acts 23:34–36); this is a solemn assembly with a *silentium* (John 7:2, 37); Num. 18:15–19; Deut. 15:19–20; Josh. 23–24; Judg. 21:19; 1 Sam. 1:3, 21; 10:8; 11:14–15; 12:17 ("wheat harvest" = Fall Ingathering); 2 Sam. 6:17–19; 1 Kgs. 6:1, 38; 8:1–66; 12:26–33; 2 Kgs. 23:2–3, 23; Ezra 3:1–6; Neh. 7:73; 8:2; 14–18; Deut. 31:10–12; 1 Esdras 5:48–53; 8:41–53; 9:5–6 (3 Ezra); 2 Macc. 1:9; Josephus, *Antiquities* 1.3.3 (81); 3.10.1–3 (237–43). On the observance of the law of Moses by Book of Mormon prophets and peoples, see Welch, in *Temples of the Ancient World*, 1994, 301–19, and the sources cited there.

2:4 *who had brought them out of the land of Jerusalem.* This designation of the Lord is a modification of the description of God as the one who brought the children of Israel out of the land of Egypt and occurs over fifty times in the OT: Ex. 12:17; 16:6; 20:2; 29:46; Lev. 19:36; 22:33; 23:43; 25:42, 45; 26:13, 45; Num. 15:41; Deut. 1:27; 5:6; 6:12; 8:14; 13:5, 10; 20:1; 29:25; Josh. 24:17; Judg. 2:12; 1 Sam. 12:6; 1 Kgs. 8:21; 9:9; 2 Kgs. 17:7, 36; 2 Chron. 6:5; 7:22; Ps. 81:10; Jer. 2:6; 7:22; 11:4, 7; 16:14; 23:7; 32:21; 34:13; Ezek. 20:10; Dan. 9:15; Amos 9:7; Micah 6:4. See also notes on Mosiah 1:11, *land of Jerusalem,* above.

delivered them out of the hands of their enemies. This phrase or variations thereof occur a number of times (Judg. 2:18; 8:34; 1 Sam. 12:10, 11; 22:1; 2 Sam. 22:18; 2 Kgs. 17:39; Ezra 8:31; Ps.

18:17, 48; 31:15; 59:1; 78:42; 143:9). Alma 45:1 reads "the people of Nephi were exceedingly rejoiced, because the Lord had again delivered them out of the hands of their enemies; therefore they gave thanks unto the Lord their God"; see also Alma 29:9–12 (with New Year marked at Alma 28:1–30:4); 1 Sam. 7:14; 14:48.

had appointed. The same Lord God who had delivered them out of the hands of their enemies had appointed just men. B. H. Roberts says of Joseph Smith, "He claimed to have received revelation from God; the visitation of angels, who conferred upon him a holy Priesthood, a divine commission, by virtue of which he was appointed to preach the Gospel and re-establish the Church of Jesus Christ on earth" (*Defense of the Faith and the Saints,* 1907–12, 2:437).

just men. This was the highest praise of a Nephite for a *ṣaddîq,* leader (see Words of Mormon 1:17; Enos 1:1; Omni 1:25; Mosiah 19:17; 23:17; 29:13; Alma 3:6; 13:26; 20:15; 63:2; 3 Ne. 8:1). *Just* means righteous, charitable, good, and is a primary virtue in the Psalms (see Ps. 7:9).

rejoice. This time of festival and convocation was typically a time of joy.

be filled with love towards God and all men. Benjamin is defining the love of the higher law and in so doing answers the question, "How do you get so good that you can love people whether they deserve it or whether they don't" (Rector, *BYU Firesides and Devotionals,* 1984, 114). See also John 15:10–12, "If ye keep my commandments, ye shall abide in my love; . . . that my joy might remain in you, and that your joy might be full . . . love one another, as I have loved you" (see also Wisdom of Solomon 3:9; 6:18–19; John 14:15–16; Rom. 13:10; 1 Jn. 2:3–5); Acts 24:16, "toward God, and toward men."

2:5 *up to the temple.* Compare Deut. 12:5–6, "unto the place which the Lord your God shall choose out of all your tribes to put his name"; Mosiah 7:17; 25:1–7; Alma 2:1–7; 2:8–10; 20:9–12; 3 Ne. 3:13, 14; 4:4. Paul Hyde finds that Benjamin's speech has 132 elements that identify it as a temple address. Notable are the elements on the desire to become clean from the sins of their generation

(2:27); Benjamin mentions his garments (2:28); gives instruction on creation and the nature of God (2:20–21, 23; 3:8; 4:9); the breath of life (2:21, 23); the acquisition of knowledge (4:6, 11–12); teachings on the fall of Adam (3:11, 16, 19, 26; 4:6–7); man's state as the dust of the earth (2:25; 4:2); witnesses (2:14); the law of sacrifice and obedience (2:3, 22, 34; 5:5); admonition to give heed in order to stay out of the power of enemies, (2:30–33); messengers sent from the presence of God (3:13); reference to divers unholy and impure practices (4:29); the law of consecration (4:16, 21, 26); the giving of a name (5:8–9, 11, 14); and the promise of sealing (5:15). (Paul Hyde letter to John Welch). For other temple elements, see this volume, pp. 299–300, 309, and Welch, in *Temples of the Ancient World*, 348–60.

pitched their tents round about. In Ex. 33:7–11, Moses pitched the tabernacle outside the camp and all who sought the Lord took their tents and went out of the camp. They stayed "every man at his tent door" and watched while Moses entered the tabernacle and spoke with the Lord. Note also that there was a pillar of cloud at the front of the tabernacle and "all the people rose up and worshipped, every man in his tent door." Some have seen this as the historical background of the booths. See also Num. 1:52–2:34; Neh. 8:14–17. "As the word *tent* can also mean household or people, . . . in a very real sense the families of Benjamin's colony turned toward the temple" (D.06, 51).

according to his family . . . separate one from another. The separation of families into booths or tents was a Feast of Tabernacles or Sukkot practice, according to the Talmud. The practice in the ancient world was that the New Year festival was to be spent dwelling in tents or booths (N.28, 299–300; see also this volume, pp. 120, 123–24, 154, 183–86). Booths represented the temporary dwellings used by the Israelites after leaving Egypt (T.49, 222). Contemporary Jews must build their own booths; the covering, usually made of palm branches, if available, should be sufficiently sparse so they are able to see the stars. This is an interesting parallel to the early Mormon tradition of building wooden tabernacles covered with pine boughs for large numbers of the saints, in both Nauvoo and Salt Lake, to assemble and hear the word of the Lord (W.57); this puts us in mind of Gordon B. Hinckley's announcement regarding the new assembly building (see *Ensign*, May 1996, 65). In Lev. 25:10, the jubilee celebration calls for assembly "every man unto his family."

and their sons, and their daughters. See Gen. 36:6, "his wives, and his sons, and his daughters, and all the persons of his house"; 1 Sam. 30:3; 2 Chron. 31:18; Deut. 31:12.

2:6 *towards the temple.* Ex. 33:8–10 confirms the tradition of having the opening of the tent toward the tabernacle, as was found in the camp of Israel (T.49, 223). Just as the Jewish synagogues were oriented toward the temple in Jerusalem as the focus of their prayers, Mohammed ordered his followers, wherever they were, to pray toward Jerusalem. Only when the Jews failed to convert did Mohammed change the focus of his followers to Mecca.

remain in their tents. See Ex. 33:8, 10, "when Moses went out unto the tabernacle [*hā-ʾōhel*], . . . all the people rose up, and stood every man at his tent [*ʾōhālô*] door, and looked after Moses, . . . And all the people saw the cloudy pillar stand at the tabernacle door: and all the people rose up and worshipped, every man in his tent door"; see also Ex. 18:7; Lev. 14:8; Num. 11:10; 16:26–27; Deut. 1:27; 33:18; Josh. 3:14; 7:21–23; Hosea 12:9; Ps. 27:5, *sukkô* "his pavilion"; Ps. 78:60, *ʾōhālô* "his tabernacle"; Hebrew *ʾōhel* "tent" of the wilderness ≅ *sukkāh* "booth" of the Law, as in Lev. 23:42–43, "Ye shall dwell in booths seven days; all that are Israelites born shall dwell in booths [*sukkôt*]: That your generations may know that I made the children of Israel to dwell in booths, when I brought them out of the land of Egypt"; Neh. 8:14–18; note the use of dwelling in pavilions and tabernacles in 1 Kgs. 20:12, 16; Job 5:24; Prov. 14:11; Mal. 2:12; see also Gen. 9:27; 1 Kgs. 8:66; 1 Chron. 20:1; Job 8:22; Jer. 4:20; 10:20; 30:18; Ps. 52:5; 78:55; 84:10; 120:5; Ugaritic Texts 128:3:18–19; 2 Aqhat V:32–33; Josephus, *Antiquities* 8.4.5 (123). For a discussion on tents, see this volume, pp. 120, 123–24, 154, 183–86; and the notes on Mosiah 2:4, *according to his family.*

2:7 *caused a tower to be erected.* The significance of Benjamin's tower is more than just a platform to enable his voice to carry farther: In Neh. 8, Ezra caused the people to gather and build a wooden structure (called a pulpit in the KJV, the Hebrew word is most often translated "tower") from which he read the book of the law to the people on the first day of the seventh month (the beginning of the autumnal feast). He also sent teachers around who "caused the people to understand the law: and the people stood in their place" (Neh. 8:7). These teachers "read in the book in the law of God distinctly, and gave the sense, and caused them to understand the reading" (Neh. 8:8). During this ceremony, "Ezra blessed the Lord, the great God. And all the people answered, Amen, Amen, with lifting up their hands: and they bowed their heads, and worshipped the Lord with their faces to the ground" (Neh. 8:6; see notes on Mosiah 4:1, *fallen to the earth,* below). In the course of this festival, Ezra read about the feast of booths and had the Israelites gather branches and construct booths; see also Hebrew *ʿammūd,* "pillar, standing-place" (2 Kgs. 11:14; 23:3; New English Bible with Apocrypha "dais") at the temple, for the coronation of Jehoash, 2 Kgs. 11:17: "And Jehoiada made a covenant between the Lord and the king and the people, that they should be the Lord's people; between the king also and the people"; renewal of covenant under King Josiah, 23:1–3: "And the king sent, and they gathered unto him all the elders of Judah and of Jerusalem. And the king went up into the house of the Lord, and all the men of Judah and all the inhabitants of Jerusalem with him, . . . and he read in their ears all the words of the book of the covenant which was found in the house of the Lord . . . and made a covenant before the Lord, . . . to keep his commandments. . . . And all the people stood to the covenant" (see also 2 Chron. 23:13; 34:29–32; Deut. 17:14–20); Neh. 8:4, "Ezra the scribe stood upon a pulpit of wood" = Hebrew *migdāl-ʿēṣ;* 1 Esdras (3 Ezra) 9:42, "And Esdras the priest and reader of the law stood up upon a pulpit of wood"; Isa. 2:15; Neh. 3:25–27; note the sixty-cubit-high stone Jewish temple tower of Onias 4 in Egypt (Josephus, *Wars* 7.10.3 [427], Greek *pyrgos*); *bima* or *ʿalmemar* (= Moslem *ʿal-minbar,* not to mention *minaret,* or Vedic *yupa*), and on the "Portion of the King" spoken from a similar pulpit in the temple; see also Alma 31:21, *"rameumptom . . . holy stand,"* whereon a kind of abbreviated Jewish *amidah*, "standing (prayer)," is recited by the Zoramites; see also Mosiah 11:13; the tower of Babel in Ether 1:3; Gen. 11:4–5; 35:21. Compare the wooden platform used by the king according to the Mishnah (T.49, 206). The fact that Benjamin had a tower constructed correlates with the platform constructed for the Feast of Tabernacles in Neh. 8:4, called a *migdāl*, which is the normal Hebrew word for tower (T.48, 229). In addition the Nephite tower can be equated with a tower and altar discovered at Adam-ondi-Ahman and identified by Joseph Smith as Nephite (Gentry, *BYUS* 13/4, 1973, 570). Nathan the Babylonian gives an account of the wooden tower built for the installation of the Exilarch (this volume, pp. 123–24). The tower in the vineyard, described in Isa. 5:1–7 and quoted by Christ in Matt. 21:33–35, has been seen as the temple (Tvedtnes, in *Temples of the Ancient World*, 700 n. 101). The Shepherd of Hermas uses the same imagery of the tower representing the church (ibid., 674). Further information on the tower can be found in this volume, pp. 245–47.

2:8 *from the tower.* In Hebrew, the Bible places the king *upon*, rather than *beside*, a pillar or platform at the time of his coronation. (S.44, 2). John M. Lundquist points out that the pillar, whether stone, wood, or bronze, is a sign of the covenant between the king and his society (in *Temples of the Ancient World*, 1994, 284–86). The pillar may have been used as a pedestal.

written and sent forth. Eugene England uses this scripture to attest to the success of Benjamin and his father in "making language an effective resource" (E.07, 28–29).

receive his words. There is a connection here between Benjamin receiving the words of the angel and the reading of the law found in Deut. 31:11, "When all Israel is come to appear before the Lord thy God in the place which he shall choose, thou shalt read this law before all Israel in their hearing"; see also 1 Esdras (3 Ezra) 9:40, "Esdras the chief priest brought the law unto the whole multitude, . . . to hear the law in the first day of the seventh month."

Benjamin's Speech: Part 1

Indebtedness to the Heavenly King (Mosiah 2:9–28)

⁹And these are the words which he spake and caused to be written, saying: My brethren, all ye that have assembled yourselves together, you that can hear my words which I shall speak unto you •this day; for I have not commanded you to come up hither to trifle with the words which I shall speak, but that •you should hearken unto me, and •open your ears that ye may hear, and your hearts that ye may understand, and your minds that the mysteries of God may be unfolded •to your view. ¹⁰I have not commanded you to come up hither •that ye should fear me, or that ye should think that I of myself am more than a mortal man. ¹¹•But I am like as yourselves, subject to all manner of infirmities in •body and mind; yet I have been •chosen by this people, and •consecrated by my father, and was •suffered by the hand of the Lord that I should be a ruler and a king over this people; and have been •kept and preserved by his •matchless power, to serve you with all the •might, mind and strength which the Lord hath granted unto me. ¹²I say unto you that as I have been suffered to spend my days in your service, even up to this time, and have •not sought gold nor silver nor any manner of riches of you; ¹³•Neither have I suffered that ye should be confined in dungeons, nor that ye should •make slaves one of another, nor that ye should •murder, or plunder, or steal, or commit adultery; nor even have I suffered that ye should commit any manner of wickedness, and •have taught you that ye should keep the commandments of the Lord, in all things which he hath commanded you—¹⁴And even I, myself, have labored •with mine own hands that I

might serve you, and that *ye should not be laden with taxes, and that there should nothing come upon you which was *grievous to be borne—and of all these things which I have spoken, ye yourselves are *witnesses this day. [15]Yet, my brethren, I have not done these things *that I might boast, neither do I tell these things that thereby I might accuse you; but I tell you these things *that ye may know that I can answer a *clear conscience *before God this day. [16]Behold, I say unto you that because I said unto you that I had spent my days in your service, *I do not desire to boast, for I have only been in the service of God. [17]And behold, I tell you these things that ye may *learn wisdom; that ye may learn that when ye are in the service of your fellow beings ye are *only in the *service of your God. [18]Behold, ye have called me your king; and if I, whom ye call your king, do labor to serve you, then ought not ye to labor to *serve one an-

other? [19]And behold also, if I, whom ye call your king, who has spent his days in your service, and yet has been in the service of God, do merit any thanks from you, O how you ought to *thank your heavenly King! [20]I say unto you, my brethren, that if you should render all the *thanks and praise which your *whole soul has power to possess, to that God who has *created you, and has kept and preserved you, and has caused that ye should rejoice, and has granted that ye should live in *peace one with another—[21]I say unto you that if ye should serve him who has *created you from the beginning, and is preserving you from day to day, *by lending you breath, that ye may *live and move and do *according to your own will, and even supporting you from one moment to another—I say, if ye should serve him with all your whole souls yet ye would be *unprofitable servants. [22]And behold, all that he requires of you is to keep his commandments; and he has promised you that *if ye would keep his commandments ye should prosper in the land; and *he never doth vary from that which he hath said; therefore, if ye do keep his commandments he doth bless you and prosper you. ²³And now, in the first place, *he hath created you, and granted unto you your lives, for which ye are *indebted unto him. ²⁴And secondly, he doth require that ye should do as he hath commanded you; for which if ye do, he *doth immediately bless you; and therefore he hath paid you. And ye are still indebted unto him, and are, and will be, forever and ever; therefore, *of what have ye to boast? ²⁵And now I ask, *can ye say aught of yourselves? I answer you, Nay. *Ye cannot say that ye are even as much as the dust of the earth; yet ye were created of the dust of the earth; but behold, *it belongeth to him who created you. ²⁶And I, even I, whom ye call your king, am *no better than ye yourselves are; for *I am also of the dust. And ye behold that *I am old, and am about to *yield up this mortal frame *to its mother earth. ²⁷Therefore, as I said unto you that I had served you, *walking with a clear conscience before God, even so I at this time have caused that ye should assemble yourselves together, that I might be found blameless, and that your *blood should not come upon me, when *I shall stand to be judged of God of the things whereof he hath commanded me concerning you. ²⁸I say unto you that I have caused that ye should assemble yourselves together that I might *rid my garments of your blood, at this period of time when I am about to go down to my grave, that I might go down in peace, and my immortal spirit may join the *choirs above in singing the *praises of a just God.

2:9 *this day.* This phrase is used here and four other times in Benjamin's speech, it appears to be an important covenantal marker, occurring as it does at ritual and covenantal high points in the text. It is used in connection with assemblies called by Jacob and Alma in the Book of Mormon and as the Hebrew word *etzem,* used only in connection with Yom Kippur, Shavuot, and as a remembrance of the Exodus (W.54).

you should hearken unto me. Benjamin is signaling that his message is not to be taken lightly. Benjamin wants their minds open "that the mysteries of God may be unfolded to your view" (Mosiah 2:9). This is "a *silentium,* which is the proper designation for a solemn assembly in the presence of the Byzantine Emperor; it is taken from the formula with which meetings are formally opened in many Christian churches: 'The Lord is in his holy temple: let all the earth keep silence [lit. "hush"] before him.' Habakkuk 2:20." (N.28, 300, 503 n.10). Israel Knohl, quoting Yehezkel Kaufmann "who laid down the foundations for the discussion of the issue of the place of prayer in the Priestly Temple," points out that silence was the rule in the temple, since no reference was made "to the spoken word in describing temple rites. All the various acts of the priest are performed in silence. . . . Even prayer is absent. . . . Therewith the Israelite cult became a domain of silence, . . . [an] awe of holiness" (*Journal of Biblical Literature* 115/1, 1996, 17).

open your ears that ye may ear, and your hearts that ye may understand, and your minds. In Deut. 29:4, Moses tells his people that the Lord had not yet given them a heart to perceive, eyes to see, or ears to hear. In Isa. 6:10, Isaiah is told by the Lord to "make the heart of this people fat, and make their ears heavy, and shut their eyes, lest they see with their eyes, and hear with their ears, and understand with their heart." The Savior paraphrased Isaiah in Matt. 13:15, and the Nephites had access to this passage from the plates of Laban as demonstrated by Nephi quoting it in 2 Ne. 16:10. Although Benjamin substitutes "minds" for "eyes," the comparison is clear, which brings an interesting Hebrew word pair to light: "eye(s) / / heart" can be found in Isa. 44:18; Ps. 73:7;

Prov. 4:21; 21:4; 23:33; Koh. 2:10; and Sirach 43:18; see *JBMS* 4/2, 1995, 44–46.

to your view. "The word *view* may be a key word to understanding the mystery the people receive. Jacob mentions this view: 'We would to God that we could persuade all men . . . to believe in Christ, and *view* his death, and suffer his cross' (Jacob 1:8). Jacob, implying that coming to Christ involves a kind of participation in the Savior's atonement, invites men from a casual performance of the Gospel into a visceral experience. . . . The Gospel is organized around various symbolic 'viewings' of the atonement of the Son of God" (M. Catherine Thomas, unpublished paper).

2:10 *that ye should fear me.* If the Nephites are indeed celebrating a Feast of Tabernacles, then certainly Benjamin would feel it is his duty to motivate the Nephites to fear God. Additional evidence helps to demonstrate that this may be his purpose. Passages in Deuteronomy that emphasize fearing God are significantly similar to those in Benjamin's discourse: Deut. 4:10; 5:29; 6:1–3, 22–24; see also Deut. 6:13; Lev. 25:43–46 for the concept of fearing God and serving him. For further discussion of fear, see this volume, pp. 174, 179; and the notes on Mosiah 3:7, *anguish;* 3:19, *natural man;* 4:1, *fallen to the earth;* 4:2, *mercy,* below.

2:11 *But I am like as yourselves.* In the Paragraph of the King (Deut. 17:14–20), the king was not to have "his heart . . . lifted up above his brethren"; for a discussion of God as king, see this volume, pp. 167–68, 188–89.

body and mind. This pair of words occurs here and in Alma 17:5.

chosen by this people. In the OT it was God who was said to have chosen the king who was then acclaimed by the people (1 Sam. 10:24). In the Book of Mormon the people played a more direct role in the choice of their king (2 Nephi 5:18), and had even greater power over the selection of their chief judges (Mosiah 29:25; Alma 4:16; 10:24; 60:1). While Benjamin says that he was chosen by his people to be king, he affirms that he had been commanded by God to declare Mosiah to be king (1:10; 2:30). Both divine investiture and popular acclamation played a role. See also notes on Mosiah 1:10, *king and a ruler,* above.

consecrated. Information on anointing can be found in this volume, pp. 249–50; see also the notes on Mosiah 6:3, *consecrated his son,* below; and TG, "Consecrate" and "Consecration."

suffered by the hand of the Lord. Corresponds to Deuteronomy 17:20 in the Paragraph of the King (T.49, 224).

kept and preserved. These words occur in 2 Ne. 25:21; Omni 1:6; Mosiah 1:5; 2:20; 28:11, 15; Alma 9:22; 37:4. They do not appear in this form together in the KJV but they are found in the present tense "keep" (Hebrew root *ŠMR) and "preserve" (Hebrew root *NṢR) in parallel passages in Ps. 12:7; 140:4; Prov. 2:8, 11; 4:6, and in the Book of Mormon in Mosiah 28:20; Alma 37:14; 44:4; D&C 117:16. Correlation is found here with a traditional rabbinic prayer, "known as Shehecheyanu. (Praised [or Blessed] art Thou, Lord our God, King of the Universe, who has kept us [alive], and hast preserved us, and enabled us to reach this season; for more on the *She-hecheyanu,* see this volume p. 190.) This prayer is recited on eating first fruits, on doing things for the first time, and at certain prescribed times, including the first day of every festival" (B.03, 3); see Mosiah 7:20; Num. 6:24, "The Lord bless thee, and keep thee" (beginning of priestly Day of Atonement blessing); Ps. 41:2, "The Lord will preserve him, and keep him alive; and he shall be blessed"; and Neh. 9:6; Wisdom of Solomon 11:25. See also notes on Mosiah 2:20, *created . . . prepared,* below.

matchless power. This phrase is found seven times in the Book of Mormon (1 Ne. 17:42; Mosiah 1:13; 2:11; 4:6; Alma 9:11; 49:28; Hel. 4:25). It does not appear in the KJV. The closest phrase in the KJV is "none . . . like" which is often used in reference to God. Interestingly, the phrase "none . . . like" only occurs once in the Book of Mormon in 2 Ne. 25:5, where the words are separated by a long phrase. See also the notes on Mosiah 1:13 and 4:6, *power.*

might, mind and strength. This phrase first appears in 2 Ne. 25:29. It also appears in Alma 39:13; Moro. 10:32; D&C 4:2; 11:20; 33:7; 59:5; 98:47. In addition, "with all thy heart, and with all thy soul, and with all thy mind" is found in Matt. 22:37; "with all thy heart, and with all thy soul, and with all thy mind and with all thy strength" in Mark 12:30; "with all thy heart, and with all thy soul, and with all thy strength" in Luke 10:27; Deut. 11:13 has "love the Lord your God, and . . . serve him with all your heart and with all your soul"; see also Josh. 22:5. As Benjamin declares himself a servant to the Nephites, so too do the Nephites have an obligation to serve God.

2:12 *not sought gold nor silver.* An integral part of the Paragraph of the King (Deut. 17:14–20) was the warning to kings not to use their power to gain wealth and satisfy their own lusts: "neither shall he greatly multiply to himself silver and gold" (Deut. 17:17). Benjamin here asserts that he has not abused his power (T.49, 225). In Acts 20:33 is found "I have coveted no man's silver, or gold, or apparel."

2:13 *Neither have I suffered.* Benjamin is making a negative confession, a list of wrongs that he, as a king, has not committed (see this volume, p. 172). In 1 Sam. 12:1–15, Samuel makes a similar negative confession: "Whose ox have I taken? or whose ass have I taken? or whom have I defrauded? whom have I oppressed?" (1 Sam. 12:3). Benjamin's speech contains many clues about legal concepts and practices operative in his kingdom and legal system: evidence that Benjamin indeed enforced the law of Moses as it applied in his land includes such factors as the limitation of royal power; prohibitions against burdensome taxation, confining in dungeons, making slaves of one another, murder, plunder, stealing, adultery, and any manner of wickedness; Hebrew attitudes toward property are reflected in the statement that the earth belongs to God (Mosiah 2:25); Benjamin divided humans into six ages—infants, little children, children, young men, men, and old men—perhaps each one having particular legal status; as in Jewish law, legal liability requires a warning (Mosiah 2:36), and the mention of those who have ignorantly sinned (see Mosiah 3:11) brings into question mental capacity; as with Hebrew law, Benjamin's law placed a high value on oral testimony (Mosiah 3:23–24); the law known to Benjamin also implied duties: to care for children (Mosiah 4:14–15) and to give to the beggar (Mosiah 4:16–23), together with placing duties on the poor, "who have not and yet have sufficient," not to covet (Mosiah 4:25); also, the duty to return the thing borrowed (see the notes on Mosiah 4:28, and this volume, p. 195), and to feed stray livestock (Mosiah 5:14; see also Ex. 23:4); for a discussion of righteous administration and the role of the king, see this volume, pp. 27–30, 31–42, 48–50, 234–38.

make slaves one of another. For information on slavery, see this volume, pp. 40, 58, and notes on Mosiah 2:41, *state of never-ending happiness,* below.

murder, or plunder, or steal, or commit adultery, . . . wickedness. This specific list of sins is repeated in Alma 23:3 and Hel. 6:23. A partial list consisting *of murder, plunder, steal, bear false witness against,* and *do all manner of iniquity* is in Hel. 7:21. Ether 8:16 has *murder, plunder, lie, commit all manner of wickedness and whoredoms.* See also 2 Ne. 26:32; Alma 1:32; 16:18, 23; 30:10; for a discussion of these lists of prohibitions, see this volume, pp. 40–41, 61–62.

have taught you that ye should keep the commandments of the Lord, in all things which he hath commanded you. Another requirement of the king in Israel was that he possess a copy of the book of the law and read from it every day: "that he may learn to fear the Lord his God, to keep all the words of this law and these statutes, to do them: . . . and that he turn not aside from the commandment" (Deut. 17:19); see also 1Q22 I–II, "[And God spoke] to Moses . . . . Interpret [for the heads of] families of the Levites and for all the [priests] and decree to the sons of Israel the words of the Law which I commanded [you] on Mount Sinai to decree to them" (translations of DSS by García Martínez). For further discussion of fear, see this volume, pp. 174, 179, and the notes on Mosiah 3:7, *anguish;* 3:19, *natural man;* 4:1, *fallen to the earth;* 4:2, *mercy,* below. For further information on commandments, see the notes on Mosiah 1:7, *commandments,* above.

2:14 *with mine own hands.* The theme of the Lord's servants ministering or laboring with their own hands is also found in connection with Paul's activities in Acts 20:34; 1 Cor. 4:12.

ye should not be laden with taxes. The Lord through Samuel warned Israel that any king they set up over themselves would take their fields, vineyards, olive groves, a tenth of their seed, a tenth of their sheep, etc. (1 Sam. 8:10–18). Further comments on conflicting views of kingship can be found in this volume, pp. 234–44.

grievous to be borne. This phrase occurs in Matt. 23:4; Luke 11:46; 1 Ne. 17:25; Mosiah 7:15, 23; Ether 10:5 (the last three are specifically associated with taxes as well). See also Deut. 17:16–17; Neh. 5:14–15; Sirach 46:19.

witnesses this day. This phrase is found in Mosiah 7:21; Ruth 4:9–10. The theme of witnesses is found in Josh. 24:22; 1 Sam. 12:5; Neh. 10:29; 2 Cor. 11:19; 1 Thes. 4:9; for notes on witnesses, see this volume, pp. 226, 228.

2:15 *that I might boast.* Benjamin was not motivated in his *deeds* by a desire to boast. The pitfalls of having one's heart lifted up in pride because of power or riches are found in Deut. 8:12–14; 17:20; Jer. 9:23. See also Mosiah 2:16, *I do not desire to boast,* below; and this volume, p. 227.

that ye may know. See Ex. 10:2; 11:7; 31:13; Josh. 3:4; Job 19:29; Isa. 43:10; Jer. 44:29; Ezek. 20:20; Micah 6:5; Matt. 9:6; Mark 2:10; Luke 5:24; John 10:38; 19:4; Eph. 1:18; Col. 4:6; 1 Jn. 5:13; Mosiah 17:9; 24:14; 3 Ne. 11:14; 21:1; 29:1–2; Morm. 3:20; Ether 2:11; Moro. 7:15, 19; 9:1; D&C 41:3; 43:8.

clear conscience. Used here and in Mosiah 2:27.

before God this day. Acts 23:1, "in all good conscience before God until this day"; see also 1 Pet. 3:21; 1 Sam. 12:2–5.

2:16 *I do not desire to boast.* Benjamin's humility and modesty are apparent throughout his speech. He was unconcerned with projecting his political image because he had Christ's image in his countenance. Benjamin is an example to us as we try to tame our egotistic selves (M.15, 12).

2:16–25; 38–40 Concerning moral persuasion and the biblical use of motive clauses, Laramie Merritt points out that motive clauses are "grammatically subordinate sentences in which the motivation for the commandment is given. . . . [which] preach obedience, . . . explain how the law developed and help people understand to what ends commandments are given." In these verses Benjamin uses motive clauses to instill a sense of debt and gratitude in his people, telling "how men acquire this debt" and warning "what happens when the demands of justice are not satisfied" (Welch, *BYU Law Papers*, 21 April 1994).

2:17 *learn wisdom.* See 2 Ne. 28:30; Alma 32:12; 37:35; 38:9; D&C 97:1; 136:32. In the same way that Benjamin is teaching that wisdom is knowing that to serve one's fellow beings is serving God, so Moses in Deut. 4:6 teaches that wisdom was keeping and doing God's judgments.

only. The word may mean "simply," "truly," or "merely." The context points, however, to the sense of "merely." See this volume, pp. 67–69.

service of your God. King Benjamin's statements on service are fairly unique. Similar statements are only found from the Savior in Matt. 25:40, "Inasmuch as ye have done it unto one of the least of these my brethren, ye have done it unto me," and from John in 1 Jn. 4:20, "for he that loveth not his brother whom he hath seen, how can he love God whom he hath not seen?" That this service is essential to salvation has been established by Robert Millet, "Love of man is vitally related to love of God; the Saints can remain clean through service to God. This service is essential to salvation" (M.21, 238). Theodore Burton also quoted this scripture as an example of how we repay the great debt we owe Christ: "[Mosiah 2:17] explains how we *can* repay Jesus Christ for his great mercy to us. His sacrifice atoned even for our personal sins and makes mercy available to you and to me. . . . This service . . . can include significant good works that could compensate Jesus for his restitution made for us" (*BYU Firesides and Devotionals*, 1984–85, 99). Susan Easton Black refers to the establishment of government: "As an example of service to humanity being service to God, Benjamin established his civil government based on the commandments of God. This teaching reflects the Savior's comment in Matt. 25:40 that 'Inasmuch as ye have done it unto the least of one of these my brethren, ye have done it unto me'"

(B.02, 40–41). Robert Millet and Joseph F. McConkie explain that "To stain our clothes and soil our hands in the service of others is but to cleanse our own souls" (M.18, 137). See also notes on Mosiah 4:14, *serve the devil,* below.

service. Regarding service, servitude, indebtedness, and slavery, see further pp. 40, 58 in this volume. If Benjamin's speech fell on a jubilee year, then Alma 30:4 and Hel. 6:14 may be the next such jubilees; Lev. 25:8–55 requires manumission of Hebrew bondservants at jubilee, while Ex. 21:2 requires the release at the sabbatical; see notes on Mosiah 5:8, *made free,* below; see also Matt. 25:34–45. The theme of service is found in Neh. 2:3; Ezra 6:18; Rom. 9:4; Heb. 9:6, 21. See also Mosiah 4:15; Ex. 3:12; 10:26; Num. 3:7–8; 8:11; Josh. 22:27; 2 Chron. 8:14; Mal. 3:14; TB ʾAḇot 1:2 "The world stands upon three things: upon the *Torah,* upon the temple service [ʿaḇodah "work"], and upon deeds of loving kindness"; 1Q22 III on the sabbatical year. For comments on service, see this volume, pp. 11–13, 67–69, 77–82, 334–36, 412–16.

2:18 *serve one another.* This phrase is found in Gal. 5:13; see also John 13:13–15; Acts 20:35.

2:19 *thank your heavenly King.* Hugh Nibley emphasizes that God is the real king and that this "is the theme of the king's address from the tower" (N.25, 455). For information on kingship, see this volume, pp. 299, 323–24; for comments on the nature of God, see this volume, pp. 234–54; for a discussion on humility, see this volume, pp. 11, 32–33, 432–35.

2:20 *thanks and praise.* These two words (or *thank* and *praise*) occur together in 1 Chron. 16:4, 35; 23:30; 25:3; 29:13; 2 Chron. 31:2; Neh. 12:24; Ps. 30:12; 35:18; 79:13; 106:1; Dan. 2:23; Alma 26:8; Ether 6:9. For a discussion of this phrase, see this volume, pp. 69, 74, 78, 169, 189–90, 334.

whole soul. This phrase is found in Jer. 32:41; 2 Ne. 25:29; Enos 1:9; Omni 1:26; W of M 1:18; Mosiah 2:21; 26:14.

created . . . preserved. This word pair is found only here and in the next verse (Mosiah 2:21). The theme of *kept and preserved* is found in 1Q22 IV. The first part of the Qumran ceremony, referred to at the beginning of the discussion on Mosiah 5:5, *covenant*, below, required a blessing of God and his works. The counterpart is found in 1QS I 18–20; 4Q*Barki Nafshi*. Benjamin is breaking down pride, "The proud, so far as their own lives are concerned, along with those whom they adversely affect, mock the plan of salvation (Jacob 6:8). Those who boast of their independence from God are like the goldfish in a bowl who regards himself as self-sufficient" (Maxwell, *Meek and Lowly*, 59).

peace one with another. This phrase is found in Mark 9:50; similar phrases occur in 2 Cor. 13:11; Lev. 26:6; Num. 6:26, "and give thee peace" (end of priestly Day of Atonement blessing).

2:21 *created you from the beginning*. Similar phrases are also found in Mosiah 7:27; Alma 18:32, 34; Ether 3:15.

by lending you breath. This phrase is unique to Benjamin, who is again emphasizing our dependence on God: "some of us nevertheless feel as though we own ourselves, our time, our talents, and our possessions; these are signs of our self-sufficiency. Actually, God lends us breath and sustains us from moment to moment" (M.17, 93). See further this volume, pp. 140–41, 182, 191, 258.

live and move. This word pair appears also in the KJV in Gen. 1:21, 28; 9:3; Lev. 11:46; Ezek. 47:9; Acts 17:28, and in D&C 45:1.

according to your own will. In Leviticus freewill offerings are made "at your own will," Lev. 19:5; 22:19, 29.

unprofitable servants. One interpretation of Benjamin's intent in using this phrase is that unprofitable servants are those who consume more than they produce. Since, in Mosiah 4:19, Benjamin refers to temporal blessings, of which we have earned nothing, we have not even earned our own keep and are therefore unprofitable servants (N.24, 110). Perhaps "at first reading [unprofitable servants] may sound harsh, deprecating, and discouraging, for surely our service to God is significant. But when our service is compared with our blessings, an 'outside audit,' said Benjamin in effect, would show us ever to be in arrears. . . . Furthermore, our service is made possible by the elements which make up our natural bodies, but these belong to God" (M.16, 10). Profit has been defined as a word implying "personal gain or benefit. . . . God is perfect—in knowledge, power, influence, and attributes. He is the Creator of *all* things. . . . We must somehow disabuse ourselves of any notion that we can bring personal profit to God by our actions. That would make God indebted to men, which is unthinkable" (M.20, 1:12). An interesting parallel to Benjamin's expression that "yet ye would be unprofitable servants" is found in the Nishmat prayer at the conclusion of the Hallel (Grace after Passover meal): "Were our mouths as full of song as the sea, and our tongues as full of jubilation as its multitudes of waves, and our lips as full of praise as the breadth of the heavens, and our eyes as brilliant as the sun and the moon, and our hands as outspread in prayer as the eagles of the sky and our feet as swift as the deer—we still could not sufficiently thank You." The phrase *unprofitable servant* or *servants* is found in Matt. 25:30; Luke 17:10; Mosiah 22:4.

2:22 *if ye would keep his commandments ye should prosper in the land.* A requirement of a king was to have the law of Moses, here written on the brass plates of Laban (T.49, 225–26). Promised blessings of prosperity in the land associated with keeping the commandments are found in Deut. 11:8; 30:16; 1 Chron. 28:8; 1 Ne. 2:20; 4:14; 17:13; 2 Ne. 1:9, 20, 32; 3:2; 4:4; Jarom 1:9; Mosiah 1:7; 2:31; Alma 9:13; 36:1, 30; 37:13; 38:1; 48:25; 50:20; Hel. 3:20. In 1 Kgs. 2:3 the promise for keeping the commandments is that "thou mayest prosper in all that thou doest." See Deut. 10:12; Mosiah 2:24. Regarding *prosper in the land,* note the presentation of the *wedjat eye,* "prosperity," at the Egyptian *sed*-festival/jubilee. One of the blessings of obedience has been linked to the requirement to bring the gospel to the Lamanites (Pratt, *JD*, 17:300). In 1947 at April general conference, Spencer W. Kimball said, "little prosperity has come to the Navajo and little can come until we Gentiles, their 'nursing fathers,' help to train them" (Conference Report, April 1947, 150). Notably, the time of prosperity during and following Benjamin's reign led indirectly to the highly successful mission of Benjamin's grandsons to the Lamanites. For a discussion on the blessings of obedience, see this volume, pp. 133–34, 281–82.

he never doth vary from that which he hath said. A variant of this phrase is found in Alma 7:20 and D&C 3:2. The second part of the Qumran ceremony referred to at the beginning of the notes on Mosiah 5:5, *covenant,* was for priests to recount God's mighty works and his favors toward Israel; see 1QS I 21–22.

2:23 *he hath created you.* Benjamin is commenting on the divine nature of our creation, "each of us would have a body of flesh and bones. [Our earthly parents] would provide it for us, obviously with the help of our Heavenly Father, who, I believe, has a hand in when we come and the fact that we do come" (Rector, *BYU Firesides and Devotionals,* 1981, 18). See also the notes on Mosiah 2:20, *created . . . preserved,* above.

indebted. This word appears in Benjamin's speech three times: here and in 2:24, 34. It also appears in the KJV in Luke 11:4 but nowhere else in the scriptures in this form. See also notes on Mosiah 2:34, *eternally indebted,* below.

2:24 *doth immediately bless you.* Drawing another parallel to 1Q22 II–III, there the Lord recounts the blessings he will give the children of Israel once they cross the Jordan river, if they keep his commandments: "[And when you cross the Jordan] for me to give you large [and good] cities, houses full of every [wealth, vineyards and olive groves] which you [did not plant, wel]ls bored which you did not dig, and you eat and become replete. . . . [God will bless you, forgiving you your si]ns." See also the notes on Mosiah 2:36, *blessed, prospered, and preserved,* below.

of what have ye to boast? If the king cannot boast, how much less can common people?

2:25 *can ye say aught of yourselves?* "God asks only two things: first to recognize his gifts for what they are, and not to take credit to ourselves" (N.24, 109; see this volume, p. 128).

Ye cannot say that ye are even as much as the dust of the earth. Equating man with dust in a way that emphasizes man's humble state is found in Gen. 3:19; 18:27; Job 34:15; Ps. 103:14; Eccl. 3:20; 12:7; Mosiah 2:26; 4:2; Hel. 12:7–8. That man is "created of the dust of the earth" is found in Gen. 2:7; Morm. 9:17; D&C 77:12;

Abr. 5:7. In Jacob 2:21 we find the idea of God creating man from the dust of the earth so that he can obey God's commandments, similar to verses 22–24 above; see also this volume, pp. 2, 261–64; and the notes on Mosiah 2:13; 2:26; 4:2, *commandments*.

it belongeth to him who created you. This has similarities with Lev. 25:23, "The land shall not be sold for ever: for the land is mine; for ye are strangers and sojourners with me." See also notes on Mosiah 2:13, *neither have I suffered*, and 4:2, *less than the dust of the earth*.

2:26 *no better than ye.* Benjamin begins his discourse on an economic note and sees the keynote as "absolute equality" (N.29, 225).

I am also of the dust. See this volume, pp. 261–64.

I am old. For information on Benjamin's age, see this volume, p. 27.

yield up this mortal frame. This phrase is not found in the KJV. It appears nine times in the Book of Mormon: here and in Alma 52:25; Hel. 5:52; 14:21, 25; 3 Ne. 3:6, 7; 4:16, 27.

to its mother earth. This phrase is also found in 2 Ne. 9:7; Morm. 6:15. In both instances the context is also of the dead returning to the mother earth.

2:27 *walking . . . before God.* This phrase or variations of it occur a large number of times: Gen. 17:1; 24:48; 48:15; 1 Sam. 2:30, 35; 12:2; 1 Kgs. 2:4; 3:6; 8:23, 25 (twice); 2 Kgs. 20:3; 2 Chron. 6:14, 16; 7:17; Ps. 56:13; 116:9; Isa. 38:3; Mal. 3:14; 1 Ne. 16:3; Mosiah 4:26; 18:29; 26:37; Alma 1:1; 5:27; 7:22; 45:24; 53:21; 63:2; Hel. 6:34; 15:5; 16:10; 3 Ne. 24:14; Ether 6:17, 30; D&C 5:21; 18:31; 20:69; 21:4; 25:2; 46:7; 68:28; 109:1; Moses 5:26.

blood should not come upon me. See Alma 5:22; 60:13; Isa. 1:15; 59:3; Jer. 26:14–15, Lam. 4:13; Ezek. 3:18–20; 33:1–9; Acts 5:28; 18:6; 20:26. See also the notes on Mosiah 2:28, *rid my garments of your blood*, below.

I shall stand to be judged of God. The king is subject to the rule of God (see Deut. 17:14–20; D&C 134:1).

2:28 *rid my garments of your blood.* Benjamin's use of the key words of garments and blood signal this as a temple oration. Jacob used a similar phrase at the temple of Nephi, "Behold, I take off my garments, and I shake them before you; . . . I shook your iniquities from my soul, . . . I stand with brightness before him, and am rid of your blood" (2 Ne. 9:44). He also said "And we did magnify our office unto the Lord, taking upon us the responsibility, answering the sins of the people upon our own heads if we did not teach them the word of God with all diligence; wherefore, by laboring with our might their blood might not come upon our garments; otherwise their blood would come upon our garments, and we would not be found spotless at the last day" (Jacob 1:19). Later Mormon wrote, "And these things are written that we may rid our garments of the blood of our brethren, who have dwindled in unbelief" (Morm. 9:35). His son Moroni wrote "And now I, Moroni, bid farewell unto the Gentiles, yea, and also unto my brethren whom I love, until we shall meet before the judgment-seat of Christ where all men shall know that my garments are not spotted with your blood" (Ether 12:38). Finally the Three Witnesses adopted this phrase for their testimony, "And we know that if we are faithful in Christ, we shall rid our garments of the blood of all men, and be found spotless before the judgment-seat of Christ." Compare Acts 20:26; Rev. 7:14. For more on guilt, see this volume, pp. 133, 164–67; see also the notes on Mosiah 2:32, *list to obey,* and 2:38, *enemy to God.*

choirs above. Compare the concourse of angels (1 Ne. 1:8); see also Welch, in *The Book of Mormon: First Nephi,* 1988, 36.

praises of a just God. Similar phrases are found in 1 Ne. 1:8; Morm. 7:7; Isa. 6:1, 3; *Testament of Levi* 3:8; *Testament of Abraham* 20:12; *1 Enoch* 39:12; *2 Enoch* 17:1; 19:3; 20:4; 21:1; 42:4; 1 Tim. 1:17.

The Coronation Announcement (Mosiah 2:29–30)

²⁹And moreover, I say unto you that I have caused that ye should assemble yourselves together, that I might declare unto you that I can •no longer be your teacher, nor your king; ³⁰For even at this time, my whole

frame doth tremble exceedingly while attempting to speak unto you; but the Lord God doth support me, and hath suffered me that I should speak unto you, and hath commanded me that I should declare unto you this day, that *my son Mosiah is a king and a ruler over you.

2:29 *no longer be your teacher.* "Now one of the best-known aspects of the year-drama is the ritual descent of the king to the underworld—he is ritually overcome by death, and then ritually resurrected or (as in the Egyptian *Sed* festival) revived in the person of his son and successor, while his soul goes to join the blessed ones above. All this, we believe, is clearly indicated in King Benjamin's farewell" (N.28, 302–3). For further discussion on this speech as a farewell address, see this volume, chapter 4.

2:30 *my son Mosiah is a king and a ruler.* This pronouncement is a formal declaration, probably accompanied by formalities, presentation to the people, and acclamation by the assembly. On the selection of the king by God and the people, see notes on Mosiah 2:11, *chosen by this people,* above.

Benjamin's Speech: Part 2

Obedience to God and King (Mosiah 2:31–41)

[31]And now, my brethren, I would that ye should do *as ye have hitherto done. As ye have kept my commandments, *and also the commandments of my father, and have prospered, and have been kept from falling into the hands of your enemies, even so if ye shall keep the commandments of my son, or the *commandments of God which shall be delivered unto you by him, ye shall prosper in the land, and your enemies shall have *no power over you. [32]But, O my people, beware lest there shall arise contentions among you, and ye *list to obey the *evil spirit, which

was spoken of by my father Mosiah. ³³For behold, there is a •wo pronounced upon him who •listeth to obey that spirit; for if he listeth to obey him, and remaineth and •dieth in his sins, the same •drinketh damnation to his own soul; for he receiveth for his •wages an •everlasting punishment, having transgressed the law of God •contrary to his own knowledge. ³⁴I say unto you, that there are not any among you, except it be your little children that have not been taught concerning these things, but what knoweth that ye are •eternally indebted to your heavenly Father, to render to him all that you •have and are; and also have been taught concerning the records which contain the prophecies which have been spoken by the •holy prophets, even down to the time our father, Lehi, left Jerusalem; ³⁵And also, all that has been spoken by our fathers until now. And behold, also, they spake that which was commanded

them of the Lord; therefore, •they are just and true. ³⁶And now, I say unto you, my brethren, that •after ye have known and have been taught all these things, if ye should transgress and go contrary to that which has been spoken, that ye do withdraw yourselves from the Spirit of the Lord, that it may have •no place in you to guide you in wisdom's paths that ye may be •blessed, prospered, and preserved—³⁷I say unto you, that the man that doeth this, the same cometh out in •open rebellion against God; therefore he listeth to obey the evil spirit, and becometh an •enemy to all righteousness; therefore, the Lord has no place in him, for he dwelleth not in •unholy temples. ³⁸Therefore •if that man repenteth not, and remaineth and dieth an •enemy to God, the •demands of divine justice do awaken his •immortal soul to a •lively sense of his own guilt, which doth cause him •to shrink from the presence of the Lord, and doth fill his breast with *guilt, and pain, and anguish, which is *like an unquenchable fire, whose flame ascendeth up forever and ever. ³⁹And now I say unto you, that *mercy hath no claim on that man; therefore his final doom is to endure a never-ending torment. ⁴⁰O, all *ye old men, and also ye *young men, and you little children who can understand my words, for I have spoken plainly unto you that ye might understand, I pray that ye should *awake to a remembrance of the awful situation of those that have *fallen into transgression. ⁴¹And moreover, I would desire that ye should consider on the blessed and happy state of those that keep the commandments of God. For behold, they are *blessed in all things, both *temporal and spiritual; and if they *hold out faithful to the end they are *received into heaven, that thereby they may *dwell with God in a *state of never-ending happiness. *O remember, remember that these things are true; for the *Lord God hath spoken it.

2:31 *as ye have hitherto done.* When a new king was installed the old order was dissolved, which necessitated reestablishing the public order.

and also the commandments of my father. By citing two generations of success in his dynasty, Benjamin seeks to insure his son's new position as king. Looking back to Mosiah₁ would have been especially important in continuing the alliegance of the people of Zarahemla who had participated in appointing him king and thereby had agreed to obey Mosiah₁ (Omni 1:19).

commandments of God. One of the six ceremonial components of an Israelite covenant speech is the commandment to obey the law. Although specific reference to the stone tablets at Sinai was not included in Benjamin's speech, Benjamin admonished obedience to a particular body of Nephite legal and religious law (K.11, 106). See also the notes on Mosiah 1:7; 2:13, *commandments,* above; 5:5, *covenant,* below.

no power over you. A similar promise as a result of obedience is found in Lev. 26:3–8, "Ye shall . . . dwell in your land safely. . . . And ye shall chase your enemies, and they shall fall before you by the sword." It would appear that this blessing has a concomitant curse—the woe pronounced on those who "list to obey" the evil spirit. A correlation can be drawn between Benjamin's promise and Moses' blessing / curse on the Levites in Deut. 33:11, which Christensen translates as "Cursed be their anger, for it is fierce; and their wrath, for it is cruel" (*ZAW* 101, 1989, 282). See also notes on Mosiah 1:7, *promises,* above.

2:32 *list to obey.* Benjamin, by using the phrase *list to obey,* is talking about a conscious decision, an exercise of agency which leads to actions "contrary to . . . knowledge" and a state of "open rebellion." This is *pesha* referred to in the discussion on *suffered in ignorance,* Mosiah 1:3. During Yom Kippur, which according to Lev. 16:29 is set on the tenth day of the seventh month (therefore during the same New Year season), the sacrifice of the goats takes place. This entails the sacrifice of two goats—one is designated as the Lord's goat, and the other the *scapegoat* or the Azazel goat (Lev. 16:7–10). The scapegoat, which is on the high priest's left hand, provides an interesting antecedent for Benjamin's concepts of listing to obey and open rebellion. According to Milgrom, when the purified high priest laid his hand on the live scapegoat, he transferred the "*ʿăwōnōt* 'iniquities'—the causes of the sanctuary's impurities, all of Israel's sins, ritual and moral alike, of priests and laity alike" (*Anchor Bible: Leviticus 1–16,* 1044). The sins to which Benjamin refers are intentional; hence the term "contrary to his own knowledge." Repentance would not normally be available to those who committed such sins, unless they had "subsequent remorse . . . that is responsible for converting [their] deliberate sin into an inadvertence, expiable by sacrifice" (ibid., 295). The sacrifice of the Azazel goat, then, would cover those who were in a state of rebellion only if they repented; for further discussion on the scapegoat ritual and sacrifice, see this volume, pp. 164, 176–79; and the notes on Mosiah 5:9–10, 12, *right hand of God . . . left hand of God,* above. "The sacrifice of Yom Kippur requires prior restitution for sins committed. If such restitution is not made, the Yom Kippur liturgy is considered effective for the community as a whole, but not for those individuals who have failed to make rectification. Until such restitution is made, those individuals are considered cut off from the community" (Anderson and Culbertson, *Anglican Theological Review* 68/4, 1986, 312–13). Ancient Israel had a community relationship with God, "Guilt . . . derives not only from the sin which each and every individual has committed, but also from the corporate guilt of past generations. Individual responsibility for sin . . . does not alter the fact that the guilt for sin either in the past or in the present rests on the whole community. The Old Testament does not preach a religious individualism in which a man can stand in a private and personal relationship with God" (Mayes, *Irish Theological Quarterly*, 15/3, 1973, 252; for more on guilt, see this volume, pp. 133, 164–67; see also the notes on Mosiah 2:28, *rid my garments;* 2:38, *enemy to God*). Benjamin says that if the sinner does not make restitution "and remaineth and dieth an enemy to God . . . his final doom is to endure a never-ending torment" (Mosiah 2:38–39; see the notes on Mosiah 2:38, *unquenchable fire,* and 3:27, *fire and brimstone,* above). An obvious parallel is Mosiah 3:11, in that the atonement is available to all who repent and have faith on the Lord Jesus Christ. In the comparison between Benjamin's speech and the initiation covenant ceremony at Qumran, the third part of the ceremony is "Levites recount the sins and rebellions of the sons of Israel under the dominion of Belial" (1QS I 22–23). See the discussion on contention in this volume, pp. 130–35.

evil spirit. This term is used in the KJV OT in connection with Saul in 1 Sam. 19:9–11. It also appears in the NT in Acts 19:15–16. In the Book of Mormon it is also found in 2 Ne. 32:8; Mosiah 2:37; 4:14. See the discussion in this volume, pp. 340–41.

2:33 *wo*. Did this *wo* take the form of a curse, a ban, or shame? Compare Jacob's pronouncement of woes in 2 Ne. 9:27–38. See also the notes on Mosiah 4:23, *wo be unto that man,* below.

listeth. List means "to incline" not "to listen." See also Mosiah 2:32, *listeth to obey,* above.

dieth in his sins. Dying in sins is mentioned in the KJV in Ezek. 3:20; 18:24; John 8:21, 24 (twice), and in the Book of Mormon in 2 Ne. 9:38; Mosiah 15:26; Alma 12:16.

drinketh damnation to his own soul. A very interesting phrase that Benjamin used three times, here and in Mosiah 3:18, 25. Variants appear in 1 Cor. 11:29 and in 3 Ne. 18:25, referring to those who partake of the sacrament unworthily. A number of similar phrases also occur—"to drink wrath" or "to drink of the cup of wrath." Benjamin used this in Mosiah 3:26; 5:5, and it appears in Job 21:20 in the OT and in Rev. 14:8, 10; 16:19; 18:3 in the NT, also in D&C 35:11; 43:26; 88:94. In Isa. 51:17, 22 is found "cup of fury." The Hebrew of the Isaiah passages is identical to that of Job. The Isaiah passages are repeated in 2 Ne. 8:17, 22, indicating that Benjamin was probably familiar with them. Finally, one is reminded of the trial of bitter waters to test for infidelity in Num. 5:11–31. The *Dictionary of New Testament Theology,* under "Redemption," contrasts the cup of wrath (Mosiah 3:26) with the cup of salvation.

wages. Punishment for sin is described as *wages* in Rom. 6:23; Alma 3:27; 5:42; Morm. 8:19; D&C 29:45. In Alma 3:27 and D&C 29:45 the *wages* are connected with "listing to obey" (see discussion on Mosiah 2:32).

everlasting punishment. This phrase is found in Mosiah 27:31; Matt. 25:46; 4 Macc. 12:12, 18; 18:5; *Testament of Gad* 7:6; *Testament of Benjamin* 7:5; see also Matt. 25:41, "everlasting fire." See TG, "Eternal."

contrary to his own knowledge. A similar phrase is found in Alma 9:23, again in connection with the Nephites, at which time Alma warns that it would "be far more tolerable for the Lamanites than them"; see also the consequences of transgressing against knowledge in Lev. 26:21, 27–28; Heb. 10:26; 2 Pet. 2:21; see also the discussion on Mosiah 2:32.

2:34 *eternally indebted.* This point was previously established by Benjamin with the words "forever and ever" (Mosiah 2:24).

Referring to the term in the Lord's Prayer (Matt. 5:13, Luke 14:34), Matthew Black points out that "the Aramaic term *ḥobha*, 'debt' or 'sin' . . . is the equivalent of *ḥayyabha*, 'debtor' or 'sinner.'" He explains further, "'Sin' was conceived of in terms of a debt; we may compare the parable of the Unforgiving Debtor" (*An Aramaic Approach to the Gospels and Acts*, 1946, 102). See also notes on Mosiah 1:3, *suffered in ignorance*; 2:32, *list to obey*, above; and 3:11, *ignorantly sinned*, below. See also TG, "Debt."

have and are. See this volume, pp. 12–13.

holy prophets. W of M 1:16; see also 2 Pet. 3:2; Luke 1:70; Acts 3:21; Rev. 22:6; 2 Baruch 85:1; see notes on Mosiah 3:13, *holy prophets*, below.

2:35 *they are just and true.* See also Rev. 15:3; 1 Ne. 14:23; Alma 18:34; 29:8; 3 Ne. 5:18; Moro. 10:6; D&C 20:30–31; 76:53. See also notes on Mosiah 4:12, *just and true*, below.

2:36 *after ye have known and have been taught all these things.* Knowledge puts people on notice, makes them legally and morally responsible. See notes on Mosiah 3:21, *none shall be found blameless*, below.

no place in you. This phrase is found in John 8:37, referring to the word of the Lord; Alma 34:35; Hel. 6:35; 13:8.

blessed, prospered, and preserved. *Blessed* and *prospered* occur as a word pair in Mosiah 25:24; 3 Ne. 5:22; 4 Ne. 1:18; Ether 10:28. See also the blessings in 1Q22 II–III cited in the notes on Mosiah 2:24, *doth immediately bless you*, above.

2:37 *open rebellion against God.* This phrase also is found in Alma 3:18 and Morm. 2:15; Welch defines this as the state of those who transgress the law contrary to their own knowledge in *Reexploring*, 62–63; see also the discussion on Mosiah 2:32, *list to obey*; and in this volume, pp. 72–73, *essence of sin.*

enemy to all righteousness. This phrase also occurs in Mosiah 4:14; Alma 34:23; *enemy of all righteousness* is found in Moro. 9:6; Acts 13:10; Sirach 1:30.

unholy temples. See also Alma 7:21; 34:36; Hel. 4:24; D&C

97:17; Lev. 26:11; John 2:19–21; 14:17; Acts 7:48–50; 17:24; 1 Cor. 3:16–17; 6:19–20; 2 Cor. 6:16; Eph. 2:21–22.

2:38 *if that man repenteth not.* Repentance is the only way out.

enemy to God. Benjamin used this phrase here and in Mosiah 3:19. Abinadi used it twice in Mosiah 16:5. It also appears in Mosiah 27:9 and Moro. 7:12. It is also used in the KJV in Lev. 26:14–17 and James 4:4. See the discussion on guilt, this volume, pp. 133, 164–67; see also the notes on Mosiah 2:28, *rid my garments,* and 2:32, *list to obey;* see also the notes on Mosiah 3:19, *putteth off the natural man,* below.

demands of divine justice. The *demands of justice* are mentioned in 2 Ne. 9:26; Mosiah 15:9; Alma 34:16; 42:15, 24. Notice that the *demands of justice* are set against the claims of mercy.

immortal soul. Benjamin recognized the individual existence of souls which cannot die.

lively sense. A vivid expression.

to shrink from the presence of the Lord. "The wicked and rebellious may suffer some anguish of conscience in this life (Alma 38:8; D&C 124:52), but the great penalty for their rebellion is in the future" (McConkie, *Mormon Doctrine,* 1979, 38). The angel uses this phrase when speaking to Benjamin in Mosiah 3:25. The phrase *the presence of the Lord* may be a temple expression; hence also "unholy temples" (Mosiah 2:37).

guilt, and pain, and anguish. This is a tripartite expression; cf. *thoughts, words, deeds* (Mosiah 4:30); *mind, body, spirit* (Alma 17:5).

like an unquenchable fire, whose flame ascendeth up forever and ever. This phrase is very similar to another passage in Benjamin's address: Mosiah 3:27, "And their torment is as a lake of fire and brimstone, whose flames are unquenchable, and whose smoke ascendeth up forever and ever." They are both similar to a passage in Jacob 6:10, "And according to the power of justice, for justice cannot be denied, ye must go away into that lake of fire and brimstone, whose flames are unquenchable, and whose smoke ascendeth up forever and ever, which lake of fire and brimstone is endless torment." The last part of this verse "endless torment" finds a parallel in Mosiah 2:39, "never-ending torment." The description of "endless torment" as "fire and brimstone" was also used by Jacob twice in 2 Ne. 9:19 and 26 and by Nephi in 2 Ne. 28:23. In D&C 76:44 the phrase is "and the fire is not quenched," which is their torment. The idea of never-ending torment is also found in Rev. 14:10–11; 20:10; D&C 19:6. The curse of wrath and torment is also found in 1Q22 II, "[Be] very [careful], for your lives, [to keep them, lest] the wrath [of your God] against you be enkindled and reach you, and it closes the skies above, which make rain fall upon you, and [the water] from under[neath the earth which gives you [the harv]est." See also notes on Mosiah 3:27, *lake of fire and brimstone,* below.

2:39 *mercy . . . claim.* Jacob, in speaking of the atonement in 2 Ne. 9:25, declared that the "mercies of the Holy One of Israel have claim upon them." Benjamin used the phrase here and in Mosiah 3:26. Later, Alma used *mercy* as the subject of the verb *claim* five times while teaching Corianton in Alma 42:21–24 and 31. It also appears in D&C 88:40. *Mercy* is also the object of the verb *claim* in Alma 12:34 and in Moro. 7:27.

2:40 *ye old men, and also ye young men, and you little children.* No women are mentioned here, although they were present (Mosiah 2:5).

young men. On the question of the age of the *young men,* Fred Woods has analyzed the comparable term in 2 Kgs. 2:23, *nᵉʿārîm qᵉṭannîm,* "children or small boys" but "imprecise with regard to exact age," with *yᵉlāḏîm,* "children," cited in 2 Kings 24, and compared them with Gen. 37:2 in which Joseph is called a *naʿar* at the age of seventeen. His conclusion is "that the age of the youths designated by these combined words would probably fall slightly under twenty years (*BYUS* 32/3, 1992, 48).

awake to a remembrance of the awful situation. The word *awful* appears 45 times in the Book of Mormon but nowhere else in scripture. Usually it describes hell, guilt, wickedness, fear, chains, or the state or situation of the wicked. In Ether 8:24, Moroni used the similar phrase "awake to a sense of your awful situation." For more information on *fear,* see notes on Mosiah 1:7, *keep the com-*

mandments; 2:10, *that ye should fear me;* 4:1, *fear of the Lord.* For remembrance, see the notes on Mosiah 1:16; 2:41; 4:11, 30; 6:3. See also the notes on Mosiah 3:25, *awful view of their own guilt,* below.

fallen into transgression. This phrase is found almost exclusively in the Book of Mormon: Enos 1:13; Jarom 1:10; Mosiah 1:13; 7:25; 15:13; Alma 9:23; 10:19; 24:30; 44:4; 46:21, 22; Hel. 3:16; 4:26; 3 Ne. 6:5. It is also found in D&C 5:32.

2:41 *blessed in all things.* Abraham is described as being "blessed in all things" in Gen. 24:1; hence, Benjamin is promising his people the blessings of Abraham.

temporal and spiritual. See also 1 Ne. 15:32; 22:3; 2 Ne. 2:5; Alma 7:23; 12:16. Contrast this with the phrase "[he who drinks] damnation to his own soul" (2:33). The cup of salvation is that of a "material deliverance attended by spiritual blessings" (*Dictionary of New Testament Theology,* 208).

hold out faithful to the end. This is also found in D&C 6:13. Variations are in Alma 5:13, "faithful until the end" and D&C 31:13 and 81:6, "faithful unto the end"; Rev. 2:10 has "be thou faithful unto death, and I will give thee a crown of life."

received into heaven. In the KJV in Mark 16:19 the Lord is "received up into heaven" and in Acts 10:16, in Peter's vision of the unclean beasts, the vessel which held them is "received up into heaven."

dwell with God. This phrase and variations are found in 1 Ne. 10:21; 15:35; Mosiah 15:23; Alma 24:22; Morm. 9:4; Moro. 8:26. Similar phrases are also found in 2 Ne. 2:8; Morm. 7:7; 9:3; D&C 76:62; 133:35; Moses 6:57.

state of never-ending happiness. Benjamin is perhaps aluding to the choice made by a Hebrew slave at the end of his six-year term of servitude, after which a slave—and we are all debt-servants in Benjamin's mind—could decide to become a permanent slave because of his love for his master (Ex. 21:5). "Dwelling with God in a *state of never-ending happiness* seems suggestive of the temporary slave's choice to become a permanent part of his master's household" (Cannon, *BYU Law Papers,* 1995). For information on slavery, see this volume pp. 40, 58, and the notes on Mosiah 2:13, *make slaves one of another,* above.

O remember, remember. Remember is used often in the scriptures, but in only five places in this same format: Alma 37:13; Hel. 5:9, 12; 14:30; D&C 3:3. In Hel. 5:9 the repetition may actually be a conscious device, for Helaman implores his sons, "O remember, remember, my sons, the words which king Benjamin spake"; see also the notes on the notes on Mosiah 1:16; 4:11, 30; 6:3 on remembering.

Lord God hath spoken it. See also Morm. 8:26; 1 Kgs. 14:11; Isa. 22:25; 25:8; Joel 3:8 (MT 4:8); Obad. 1:18, "for the Lord hath spoken it." This declaration formally and overtly marks the end of this section of the speech. See notes on Mosiah 3:27, *Thus hath the Lord commanded me,* below.

Benjamin's Speech: Part 3

The Name of the Lord Omnipotent (Mosiah 3:1–10)

3:1And •again •my brethren, •I would call your attention, for I have •somewhat more to speak unto you; for behold, I have things to tell you concerning that •which is to come. 2And the things which I shall tell you are •made known unto me by an •angel from God. And he said unto me: •Awake; and I awoke, and behold he •stood before me. 3And he said unto me:

Awake, and hear the words which I shall tell thee; for behold, I am come to declare unto you the •glad tidings of great joy. 4For the Lord hath •heard thy prayers, and hath •judged of thy righteousness, and •hath sent me to declare unto thee that thou •mayest rejoice; and that thou mayest declare unto thy people, that they may also be filled with joy. 5•For behold, the time cometh, and is not far distant, that with power, the •Lord Omnipotent who •reigneth, who was, and is •from all eternity to all eternity, •shall come down from heaven among the children of men, and shall dwell in a •tabernacle of clay, and shall go forth amongst men, working mighty miracles, such as *healing the sick, raising the dead, causing the lame to walk, the blind to receive their sight, and the deaf to hear, and curing all manner of diseases. ⁶And he shall cast out devils, or the *evil spirits which dwell in the *hearts of the children of men. ⁷And lo, he shall suffer *temptations, and pain of body, *hunger, thirst, and fatigue, *even more than man can suffer, except it be *unto death; for behold, *blood cometh from every pore, so great shall be his *anguish for the *wickedness and the abominations of his people. ⁸And he shall be called *Jesus Christ, the Son of God, the Father of heaven and earth, the Creator of all things *from the beginning; and *his mother shall be called Mary. ⁹And lo, he *cometh unto his own, *that salvation might come unto the children of men even *through faith on his name; and even after all this they shall consider him a man, and say that *he hath a devil, and shall *scourge him, and shall *crucify him. ¹⁰And he shall rise the *third day *from the dead; and behold, he *standeth to judge the world; and behold, all these things are done that a *righteous judgment might come upon the children of men.

3:1 *again*. It is possible that a break or pause occurred between the ending of section 2 and the beginning of section 3.

my brethren. Benjamin referred to the men in his kingdom as his "brothers." This is consistent not only with the overall concept of Israel as a family or household of God with God as the father, but it is also consonant with the legal requirement of Deut. 17:15, that the king shall be "one from among thy brethren." See the notes on Mosiah 1:5, *brethren*; 1:13, *weak like unto their brethren*.

I would call your attention. Benjamin alone uses this phrase; it appears here and in Mosiah 4:4. In the KJV the verb *hear* is used often to express the same idea: Num. 12:6; 16:8; Deut. 6:3–4, etc.

somewhat . . . speak . . . concerning. This expression is unique to the Book of Mormon, being found in 2 Ne. 6:8; 25:1; Omni 1:12, 27; W of M 1:3; Alma 54:6; 56:2; Ether 12:6; compare 1 Kgs. 2:14, "moreover, I have somewhat to say unto thee."

which is to come. Eph. 1:21; "that which is to come" (1 Tim. 4:8). This formulation is used seven times in the Book of Mormon: Mosiah 3:1; 4:11; 5:3; Alma 5:48; 21:8; 51:40; Hel. 8:23.

3:2 *made known unto me by an angel.* The formulation "angels making known" does not appear in the KJV. It is found in the Book of Mormon in 1 Ne. 14:29; Alma 11:31; 13:26; 36:5; 40:11. The concept of a heavenly messenger appearing to impart wisdom and give a divine commission is found in the literature on enthroning a Mesopotamian king to whom is revealed "the great mystery of heaven and earth, the hidden things, . . . the hidden knowledge possessed by the gods" (Widengren, *The Ascension of the Apostle and the Heavenly Book,* 1950, 20). A parallel can be drawn with Ezek. 2:9–3:2, the calling of the prophet and the imparting of knowledge in the form of a roll of a book (ibid., 331–32). Moses, too, "is elevated above the human sphere, and, in Samaritan literature thought to be pre-existent and divine, ascends to heaven . . . the bringer of divine revelation" (ibid., 46–47). Messages delivered or introduced by angels are common in scriptural and pseudepigraphic literature. In the Book of Mormon, see for example 1 Ne. 8 (Lehi led by an angelic guide), 1 Ne. 11 (Nephi's vision directed by an angelic escort). See also Ezek. 40–48 (Ezekiel's vision); Zech. 1–6 (Zechariah's vision). From the books of Enoch and other texts involving angelic escorts, see 1 Enoch 1:2–9; 17:1–19:3; 21:1–36:4; 72:1–82:20; 108:5–15; 2 Enoch 1:4–10; 3:1–22:11; 37:1–38:2; 3 Enoch 4–48:10; Moses 6:26–36. On the phenomenon of the angelic escort in general, see Davis, *Journal of Theological Studies* 45/2, 1994, 479–503.

angel . . . Awake. The story of a prophet being awakened by a heavenly being who has a message for him is also found in the calling of Samuel (1 Sam. 3:1–18). Other instances of visions occur at waking or soon afterwards: two of Daniel's visions (Dan. 8:18; 10:7–11) and one of Zechariah's (Zech. 4:1–2). For information about the angel, see this volume, pp. 65–66, 112–13, 283–87, 406 n.

63; see also the notes on Mosiah 3:4, *hath sent me* and *mayest rejoice*, and 4:11, *spoken by the mouth of the angel*, below.

Awake. Susan Easton Black sees this awakening as the transition from slumbering in the types and shadows of the law of Moses to finding the gospel of Christ (B.02, 43).

stood before me. See also Dan. 8:15; 10:15–16; Zech. 4:1; Acts 10:30.

3:3 *glad tidings of great joy. Glad tidings* is not found in the KJV OT but appears in the NT: Luke 1:19; 8:2; Acts 13:32; Rom. 10:15. In the Book of Mormon the phrase appears in Alma 13:22–23; 39:15–16, 19; Hel. 13:7; 16:14; 3 Ne. 1:26. A similar phrase, "good tidings," occurs in 2 Sam. 4:10; 18:27; 1 Kgs. 1:42; 2 Kgs. 7:9; Isa. 40:9 (twice); 41:27; 52:7; 61:1; Nahum 1:15; Luke 2:10; 1 Thes. 3:6; Mosiah 12:21; 15:14, 18; 27:37; Hel. 5:29; 3 Ne. 20:40. *Glad tidings of great joy* is not found in the KJV, but it appears here, in Alma 13:22 and Hel. 16:14. It is also found three times in the D&C. In Alma 13:22, Alma specifically affirms Benjamin's testimony, declaring that the "glad tidings of great joy" are proclaimed by the voice of the Lord or "by the mouth of angels." See also Isa. 52:7, "How beautiful upon the mountains are the feet of him [Nahum 1:15; 1 Ne. 13:37; Mosiah 12:20–21, 32–33, 15:15–18, 3 Ne. 20:40] that bringeth good tidings, that publisheth peace"; Isa. 52:9, "Break forth into joy"; 1 Esdras (3 Ezra) 9:53–54. See also the notes on Mosiah 3:4, *mayest rejoice*, and 4:11, *exceedingly great joy.*

3:4 *heard thy prayers.* Benjamin had been praying to receive further light and knowledge about the items revealed to him. This is significant for at least two reasons: first, God usually does not reveal important information to people unless they make a petition asking for it (1 Ne. 15:8; Matt. 7:7), and second, prophets often make requests, known as intercessory prayers, pleading with the Lord on behalf of their people. Thus, for example, Lehi prayed "on behalf of his people" (1 Ne. 1:5), and Enos poured out his soul on behalf of the Nephites and Lamanites (Enos 1:9–17). Because the revelation given to Benjamin deals with the salvation and welfare of his people in general, it is reasonable to assume that Benjamin's prayer was an intercessory prayer offered on behalf of others. Such efforts by prophets to intercede at the throne of God on behalf of their people have been identified as one of the notable functions of classic Israelite prophecy. See Welch, in *The Book of Mormon: First Nephi*, 1988, 38–39. Compare *Encyclopedia Judaica*, 13:1170. Prophetic intercessory functions were served by other prophets such as Abraham (Gen. 20:7), Samuel (1 Sam. 7:5–9), and Jeremiah (Jer. 14:11).

judged of thy righteousness. God judges not only the transgressions but also the righteousness of his children. Throughout the book of Psalms, the sentiment of the righteous is to invite and desire, not to fear and worry about, the judgment of God. Judging was seen as a positive attribute of God in biblical times. For an insightful discussion of the concept of judgment in the Psalms, see Lewis, *Reflections on the Psalms*, 1938, 15–22.

hath sent me. Angels, prophets, and apostles are *sent* as authorized agents to carry specific messages from the Lord. The word *missionary* literally means one who is sent (from the Latin, *mitto*). In this case, being sent involves more than merely acting as a delivery boy; it implies full authority to act on behalf of the sender, with the accompanying obligation to deliver the message verbatim and to fulfill the delegated assignment precisely. See also the notes on Mosiah 3:2, *angel . . . Awake*, and 3:4, *mayest rejoice*.

mayest rejoice. The angel was sent with instructions to give King Benjamin permission to rejoice and to tell his people that they may also be filled with joy. Evidently more is involved here than a mere expression of happiness. Just as "joy" in 2 Ne. 2:25 embraces the attainment of the full purpose of life, "Man is that he might have joy," so here the angel announces the good news of the eternal gospel that Benjamin and his people may rejoice and be filled with joy, that is that they have attained and shall fulfill the measure of their creation and shall enjoy all the blessings of the atonement of Jesus Christ through the gift and power of God and their righteous obedience. B. H. Roberts describes it as the joy that "will arise from a consciousness of moral, spiritual, and physical strength; of strength gained in conflict" (*The Truth, the Way, the Life*, 1996, 266, and in general, 265–67). Talking of the change in fortunes as a result of the Depression, President Kimball contrasts the worldly pleasures obtained from spending material wealth with the joy that comes from spending time with family: "Having lost their expensive cars, or unable to purchase gasoline for them, groups remained at home and found real joy in family associations and in teaching the children the way of life" *(The Teachings of Spencer W. Kimball,* 1982, 354). Millet and McConkie describe this joy as when one receives a remission of sins, he "delights in fellowship with those of the household of faith; his confidence once again begins to wax strong in the presence of the Lord; the word of the Lord becomes sweet to the taste; and the strength of the Lord enables him to bear life's burdens with perspective" (M.18, 158). For further information on remission of sins, see this volume, pp. 16, 197–98. See also the notes on Mosiah 2:32, *list to obey;* 2:34, *eternally indebted;* 3:11, *ignorantly sinned;* 3:13, *remission of their sins;* 4:26, *retaining a remission;* 4:28, *cause thy neighbor.*

3:5–10 *For behold, the time cometh.* Messianic expectations in ancient Israel are not limited to those found in the Book of Mormon; both Zechariah and Haggai saw in Zerubbabel a partial fulfillment of Messianic prophecies, implying that older Messianic prophecies were common knowledge at that time (van der Woude, *ZAW* 100, 1988, 138–40). The Dead Sea Scrolls contain Messianic references: Paolo Sacchi, after first defining Messianism and citing specifically 2 Sam. 7, Isa. 11:1–5, Jer. 23:5, Zech. 3:8, 6:12, Ezek. 34:23–24, 37:25; 45:9, and generally Chronicles, Job, Ruth and Jonah, highlights those details in 11QMelch, in which the eschatalogical leader of the sons of light appears as a "superhuman figure." Sacchi sees this exposition of the role of the Messiah as a "new form" of Messianism dating from about 200 B.C., again showing that Messianic expectations had been in existence for a long time (*ZAW* 100, 1988, 201–9). In contrast to the NT declaration in John 4:25–26; 6:69; 20:31, which is *"clear, . . .* the Book of Mormon is *emphatic"* (Maxwell, *Not My Will, but Thine,* 1988, 45). For a discussion of the angel's preview of Christ's life, see this volume, pp. 343–54.

3:5 *Lord Omnipotent.* Benjamin uses this phrase five times; it is found only in his speech in the Book of Mormon: Mosiah 3:17–18, 21; 5:2, 15. In the KJV it is found only in Rev. 19:6. As a king, a potentate with great power, Benjamin related especially to the idea of God's power and omnipotence.

the Lord . . . reigneth. Also found in 1 Chron. 16:31; Ps. 47:8; 93:1; 96:10; 97:1; 99:1; Isa. 52:7; Rev. 19:6; Mosiah 12:21; 15:14; 27:37; 3 Ne. 20:40 (quoting Isaiah).

from all eternity to all eternity. Also found in Alma 13:7 and Moro. 8:18; D&C 39:1; Moses 6:67; 7:29, 31. According to this formulation, eternity is without beginning as well as without end. In the KJV a portion of this idea is expressed with the word *everlasting:* Ps. 41:13; 90:2; 103:17; 106:48; see also Moro. 7:22.

shall come down. The condescension of the Lord from heaven to dwell in a mortal body was a consistent element of Nephite messianic expectation. Lehi saw "One descending out of the midst of heaven" (1 Ne. 1:9), and Nephi was asked by the angel, "Knowest thou the condescension of God?" (1 Ne. 11:16). Essential to the Christology taught by early Book of Mormon prophets was the understanding that God himself, "Who was, and is from all eternity to all eternity," would humble himself and become mortal. See Millet, in *The Book of Mormon: First Nephi*, 1988, 167–69.

tabernacle of clay. See also Alma 7:11–12. The phrase *tabernacle of clay* is unique to the Book of Mormon, used only here by Benjamin and by Mormon in Moro. 9:6.

healing the sick, raising the dead, causing the lame to walk, the blind to receive their sight. A fragment from the Dead Sea Scrolls (4Q251), from about 100 B.C., contains the following similar messianic expectations: "And when the Messiah comes then he will heal the sick [make the blind see], raise [or resurrect] the dead, and to the poor announce glad tidings." See Wise and Tabor, *Biblical Archaeology Review* 18/6, 1992, 60–65; see also García Martínez, *LDS Perspectives on the Dead Sea Scrolls*, 1997, 131–32. For a text to speak more than a hundred years before the time of Christ so explicitly about the miracles to be performed by the Messiah is news to most of the world; but to those who see continuity between the Old Testament and the New, this text, which named three of the four points also found in Mosiah 3:5, sounds quite familiar. Compare Matt. 11:5 and Luke 7:22 (blind receive sight, lame walk, lepers cleansed, deaf hear, dead raised, and the poor have the gospel preached to them); and Matt. 15:32 (dumb speak, maimed whole, lame walk, blind see). See also Isa. 35:5–6, "Then the eyes of the blind shall be opened, and the ears of the deaf shall be unstopped"; Luke 4:18–19; Isa. 61:1–2, which is a sabbatical and jubilee proclamation; see also Lev. 25:10; Sirach 48:5. Christ's ministry was revealed to Benjamin as a continuous series of examples of service (B.02, 41).

3:6 *evil spirits.* See Matt. 10:8, "Heal the sick, cleanse the lepers, raise the dead, cast out devils"; 10:1, "power against unclean spirits, to cast them out, and to heal all manner of sickness, and all manner of disease"; Luke 9:1, "power and authority over all devils, and to cure diseases"; see also Matt. 9:32–35; 12:22, 24; 11QPsAp IV 15.

hearts of the children of men. This phrase is found in 2 Chron. 6:30; Prov. 15:11.

3:7 *temptations.* Benjamin's report that Christ "shall suffer temptations" calls to mind the temptations of Jesus in Matt. 4:1–11 and Luke 4:1–12. The Greek word for temptation comes from the verb *peirazo*, whose meanings include to attempt, to try to do a thing, to test (either with good or bad intent), as well as to tempt. Thus the sufferings endured by Jesus during his forty days in the wilderness were as much a test as a temptation. Benjamin's reference to the sufferings of hunger, thirst, and fatigue seem to focus on the forty-day period of trial in the wilderness, whereas the "pain of body" relates more to the suffering in the Garden of Gethsemane, so great that "blood cometh from every pore."

hunger, thirst, and fatigue. These words first appear in 1 Ne. 16:35. They are also found here and in Mosiah 7:16; Alma 17:5; 60:3.

even more than man can suffer. Benjamin is confirming the great suffering of the Savior, "Any theology which teaches that there were some things he did not suffer is a falsification of his life" (M.14, 6). See also TG, "Jesus Christ, Redeemer."

unto death. See also Matt. 26:38, "My soul is exceeding sorrowful, even unto death"; Mark 14:34; Sirach 37:2.

blood cometh from every pore. This prophesies the event reported in Luke 22:44 that "his sweat was as it were great drops of blood." Benjamin, in his declaration of the suffering of Christ in Gethsemane and in keeping with the role of the Book of Mormon as "Another Testament of Jesus Christ," affirms the literal nature of Luke's description. This verse in Luke is unique to his Gospel, and since the times of the Ante-Nicene Fathers, lines have been drawn as to whether this verse was symbolic or literal. Some assert, "in using the expression 'as it were great drops of blood,' he does not declare the drops of sweat to have been actually drops of blood" (Dionysius, *Ante-Nicene Fathers*, 6:115); others saw it literally, "And in an agony He sweats blood, and is strengthened by an angel" (Hippolytus, *Ante-Nicene Fathers*, 5:230). Modern commentators have noted, "Cases are known in which the blood, violently agitated by grief, ends by penetrating through the vessels which inclose it, and driven outward, escapes with the sweat through the transpiratory glands" (Godet, *Commentary on Luke*, 1981, 476). Further uncertainty about Luke 22:43–44, however, arises because these words are not present in the earliest NT manuscripts of Luke. Joseph Fitzmyer concludes, nevertheless, that there can be at least "no doubt that a tradition about Jesus' agony in the garden as found in these verses [Luke 22:43–44] is ancient" (*Luke*, 1985, 1443). Raymond E. Brown evaluates textual, stylistic, structure, scribal, and other evidence and concludes: "While clearly the evidence available does not settle the issue of whether Luke wrote 22:43–44, in my judgment the overall import of the five types of evidence or reasoning discussed above favors Lucan authorship" (*SBL 1992 Seminar Papers*, 159); see further the scholarly sources cited by Brown. In 1Q22 IV the blood symbolism is used for remembrance, "[And you shall] take [the blood and] pour [it] on the earth . . . and it will be forgiven them." See also Luke 22:44; Matt. 26:28; Rom. 5:9; Eph. 2:16; Heb. 2:9; 9:28;

1 Pet. 2:21, 24; 3:18; 1 Jn. 1:7; 1 Ne. 11:33; Hel. 5:9; 3 Ne. 11:14; Moro. 10:33. For further discussion of the sweat of blood and suffering, see this volume, pp. 14, 172, 175–76, 347.

anguish. The anguish of Jesus was not only physical but also mental and spiritual. The word *anguish* comes from the German word *Angst,* meaning fear, worry, or concern, and is related to the words anxiety and anger, describing mental as well as physical states.

wickedness and . . . abominations. This is a very common word pair in the Book of Mormon. It occurs 46 times: 1 Ne. 1:19; 14:4, 12; 27:8; 28:14, 17; Jacob 2:10, 31; Mosiah 3:7; 7:26; 11:20; 29:18; Alma 4:3; 21:3; 37:21, 23; 37:29 (twice); Hel. 4:11; 6:24, 34; 7:27; 9:23; 13:14–17; 3 Ne. 2:3; 7:15; 9:7–8, 10–12; 30:2; 4 Ne. 1:39; Morm. 2:18 (3), 27, 3:11; Ether 14:25; Moro. 9:15. It is also found in D&C 10:21; 45:12. The theme of abomination of the people is found in 1Q22 I, "they will desert me and ch[oose the sins of the na]tions, their abominations and their disreputable acts."

3:8 *Jesus Christ, the Son of God, the Father of heaven and earth, the Creator of all things from the beginning.* This title is repeated verbatim in Hel. 14:12. In 3 Ne. 9:15, Christ uses most of the elements contained in this title but not in exactly the same way. Ether 4:7 has a title that is similar but not identical. For *Son of God* see Mark 1:1; Dan. 3:25; Matt. 1:21, 23; 4:6–7; Luke 1:31–33, 70; 2:21, 30; 24:27; John 5:39, 46–47; 12:41; Acts 3:18, 21, 24; 20:22–23; 1 Pet. 1:10–11; 2 Esdras 7:28–29 (4 Ezra); 1 Ne. 10:4–7; 11:18; 2 Ne. 25:19–20, Mosiah 15:1–9; Alma 5:48; 7:10; 3 Ne. 20:24; for the specific name of a king of Judah given centuries before his birth, see 1 Kgs. 13:2; 2 Kgs. 21:24 (Josiah); see also Isa. 44:28; 45:1 (Cyrus). For notes on the creation, see this volume, pp. 169–70.

from the beginning. See also Isa. 9:6; Jonah 1:9; John 1:1–3, 17–18; Acts 4:24; 1 Jn. 5:7; 2 Ne. 2:14; Jacob 2:5; Mosiah 4:2, 9; 7:27; 15:2–4; Hel. 14:12; 16:18; Judith 13:18.

his mother shall be called Mary. The name Mary was a common Jewish name. In Hebrew it is spelled Miriam, notably also the name of the sister of Moses (Num. 26:59). The name in Hebrew means "one who is exalted." In other words, the mother of the Savior would be called "one who is exalted."

3:9 *cometh unto his own.* See John 1:11, "He came unto his own."

that salvation might come. The Hebrew word for salvation is *yᵉšû῾āh*. In Hebrew prophecy, the name *Jehovah* was often equated with salvation. "The Lord [is] my strength and song, and he is become my salvation: he [is] my God" (Ex. 15:2; see also Ps. 27:1; 118:14; Isa. 12:2). Thus the parallelism in Benjamin's text is strong: "*He* cometh unto his own // that *salvation* might come unto the children of men."

through faith on his name. The earliest reference to faith on God's name is Acts 3:16. In the OT, names were often symbolic, so that having faith on the name of God can be associated with the reverence attached to it. In the Hebrew scriptures, the name of God was represented by the Tetragrammaton YHWH and pronounced *adonai*. Thus it may be said that the name represented the concept of God. For further information on names, see Barr, *Bulletin of the John Rylands Library* 52/1, 1969, 11–29; Madsen, in *By Study and Also by Faith*, 1990, 458–81. See also notes on Mosiah 5:8, *take upon you the name of Christ*, below.

he hath a devil. Fulfillment of this prophecy is found in John 10:20; see also Matt. 12:24. Bruce R. McConkie describes this argument as "an affirmative denial of [Christ's] Messiahship" (*The Mortal Messiah*, 3:167).

scourge. According to Webster's 1828 dictionary, to *scourge* means to whip severely, lash; or to punish with severity; to chastise; to afflict for sins or faults, and with the purpose of correction." Deut. 25:3 allowed a convicted party to be beaten, but not in excess of forty stripes or blows.

crucify. Crucifixion was not only a Roman form of punishment but is attested as well as a Hebrew mode of execution. Deut. 21:22 provides for execution in capital cases: "And if a man hath committed a sin worthy of death, and he be to be put to death, and thou hang him on a tree . . ." Although this passage is ambiguous, whether hanging on a tree was a mode of execution or simply displaying the body after stoning, passages from the Dead

Sea Scrolls make it clear that crucifixion was used by Jews as a mode of execution before Roman times. Tvedtnes, *Insights*, April 1997, 2. See *Temple Scroll* (11Q19) LXIV 6–13 in García Martínez, *The Dead Sea Scrolls Translated*, 1996, 178; *Pesher Nahum*, frgs. 3–4 I 7–8, in ibid., 196; 3 Ne. 4:28.

3:10 *third day.* Jesus had prophesied that he would rise on the third day. The third day is significant in many OT accounts. For example, Moses told the people at Sinai to purify themselves "and be ready against the third day; for the third day the Lord will come down in the sight of all the people upon Mt. Sinai" (Ex. 19:11); Jonah was in the depths of the sea, "in the belly of the fish three days and three nights" (Jonah 1:17). See Howton, *Scottish Journal of Theology* 15/3, 1962, 288–304; Walker, *Novum Testamentum* 5, 1960, 261–62; Landes, *Journal of Biblical Literature* 86/4, 1967, 446–50.

from the dead. See Matt. 20:19, "and to scourge, and to crucify him: and the third day he shall rise again"; Mark 10:34, "and shall scourge him, and shall spit upon him, and shall kill him: and the third day he shall rise again"; see also Matt. 28:7; Luke 18:33; 1 Ne. 19:10; 2 Ne. 25:13; Mosiah 3:7; 5:12; Hel. 14:20, 27, 3 Ne. 10:9; 4 Macc. 6:1–29; Wisdom of Solomon 10:5. See also the notes on Mosiah 3:9, *scourge*, above.

standeth to judge the world. In ancient Israel, judges stood to render judgment; God as the *judge of the world* is a theme found in Moses' speech in 1Q22 IV; see also notes on Mosiah 3:24, *judge.*

righteous judgment. The death and resurrection of Jesus was essential in order to make a righteous judgment possible.

Benjamin's Speech: Part 4

The Atonement of the Lord Omnipotent (Mosiah 3:11–27)

¹¹For behold, and also •his blood atoneth for the sins of those who have fallen by the •transgression of Adam, who have died •not knowing the will of God concerning them, or who have •ignorantly sinned.

¹²But wo, wo unto him who knoweth that he *rebelleth against God! For salvation cometh to none such except it be *through repentance and *faith on the Lord Jesus Christ. ¹³And the Lord God hath sent his *holy prophets *among all the children of men, to declare these things to *every kindred, nation, and tongue, that thereby whosoever should *believe that Christ should come, the same might receive *remission of their sins, and *rejoice with exceedingly great joy, even as though he had already come among them. ¹⁴Yet the Lord God saw that his people were a *stiff-necked people, and he *appointed unto them a law, even the *law of Moses. ¹⁵And *many signs, and wonders, and *types, and shadows showed he unto them, concerning his coming; and also holy prophets spake unto them concerning his coming; and yet they *hardened their hearts, and understood not that the *law of Moses availeth nothing except it were through the atonement of his blood. ¹⁶And even if it were possible that *little children could sin they could not be saved; but I say unto you they are blessed; for behold, *as in Adam, or by nature, they fall, even so the blood of Christ *atoneth for their sins. ¹⁷And moreover, I say unto you, that there shall be *no other name given nor any other way nor means whereby *salvation can come unto the children of men, only in and through the name of Christ, the Lord Omnipotent. ¹⁸For behold he judgeth, and his *judgment is just; and the *infant perisheth not that dieth in his infancy; but men *drink damnation to their own souls except they humble themselves and become as *little children, and believe that salvation was, and is, and is to come, in and *through the atoning blood of Christ, the Lord Omnipotent. ¹⁹For the natural man is an *enemy to God, and has been from the fall of Adam,

and will be, forever and ever, unless he yields to the enticings of the Holy Spirit, and *putteth off the natural man and becometh a saint through the atonement of Christ the Lord, and becometh as a child, *submissive, *meek, *humble, *patient, *full of love, *willing to submit to all things which the Lord seeth fit to inflict upon him, even as a child doth *submit to his father. ²⁰And moreover, I say unto you, that the time shall come when the *knowledge of the Savior shall spread throughout every nation, kindred, tongue, and people. ²¹And behold, when that time cometh, *none shall be found blameless before God, except it be little children, only through repentance and faith on the name of the Lord God Omnipotent. ²²And even at this time, when thou shalt have taught thy people the things which the Lord thy God hath commanded thee, even then are they found no more blameless in the sight of God, only according to

the words which I have spoken unto thee. ²³And now *I have spoken the words which the Lord God hath commanded me. ²⁴And thus saith the Lord: They shall *stand as a bright testimony against this people, at the judgment day; whereof they shall be *judged, every man according to his works, whether they be good, or whether they be evil. ²⁵And if they be evil they are *consigned to an *awful view of their own guilt and abominations, which doth cause them to shrink from the *presence of the Lord into a state of misery and *endless torment, from whence they can *no more return; therefore they have drunk damnation to their own souls. ²⁶Therefore, they have drunk out of the cup of the *wrath of God, which *justice could no more deny unto them than it could deny that Adam should fall because of his partaking of the forbidden fruit; therefore, mercy could have claim on them no more forever. ²⁷And their

•torment is as a •lake of fire
and brimstone, whose
flames are unquenchable,
and whose smoke ascendeth

up •forever and ever. •Thus
hath the Lord commanded
me. •Amen.

3:11 *his blood atoneth.* In discussing the atoning blood of
Christ, Benjamin refers to the full range of atoning concepts under the law of Moses and focuses on Christ's blood actually being
spilt (W.53, 232). In addition, one may compare the blood of the
covenant sprinkled on the people by Moses at the first Sukkot
(T.49, 222). The words *blood* and *atone/atonement* do not occur together often in the scriptures. In the KJV OT they are found in Ex.
30:10; Lev. 12:7; 16:18, 27; 17:11; 2 Chron. 29:24. The passages in
Ex. 30 and Lev. 16 have reference to the Day of Atonement (see
this volume, pp. 174–83). In the NT the concept of atoning blood
is found in Matt. 20:28; Rom. 5:10–11; 1 Tim. 2:5–6; Rev. 1:5. Heb.
13:10–13 clearly equates the sin offering of Ex. 29:10–14 with the
atonement of Jesus—including the casting out of the "scapegoat"
(see also Matt. 21:39; John 19:17–18; Heb. 10:6, 10; 4 Macc. 6:29).
Benjamin uses this combination of blood and atonement three
times: Mosiah 3:11, 15, 16. Compare Alma 21:9; 24:13; 34:11; and
D&C 76:69. The symbolism of the blood of atonement is found in
Moses' speech in 1Q22 IV. For further discussion of the law of
Moses and the atonement of Christ, see this volume, pp. 99, 176–
77; and generally chapter 5; see also the notes on Mosiah 1:3, *suffered in ignorance;* 2:32, *list to obey;* 2:34, *eternally indebted.*

transgression of Adam. The word transgression means literally
"walking across" from the Latin *trans,* across, and *gredi,* a step.
Dallin Oaks explains that Adam and Eve "were in a transitional
state, no longer in the spirit world but with physical bodies not
yet subject to death and not yet capable of procreation." Therefore they "could not fulfill the Father's first commandment [be
fruitful and multiply] without transgressing the barrier between
the bliss of the Garden of Eden and the terrible trials and wonderful opportunities of mortal life" (*Ensign,* Nov. 1993, 73). "In order
to obey the command of God to multiply and people the earth,

Adam and Eve transgressed the law. Their deliberate action resulted in their fall" (Bailey, "Adam: LDS Sources," in *Encyclopedia of Mormonism*, 1:16). Robert J. Matthews explains that "The creation of the earth was a multistep process in which the fall of Adam and Eve and their expulsion from the Garden of Eden were the final necessary steps in bringing about the mortal condition. . . . The Fall was a benefit to mankind. It was part of the Father's plan" (Matthews, "Fall of Adam," in *Encyclopedia of Mormonism*, 2:485–86). Benjamin makes it clear that the transgression of Adam led to the fall, which created the possibility of sin, and that the blood of Christ atones for the sins of those who have fallen by the transgression of Adam, which was a necessary part of the plan of salvation. Compare Rom. 5:14, "Adam's transgression." See the notes on Mosiah 3:7, *blood cometh from evey pore.*

not knowing the will of God. People who live and die never knowing the will of God concerning them are reconciled to God through the atoning blood of Christ. Apparently, this refers to people who never knew the will or law of God expressly. Jewish law assumed that all people knew a portion of God's will concerning all humanity and that all people were naturally knowledgeable of the requirements imposed upon all mankind by the covenant made by God with Noah, which covered such things as the Noachide prohibition against murder (Gen. 9:6).

ignorantly sinned. An important concern under the law of Moses was atoning for sins that a person committed ignorantly or unwittingly. While modern theologies would be less inclined to consider ignorant transgressions to be sins at all, the law of Moses included provisions for atoning for sins that were committed ignorantly. See Welch, *JBMS* 1/1, 1992, 119–41. Benjamin here includes the concept of inadvertent sins. This idea is repeated in 3 Ne. 6:18, where it is contrasted with the concept of rebelling, as it is in Mosiah 3:12. The ancient mind included in its concept of sin unintentional transgressions, accidents, errors, or misjudgments: "Impurity could result, for example, from any direct or indirect contact with a corpse, even if the person was unaware of the contact. . . . Inadvertent sins . . . stood at the crux of the

concept of expiation and atonement in the ancient system of sacrifices" (W.55, 2). See also the notes on on Mosiah 1:3, *suffered in
ignorance*; 2:32, *list to obey*; 2:34, *eternally indebted*; 3:11, *his blood
atoneth*.

3:12 *rebelleth against God*. This is a most serious sin. It appears
often in the OT: Deut. 1:26; 9:23; Josh. 22:16, 19, 22, 29; 1 Sam.
12:14; Ps. 5:10; 107:11; Dan. 9:9; Hosea 13:16. The phrase is not
found in the KJV NT. It is found in the Book of Mormon: Jacob 1:8;
Mosiah 2:37; 3:12; 15:26; 16:5; 27:11; Alma 3:18; 10:6; 36:13; 62:2;
Hel. 8:25; 3 Ne. 6:18. See also the notes on Mosiah 2:32, *list to obey*;
3:19, *enemy to God*.

through repentance and faith. This phrase is found here and in
Mosiah 3:21. Variants include "baptized unto repentance,
through faith" in Alma 9:27, and "through faith and repentance"
in Alma 22:14. For comments on repentance, see this volume, pp.
177, 181, 227, 350–54, 446–51.

faith on the Lord Jesus Christ. This concept is also found in Acts
16:31, "Believe on the Lord Jesus Christ."

3:13 *holy prophets*. The description of prophets as *holy* is found
28 times in the Book of Mormon, 5 times in the D&C and 4 times
in the NT. In most cases the reference is to revelation given from
their mouths. Holiness was usually understood in the OT as referring to the sancta in the temple, the domain of the priests. It
appears that the Nephites did not rigidly distinguish the priestly
domain from the prophetic realm. See the notes on Mosiah 2:34,
holy prophets, above.

among all the children of men. The implication is that prophets
of God have been among all people in all lands of the world.
George Q. Cannon said, "There have been many faithful men in
all nations and among all people unto whom God has given great
light and knowledge. He gave light and knowledge to Luther and
Calvin and Melancthon and Cranmer and George Whitefield and
John Wesley and Edward Irving and Alexander Campbell and to
Confucius, Socrates and Plato and many other philosophers and
teachers" (*Writings of LDS General Authorities*, 1965, 1:308).

every kindred, nation, and tongue. Usually the word *people* is added to this group, which usually begins with *nation* instead of *kindred.* See Rev. 5:9; 14:6; 1 Ne. 19:17; 2 Ne. 26:13; Mosiah 3:20; 15:28; 16:1; Alma 9:20; 37:4; 45:16; D&C 10:51; 77:8, 11; 98:33; 133:37. See also the notes on Mosiah 3:20, *knowledge of a Savior.*

believe that Christ should come. These "holy prophets" would declare not only ethical teachings or predictions about the future, but would give sufficient knowledge that "whosoever should believe that Christ should come" would be forgiven of sins.

remission of their sins. This phrase is found in Acts 10:43, "Whosoever believeth in him shall receive remission of sins." For further information on remission of sins, see this volume, pp. 16, 197–98. See also the notes on Mosiah 2:32, *list to obey;* 2:34, *eternally indebted;* 3:4, *mayest rejoice;* 3:11, *ignorantly sinned;* 4:26, *retaining a remission;* 4:28, *cause thy neighbor.*

rejoice with exceedingly great joy. See also Matt. 2:10, "rejoiced with exceeding great joy." See also the notes on Mosiah 3:3, *glad tidings of great joy;* 3:4, *mayest rejoice;* 4:11, *exceedingly great joy;* and this volume, pp. 284–86, 288–89.

3:14 *stiffnecked.* This term appears in the KJV, mostly in Exodus and Deuteronomy, referring to the children of Israel: Ex. 32:9; 33:3, 5; 34:9; Deut. 9:6, 13; 10:16; 31:27; 2 Chron. 30:8 (referring to the Israelites at the time of Moses); Acts 7:51 (paraphrasing Deut. 10:16). It appears no less than 25 times in the Book of Mormon.

appointed unto them a law. Webster's 1828 dictionary includes an entry under *appoint* that refers directly to biblical phraseology; *appoint* means "to constitute, ordain, or fix by decree, order or decision," so that when Benjamin uses this phrase, it is in the same sense as "Or will I receive at your hands that which I have not appointed?" (D&C 132:10), i.e., that the law is ordained by God.

law of Moses. The phrase *law of Moses* appears in biblical texts as early as Joshua 8:31. The law of Moses embodies not only the rules of sacrifice, but also the Ten Commandments (Ex. 20), the civil and ethical teachings of the Code of the Covenant (Ex. 21–23), the laws of chastity, holiness, and consecration in the book of

Leviticus, and many rules of charity, kindness, and purity found in Deuteronomy. Because the people were "stiffnecked," the law of Moses needed to spell out these exalted concepts in more explicit and sometimes mundane terms, together with stringent punishments for transgression. This does not mean, however, that the principles promoted by the law of Moses were retrograde or defective, even though they did not constitute the fullness of the gospel of Jesus Christ.

3:15 *many signs and wonders.* It is interesting that these phrases appear together and in a verse that mentions the law of Moses. *Signs and wonders* (miracles) are both used often in the KJV OT in connection with the story of Moses and Pharaoh. Benjamin's text, in using these words and *stiffnecked* in the previous verse, harks back to the experience of the Israelites at the time when the law of Moses was received. See also variations on this theme in Deut. 4:34; 7:19; Acts 5:12; 2 Cor. 12:12; Heb. 2:4; Wisdom of Solomon 10:16; Hel. 16:13.

types, and shadows. This phrase shows that "the foretelling role of the law of Moses is made more clear in the plain and precious Book of Mormon" (Maxwell, *But for a Small Moment*, 1986, 46); "Knowing that the God they worship is a being in whom there is no variableness, neither shadow of turning from that course which he has and shall pursue everlastingly, it is no surprise to spiritually literate souls to learn that the prophecies of the First Coming are but types and shadows of similar revelations relative to the Second Coming" (McConkie, *Promised Messiah*, 1978, 31). And further, "There are in the Feast of Tabernacles more ceremonies that center in Christ, more similitudes that tell of his life and ministry, and more types and shadows that testify of him and his redeeming sacrifice than in any of the other feasts. In a general sense, the Feast of Tabernacles has all that the other feasts had, and a great deal more that is unique, distinctive, and reserved for this most joyous of all festive occasions" (McConkie, *Mortal Messiah*, 1978, 177–78; see also *Mormon Doctrine* and *Encyclopedia of Mormonism* under "Types and Shadows"). Looking at types and shadows as a form, "To the modern and the western mind all this over-obvious dwelling on types and shadows seems a bit over-done, but not to the ancient or Oriental mind. The whole Arabic language is one long commentary on the deep-seated feeling, so foreign to us but so characteristic of people who speak synthetic languages, that if things are alike they are the same" (Nibley, *An Approach to the Book of Mormon*, 212). In addition, "Divination of the future is an essential and unfailing part of the year-rite and royal succession everywhere, especially in the Old World, but again Benjamin gives it a spiritualized turn, and what he prophesies is the earthly mission of the Savior, the signs and wonders shown the ancients, being according to him 'types and shadows showed . . . unto them concerning his coming'" (ibid., 303–4).

hardened their hearts. Becoming hard-hearted means losing sight of the purpose and spirit of the law. It also has to do with becoming stubborn, proud, and unwilling to obey the word of the Lord. Pharaoh hardened his heart (Ex. 7:14), and likewise the people of Israel hardened their hearts even though they too were shown many signs and wonders.

law of Moses availeth nothing. Although the Nephites knew that the law of Moses by itself would ultimately avail nothing, they continued to observe the law of Moses strictly. See Welch, in *Temples of the Ancient World*, 1994, 302–9.

3:16 *little children.* This is the first time that the salvation of little children, as a group apart from the children of men, is mentioned in the Book of Mormon. This point of Nephite doctrine is stated extensively in Mormon's letter to Moroni (Moro. 8). Commenting on this, Calvin Rudd says that, "Before that time [of accountability] they are considered 'infants' or 'little children' and are not required to be baptized. They are considered 'alive in Christ' and are 'whole' (Moro. 8:8–12; JST, Matt. 18:10–11)" ("Children: Salvation of Children," in *Encyclopedia of Mormonism*, 1:267). Joseph Smith said, "The doctrine of baptizing children, or sprinkling them, or they must welter in hell, is a doctrine not true, not supported in Holy Writ, and is not consistent with the character of God. All children are redeemed by the blood of Jesus Christ, and the moment that children leave this world, they are taken to the bosom of Abraham" (*TPJS*, 4:197).

as in Adam, or by nature, they fall, even so the blood of Christ.
These words show that "we are descendants of Adam; we all
have a common father. . . . The blessings of the fall have passed
upon all men; all can be redeemed because Adam fell and Christ
came" (McConkie, *BYU Firesides and Devotionals,* 1982, 30). The
phrase is similar to 1 Cor. 15:22, "For as in Adam all die, even so
in Christ shall all be made alive." The pairing of Adam and Christ
in the plan of salvation is also found in Mosiah 3:19; Alma 22:13;
40:18; Morm. 9:12; Moro. 8:8.

atoneth for their sins. Compare 1 Jn. 1:7, "the blood of Jesus
Christ . . . cleanseth us from all sin"; see also Lev. 17:11; Isa. 53:5,
10–11; Matt. 20:28; Mark 10:45; Rom. 5:6–21; 1 Cor. 10:16; Eph.
2:13; Heb. 9:12, 14; 1 Pet. 1:19; Rev. 1:5; compare *Testament of Benjamin* 3:8; 2 Macc. 12:44–45; *4 Macc.* 6:28–30; 17:21–22; 1QS V 6; V
3–4, 10; IX 4.

3:17 *no other name.* For the ancient Israelites, of necessity,
types and shadows replaced clear revealed light; for the Nephites
no symbolic replacement took place, but the name was given
(B.02, 42). Nibley explains, "Why the name? Because he is all we
have. The account of him is the story—the name we refer to. You
have no identity without your name" (N.25, 469). For a further
discussion of the name, see this volume, pp. 46, 179–80, 252–53,
286–87; and notes to Mosiah 3:9, *through faith on his name;* 5:8, *no
other name given.*

salvation . . . in and through the name of Christ. The idea of gaining salvation only through the name of Christ occurs in the NT. In
Acts 4:12 we read "Neither is there salvation in any other: for
there is none other name under heaven given among men,
whereby we must be saved." This idea occurs often in the Book of
Mormon, especially in King Benjamin's speech. See Mosiah 3:9,
17; 5:8; Alma 11:40; 26:35; 34:15; D&C 109:4; 6:52.

3:18 *judgment is just.* This phrase is also found in Mosiah
29:12, "the judgments of God are always just," and in John 5:30, "I
judge: and my judgment is just."

infant perisheth not. This phrase is unique to Benjamin.

drink damnation. The sense here is that *damnation* is the equivalent of the "dregs of the bitter cup" in Alma 40:25–26 and the "wine of the wrath of God" in Rev. 14:8–11. Bruce R. McConkie says that "agency, which is the law of choosing between opposites, requires both rewards and punishments. But both of these come in varying degrees. The better man's works, the higher his reward will be; and the more evil his deeds, the greater his punishment. The highest reward is eternal life for the sons of God, and the greatest condemnation is eternal damnation for the sons of perdition" (*A New Witness for the Articles of Faith*, 1985, 96).

little children. The concept of becoming as a little child is found in Matt. 18:3–4, "Except ye be converted, and become as little children, ye shall not enter into the kingdom of heaven." "Why the emphasis on children? . . . Children will accept the gospel. They will accept the plan and obey and will offer no resistance" (N.25, 469). See this volume, p. 447–48.

through the atoning blood of Christ. See the discussion of the atonement in this volume, pp. 99, 176–77, 420–26; generally chapter 5; and the notes on Mosiah 3:7, *blood cometh from every pore,* and 4:2, *apply the atoning blood of Christ.*

3:19 *enemy to God.* See the discussion on the *natural man* below, and Rom. 8:7–9; 1 Cor. 2:14; James 4:4; Wisdom of Solomon 13:1. See also notes on Mosiah 2:38, *enemy to God,* above.

putteth off the natural man. Essentially, the natural man is the unrepentant person; see also Alma 26:21. Definitions of the natural man vary on the question of proactivity: one view is that "the natural man is the earthy man who has allowed rude animal passions to overshadow his spiritual inclinations" (K.12, 112); another commentator sees "natural men and women [as] unregenerated beings who remain in their fallen condition, who may be upright and moral with regard to the world, but who have not hearkened sufficiently to the Light of Christ to be led to the gospel" (M.23, 74). A further view concentrates on man's willful rebellion against his spiritual nature: "Mormonism teaches that man is essentially good by nature. The moral nature of man cannot be described in terms of the 'fall,' since all pre-earth men were capable of evil in its definition of that which is contrary to the will of God; 'natural' is the opposite of 'spiritual,' meaning those who have chosen to disobey God; sin has to do with acts" (B.04, 57–61). Since infants are in full fellowship with God, they can only become *natural men* because they will not hearken to the voice of the Lord (B.05, 1095). Similarly, "people are basically good" with a tendency to do right; evil is against our nature (P.32, 73); Marion G. Romney affirms this: "Men are by nature of the spirit. They are natural born spirit children of God. . . . Those who reject the guidance of the Spirit and in rebellion yield to the temptations of the Evil One become carnal, sensual, and devilish" (*BYU Speeches of the Year*, 1961, 4). The natural man is "contrasted with the man of Christ" (A.01, 30). Referring to the effect of the atonement on the fall, "the natural man, which is Adam, is conquered by the perfect man, which is Christ; and thus 'all mankind may be saved by obedience to the laws and ordinances of the gospel' (Third Article of Faith)" (McConkie, *BYU Firesides and Devotionals*, 1982, 30). M. Catherine Thomas interprets Benjamin's understanding of the natural man as follows: "Resistance to our spiritual natures manifests itself as guilt, despair, resentment, self-pity, fear, depression, feelings of victimization, fear over the scarcity of needed things, and other forms of distress. These are all functions of the fallen self, and we all necessarily experience them. . . . King Benjamin called this fallen self the natural man" (*BYU Firesides and Devotionals*, 1995, 47). Making the change from the natural man requires "Changing fallen human nature from evil to good . . . the cessation of feeding the evil desire, which will cause that evil desire to die" (R.34, 102); "The spirit is law-abiding and truth-seeking, but the 'flesh' is corrupt and untamed. It must be disciplined. . . . The 'evil' in fallen man must be interpreted in terms of the holiness that characterizes God and those who become like him. . . . The natural man is every man who is in a state of sin" (T.47, 77–78). Finally, Neal A. Maxwell notes, "Too often when we seek to excuse ourselves, it is, ironically, the 'natural man' we are excusing. Yet scriptures inform us 'the natural man' is to be 'put off.' . . . 'He' certainly should not be 'kept on' because of a mistaken sense that the natural man constitutes our individuality" (*BYU Firesides and Devotionals*, 1992, 105), and "Such is the scope of putting off the burdensome natural man who is naturally selfish. So much of our fatigue in fact comes from carrying that needless load. This heaviness of the natural man prevents us from doing our Christian calisthenics; so we end up too swollen with selfishness to pass through the narrow needle's eye" (*Men and Women of Christ*, 1991, 31). With regard to *putting off*, Logion 37 of the *Gospel of Thomas* reads, "His disciples said, 'When will You become revealed to us and when shall we see You?' Jesus said, 'When you disrobe without being ashamed and take up your garments and place them under your feet like little children and tread on them, then [will you see] the Son of the Living One, and you will not be afraid.'" Jonathan Smith sees the undressing and nudity as a sign of being reborn. Treading upon the garments is a "specific reference to prebaptismal exorcism." The garments refer ultimately back to Adam and Eve, and to tread on them "is a renunciation of sin, flesh, and the world" (*History of Religions* 5:237–38). Thus putting off the natural man is a renunciation of the natural man so that we can become "blameless before God." Other references to the natural man are found in D&C 67:12; Moses 1:14. The only reference to natural man in the KJV Bible is in 1 Cor. 2:14; Col. 3:9 has "put off the old man"; see also Eph. 4:22; Col. 2:11. Comments on the natural man in this volume can be found at pp. 17–18, 128–30, 352–54, 427–32, 466–67.

submissive, meek, humble, patient, full of love. Neal A. Maxwell sees these attributes as "*eternal* and *portable!* Being portable, to the degree developed, they will go with us through the veil of death, and still later they will rise with us in the Resurrection" (*BYU Firesides and Devotionals*, 1992, 104). Similar, though not identical, lists are found in Alma 7:23; 13:28. On being *submissive*, see this volume pp. 10–12, 13, 33, 44, 52–54.

meek. Neal A. Maxwell, commenting on the Savior's meekness, says, "If our emulation of Him is to be serious, amid rampant egoism, we should ponder how, through 'all of these things,' He was so self-disciplined and how His self-discipline was aided by

His meekness. Meekness can be a great help to us all in coping with the injustices of life and also in avoiding the abuse of authority and power, to which tendency most succumb—except the meek" (*Even As I Am*, 1985, 20–21; see also this volume, pp. 18–20).

humble. The Hebrew word that most nearly describes the state of humility required to put off the natural man is *šēpel rûaḥ*, "lowly of spirit" (see Prov. 16:19; 29:23). In Greek only one word is used for being humble, *tapeinos*, also meaning "lowly of spirit."

patient. The Hebrew *ʾārēk* means "slow to anger."

full of love. Neal A. Maxwell adds this to the qualities of sainthood and discipleship that Benjamin details in this verse, equating it with Alma 7:23 and phrases such as "humble and submissive," "easy to be entreated," "full of patience and long-suffering" (*We Will Prove Them Herewith*, 1982, 61). We are reminded of the Savior's declaration that he is "filled with compassion" for his children (Mosiah 15:9; 3 Ne. 17:6–7; D&C 101:9; see also this volume, pp. 13–15).

willing to submit. Bringing this to a personal level, Harold B. Lee said, "I am aware that I have had to submit to some tests, some severe tests, before the Lord, I suppose to prove me to see if I would be willing to submit to all things whatsoever the Lord sees fit to inflict upon me, even as a little child does submit to its father" (*Improvement Era*, Jan. 1968, 26). Neal A. Maxwell has remarked extensively on this scripture, requiring that we "strip ourselves of pride in order to be obedient to Him. In that process we make ourselves so much more useful in the achievement of God's purposes among His children" (M.17, 88; see also this volume, pp. 10–12); "Further, as it must be with anyone who seeks sainthood, Paul had to be 'willing to submit to all things which the Lord seeth fit to inflict upon him'" (Maxwell, *All These Things*, 1980, 31); "We can scarcely attain that attribute of sainthood—being 'full of love'—unless we are willing to communicate by giving and receiving appropriate counsel, correction, and commendation" (ibid., 72–73). On the subject of voluntary submission, "only volunteers will trust the Guide sufficiently to follow Him in the dangerous ascent which only He can lead" (M.17, 89).

submit to his father. Jehovah rehearses these conditions of redemption to Israel in Lev. 26:40–41; the context of obedience to parents is found in Col. 3:20.

3:20 *knowledge of the Savior shall spread.* A similar prophecy is found in 1 Ne. 19:17, "Yea, and all the earth shall see the salvation of the Lord, saith the prophet; every nation, kindred, tongue and people shall be blessed," and 2 Ne. 26:13, "And that he manifesteth himself unto all those who believe in him, by the power of the Holy Ghost; yea, unto every nation, kindred, tongue, and people." See also the notes on Mosiah 3:13, *every kindred, nation, and tongue.*

3:21 *none shall be found blameless.* An important part of ancient Jewish law was the necessity of warning the people before they could be convicted of a transgression. The Talmud required evidence in court that a person had been specifically warned immediately prior to committing a crime before that person could be convicted and put to death. The angel's point that the knowledge of a Savior shall spread throughout the world, therefore, has legal significance connected with the fact that "none shall be found blameless," for all have been warned. On the necessity of warning as a part of a prosecutor's case under Jewish law, see Elon, *The Principles of Jewish Law,* 1975, 473.

3:23 *I have spoken the words.* The angel emphasized that he had delivered *the* very *words* that he had been commanded to deliver. "From the fact that many ancient Near Eastern accounts show the messenger delivering the identical words he received from the council, it has been concluded that it was apparently important to these people that 'the message [be] delivered in precisely the same words that had been given to the divine couriers'" (Welch, in *The Book of Mormon: First Nephi,* 1988, 40, citing Mullen, *The Divine Counsel in Canaanite and Early Hebrew Literature,* 1980, 209–10).

3:24 *stand as a bright testimony.* The concept of words standing as a testimony also appears in 2 Ne. 25:28; Mosiah 17:10; Alma 39:8; Ether 5:4.

judged, every man according to his works, whether they be good, or whether they be evil. This is very similar to phrases in Mosiah 16:10; Alma 11:44; 3 Ne. 26:4; 27:14; Morm. 3:20; see also Ps. 62:12; Sirach 16:12, 14; 35:19; John 12:48–49; Rev. 20:13. For more on *according to his works,* see the notes on Mosiah 4:13, *that which is his due;* 4:28, *the thing that he borroweth,* below. For more on *judging,* see Mosiah 3:10, *standeth to judge the world,* above.

3:25 *consigned.* This word appears only in the Book of Mormon and is most often used in describing the state of the wicked: Alma 9:11; 28:11; 40:26; 42:1, 14; 50:22; Hel. 7:9; 12:26.

awful view of their own guilt. Benjamin refers here to the supposition that "in the final judgment we judge ourselves" (E.07, 31). See also the notes on Mosiah 2:40, *awake to a remembrance of the awful situation.*

presence of the Lord. Variations on this phrase are found in Gen. 4:16; Job 1:12; 2:7; Jonah 1:3, 10; Acts 3:19.

endless. On the word *endless* as an attribute and name of God, see D&C 19:10. See also the notes on Mosiah 3:27, *torment* and *fire and brimstone.*

no more return. Describing the world of the dead as a place from which no one can return is a common practice, not only in the Book of Mormon (see 2 Ne. 1:14), but also throughout ancient Near Eastern literature. See Smith, "Shakespeare and the Book of Mormon," FARMS, 1980.

3:26 *wrath of God.* Rev. 14:10 reads, "shall drink of the wine of the wrath of God, . . . the cup of his indignation"; Jer. 25:15 has "the wine cup of this fury . . . to drink it"; see also Rev. 14:19; 16:19, "the cup of the wine of the fierceness of his wrath"; Ps. 11:6; Isa. 51:17, 22; 75:8; 2 Ne. 8:17, 22.

justice . . . mercy. On the operation and conjunction of justice and mercy as divine attributes, see Alma 42.

3:27 *torment.* When Alma underwent his conversion, he reported that he was "racked, even with the pains of a damned soul . . . racked with torment" (Alma 36:16–17). The torment was spiritual and emotional but was also experienced as physical. In

Revelation, torment is described as "the torment of a scorpion, when he striketh a man" (Rev. 9:5). In the Book of Mormon, torment is often described as endless, which is a synonym for God's torment (D&C 19:10). See the notes on Mosiah 3:25, *endless torment*.

lake of fire and brimstone. It is interesting that the metaphor for hell is culturally determined by the worst conditions or imagination of a particular culture. For instance, in Tibet and Japan hell is represented by a mountain of nails and a river of boiling lead, while in Scandinavian countries it is intense cold. It could thus be inferred that the images of fire and brimstone were influenced by some familiarity with volcanic activity. In Gen. 19:24, we read that "the Lord rained upon Sodom and upon Gomorrah brimstone and fire." In the Book of Mormon this phrase is used as a simile, whereas in the OT and in the book of Revelation, it is used in a literal sense. On this metaphor, Kevin Christensen writes, "How should we understand the Book of Mormon descriptions of punishments, as prophets mention 'unquenchable fires,' or 'the everlasting gulf of misery,' or the 'lake of fire and brimstone?' In several cases, such terms are express metaphors for intense shame and guilt (see Mosiah 3:25, Alma 12:17; and D&C 19). The 'awful gulf' (1 Ne. 15:28) represents hell and separation from God. Nephi's brothers ask whether the symbols represent 'the torment of the body in the days of probation, or doth it mean the final state of the soul after the death of the temporal body, or doth it speak of things which are temporal?' (1 Ne. 15:31)" (*JBMS* 2/1, 1993, 16). Brigham Young explained, "We believe that all will be damned who do not receive the gospel of Jesus Christ; but we do not believe that they will go into a lake which burns with brimstone and fire, and suffer unnamed and unheard of torments, inflicted by cruel and malicious devils to all eternity. The sectarian doctrine of final rewards and punishments is as strange to me as their bodiless, partless, and passionless God" (*JD*, 11:125–26); "Fire and brimstone characterize the person, not the place" (Turner, "Sons of Perdition," in *Encyclopedia of Mormonism*, 3:1391). Benjamin's concept of hell appears to be that of Gehenna, the place of punishment, rather than the broader hell or Hades. Richard

Bauckhaum differentiates between the concept of hell as Hades and as Gehenna. Hades "retains its close association with death and is not confused with the place of eternal torment for the wicked after the day of judgment, which was usually known as Gehenna" (*Anchor Bible Dictionary*, 3:14). Duane Watson elucidates, "By at least the 1st century c.e. there emerged a metaphorical understanding of Gehenna as the place of judgment by fire for all wicked everywhere (*Sib. Or.* 1.100–103)" and "This association of fiery judgment and Gehenna was once attributed to the influence of the Iranian Avestan doctrine of the ultimate judgment of the wicked in a stream of molten metal (*Yasna* 31.3; 5.19). However, the Zoroastrian molten metal was purgatorial, not penal" (*Anchor Bible Dictionary*, 2:927–28). Afonso categorizes the abode of the dead as the Netherworld, adding the term Sheol, the etymology of which is "obscure." An interesting comment is that "For Israel, however, the Lord rules over the whole universe, His sovereignty extends from heaven to Sheol (Ps. 139: Job 26:6; cf. Ps. 90:2; 102:26–28). However, there is no communication between the dead and the Lord (Ps. 88:6); no praise to the Lord comes from the netherworld (Isa. 38:18; Ps. 30:10; 88:12–13)" (*Encyclopedia Judaica*, 12:997). See also notes on Mosiah 2:38, *like an unquenchable fire*; 3:25, *awful view* and *endless torment*.

forever and ever. Eternal torment is treated in 2 Ne. 9:16; Rev. 14:10–11, "shall be tormented with fire and brimstone. . . . And the smoke of their torment ascendeth up for ever and ever"; Rev. 20:10, "the lake of fire and brimstone, . . . and shall be tormented day and night for ever and ever"; Matt. 3:12, "he will burn up the chaff with unquenchable fire"; see also Lev. 26:14, 16; *1 Enoch* 48:9; 3 Macc. 2:5; Luke 3:17; Rev. 19:20; 20:14–15, 21:8; 2 Ne. 9:16; 1Q22 II. See also the notes on Mosiah 3:25, *endless torment*.

Thus hath the Lord commanded me. See the notes on Mosiah 2:41, *Lord God hath spoken it*. Again this phrase brings to an end this section of Benjamin's speech.

Amen. "The Hebrew word, meaning 'truly,' is transliterated into Greek in the New Testament, and thence to the English Bible. . . . The Hebrew infinitive conveys the notions 'to conform, support, uphold, be faithful, firm.' In antiquity the expression carried the weight of an oath" (McKinlay, "Amen," in *Encyclopedia of Mormonism*, 1:38).

The Declaration of the People (Mosiah 4:1–3)

⁴:¹And now, it came to pass that when king Benjamin had •made an end of speaking the words which had been delivered unto him by the angel of the Lord, that he •cast his eyes round about on the multitude, and behold they had •fallen to the earth, for the •fear of the Lord had come upon them. ²And they had viewed themselves in their own •carnal state, even •less than the dust of the earth. And they •all cried aloud with one voice, saying: •O have mercy, and •apply the atoning blood of Christ that we may receive •forgiveness of our sins, and our •hearts may be purified; for we •believe in Jesus Christ, the Son of God, who •created heaven and earth, and all things; •who shall come down among the children of men. ³And it came to pass that after they had spoken these words •the Spirit of the Lord came upon them, and they were •filled with joy, having received a •remission of their sins, and having •peace of conscience, because of the •exceeding faith which they had in Jesus Christ who should come, according to the words which king Benjamin had spoken unto them.

4:1 *made an end of speaking the words.* See also Num. 16:31; Judg. 15:17; 1 Sam. 24:16; Jer. 26:8; 43:1; Mosiah 8:1, 19; 25:14, 17; Alma 6:1; 14:1.

cast his eyes. Instead of *looking* somewhere, Book of Mormon figures often *cast* their eyes about in order to see. This phrase is also found in the KJV: Gen. 39:7; Neh. 6:16; but it is much more common in the Book of Mormon: 1 Ne. 8:13, 17, 25; 2 Ne. 25:20; Mosiah 19:6; Alma 33:21–22; Hel. 5:43, 48; 3 Ne. 11:3, 8; 15:1; 17:5, 24; 23:8; also Moses 1:27. Similar phrases can be found, such as "lifting" the eyes: Gen. 13:10, 14; 18:2; 22:4, 13, 63; 24:64; 31:10, 12; 33:1, 5; 37:25; 43:29; Ex. 14:10; Num. 24:2; Deut. 3:27; 4:19; Josh. 5:13; Judg. 19:17; 1 Sam. 6:13; 2 Sam. 13:34; 18:24; 2 Kgs. 19:22; 1 Chron. 21:16; Job 2:12; Ps. 121:1; 123:1; Isa. 37:23; 40:26; 49:18; 51:6; 60:4; Jer. 3:2; 13:20; Ezek. 8:5; 18:6, 12, 15; 23:27; 33:25; Dan. 4:34; 8:3; 10:5; Zech. 1:18; 2:1; 5:1, 5, 9; 6:1; Matt. 17:8; Luke 6:20; 16:23; 18:13; John 4:35; 6:5; 11:41; 17:1; 1 Ne. 21:18; 2 Ne. 8:6; Hel. 5:36; D&C 104:18; Moses 1:24; or "setting eyes" on something: Gen. 44:21; Ps. 17:11; Prov. 23:5; Jer. 24:6; Amos 9:4; and Acts 13:9.

fallen to the earth. Nibley correlates this act with "the Year Rite proskynesis required on the day of coronation when all the human race demonstrated its submission to divine authority" (N.28, 304). With regard to the outward display of repentance, "how beautiful the day when a person's conversion brings him to his knees before God in repentant awareness and a determination to qualify according to God's commandments" (Cannon and Pinegar, *The Mighty Change,* 1978, 39). Falling to the ground either because of fear or worship occurs in Gen. 44:14, when Judah and his brethren returned to the palace of the Egyptian official whom they did not recognize as Joseph; in Lev. 9:23–24, the people fell in fear and obeisance when the fire consumed the altar; in Num. 16:20–22, the people fell to the ground in fear of reprisal for sin, after which Moses asked for mercy for them; Deut. 9:18–25 recounts how Moses fell down before the Lord for forty days and forty nights for the sins of Israel; in the NT, Matt. 17:5–7, the disciples fell to the ground when the voice from the cloud proclaimed the divine Sonship of Christ; see also 1 Esdras 9:47; Sirach 50:17. "Confession of sin and unworthiness by the initiate" is a part of the Qumran initiation ceremony and is found in 1QS I 24–II 1.

fear of the Lord. This phrase can be found 45 times in the scriptures: 1 Sam. 11:7; 2 Chron. 14:14; 17:10; 19:7, 9; Job 28:28; Ps. 19:9; 34:11; Prov. 1:7, 29; 2:5; 8:13; 9:10; 10:27; 14:26–27; 15:16, 33; 16:6; 19:23; 22:4; 23:17; Isa. 2:10, 19, 21; 11:2–3; 33:6; Acts 9:31; 2 Ne. 12:10, 19, 21; 21:2–3; Enos 1:23; Mosiah 29:30; Alma 19:15; 36:7; Moses 7:17; JST Gen. 7:21; JST Isa. 2:10, 19, 21. Key ideas associated with the fear of the Lord are that it stops enemies of the Lord from bothering his people; it motivates righteousness, calling on the Lord for help, or repentance; it is the beginning of wisdom and knowledge; it can be taught and learned; it must be chosen; and it comes upon people at judgment times. This fear is a desire "to be free from sinning . . . willing to forego eating and drinking, sleep and rest, riches and honors, even life itself in the quest for freedom from transgressing against . . . God. . . . [It] is not a motive open to atheists and agnostics" (Riddle, *BYU Firesides and Devotionals*, 1987, 168). For more information on *fear*, see notes on Mosiah 1:7, *keep the commandments*; 2:10, *that ye should fear me*; 2:40, *awake to a remembrance*.

4:2 *carnal state*, or *carnal nature*. This phrase occurs only in the Book of Mormon and is found in Mosiah 16:5; 26:4; 27:25; Alma 22:13; and 41:11. A carnal state is often also associated with being in a sinful or fallen state. See the notes on Mosiah 3:19, *natural man*.

less than the dust of the earth. This phrase is repeated in Hel. 12:7. See note on Mosiah 2:25, *Ye cannot say*, above.

all cried aloud with one voice. In the ancient world, "the *ḥazzān*, the *praecentor*, or *stasiarch*, would be handed a piece of paper, . . . then the emperor . . . or someone else would tell him what he wanted the people to chant." Referring to the account of Nathan the Babylonian, "the whole thing is directed by the man on the tower. The old man, the *praecentor*, comes down, they ask questions, the king interprets the law to them, and they all answer together. . . . It isn't as if they all spontaneously recited this whole thing in one voice. It says it was in one voice, but that's the way it was done" (N.25, 471). See also the notes on Mosiah 5:6, *righteous covenant*, below.

O have mercy. Other instances in which people have asked for mercy and forgiveness for their sins are Ps. 51:1–2, "blot out my transgressions. Wash me thoroughly from mine iniquity, and cleanse me from my sin"; Ps. 25:7, "Remember not the sins of my youth"; Ps. 33:22, "Let thy mercy, O Lord, be upon us, according as we hope in thee"; and Ps. 85:7, "Show us thy mercy, O Lord, and grant us thy salvation." First Baruch 1:13–14 has another example of confession at the temple: "Also pray for us to the Lord our God, for we have sinned against the Lord our God and the wrath and anger of the Lord have not turned from us until this day.... Make confession in the house of the Lord on the day of the feast and during the days of the solemn assembly." In 1 Baruch 3:1–8 we read, "O Lord of Hosts, God of Israel, a soul in anguish and a troubled spirit cry to you. Listen, O Lord, and have mercy upon us, because we have sinned against you. You live for ever but we perish continually. O Lord of Hosts, God of Israel, listen to the prayer of the dead ones of Israel and of the children of those who sinned against you and who did not obey the Lord their God so that the evil has clung to us. Remember not the iniquities of our ancestors but remember your power and your name at this time. For you are the Lord our God, and we shall praise you, O Lord. You have put fear of you in our hearts that we would call upon your name, we shall therefore praise you in our captivity, reminding ourselves of all the wrongdoing of our ancestors who sinned against you. Behold, in our captivity where you have banished us we are at this day an object of reproach, curse and repugnance because of all the iniquities of our ancestors who rebelled against the Lord our God" (translations from 1 Baruch are by Emanuel Tov). See also the notes on Mosiah 5:2, *with one voice saying,* below.

apply the atoning blood of Christ. See Hel. 5:9, and the notes on Mosiah 3:7, *blood cometh from every pore;* 3:18, *through the atoning blood of Christ,* above. See also pp. 176–77 in this volume.

forgiveness of our sins. See further the notes on Mosiah 2:32, *list to obey;* 2:34, *eternally indebted;* 3:11, *ignorantly sinned;* 4:26, *from day to day;* 4:28, *cause thy neighbor.*

hearts may be purified. The need to purify one's heart is written about in Acts 15:9; James 4:8; Hel. 3:35; D&C 88:74; and 112:28. This can be tied in with the need for having a pure heart, which is found numerous times throughout the scriptures. See Ps. 24:4; Matt. 5:8; 1 Tim. 1:5; 2 Tim. 2:22; 1 Pet. 1:22; Jacob 2:10; 3:1–3; Alma 5:19; 3 Ne. 12:8; D&C 41:11; 5:18; 97:16, 21; 101:18; 122:2; 123:11; 124:54; 136:11. The word that is translated as "pure" in Ps. 24:4 is often translated as "clean." The phrase *clean heart* occurs in Ps. 51:10; 73:1; Prov. 20:9.

believe in Jesus Christ. "What is needed is faith in Christ and faith enough to repent" (W.56, 7). This declaration by the people echoes the specific words of the name given to them by Benjamin in Mosiah 3:8.

created heaven and earth. See Mosiah 3:8; 5:15; 1Q22 I.

who shall come down among the children of men. See Mosiah 3:5; 7:27; 13:34; 15:1; 17:8. The same phrase appears in D&C 65:5, but in reference to the second coming.

4:3 *the Spirit of the Lord came upon them.* This idea is found in Num. 24:2; Judg. 3:10; 6:34; 11:29; 14:6, 19; 15:14; 1 Sam. 10:6, 10; 11:6; 16:13; 19:23; 1 Chron. 12:18; 2 Chron. 15:1; 24:20; Ezek. 11:5; 1 Ne. 13:12; 22:2.

filled with joy. See Acts 13:52; Rom. 15:13; 2 Tim. 1:4; 1 Ne. 5:1; 8:12; Mosiah 3:4; 4:20; 21:24; 25:8; Alma 4:14; 19:30; 22:15; 29:10; 36:20; 57:36; 62:1; Hel. 3:35; 5:44; 3 Ne. 17:17; D&C 11:13; 75:21; JS–H: Oliver Cowdery footnote. "This is a marvelously happy event. . . . [Christ] is ready to bring us back into the great eternal order of things. . . . Now [Benjamin's people] have a glimpse of it, they are filled with joy" (N.25, 471).

remission of their sins. See Matt. 26:28; Mark 1:4; Luke 1:77; 3:3; 24:47; Acts 2:38; 10:43–44; Rom. 3:25; 2 Ne. 25:26; 31:17; Enos 1:2; Mosiah 3:13; 4:11–12, 20, 26; 15:11; Alma 4:14; 7:6; 12:34; 13:16; 30:16; 38:8; Hel. 14:13; 3 Ne. 1:23; 7:16, 23, 25; 12:2; 30:2; Moro. 3:3; 8:11, 25–26; 10:33; D&C 13:11; 19:31; 20:5, 37; 21:8–9; 27:2; 33:11; 49:13; 53:3; 55:1–2; 68:27; 84:27, 64, 74; 107:20; 137:6; 138:33; JS–H 1:68–69; A of F 1:4; 1Q22 III. On the repentance process, see this volume, pp. 357–59, 448–51. For further information on remission of sins, see this volume, pp. 16, 197–98. See also the notes on Mosiah 2:32, *list to obey;* 2:34, *eternally indebted;* 3:4, *mayest rejoice;* 3:11, *ignorantly sinned;* 4:26, *retaining a remission;* 4:28, *cause thy neighbor.*

peace of conscience. Benjamin refers to his having a clear conscience in Mosiah 2:15, 27, but the idea of *peace of conscience* is perhaps best represented by "a conscience void of offence towards God" (Acts 24:16; see also D&C 135:4).

exceeding faith. This is the faith that enables men to work mighty wonders (2 Ne. 3:24), it is that with which the pure in heart pray (Jacob 3:1), and the quality of those called to the priesthood after the order of the Son (Alma 13:3), as was exhibited by the brother of Jared so that the finger of God was visible to him (Ether 3:6–9).

Benjamin's Speech: Part 5

The Goodness of the Lord Omnipotent (Mosiah 4:4–12)

[4]And king Benjamin again *opened his mouth and began to speak unto them, saying: *My friends and my brethren, my kindred and my people, I would again call your attention, that ye may hear and understand the remainder of my words which I shall speak unto you. [5]For behold, if the *knowledge of the goodness of God at this time has awakened you to *a sense of your nothingness, and your *worthless and *fallen state—[6]I say unto you, if ye have come to a knowledge of the *goodness of God, and his *matchless power, and his *wisdom, and his patience, and his *long-suffering towards the children of men; and also, the atonement which has been prepared from the *foundation of the world, that thereby salvation might come to him that should put his *trust in the Lord, and should be *diligent in keeping his commandments, and *continue in the faith even unto the end of his life, I mean the life of the *mortal body—[7]I say, that this is the man who *receiveth *salvation, through the atonement which was prepared from the foundation of the world for all mankind, which ever were since the fall of Adam, or *who are, or who ever shall be, even unto the *end of the world. [8]And this is the means whereby salvation cometh. And there is *none other salvation save this which hath been spoken of; neither are there any *conditions whereby man can be saved except the conditions

which I have told you. ⁹•Believe in God; believe that he is, and •that he created all things, both in heaven and in earth; believe that he has •all wisdom, and all power, both •in heaven and in earth; believe that •man doth not comprehend all the things which the Lord can comprehend. ¹⁰And again, believe that ye must repent of your sins and forsake them, and •humble yourselves before God; and •ask in sincerity of heart that he would forgive you; and now, if you believe all these things •see that ye do them. ¹¹And again I say unto you as •I have said before, that as ye have come to the knowledge of the •glory of God, or if ye have known of his goodness and have tasted of his love, and have received a remission of your sins, which causeth such •exceedingly great joy in your souls, even so I would that ye should remember, and •always retain in remembrance, the greatness of God, and your own nothingness, and his •goodness and long-suffering towards you, •unworthy creatures, and humble yourselves even in the •depths of humility, •calling on the name of the Lord daily, and standing •steadfastly in the faith of •that which is to come, which was •spoken by the mouth of the angel. ¹²And behold, I say unto you that if ye do this ye shall •always rejoice, and be filled with the •love of God, and always •retain a remission of your sins; and ye shall grow in the •knowledge of the glory of him that created you, or in the knowledge of •that which is just and true.

4:4 *opened his mouth and began.* "It's a conversation. It's an antiphonal between the king and the people" (N.25, 471).

My friends and my brethren, my kindred and my people. Benjamin addresses his audience as friends, brothers, kinsmen, and his subjects. In so doing, he recognizes a fourfold spectrum of interpersonal relationships based on the bonds of social friendship, obligations of religious covenantal relationships, family bloodlines, and governmental authority. See the notes on Mosiah 1:1, *belonged to King Benjamin;* 1:5, *brethren;* 1:13, *weak like unto their brethren;* and 3:1, *my brethren.*

4:5 *knowledge of the goodness of God.* A few writers speak of knowing of the goodness of God. See Ps. 52:1; Rom. 2:4; Wisdom of Solomon 11:23; 1 Ne. 1:1; 5:4; Mosiah 4:6, 11; 5:3; 25:10; 27:22. For comments on the goodness of God, see this volume, pp. 257–58, 354–58.

a sense of your nothingness. Again Benjamin remarks on the nothingness of mankind, but now as part of the process of repentance, "such realization reminds all of us of our puniness before God and fosters feelings of humility—placing us in a teachable frame of mind" (Asay, *BYU Firesides and Devotionals,* 1991, 161). Hugh Nibley adds that "I don't think that would offend them at all. If you were in the presence of celestial glory, you would certainly feel that way and you wouldn't feel at all insulted. They don't feel like crawling under rocks though. They feel pretty good about it" (N.25, 471). The relationship of man to God can be explained in terms of Moses' experience, "What he saw confirmed man's worth in the sight of God even though, comparatively speaking, a meek man may feel he is 'nothing' (see Mosiah 4:5). In God's plans, man, as God's child, is as 'everything' to him. Our loving, redeeming Father has so said, declaring to an overwhelmed and meek Moses: [Moses 1:39]" (Maxwell, *Behold, I Say unto You, I Cannot Say the Smallest Part Which I Feel,* 1973, 87). See this volume, pp. 126–30, 180, 190.

worthless. On Benjamin's discussion of the worthlessness and the fallen state of the human condition, see the explanation in Mosiah 2:21. Humans are less than the dust of the earth because they are created out of the dust and it belongs to God, and for every act of obedience God blesses man and therefore man remains entirely in God's debt. Having a sense of one's present state of nothingness, however, does not imply that man has no potential for becoming redeemed and exalted through the merits of the Savior.

fallen state. This phrase occurs in 1 Ne. 10:6; 2 Ne. 25:17; Mosiah 16:4–5; 27:25; and Alma 42:12. See also the notes on Mosiah 4:2, *carnal state.*

4:6 *goodness of God.* The goodness of God is one of his primary attributes. See Matt. 19:17, "there is none good but one, that is, God." See also notes on Mosiah 4:5, *knowledge of the goodness of God.*

matchless power. The Lord is described as having *matchless power* in 1 Ne. 17:42; Mosiah 1:13; 2:11; Alma 9:11; Alma 49:28; Hel. 4:25. See also the notes on Mosiah 1:13, *matchless and marvellous power,* and 2:11, *matchless power.*

wisdom. Benjamin includes among the attributes of God his goodness, power, wisdom, patience, and long-suffering love toward his children. "Let us here observe, that three things are necessary in order that any rational and intelligent being may exercise faith in God unto life and salvation. First, the idea that he actually exists. Secondly, a correct idea of his character, perfections, and attributes. Thirdly, an actual knowledge that the course of life which he is pursuing is according to his will"(*Lectures on Faith,* comp. N. B. Lundwall, n.d., 33). On the divine attributes of God, see Roberts, *The Truth, the Way, the Life,* 1996, 413–22.

long-suffering. See 1 Ne. 19:9; Mosiah 4:11; Alma 5:6; 9:11, 26; 26:16; 42:30; Morm. 2:12; Moro. 9:25; D&C 138:28; JST 1 Pet. 3:20; JST 2 Pet. 3:15. In the KJV NT see Col. 1:11. See also the notes on Mosiah 3:18, *full of love,* and 3:19 generally for the attributes of Christ that are to be emulated.

foundation of the world. See 2 Ne. 27:10; Mosiah 15:19; 18:13; Alma 12:25; 13:7; Hel. 5:47; 3 Ne. 1:14; Eth. 4:14, 15, 19; Moro. 8:12; Matt. 13:35; 25:34; Luke 11:50; Heb. 4:3; 1 Pet. 1:19–20; Rev. 13:8; 17:8.

trust in the Lord. Prov. 29:25, "whoso putteth his trust in the Lord shall be safe"; Ps. 4:5, "put your trust in the Lord"; 71:1, "In thee, O Lord, do I put my trust."

diligent in keeping his commandments. For Benjamin, salvation is conditioned on trusting in the Lord, being diligent in keeping his commandments, and continuing in faith to the end of mortal life.

continue in the faith. See Acts 14:22; Col. 1:23; 1 Tim. 2:15.

mortal body. See Rom. 6:12; 8:11.

4:7–12 *receiveth salvation.* Another part of the Qumran ceremony of initiation involves "the blessing of those who are among the lot of God by the priests" in 1QS II 1–4. In a similar way, Benjamin is recounting the blessings that come to those who enter into the covenant.

4:7 *salvation.* "These verses [6–7] constitute a marvelous summary of the plan of salvation. A knowledge of God, his attributes, the central role of the Atonement, the necessity of keeping the commandments and enduring to the end—all these are mentioned. Further, we are taught that the Atonement comes in answer to the Fall. That is, Christ atoned for all 'since the fall of Adam.' Those who have postulated the existence of pre-Adamites create the theological difficulty of having creatures not subject to the Fall and therefore not eligible for the redeeming effects of the Atonement" (M.18, 159–60).

who are, or who ever shall be. See also Rev. 1:4, 8, "which is, and which was, and which is to come."

end of the world. Dan. 6:26, "shall be even unto the end"; Matt. 28:20, "even unto the end of the world."

4:8 *none other salvation.* The supreme sacrifice that is required of us is not a "blood atonement," rather it is nothing less than a willingness to part with our most precious possession (N.27, 588–91). See also Mosiah 3:17; Mark 12:32; Acts 4:12.

conditions whereby man can be saved. These are also discussed in Alma 5:10; Hel. 5:11. "We do not barter where salvation is concerned" (M.18, 160).

4:9 *Believe in God.* Benjamin lists six things that a person must believe. In a way, this verse comprises a basic statement of the Nephite faith. Benjamin exhorted people to believe (1) in God, (2) that he created all things, (3) that he is omniscient and (4) omnipotent, (5) that man cannot comprehend all that God can comprehend, and (6) that man must fully repent. See this volume, pp. 70–71; for a discussion of Benjamin's steps to build faith in God, see this volume, pp. 75–76; for a discussion of the nature of God, see this volume, pp. 10, 71, 253–54.

that he created all things. See Eph. 3:9; Rev. 4:11; 3 Macc. 2:3; Sirach 18:1; Wisdom of Solomon 1:14.

all wisdom . . . all power. God has *all wisdom.* See Alma 26:35; Abr. 3:21. One might make a distinction between being all-wise and being omniscient. God has *all power*—see Matt. 28:18; 1 Ne. 9:6; Alma 12:15; Alma 26:35; Morm. 5:23; Ether 3:4; Moro. 8:28; D&C 19:3; 61:1; 84:28; 93:17; 100:1; Moses 6:61; man is unable to comprehend all that God does—see Job 27:5; Micah 4:12; Morm. 9:16; D&C 121:12; Isa. 55:8–9; Wisdom of Solomon 17:1; Rom. 11:33–34, 2 Baruch 14:8–9. For a discussion of power, see this volume, pp. 134–35.

in heaven and in earth. See also Dan. 6:27, "in heaven and in earth"; Ps. 113:6, "in heaven, and in the earth!" See also Ps. 135:6; Matt. 28:18, "in heaven, and in earth"; Alma 44:5; 1Q22 I, "[Take] the heavens and the [earth as witnesses]."

man doth not comprehend all the things which the Lord can comprehend. See Isa. 55:8–9; Wisdom of Solomon 17:1; Rom. 11:33–34; 2 Baruch 14:8–9.

4:10 *humble yourselves before God.* See 2 Chron. 34:27, "and thou didst humble thyself before God"; 2 Kgs. 22:19, "and thou hast humbled thyself before the Lord"; Ex. 10:3; 1 Kgs. 21:29; 2 Chron. 33:12, 23; Acts 20:19; James 4:10; 1 Pet. 5:6.

ask in sincerity of heart. See Hel. 3:27; Moro. 10:4; D&C 5:24.

see that ye do them. Benjamin is adding the injunction that works are necessary to the exercise of faith, "I have said that we show our faith even to ourselves by our works. . . . Turning this statement [Mosiah 4:10] around, we may also say, if you do all these things, see (or recognize or acknowledge to yourself) that ye believe them. We need to trust what our own good deeds tell us about ourselves" (Rasmussen, *Lectures on Faith in Historical Perspective,* 15:169–70). Neal A. Maxwell applies this instruction: "The same challenge persists for the disciple in each age: to conform his life to the requirements of the Realm of which he would be a citizen" (*The Smallest Part,* 1973, 41). Dallin Oaks described this section of King Benjamin's speech as the "therefore what," the action to be taken following the instruction (see *Ensign,* Nov. 1997, 72). See also John 13:17.

4:11 *I have said before.* Benjamin is employing deliberate repetition; see the discussion of parallelism and chiasmus in chapter 11 of this volume.

glory of God. This phrase occurs in Ps. 19:1; Prov. 25:2; John 11:4, 40; Acts 7:55; Rom. 3:23; 5:2; 15:7; 1 Cor. 10:31; 11:7; 2 Cor. 1:20; 4:6, 15; Philip. 2:11; Rev. 15:8; 21:11, 23; 2 Ne. 1:25; 27:16; Mosiah 27:22; Alma 19:6; Morm. 9:5; D&C 4:5; 76:70; 82:19; 88:116; 93:36; 135:6; Moses 1:2; JST Isa. 29:21; JST Matt. 6:22.

exceedingly great joy. See the notes on Mosiah 3:3, *glad tidings of great joy;* 3:4, *mayest rejoice;* 4:11, *exceedingly great joy;* and this volume, pp. 284–86, 288–89.

always retain in remembrance. One of Benjamin's favorite phrases is *always retain.* It is not enough to obtain knowledge; one must *always retain* in remembrance these things. Likewise, it is not enough to be forgiven, one must *retain* a remission of one's sins (Mosiah 4:26). Compare "Let thine heart retain my words: keep my commandments, and live" (Prov. 4:4); "And even as they did not like to retain God in [their] knowledge, God gave them over to a reprobate mind, to do those things which are not convenient" (Rom. 1:28). See the notes on on Mosiah 1:16, 17; 2:41; 4:30; 6:3 on remembering. For further information on remission of sins, see this volume, pp. 16, 197–98. See also the notes on Mosiah 2:32, *list to obey;* 2:34, *eternally indebted;* 3:4, *mayest rejoice;* 3:11, *ignorantly sinned;* 3:13, *remission of their sins;* 4:26, *retaining a remission;* 4:28, *cause thy neighbor.*

goodness and long-suffering. Compare 1 Baruch 2:27–28, "Yet you have treated us, O Lord our God, with all your goodness and great mercy." See also the notes on Mosiah 4:6, *long-suffering.*

unworthy creatures. See Sirach 16:16–17.

depths of humility. This phrase is used a few times: 2 Ne. 9:42; Mosiah 21:14; Alma 62:41; Hel. 6:5; 3 Ne. 12:2; JST Matt. 5:4. See also 2 Ne. 17:11; Alma 63:8.

calling on the name of the Lord daily. Benjamin emphasizes the importance of daily religious observance, not just once a week or on special occasions. Abinadi also emphasized daily observance of the law of Moses (see Mosiah 13:30), which may be reminiscent of the daily sacrifices offered in the temple in Jerusalem. See Welch, in *Temples of the Ancient World*, 1994, 305–6. Variants of this phrase are found in Gen. 4:26; 2 Kgs. 5:11; Ps. 88:9; 116:13, 17; Joel 2:32; Zeph. 3:9; Neh. 1:6; Acts 2:21; 22:16; Rom. 10:13; 2 Ne. 9:52; 33:3; Alma 34:21.

steadfastly in the faith. This idea is used a few other times. See Alma 1:25; Hel. 15:8; Ether 12:4.

that which is to come. This phrase occurs in Eph. 1:21; 1 Tim. 4:8; Mosiah 3:1; 5:3; Alma 5:48; 21:8; 58:40; Hel. 8:23; D&C 1:12; 104:51; 128:21. Similar phrases can be found in Isa. 41:22; 42:23; 45:11.

spoken by the mouth of the angel. This phrase seems odd to English speakers, since we would just say that the angel spoke it, not his mouth. But the mouth is continually associated with words in the OT. Things are declared or spoken by the mouth: 1 Kgs. 22:13; 2 Chron. 36:22; Ps. 17:10; 49:3; 66:14; 145:21; Prov. 8:7; Isa. 1:20; 40:5; 58:14; Jer. 9:12; 23:16; 36:4; Micah 4:4; Matt. 12:34; Acts 3:21; 1 Ne. 3:20; 5:13; 2 Ne. 9:2; 25:1; Mosiah 18:19; Alma 5:11; 7:1; 13:26; 3 Ne. 1:13; Ether 1:39; 15:3; D&C 27:6; 29:21; 43:30; 84:2; 109:45; 110:14. God put words in people's mouths; see Num. 22:38; 23:5, 12; Deut. 18:18; 2 Sam. 14:3, 19; Jer. 5:14. For similar phrases see Deut. 32:1; Job 8:2. For more information on the angel, see this volume, pp. 65–66, 112–13, 283–87, 406 n.63; see also the notes on Mosiah 3:2, *angel . . . Awake;* 3:4, *hath sent me,* and *mayest rejoice.*

4:12 *always rejoice.* Benjamin emphasizes the daily or continual rejoicing that comes with and from daily righteousness.

love of God. This phrase is repeated in Luke 11:42; John 5:42; Rom. 5:5; 8:39; 2 Cor. 13:14; 2 Thes. 3:5; Titus 3:4; 1 Jn. 2:5; 1 Jn. 3:16, 17; 4:9; 5:3; Jude 1:21; 1 Ne. 11:22, 25; 2 Ne. 31:20; Jacob 7:23; Alma 13:29; 4 Ne. 1:15; Morm. 3:12. *Love of Christ* appears in Eph. 3:19.

retain a remission. Giving to the poor is a step in the repentance process. Benjamin is advocating a "modest life of practical wisdom, not the life of frantic fanaticism," which will enable us to grow incrementally and retain a remission of our sins (H.10, 165). For further information on remission of sins, see this volume, pp. 16, 197–98. See also the notes on Mosiah 2:32, *list to obey;* 2:34, *eternally indebted;* 3:4, *mayest rejoice;* 3:11, *ignorantly sinned;* 3:13, *re-mission of their sins;* 4:26, *retaining a remission;* 4:28, *cause thy neighbor.*

knowledge of the glory of him. See Hab. 2:14, "with the knowl-edge of the glory of the Lord"; 2 Cor. 4:6, "of the knowledge of the glory of God."

that which is just and true. See Rev. 15:3, "just and true"; Col. 4:1, "that which is just and equal"; 1 Enoch 25:5; 27:3. See also notes on Mosiah 2:35, *just and true,* above.

Benjamin's Speech: Part 6

Stipulations of the Covenant (Mosiah 4:13–30)

¹³And ye will not have a mind •to injure one another, but to •live peaceably, and to render to every man accord-ing to •that which is his due. ¹⁴And ye will not •suffer your children that they go •hungry, or naked; neither will ye suffer that they •transgress the laws of God, and •fight and quarrel one with another, and •serve the devil, who is •the master of sin, or who is the •evil spirit which hath been spoken of by our fathers, he being an •enemy to all righteousness. ¹⁵But ye will •teach them to •walk in the ways of truth and soberness; ye will teach them to •love one another, and to •serve one another.

¹⁶And also, ye yourselves will •succor those that stand in need of your succor; ye will •administer of your substance unto him that standeth in need; and ye will •not suffer that the beg-gar putteth up his petition to you in vain, and •turn him out to perish. ¹⁷Perhaps thou shalt say: The man has •brought upon himself his misery; therefore I will stay my hand, and will not give unto him of my food, nor impart unto him of my sub-stance that he may not suf-fer, for his punishments are just—¹⁸But I say unto you, O man, whosoever doeth this the same hath great cause to repent; and except he repent-

eth of that which he hath done •he perisheth forever, and hath •no interest in the kingdom of God. [19]For behold, •are we not all beggars? Do we not •all depend upon the same Being, even God, for all the substance which we have, for •both food and raiment, and •for gold, and for silver, and for all the riches which we have of every kind? [20]And behold, even at this time, ye have been calling on his name, and •begging for a remission of your sins. And has he suffered that ye have begged in vain? Nay; he has •poured out his Spirit upon you, and has caused that your hearts should be filled with joy, and has caused that your •mouths should be stopped that ye could not find utterance, so exceedingly great was your joy. [21]And now, •if God, who has created you, on whom you are •dependent for your lives and for all that ye have and are, doth grant unto you whatsoever ye •ask that is right, in faith, believing that ye

shall receive, O then, how ye ought to impart of the substance that ye have •one to another. [22]•And if ye judge the man who putteth up his petition to you for your substance that he perish not, and condemn him, •how much more just will be •your condemnation for withholding your substance, which •doth not belong to you but to God, to whom also your life belongeth; and •yet ye put up no petition, nor repent of the thing which thou hast done. [23]I say unto you, •wo be unto that man, for his •substance shall perish with him; and now, I say these things unto those who are rich as pertaining to the things of this world. [24]And again, •I say unto the poor, ye who have not and yet have sufficient, that ye remain from day to day; I mean all you who deny the beggar, because ye have not; I would that ye •say in your hearts that: •I give not because I have not, but if I had I would give. [25]And now, if ye say this in your hearts ye *remain guiltless, otherwise ye are condemned; and your condemnation is just for *ye covet that which ye have not received. ²⁶And now, for the sake of these things which I have spoken unto you—that is, for the sake of *retaining a remission of your sins *from day to day, that ye may walk guiltless before God—I would that ye should impart of your substance to the poor, every man *according to that which he hath, such as *feeding the hungry, clothing the naked, *visiting the sick and *administering to their relief, *both spiritually and temporally, *according to their wants. ²⁷And see that all these things are done *in wisdom and order; for it is not requisite that a man should run faster than he has strength. And again, it is expedient that he should be diligent, that thereby he *might win the prize; therefore, all things must be done in order. ²⁸And I would that ye should remember, that whosoever among you borroweth of his neighbor should return *the thing that he borroweth, according as he doth agree, or else thou shalt commit sin; and perhaps thou shalt *cause thy neighbor to commit sin also. ²⁹And *finally, I cannot tell you *all the things whereby ye may commit sin; for there are divers ways and means, even so many that I cannot number them. ³⁰But this much I can tell you, that if ye do not *watch yourselves, and *your thoughts, and your words, and your deeds, and *observe the commandments of God, and continue in the faith of what ye have heard concerning the *coming of our Lord, even unto the *end of your lives, ye must perish. And now, O man, *remember, and perish not.

4:13 *to injure one another.* See Lev. 25:14, 17. Benjamin is calling for a paradigm shift to a moral life, so that it is not just a question of cleaning up pollutions but becoming a moral society in order that his people will be able to make commitments at or in the temple, which will be followed by the temple blessings given to a covenant people. In a similar way, in a translation of Hag. 2:10–19, David Hildebrand points out a contrast between the life before "this day" and thereafter. He sees the sacrifice as being not one just of ritual purification, but also of ethical purification; in other words, it is a call for a moral change of heart in order to be worthy of being a temple people. Once this has been accomplished, Hildebrand translates Hag. 2:19 as, "From this day on, I will bless you," implying blessings for obedience to moral behavior (*Vestus Testamentum* 39/2, 1989, 154–68).

live peaceably. See Lev. 26:6; Matt. 5:38–41; Rom. 12:18.

that which is his due. See the notes on Mosiah 4:28, *the thing that he borroweth*; 3:24, *according to his works*; and this volume, pp. 193–95; see also Prov. 24:12, "render to every man according to his works"; Rom. 2:6, "render to every man according to his deeds"; Ps. 62:12; see also Lev. 25:15–16, 50; 1 Cor. 4:5; Sirach 16:14.

4:14 *suffer your children.* Nibley asks, "Why the emphasis on little children, because they are the only segment of society that offers no resistance to the message, because they are not guilt-ridden, naive. We have a subconscious burden of guilt. . . . Only the children are blameless because the others can save themselves. . . . 40,000 children die of hunger and hunger-related diseases every day; something is wrong here; that's something to be afraid of" (N.25, 467–74). For a discussion of instructions to parents, see this volume, pp. 366, 435–39. For further information see TG, "Family, Children, Responsiblities toward."

hungry, or naked. See Matt. 10:42; 25:40; 1 Esdras (3 Ezra) 9:51.

transgress the laws. See Rom. 2:27; Alma 1:32; Alma 60:33.

fight and quarrel with one another. The behavior of children was regulated under the law of Moses. A son who struck his father was liable to be put to death (Ex. 21:15), and a rebellious and stubborn son could be brought before the elders and also executed (Deut. 21:18–21). Benjamin recognizes that fighting and quarreling of any kind is a precursor to such pugnaciousness, and thus he requires his people by way of covenant, not to allow their children to fight and quarrel one with another.

serve the devil. Just as Benjamin has spoken about serving God and being in the *service* of one's fellowman, he now declares that misconduct results in *serving* the devil. Benjamin's words would probably have been understood in the strong sense of serving, namely becoming a servant to or a slave of the devil. See the discussion of the word *service* in connection with Mosiah 2:17, above.

the master of sin. See John 8:34, "servant of sin"; Rom. 6:20; 2 Pet. 2:19.

evil spirit. See Mosiah 2:32. Here again the evil spirit is described as the source of contention.

enemy to all righteousness. Reference this phrase with the discussion on the *natural man* in Mosiah 3:19 and *rebellion* in Mosiah 2:32–37. See also Acts 13:10, "thou child of the devil, thou enemy of all righteousness."

4:15 *teach them.* See this volume pp. 366, 435–39; and notes on Mosiah 1:2, *all the language of his fathers.*

walk in the ways of truth and soberness. The definition of the word *sober* means far more than avoiding drunkenness. Sobriety includes being alert, having good judgment, and exercising practical wisdom. See Ps. 119:30; 2 Pet. 2:2. "Way of God in truth" appears in Matt. 22:16 and Mark 12:14. The idea of walking in truth can be found in 1 Kgs. 2:4; 3:6; 2 Kgs. 20:3; Ps. 26:3; 86:11; Isa. 38:3; 2 Jn. 1:4; 3 Jn. 1:3–4; Hel. 6:34. See also Acts 26:25, "of truth and soberness"; Deut. 31:13; Prov. 2:13 (2:20); Eccl. 11:9; Isa. 8:11 (2 Ne. 18:11); Judith 10:13.

love one another. See Rom. 13:8; 1 Cor. 13; 1 Thes. 4:9; 1 Jn. 4:11.

serve one another. See Mosiah 2:18 (16–21); Hosea 6:6; Gal. 5:13; TB ʾAḇot 1:2.

4:16 *succor.* The word *succor* means to aid, assist, and to provide relief to someone in need. It apparently comes from the words *sub-* and *cur,* literally meaning "to go beneath" or "to run to help or assist." See Holland, "Come unto Me," CES Fireside, delivered at Brigham Young University, 2 March 1997.

administer. This is a fairly formal term, appropriate to priestly administrations or the services of a minister. Administration implies loving, righteous, organized, and effective service. It requires more than simply the act of giving.

not suffer that the beggar putteth up his petition to you in vain. Benjamin's stern and emphatic instructions on giving to the poor are borne out by rabbinic commentary (*Rabbinic Anthology*): "But how does he who follows after righteousness find righteousness? Because God will give him money to do charity with it to men worthy of charity, so that he may receive reward" (§804); "He who gives alms in secret is greater than Moses" (§1137); "All the almsgiving and loving deeds which the Israelites do in this world are great advocates between them and their Father in heaven. Great is almsgiving, for it brings the Redemption nearer" (§1142); "The door which is not open to charity is open to the doctor [i.e., those who do not give charity when in health, either will fall ill or promise to give when sick]" (§1139). Modern commentators have said, "That doesn't sound very optional, does it? After we have done all the good things we have been called to do with as much sincerity as we have to commit to the cause, if we do not take a lively interest in those who have special needs, then we do not meet the conditions [of readiness to meet the Lord]" (Hanks, *BYU Firesides and Devotionals,* 1982, 39). Nibley, commenting on a news report of people dying of starvation on the sidewalks of San Francisco adds, "What is going on here? What a society when it comes to that" (N.25, 474). See also the notes on Mosiah 4:19, *are we not all beggars.*

turn him out to perish. See Deut. 15:7–8, "thou shalt not harden thine heart, nor shut thine hand from thy poor brother"; 1 Jn. 3:17, "whoso hath this world's good, and seeth his brother have need, and shutteth up his bowels of compassion from him, how dwelleth the love of God in him?" See also Lev. 25:35; Prov. 21:13; Acts 20:35; 1 Esdras (3 Ezra) 9:51, 54.

4:17 *brought upon himself.* Jewish law discusses the causes of poverty and the conditions under which one may or may not withhold charity because the poor person has brought upon him or herself an impoverished condition. See Mishnah, *Peʾah* 7–9;

Ḥullin 134a. Tobit 4:16 cautions against giving alms grudgingly. In Jewish law, charity is said to be "a legal obligation" (Falk, *Law and Religion*, 1981, 92).

4:18 *he perisheth forever.* Poverty in the ancient world was not only a matter of deprivation of life's comforts and luxuries, but usually was a matter of life and death itself. Human beings in the ancient world were particularly vulnerable to starvation, disease, the ravages of war, and the vicissitudes of weather. Turning away a beggar indeed was setting him out to perish, to die, to be destroyed.

no interest in the kingdom of God. Brigham Young offers an explanation of this state of rebellion: "I wish the people to understand that they have no interest apart from the Lord our God. The moment you have a divided interest, that moment you sever yourselves from eternal principles" (*Discourses of Brigham Young*, 283).

4:19 *are we not all beggars.* Again, Benjamin's emphatic insistence on our nothingness compared to God causes comment, "This stings a lot of people; they don't like it at all. They try to give it an allegorical or symbolic interpretation—spiritually beggars, etc. . . . I am talking about goods and substance and going hungry . . . [not] about what you call spiritual things" (N.25, 474). See also Prov. 22:2; 2 Esdras (4 Ezra) 16:40; see also this volume, pp. 15, 74, 80, 129; and the notes on Mosiah 2:13, *neither have I suffered;* 4:16, *not suffer that the beggar.*

all depend on the same Being. Benjamin returns here to the crucial point that he made at the beginning of his speech, namely that all people are totally dependent upon God for all of their substance and daily sustenance. As a result, all human beings are morally obligated to give to their fellow beings, because all are beggars before God. A similar moral basis underlies the law and ethic of the book of Deuteronomy.

both food and raiment. Food and *raiment* appear as a word pair in several Hebrew texts. The term *raiment* includes any kind of clothing. See Deut. 10:18; 1 Tim. 6:8. See also the notes on Mosiah 4:19, *unprofitable servants.*

for gold, and for silver. Gold and *silver* appear frequently as a word pair in biblical texts. It operates here as a hendiadys or merism, encompassing all forms of wealth. See 2 Chron. 32:27, "for silver, and for gold, and for precious stones, . . . and for all manner of pleasant jewels."

4:20 *begging for a remission of your sins.* Benjamin uses a dramatic word here. More than simply asking for forgiveness, people must *beg* for forgiveness. Benjamin expects religious people to see themselves as beggars before God, impoverished, in utter need, and wholly dependent upon the loving kindness of God. For further information on remission of sins, see this volume, pp. 16, 197–98. See also the notes on Mosiah 2:32, *list to obey;* 2:34, *eternally indebted;* 3:4, *mayest rejoice;* 3:11, *ignorantly sinned;* 3:13, *remission of their sins;* 4:26, *retaining a remission;* 4:28, *cause thy neighbor.*

poured out his Spirit upon you. Almost always it is the Spirit of the Lord that is being poured. Rarely it will be something else, like the spirit of sleep or grace. See Prov. 1:23; Isa. 29:10; 32:15; 44:3; Ezek. 39:29; Joel 2:28–29 (MT 3:1–2); Zech. 12:10; Acts 2:17–18; 2 Ne. 27:5; Jacob 7:8; Mosiah 18:10, 12–13; 25:24; Alma 8:10; 16:16; 19:14, 36; Hel. 6:36; 3 Ne. 12:6; D&C 19:38; 27:18; 44:2; 95:4.

mouths should be stopped. Benjamin describes here an experience of joy so profound that it leaves one utterly speechless. Such joy is the result of a depth of need that is desperately urgent, followed by a resolution of that problem that is so sudden and complete that it leaves the person overwhelmed and unprepared as to what to do or say next. Spiritual experiences often come most powerfully when they are least anticipated, unpremeditated, and most unexpected.

4:21 *if God. . . .* Benjamin's logic here is similar to that in Mosiah 2:18–19. His moral argument is one of transferred obligation. If God, or if Benjamin as king, do certain things, then how much more are their subjects, who owe them various duties, obligated to do likewise.

dependent. Nibley says emphatically, "No one is independent" (N.29, 227–28).

ask . . . receive. The idea of receiving from the Lord what you ask is preserved in Matt. 7:7–8; 21:22; John 14:13–14; 16:24 (this verse also ties the idea in with being full of joy, as does Mosiah 4:21); James 1:6; 5:16; 1 Jn. 3:22; 1 Ne. 15:11; Enos 1:15; 3 Ne. 18:20; 27:29; Moro. 7:26; D&C 4:7; 6:5; 8:1; 11:5; 14:5, 8; 18:18; 29:6; 42:61; 49:26; 66:9; 75:27; 88:63; 103:31, 35; 124:95, 97; Moses 6:52; Midrash *Pesiqta' deRab Kahana'* 176a; see also TB *Megilla* 12b. For a discussion on prayer and *receive what is right*, see this volume, pp. 9–19.

one to another. See Deut. 15:10–11, "Thou shalt open thine hand wide unto thy brother, to thy poor, and to thy needy, in thy land"; Lev. 25:35–36; Luke 6:33; 1 Esdras (3 Ezra) 9:51, 54.

4:22 *And if ye judge.* Such judging need not be formal; see "judge not" (Matt. 7:1–2; 3 Ne. 14:1–2).

how much more just. This form of argumentation is called *a fortiori*, using an argument for a smaller or lesser group to apply to a larger or greater group; for instance, B. H. Roberts tell us that "we may get arguments dealing with the nature of the Deity, as e.g. the interesting *a fortiori* argument from creature to Creator in Ps. 94" (*Seventy's Course in Theology, Third Year,* 1994, 27).

your condemnation. This is a strong indictment by Benjamin against judging. In TB *ʾAḇot* 2:3, Rab Hillel said "Do not judge your fellow man until you have been in his place" (used in connection with *Kol-nidre* of *Yom Kippur* / the Day of Atonement), i.e., forgive and be forgiven; see the Rambam (Maimonides), *Yad* (*Mishne Tora*), *Matnot ʿAniyim,* 10:1–14, on the eight-stage ladder of *ṣᵉdāqāh*, "charity" ("righteousness"), especially the injunction to be a cheerful giver—else the giving is in vain (Prov. 22:2, 9; 2 Cor. 9:7; 1 Esdras [3 Ezra] 9:54; Tobit 4:7–11, 16; 12:8–9; Sirach 4:1–10). On the requisite works of charity, see Matt. 19:16–30; Mark 10:17–31; Luke 12:33; 14:33; 18:18–30; 2 Cor. 8:11–15; James 2:14–18; 1 Jn. 3:17–18. Philo Judaeus translated the Hebrew of *ṣᵉdāqāh* "righteousness; charity" as Greek *philanthropia* (*De Cherubim* 99); see also TB *ʾAḇot* 1:6, "Judge everyone with the scale weighted in his favor," and 2:7, "The more charity, the more peace"; TB *Ketubot* 66b–68a, *Sukka* 49b, *Baba Batra* 9a-10a, *Pesahim* 49a *Baraita*; TY Peʾah 1:1, 15c; Midrash *Pesiqta' deRab Kahana'*

28:13; 13:1; Matt. 5:42; 6:1; 7:1–2; Luke 6:37–38; Lev. 25:35–37; Deut. 15:7–8; Wisdom of Solomon 12:22; 3 Ne. 12:42.

doth not belong to you but to God. Withholding charity from those in need "is stealing, holding on" to God's property (N.29, 229).

yet ye put up no petition. In other words, people put up no petition to God for their basic sustenance, the life they enjoy, the breath they breathe from day to day. Truly, most things that we receive from God are given to us without any petition or asking on our part.

4:23 *wo be unto that man.* The *wo* uttered here in connection with withholding substance and in 4:25 regarding denying the beggar parallels further parts of the initiation ceremony at Qumran, "Cursing of the lot of Belial, his works (and all associated with him) pronounced by Levites and confirmed by those entering the covenant by saying the solemn 'Amen, Amen,'" in 1QS II 11–18. See also the notes on Mosiah 2:33, *wo.*

substance shall perish with him. For this concept see also Dan. 5:16–17; Acts 8:20.

4:24 *I say unto the poor.* Benjamin also imposes moral obligations on the poor who would ask for, and presumably receive, sustenance and support. Jewish law imposed obligations on the recipients of charity, especially requiring them to be in actual need before accepting charity (Mishnah *Peʾah* 9).

say in your hearts. It is sufficient to say such things in one's heart. It is not necessary that they be said aloud (Deut. 15:9). God looks upon the heart and judges (1 Sam. 16:7). Jesus also taught that the seat of morality is essentially in the heart (Matt. 5:28).

I give not because I have not. At times the desire of our hearts can be accepted as the deed, only when action is truly impossible, and only when the deed is not an ordinance of the gospel (O.30, 30–31).

4:25–26 *remain guiltless . . . walk guiltless.* Alma 7:22 contains the phrase "walk blameless before him [God]." The idea of walking before the Lord can be found in Gen. 17:1; 1 Sam. 2:30, 35; 1 Kgs. 2:4; 8:23, 25; 9:4; 2 Chron. 6:14, 16; 7:17; Ps. 56:13; 116:9; 1 Ne. 16:3;

Mosiah 18:29; Alma 45:24; 53:21; 63:2; Hel. 6:34; 15:5; Ether 6:17, 30; D&C 5:21; 18:31; 20:69; 25:2; 68:28; 109:1. The most common phrase in all of these is to "walk uprightly before the Lord."

4:25 *ye covet that which ye have not received.* "Thou shalt not covet" is the tenth commandment in the Decalogue (Ex. 20:17; Deut. 5:21; see also Rom. 7:7; 13:9; Mosiah 13:24). One of the many problems with coveting is that it fundamentally denies that all things belong to God. Just as the giver must accept God's ultimate ownership in order to share his wealth properly with the poor, the poor must receive it in the same spirit, recognizing the same dependence of all people on God.

4:26 *retaining a remission of your sins.* For further information on remission of sins, see this volume, pp. 16, 197–98. See also the notes on Mosiah 2:32, *list to obey;* 2:34, *eternally indebted;* 3:4, *mayest rejoice;* 3:11, *ignorantly sinned;* 3:13, *remission of their sins;* 4:28, *cause thy neighbor.* For other blessings that come from remembering the poor, see Ps. 41:1–3.

from day to day. Retaining a remission of one's sin is a daily process. Repeating the transgression itself causes the weight of the former sins to return (D&C 82:7). Moreover, failure to serve others in need is essentially unbecoming, for a recipient of remission has been the beneficiary of the gift of God.

according to that which he hath. TB *Arakin* 8:4; TY *Pe'ah* 1:1, 15b, 23, place reasonable limits on giving.

feeding the hungry, clothing the naked. Benjamin focuses mainly on the importance of filling two needs: feeding the hungry and clothing the naked. Compare Isa. 58:7; Ezek. 18:7. He does not require his subjects to achieve complete economic equality or a pro rata distribution of wealth. Nevertheless, Book of Mormon economic doctrine generally advocates and promotes an equal distribution of wealth among people. Indeed, communities prosper most when wealth is most evenly distributed among its members. See Robison, *JBMS* 1/1, 1992, 35–53.

visiting the sick. See Jacob 2:19; Alma 4:12–13; Matt. 25:35–36; further references are found in Matt. 25:37–44; Tobit 4:16; Josephus, *Wars* 6.5.3 (307).

administering to their relief. This phrase is found a few times in the scriptures. It is connected with helping the needy in Jacob 2:19; D&C 38:35; 44:6. In Alma 60:30 it is used to mean helping in times of war; in 1Q22 III it is specific to the sabbatical year and part of Moses' speech. On the sabbatical year, see this volume, pp. 190–93.

both spiritually and temporally. The dichotomy between spiritual and temporal ideas appears elsewhere in the Book of Mormon. See 1 Ne. 22:1–3. It is unclear exactly how the Nephites conceptualized this dichotomy, but for Benjamin's purposes, people were required to feed and protect the human spirit and mind, as well as body.

according to their wants. This phrase can be found in Alma 35:9; D&C 42:33; 51:8. It is written as "their wants and needs" in Mosiah 18:29; D&C 51:3; 82:17.

4:27 *in wisdom and order.* A comparable phrase is found in 1 Cor. 14:40, "Let all things be done decently and in order." For discussion on *wisdom and order,* see this volume, pp. 8–10, 16, 366.

might win the prize. A similar expression can be found in 1 Cor. 9:24; Philip. 3:14.

4:28 *the thing that he borroweth.* Under Israelite law, failure to return that which a person has borrowed was the equivalent of theft. See Jackson, *Theft in Early Jewish Law,* 1972, 17–18, 91. Jewish law placed no significance on the fact that the person had received the possession of property lawfully, whereas Anglo-American common law makes the taking of property a crime only if a person possesses that property unlawfully (Chitty, *A Practical Treatise on the Criminal Law,* 1978, 4:917; "Larceny," *American Jurisprudence,* 50:160). It was also important for a person under ancient law to return exactly what he had borrowed; otherwise a dispute could ensue over whether the value of the returned object was equal to the value of the borrowed object. Accordingly, in the laws of Eshnunna 18–21, repayment of a loan had to be made in the kind of property stipulated in the loan document, and thus, presumably, a lender could require the borrower to return precisely the thing or the kind of thing that had been borrowed. Returning specific property to its proper owner was also a major concern at the time of jubilee (Lev. 25:25–34). See also the notes on Mosiah 2:13, *neither have I suffered;* 4:13, *that which is his due;* and this volume, pp.193–95.

cause thy neighbor to commit sin. Failure to return the exact object borrowed could result in a lawsuit and therefore might cause the lender to commit sin in enforcing his legal rights, by overstating his case, or by wrongfully employing self-help to collect his property. Benjamin desired to avoid both the problems of the delinquent debtor and the problems of the overzealous creditor. For further information on remission of sins, see this volume, pp. 16, 197–98. See also the notes on Mosiah 2:32, *list to obey;* 2:34, *eternally indebted;* 3:4, *mayest rejoice;* 3:11, *ignorantly sinned;* 3:13, *remission of their sins;* 4:26, *retaining a remission;* 4:28, *cause thy neighbor.*

4:29 *finally.* For comment on final warnings, see this volume, pp. 97–98.

all the things whereby ye may commit sin. Benjamin recognized that it was impossible to number all the commandments in the Torah. Jewish law eventually identified 613 commandments. The Book of Mormon does not take such an approach to the law of God.

4:30 *watch yourselves.* The verb for *watch* most likely comes from the Hebrew root *ŠMR, which means "to watch or keep." *Keeping oneself,* using this root, occurs in Ps. 18:23; 2 Sam. 22:24.

your thoughts, and your words, and your deeds. Nibley points out that "these are the three things you produce: thoughts, words, and deeds" (N.25, 480). Alma says that people will be judged according to these three elements (Alma 12:14).

observe the commandments of God. This idea of observing can be found in Ex. 34:11; Num. 15:22; Deut. 5:32; 6:25; 8:1; 12:28, 32; 15:5; 24:8; 28:1, 13, 15; 32:46; Josh. 1:7; 2 Kgs. 17:37; 21:8; 2 Chron. 7:17; Neh. 1:5.

coming of our Lord. See 1 Cor. 1:7; 1 Thes. 3:13; 2 Thes. 2:1; 2 Pet. 1:16.

end of your lives. A variant of this phrase is found in Deut.

11:12, "even unto the end of the year"; Matt. 28:20, "even unto the end of the world."

remember, and perish not. "Remembrance is a saving principle of the gospel and a distinctive aspect of Israelite mentality" (M.19, 127). The Hebrew word *zākôr* not only means "to remember," but also "to obey." *Reexploring,* pp. 127–29. See also this volume, p. 170, and the notes on Mosiah 1:16; 2:41; 4:11; 6:3 on remembering.

The Covenantal Response of the People (Mosiah 5:1–5)

⁵:¹And now, it came to pass that when king Benjamin had thus spoken to his people, *he sent among them, *desiring to know of his people if they believed the words which he had spoken unto them. ²And they all cried *with one voice, saying: Yea, we believe all the words which thou hast spoken unto us; and also, *we know of their surety and truth, because of the Spirit of the Lord Omnipotent, which has wrought a *mighty change in us, or in our hearts, that we have *no more disposition to do evil, but to do good continually. ³And we, ourselves, also, through the *infinite goodness of God, and the *manifestations of his Spirit, have *great views of that which is to come; and were it *expedient, we could *prophesy of all things. ⁴And it is the faith which we have had on the things which our king has spoken unto us that has brought us to this great knowledge, whereby we do rejoice with *such exceedingly great joy. ⁵And we are willing to *enter into a covenant with our God *to do his will, and to be *obedient to his commandments in all things that *he shall command us, all the *remainder of our days, that we may not bring upon ourselves a never-ending torment, as has been spoken by the angel, that we may not drink out of the *cup of the wrath of God.

5:1 *he sent among them.* Because not all of the people were under the sound of Benjamin's voice, he apparently had to send priests or officers to obtain the response of his people.

desiring to know. This is a common phrase in the Book of Mormon, variations of which appear fourteen times: 1 Ne. 2:16; 11:1; 15:6; 2 Ne. 5:33; Mosiah 7:10; 12:25; 29:1; Alma 19:3; 22:3; 32:24; 33:1; 60:6 (twice); D&C 15:4; 16:4; 18:1; 49:2; it appears nowhere in the Bible.

5:2 *with one voice, saying.* This phrase in Mosiah is used when a people make a covenant as a group and individually. It is used similarly in Ex. 24:3. It is also used when a group praises or calls on God for help. It is the *acclamatio*, also part of the year-rite (N.28, 305). In Acts 4:24 the phrase "with one accord" has the same basic meaning. See Neh. 10:29; Acts 19:34; Mosiah 4:2; Alma 43:49; 3 Ne. 4:30; 20:9; 1 Esdras (3 Ezra) 9:47; Sirach 50:17.

we know of their surety. To know something "of a surety" is to know it firmly, steadfastly, and faithfully. This word is related, in ancient legal contexts, with the idea of suretyship (Kittle, *Theological Dictionary of the New Testament* 1:602). A surety is a guarantor. When something is assured or has a surety standing behind it, the guarantor agrees to step in and make good any losses or to compensate for any shortfalls. Some guarantors or insurers, of course, are compensated, but the legal concept of suretyship is Anglo-American common law, developed out of the assumption that the surety was gratuitous and uncompensated.

mighty change. When Benjamin speaks about a *mighty change,* one might consider the process involved in achieving it. One view is that this comes about by extending the love and grace the Lord has given us to others (H.10, 164); it also involves repentance, and it is "not just a change of actions, but a change of heart. . . . Part of this mighty change of heart is to feel godly sorrow for our sins. This is what is meant by a broken heart and a contrite spirit. . . . This mighty change, which is brought about only through faith in Jesus Christ and through the operation of the Spirit upon us . . . is likened to a new birth" (Benson, *Ensign,* Oct. 1989, 2–5). Our responsibility is not just to ourselves, "In a spiritual sense, repentance and growth require the flowering of our fellows, and we must aid and abet 'the mighty change.' Encouraging communications will not only stretch the shy, but the able also, who possess additional but unused abilities" (Maxwell, *All These Things*, 1980, 83). Benjamin is also talking about the process of sanctification, "They humbled themselves and prayed mightily that God would apply the atoning blood of Christ and purify their hearts. The Spirit came upon them and filled them with joy; a mighty change came into their hearts and they had 'no more disposition to do evil, but to do good continually'" (Ott, "Sanctification," in *Encyclopedia of Mormonism*, 3:1259–60). See also Alma 5:14. For a discussion of *mighty change*, see this volume, pp. 44, 284–85, 288–90, 443–46.

no more disposition to do evil. The mark of full conversion is that a person's desires are changed. Sin is no longer attractive. The long-term losses and eternal consequences are seen as if in the present, and therefore short-term values are seen for what they really are. Unholy practices and transgressions offensive to God are not looked upon with the least degree of allowance as one comes to view matters from a divine perspective. See D&C 1:31.

5:3 *infinite goodness.* This phrase occurs in 2 Ne. 1:10; Hel. 12:1; Moro. 8:3. The same idea is expressed in Mosiah 28:4 with the phrase *infinite mercy.* Similar ideas are found in the KJV, for instance, "the Lord is good, his mercy endureth forever" in 1 Chron. 16:34, 41; 2 Chron. 5:13; 7:3, 6; 20:21; Ezra 3:11; Ps. 106:1; 107:1; 118:1–4, 29; 136:1–26; Jer. 33:11. The earliest of these uses, with the possible exception of the Psalms, is from Jeremiah. The phrase *endureth forever* comes from the Hebrew word *olam*, which means "without end," "eternal," or "infinite." The idea is the same and could well be translated "infinite." Similar phrases are found in 1 Kgs. 10:9; Ps. 25:6; 52:8; 89:2; Hosea 2:19.

manifestations of his Spirit. A *manifestation* is literally something brought to hand (*manus*). Therefore it is open and plain, and is as direct and immediate as a handshake or an event at hand. Benjamin's people received great manifestations, experiencing open, intimate revelations. For a discussion on revelation, see this volume, pp. 8–10, 31–32, 64–66, 100.

great views. A full response to a powerful spiritual experience often includes the expansive view opened to the soul. For example, Moses viewed the entire world (Moses 1); to Nephi on the mountain great expanses were unfolded to his view (1 Ne. 11); Micaiah saw all Israel (1 Kgs. 22:17).

expedient. The word *expedient* is often associated in the Book of Mormon, not with efficiency or expediency in a modern sense, but usually with the atonement. See, for example, Alma 34:13.

prophesy of all things. This does not necessarily mean foretelling the entire future. The word prophecy also refers to "speaking forth" or speaking freely, and in that sense Benjamin's people were so filled with the spirit that words of joy gushed forth.

5:4 *such exceedingly great joy.* The joy here is expressed as a result of faith in King Benjamin's words, given him by an angel; a similar phrase is used in Matt. 2:10 when the three kings saw the star and knew the words of the angel were true.

5:5 *enter into a covenant with our God . . . to be obedient to his commandments.* Benjamin is here signaling the terms of the covenant. According to the *Dictionary of New Testament Theology,* the six elements involved in covenant making are (1) the preamble mentioning the names of the partners; (2) a preliminary history of the relationship of those entering the covenant; (3) a basic declaration about the future relationship of the partners; (4) details of the new relationship; (5) an invocation of the respective gods worshipped by both sides to act as witnesses; (6) a pronouncement of curse and blessing ("Covenant"). Stephen Pfann has reconstructed from 1QS and other parts of the Dead Sea Scrolls a sequence of steps that may have comprised the initiation ceremony at Qumran (paper given at the July 1996 Dead Sea Scroll Convention in Provo, Utah). These steps have their counterparts in Benjamin's speech; see notes above for Mosiah 2:20–24, 32–33; 4:1–4; 7–11; 23–25; 5:11–12, 15; 6:3. The *Dictionary of New Testament Theology* also points out that Martin Noth "has drawn attention to the most recent textual finds, which show that the covenant was mediated by a third party between the two sides." In this case the covenantal relationship exists between the people, their king, and God (see Mosiah 2:31). For a recent study of the OT background on covenant making, the role of covenant in creating the identity of a people, the manifestation of divine presence in guaranteeing covenant validity and boundaries, covenant promises and relationships, see Christiansen, *The Covenant in Judaism and Paul,* 1995. On covenant, see this volume, pp. 295–97; on relationship with God the Father and Jesus Christ, see this volume, pp. 167–69, 235, 243–44, 253–61. On the nature of God, see the notes on Mosiah 3:11, *not knowing the will of God;* and this volume, pp. 10, 71, 253–54. The idea of entering into a covenant with God is found often throughout the scriptures; see Deut. 29:12; 2 Chron. 15:12; Ezek. 16:8 (in this passage it is God who enters into a covenant with his people); Mosiah 18:10; 21:31–32; Alma 7:15; D&C 5:3. For the idea of entering into a covenant with someone other than God, see Jer. 34:10; Mosiah 6:2; 18:13; Alma 43:11; 44:15, 20; 46:20, 31, 35; 53:15–18; 62:16–17; Hel. 1:11; 2:3; 6:21–22; 3 Ne. 5:4–5; 6:3, 28–29; 7:11; D&C 132:7. *Covenant* occurs with equal frequency in the Dead Sea Scrolls (as the Hebrew *bᵊrît*), appearing fully 32 times in the *Rule of the Community* alone. Baltzer, in *The Covenant Formulary,* 1971, views the *Rule of the Community* as a covenant document, exhibiting the following sections: (1) preamble: God and the community, representing Israel wandering in the wilderness, 1QS I 1–5, participants in the covenant; (2) review of God's relations with Israel; (3) terms of the covenant, 1QS V–XI; (4) formal witness, 1QS I 5–II 4; (5) blessings and curses, 1QS II 5–26; IX 22–27; (6) recitation and deposit of the covenant. The association of a covenant with keeping or obeying the commandments can be found in Deut. 7:9; 2 Kgs. 23:3; 2 Chron. 34:31; Neh. 1:5; Ps. 103:18; Dan. 9:4; Mosiah 6:1; 18:10; 21:31–32; Alma 7:15; 60:34; D&C 5:28; 136:2; JST Gen. 9:21; 1 Esdras (3 Ezra) 9:47, 50; this is the *acclamatio* of the year-rite, but can be applied to any covenantal reaffirmation. In his speech in 1Q22 III, Moses says, "Keep al[l the words of] this covenant [carrying them out.]" For further comments on Benjamin's covenant with his people and God, see this volume, pp. 102, 187–88, 199–200, 295–97.

to do his will. The people were willing to entirely submit their desires to the will of the Father and to covenant to do his will. See the Lord's Prayer, "Thy will be done" (Matt. 6:10; 3 Ne. 13:10) and Jesus' utterance in the Garden of Gethsemane, "Not my will, but thine, be done" (Luke 22:42).

5:5–12 *obedient; name of Christ; remember to retain.* In these verses, Benjamin incorporates the three promises that are the essential elements of the sacramental prayers (W.52, 286).

he shall command us. See 3 Ne. 18:10–11; Moro. 4:3; Ex. 24:3; see also Heb. 13:21, "to do his will."

remainder of our days. Variants are found in Deut. 31:12–13, "and observe to do all the words of this law . . . as long as ye live"; 1 Sam. 12:4–5; 3 Ne. 18:7; Moro. 4:3; 5:2.

cup of the wrath of God. See Mosiah 3:26; Isa. 51:17, "the cup of his fury"; Rev. 14:10, "drink of the wine of the wrath of God"; see also Rev. 14:8, 19; 15:7; 2 Ne. 8:17, 22; 3 Ne. 18:8–9; Moro. 5:1–2.

Benjamin's Speech: Part 7

The Covenantal Relationship (Mosiah 5:6–15)

⁶And now, these are the words which king Benjamin desired of them; and therefore he said unto them: Ye have spoken the words that I desired; and the covenant which ye have made is •a righteous covenant. ⁷And now, because of the covenant which ye have made ye shall be •called the •children of Christ, his sons, and his daughters; for behold, this day he hath •spiritually begotten you; for ye say that •your hearts are changed through faith on his name; therefore, ye are born of him and have become his sons and his daughters. ⁸And •under this head ye are •made free, and there is no other head whereby ye can be made free. There is •no

other name given *whereby salvation cometh; therefore, I would that ye should *take upon you the name of Christ, all you that have entered into the covenant with God that ye should be obedient unto the end of your lives. [9]And it shall come to pass that whosoever doeth this shall be found at the *right hand of God, for he shall *know the name by which he is called; for he shall be called by the name of Christ. [10]And now it shall come to pass, that whosoever shall not take upon him the name of Christ must be called by some other name; therefore, he findeth himself on the *left hand of God. [11]And I would that ye should remember also, that this is the name that I said I should give unto you that never should be *blotted out, except it be through transgression; therefore, take heed that ye do not transgress, that the name be not blotted out of your hearts. [12]I say unto you, I would that ye should *remember to retain the name *written always in your hearts, that ye are not found on the left hand of God, but that ye *hear and know the voice by which ye shall be called, and also, the name by which he shall call you. [13]For how knoweth a man *the master whom he has not served, and who is a *stranger unto him, and is *far from the thoughts and intents of his heart? [14]And again, doth a man *take an ass which belongeth to his *neighbor, and keep him? I say unto you, Nay; he will not even suffer that he shall feed among his *flocks, but will drive him away, and cast him out. I say unto you, that even so shall it be among you if ye know not the name by which ye are called. [15]Therefore, I would that ye should be *steadfast and immovable, *always abounding in good works, that Christ, the Lord God Omnipotent, may *seal you his, that you may be *brought to heaven, that ye may have *everlasting salvation and eternal life, through the *wisdom, and power, and justice, and mercy of him who *created all things, in heaven and in earth, who is *God above all. Amen.

5:6 *a righteous covenent.* Joseph F. Smith commented on this scripture: "Surely, it is a righteous covenant. It could not be other than a righteous covenant; for the covenant was with God, to do His will, to be obedient to His commandments in all things all the remainder of their days" (Conference Report, April 1898, 66). Thus it can be said that an unrighteous covenant would involve not doing God's will or not obeying his commandments.

5:7–12 *called the children of Christ* (taking the name of Christ). Benjamin completes the covenant by having his people take upon themselves the name of Christ, "With a new name comes a new identity, and a new self-definition. Names associated with ordinances are not mere sounds, but have divine power concentrated in them. Through exceeding faith and repentance (Alma 13:11– 12) and through priesthood ordinances (D&C 84:20–22), one learns how to gain access to the enabling power of Jesus Christ and to take upon himself the name, the nature, and the power of Christ. . . . It is through the divine name that one gains the power to take on the divine nature and, indeed, to be assimilated to Christ and the Father" (M. Catherine Thomas, unpublished paper). The OT conception of a name does not make a distinction between the name and the nature of the thing named; to know the name of something is to understand its nature. In the NT Peter and John were asked, "By what power, or by what name, have ye done this?" (Acts 4:7).

5:7 *children of Christ, his sons, and his daughters.* Becoming children of Christ is recognized in modern LDS doctrine as the divine investiture of authority: "Christ is also our Father because his Father has given him of his fulness; that is, he has received a fulness of the glory of the Father" (Smith, *Doctrines of Salvation*, 1:294). Neal A. Maxwell explains, "Jesus is even described as the Father, because under Elohim's direction he is the Father-Creator of this and other worlds (see D&C 76:24). Furthermore, He is the Father of all who are born again spiritually. When we take upon ourselves His name and covenant to keep His commandments, it is then that we become His sons and daughters, 'the children of Christ'" (*Men and Women of Christ*, 1991, 37). Bruce R. McConkie links this concept to being born again: "In setting forth that all men must be born again to gain salvation, we have seen that this means they must be 'born of God, changed from their carnal and fallen state, to a state of righteousness, being redeemed of God, becoming his sons and daughters' (Mosiah 27:25). Whose sons and whose daughters do we become when we are born again? Who is our new Father? The answer is, Christ is our Father; we become his children by adoption; he makes us members of his family. Nowhere is this set forth better than in the words of King Benjamin to his Nephite subjects" (*The Promised Messiah*, 1978, 352). See also 3 Ne. 9:17; Mormon 9:26.

spiritually begotten. See Ps. 2:7; Acts 13:33; Heb. 1:5, "this day have I begotten thee"; also 2 Cor. 6:18, "and ye shall be my sons and daughters, saith the Lord Almighty." See this volume, pp. 125, 283–90, 447–48.

your hearts are changed through faith on his name. This is how Benjamin proposes his people make the *mighty change* spoken of in Mosiah 5:2. The idea of having one's heart changed occurs once in the OT, in a vision of Daniel about King Nebuchadnezzar becoming like a beast. In Dan. 4:16 a heavenly messenger says to "let his heart be changed from man's, and let a beast's heart be given unto him." The only other book of scripture in which this phrase occurs is the Book of Mormon, where it is a common concept. The idea of having one's heart changed by God occurs in Mosiah 5:2, 7; Alma 5:7, 12–14, 26; 19:33; Hel. 15:7. On the changing of hearts through faith on Christ, "As we earnestly strive to become one with Him, being swallowed up in His purposes, we come to resemble Him. Christ who has saved us thus becomes the father of our salvation, and we have His image increasingly in our countenances and conduct" (Maxwell, *Men and Women*, 1991, 49).

5:8 *under this head.* Jesus is referred to as a *head*, perhaps referring to his station as the head of this family of believers or the leader of its priesthood order.

made free. See notes on Mosiah 2:17, *service.*

no other name given. "The only way a person can come back or be exalted into the presence of God the Eternal Father . . . is through Jesus Christ. . . . That is why the scriptures in so many places state that there is only one name given by which mankind can be saved, or, better stated, exalted into the presence of God the Father. . . . We can take upon ourselves this holy name only by means of a covenant with God . . . in the waters of baptism. We thus take upon ourselves a new and holy name" (Burton, *BYU Firesides and Devotionals,* 1989, 174). Further references to the name of Christ are in Mosiah 3:17; 5:9–10; 6:2; 25:23; 26:18; 3 Ne. 18:11; Moro. 4:3; 5:2; 2 Tim. 2:19; 1 Pet. 4:14; Sirach 23:10; this volume, pp. 58, 243, 252–53, 286, 290–91, 296.

whereby salvation cometh. See Acts 4:12, "Neither is there salvation in any other: for there is none other name under heaven given among men, whereby we must be saved."

take upon you the name of Christ. Compare Num. 6:27. On the importance of taking upon oneself a new name in connection with covenant making, see Madsen, in *By Study and Also by Faith,* 1990, 458–81. See the notes on Mosiah 3:2, *through faith on his name.*

5:9–10, 12 *right hand of God . . . left hand of God.* In referring to the right and left hand of God, Benjamin is equating the name he is giving them which puts them on the right hand of God, rather than some other name which would put them on the left hand of God, with the scapegoat ritual (see Lev. 16 and the notes on Mosiah 2:32, *list to obey*). Sorenson makes a comparison with the "head" that makes one free, saying "one might imagine that [Benjamin] looked to his right at the head of the sacrificial animal that symbolized Christ and whose blood would be used in purifying the people" (S.42, 1). The idea of the right and left hand of God occurs often. Sometimes the distinction is made as to whether it is good to be on the right hand of God as opposed to the left, and sometimes not. Being found on the right hand of God is associated with receiving exaltation, and Christ is most often the one found on the right hand of God. The name Benjamin means "son of the right" (see this volume, pp. 25–26). The phrase *left hand of God* appears only twice in the Book of Mormon, both times here in this chiastic passage. Being on the left hand was a negative, inauspicious, or sinister thing. The preferred son stood on the right hand of the father. "There are a few instances where left has a negative connotation: 'A wise man's heart inclines him toward the right, but a fool's heart toward the left' (Eccl. 10:2). . . . Left-handedness was unusual in ancient Israel" (*Anchor Bible Dictionary*, 4:274). As the ancient person oriented himself to the east, favorable and warm regions were to the south on his right, but dark and cold regions were to the north on his left (see Richard C. Martin, "Left and Right," in *The Encyclopedia of Religion*, ed. Eliade, 1995, 496; Needham, ed. *Right and Left: Essays on Dual Symbolic Classification*, 1973). For references to there being a difference whether one is on the right or the left, see Ps. 98:1; Matt. 22:44; Mark 12:36; Mark 16:19; Luke 20:42; 22:69; Acts 2:33–34; 7:55–56; Rom. 8:34; Col. 3:1; Heb. 10:12; 12:2; 1 Pet. 3:22; Alma 5:58; 28:12; Hel. 3:30; Ether 12:4; Moro. 7:27; 9:26; D&C 76:23; 104:7; Moses 7:56; JS–M 1:1; and JST Gen. 7:63–64. For equality of position—right hand or left—see 1 Kgs. 22:19, "all the host of heaven standing by him [the Lord] on his right hand and on his left"; see also 2 Chron. 18:18.

5:9 *know the name by which he is called.* Knowing the name and knowing God are often synonymous in the scriptures and are essential parts of salvation. "And they shall put my name upon the children of Israel; and I will bless them" (Num. 6:27). "Every one that is called by my name: for I have created him for my glory" (Isa. 43:7). Many will claim to know the name, but in fact will not: "Many will say to me in that day, Lord, Lord, have we not prophesied in they name? And in thy name hath cast out devils? And in thy name done many wonderful works? And then will I profess unto them, I never knew you: Depart from me, ye that work iniquity" (Matt. 7:22–23). Likewise, the five foolish virgins seek to enter the banquet hall, but they will be told: "Verily I say unto you, I know you not" (Matt. 25:12). See also the notes on Mosiah 1:11; 3:8; and 5:8 on the name of Christ.

5:10–12 For the chiastic nature of these verses, see this volume, pp. 69, 370–73.

5:11 *blotted out.* This phrase occurs in Ps. 109:13, in which the wicked will have their posterity cut off and their name blotted out. It is also found in Num. 5:23; Deut. 9:14; 29:20; 2 Kgs. 14:27; Rev. 3:5; Mosiah 1:12; 26:36; Alma 1:24; 5:57; 6:3; Moro. 6:7; D&C 20:83. But the idea is preserved in many places with phrases such as having one's name cut off or destroyed. See Josh. 7:9; 1 Sam. 24:21; Ps. 83:4; Isa. 14:22 (see also 2 Ne. 24:22); 48:19 (see also 1 Ne. 20:19); 56:5; Jer. 11:19; JST Zeph. 1:4. This idea, though the actual word *name* may not be used, is often implied in reference to being blotted out from the book of life. See Ex. 32:32–33; Deut. 25:19; Ps. 69:28. The part of the Qumran initiation ceremony dealing with cursing (see notes on Mosiah 4:23, *wo be unto that man*) has to do with excommunication of unfaithful members and correlates to the names of the covenant makers being blotted out through transgression (1QS II 11–18). For *blotted out,* see also the notes on Mosiah 1:12.

5:12 *remember . . . always.* Either always remembering something or always remembering to do something is a frequent theme in the Book of Mormon. See also the notes on Mosiah 1:16; 2:41; 4:11, 30; 5:12; 6:3 on remembering. References can be found in 1 Ne. 15:25; Mosiah 4:11; Alma 29:12; 3 Ne. 18:7, 11; Moro. 4:3; 5:2; D&C 20:77, 79; 46:8, 10.

written always in your hearts. This idea is found frequently in the KJV, especially the idea of the Lord's people having his law written in their hearts. See Prov. 3:3; 7:3; JST Isa. 51:7; Jer. 17:1; 31:33; Rom. 2:15; 2 Cor. 3:2–3; Heb. 8:10; 10:16. For the Lord's saying in the Book of Mormon, as he did in the OT, that his people had his law written in their hearts, see 2 Ne. 8:7. In Mosiah 13:11, Abinadi accuses Noah and his people of not having the commandments written in their heart.

hear and know the voice. The ultimate benefit of service is that a person thereby learns to recognize the voice of the master whom he serves. "Service is not something we endure on this earth so we can earn the right to live in the celestial kingdom. Service is the very fiber of which an exalted life in the celestial kingdom is made" (Romney, *Ensign*, Nov. 1982, 93).

5:13 *the master whom he has not served.* This is an important concept: "If we are not serving Jesus, and if he is not in our thoughts and hearts, then the things of the world will draw us instead to them! Moreover, the things of the world need not be sinister in order to be diverting and consuming" (Maxwell, *BYU Firesides and Devotionals*, 1992, 105; see also this volume, pp. 10–12).

5:13–14 *stranger . . . neighbor.* In Moses's speech in 1Q22 III, Moses gives instructions on the treatment of neighbors or brothers and strangers or foreigners/aliens.

far from the thoughts and intents of his heart. God judges by looking upon the intents and thoughts of the heart. Alma realized that we will be judged by our words, our deeds, and our thoughts (Alma 12:14).

5:14 *take an ass.* See Ex. 13:13; 34:20, "And every firstling of an ass thou shalt redeem with a lamb; and if thou wilt not redeem it, then thou shalt break his neck"; the ass is ritually unclean according to the Mosaic Code, Lev. 11:1–8; Deut. 14:3–8. In typical ancient Near Eastern covenant-making fashion, and in accordance with Deut. 11:26–28 and 27:14–26, Benjamin ends his covenant ceremony by pronouncing a blessing and a curse. Here, Benjamin compares the fate of the disobedient person with that of an ass that tries to live and eat where he does not belong. To what extent can Benjamin's reference to the ass in this ritual context be connected with any other ancient ceremonial practices? If Benjamin had spoken of a goat instead of an ass, a connection with the Israelite Day of Atonement ritual would have been obvious (Lev. 16:10). Benjamin does not, however, speak of a goat. Nor does he say that the ass, which shall be driven away and cast out, shall bear the sins of the people. Undoubtedly he does not make use of the traditional scapegoat for the simple reason that using an animal to carry away the sins of the people would be inconsistent with the understanding now revealed through Benjamin that only the blood of Christ (Mosiah 3:18–19, 21) atones for sin. The scapegoat ritual, although probably remaining symbolically meaningful to Benjamin, had been superseded. Thus it is suggested that Benjamin intentionally avoided any reference to a goat in this context but spoke instead of an ass, as several reasons may elucidate: (1) Benjamin may have felt a need to refer to some kind of animal in the place of the scapegoat, and the ass proved more suitable than other candidates, such as sheep, which were symbols of obedient followers, and even of the Lord himself (1 Ne. 10:10). (2) The fabled stubbornness of the ass could have been, in Benjamin's mind, a good characterization of the rebelliousness of sinners, those that "remaineth and dieth an enemy to God" (Mosiah 2:38). Other traditions, however, could have led Benjamin to consider the ass to be adequately endowed with strong innate virtues, enabling the ass to please his master, but at the same time to be characteristically foolish, foreign, and stubborn. (3) The ass appears to have had significance among the Israelite descendants of Joseph who was sold into Egypt, and perhaps it therefore had particular meaning to the posterity of Lehi who was from that lineage. The Hebrew word *lᵉḥî* means "jawbone" or "cheekbone," words which have many direct associations with asses. (4) That the ass was used in covenant rituals in the ancient Near East generally is addressed in Hiller's book, *Covenant: The History of a Biblical Idea,* 1969, 40–41. (5) The ass was uniquely "redeemable"; see Ex. 13:13 and 34:20. If any of these ideas has merit, Benjamin might have drawn upon these traditions in creating a powerful analogy here, leading to this interpretation: if Joseph is associated with the ass, then his descendants would constitute the "flock" to which Benjamin refers. Thus the sinner is likened to a foreign or wild ass, who is not permitted to eat with the asses of the master. The idea that the "flock" here is a flock of asses is consistent with the verse which immediately precede Benjamin's expulsion simile (Mosiah 5:13). This implies that the "flock" is not a flock of passive animals, but must be a group of animals capable of rendering useful service to the master. A group of asses would symbolize such a group of servants bearing the burdens of the master. The concept of feeding another man's animals when they stray into your land is part of the law. See notes on Mosiah 2:13, *neither have I.*

flocks. The question of what animals the Nephites had in their flocks is complicated. "Twelve creatures are specified in the Book of Mormon: ass, cow, dog, goat, wild goat, horse, sheep, ox, swine, elephant, 'curelom,' and 'cumom.' . . . Some animals were included in the flocks and herds that the Nephites began to raise (2 Ne. 5:11). . . . Still, goats, wild goats, and horses that the early Nephites were said to 'raise' were not included in either the flocks or herds (Enos 1:21). . . . Present knowledge of the species in Mesoamerica indicates that there were enough of the right sorts of animals in that setting that all twelve of the Book of Mormon's beasts can be plausibly accounted for" (Sorenson, *An Ancient American Setting for the Book of Mormon,* 1985, 288–91).

5:15 *steadfast and immovable.* Benjamin, as part of changing the moral paradigm of his people so that they might be a temple people, is stipulating behavior. "The pattern is less a matter of error-free obedience to multiple commandments than it is a basic *attitude* that helps us cope patiently with our failings" (H.10, 163). The only way to remove the bonded name is through transgression (B.02, 46). The phrase *steadfast and immovable* also occurs in 1 Cor. 15:58; 2 Cor. 9:8; 1 Ne. 2:10; Alma 1:25; 3 Ne. 6:14.

always abounding in good works. Neal A. Maxwell explained, "the works we are to do are those things which He did—and of which he told us to go and 'do likewise'" (Maxwell, *Even As I Am,* 1985, 31–32). He further elucidated, "Faith, hope, and charity draw to them other needed virtues, such as patience and temperance. We will be abounding in good works if we have faith, hope, and charity (Alma 7:24), because, knowing that there is divine purpose in life and personal accountability, we also know that what we do really matters" (Maxwell, *Notwithstanding My Weakness,* 1981, 48–49). See also Ether 12:4.

seal you his . . . everlasting salvation and eternal life. See John 6:27; 2 Cor. 1:22; Eph. 4:30; 2 Tim. 2:19; Rev. 7:2–8; 9:4; D&C 68:12; 77:8–9, 11; 124:124; 131:5. In Alma 34:35 we read that it is possible to be sealed unto Satan. The phrase *everlasting salvation* occurs in Isa. 45:17; Alma 26:15; D&C 6:3; 11:3; 12:3; and 43:25. This phrase refers to the Jewish New Year (*Rosh ha-Shanah*) and Day of Atonement (*Yom Kippur*) greeting: "May you be inscribed for a good sealing!" The closing of the Qumran initiation ceremony, the Maskil's closing blessing of the community is given in 1QSb IV 25–26, which reads, "You shall be around, serving in the temple of the kingdom, sharing the lot with the angels of the face and the Council of the Community [. . .] for eternal time and for all the perpetual periods."

brought to heaven. Hugh Nibley comments on the change in tone, "Notice the last verse of the preceding chapter, verse 15. It ends on a very upbeat affair. This is an interesting thing about this meeting. This was at the end of the very brilliant reign of Benjamin, who has made them victorious over their enemies and assured prosperity in the land. Things were going wonderfully. They are at the peak of their power, glory, and influence. It must have been a splendid affair, and all Benjamin does during his whole speech is to throw cold water on their pride, etc. Don't get any ideas that you are anybody at all. He really cuts them down to size again and again. . . . We are less than the dust. We are nothing and have no right to claim anything at all. He goes on and on; that's the whole theme. Then when he gets to the end of his speech, it's upbeat" (*Teachings of the Book of Mormon*, 2:9).

everlasting salvation. "And because it is the power of God that saves men, it includes both what the Lord does for us and what we must do for ourselves to be saved. On his part it is the atonement; on our part it is obedience to all that is given us of God. Thus the gospel includes every truth, every principle, every law—all that men must believe and know. Thus it includes every ordinance, every rite, every performance—all that men must do to please their Maker. Thus it includes every priesthood, every key, every power—all that men must receive to have their acts bound on earth and sealed eternally in the heavens. The fulness of the everlasting gospel, meaning all that is needed to enable men to gain a fulness of *everlasting salvation*, has been given of God in successive dispensations" (McConkie, *The Millennial Messiah*, 1982, 98).

wisdom, and power, and justice, and mercy. God is ascribed as having the attributes of wisdom, mercy, power, and justice. While there are many passages in which he is ascribed one of these attributes separately, several of them are combined in the following references: Ps. 136:5; Prov. 1:3; Jer. 10:12; 51:15; 1 Cor. 1:24; Rev. 5:12; 7:12; 2 Ne. 2:12; 9:8; Jacob 4:10; Mosiah 4:6, 9; Alma 26:29, 35; 31:35; Moses 6:61. Many similar references can be found in the Dead Sea Scrolls.

created all things, in heaven and in earth. Notice this reference to God, harking back to elements in the new and sacred name given in Mosiah 3:8. With this compare ʾēl ʿelyôn qôneh šāmayim wāʾāreṣ, translated as "God most high, creator of heaven and earth" (see Habel, *Journal of Biblical Literature* 91, 1972, 321–37), or "God most high, lord / possessor of heaven and earth (in the traditional-revisionist reflections of Lipinski, "qānāh," *Theologisches Wörterbuch zum Alten Testament*, 1993, 7:67–68. This phrase is also to be compared with the Phoenician-Picture Hittite Inscription of Azitawadda from Karatepe (see Donner and Röllig, *Kanaanäische und Aramäische Inschriften*, 1973, 26:III:18, vol. 1:6), and in a neo-Punic inscription from Leptis (see ibid., 129:1, vol. 1:25). Elkunirša is also to be found in a Canaanite myth found in Hittite tablets from Boghazköy (see Hoffner, *Revue hittite et asianique* 23, 1965, 5-16; cf. also the discussion of these materials in Pope, *El in the Ugaritic Texts*, 1955, 51–52, and Astour, *Hellenosemitica: An Ethnic and Cultural Study in West Semitic Impact on Mycenaean Greece*, 1967, 206, where they are connected with figures in Mycenaean-Greek myth and legend). The concept of God in heaven and on the earth is found in Gen. 1:1; JST Gen. 1:3; 2:6; Josh. 2:11; 1 Chron. 29:11; Ps. 113:6; 135:6; Dan. 6:27; Joel 2:30; Matt. 28:18; Col. 1:16; Rev. 10:6; Mosiah 4:2, 9; Alma 18:28; 22:10; Morm. 9:17; Moses 2:1; 3:4–5.

God above all. "This designation [Most High] connotes a state of supreme exaltation in rank, power, and dignity; it indicates that each of these Gods is God above all. Obviously the Father is the Most High God in the literal sense for he is the God of the Son as well as the God of all men. (John 20:17.) The Son, however, is the Most High God in the sense that by divine investiture of authority, he is endowed with the power and authority of the Father, speaks in his name as though he were the Father, and therefore (having the fulness of the Father) he thinks it 'not robbery to be equal with God' (Philip. 2:6)" (McConkie, *Mormon Doctrine*, 1996, 516). See 2 Chron. 2:5; 1 Ne. 13:30.

Epilogue (Mosiah 6:1–7)

⁶ʼ¹And now, king Benjamin thought it was expedient, after having finished speaking to the people, that he should •take the names of all those who had entered into a covenant with God to •keep his commandments. ²And it came to pass that there was not one soul, except it were little children, but who had entered into the covenant and had taken upon them the name of Christ. ³And again, it came to pass that when king Benjamin had made an end of all these things, and had •consecrated his son Mosiah to be •a ruler and a •king over his people, and had given him •all the charges concerning the kingdom, and also had appointed •priests to teach the people, that thereby they might •hear and know the commandments of God, and to •stir them up in remembrance of •the oath which they had made, he dismissed the multitude, and they returned, every one, •according to their families, •to their own houses.

⁴And Mosiah began to reign •in his father's stead. And he began to reign in the •thirtieth year of his age, making in the whole, •about four hundred and seventy-six years from the time that

Lehi left Jerusalem. ⁵And king Benjamin lived three years ⸱and he died. ⁶And it came to pass that king ⸱Mosiah did walk in the ways of the Lord, and did observe his ⸱judgments and his statutes, and did keep his commandments in all things whatsoever he commanded him. ⁷And king Mosiah did cause his people that they should ⸱till the earth. And he also, himself, did till the earth, that thereby he might not become burdensome to his people, that he might do according to that which his father had done in all things. And there was ⸱no contention among all his people for the space of three years.

6:1 *take the names.* This correlates to the recording of names of covenanters in ancient Israel (T.49, 224). Censuses were taken in ancient Israel, and six are recorded in the OT: Moses' first census (Num. 1:46; 3:39; Ex. 38:26), Moses' second census (Num. 26:51), King David's first census (2 Sam. 24:9), King David's second census (1 Chron. 21:5), Solomon's census of foreigners (2 Chron. 2:17), and the census after the return from the Exile (Ezra 2:64–65). With the possible exception of Ezra's census and Solomon's census of foreigners, only men were numbered (Slattery, *Bible Review* 6/3, June 1992, 16). Stephen Pfann includes census taking, with oaths and immersions, as part of the initiation ceremony into the community at Qumran. 1QS III 11–12 reads, "In this way he will be admitted by means of atonement pleasing to God, and for him it will be the covenant of an everlasting Community." See also Josephus, *Wars* 2.139–42; notes on Mosiah 2:2, *he never doth vary*, above.

keep his commandments. See Deut. 28:45; 29:12 (29:9–14); 30:10; Ezek. 16:8; Neh. 10:29; 1 Esdras (3 Ezra) 9:47, 50; Mosiah 5:5; 18:10.

6:3 *consecrated his son . . . to be . . . a king.* See Judg. 9:8, 15; 1 Sam. 2:10; 15:1, 17; 26:16; 2 Sam. 2:4, 7; 3:39; 5:3, 17; 12:7; 22:51; 1 Kgs. 1:34, 39, 45; 5:1; 19:15–16; 2 Kgs. 9:3, 6, 12; 11:12; 23:30; 1 Chron. 11:3; 14:8; 29:22; 2 Chron. 23:11; Ps. 18:50; Jacob 1:9;

Mosiah 2:11; Alma 2:9; Ether 6:22, 27; 9:4, 14–15; 10:10, 16. See also this volume, pp. 238–39, 247–50; and the notes on Mosiah 2:11, *consecrated.*

a ruler and a king. These words and similar forms often appear as a word pair. For example, in 1 Ne. 2:22, ruler: teacher; in 1 Ne 16:38 and Mosiah 2:11, ruler: king; in Jacob 1:9, Mosiah 1:10, 2:30, and 23:39, king: ruler. These expressions seem to qualify or delimit the concept of kingship among the Nephites: "So far he will go in the traditional claim to divine rule, but no farther: he has been elected by acclamation of the people, as the king always must at the Great Assembly, and the Lord has 'suffered' him to be a ruler and a king. In all this part of his speech concerning his own status, Benjamin is plainly aware of the conventional claims of kingship, which he is consciously renouncing" (Nibley, *An Approach to the Book of Mormon*, 1988, 300–301).

king over his people. See Mosiah 2:4; 23:13; 1 Sam. 15:1, "anoint thee to be king over his people"; 1 Kgs. 1:35; 19:15; 2 Chron. 11:22; see also Lev. 16:32; Ex. 18:21; 1 Sam. 11:14–15; 12:13–16; 2 Sam. 3:17; 7:8; 1 Chron. 28:4; 2 Chron. 6:5; 7:18; 9:8; Acts 7:35; 13:22.

all the charges. In coronation ceremonies, the old king or some other authority typically charged the new king with responsiblity for the affairs of the kingdom. David charged Solomon to discharge all his obligations as king (1 Kgs. 2:1–9).

priests to teach the people. See 2 Chron. 17:8–9, "And with them he sent Levites, . . . priests. And they taught in Judah, and had the book of the law of the Lord with them, and went about throughout all the cities of Judah, and taught the people"; see also Ezra 7:13–26; 1 Esdras (3 Ezra) 9:48–49, 53; 1 Ne. 12:8; 2 Ne. 5:26; 6:2; Jacob 1:18–19; Mosiah 2:4; 8:3; 25:19–21; 3 Ne. 13:25; 1Q22 I.

hear. Hearing the law implies a regular oral recitation of the law. See Deut. 31:10–13.

stir them up in remembrance. See the notes on Mosiah 1:16; 2:41; 4:11, 30; 5:12 on remembering.

the oath which they had made. Oaths would have been sworn in connection with the making of covenants.

according to their families. See Mosiah 2:5; Num. 4:49, "every one according to his service, and according to his burden"; Num. 15:12, "every one according to their number" (4:29, "number them after their families, by the house of their fathers"); 2 Kgs. 23:35, "every one according to his taxation"; Gen. 36:40; 47:12; Num. 26:50; Josh. 13:15.

to their own houses. The fact that the people returned to their houses is noteworthy. At the end of this assembly or coronation festival it was no longer necessary to dwell in tents.

6:4 *in his father's stead.* A similar phrase is found in Lev. 16:32, "consecrate . . . in his father's stead"; see also 2 Kgs. 23:30; 2 Chron. 36:1.

thirtieth year of his age. That is, twenty-nine years of age; see Jer. 1:2, "in the thirteenth year of his reign"; Mosiah 9:14.

about four hundred and seventy-six years. The date is imprecise. Apparently the Nephite chronologers were not sure exactly how many years had transpired between the time of Lehi and the time of Benjamin. Nevertheless, during this period, the Nephites were exceedingly strict in keeping the law of Moses, apparently including its calendrical requirements (Jarom 1:5). Later, they would know exactly how many years there were between King Benjamin and the coming of Christ, but it may have been necessary for them to use this approximate number in order to create a precise 600 years, consistent with the prophecies that Christ would come 600 years after Lehi had left Jerusalem.

6:5 *and he died.* Benjamin was possibly about seventy-five years old at his death. See this volume, p. 27.

6:6 *Mosiah did walk in the ways of the Lord.* The idea of walking in the Lord's way is a continual theme in the scriptures. See Deut. 5:33; 8:6; 10:12; 11:22; 13:5; 19:9; 26:17; 28:9; 30:16; Josh. 22:5; Judg. 2:17, 22; 1 Kgs. 2:3; 11:33; 2 Kgs. 21:22; 2 Chron. 6:16; Ps. 86:11; 119:1; 128:1; Isa. 2:3; 42:24; Jer. 6:16; 7:23; 42:3; Hosea 14:9; Micah 4:2; Zech. 3:7; 2 Ne. 12:3; Mosiah 23:14; 29:43; Alma 7:9; 25:14; 41:8; Ether 10:2. Many references to this can also be found in the Dead Sea Scrolls. The fact that so many references come from

Deuteronomy signals a heavy influence on Book of Mormon teachers and writers.

judgments; statutes; commandments. These three expressions occur frequently together in the OT, alluding to the idea that they are distinct; see Lev. 26:15; Deut. 5:31; 6:1; 7:11; 8:11; 11:1; 26:17; 30:16; 1 Kgs. 2:3; 6:12; 8:58; 2 Chron. 19:10; Neh. 1:7; 9:13; 10:29; 1 Ne. 17:22; 2 Ne. 5:10; Alma 8:17; 58:40; Hel. 3:20; 15:5. Again the large number of Deuteronomy references is significant. These three words probably correspond to the Hebrew *mishpatim, huqqot,* and *mitzvot.* See Welch, *Reexploring,* pp. 62–65.

6:7 *till the earth.* The fact that the king needed to cause the people to return to farming may indicate the close of a sabbatical or jubilee year in which the land had lain fallow.

no contention. There being no contention in the land is a Book of Mormon phenomenon rarely chronicled, and is found in Mosiah 1:1; 6:7; Hel. 3:1–2; 4 Ne. 1:13, 15, 18.

BIBLIOGRAPHY TO THE APPENDIX

A.01. Anderson, Kenneth W. "What Parents Should Teach Their Children from the Book of Mosiah." In *The Book of Mormon: Mosiah, Salvation Only through Christ*, ed. Monte S. Nyman and Charles D. Tate Jr., 23–36. Provo, Utah: BYU Religious Studies Center, 1991.

B.02. Black, Susan Easton. "King Benjamin: In the Service of Your God." In *The Book of Mormon: Mosiah, Salvation Only through Christ*, ed. Monte S. Nyman and Charles D. Tate Jr., 37–48. Provo, Utah: BYU Religious Studies Center, 1991.

B.03. Boruchowitz, David E. "Who Hast Kept Us and Preserved Us," unpublished manuscript.

B.04. Boyd, George T. "A Mormon Concept of Man." *Dialogue* 3/1 (1968): 55–71.

B.05. Burton, Alma P. "The Natural Man . . . An Enemy to God?" *Improvement Era* (December 1965): 1094–95, 1182–83; (January 1966): 26–27, 63.

D.06. Donaldson, Lee L. "Benjamin and Noah: The Principle of Dominion." In *The Book of Mormon: Mosiah, Salvation Only through Christ*, ed. Monte S. Nyman and Charles D. Tate Jr., 49–58. Provo, Utah: BYU Religious Studies Center, 1991.

E.07. England, Eugene. "Benjamin, the Great King." *Ensign* (December 1976): 26–31.

E.08. England, Eugene. "'Means unto Repentance': Unique Book of Mormon Insights into Christ's At-one-ment." In *Rediscovering the Book of Mormon*, ed. John L. Sorenson and Melvin J. Thorne, 153–67. Salt Lake City: Deseret Book and FARMS, 1991.

E.09. England, Eugene. "Why Nephi Killed Laban: Reflections on the Truth of the Book of Mormon." *Dialogue* 22/3 (1989): 32–51.

H.10. Hafen, Bruce C., and Marie K. Hafen. "Ten Insights from King Benjamin about the Atonement," 160–67. In *The Belonging Heart: The Atonement and Relationships with God and Family*. Salt Lake City: Deseret Book, 1994.

K.11. Kerr, Todd R. "Ancient Aspects of Nephite Kingship in the Book of Mormon." *Journal of Book of Mormon Studies* 1/1 (1992): 85–118.

K.12. Kimball, Spencer W. "Ocean Currents and Family Influences." *Ensign* (November 1974): 110–13.

L.13. Lund, Gerald N. "Divine Indebtedness and the Atonement." In *The Book of Mormon: Mosiah, Salvation Only through Christ*, ed. Monte S. Nyman and Charles D. Tate Jr., 73–90. Provo, Utah: BYU Religious Studies Center, 1991.

M.14. Madsen, Truman G. "The Commanding Image of Christ." Address given to the Brigham Young University student body, 16 November 1965.

M.15. Maxwell, Neal A. "The Children of Christ." In *The Book of Mormon: Mosiah, Salvation Only through Christ*, ed. Monte S. Nyman and Charles D. Tate Jr., 1–22. Provo, Utah: BYU Religious Studies Center, 1991.

M.16. Maxwell, Neal A. "King Benjamin's Manual of Discipleship." *Ensign* (January 1992): 8–13.

M.17. Maxwell, Neal A. "Willing to Submit." In *"Not My Will, But Thine,"* 87–111. Salt Lake City: Bookcraft, 1968.

M.18. McConkie, Joseph Fielding, and Robert L. Millet. *Jacob through Mosiah*. Vol. 2 of *Doctrinal Commentary on the Book of Mormon*, 127–80. Salt Lake City: Bookcraft, 1988.

M.19. Midgley, Louis C. "O Man, Remember and Perish Not." In *Reexploring the Book of Mormon*, ed. John W. Welch, 127–29. Salt Lake City: Deseret Book and FARMS, 1992.

M.20. Millet, Robert L. "Benjamin: King, Prophet, Theologian." Video transcript, 2 parts, Provo, Utah: FARMS, 1996.

M.21. Millet, Robert L. "Growing in the Pure Love of Christ." In *The Power of the Word: Saving Doctrines from the Book of Mormon*, 230–48. Salt Lake City: Deseret Book, 1994.

M.22. Millet, Robert L. "The Natural Man: An Enemy to God." In *The Book of Mormon: Mosiah, Salvation Only through Christ*, ed. Monte S. Nyman and Charles D.

Tate Jr., 139–60. Provo, Utah: BYU Religious Studies Center, 1991.

M.23. Millet, Robert L. "Putting Off the Natural Man." In *The Power of the Word: Saving Doctrines from the Book of Mormon,* 70–86. Salt Lake City: Deseret Book, 1994.

N.24. Nibley, Hugh W. "Gifts." In *Approaching Zion,* 85–117. Salt Lake City: Deseret Book and FARMS, 1989.

N.25. Nibley, Hugh W. "King Benjamin's Speech." In *Teachings of the Book of Mormon: Semester 1,* 437–82. Provo, Utah: FARMS, 1993.

N.26. Nibley, Hugh W. "Kingship: Covenants." In *Teachings of the Book of Mormon: Semester 2,* 1–15. Provo, Utah: FARMS, 1993.

N.27. Nibley, Hugh W. "The Meaning of the Atonement." In *Approaching Zion,* 554–614. Salt Lake City: Deseret Book and FARMS, 1989.

N.28. Nibley, Hugh W. "Old World Ritual in the New World." In *An Approach to the Book of Mormon,* 3rd ed., 295–310. Salt Lake City: Deseret Book and FARMS, 1988.

N.29. Nibley, Hugh W. "Work We Must, but the Lunch Is Free." In *Approaching Zion,* 202–51. Salt Lake City: Deseret Book and FARMS, 1989.

O.30. Oaks, Dallin H. "The Desires of Our Hearts." In *BYU Fireside and Devotional Speeches, 1985–86,* 27–31. Provo, Utah: Brigham Young University, 1986.

O.31. Ostler, Blake T. "The Covenant Tradition in the Book of Mormon." In *Rediscovering the Book of Mormon,* ed. John L. Sorenson and Melvin J. Thorne, 230–40. Salt Lake City: Deseret Book and FARMS, 1991.

P.32.   Packer, Boyd K. "We Are Children of God." In *Teach Ye Diligently*, 72–73. Salt Lake City: Deseret Book, 1975.

P.33.   Pew, W. Ralph. "For the Sake of Retaining a Remission of Your Sins." In *The Book of Mormon: Mosiah, Salvation Only through Christ*, ed. Monte S. Nyman and Charles D. Tate Jr., 227–60. Provo, Utah: BYU Religious Studies Center, 1991.

R.34.   Rector, Hartman, Jr. "From Weakness to Strength." *Improvement Era* (June 1970): 102–3.

R.35.   Ricks, Stephen D. "Benjamin." In *Encyclopedia of Mormonism*, ed. Daniel H. Ludlow, 1:99–100. New York: Macmillan, 1992.

R.36.   Ricks, Stephen D. "The Coronation of Kings." In *Reexploring the Book of Mormon*, ed. John W. Welch, 124–26. Salt Lake City: Deseret Book and FARMS, 1992.

R.37.   Ricks, Stephen D. "The Ideology of Kingship in Mosiah 1–6." In *Reexploring the Book of Mormon*, ed. John W. Welch, 114–16. Salt Lake City: Deseret Book and FARMS, 1992.

R.38.   Ricks, Stephen D. "Kings, Coronation, and Covenant in Mosiah 1–6." In *Rediscovering the Book of Mormon*, ed. John L. Sorenson and Melvin J. Thorne, 209–19. Salt Lake City: Deseret Book and FARMS, 1991.

R.39.   Ricks, Stephen D. "The Treaty/Covenant Pattern in King Benjamin's Address." Provo, Utah: FARMS, 1983.

R.40.   Roper, Matthew. "A Black Hole That's Not So Black." *Review of Books on the Book of Mormon* 6/2 (1994): 156–203.

R.41.   Rust, Richard D. "'Know the Covenants of the Lord': Sermons." *In Feasting on the Word,* 101–43. Salt Lake City: Deseret Book and FARMS, 1997.

S.42.   Sorenson, John L. "On the Right or Left: Benjamin and the Scapegoat." *Insights* (January 1995): 1.

S.43.   Szink, Terry L. "Benjamin's Tower and Old Testament Pillars." FARMS Update, *Insights* (October 1995): 2.

S.44.   Szink, Terry L. "Upon the Tower of Benjamin." FARMS Update, *Insights* (August 1995): 2.

T.45.   Thomasson, Gordon C. "Mosiah: The Complex Symbolism and Symbolic Complex of Kingship in the Book of Mormon." *Journal of Book of Mormon Studies* 2/1 (1993): 21–38.

T.46.   Turner, Rodney. "The Great Conversion: (Mosiah 1–6)." In *1 Nephi to Alma 29.* Vol. 7 of *Studies in Scripture,* ed. Kent P. Jackson, 205–29. Salt Lake City: Deseret Book, 1987.

T.47.   Turner, Rodney. "The Moral Dimensions of Man: A Scriptural View." *Dialogue* 3/1 (1968): 72–82.

T.48.   Tvedtnes, John A. Review of *Answering Mormon Scholars: A Response to Criticism of the Book "Covering up the Black Hole in the Book of Mormon."* Vol. 1. By Jerald and Sandra Tanner. *Review of Books on the Book of Mormon* 6/2 (1994): 204–49.

T.49.   Tvedtnes, John A. "King Benjamin and the Feast of Tabernacles." In *By Study and Also by Faith,* ed. John M. Lundquist and Stephen D. Ricks, 2:197–237. Salt Lake City: Deseret Book and FARMS, 1990.

W.50. Welch, John W. "Benjamin's Speech: A Classic Ancient Farewell Address." In *Reexploring the Book of Mormon*, ed. John W. Welch, 120–23. Salt Lake City: Deseret Book and FARMS, 1992.

W.51. Welch, John W. "King Benjamin's Speech in the Context of Ancient Israelite Festivals." Provo, Utah: FARMS, 1985.

W.52. Welch, John W. "Our Nephite Sacrament Prayers." In *Reexploring the Book of Mormon*, ed. John W. Welch, 286–89. Salt Lake City: Deseret Book and FARMS, 1992.

W.53. Welch, John W. "Ten Testimonies of Jesus Christ from the Book of Mormon." In *Doctrines of the Book of Mormon: The 1991 Sperry Symposium*, ed. Bruce A. Van Orden and Brent A. Top, 223–42. Salt Lake City: Deseret Book, 1992.

W.54. Welch, John W. "This Day." In *Reexploring the Book of Mormon*, ed. John W. Welch, 117–19. Salt Lake City: Deseret Book and FARMS, 1992.

W.55. Welch, John W. "Unintentional Sin in Benjamin's Discourse." FARMS Update, *Insights* (April 1996): 2.

W.56. Wells, Robert E. "The Liahona Triad." In *Doctrines of the Book of Mormon: The 1991 Sperry Symposium*, ed. Bruce A. Van Orden and Brent A Top, 1–15. Salt Lake City: Deseret Book, 1992.

W.57. Whitney, Orson F. Conference Report, April 1909, 15.

CONTRIBUTORS

Daryl R. Hague, J.D., is a Spanish instructor at Brigham Young University.

Neal A. Maxwell is a member of the Quorum of the Twelve Apostles of the Church of Jesus Christ of Latter-day Saints.

Hugh W. Nibley is emeritus professor of ancient studies at Brigham Young University.

Stephen D. Ricks is professor of Hebrew and Semitic languages at Brigham Young University.

Terrence L. Szink is an instructor of ancient scripture at Brigham Young University.

M. Catherine Thomas is assistant professor of ancient scripture at Brigham Young University and is currently serving in the Argentina Mendoza Mission for the Church of Jesus Christ of Latter-day Saints.

Bruce A. Van Orden is professor of church history and doctrine at Brigham Young University.

John W. Welch is Robert K. Thomas Professor of Law at Brigham Young University and serves as the editor in chief of *BYU Studies*.

SCRIPTURE INDEX
FOR CHAPTERS 1–12

Exodus (*continued*)

24:11 p. 310
29:4 p. 267 n. 23
33:7–11 p. 218 n. 131
33:8 p. 185
34:1–2 JST p. 294 n.12
34:18–23 p. 150
34:20 p. 215 n. 107
34:22 p. 183
40:12 p. 267 n. 23

Leviticus

4:6, 17 p. 213 n. 92
8:11 p. 213 n. 92
14:7, 16, 27, 51 p. 213 n. 92
16 p. 212 n. 89
16:7–10 p. 177
16:8 p. 214 n. 105
16:14, 19 p. 213 n. 92
16:16–20 p. 176
16:21, 33 p. 176
16:29–31 p. 180
16:34 p. 176
19:18 pp. 81, 167
23 p. 150
23:23–25 p. 170
23:24 pp. 162, 208 n. 33
23:24–25 p. 164
23:26 p. 213 n. 90
23:26–32 p. 212 n. 89
23:27–32 p. 180
23:29 p. 180
23:33–34 p. 183
23:39 p. 183
23:41–44 p. 185
23:42–43 p. 119
23:43 p. 185
24:17–21 p. 87 n. 30
25:8–17 p. 401 n. 18
25:8–55 p. 375
25:10 pp. 193–95, 222 n. 162, 375

25:14, 17 p. 195
25:15–16 p. 195
25:18–19 p. 195
25:25–55 p. 58
25:35 p. 195
25:38 p. 195
25:42 p. 375
25:50 p. 195
25:55 p. 375
26:3 p. 376
26:40–42 p. 375

Numbers

6:24–26 p. 309
6:27 p. 309
8:25 p. 153
15:27–29 p. 176
15:30–31 p. 177
28–29 p. 150
29:1 p. 162
29:7–11 p. 212 n. 89
29:12 p. 183
29:12–34 p. 186
29:12–38 p. 183

Deuteronomy

4 p. 41
5:24 p. 166
6:5 p. 402 n. 25
6:8 p. 309
10:12 p. 79
12:6 p. 208 n. 39
12:17 p. 119
12:18 p. 119
15:1–2 p. 191
15:1–6 p. 58
15:3–4 p. 191
15:4 p. 60
15:6 p. 191
15:7 p. 60
15:7–18 p. 191

Luke (*continued*)

22:19 p. 303
22:20 p. 303
22:21, 34 p. 93
22:25–38 p. 92

John

1:42 p. 273 n. 60
3:16 p. 141
5:19 p. 18
7:2 p. 183
7:16 p. 18
8:33 p. 372
17:19 p. 281

Acts

13:9 p. 273 n. 60
20:36–38 p. 92

Romans

2:4 p. 13
3:25 p. 308
6:6 p. 467
7:12 p. 79
8:5 p. 11
8:26 p. 9
15:7 p. 143

1 Corinthians

1:23 p. 8
2:14 p. 18
2:16 p. 11
11:24 p. 303

Colossians

3:9 p. 17

Hebrews

6:7 p. 143
7:1–24 p. 301

9:4 p. 313 n. 13
9:7 p. 176
11:10 p. 280
11:10, 16 p. 282

1 John

3:9 JST p. 289

Revelation

2:17 pp. 273 n. 60, 313 n. 13
3:12 p. 294 n. 17
8–9 p. 163
14:1 p. 294 n. 17

Book of Mormon

1 Nephi

5:9 p. 186
7:14 p. 40
7:22 p. 186
10:16 p. 185
11:21 p. 312 n. 7
11:31–33 p. 407 n. 63
11:35 p. 8
13:29 p. 5
13:40 p. 312 n. 7
14:1 p. 5
14:17 p. 311 n. 6
17:23–43 p. 219 n. 139
21:26 p. 310
22:3 p. 35
22:13 p. 310

2 Nephi

1–4 p. 104
2:11 p. 83
2:21 p. 138
4:21 p. 284
5:10 p. 150
5:16 p. 308
5:18 p. 241

5:26 pp. 31, 249
6:18 p. 310
8:17 p. 303
9:6 p. 467
9:7 pp. 128, 144
9:44 pp. 34, 99
19:6 p. 312 n. 7
25:12 p. 312 n. 7
25:18, 28 p. 407 n. 63
25:22 p. 2
25:24 p. 151
25:24–27 p. 407 nn. 63, 72
26:20 p. 8
27:20–21 p. 19
28:19 p. 5
31–33 p. 104
31:2 p. 34
31:13–14 p. 287
31:15 p. 19
32:2–3 p. 287
32:3 p. 2
32:7 p. 138
32:8 pp. 35, 214 n. 105
32:9 p. 313 n. 9

Jacob

1:2 p. 116 n. 10
1:9 p. 250
1:10–11 p. 253
1:11 pp. 50 n. 2, 240
1:19 p. 34
2:2 p. 34
4–6 p. 104
4:5 p. 313 n. 9
4:13 p. 6
4:18 p. 138
7:22 p. 311 n. 6

Enos

1:15 p. 313 n. 9
1:27 p. 104

Jarom

1:5 p. 153

Omni

1:2 p. 31
1:4–11 p. 31
1:12 p. 30
1:14 p. 48
1:17 pp. 7, 36
1:18 p. 36
1:19 p. 48
1:20 p. 294 n. 8
1:23 pp. 24, 27
1:23–24 p. 29
1:24 p. 28
1:25 pp. 11, 25, 50
1:30 p. 31

Words of Mormon

1:10 p. 30
1:10–18 p. 28
1:12–16 p. 236
1:13 pp. 2, 28
1:13–14 p. 283
1:14 p. 30
1:16 pp. 3, 30
1:16–17 p. 31
1:17 pp. 3, 11, 31, 287
1:18 pp. 3, 12, 31, 50, 237, 283

Mosiah

1:1–2:8 p. 326
1:2 pp. 33, 37, 238
1:2–3 pp. 4, 436
1:2–7 p. 436
1:3 p. 33
1:3, 6, 7 p. 170
1:4 p. 37
1:5 pp. 7, 33, 427
1:6 p. 4

Mosiah (continued)

1:7 pp. 34, 248, 440
1:8 p. 4
1:9 pp. 96, 239
1:9–10 p. 95
1:9–12 p. 245
1:10 pp. 48, 172, 184, 193, 235, 238, 243
1:10–13 p. 96
1:10–15 p. 48
1:10–18 p. 95
1:11 pp. 58, 180, 186, 243, 284, 290
1:11–12 p. 286
1:12 p. 113
1:13 p. 113
1:15 pp. 99, 455
1:15–16 pp. 101, 234, 248
1:16 pp. 35, 99, 211 n. 77, 294 n. 8
1:17 p. 170
1:18 pp. 184, 193, 245
2:1 pp. 95, 119
2:1–10 p. 238
2:3 pp. 102, 125, 164, 186, 231
2:4 pp. 30, 122, 284, 440
2:5 pp. 120, 154, 184, 193, 402 n. 18, 436
2:5–6 pp. 230–31
2:6 pp. 184–86
2:7 p. 245
2:8 pp. 186, 193
2:8–9 p. 260
2:9 pp. 5, 95–96, 162, 193, 228, 257, 278, 329, 454–55
2:9, 11, 13–14 p. 329
2:9–13 p. 451
2:9, 27 p. 184
2:9–28 pp. 325–26
2:9, 40–41 p. 97
2:9–41 p. 464

2:10 pp. 126, 404 n. 44
2:10–11, 26 p. 69
2:11 pp. 27, 126, 173, 249, 262, 329, 402 n. 21, 403 n. 35, 404 n. 43
2:11–14 p. 34
2:11, 20–21 p. 168
2:11, 26 p. 252
2:12 pp. 60, 123
2:12, 14 p. 436
2:12–14 pp. 96, 242
2:13 pp. 40, 45, 58, 61, 192, 228, 236, 244, 375
2:13, 22, 31, 41 p. 187
2:14 pp. 33, 40, 167, 228, 329
2:15 pp. 96; 227–29; 404 nn. 40, 46
2:15, 17 p. 8
2:16 pp. 68, 471
2:16–17 pp. 329, 375, 413
2:16–18 p. 464
2:17 pp. 67–68, 73, 211 n. 77, 412–13, 427, 433, 437, 458, 462
2:17–18 p. 243
2:17–19, 21 p. 67
2:18 pp. 77, 96, 235, 317, 367, 369, 405 n. 49
2:18–19 pp. 77, 171, 335, 367, 374
2:19 pp. 18; 71; 162; 167–69; 189–90; 234; 252; 319; 368; 374; 404 n. 42; 405 nn. 48–49; 455
2:19, 21 p. 258
2:19–25 p. 230
2:19–26 p. 472
2:20 pp. 44, 74, 134, 169, 334
2:20–21 pp. 69, 73, 170, 190
2:20–23 p. 171
2:20–24 p. 433
2:20–25 pp. 1, 262
2:20–26 p. 212 n. 88
2:21 pp. 237, 433, 471

For further scripture references and cross-references organized under the words and phrases in each verse of Benjamin's speech, see the appendix, pp. 479–616.

Subject Index

atonement (*continued*)
emphasis on, in Benjamin's
address 14
essential in overcoming the
natural man 429
indebtedness created
through the 80
and the law 347
as most important event in
world history 429
necessity for 140, 420–21
necessity of pain in 140–41
questions pertaining to the
138–42
repeated mention of 154
ritual, at the temple 174
role of
in absolving man of sin 348
in judgment 79–80
valid for all ages 353
vicarious nature of 141–43
authority in oratory 64–66
autumn festival complex 159

Babylonia, coronation of the
Exilarch in 123
balance
of equivalent words and
phrases 334
exhortation toward 16
keeping life's demands in 453
between pace and diligence
471
Ballard, M. Russell 439, 453
Bangerter, W. Grant 447
baptism, as beginning of
spiritual rebirth 288
Beatitudes 359
beggars, state of mind in
approaching 361
beginnings, time of 196–98

belonging to one's king 481
Benjamin
achievements of 49–50
as antithesis of King Noah 24
character of 2–3, 50, 53–54
n. 28
chronology of 27
as a classicist 38–39
clear conscience of 8
as commander-in-chief 29
congregation of, held
spellbound 124
as conservator 35–36
consolidation by, of lands and
people of Zarahemla 28
counseling techniques of 76
as an examplar 235
as an example of consecration 12–13
as an example of a righteous
ruler 241
as father 4, 38
as founding father 41–42
as a great Nephite king 24
as holder of Holy Priest-
hood 10
as a holy and just man 11
humility of 472
influence of, on later generations 42–48, 60–62
as judge 236
as keeper of the records 30–31
as legalist 39–41
lineage and date of birth of,
unknown 25
as linguist 36–37
logic of 77–82
meekness of 3, 18–19
as military leader 29
as a model disciple 11
name of 25–27

claim to, by subgroup in
Zarahemla 49
and covenant 243
divergence of, between
theory and practice 240
as a divine election in
ancient Near East 238
expediency of 24
of God 167–69
insignia of 247–49
institution of, abandoned
by Nephites 49
meaning of 234–37
objections to 239, 241
perils of 239, 242
renewal of, at akitu festival
171
symbols of 35, 248
knowledge
leading to action 354
responsibility for own 354
Kurz, William S. 89

Laban, sword of 29
Lamanites
invasion by 28
war against 283
land
leaving fallow in sabbatical
years 191–92
ownership of 194
language
of fathers taught to
Benjamin's sons 37
and literature of prophets of
Israel 39
Nephite, taught to
Mulekites 36
law
Benjamin's public laws 45

and commitment to 187–88
reading of the 192–93, 246
on Sukkot 187
receipt of, by Mosiah 248
law of Moses 147, 158, 507–8,
557–58
blended with Christianity
59–60
fulfillment of 151, 298
giving of 187
observance of, by Lehi and
his descendants 150–51
observance of holy days
required by 150
sacrifice in 186
leaders, secular, consistency in
behavior of 3
leadership 73
Lee, Harold B. 413, 449
left hand of God 604–5
legal formula, Nephite 44–45, 61
legal practices among
Benjamin's people 39–41,
520–21
lender, duty of, to accept proper
repayment 222 n. 165
life, coming to, associated with
covenant making and
keeping 262
Limhi, people of
as hearers of Benjamin's
words 43
numbered among the
Nephites 43
as participants of the
covenant 53 n. 25
literary analysis 377–400
Lord
emulation of 11
as the heavenly king 71

Muilenburg, James 316
Mulekites, dissatisfaction of,
    with Nephite rule 49
mysteries 277–94
    of God, understanding 278,
        488
    of heaven 138
    as plain and precious things
        required for salvation and
        exaltation 7

naked, caring for 98
name
    acquisition of 372
    of Christ
        petitioning in 302
        reception of 291
        taking upon oneself 296
        willingness to take the 291
    giving of 286
    new
        at coronation 252–53
        at enthronement 273 n. 60
        bestowal of 254
        conferred upon Mosiah
            and the people 234
        given to the people 58, 125
        given at transition 273 n. 60
    of God
        pronouncement of 179–80
        reverent behavior toward
            216 n. 114
        taking upon oneself 309
    remembering the, by which
        they were called 4
names
    blotting out of 114
    of covenanters recorded 260

natalia 125
Nathan the Babylonian,
    writings of 123–26
natural man 128–29, 352, 429
    descriptions of 427
    difficulties in teaching 17
    as an enemy of God 427
    progression of, toward
        becoming a saint 348
    putting off of 13, 17–18,
        114, 561–63
    understanding the 18
necessities of life, dependence
    on God for 15
needy, providing for 366
negative confession 172, 520
Nelson, Russell M. 436
Nephi and Lehi, taught by
    father Helaman words of
    King Benjamin 45
Nephite civilization, flourish-
    ing of 42
New Year 160–74
    Israelite
        themes appropriate to 200
        themes of, similar to King
            Benjamin's speech 174
    observation of 160
    as time for coronation of
        king 170
    as a time of judgment 164–67
    as time to recall creation 169
    as time for renewal of the
        covenant 170
New Year's Day, killing of a
    king on 212 n. 85
New Year's festival at Babylon
    172

THE FOUNDATION FOR ANCIENT
RESEARCH AND MORMON STUDIES
(FARMS)

The Foundation for Ancient Research and Mormon Studies encourages and supports research and publication about the Book of Mormon, Another Testament of Jesus Christ, and other ancient scriptures.

FARMS is a nonprofit, tax-exempt educational foundation, affiliated with Brigham Young University. Its main research interests in the scriptures include ancient history, language, literature, culture, geography, politics, religion, and law. Although research on such subjects is of secondary importance when compared with the spiritual and eternal messages of the scriptures, solid scholarly research can supply certain kinds of useful information, even if only tentatively, concerning many significant and interesting questions about the ancient backgrounds, origins, composition, and meanings of scripture.

The work of the Foundation rests on the premise that the Book of Mormon and other scriptures were written by prophets of God. Belief in this premise—in the divinity of scripture—is a matter of faith. Religious truths require divine witness to establish the faith of the believer. While scholarly research cannot replace that witness, such studies may reinforce and encourage individual testimonies by fostering understanding and appreciation of the scriptures. It is hoped that this information will help people to "come unto Christ" (Jacob 1:7) and to understand and take more seriously these ancient witnesses of the atonement of Jesus Christ, the Son of God.

The Foundation works to make interim and final reports about its research available widely, promptly, and economically, both in scholarly and popular formats. FARMS publishes information about the Book of Mormon and other ancient scripture in the *Insights* newsletter; books and research papers; *FARMS Review of Books; Journal of Book of Mormon Studies;* reprints of published scholarly papers; and videos and audiotapes. FARMS also supports the preparation of the *Collected Works of Hugh Nibley*.

To facilitate the sharing of information, FARMS sponsors lectures, seminars, symposia, firesides, and radio and television broadcasts in which research findings are communicated to working scholars and to anyone interested in faithful, reliable information about the scriptures. Through Research Press, a publishing arm of the Foundation, FARMS publishes materials addressed primarily to working scholars.

For more information about the Foundation and its activities, contact the FARMS office at 1-800-327-6715 or (801) 373-5111.